FRONTYARD BACKYARD

Perspectives on Underdevelopment Series

Perpetuating Poverty
The Political Economy of Canadian Foreign Aid
by Robert Carty and Virginia Smith

Bitter Grounds
Roots of Revolt in Central America, 2nd edition
by Liisa North

Ties That Bind
Canada and the Third World
edited by Robert Clarke and Richard Swift

Banking on Poverty
The Global Impact of the IMF and World Bank
edited by Jill Torrie

FRONTYARD BACKYARD

THE AMERICAS IN THE GLOBAL CRISIS

Edited by John Holmes & Colin Leys

between the lines

Published by Between The Lines
229 College St.,
Toronto, Ontario
M5T 1R4 Canada

Cover design by Goodness Graphics

Typeset by Canadian Composition

Printed in Canada

Between The Lines receives financial assistance from the Canada Council and the Ontario Arts Council.

Canadian Cataloguing in Publication Data

Main entry under title:

Frontyard/backyard

(Perspectives on underdevelopment)
ISBN 0-919946-78-X (bound) ISBN 0-919946-79-8 (pbk.)

1. International economic relations. 2. America — Economic conditions — 20th century. 3. Economic development. 4. America — politics and government — 20th century. I. Holmes, John, 1954- . II. Leys, Colin, 1931- . III. Series.

HF1412.F76 1987 337 C87-093501-1

Contents

Preface

U.S. POLITICIANS sometimes refer to Central America and the Caribbean as the United States' "backyard." Like any backyard, what happens in the Caribbean Basin (as the whole region has come to be called, emphasizing its preeminent place in U.S. strategic thinking) is largely a product of what happens, or fails to happen, in the frontyard. This book explores some of the relationships between what is going on in the United States' frontyard — including the Canadian part of the yard, since the book is the result of a Canadian project — and its backyard.

Two issues dominated political and economic life in the western hemisphere during the first half of the 1980s: the contraction and restructuring of industrial production in North America; and political struggle in Central America and the Caribbean. Although on the surface, and certainly as they are discussed in the media, these two issues may appear to be separate and unconnected, in fact they are closely linked aspects of the contemporary crisis in the world economy. The basic assumption of this book is that the current global economic crisis was produced by the exhaustion of the model of accumulation which sustained the long post-war boom and by the ways in which international capital manoeuvred to weather this period of constrained profitability. The "monetarist shock" of the late 1970s was a logical outcome of these efforts.

In North America the effects have included the "de-industrialization" of certain regions and the radical restructuring of production in many manufacturing sectors. During the restructuring process, the "liberal consensus," which had been established after World War II by the Democrats in the U.S. and the Liberals in Canada, and which characterized politics in these two countries throughout the post-war boom, was undermined and replaced by the politics of the radical right. The ascendancy of Reaganism in the United States intensified the ideological and military conflict in Central America and the Caribbean, where the same global crisis had previously produced a strong groundswell of support for popular left-wing forces.

The individual chapters in the book examine these linked developments at the international, national, and regional levels, beginning with an analysis of the global crisis. Subsequent chapters focus on three interrelated aspects of the response to the crisis: "de-industrialization" in the United States and Canada, and its economic, social and political consequences; U.S. and Canadian policy in Central America and the Caribbean during the post-war period; and, finally, the implications these developments hold for popular movements in three particular countries of the region (Grenada, Jamaica, and Nicaragua). In the introductory essay we spell out some of the interconnections between these different levels of analysis — as well as between the economic and the political developments involved.

With one exception the chapters are revised versions of papers first presented to a workshop held in May 1984, at Kingston, Ontario, under the auspices of the Programme of Studies in International and National Development at Queen's University. The workshop theme was "Development in the 1980s: Canada in the Western Hemisphere." Clive Thomas' paper originated as a public lecture given in association with the workshop. The workshop was made possible by a grant from the Social Sciences and Humanities Research Council of Canada, with additional financial support from the School of Graduate Studies and Research at Queen's University.

We owe a large debt of gratitude to the discussants and other participants at the workshop, and to many other individuals for their help both in planning and running the workshop and for subsequent editorial assistance; in particular, Laurie Adkin, Jim Cannon, Bryant Fairley, Cynthia Guttman, Banu Helvacioglu, Rene Hogarthy, Catherine Hyett, Fred Judson, George Lovell, Patricia O'Reilly, David O'Toole, Devanand Ramnarine, and Usha Thakur. We would also like to thank Bernice Gallagher for typing the manuscript, Ross Hough for redrafting the graphs for publication, and, at Between The Lines, Catherine Edwards for her help in copy-editing and Robert Clarke for his editorial guidance and encouragement.

Colin Leys and John Holmes
Kingston, Ontario.
November 1986

Chapter 1

Introduction

John Holmes and Colin Leys

OVER THE LAST FIFTEEN years the global economy has been going through a period of major restructuring that has had profound effects on every region of the world.[1] By the beginning of the 1970s, the relatively stable period of accumulation that had characterized the first twenty years or so of the post-war period had come to an end.

During the 1970s and early 1980s the manufacturing sectors in virtually all of the countries of the Organization for Economic Cooperation and Development (OECD) displayed the same symptoms: a drastic slowdown in productivity growth, declining industrial employment, stagnating industrial output, and sharply rising unit labour costs.[2] Over the last ten years falling profit rates and intensifying international competition have forced many individual firms, and in some cases whole industrial sectors, to undertake large-scale restructuring of production. The advanced economies have experienced intense pressure to reduce both their levels of public sector borrowing and their expenditures; the fragile economies of many underdeveloped countries have been devastated by rapidly deteriorating terms of trade; and several of the Newly Industrializing Countries (NICs), which had been experiencing rapid economic growth, are faced with debt crises and growing political tensions.

The scale and nature of the recent restructuring of the world economy are qualitatively different from the relatively stable processes of restructuring associated with "normal" business cycles. A growing number of writers argue that the world economy is in the middle of the third "long swing" crisis of the past hundred years, and that the restructuring currently underway is an attempt to find a "solution" that will mark the emergence of a new and qualitatively different phase in capitalist development. Mandel, for example, identifies the onset of the crisis with the exhaustion of the expansionary phase of the fourth Kondratieff "long wave."[3] Writers of the French regulation school identify the crisis with a breakdown in the mode of regulation, which provided the underpinnings for the regime of accumulation that they call Fordism.[4] In the United States, political economists Gordon, Edwards, and Reich equate the crisis with the decay phase of the most recent "social structure of accumulation" — a concept similar to the "regime of accumulation" formulated by the authors of the French regulation school.[5] While these writers differ, often substantially, in the details of their analyses, they reach a general agreement about certain aspects of the crisis. They agree that the crisis developed during the late 1960s, and that an interpretation needs to situate the crisis in the broader historical context of the development and subsequent exhaustion of the long post-war economic boom. They also agree on the fact that this period of restructuring represents a major rupture in the history of capitalist development.

The French regulation school's interpretation of the post-war period is valuable for a number of reasons. For one thing, the key analytical concepts contained in the phrases "regime of accumulation" and "mode of regulation" stress the links between production and consumption. During periods of major rupture, restructuring is not limited to the transformation of the technical and social organization of production, but encompasses the transformation of consumption patterns and a whole range of economic, social, and political institutional forms. Secondly, this account makes explicit the connections between different aspects of the crisis manifested at both the international and the national levels — aspects too often considered to be unrelated. The analysis of the French regulation school, represented in this volume by Alain Lipietz, links, for example, the economic effects of the crisis experienced in North America and Western Europe, the economic development and subsequent debt crises and internal political conflicts that have characterized the recent history of the NICs, and the political and military consequences of the erosion of U.S. economic and political hegemony.

The work of the French regulation school is best known to English-language readers through the work of Michel Aglietta in his book *A Theory of Capitalist Regulation* (1979), and through Alain Lipietz's analyses of the current crisis, which have appeared in English-language journals.[6] Aglietta sought to provide an analysis of the political economic development of the United States after the mid-nineteenth century. In an attempt to comprehend both the transformation of production and consumption norms that characterized the post-war period of capitalist accumulation and reproduction in the United States, Aglietta employs the concepts of "regime of accumulation" and "mode of regulation." He uses the term regime of accumulation to describe periods of relatively stable and sustained accumulation in which there is:

> a systematic mode of distribution and reallocation of the social product, which brings about a long run correspondence between the changing conditions of production (volume of capital investment, distribution among the different branches, and production norms) and the changing conditions of final consumption (consumption norms of wage-earners and other social classes, collective expenditures and so on).[7]

The concept thus stresses the relationship that exists between production and consumption. Aglietta recognizes that regimes of accumulation do not automatically and instantaneously come into being, but are conditional upon the emergence and coalescence of various institutional forms that provide the necessary social "cohesion."

Aglietta's second concept, mode of regulation:

> refers to the ensemble of institutional forms, networks, and explicit or implicit norms which assure compatibility of market behaviour within a regime of accumulation, in keeping with the actual pattern of social relations, and beyond (or even through) the contradictory, conflictual nature of relations among economic agents and social groups.[8]

Looking at the case of the United States, Aglietta identifies a succession of different regimes of accumulation. He calls the most recent the "regime of intensive accumulation," or Fordism, which provided the economic, social, and political foundation for the long post-war economic boom. Although most of the analyses in the subsequent chapters are not couched explicitly within the framework of the French regulation school, they do all focus on the political and economic consequences of the global crisis. Aglietta and Lipietz see those consequences as integrally connected to the breakdown of Fordism.

In his essay here Lipietz refines and extends his previous analyses of the globalization of the crisis of Fordism. He argues that the long post-war boom in North America and Western Europe was due to a combination of the extension of "Fordist" (that is, mechanized mass-production) techniques of production to many sectors of consumer goods production, and the expansion of mass consumption and a sharp rise in working-class standards of living. He emphasizes two points: first, the significance of rising rates of labour productivity, and the link between this growth and an accompanying growth in real wages; and second, the fact that the modes of regulation that determined the different varieties of Fordism in the advanced capitalist economies were internal to each national economy. Analogous mechanisms and institutions for regulating the interaction between national economies at the international level developed only in the most rudimentary forms.

The onset of crisis in the late 1960s resulted from a breakdown of Fordism. Two factors in particular play an important role in an understanding of the crisis that developed: the slowdown in labour productivity growth and the intensification of international competition.

Various analysts have suggested a number of reasons for the dramatic slowdown in productivity growth that occurred after 1973. In the labour process, the *potential* productivity of labour is determined by technology used at any particular point in time, while the *actual* productivity depends on how hard and fast workers can be made to work, and by the extent of the market. Some writers suggest that as Fordist principles of work organization became fully implemented across whole sectors of industrial production, it was inevitable that the growth in labour productivity would begin to slow down as the technical limits to potential productivity using Fordist techniques began to be reached.[9] Lipietz and other writers argue, however, that the slowdown in labour productivity growth did not stem primarily from the limits of potential productivity under Fordist technology, but rather from the failure of Fordist principles of labour organization. This failure resulted from the resistance of workers on the shopfloor to further intensification of production by management when managers attempted to force actual productivity as close as possible to potential productivity. These writers argue that the slowdown in productivity growth was the result of intensified class struggle at the point of production, manifested in the wave of "wildcat" strikes and other forms of production disruption that reemerged in North America in the late 1960s after twenty years of relative labour peace.[10]

Yet another group of writers suggest that the slowdown in productivity was linked to a slowing down of growth in consumer demand in certain sectors due to the relative saturation of the market. They argue that just as a rapid growth in demand tends to facilitate sharp increases in productivity growth in production, slowdowns in the growth of demand tend to act as a brake on productivity growth.[11] Sabel and Piore locate the cause of the crisis of Fordism in the breakdown of mass markets, arguing that the markets for many products are such that the products are not amenable to mass production and, more importantly, that consumer reaction against mass-produced and standardized products has led to market fragmentation and increasingly differentiated products.[12] Consequently, product quality, variety, and innovation have become important competitive strategies. The ability to produce a range of different products at the lowest total cost is becoming more important than reducing the unit cost of any one product to the technically attainable minimum (one of the hallmarks of Fordist production methods).

The full explanation perhaps lies in a combination of all these factors, but there is no disputing the fact that in North America the slowdown in productivity growth was dramatic.[13] In turn, this slowdown led to a decline in profitability as unit labour costs escalated rapidly and as further capital expenditures on new production equipment failed to be offset by corresponding increases in labour productivity. In the period after 1973, for example, Canadian manufacturing experienced both slower growth in labour productivity and increased rates of capital intensification, in sharp contrast to the period from 1946 to 1973, during which the rate of growth in capital intensity had been roughly matched by the rate of growth in labour productivity.[14]

The intensification of international competition resulted in large measure from the very success of Fordism within the advanced industrial economies. Throughout the 1950s and early 1960s the rapid growth in domestic output in the consumption goods sectors in North America and Western Europe was generally absorbed by growing domestic markets. However, by the early 1970s the tendency towards ever-expanding production spilled over national boundaries as competition intensified among OECD countries for each others' lucrative markets. The existence of surplus capacity on a world scale, and of substantial variations in unit costs of production between different national producers, threatened to create serious dislocations in the world economy. Large segments of secondary manufacturing industry in countries such as Canada and the United States, which had comparatively high unit costs of production, were particularly threatened by these developments, and began to undergo wholesale restructuring.

Restructuring is clearly a two-sided (although, we hasten to add, not normally a zero sum) process, in that it brings into being new plants, production methods, and jobs, at the same time as it displaces the old. However, the two sides of this process are rarely synchronized in time or space, and the industrial economies of North America and Western Europe have been dominated by the displacement effects of restructuring. Aggregate measures of output, exports, investment, productivity, and employment all point to a cumulative weakening of the relative, and in some instances, the absolute position of manufacturing in these economies. Many traditional manufacturing sectors and industrial regions have experienced disinvestment and rationalization manifested in plant closings, high rates of job loss and unemployment, and the economic and social dislocation of communities. An obvious political consequence was the breakdown of the liberal consensus (in Canada and the United States) and the social-democratic consensus (in Western Europe), which was followed by the rise of neo-conservatism, leading ultimately to the monetarist deflation that brought on the global recession. The four chapters by Niosi and Faucher, Bellon, Holmes, and Gagnon and Montcalm examine some of the economic and political effects of this experience on the United States and Canada.

With the much-heralded recovery of the U.S. economy (a recovery that increasingly appears to be fragile and short-lived) it is easy to lose sight of the far-reaching economic changes that occurred in North America during the 1970s and early 1980s; changes that have contributed to shifts both in the political climate within North America and to the decline of U.S. hegemony internationally. In chapter 3, Jorge Niosi and Philippe Faucher document the economic decline of the United States and Canada. As they observe, the term "de-industrialization" is ambiguous. Some writers argue that de-industrialization occurs when a national economy is unable to produce sufficient manufactured goods to cover domestic consumption either directly or indirectly through trade.[15] They define an efficient manufacturing sector "as one which, currently as well as potentially, not only satisfies the demand of consumers at home but is also able to sell enough of its products abroad to pay for the nation's import requirements,"[16] and hold that de-industrialization occurs when there is a significant movement away from this position.[17]

However, many writers define de-industrialization in terms of a decline of manufacturing employment. Part of the conventional wisdom of orthodox economics is that there is a long-run tendency in advanced industrial economies for employment in the manufacturing sector to decline relative to employment in the service sector.[18] A number of mechanisms have been posited to account for this tendency. It has been argued, for instance, that since productivity tends to grow relatively slowly in services compared to manufacturing, this means that even with no change in the relative pattern of demand for services and manufactured goods there will still be a change in the pattern of employment over time. In addition, it is argued that the income elasticity of demand is greater for services than for manufactured goods. So, as real incomes rise, the composition of demand will shift in favour of services. In the long run the combination of these mechanisms will lead to the development of the so-called "post-industrial service economy" and in this sense de-industrialization is inevitable.

However, the recent decline in manufacturing activity that has been experienced in a number of advanced industrial economies is not simply the outcome of such general long-run economic tendencies. For example, in the United Kingdom it is not the relative decline but the absolute decline in manufacturing employment that is the most worrying and distinctive feature of de-industrialization. By early 1982 total industrial employment in Britain had fallen from its peak level in 1966 by over four million people, three-quarters of whom had been displaced from employment in manufacturing. Over the same period employment in the service sector increased by just over one million; the result has been an increase of nearly three million officially unemployed people. Niosi and Faucher show that in the United States and Canada, while there has been a *relative* shift in both output and employment from the goods producing sectors (particularly from manufacturing) to the service sectors since the late 1960s, there was not, at least until the 1981 recession, a massive *absolute* loss of manufacturing employment such as occurred in the United Kingdom. However, using other measures of economic decline, the data compiled by Niosi and Faucher clearly document the simultaneous industrial, commercial, and financial decline of the United States, the industrial decline of the Canadian economy, and the steadily worsening position of the

North American economy with respect to international patterns and balances of trade.

There have also been some significant shifts in the nature of employment and the composition of the labour force in North America which can be highlighted using the Canadian data:

(1) Although manufacturing has represented a progressively declining relative share of total employment in Canada since 1962 it is only after 1977 that a general trend towards an absolute decline in manufacturing employment becomes clear.
(2) Of the almost 600,000 jobs lost in the 1981-82 recession, 54 per cent were from the manufacturing sector and a further 15 per cent were from the non-agricultural primary sector. It is estimated that in Canada over 80 per cent of the increase in unemployment in 1982 was due to declines in employment, rather than to growth in the work force. This is in contrast to the United States where strong growth in the work force accounted for over 75 per cent of the observed increase in unemployment during 1982. In fact, during the 1970s jobs were created in the United States at twice the rate of the previous three decades.
(3) Two changes in the composition of the labour force during this period should be emphasized. Female employment continued to increase throughout the period, even during the 1981-82 recession, and there was a significant shift towards part-time work. By 1983 over 85 per cent of all part-time jobs were in service sectors and adult females and youths almost equally shared 92 per cent of part-time employment.[19]

It seems, therefore, that a shift is occurring from more highly paid, full-time, male employment in manufacturing to lower paid, part-time, female, and youth employment in the service sector. In turn, there is mounting evidence in North America that a bipolar distribution of household income is emerging: the so-called "missing middle" phenomenon. A study analyzing employment and income changes in Pittsburgh argues, "Pittsburgh's heavy industrial growth produced a well-paid unionized blue collar middle class with a distinctive lifestyle. Yet since 1960 the shifting industrial and occupational mix has been producing progressively greater inequality." The study notes, "Declining sectors have the heaviest concentrations of middle income jobs; growing sectors have earnings distributions split between the top and the bottom earnings categories."[20] Such changes clearly have significant implications for the consumption sphere and, in particular, for the reorganization and restructuring of the retailing and personal service sectors. If one accepts the conceptual framework provided by the French regulation school, these developments may provide some clues to the shape and form of a new mode of regulation.

The extent to which manufacturing employment recovered in the wake of the 1981-82 recession is unclear. Obviously, job loss or even net employment change should not be equated with industrial decline and reduced output. For example, a sharp increase in labour productivity resulting from technological change may well result in an expansion of output with a constant or even declining labour force. In addition to job losses in heavy manufacturing, recent years have also witnessed significant increases in capital investment, major technical changes, and dramatic increases in labour productivity in some "leading" industrial sectors (see, for example, the evidence of the Canadian auto industry presented by Holmes in chapter 5). The massive shakeout of labour, coupled with gains in labour productivity made possible as a result of investments in new technology, has enabled firms to meet moderate expansions of demand without any substantial increases in employment. In Canada in 1983 labour productivity in manufacturing (measured by output per person-hour) increased by 6.4 per cent (the highest annual increase since 1971) and unit labour costs increased by a mere 0.3 per cent. In 1984 the corresponding figures were 4.0 per cent and minus 2.3 per cent respectively, yet high rates of unemployment persisted.[21] This pattern clearly raises fundamental questions about the future economic and social structure of North American society.

Niosi and Faucher also highlight the historical weakness of the Canadian manufacturing sector. In comparison with other so-called advanced economies (the OECD countries, for example) Canada has a strikingly different economic structure, which is reflected in employment, output, and trade figures and which results from the "peculiar" position of Canada within earlier international divisions of labour.[22] Its economic development has tended to overemphasize the extraction and semi-processing of raw materials and to have underemphasized the industrial production of finished products.[23] On the one hand, Canada was (and remains) a major source of raw materials, initially for Britain and, later, for other OECD countries, particularly the United States and Japan. On the other hand, the fact that wages in Canada have been relatively high has led to the development of an affluent domestic market for consumption goods. This market coupled with tariff protection permitted the development of import substitution industries in the consumption goods sectors to a degree that was "inconceivable on the periphery of the world economy and thereby confirmed the basically developed nature of the Canadian economy."[24] The Canadian economy supplies raw materials and semi-finished products to other industrialized countries within the OECD and is susceptible to fluctuations in the levels of demand and terms of trade for these materials; it produces consumption goods for a limited domestic market with virtually no export of these goods (with the specially negotiated exception of automotive products to the United States); and it imports both consumption goods and large volumes of capital goods.

The chapter here by Bertrand Bellon examines changes in federal industrial policy in the United States in response to one of the most striking features of the collapse of Fordism; the declining competitiveness of U.S. industry in the face of fierce international competition and rapidly escalating production costs. These circumstances have created tremendous political pressure for government to adopt an increasingly protectionist stance. However, many commentators argue that protectionism should only be viewed as a temporary measure to create sufficient breathing space to allow the sweeping restructuring of U.S. industrial sectors such as autos, steel, and electronic consumer goods. They say this restructuring is necessary if these sectors are to become internationally competitive. Bellon begins by describing the surprisingly large size and scope of existing federal support for private capital in the form of financial transfers and legal and administrative intervention. The main focus of the chapter is an analysis of the current debate over the form that federal industrial policy in the United States should take in order to most efficiently restructure and restore the international competitiveness of the U.S. manufacturing industry. In particular, Bellon focusses on the different positions taken in this debate by financial interests, large capital, small firms, and the unions.

This discussion of current and possible future industrial policy responses to industrial decline in North America, coupled with the persistence of high rates of unemployment even during the present recovery in industrial output, once again highlights the issues raised by Lipietz in chapter 2, in his discussion of possible escape routes from the global crisis of Fordism. One of the initial responses of industrial capital to the crisis was to further internationalize production. This process has been widely discussed (and possibly overemphasized) in the literature on the so-called new international division of labour.[25] However, as Lipietz points out, this strategy proved to be a dead-end: while the geographic relocation of industrial production that occurred in the 1970s may have helped decrease the average cost of labour, it did not bring about a significant expansion in markets (rather the opposite, in fact) or lead to increases in productivity. Consequently it did not resolve the crisis of Fordism and the problem of how to give new impetus to productivity and to consumption on a worldwide scale; it merely shifted the crisis of Fordism from a limited arena in certain "advanced" countries to a global arena.

The recent introduction of industrial robotics and other microelectronic-based process technologies has created the potential for a radical restructuring of the labour process.[26] The use of electronic process control in manufacturing enables increases in potential productivity levels through the maximum coordination of material transfers on the assembly line. This reduces queuing and deadtime, enables tight quality control, facilitates the twenty-four hour utilization of plant and equipment, and permits the "mass production of diversity." Perhaps the most important feature of industrial robotics and numerically controlled machine tools is their flexibility, which allows small batches of different products to be treated as identical elements of a single mass production run. One consequence of this is the severing of the link between lowering unit costs and lengthening production runs, a link based on economies of scale, a marked characteristic of Fordist production. A second consequence of flexibility is that because industrial robots and numerically controlled machine tools are easily and quickly reprogrammed, the rate of obsolescence of capital goods has been significantly reduced. Although evidence suggests that fairly large gains in labour productivity are possible through the implementation of these new technologies, simply transforming the techniques of production does not constitute the formation of a new mode of regulation. The question of how to "match" consumption with the increase in output that increased labour productivity will bring remains to be solved.

This point is underscored by the contradictions implicit in the idea of "re-industrialization" — an idea currently popular in North America and advocated in various forms by analysts of many different political stripes. Re-industrialization appears to offer something for everyone by implying that a sharp upturn in manufacturing employment is possible if only the right "industrial policy mix" can be found.

The proponents of re-industrialization strategies all agree on the need to increase labour productivity. However, any policy to remove the obstacles to productivity growth and to encourage the use of these new technologies will only accelerate the trend to produce more with less human labour and total effective demand will continue to stagnate (in fact, the total number of person-hours worked in Canadian manufacturing has barely risen in the last twenty years while output has increased by over 80 per cent). To quote Fred Block:

> As long as employers continue to have strong incentives to produce goods more cheaply, it seems highly unlikely that any program of 'reindustrialization' will increase manufacturing person hours. The choice of particular policies — protection of older industries versus support for high technology firms — is likely to influence only the rate at which manufacturing employment declines.[27]

As Lipietz suggests, one possibility is that any new mode of regulation that emerges from the present crisis must include either a new "functional form" — other than the wage as we now know it — for apportioning a share of the social product to the mass of the population, or a dramatic decrease in individual work time with no loss of real wages.[28] There are also other scenarios (only hinted at by Lipietz) which are extremely grim.

Chapter 5 by Holmes and chapter 6 by Gagnon and Montcalm emphasize the complexity and unevenness of the effects of restructuring on one Canadian industrial sector and one Canadian region respectively. Holmes' analysis of the post-1960 restructuring and reorganization of production in the automobile industry, one of Canada's most important manufacturing sectors, is set explicitly within the theoretical framework provided by Lipietz and the French regulation school. The development of the Canadian auto industry in the post-war period demonstrates both the nature and the limits of Fordism. The chapter also stresses the geographically uneven nature of the restructuring process by pointing out that although the Canadian auto industry has been part of an integrated North American automobile industry since the mid-1960s, it is misleading to assume that developments in the "Canadian" portion of the industry will simply mirror changes in the "U.S." industry. For example, the most recent phase of restructuring in the North American auto industry has produced sharply different effects (particularly in terms of employment and output levels) in the two countries and in the short term at least has left the auto industry in a stronger position in Canada than in the United States. Predictions of the imminent demise of the auto industry in Canada, common a few years ago, appear to have been premature, underscoring the difficulties involved in trying to decipher the changes under discussion here.[29]

Uneven geographical development is also a theme running through the chapter by Alain Gagnon and Mary Beth Montcalm, who examine some of the political consequences of the economic crisis within one region of North America: Quebec. The long-term implications of the crisis for North America are apt to be obscured by the effects of the crisis in aggravating longstanding social and political issues. In Canada this means, above all, the chronically vexed question of regionalism, most notably that of Quebec. Gagnon and Montcalm examine the contemporary realignment of class and political relations within Quebec in the context of the restructuring of both the North American and world economies. They note that the relative decline of the Quebec economy, based heavily on primary resource industries and older manufacturing sectors such as textiles, and Quebec's increasing economic "peripheralization", are not of recent origin. However, the effects of this decline were masked in the 1960s and 1970s by the rapid expansion of the state sector which also supported the rise of a new middle class. The new social stratum was an important element in the political alliance which first returned the nationalist Parti québécois (PQ) to power. However, in the face of deepening economic crisis, the PQ government was forced to reduce government borrowing and spending, which led to a widening gap between the interests of the new middle class and those of the party. Gagnon and Montcalm go on to explore other elements of the major realignment of the Quebec power structure which is occurring in the context of shifting class alliances, in turn a response to the global crisis and Quebec's peripheral position within the world economy. The eventual outcome was a split in the PQ, leading to the retirement of the party's charismatic founder and leader, René Levesque, in 1985, following a series of resignations from his cabinet over the party's gradual abandonment of the goal of independence for Quebec, its original raison d'être. Finally, in December 1985, the PQ was overwhelmingly defeated in an election by the provincial Liberal Party, led by the same Robert Bourassa whose uninspired machine politics had led nine years earlier to his party's crushing defeat by the PQ, and to his personal eclipse as leader. The political impact of the economic crisis in Canada could not have had a more dramatic expression than such a complete — if not necessarily final — setback to the dream of a "Québec libre".

Yet the shift in the balance of political forces resulting from the economic crisis was hardly less profound in the rest of Canada, and was even more profound in the United States, with immense consequences for the rest of the world, and especially for the United States' "backyard".

The political effects of the economic crisis, experienced in the form of sectoral or regional decline, falling business profits, and — for many people — stagnant or declining real incomes, led to mounting pressure from business organizations and from the middle class to reduce taxes by cutting state spending (or at least those forms of state spending which the exponents of "market doctrine" saw as creating "supply-side" obstacles to growth, that is, spending on income maintenance for the unemployed, single parents, the aged poor, and so on). A sustained campaign against Keynesian economic management, unionized labour, and welfare state spending gradually undermined the broad political consensus that had formerly sustained the parties most identified with the post-war settlement — the Democrats in the United States and the Liberals in Canada. As well as recapturing the presidency, for the first time in twenty-five years the Republicans also displaced the Democrats in the Senate in the watershed elections of 1980; and the Progressive Conservatives finally displaced the Liberals in the Canadian general election of 1984.

In the U.S. case, the country's growing economic weakness was mirrored in loss of international influence. Failure in Vietnam and the humiliation of the Teheran hostages incident led to growing popular support for Reagan's belligerent "new patriotism"; and the invasion of Grenada in 1983 was widely seen, and approved, in the United States as a reassertion of the country's proper international authority. The invasion also fitted into the framework of the President's "Caribbean Basin Initiative", announced early in 1982: a package of bilateral military and economic measures designed to link the Caribbean and Central America more closely to U.S. markets, and to foster economic growth based on the private sector; and to assert, in effect, a new doctrine of U.S. hegemony in the region. The initiative, significantly, excluded Cuba, Grenada, and Nicaragua — all of them represented as bridgeheads for Soviet expansion. The doctrine had the explicit aim of preventing any new left-wing regimes from coming to power in the region, and the implicit aim — less and less concealed as time went on — of overthrowing regimes that were unacceptable to the United States, and particularly the Sandinista regime in Nicaragua.

As Petras and Morley show in chapter 7, these policies were really less novel than they may have at first appeared; they were in line with traditional U.S. policies in the region, sustained regardless of the party in power in Washington. Nevertheless, the sharp accentuation of U.S. reliance on military means for the pursuit of its interests in the region since 1980 has been explicitly linked by the Reagan administration to the need to reassert U.S. authority following its decline in the two previous decades. On the other hand, as Petras and Morley also indicate, there is a tension between U.S. military and economic interests, with the economic generally subordinate to the military. There is a corresponding tension between U.S. military interests and Canadian economic interests in the region — or there was so long as the Liberals remained in office in Ottawa. Yet in spite of this tension Canadian interests have always been subordinate to those of the United States, in this as in other fields, because of Canada's economic and military dependence on the United States.

In this respect, Petras and Morley confirm other recent research that reports a significant change in Canada's self-definition as an actor in world affairs. The change started to take place before the end of the Liberal era in Ottawa, but has been considerably reinforced since. In the Liberals' last decade in power significant differences between Canada and the United States in foreign affairs became less frequent, and Canadian aid policy similarly became more and more explicitly subordinated to Canadian trade promotion.[30] By 1985, under the Progressive Conservative government of Brian Mulroney, and in the face of rising protectionist sentiments in the United States, free trade with its neighbour had become the main goal of Canadian foreign policy. The ultimate rationale of Canada's "new realism" in foreign policy, under the impact of the global crisis, was summed up by the Macdonald Commission on the Economic Union and Development Prospects for Canada, appointed by the Liberals in 1982 and reporting to the Conservatives in 1985:

> Our trade dependence on the American market, which has evolved, in spite of our efforts at diversification, over recent decades, has convinced the Commission that we must concentrate our efforts on obtaining secure access to the American market, on which continental economic forces have made us increasingly dependent. We cannot cut back significantly our trading integration with the United States without risking severe economic dislocation, cessation of economic growth, and a resultant political instability.[31]

Given this overriding goal, endorsed by the Mulroney government, it could not be expected that in the future, any more than in the past, Canadian interests in Central America or the Caribbean (where Canadian interests are extensive, and which has the highest level of Canadian aid per capita of any area of the Third World) would be allowed to give rise to significant differences with the United States.

Before 1984, while the Liberals under Trudeau were still in office, the incoming Reagan administration in Washington could not be sure of this; and the U.S. government conspicuously failed to consult Canada, the most important interested Commonwealth country, before it invaded Grenada — another Commonwealth country — in October 1983. Yet as Clive Thomas shows in chapter 8, while the opportunity to invade was welcomed by the Reagan administration, this was not the most significant aspect of the Grenada crisis. Its chief significance lay rather in the failure of the leadership of the Grenadian revolution, the New Jewel Movement, to keep faith with the democratic tradition that constitutes, ultimately, the Caribbean region's chief hope for a legitimate and successful project of independent development. The fact that the interests of the United States and Canada, as the two major neighbours and trading partners of the Caribbean countries, were increasingly fused, as the impact of the global crisis led Canada to adopt an increasingly close dependence on the United States, meant that anti-imperialist movements in the region confronted a de facto and increasingly de jure unity on the part of the external forces ranged against them. In the face of this alliance the unity of the popular forces pressing for an independent course of development in the region became all-important.

During the 1970s this unity was growing, as popular sentiment throughout the whole region moved more or less continuously leftwards. As the crisis of Fordism developed to the North, the markets for the commodities of Central America and the Caribbean contracted and the terms of trade for countries in the region declined. Those countries' debts escalated out of control and even that most ambivalent of trades, tourism, stagnated. In response, a region-wide movement for economic and political emancipation developed, based on political pluralism, but with a strong emphasis on regional cooperation and non-alignment. This movement had united a broad range of social forces and had further isolated and marginalized the groups and individuals most closely linked to foreign interests — local traders, real estate owners, small manufacturers, and the more colonially-minded state and transnational bureaucrats in the local capitals.

As the 1970s drew to a close the strength of the popular movement for change — and the weakness and vacillation of the forces opposed to change, both in the region and in the United States — were dramatically demonstrated in the success of the New Jewel Movement's coup in Grenada in March 1979, and the triumph of the popular uprising led by the Sandinista National Liberation Front (FSLN) in Nicaragua the following July. Further evidence of the shift was the sharp turn to the left of the People's National Party (PNP) government in Jamaica after 1974, and later, the dramatic advance of the popular struggle grouped under the Democratic Revolutionary Front (FDR) in El Salvador.[32]

In every case the issue of democracy was central. On the one hand, pro-imperialist social forces had been discredited — most obviously the corrupt and violent regimes of Gairy in Grenada and Somoza in Nicaragua; on the other, progressive leaderships had increasingly succeeded in uniting a wide range of working class, peasant, middle-class, and non-class forces (including church forces) into a broad movement for change. The question was whether these alliances could be sustained and developed so as to provide firm popular support for long-term strategies of economic development and social and political emancipation, in the face of increasingly unrestrained hostility from opposition elements with U.S. backing. In two of the three cases reviewed here — Grenada and Jamaica — this requirement was not met, with disastrous consequences for the region as a whole. In the case of Nicaragua, the requirement was met; the Sandinista leadership demonstrated the immense potential of a political strategy based on a genuine pluralism, and on unremitting efforts to involve ordinary people in their own development.

In Grenada, following independence in 1974, the regime of Eric Gairy presided over economic decline combined with gross corruption, which in the context of the world economic recession eventually created the conditions for the virtually bloodless coup by forty "combatants" of the New Jewel Movement in March 1979. With Cuban help the NJM regime immediately embarked on a program of radical economic development. By the end of 1982 it seemed to be achieving a large measure of success, with a wide range of popular participation and support. The regime came under increasing diplomatic and economic pressure from the Reagan administration after 1981 (signalled openly by Grenada's exclusion from the Caribbean Basin Initiative) and this undoubtedly contributed to its eventual collapse. (One of the issues dividing the NJM leadership was the level of concessions that should be offered to the United States to try to neutralize its opposition, though in fact the Reagan administration's opposition was ideological and non-negotiable.) But the final destruction of the Grenadian revolution was self-inflicted: the murder of Maurice Bishop and many of his closest colleagues in October 1983 cannot be explained by primarily external causes.

Why then did the NJM revolution, which had captured the imagination of so many people who dreamed of an alternative to the dependent and unpromising forms of development so far experienced in the Caribbean, "implode" (to use Thomas' apt word)? What are the likely long-term effects on the region as a whole? Thomas argues that the cause was a fatal insensitivity to the content and forms of pluralist democracy, which are so central to the region's hard-won political heritage. This was an insensitivity on the part not only of many NJM leaders and activists, but also of the region's left intelligentsia, and its consequences are even more profound than the new opening which the murder of Bishop gave for the reassertion of U.S. regional hegemony through military intervention, important though that is in itself.

The experience of Jamaica, the largest of the English-speaking Caribbean countries, is perhaps better known. Michael Manley's People's National Party government, elected in 1972, "turned to the left" in 1974 under the impact of the deepening world crisis and, in particular, in face of the opposition of the multinational companies that controlled the country's most important export, bauxite. After being re-elected in 1976 on the basis of its new radical program, however, the PNP government gradually succumbed to a mounting fiscal crisis, rapidly rising unemployment, and growing violence organized by the opposition. It was eventually heavily defeated by Edward Seaga's right-wing Jamaica Labour Party in the elections of October 1980, a result greeted with enthusiasm by the incoming Reagan administration in Washington.

Michael Kaufman's analysis of this experience is not primarily concerned with the economic problems confronting the PNP government, although these were severe enough even without the opposition of the United States (which increasingly assumed a "destabilizing" character, as Michael Manley and his colleagues in the PNP perceived it).[33] Instead, his chapter is concerned with the PNP's failure to transcend the parliamentary-statist model of politics with which the Manley government embarked on their increasingly radical course. New democratic initiatives were taken (most notably the effort to expand the role of community councils from 1976 onwards) but in general the PNP failed to grasp the need to mobilize ordinary people to undertake directly the transformation of their own lives as workers and citizens: to turn them, in Kaufman's words, "from being political consumers to being political producers". As a result the PNP government's mounting difficulties were not experienced and understood by the mass of its own supporters who became, instead, vulnerable bystanders in relation to the opposition's attacks on the government for failures they could not assess, and for which they felt no responsibility. The result was a sharp degeneration of Jamaican politics to new depths of violence and intimidation, and the restoration of a government more closely integrated than ever into the structure of U.S. regional hegemony.

The "market" orientation of Seaga's policies was conspicuously unsuccessful in producing the promised economic recovery, in spite of both the assistance offered by the Caribbean Basin Initiative and a major easing in the country's access to international loans, thanks to Washington's support in the International Monetary Fund (IMF) and the World Bank. The popularity of Seaga's JLP government steadily declined, especially following its attempt to "steal" a fresh term of office by calling a snap election based on an outdated electoral register immediately following the invasion of Grenada. The election, which the PNP boycotted, appeared to reduce rather than increase the government's legitimacy in the country. Yet the negative legacy of the 1970s in terms of popular mobilization for, and faith in, an independent strategy of development and change, had still to be overcome.

The contrast between the experiences of Grenada and Jamaica, on the one hand, and Nicaragua on the other, is sharp. While the ultimate outcome of the Nicaraguan struggle for survival in the face of the United States' economic blockade and overt, but undeclared, war, remained in the balance by the second half of the 1980s, one thing was clear: the Sandinista leadership had earned, and had set itself to retain, the support of a substantial majority of the people in whose name it was carrying on the struggle, and above all the nation's youth, who had borne the brunt of the liberation struggle itself.

From 1983 onwards the United States' campaign of blockade and destabilization put this country of two-and-a-half million inhabitants under an increasingly intolerable strain. Somoza's Nicaragua was already backward (in Central America only Honduras was poorer); it had suffered appalling losses in the war of liberation, culminating in the plunder by the Somoza family and its associates of half a billion dollars' worth of national assets (including the whole of an IMF loan granted just days before Somoza's fall); it was starved of aid by the World Bank and the Inter-American Bank, acting under U.S. pressure, and subjected to a complete U.S. trade embargo from 1985 onwards; finally, it was subjected to an increasingly ruthless terrorist war, waged by forces paid for and trained by the CIA and led by the former officers of Somoza's National Guard. It was a war that claimed thousands of civilian casualties, severely curtailed agricultural production, and forced the regime to devote more than 50 per cent of its exiguous revenues to national defence.[34]

Yet by 1986 the Reagan administration had to face the unpalatable truth that the Sandinista regime could not be brought down by even this ferocious combination of pressures, simply because its popular base, even if war-weary and frustrated, had become if anything even more implacably determined to defend the revolution. The Sandinista government distributed weapons — by 1986 the official figure was 300,000 small arms — to the population. As Tomas Borge, the Minister of the Interior, pointed out, the FLSN regime was unique among Latin America governments in being able to do this.

Fred Judson's account in chapter 10, while carefully reviewing the severity of the pressures on the Sandinista regime, focusses primarily on the various ways in which it has kept faith with its democratic principles: single-mindedly pursuing the goal of pluralism and popular alliances, of collaboration with the progressive wing of the Catholic Church, and of open elections; and also with its commitment to a mixed economy (with a definite, though not politically dominant, role for private enterprise) and to an ideologically broad range of international ties. The Nicaraguan revolution is no doubt not the popular movement's last word in the struggle for liberation in the Americas but its significance is nonetheless profound. It suggests not only that there are limits to the willingness of ordinary people to pay the price that capitalist restructuring demands, but also that there are alternatives. It suggests too that a mobilized people is capable of developing the organizational and moral resources to realize those alternatives.

Notes

1 Like the term "de-industrialization" the term "restructuring" has become a "taken-for-granted" term which is rarely defined. In economics and business the term was traditionally used to refer to the financial reorganization of capital aimed at restoring the profitability of a particular enterprise, and normally achieved through recapitalization, merger, or takeover. Recently the term has been applied to the large-scale shifts which are occurring within the world economy. The notion that restructuring occurs in an effort to restore profitability remains central. In this chapter the expression "industrial restructuring and reorganization" refers to strategies and methods used in an attempt to restore profitable accumulation. These strategies include, but are not confined to, the methods for financial restructuring noted above, changes in product technology, state initiatives designed to encourage and facilitate the restructuring of individual firms or wider sectors of production, and changes in the technical and social organization of production.

2 P. Armstrong, A. Glyn, and J. Harrison, *Capitalism Since World War II* (London: Fontana, 1984); S. Bowles, D.M. Gordon, and T. Weisskopf, *Beyond the Waste Land* (New York: Doubleday, 1983); B. Harrison and B. Bluestone, *The Deindustrialization of America* (New York: Basic Books, 1982); and I.C. Magaziner and R.B. Reich, *Minding America's Business: The Decline and Rise of the American Economy* (New York: Harcourt Brace Jovanovich, 1983).

3 E. Mandel, *Long Waves of Capitalist Development* (Cambridge: Cambridge University Press, 1980).

4 M. Aglietta, *A Theory of Capitalist Regulation: The U.S. Experience* (London: New Left Books, 1979); and A. Lipietz, "Towards Global Fordism?" *New Left Review*, 132 (1982), 133-47.

5 D.M. Gordon, R.C. Edwards, and M. Reich, *Segmented Work, Divided Workers: The Historical Transformation of Labour in the U.S.* (Cambridge: Cambridge University Press, 1982).

6 A useful overview and summary of analyses of the contemporary crisis by members of the French regulation school is contained in a recent article by De Vroey; see M. De Vroey, "A Regulation Approach Interpretation of the Contemporary Crisis," *Capital and Class*, 23 (1984), 44-66. In a brief but illuminating preface to the recently translated English edition of his *The Enchanted World*, Lipietz traces the intellectual origins and development of the regulation school, stressing the diversity of theoretical and conceptual viewpoints that exist among its members: see A. Lipietz, *The Enchanted World: Inflation, Credit and the World Crisis* (London: Verso, 1985). In this book, we associate the French regulation school primarily with the work of Aglietta and Lipietz. Also referred to here is A. Lipietz, "Towards Global Fordism? *New Left Review*, 132 (1982), 133-47; and A. Lipietz, "De la Nouvelle Division du Travail à la Crise du Fordisme Periphérique," *Espaces et Sociétés*, 44 (1984), 51-78.

7 A. Lipietz, *The Enchanted World*, xvi.

8 *Ibid.*

9 Mandel, *Long Waves*.

10 B. Palmer, *Working-Class Experience: The Rise and Reconstitution of Canadian Labour, 1800-1980* (Toronto: Butterworths, 1984), 280.

11 J. Gouverneur, *Contemporary Capitalism and Marxist Economics* (Oxford: Martin Robertson, 1983), 203.

12 C.F. Sabel, *Work and Politics: The Division of Labor in Industry* (Cambridge: Cambridge University Press, 1982); and M.J. Piore and C.F. Sabel, *The Second Industrial Divide: Possibilities for Prosperity* (New York: Basic Books, 1984).

13 In the Canadian manufacturing sector as a whole the average annual rate of growth in output per person-hour worked in the period 1961-62 to 1972-73 was 4.7 per cent. This rate fell to 1.2 per cent for the period 1973-74 to 1981-82. See the chapter by Holmes in this volume for a fuller discussion of changes in post-war labour productivity in Canada, and L.J. Fulco, "Strong Post-Recession Growth in Productivity Contributes to Slow Growth in Labor Costs," *Monthly Labor Review* (December 1984), 3-10 for comparable data on the United States.

14 U. Zohar, *Canadian Manufacturing: A Study in Productivity and Technological Change* (Toronto: James Lorimer, 1982), 31.

15 F. Blackaby, ed., *Deindustrialization* (London: NIESR and Heinemann, 1979), 263.

16 A. Singh, "U.K. Industry and the World Economy: A Case of De-industrialisation?" *Cambridge Journal of Economics*, 1 (1977), 128.

17 The Economic Council of Canada uses this kind of definition to dismiss claims that Canada is de-industrializing and to further promote its ideological pursuit of free trade. They use normalized trade balance figures to argue that in relative terms Canadian fully manufactured end products have held their own, in the sense that the deficit as a proportion of total trade in fully manufactured end products has remained relatively constant. Furthermore, they argue that what has happened is that under a regime of declining trade barriers import penetration has increased in some spheres and export success has been experienced in others, producing greater specialization but not necessarily any new loss. Thus, the Economic Council is able to conclude that "...in sum, the manufacturing sector has not withered, and is not withering in the face of increased competition...the upshot of this is that Canada is a far cry from deindustrialization. In our considered judgment there is no evidence of this process even beginning." Economic Council of Canada, *The Bottom Line* (Ottawa: Economic Council, 1984), 104. Note that this conclusion, while denying that Canada is experiencing de-industrialization does not preclude (and in fact strongly implies) that Canadian manufacturing nevertheless has been, and is, experiencing a period of significant industrial reorganization and restructuring.

18 C.J.F. Brown and T.D. Sheriff, "De-Industrialization: A Background Paper," in Blackaby, *Deindustrialization*.

19 Canada, Department of Finance, *Economic Review*, (Ottawa: Ministry of Supply and Services, 1983), 33.

20 B.J.L. Berry and S. Elster, "What Lies Ahead for Urban America?" Paper presented at The Metropolis: A Conference in Honour of Hans Blumenfeld, University of Toronto, November 1983, (unpublished paper), 6.

21 Statistics Canada *Daily*, March 25, 1985.

22 How "peculiar" is the Canadian social formation in this respect? There is a good case to be made that Canada's economic development and structure bear a number of striking similarities to those of Australia, New Zealand, and (possibly, at least until the late inter-war years) Argentina and Uruguay: that small group of social formations labelled the "dominion capitalist social formations" by P. Ehrensaft and W. Armstrong, "Le Capitalisme de Dominion: le Canada, L'Australie, la Nouvelle-Zélande, l'Argentine et Uruguay," *Les Cahiers du Socialisme*, 3 (1970), 162-217. One of the more sensitive and insightful analyses of Canada's position

within the new international division of labour is provided by D. Ethier, "L'Économie political canadienne et la nouvelle division internationale du travail," in D. Cameron and F. Houle, eds., *Canada and the New International Division of Labour* (Ottawa: University of Ottawa Press, 1985), who also draws upon the ideas of the regulation school.

23 G. Williams, *Not for Export: Toward a Political Economy of Canada's Arrested Industrialization* (Toronto: McClelland and Stewart, 1983).

24 *Ibid.*, 15.

25 R. Jenkins, "Divisions Over the International Division of Labour," *Capital and Class*, 22 (1984), 28-58.

26 The technical and social restructuring of the labour process that is currently underway really is radical and goes far beyond the changes which a number of French political economists began to write about in the late 1970s under the rubric of "neo-Fordist methods of production": C. Palloix, "The Labour Process from Fordism to Neo-Fordism," in *The Labour Process and Class Strategies* (London: Stage 1, 1978), 46-65; and B. Coriot, "The Restructuring of the Assembly Line: A New Economy of Time and Control," *Capital and Class*, 11 (1980), 34-43. See J. Holmes, "The Impact of Technical Change on the Organization and Locational Structure of Automobile Production in Canada," in K. Chapman and G. Humphreys, eds., *Technical Change, Employment and Regional Policy* (Oxford: Basil Blackwell, 1987), for a discussion of the impacts of recent technical change on the labour process in the auto industry.

27 F. Block, "The Myth of Reindustrialization", *Socialist Review*, 14, 1, 59-76, esp. 69.

28 It is interesting to note that two recent major labour disputes in the auto industry — the 1984 strikes by I.G. Metall against the carmakers in West Germany and by the UAW against GM in Canada — centred on demands from the workers for reduced working time with no loss of real income. The problem associated with the introduction of new technology under capitalist social relations of production, which almost inevitably leads workers to adopt a defensive and seemingly reactionary stance in defence of their own immediate personal economic interests, is aptly summed up in the following quotation from the *Economist*, "...easy transition to the higher incomes and more leisure that new technology offers is hampered in two ways. First, workers are not capitalists, if they were part owners of the companies they worked for, they would welcome new inventions that displaced jobs; progress would mean less work without loss of income. While workers depend entirely on wages it is in their interests to resist": quoted in *The Globe and Mail*, Toronto, April 6, 1984. Put more succinctly, and to quote one of my grandfather's favourite slogans: "Technical change under capitalism means unemployment; under socialism more spare time!"

29 R. Perry, *The Future of Canada's Auto Industry* (Toronto: James Lorimer, 1982); and M. Van Ameringen, "The Restructuring of the Canadian Automobile Industry," in Cameron and Houle, *Canada and the New International Division of Labour*, 267-87.

30 R.C. Pratt, "Canadian Policy Towards the Third World: Basis for an Explanation," *Studies in Political Economy*, 13 (1984), 27-55; and L. Freeman, "The Effect of the World Crisis in Canada: Involvement in Africa," *Studies in Political Economy*, 17 (1985), 107-39.

31 D. Macdonald, *Report of the Royal Commission on the Economic Union and Development Prospects for Canada* (Ottawa: Ministry of Supply and Services, 1985), 71.

32 F. Ambursley and R. Cohen, *Crisis in the Caribbean* (London: Heinemann Educational Books, 1983).

33 M. Manley, *Jamaica: Struggle in the Periphery* (London: Third World Media, 1982).

34 T. Hayter and C. Watson, *Aid: Rhetoric and Reality* (London: Pluto Press, 1985), 51-52.

Chapter 2

The Globalization of the General Crisis of Fordism, 1967-84

Alain Lipietz

In 1976, the Parisian publisher Dunod published two collections of economic articles, one "neo-classical", the other "Marxist" or "radical". They were respectively titled *Fluctuation in a Prosperous Economy* and *Rupture of an Economic System*, and history, unfortunately, has vindicated the latter. No one any longer contests the duration and the depth of the crisis, and in spite of the spectacular but fragile U.S. upturn, very few observers today would risk announcing that the end of the tunnel is in sight.

Yet the crisis officially begun by the first "oil shock" in 1974 (although the warning signals could, in retrospect, be seen in the ten previous years) is quite different from the 1930s depression. Since in many Organization for Economic Cooperation and Development (OECD) countries the average rate of growth remains high, some analysts have argued that the post-1974 crisis amounts to nothing more than a succession of more or less contingent shocks in a progressive evolution which, when all is said and done, has been mastered. To make this argument, however, is to ignore the intolerable poverty accumulating at the end of the chain in the Third World, and the pockets of poverty in the most prosperous metropoles. It is to ignore the immensity of the mutations that are occurring. Above all, it is to ignore the increasing spread of feelings of uncertainty about the future, in contrast to the straightforward expectations which accompanied the mode of development of the glorious post-war years. "The old is dying; the new has not yet been able to be born": in economics too, Gramsci's formulation aptly grasps the essence of the crisis.

This essay seeks to sketch broadly the painful process of gestation which is occurring, using as a starting point some recent studies sometimes designated the "French school of regulation." These recent works are imperfect in nature; if they have in my view succeeded in advancing considerably the analysis of the roots of the crisis as it manifests itself *country by country* (especially in the United States and in France),[1] the methodology which they propose suffers from lacunae as far as the international, or global, dimensions of its application is concerned, and for deep-seated reasons, as will be shown. Some recent extensions of this theoretical orientation[2] nonetheless offer a sketch of such developments, which will be presented in the following text.

In the first section, the elements of the problematic will be reviewed in terms of "regime of accumulation" and "mode of regulation". This will serve to establish our point of departure: the Fordist model of development, with its international aspects. In the second section, the system's entry into crisis from 1967 to 1974 will be analyzed. The third section will present a transitional regime which schematically links the two oil shocks, a regime characterized by "Keynesian management" of the crisis in the developed countries, and the take-off of "peripheral Fordism". The fourth section will measure the damage done by the "monetarist shock". A fifth and concluding section will underline the scale of the problems remaining to be resolved before one can speak of "emerging from the crisis".

A Well-Regulated Regime of Accumulation: Fordism

To understand the crisis — to understand that it cannot be reduced to some shocks caused by the carelessness of rulers (monetary laxity) or the sudden greed of some of the groups sharing the total world product (the trade unions of the centre countries or the rentiers of OPEC) — is to understand how "the old which is dying" used to work in the glory of its maturity, in the epoch which President Johnson called "the U.S. summer". We must still understand what had to be made to work.

The Contradictions of Capitalist Accumulation

The capitalist mode of production is a combination of two fundamental relations: the market relation and the wage relation.

- *Market relation* The owners of means of production offer on the market the products of the labour processes which they have initiated. The products of these labours, independent from each other, thus appear as value which must be socially validated by exchange for cash; this is "realization", or sale.

- *Wage relation* The owners of these means of production buy the labour power of wage-workers, in exchange for a sum of cash which represents a value less than that which they produce; the difference is surplus value.

Individually, the capitalist, the owner of a sum of money, exchanges it for means of production, in particular fixed capital (that is, investment) and labour power. The capitalist organizes the process of production, sells the merchandise, and *reaccumulates* capital and surplus value. The initial value which the capitalist possesses is thus *value in process*, which grows over time *if it has been put to use correctly and valorized*. Symmetrically, the wage-worker spends the wage earned, and thereby reconstitutes his or her labour power for the following cycle: on the one hand the wage relation, and on the other, the market division of labour, are thus reproduced.

Subject to certain limits the rate of profit (the surplus value accruing to capital) is positively related to the rate of surplus value (the relation of surplus value to value added), and negatively to the "composition of capital" (the relation of value added to capital employed). These two factors themselves depend on norms of production (which define productivity and the coefficient of fixed capital per capita) and norms of consumption of the wage-workers.

Socially, the reproduction of the whole presents itself as follows: "values-in-process-capitals" march alongside each other, exchanging goods with each other, or exchanging goods for those very special values-in-process which are wage revenues. How is it possible that this interlacing of autonomous processes weaves a coherent social product, where all the private employments of labour (by means of the expenditure of capital) are affirmed as valid? As in every social relation, the acquired experience of the possibility of a solution is in itself one of the bases of the solution. The capitalist, by virtue of acquisitions (previous revenues) and a knowledge of the market (tested in the previous periods) bets that it is all right to review the wage relation, to buy more constant capital, and by this very fact already contributes to the validation of the products of colleagues and of the labour power offered by the wage-earning class. The conditions inherited from the past and the expectation of a continuing future are the conditions of the present social bond. The continuity of accumulation, the habits acquired regarding an allocation which is equilibrated between the different branches of the division of labour, and the expectations with regard to the social orientations of the transformations of the norms of production and consumption, all combine to dominate the private bets of entrepreneurs (and their bankers) like an immanent force, laying the foundations of a "social mould," which is called in this context a *regime of accumulation*.

The regime of accumulation is a systematic mode of dividing and reallocating the social product. Over a long period a certain match is achieved between the transformation of the conditions of production (volume of capital employed, distribution between branches, and norms of production) and transformations in the conditions of final consumption (norms of consumption of the wage-workers and the other social classes, and collective expenditures).

Once accumulation expands, the growth of output of production goods and consumption goods must match the growth of capital commitments and the growth of purchasing power of wage-earners. It is thus convenient to summarize the coherence of a regime of accumulation by means of a reproduction scheme describing from period to period the allocation of capital (and through it, labour) between the two fundamental departments of the production of use values defined solely by their social function (Department 1: production goods which reproduce the monopoly of capitalist property; and Department 2: consumption goods which reproduce the free workers' subsistence). The reproduction scheme forms a kind of skeleton for the different regimes of accumulation, an outline of its formal coherence.

Within this conceptualization, there appear several typical regimes of accumulation: among these can be distinguished extensive accumulation (simple homothetic growth of the two departments validating each other), intensive accumulation without mass production (where the expansion of constant capital alone validates the growth of Department 1), and intensive accumulation with growing mass consumption. This stylized representation, however, calls for some refinements before its application to an analysis of a concrete regime of accumulation.

Every concrete regime of accumulation is in effect surrounded by an "exterior", in two senses of the word. First, all the production in any national community is not governed by capitalist relations. To begin with the reproduction of labour power, it may be observed that the patriarchal social relation, or domestic mode of production, or sexism, assures its reproduction, using the "means of reproduction" which its wages purchase.

Another dimension appears when the economic relations between communities organized by capitalism are taken into account. Historically, the first practices that can be identified as forming "capitalist relations" commonly crossed the frontiers of feudal or tributary states. But the modern nation-state, conceived of as a community of individuals linked by a social contract, developed with the generalization of market practices. It was in this framework that the wage relation was codified and institutionalized, in the shadow of the sovereignty of the state, cemented by the history of civil and foreign wars. It was at the level of the nation-state that the social contradictions were regulated, and, therefore, at this level that the coherence of true regimes of accumulation was gradually affirmed, the unification of states and the "densification" of regimes of accumulation mutually supporting each other.

The "creation of the internal market" by the development of capitalist relations never led to the disappearance of international exchanges: according to the evolution of the regimes of accumulation they were restricted or extended in importance. So it is useful for an analysis of a national regime of accumulation to isolate an "export department"[3] whose revenues support the financing of the purchase abroad of "Department 1" or "Department 2" use values. From a certain angle one can even speak of "world regimes of accumulation".

These, then, are the bases of the "social mould". It remains true that regimes of accumulation do not materialize by themselves. The problem is to know what coercive forces and what institutional forms will assure the coherence of the strategies and expectations of the agents of the capitalist market economy, making them converge towards the realization of the schema of reproduction.

The problem of regulation thus emerges. A *mode of regulation* can be defined as the ensemble of institutional forms, networks, and explicit or implicit norms, which assure the compatibility of behaviours in the framework of a regime of accumulation, in conformity with the state of the social relations, and thereby with the contradictions and the conflictual character of the relations between agents and social groups.

In the capitalist mode of production, the forms of regulation must at the very least deal with:

- the regulation of the wage relation (fixing the norms of working hours, of the intensity of work, of the value of labour power, the norm of consumption for wage earners, the reproduction of the hierarchy of qualifications and of the segmentation of the labour market, the division between direct and indirect wages, etc.).
- the regulation of the reallocation of money-capital set free by the validation of goods in this or that branch and according to this or that degree of intensification of the composition of capital.
- the reproduction of the management of currency, its issue, its circulation, its forms of productive employment, etc.
- the forms of state intervention, from the juridical to the economic.

It is considered to be of great heuristic utility to polarize two modes of regulation characterized by contrasting institutional forms, according to whether the hazardous social validation of the goods and labour power offered was simply established *ex-post*, or whether the high probability of its realization was integrated *ex-ante* in the behaviour of agents. In the first case, the values-in-process make the "dangerous leap" of the metamorphosis into money one by one, or they are eliminated. In the second case, on the contrary, the values-in-process integrate their own growth with the transformation of the social norms of production and exchange in order to steer their own metamorphoses. At one extreme, labour power will be sold on a daily basis, at a price depending on market pressures, or it will be unable to reproduce itself. At the other extreme, not only will it be guaranteed a minimum income, but it will lease itself to a particular entrepreneur on a multi-year contract, integrating the changes anticipated in the economic environment.

It is impossible to retrace here, even briefly, the complex history of capitalist development models characterized by a regime of accumulation, itself rooted in a dominant form of organization of the immediate process of production,[4] and a mode of regulation. Let us come directly to the point of departure of our more limited canvas: the Fordist model, as it was consolidated in the developed capitalist countries at the end of World War II.

The Fordist Model in its Golden Age

In the 1920s, a revolutionary mode of organization of work was generalized in the United States, and partially in Europe: Taylorism. It consisted in expropriating, by a gigantic and capillary deepening of the capitalist control of the labour process, the collective know-how of the workers, a know-how henceforth systematized by engineers and technicians according to the methods of the "Scientific Management of Work". A further step was the incorporation of this know-how into the automatic systems of machines, which then dictated the method of work to the workers, who had thus been robbed of initiative: this was the productive watershed of Fordism.[5]

In the inter-war years, the development of Taylorism and embryonic Fordism provoked the first big wave of intensive accumulation. Productivity grew at the rate of 6 per cent per year (three times the average rate of the nineteenth century), but the growth of purchasing power remained mediocre. This scissors effect, very favourable to the rate of profit via a raising of the rate of exploitation which was in no way offset by the growth of the composition of capital, which remained modest, provoked an unprecedented crisis of overproduction: the crisis of the 1930s. It was more than a question of the "low point" of the cycle. Competitive regulation was no longer adequate to intensive accumulation. This big crisis of the 1930s can therefore be characterized as both the first crisis of intensive accumulation and the last crisis of competitive regulation.

After the reconstruction of Europe (by its nature, mainly extensive) and the Korean War, the OECD countries underwent a new intensive expansion, which lasted this time for twenty years. During this expansion, productivity increased again considerably, as did fixed capital per head, but this time the increase in the purchasing power of wage-earners (productive and unproductive) parallelled almost exactly the rise in productivity. As this rise in productivity affected the two departments more or less equally, the organic composition of capital remained roughly unaltered, as did the rate of exploitation.

These results, although they must be qualified, allow the broad outlines of the "Golden Age" to emerge. In this "Golden Age" model:

- The rates of growth of the global technical composition of capital (that is, approximately, of fixed capital per capita) and of the productivity of Department 1 are the same. This "counter-tendency" to the rise of the technical composition of capital inhibits the tendency of the value composition of capital to increase.
- The rates of growth of consumption of wage-earners, and of the productivity of Department 2, are the same. The "counter-tendency" of the rate of profit to fall, which the rise in the rate of exploitation would have constituted, was certainly inhibited, but by the same fact so was the tendency towards a crisis of under-consumption. Since the organic composition of capital did not vary, the general rate of profit remained stable, and accumulation could therefore follow a regular rhythm.

These two conditions held, approximately, in the developed countries up to the middle of the 1960s. Nothing assured a priori that this would be so.

The first condition was verified in near-miraculous fashion,[6] and in fact statistical data show that it was decreasingly verified during the 1960s in the main industrialized countries. On the other hand, the second condition was assured more or less explicitly by a policy of regulation of the wage relation: mass production was accompanied by mass consumption, thus realizing the full development of Fordism. This partial regulation was one among a set of institutional forms which constitutes a variant of monopolistic regulation.

Schematically, the mode of regulation which was consolidated after 1945 combined the following institutional forms.

A collective "contractualization" of the direct wage. The worker did not need to negotiate day by day, individually, the sale of his or her labour power. Collective agreements covered the majority of the wage-earners, so that the employers could agree among themselves (and incidentally with the trade unions) on the wage increases which would be imposed on all, at the level of a region or a country. To complete this obligation of "sharing the fruits of growth" a "guaranteed minimum wage" was established.

The welfare state: social security plus a system of unemployment insurance. It insured every wage-earner, and then nearly all of the population, a guaranteed income immune to the risks of everyday life.

The growth of the tertiary sector. This stabilization of the wage relation was accompanied by its generalization to most activities, including those of management, of trade and finance regulation, and of control.[7]

Important modifications in the relations between banks and industrial firms. These modifications allowed firms to redirect their production from division to division, while maintaining their prices in the declining divisions.

A very important modification of the role of the state. The most important changes concerned the management of the wage relation (the management of the welfare state and of the direct wage relation), and the management of currency. Its nature was modified by a series of institutional innovations. Henceforth, the private banks freely put currency into circulation by opening lines of credit to firms and households. This "credit currency", anticipating the validity of values-in-process, and liquidated on reimbursement, is wagered on the bet that the borrowers will effectively be able to pay. The central bank, dependent on the state, conserves by a battery of mechanisms the ability to exert pressure on this freedom to create currency. It can thus facilitate credit, to stimulate business or to limit it. The last resource open to the interventionist state rests on the control of its own expenditures and of its own receipts: when business slackens, it can cut taxes and increase spending, relying on the ensuing growth to cover its deficit. Such are the instruments of "Keynesian policy".

It is the functioning of this mode of regulation, superimposed on the generalization of Fordism in the labour process, which has permitted the a priori acceptance of the two rules of the "scheme of the Golden Age" of intensive accumulation. The different countries of the OECD were thus able to experience, during a fifteen-year period, an exceptionally strong, lengthy, and regular growth. Of course, there were some downturns (the "recessions"). There were also great differences between national rates of growth, but each country experimented with and developed Fordism for its own purposes, by increasing its internal demand. The country initially most advanced, the United States, of course experienced a slower growth (but of the order of 4 per cent per year) than the countries coming more recently to Fordism. Only Great Britain, because of the strength of its craft unions and the disinterest of its financial bourgeoisie, deviated notably from the Fordist model of production, and experienced a more mediocre growth.

The Implicit Hegemony of the United States

As we have seen, the Fordist model of growth awards only secondary importance to international trade. Its engine is the internal transformation of the industrial production processes; its target is the growth of the internal market by the increase of purchasing power. "External markets" in dominated countries, the traditional form of regulation of competitive capitalism, therefore lose much of their importance.[8] In fact, the ratio of exports to the internal market in manufactured goods reached its lowest historical point towards 1965. Furthermore, internal trade developed mainly within continental blocs and within the OECD: Europe and North America (see table 1).

Tendentially, the South was limited to a role as the provider of labour and raw materials. The control of these resources was the essential task of the political and military hegemony of the United States. Of course, certain countries in Latin America and Asia attempted to latch on to the Fordist model on their own account, behind strong tariff barriers: it was the "first policy of

Table 1

Exports of Manufactured Products

(In percentages)

	1899	1913	1929	1937	1950	1959
Exported portion of manufactured products: France	33	26	25	12	23	18
Germany (1937 boundaries)	31	31	27	15	–	–
West Germany	–	–	–	17	13	23
United Kingdom	42	45	37	21	23	19
United States	5	5	6	5	5	4
Japan	25	40	29	40	29	23

Source: J. Mistral, Compétitivité et formation du capital en longue période, *Économie et Statistiques*, 97 (1977).

import substitution". This policy failed, because of its inability to attain the rate of productivity growth of the developed countries, for complex but mainly internal reasons.[9]

International economic relations are thus mainly "North-North" relations.[10] Is it possible to consider them as a regime of accumulation, as a world mode of regulation? In fact, these relations consist essentially of a vast "catching-up" movement by Europe and Japan in relation to the United States, starting from a strongly differentiated situation. This "differentiation/catching-up" constitutes itself as a regime of accumulation and a form of regulation, the basis for what Arrighi has called "the implicit hegemony of the United States".[11] Victor of World War II, with a considerable lead in industrial productivity, producing by itself 63 per cent of the gross domestic products of the five main countries (the United States, the United Kingdom, West Germany, France, and Japan) and 57 per cent of the manufactured value added in 1950, the U.S. imposed its model of development, culturally at first, then financially (with the Marshall and MacArthur plans), and finally institutionally (Bretton-Woods agreements, the creation of the General Agreement on Tariffs and Trade [GATT], the International Monetary Fund [IMF], and the OECD).

In these conditions, no form of international regulation of wage relations was necessary. In different concrete forms, the same principles ("contractualization", welfare state, growth of purchasing power) were adopted everywhere. The dollar became the international currency. This currency was in fact based on the indisputable validity of the United States' values-in-process: the productivity differential was such that U.S. capital goods, which incorporated the best norms of production, would always find buyers in Europe or Japan. The U.S. trade balance was thus systematically in surplus. The problem was rather that of Japanese and European capacity to buy capital goods from the U.S. This problem was first resolved by U.S. state loans, then more and more by the foreign investment of U.S. firms: the U.S. balance of payments was therefore structurally in deficit. These deficits constituted the basis of an international currency in xeno-dollars, a basis theoretically guaranteed by the U.S. gold reserves, but in fact, once again, by the undisputed validity of U.S. capitalist production. This became clear when, once this validity became more problematic, the United States refused to exchange the dollar balances held by foreign residents for gold.

This is not, therefore, a regime of accumulation, strictly speaking, but a world configuration which provisionally realizes the compatibility of a juxtaposition of similar accumulation regimes, differentiated by individual rates of growth and modes of international insertion. Schematically, the United States equips Europe (or Japan) in exchange for a claim on European labour power, the purchase of this labour power (by the multinational firms) in turn giving rights to U.S. capital goods, the purchase of which, linked to the accelerated generalization of Fordism, permits Europe[12] and Japan to catch up. This catching up does not occur in the "import substitution" countries of the South, because they lack sufficient social reforms.

The world economy could never surpass this level of implicit organization. There could never be institutional forms regulating world demand; and there will never be any supra-national sovereign authority regulating the money supply. The complementarities and antagonisms of the national economies would always remain *configurations* of relationships, partial and unstable, and it is only as a figure of speech that it is possible to talk about any "world regime of accumulation."[13]

From Slow Erosion to Manifest Crisis, 1967-74

If the crisis is characterized by the general slowing of the growth of manufactured production, causing a general and continuous rise in unemployment, and by the loss of regular growth, then its symptoms can be discerned as early as the recession of 1967 (see graph 1). Not only is the curve linking the high points of the world short cycles inflected slightly starting at this date, but, above all, the curve linking the low points, until then quite close and parallel (at a rate of 6.6 per cent per year) diverges significantly from it. It decreases to 4.8 per cent between 1967 and 1971 and to 2.5 per cent between 1971 and 1975.

The search for more fundamental indicators leads first, taking into account the dynamics of Fordism, to the study of manufacturing productivity. It is here, of course, that the root of the crisis of Fordism rests, a crisis which becomes generalized during the period under study. This section will examine first this general crisis, with respect to the factors all the national regimes of accumulation have in common. Then the interactions of these regimes will be considered, demonstrating their amplifying role.

The Roots of the General Crisis of Fordism

In the development of the present crisis, three different sets of phenomena and linkages must be distinguished.

(1) those that proceed from the general crisis of Fordism, and which are found in some degree in all countries that have adopted this mode of development;
(2) the amplifying linkages due to the interconnection of different socio-economic formations;
(3) the specific phenomena of each of the relevant social formations.

Graph 1
Growth in Manufacturing Production in the Market Economies 1958-80 (1970 = 100)

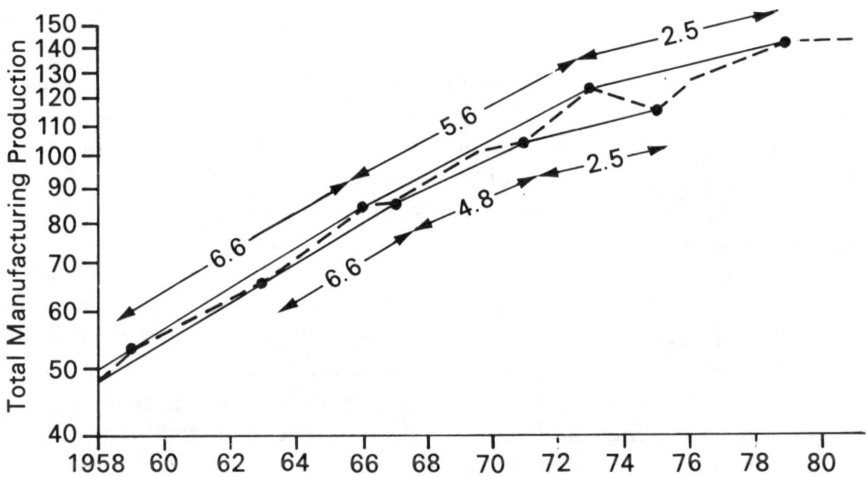

Source: CEPII, (1983)

National specificities will not be referred to here, although their study is currently one of the more fertile areas of inquiry inspired by the school of regulation.[14] The distinction between the first two types of linkages must, however, be quite clear, and its political implications are evident. If we limit ourselves to a consideration of the second set of linkages, the crisis appears to be the national monopolist regulation coming into contradiction with the internationalization of production: a way out of the crisis by a concerted expansion can be envisaged. If we consider the first type of linkage, the crisis strikes, moreover, the roots of the regime of intensive accumulation grounded on the Taylorist principles of organization of labour and on the Fordist development of mass consumption. An attempt to synthesize the two types of linkages is presented next.

The clearest symptom of the crisis of the regime of accumulation is the general slowing down of productivity gains, which occurred at the end of the 1960s, and first affected the most typically Fordist branches, such as automobile production.[15] But how does this slowing down produce a crisis?

A first approach consists of underlining the contradiction between the slowing down and the maintenance of the rise in purchasing power. The crisis would then be the result of a "profit squeeze" caused by the rise of the wage cost per unit produced. However, statistical data do not seem to confirm this diagnosis for all the industrialized countries at the start of the 1970s (with the transitory exception of Germany and Japan). More exactly, the increase of purchasing power does not manifest an autonomous acceleration, and in the rare case where it outpaces productivity gains, it is because these have slowed down (see table 2). Furthermore, if this was the origin of the crisis, a simple slowing down of direct or indirect wage increases would have been sufficient to check it.

A more convincing explanation is provided by taking into account the other component of the profitability of capital. These decreasing productivity gains required as early as the middle 1960s an increase in the value of capital per head, or, in Marxist terms, of the organic composition of capital.[16]

Table 3 indicates that productivity gains no longer compensated for the higher technical composition of capital, the volume of fixed capital per head. The "mark-up" procedures characteristic of monopolistic regulation initially compensated for this "instantaneous" decrease in the profitability of capital through a nominal rise in profits, but this led to a general increase in prices and wages, and then in the share of depreciation in the gross margin of reinvestment. This led to a tendency of greater firm indebtedness, and an increase of financial costs which, added to the rise in depreciation and in the relative price of investments, led to a latent crisis of investment capability in an inflationary environment.[17] Hence the slowing down of investment, combined with the decline in the employment generated by each new investment, led to the rise of unemployment, and also to a rise in the costs of the welfare state.

Whether one stresses the profit squeeze or the increase in the organic composition of capital, the present crisis of intensive accumulation appears as a crisis of profitability, in contrast to the crisis of 1930, which was clearly one of overproduction. The institutional forms of monopolistic regulation in fact limit the "depression spiral": the increase in the indirect wage stops the decrease in global purchasing power (in spite of the growth of unemployment), the strength of credit currency permits the survival of values-in-process (and so of firms) which would have been reduced to bankruptcy in the context of a

Table 2

Growth of Real Wages and Productivity

(mean annual growth rate)

		(1950 -1955)	(1955 -1960)	(1960 -1970)			(1970 -1974)
Great Britain	(s/p)	3,0	2,3	3,1			1,2
	Il	2,0	2,3	2,6			2,4
			(1956 -1961)	(1961 -1966)	(1966 -1970)		(1970 -1975)
United States	(s/p)		2,9	2,4	2,5		–0,2
	Il		2,3	3,6	0,9		0,3
		(1950 -1955)	(1955 -1960)	(1960 -1965)	(1965 -1970)		(1970 -1974)
West Germany	(s/p)	5,5	4,8	5,5	4,9		5,1
	Il	7,2	5,2	5,0	5,3		3,8
			(1957 -1959)*	(1959 -1964)	(1964 -1968)	(1968 -1973)	(1973 -1975)
France	(s/p)		2,4	5,6	4,5	4,9	4,2
	Il		4,1	6,1	4,8	5,4	1,8
		(1954 -1957)	(1957 -1964)		(1964 -1970)	(1970 -1973)	(1973 -1975)
Japan	(s/p)	5,8	7,7		8,6	11,6	5,6
	Il	8,6	9,4		9,6	6,5	0,5

*Old base of the National Accounts

Source: C. Lapierre-Donzel, Le partage des revenues, la formation du profit: comparaison entre les cinq grandes économies, *Statistiques et études financières,* Série Orange 44 (1980).

banking system under the gold standard. The crisis thus assumes the form of a stagnation (and not of a collapse of production) coexisting with inflation (and not a collapse of prices).

But why a slowing down of productivity? Here, the analyses we have just evoked are most clearly distinguished from the theory of "the long wave of innovations". It is indeed quite difficult to identify a slowing of technological innovation during the 1960s. On the contrary, nothing fundamentally new laid the basis of post-war growth, and transistorized computing was already well developed at the start of the 1970s. On the other hand, the successes followed by the failures first of Taylorist, then of Fordist principles of labour organization, are manifest.[18]

After half a century of Taylorism and Fordism, it has become "natural" to expect that each year a worker produces more than the year before, and "mysterious" to find that this growth is slowing. However, when Taylor and Ford invented their new methods for the organization of labour, they broke up a routine which had previously known only a few forward leaps. Their method was before all else one of discipline and extraction of know-how. After

Table 3

Annual Rates of Growth of the Technical Composition of Capital (K/N) and Industrial Productivity (Q/N)

	K/N					Q/N				
	1950 -1955	1955 -1960	1960 -1965	1965 -1970	1970 -1975	1950 -1955	1955 -1960	1960 -1965	1965 -1970	1970 -1975
Japan		5,7	11,0	10,9	11,2 9,9(c)		12,5(b)	7,8	13,1	3,5 5,4(c)
Germany . .	1,8	6,1	8,0	5,9	7,6 7,5(c)	8,5	5,4	5,4	5,4	3,2 3,3(c)
France										
old base . . .	3,2	3,5	5,7			5,1	5,6	5,1		
new base . .			4,1	4,9	5,0 4,8(c)			6,1	7,0	3,1 4,9(c)
United Kingdom . .	2,3	3,8	3,7	4,3	4,6(d) 5,0(c)	2,2	2,4	2,9	3,2	3,4(d) 5,5(c)
United States		5,0(b)	2,0	3,6	4,3 1,8(c)		2,1(b)	4,5	1,0	−0,6 2,6(c)

(a) 1951-1955 (b) 1956-1960 (c) 1970-1973 (d) 1970-1974

Source: Lapierre-Donzel, Le partage des revenues (1980).

fifty years, there remain few reasons to think that "the one best way" has not been detected, disaggregated, systematized, and generalized. The "massification" of labour finally exhausted the great font of worker knowledge. Not that there no longer exist great reserves of productivity in human ingenuity; but they can no longer be exploited by Taylorist methods, those of drudgery, of the parcellization of tasks, of operations indefinitely repeated. Furthermore, parcellization itself encountered its own limits: loss of time between operations, delays concentrated at the end of the production line, and so forth.

It is here that class struggle emerges, at the root of the slowing down of productivity: the great victory of the employers during the 1920s had undermined its own bounty. Against the factory masters, the employers, methods offices, time-keepers, and foremen and women, now rose the massified bloc of specialized workers.

The years from 1967 to 1974 were first those of a worker counteroffensive superimposed on the employers' immobile "social technology": a counteroffensive of the specialized worker avenging the defeat of the professional worker. This is the grain of truth in the assertion that the workers put capitalism into crisis, much more than did the petroleum states regaining control of their resources.

It remains to be understood how this latent crisis of Fordism, undermined on the whole by minimal changes, but ones which tend to accumulate, could degenerate into manifest recession. It is necessary to take into account the international dimension, and governmental and employer reactions.

From the Erosion of U.S. Hegemony to the First Petroleum Shock

Starting in 1967, a qualitative transformation radically modified the international configuration: the productivity of Japan and Europe (particularly of West Germany and France) closed on that of the United States (see graph 2), to the point where the differences in wage costs per unit produced became unfavourable to U.S. competitiveness, at the current value of the dollar (see graph 3). This catching up was caused both by the growth of multinational firms in Europe and by the generalization in Europe and Japan of Fordist methods: the rate of investment in these countries indeed remained much higher than the U.S. rate (see graph 4).

From that point onwards, the trade balance of the U.S. was in deficit. The mass of xeno-dollars was no longer covered by the Fort Knox gold reserves. These dollars could no longer be considered as representing a "currency-commodity" (gold), nor as representing values-in-process indisputably validated at the international level (since U.S. production was less and less competitive). The dollar thus appears overvalued.

By degrees[19] the dollar abandoned its role as a fixed point of reference, and started to float downward against all currencies. U.S. capital lost its capability for foreign investment, but the subsidiaries of its multinational firms could now finance themselves directly from external sources. On the other hand, a trade war was launched between the three poles of the world economy, of more or less equal competitiveness. The differentiated configuration of the 1950s and 1960s had been succeeded by a linkage of three poles in which the phases of expansion and recession tended directly to echo and amplify one another.

The world boom of 1973 thus in every way augured a general recession the following year. But mainly it produced extreme tension on the raw materials markets. At the same time, the blows struck at the explicit hegemony of the United States in Indochina provoked a wave of nationalism in the Third

Table 4

Levels of Productivity Per Person in Manufacturing by Sector, 1980

(base 100 United States)

	France	West Germany	United Kingdom	Japan
•Metal Industries	62	64	28	122
including:				
Metallurgy	70	91	38	137
Machinery	71	65	27	117
Electrical & Electronics Equipment	50	40	26	135
Transportation Equipment*	55	55	21	94
•Non-Metal Industries	73	70	47	59
including:				
Construction Materials	71	76	38	47
Textiles	64	69	46	48
Pulp and Paper	63	67	42	66
Chemicals	78	79	46	101
Agriculture/Food	76	48	54	43
•Manufacturing Industries	69	67	38	90

*There are rapid relative changes in this sector. Thus by 1981 Japan had overtaken the United States and had an index of 101.

Source: CEPII, (1983).

World. The Arab-Israeli war of October 1973, in this objective and subjective conjuncture, gave the petroleum exporting countries the opportunity to recover control of the fixing of oil prices, which were raised to $11 a barrel.

Theoretically, this constituted only a shift in the ownership of a minimal share of world value added.[20] In the developed countries, however, already menaced by recession and where the latent crisis of Fordism exacerbated tensions over the share-out of this value added, this sudden deduction immediately provoked an inflationist flare up in the struggle for the redefinition of the share-out. Under the pretext of a rise in inflation, employers and governments attempted, by squeezing wages and restricting credit, to impose a decrease in the purchasing power of wage-earners. The first results obtained

Graph 2
Levels of Productivity per Worker in Manufacturing Industry 1951-81, Base 100 = United States

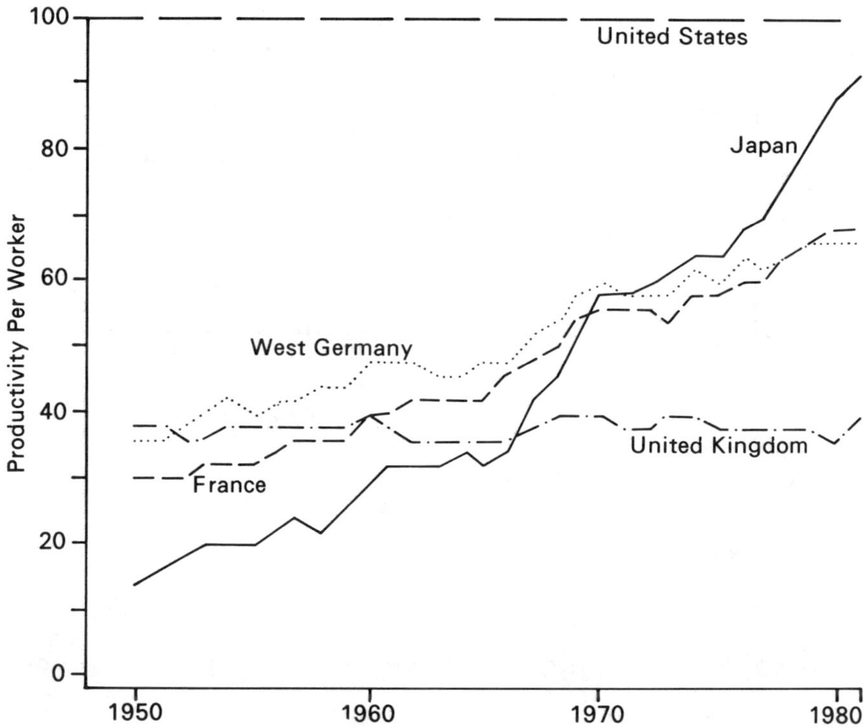

Source: CEPII, (1983)

from this strategy during 1974 produced a depression of world demand which, added to a catastrophic reduction of inventories, provoked the first great recession of the crisis.

From 1975 onward, however, worker and union resistance everywhere in the world choked off this first austerity offensive. In particular, the automatic stabilizers of the welfare state, often reinforced by the precipitate extension of unemployment insurance (all the more "generously" granted in that the dominant classes did not believe in the seriousness of the crisis) prevented a depressive spiral, guaranteeing the stability of consumption in spite of the growth of unemployment.[21] A security net thus limited the recession, and by 1975 there was a general recovery, especially since the oil deduction, financed on credit, multiplied effective world demand. Such was the strange configuration which will be examined in the following section.

Graph 3
Unit Labour Costs in Manufacturing Industry

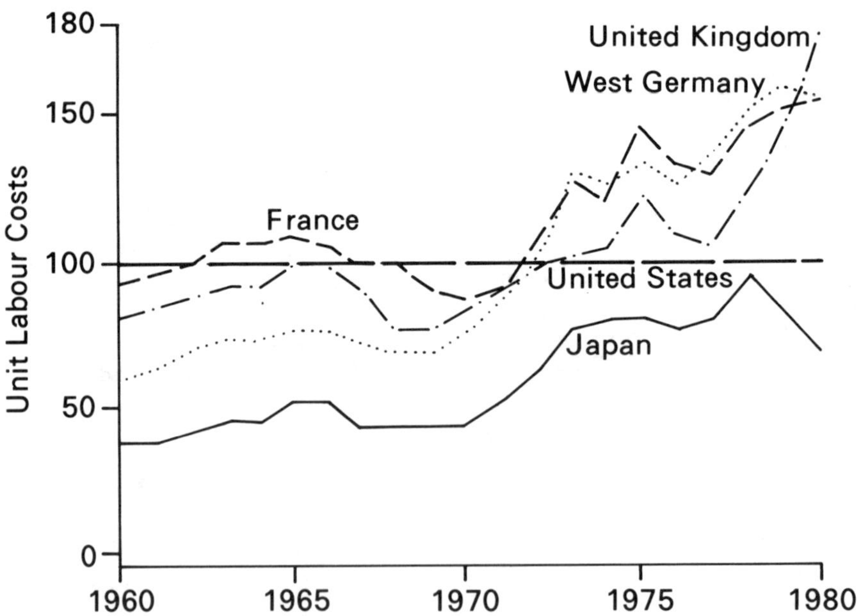

Source: CEPII, (1983)

A Transitional Configuration, 1975-79

The second half of the 1970s was marked by a strange contradiction. On the one hand, the crisis of Fordism got worse. On the other, Keynesianism survived quite honourably on its own base, at both the national and international levels. This survival is the main factor which colours the period.

Graph 4
Rates of Investment in the Manufacturing Sector
1960-81

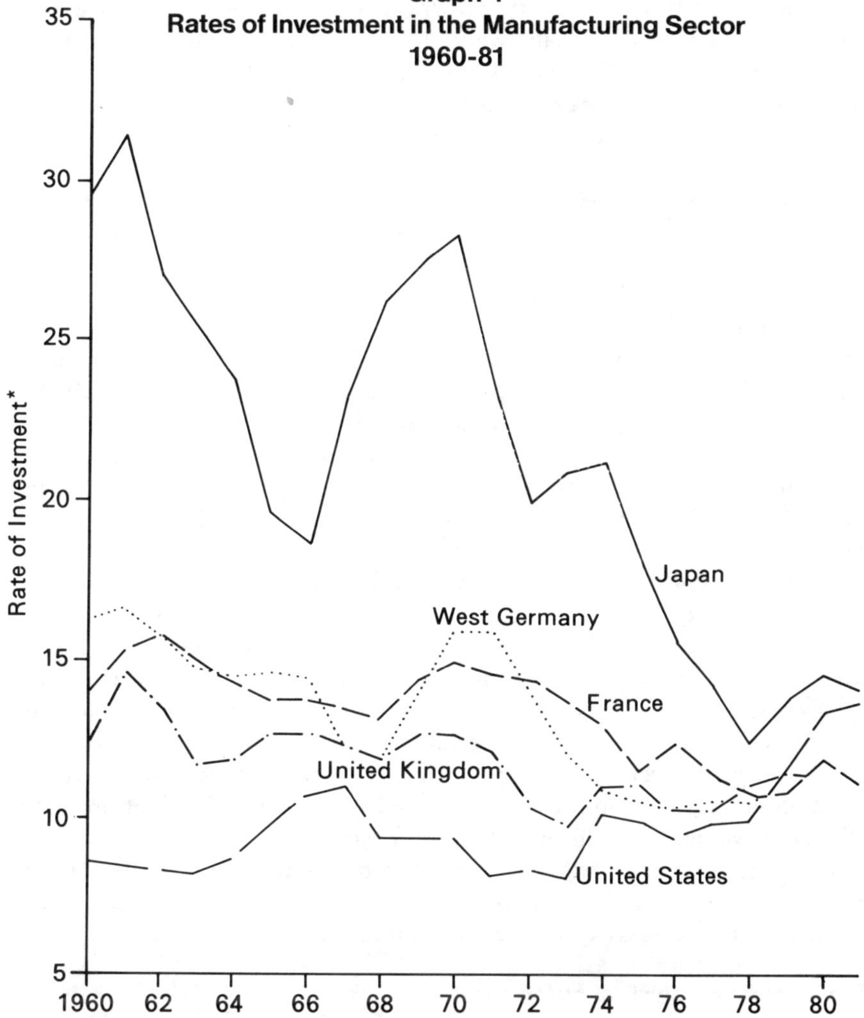

*Ratio of volume of investment to volume of gross value added (base: 100 = 1970)

Source: CEPII, (1983)

A Social-Democratic Management of the Crisis

The first phase of the management of the crisis can be described as "social-democratic". In Germany and Scandinavia, social democrats were in power, in Britain, the Labour Party's Callaghan, and in the United States, the Democrat Carter had been elected. In France, Valéry Giscard d'Estaing and Jacques Chirac organized the recovery, even though the role of political manoeuvre can not be distinguished from one of economic conviction. In general, the dominant evaluation then was that Keynesianism remained valid. It was only necessary, by borrowing (as in Sweden), or by putting world credit currency into circulation (as in the United States), to wait out the oil shock and the adjustment of supply to the distortion of the world demand structure towards the capital goods and military equipment ordered by the oil producing and exporting (OPEC) countries.

At the national level, this policy of "absorbing" the oil shock was practised in a particularly consequential manner by the Carter administration. As the main "engine" (to use the OECD expression in use at the time), the United States under Carter, at the cost of a discretionary currency increase, supplied the world with a credit currency whose validity was universally accepted, even though its international purchasing power was increasingly disputed. At the internal level, in spite of, or rather because of a marked absence of productivity gains, the United States was able to generate millions of jobs, essentially in the tertiary sector. Western Europe and especially Japan provided machines and consumer durables, not only to the United States, but also to the OPEC countries, to the eastern bloc, and especially to the countries of the South, which were adopting in turn a variant of the Fordist model.

Of course, this U.S. "monetary laxity" produced a precipitate drop in the value of the dollar which it could not cure. But this devaluation favoured domestic expansion since, taking into account the United States' low import coefficient, this laxity only caused a moderate increase in inflation. The nominal decrease in value of the dollar relative to other currencies translated into a real devaluation of U.S. costs, reestablishing the competitiveness too long compromised by overvaluation (see graph 3). That is, taking into account the inflation differentials on the one hand, and the nominal devaluation on the other, the average "bundle" of U.S. goods costs less and less, in the same currency at the current exchange rate, relative to the average "bundle" of German or French goods. Thus, compared to a U.S. "bundle" of the same price in 1970, a German one was worth 90 per cent more in 1980.

The Relative Paralysis of Europe

While the United States was preserving the growth of employment by a headlong devaluation, at the cost of stagnation in productivity, Japan pursued the same devaluation policy, with the same absence of dramatic consequences for internal inflation, and for the same reason, the low share of imports. It used this weapon to capture market shares and flood the world market with Fordist-type manufactured products (for example, cars, stereos, and optical instruments). In graph 5, these two countries are seen to be set apart from the others in terms of industrial growth. In contrast, the European countries experienced a growth still remarkable for a period of crisis, but clearly weaker than the U.S. and Japan.

The reasons for this weakness are assuredly fundamental. They are linked to the seriousness of the industrial crisis, and characterized by the heavy weight

Graph 5
Industrial Production
1965-83

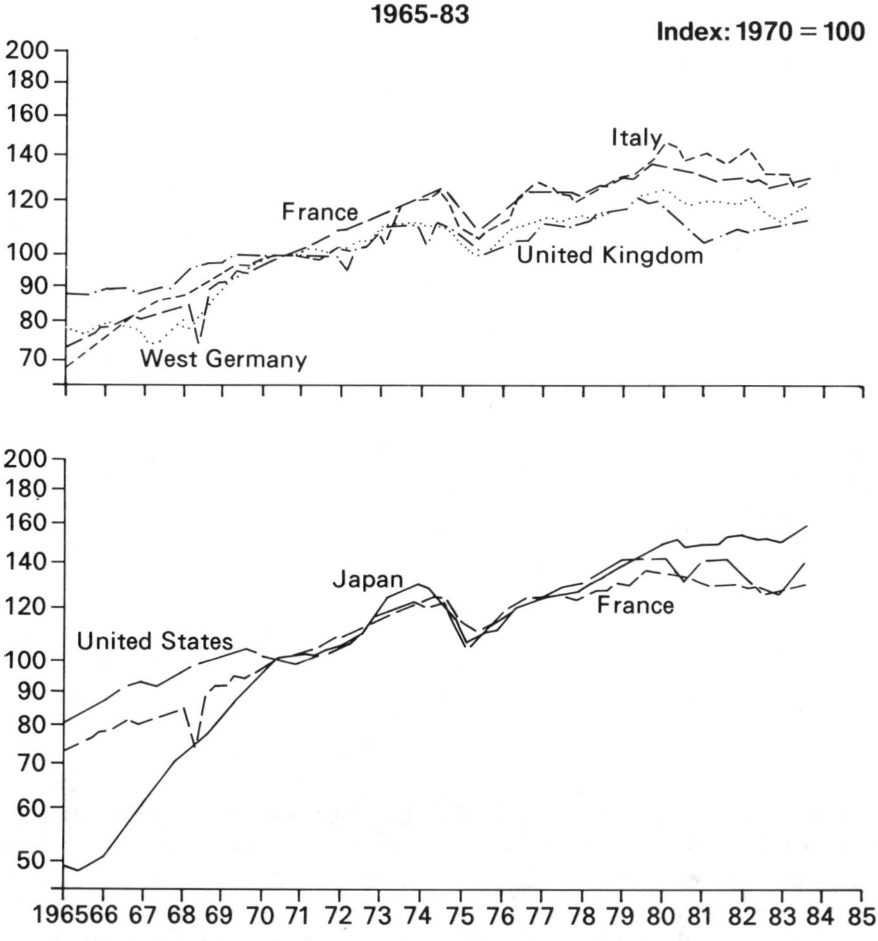

Source: Tendances de la Conjoncture (Paris: INSEE)

(in terms of capital intensity) and the great rigidity (in terms of social relations) of the European variants of Fordism. In focussing on the non-national dimensions of the crisis, we must underline an important obstacle to the implementation in Europe of the "Keynesianism plus devaluation" tactic. The obstacle consists of the perverse mechanics of "austerity internationalization".

More and more integrated at the industrial level, Europe remained fragmented into distinct nations each of which had to watch its trade balance. However, their production was becoming more and more "complementary": they had to remain each others' customers. In such conditions, devaluation loses much of its effectiveness, since "price effects" have less impact. In order to reestablish its trade balance, a country must import less, consume less, and invest less. Even for "substitutable products", price competition, in the free trade zone without a common policy such as Europe has become, imposes a strong form of protectionism: protectionism by restrictions on wages, by "competitive stagnation", or "austerity". The wage cost, determined by the "standard of living" of a given country, then acquires a new dimension: it becomes one of the determinants of international competitiveness.

The wage cost, or more exactly, the cost corrected for productivity, what is called the wage cost per unit of output, has always been, for each firm, a condition of competitiveness relative to other firms. This is why, in the 1920s, Ford could not win his bet alone. Factors such as collective agreements and the minimum wage were necessary to insure that each firm abandoned competition, in the same country, on the basis of low wages, which would have decreased national demand. But here is the hitch: there are no international collective agreements, there is not even a "European social space".

Thus, the different European countries found themselves, relative to one another, in a situation of "competitive regulation", which, earlier than anywhere else, compromised the effectiveness of internal Keynesianism. This configuration of stagnation later became general, with the second oil shock and the monetarist shock. At the time, however, this local European configuration found itself in a more favourable environment, constituting a "world Keynesianism", whose most spectacular effect was the growth of peripheral Fordism.

Peripheral Fordism

The internal logic of peripheral Fordism, which triumphed during the 1970s in a handful of "newly industrialized countries" — Mexico, Brazil, Korea, Taiwan, etc — has often been described.[22] It consists essentially of the adoption of the Fordist model of industrialization, from the perspective of the immediate labour process, but only very partially (and, at the limit, not at all) from the perspective of the regulation of the wage relation. In such conditions, "effective demand", the markets, can only be international: the NICs import the North's capital goods and sell it manufactured goods.[23] During the 1970s, this strategy seemed to encounter miraculous conditions of implementation. Schematically, this was the configuration:

- The countries of the OECD, and especially the United States, with low productivity gains and lagging investments, pursued growth through a lagging but not decreasing consumption.
- These countries financed their imports on credit, and thus permitted the expansion of an international credit currency (xeno-dollars) based on U.S. credit currency.
- This liquidity, loaned by the banks of the surplus countries (OPEC and Japan) to certain countries of the South (the NICs), permitted them to purchase on credit capital goods from the OECD.
- The NICs hoped to reimburse these loans by selling their manufactured goods to the OECD and OPEC countries. This was a "playable" option for two reasons:
  (1) the productivity gains of these "new" countries were made very rapidly (while they had slowed considerably in the North), and their hourly wage costs were five to ten times lower;
  (2) the world market continued to expand because of the "social democratic management of the crisis".

In this transitory but brittle configuration, the NICs were able to attain rates of growth in the order of 10 per cent per year, which is quite respectable for a "great crisis". Better still, their demand for capital goods from the North more than compensated for the loss of jobs in the old industrial countries resulting from their productivity gains in the consumer goods sector.

By a strange trick of history, one finds here something of a mirror image of the virtuous U.S.-Europe-Japan configuration of the 1950s. In a sense, the increase in the oil price financed by the "monetarization" of the U.S. deficit, and then recycled by the private banks towards the NICs, plays the role of a forced Marshall plan for the Third World. One must, however, insist on the extreme brittleness of this private recycling, and of the peripheral Fordist model itself. Extremely dependent on the evolution of world demand, it affected only a very limited number of countries of the South, at the same time destabilizing their internal structures.

Even before the end of the decade, the Fordist model collapsed under the weight of its own contradictions in Iran, Nigeria, Turkey, and elsewhere.

Continuation of the Crisis of Fordism and the Search for New Ways Out of It

This period was thus one of gentle management of the crisis. Productivity, production, and consumption nonetheless continued to grow, and unemployment increased only slowly. To maintain a growing consumption with a decreasing industrial work force, a slowed productivity growth required an increasing deduction from the value added to sustain the costs of the welfare state. This cost was paid by the firms, since it had been decided not to impose too great a cost on wage-earners. In France, the profit share fell from 30 per cent in the 1960s to 25 per cent in the 1970s.

This decrease in the distribution of profit shares was added to the rise in the cost of fixed capital, and hence of investments, which was accelerating inasmuch as both employers and governments were attempting to replace workers by even faster machines, and fuel-based generating plants by nuclear-based ones. If 1977 is compared to 1972, the "apparent productivity of capital" plunges, especially in the most Fordist industries. In France, for instance, it became necessary to invest 17 per cent more to produce the same value added.

Because of the welfare state and Keynesian policies, Fordism survived, but its fundamental crisis was more and more evident. It manifested itself in the contrast between an "abnormally" slow growth and an increasingly rapid inflation: "stagflation".

Under the appearance of a credit-based continuity, though, things were changing. Capitalism was exploring new ways, new arrangements for attempting to get out of the crisis.

Peripheral Fordism, the transfer of vulgarized Fordist production to low wage and low social security countries, was one of those ways. More fundamentally, in the industrialized countries themselves, the wage relation saw two great changes taking shape, the first regressive, the second potentially progressive.

The first change was the undermining of the conditions of labour power production. During the period of growth, the productivity-direct wage link had played the principal role, the welfare state a supporting one. As the role of the latter was developed, insuring a kind of permanent income to wage-earners and their families, firms attempted to free themselves from their heavy contractual obligations to their employees. The "hard core" of wage-earners (permanent workers) started to dwindle, while a world of non-status, temporary, or part-time workers proliferated. They survived mainly on state welfare handouts and, from time to time, on a wage. This was quite a profitable arrangement for individual firms, but the cost fell on the whole of the population and all firms through increases in compulsory deductions. Furthermore, this evolution accelerated the breakdown of the Fordist consensus: the last traces of "status" or of a "trade" were disappearing for young people, condemned from their entry into the labour force to a succession of "small jobs" and welfare.

The second, more interesting tendency was the search for new sources of productivity. These sources were sought at the heart of the labour process itself, both in the promise of the electronics-based "technological revolution" and in the replacement of Taylorist principles: reaggregation of tasks, individual or collective involvement through "quality-control groups", and involvement of the producers in the search for efficiency.

At the present time, the developmental stage of the crisis is evidently giving way to the next stage, one in which ways to resolve it are explored. A new principle for the organization of labour is being sought which will lay the basis for a future regime of accumulation. It is no longer a question of "catching-up" or imitating a pre-existing model (such as the United States offered in the 1950s). The spectacular leap forward in Japanese productivity, which left standing the two other competitors (West Germany and France) pursuing the U.S., is evident from that period represented in graph 2. It is even more evident when one considers the industrial sectors in detail (see table 3). Japanese capitalism did not "catch up" with the United States. It overtook it, by inventing a new, post-Fordist method of transforming the manual and intellectual producers' ingenuity into productivity.

But these seeds of the future, like Taylorism earlier, could only grow in a favourable macroeconomic and social environment. This was demonstrated, in contrast, by the monetarist shock.

A Needless Catastrophe: The Monetarist Shock

It was thus in a morose but not discouraging environment, one where industrial production had progressed relative to 1970 by 30 per cent in Germany and England, by nearly 40 per cent in the United States and France, and by 45 per cent in Japan, that the second "oil shock" occurred in 1979. The "$11 dollars a barrel" of the first shock had been largely absorbed by world inflation: the terms of trade of oil versus products of the industrial world had returned to the level at the end of the Korean War, that is, at the point of departure of Fordist growth. The increase to $34.00 dollars a barrel brutally reintroduced the vexing issue of oil rent. A return to 1974?

No, and it is not very easy to understand why. Everything was to turn out, in fact, very differently, as if the dominant classes no longer believed, or could no longer believe, in Keynesianism.

A Recess in Adjustment to the Second Petroleum Shock

Future historians will no doubt discuss interminably the chain of events which led from the second oil shock to the monetarist shock of 1981. Objective constraints had accumulated since the first shock, reducing the margins of the Keynesian game: threatening trade deficits in France and in Great Britain, and accumulated public debt in the United States, West Germany, and Japan.[24] Furthermore, international capitalist centralization had increased through the crossing of financial flows between the industrial economies, flows which were essentially destined for mergers and purchases of firms competing with one another: what Madeuf, Michalet, and Ominami call "investments without accumulation".[25] The complementarity of these economies had thus been reinforced, and the possibilities of autonomous Keynesian policies had been restrained: the European stagnation configuration had widened and deepened.

Perhaps more fundamentally, the world élites, the heads of firms and politicians of the Trilateral Commission, stopped believing in international Keynesianism. The shortcomings of this regime had become evident:

- If the "security net" of monopolistic regulation in the North prevented depression, it also constrained the redirection of production and consumption towards new norms, by the rigidity it conferred on the labour force and on the allocation of capital between sectors.
- International credit was, like all credit, based on the wager that the regime of accumulation would be reestablished, that the country issuing the currency (the United States) could unconditionally offer the equivalent in competitive goods of these monetary symbols, and that the indebted countries of peripheral Fordism would find in the North large enough outlets to repay their debts.

Towards the end of the 1970s, it was clear that none of these assumptions was valid. Growth remained sluggish, productivity gains continued to be slow, and capital per capita continued its acceleration. U.S. currency was challenged more often, and continued to lose its international purchasing power.

The accession to hegemony of monetarist or simply less Keynesian coalitions (in England with the victory of the Conservatives, in the United States with the nomination of Volker to head the Federal Reserve Bank (the Fed) prior to the election of Reagan, in West Germany with the hegemony of the Liberals in the centre-left coalition, and in France with the full implementation of Barrism after the defeat of the left in 1978) all reflect this avowal of impotence. By the simple effect of the vacuum, the ideas of liberalism reimposed themselves: the simple play of market forces would favour those firms implementing the processes of the future, would eliminate the slag of the past, would reconstitute the compatibility of behaviours.

By 1980, the change was quite clear: West Germany and France imposed on their wage-earners a downward adjustment to the oil shock, decreasing industrial production by 5 per cent. Great Britain had clearly chosen monetarism by 1979. The Fed under Volker attempted to implement the same policy, with similar results — a decrease of 7 per cent, quickly reversed in the face of electoral deadlines. Only Japan experienced a growth of 10 per cent, on wages permitted by its protectionism and the efficiency of its exporting sector: it let its currency plunge (see graph 3). But even Japanese growth would be broken by the third shock, the monetarist shock.

The Monetarist Catastrophe

With the accession of Reagan to the presidency, the United States joined Great Britain in the extreme monetarist camp. Cutting welfare spending and blocking the "pseudo-validation" through credit of the values in process based on the Fordist regime of accumulation (by cutting the issue of credit), these two coalitions erased in their respective countries within a few months the growth of the previous five years. In doing so, they started a rather complex chain reaction.[26] They not only condemned all the other countries — including France under Mitterand[27] — through the mechanism of austerity internationalization, but they also dried up the creation of international credit by erasing OPEC surpluses through the world recession they provoked. Credit became scarce and costly, and world demand was quickly decreased: peripheral Fordism found itself incapable of repaying its debts.

It is difficult to attribute the bankruptcy of the NICs (especially the Latin American ones) to the oil shock itself. The real interest rate of the developing countries (that is the rate of Euro-dollars deflated by the price of their exports, OPEC included), which had plunged to minus 30 per cent in 1974 because of the oil price increase, and had oscillated around 0 per cent from 1975 to 1978, only fell to minus 10 per cent in 1979 but went up to plus 20 per cent in 1981 and 1982. To this was added, decisively, the reduction of world demand.

However, the very imminence of the bankruptcy of the NICs added to the tangible multiplication of chains of bankruptcies in the main industrial countries and especially in the United States[28] began from July 1983 to greatly worry the U.S. administration, which relaxed monetary constraints. Too late: in August, Mexico declared a suspension of payments, signalling general insolvency. A world financial crash was close.[29] The Reagan administration abandoned monetarism in response, ordered the world banking system to accept a general rescheduling of the Third World debt, and crudely restored domestically the old Keynesianism, in an almost Kennedyist style. Tax cuts and increased defence spending produced a gigantic budget deficit, largely financed by the Federal Reserve. A "boom" largely based on household consumption (notably housing) reestablished U.S. industry in one year (1983) to its level of 1979. The considerable external deficit which resulted broke the recession in the OECD countries, with an export-based recovery in Japan, and a housing and consumption recovery in Germany.

But the issue of credit remained limited to the needs of the U.S. administration. The recovery was not enough to reconstitute the OPEC surpluses. The NICs, insolvent except for those in the Japanese sphere, were unable to repay their debts, so the multiplying mechanisms of xeno-dollar creation remained inactive. The dollar continued to be scarce and costly outside the United States. The effects of the monetarist shock were far from overcome.

As far as positive effects are concerned, they remain doubtful, even in the United States. The recovery is not based on a new model of development: it is a return to the 1970s. Inflation has certainly slowed down considerably, a result of the internal decrease of the price of imports and short-term productivity gains made by the reemployment of idle capacity. But the overvaluation of the dollar based on U.S. power, as was the case at the end of the 1960s, is liable to experience a new downfall, as happened in 1971. The contraction of traditional industries, such as the auto industry, while it has permitted an extensive rationalization, does not point in any clear way to the possibility of a new growth period based on new technologies. This is the point to be examined in the conclusion, in a necessarily abstract manner.

A Conclusion: Two Plausible Resolutions of the Crisis

Some months before his death, the futurologist Herman Kahn identified the 1983 U.S. recovery with the take-off of a new Kondratieff cycle, which would ascend until the year 2000. We are not yet there; and we can only know that the curve linking the last two "low points" (1975 and 1982) is nearly horizontal. We do not know if the curve linking 1979 to the next "high point" (1984? 1985?) will be as steeply rising as the previous one (2.5 per cent between 1973 and 1979: see graph 1).

The hypothesis of a new Kondratieff cycle is based on the emergence of new sectors around the automation-electronics revolution. The formation of a new centre of the world economy on the Pacific rim is also invoked. Let us ignore here the strange topology of this centre. If there is to be a new Kondratieff cycle, it will neither relegate New England to its periphery, nor some of the very active regions of Europe. True, it seems that a "virtuous configuration" today ties Japan and the Asiatic NICs to the rocket of U.S. recovery. But the brittleness of this recovery must be acknowledged: based on immense public (in the United States and Japan) and external (in the U.S.) deficits, it is only maintained by pumping capital out of the rest of the world, through the unprecedented real interest rates offered in the U.S. This pumping limits the European recovery, maintains Latin America in a depression, and plunges whole areas of the Third World into famine and death. No virtuous global cycle has yet emerged.

More profoundly, we must reflect on the real effects of the electronics revolution. Because, between technology and a model of development, there is a series of links, social relations. From technology to technical implementation: *the immediate relations of production* (Who decides? How is collective labour organized?). From production to the economic: *the overall socio-economic relations* (Will there be enough consumers, enough investors? What is produced? To insure what form of full employment?). In other words, a new regime of accumulation, and a new mode of regulation, especially of the wage relation (or other relations of production, why not?) remains to be invented. But this model of development must be compatible with a new *international configuration.* Let us briefly examine these three sets of problems.

What do informatics accomplish: not so much productivity gains by second of machine-time used, but the possibility of full-time use of the machines of a workshop and of making this workshop flexible.[30] A Fordist workshop, based on the double specialization of machines and persons, does not make efficient use of either of their time: waits between two operations, piling up of intermediary stocks, and disequilibrium between work stations. Automated management of the workshop permits a leap forward in the fluidity of the production process: each part arrives in time at its proper place and the elementary acts are more precisely interconnected. This is the great source of profitability that informatics create in this context. It is costly in initial investment — networks of wire-guided conveyor, central and peripheral computers — but they are utilized in full.

This is not all. Electronics above all make machine systems flexible. Automation in the workplace is not new. Machines have long been made that are capable of performing operations on their own, for example, the transmission belts of an automobile factory or press-shops. But these enormous installations could only perform one set of actions, always producing the same product. The robot can adapt itself, change tools, go from one task to another with a quick reprogramming. The robotized workshop can thus adapt itself to fluctuating demand, jumping from short production series to short production series.

A first bifurcation appears here: two axes of evolution present themselves to the post-Fordian reorganization of the labour process. The automation of the management of the production process presents the temptation to push further the break between the theoretical conception of the process and the implementing actions of the workers. These workers would become simply flesh-and-blood links in the automated process. This has been the road chosen by the majority of U.S. and some European firms. In contrast, automation can produce a partial requalifying of the workers, the practical know-how of the operators being mobilized in real time in the actual automation process. This is the road that a majority of Japanese and some European firms seem to be following. This bifurcation forms the field of a tremendous social conflict, whose stake is the negotiation of a new social compromise between the involvement of the workers and the apportionment of the new productivity gains.

For — and this is a second bifurcation — it is necessary to know whom and what these productivity gains will serve. The first variant of the post-Fordist model will mobilize even more fixed capital than aging Fordism itself. Productivity gains will be reserved for profits and the final demand will not grow. The "flexibility" of automated processes itself makes possible the profitability of massive investments, through a succession of short production series destined for the segmented and versatile consumption of a well-off clientele. But these productivity gains without any increase of mass consumption will bring about the growth of unemployment and the risk of a division of society into three parts: a dominant class benefitting from the new gadgets of the electronics revolution, a stable but limited core of permanent wage-earners, and a growing mass of uncertain workers under a weakened social security system, only able to gain transitory employment in the tertiary sector during conjunctural recoveries. This seems, again, to describe the road currently followed in the United States. The other road consists of a new negotiated apportionment of productivity gains, with mass access to new consumption goods, which require consumption time: for example, optical and acoustic cultural devices, and home computers. These relatively inexpensive goods (as compared to the automobile) call for an apportionment of productivity gains in the shape of a massive reduction of work-time.

Naturally, a model of development grounded in the mass extension of non-wage-earning activity (leisure, creativity and intellectual enrichment) may well not be very competitive in terms of hourly wage costs relative to a model grounded on the intensification of labour without any reapportionment of productivity gains. Two paths again present themselves. One would be the unending struggle for hegemony or at least for trade-balance equilibrium, through "competitive stagnation". The world would enter a new long period of stop-and-go cycles, to the rhythm of the choices of "expansion" or "retrenchment" of the hegemonic power, leading to a permanent trade war which could in turn lead to the conflictual disintegration of the world economy. Or, a path could be chosen on which international institutional forms would be put in place, permitting, in the best case, the joint adoption by interested parties of a variant of the second model (international norms relative to work-time and wages, etc.), or at least the de-linking of those nations (or communities of nations) who would adopt such a model of development, relative to those who would choose a more productivist and competitive model (protectionism on the basis of social criteria, direct control of trade balances by quotas, etc.).

In a very concrete way, the manner in which the problem of Third World indebtedness is resolved will provide us with decisive indications. Practically, the 1982 crisis was resolved by a debt moratorium of three years on the average, the IMF imposing moreover an "adjustment" of the NICs' regime of accumulation towards greater exports, in fact an "austerity" program which pushes the new middle classes back into poverty, the workers towards wretchedness, the poor towards death. We have here an illustration, at the level of international relations, of the first variant, which resembles the prophecies made by Jack London in *The Iron Heel*. Perpetual indebtedness would be a way to maintain the industrialized Third World in the role of a sweatshop, committed to the production of popular intermediary or Fordist goods, while a minority of developed countries would enter "post-industrial civilization".

The other alternative implies the de facto cancellation of the Third World debt, whether by balancing out (as for the German and Russian debts between the wars) or by the consolidation of the loaned amounts, permanently frozen like those of a shareholder. The free issue and distribution of international currency would then permit the recovery of the periphery Fordist countries on a more autonomous road, on a more self-centred regime of accumulation.

Without even mentioning a non-capitalist (or apocalyptic) resolution of the crisis, two roads are open for each question for a capitalist resolution: a repressive way of a new type, a social democratic way of a new type. Is it necessary to recall that, during the 1930s, Nazism and the New Deal also offered two solutions to the crisis? And that it took strikes, revolts, a war, and tremendous commotions on the planet for a variant of the second way to impose itself?

Notes

1 See in the United States the seminal work of M. Aglietta, *Régulation et crises du capitalisme* (Paris: Calmann-Levy, 1976), (English translation: NLB, 1979), and, based on some collective research on France in 1977, of R. Boyer and J. Mistral, *Accumulation, inflation et crise* (Paris: P.U.F., 1978) (second edition, 1983), and A. Lipietz, *Crise et inflation: pourquoi?* (Paris: Maspéro, 1979); *Le Monde enchanté: De la valeur à l'envol inflationiste* (Paris: Maspéro-La Découverte, 1983), (English translation: Verso, 1985); and *L'Audace ou l'enlisement* (Paris: Découverte, 1984).

2 This concerns mainly work done at the CEPREMAP by Boyer, Lipietz, and Mistral, and at the Centre d'Études Prospectives et d'Informations Internationales with Aglietta, Brender, and Oudiez: see for example, CEPII, *Économie mondiale: la montée des tensions* (Paris: Economica, 1983), and "Dualité, change et contraintes extérieures dans cinq économies dominantes," Économie Prospective Internationale, 13-14 (1983).

3 H. Bertrand, "La Croissance française analysée en sections productives," *Statistiques et Études Financières*, Série Orange, No. 35.

4 This prevalence has led some Marxist authors, such as Paul Sweezy and Ernest Mandel, to explain the expansion phases of capitalism (identified as the long cycles of Kondratieff) by the appearance of technical innovation clusters. Beyond the uncertainty of identification of the long cycles themselves, this explanation is criticized by the school of regulation, which prefers to identify a succession of regimes of accumulation disarticulating themselves through the effect of their own contradictions. From this perspective, techniques are themselves social relations, which only produce their economic effects in the environment determined by all the forms of regulation. One will find, however, a great convergence between these two

approaches in C. Perez's concept of "technological paradigm", expressed in her article "Structural Changes and Assimilation of New Technologies in the Economic and Social Systems," *Futures*, (1977), and great similarities with the concept of "social structure of accumulation" developed by S. Bowles, D. Gordon, and T. Weisskopf in "The Social Structure of Accumulation and the Profitability of the Postwar U.S. Economy," (1983), (unpublished).

5 B. Coriat, *L'Atelier et le chronomètre* (Paris: Bourgois, 1979).

6 It would be too complex to show here how monopolistic regulation favoured an intensive accumulation of capital. See Lipietz, *Le Monde enchanté*.

7 M. Aglietta and A. Brender, *La Configuration mondiale des années quatre-vingt: les risques d'une déflation generalisée*, CEPII (mimeo).

8 A. Lipietz, "Towards Global Fordism?" *New Left Review*, 132 (1982).

9 A. Lipietz, "New Tendency in the International Division of Labour: Regimes of Accumulation and Modes of Regulation," in A.J. Scott and M. Storper, eds. *Production, Work, Territory* (London: George Allen and Unwin, 1986).

10 In this essay, so-called socialist centralized economy countries will be totally excluded since they have a different regime of accumulation, and especially, a quite different mode of regulation. See, however, D. Leborgne and A. Lipietz, "Est, Ouest: deux modes de régulation du capitalisme," *Reflets et perspectives de la vie économique*, 4 (1983), and B. Chavance, "Les formes actuelles de crise dans les économies de type soviétique, *Critiques de l'Économie Politique*, 26/27 (1984).

11 G. Arrighi, "Une Crise d'hégémonie" in G. Arrighi, *et. al.*, *La Crise, quelle crise?* (Paris: Maspéro, 1982).

12 We consider Europe here as a bloc, but in fact a "virtuous complementarity" configuration can also be identified between the member states of the European Economic Community. Schematically, West Germany is the capital goods workshop of France and Italy, who sell consumer goods in exchange, the adjustment being done "by prices" (by changes in parity) and "by volume" (through moderate "cooling-off plans").

13 For a methodological reflection on this problem, which implies a prudent approach to the systemist vision of a "world economy", see Lipietz, "New Tendency."

14 See especially the works of the CEPII in number 13-14 (1983) of the journal *Économie Prospectives Internationales*. These works take into account the different conditions of apportionment of productivity surpluses between the manufacturing (and internationalized) sector, on the one hand, and the tertiary (and protected) sector, on the other.

15 R. Boyer, "Déterminants et évolution probable de la productivité et l'emploi: un essai de synthèse de travaux récents," CEPREMAP, No. 7922, (1979).

16 A. Lipietz, "Derrière la crise: la tendance à la baisse du taux de profit," *Revue Économique*, 33, 2, (1982).

17 Lipietz, *Le Monde enchanté*.

18 Coriat, *L'Atelier*.

19 In 1968, the abandonment of the gold pool made the dollar a forced rate currency. On August 15, 1971, its reference to gold was finally abandoned and its parity relative to the other currencies became totally floating, beginning in March 1973. This evolution became official in January 1976 under the Jamaica agreements.

20 For "classical" economic thought, the increase of ground rent presents two aspects: (1) for Ricardo, it is subtracted from capitalist profit, but we will see that the oil rent will be recycled as investments; and (2) for Malthus, it reinforces the real demand for "luxury" goods, and this is what will occur, warplanes replacing coaches! The oil shock therefore cannot be considered as an autonomous cause of the crisis; at the most it revealed the latent contradictions.

21 R. Boyer, "Origine, originalité, et enjeux de la crise actuelle en France: une comparaison avec les années trente," in *La Crise économique et sa gestion* (Montreal: Boréal Express, 1982).

22 Lipietz, "New Tendency".

23 In fact, they also continue to sell their raw materials — when they can. Further, some East bloc countries, such as Poland under Gierek, follow the same road (with the same results).

24 J. Le Dem and J. Pisani-Ferry, "Crise et politiques économiques dans les grandes économies industrielles: permanence et changement," *Critiques de l'Économie Politique*, 26/27 (1984)

25 B. Madeuf, C.A. Michalet, and C. Ominami, "D'une Crise internationale à une crise mondiale," *Critiques de l'Économie Politique*, 26/27 (1984).

26 Aglietta and Brender, *La Configuration*, and A. Lipietz, "Le Fordisme périphérique étranglé par le monétarisme central," *Actualité Économique* (English translation in *New Left Review* [June 1984]).

27 Lipietz, *L'Audace*.

28 Lipietz, *Le Monde enchanté*.

29 O. Berger, " Système bancaire international: au bord de la faillite et au coeur de la crise," *Critiques de l'Économie Politique*, 26/27 (1984).

30 B. Coriat, "Crise et électronisation de la production: robotisation d'atelier et modèle fordien d'accumulation de capital," *Critiques de l'Économie Politique*, 26/27 (1984).

Chapter 3

The Decline of North American Industry: The United States and Canada

Jorge Niosi and Philippe Faucher

THE U.S. ECONOMY has been steadily declining relative to the global economy during the last three decades. That decline, however, went virtually unnoticed until recently. Both Marxist and non-Marxist economists are divided over the importance, the explanation and, indeed, the very existence of the decline. Faced with so many different perspectives, this essay must first review some of the main contributions to the debates, and the main concepts, before going on to examine the evidence concerning the decline of the U.S. and Canadian economies (including several statistical series showing their relative position in the world economy).

After comparing several analytical perspectives with the empirical evidence, some propositions concerning past trends and the future evolution of the North American economy will be presented. Industry in the United States has been declining for the past thirty years and it now constitutes only one of the three major industrial poles (along with the European Economic Community [EEC] and Southeast Asia) of the capitalist world. However, this decline has proceeded at a slower rate during the 1980s, and at the same time several symptoms of the U.S. "disease" have become evident in Europe and Japan.

The Canadian economy is not renowned for its industrial dynamism. The well-documented shortcomings of our manufacturing structure are hardly challenged by the few success stories that are splashed all over the media. Stories of failures like those involving Tembec, Massey-Ferguson, and Bell Helicopter are familiar to the attentive observer.

Given the very close ties which bind Canadian industrial production to the U.S. economy, it is to be expected that the evolution of our industry will reflect the global economic pattern of change apparent in the United States. It would be wrong, however, to believe that because the U.S. economy is in decline, that Canada has no choice but to follow suit. It would also be incorrect to simply reproduce for Canada the analysis developed for the United States, in order to explain the causes of our domestic hardships. Even if the manifestations of the problem are similar, they are not necessarily the result of the same combination of causal factors. This is an important distinction which implies that since the challenges confronting Canadian industry are qualitatively different, they require a different set of policies than the ones applied in the U.S.

The Debates on the Decline

The literature on the economic decline of the United States, almost nonexistent before 1980, mushroomed when the growing trade deficit showed that most North American products were losing their competitive edge when measured against similar goods from Japan, Western Europe, and several newly industrialized countries. No consensus, however, has emerged from this literature. A useful starting point in an evaluation of the debates is to introduce some basic definitions.

Definitions

Deindustrialization means very different things in the studies that have been made of both the British and the U.S. economic declines. Some authors define it as a long-term fall in manufacturing employment and/or value of manufactured products as a percentage of total employment or GNP respectively.[1] This definition, however, applies to every developed country, even to those such as Japan in which manufacturing shows absolute growth, but at a slower rate than in its service sector.

In their book on the deindustrialization of the United States, Bluestone and Harrison define the process as a widespread, systematic disinvestment in the nation's basic industries.[2] Two problems arise with this definition. First, it neglects the growth of new jobs in new manufacturing industries and therefore neglects changes in the net balance of employment. Second, by introducing the investment variable, it prejudges the explanation of U.S. deindustrialization, while ignoring the fact that industrial investment has not fallen in the last fifteen years, but has shifted from traditionally basic to modern industries.[3]

A more restrictive definition is proposed by Thirlwall. According to him, deindustrialization is an absolute loss of industrial jobs, particularly in manufacturing.[4] On the basis of this definition only a few countries, including the United Kingdom and Argentina, have been deindustrializing during the last ten years, if we do not take into account the 1982-83 crisis.[5] This definition is adopted here: it is simple, precise, general, and does not anticipate the causes of the phenomena it is supposed to describe. In this essay, deindustrialization is synonymous with absolute industrial decline.

Economic decline is also an ill-defined concept. Magaziner and Reich, in their books on the U.S. decline, use several comparative economic indicators in order to measure economic decline: standards of living, unemployment rates, productivity, and per capita GDP, among others.[6] These authors are easily challenged and criticized by an examination of the available figures on alternative indicators such as the cost of living (lower in the United States than in any other industrial country), on exchange rates fluctuations (affecting GDP figures), and the internal distribution of gross national income (the U.S. being more egalitarian than most industrial capitalist nations).[7] In this text, economic decline is defined as a relative phenomenon: the long-term reduction in the relative importance of a particular country within the world economy. It can be measured by the proportion of the country's GDP in the aggregate GDP of a significant group of countries such as the OECD.

Some other definitions can be derived from this definition of economic decline. *Commercial decline* is the long-term fall in the export competitiveness of a country; it is measured by the country's value of exports as a percentage of the world's value of exports. *Relative industrial decline* is the long-term reduction of a country's gross industrial product (GIP). *Financial decline* can be understood as the falling proportion of world financing accounted for by the country's financial institutions.

The concept of *economic hegemony* has also been used, mainly by Marxists, to describe the economic decline of the United States in the capitalist world. Even among Marxists, decline in hegemony has several meanings. According to Magdoff and Sweezy, the decline in U.S. economic hegemony is essentially a monetary phenomenon, specifically, the abandonment of the dollar's convertibility into gold and the subsequent devaluation of the U.S. dollar in August 1971.[8] The decline of the dollar is explained by the chronic deficit of the U.S. balance of payments, due to the worldwide military activities of the United States, and to foreign direct investment by U.S. multinational corporations.

Wallerstein defines the decline in hegemony as the decline in the relative efficiency of the productive, commercial, and financial enterprises of the United States.[9] He refers to the declining competitiveness of U.S. industry and, more specifically, the loss of U.S. leadership in most productive activities. This latter definition for economic hegemonic decline is adopted here: it points to a larger and more complex phenomenon than the simple decline of the dollar, and besides, it refers to something different from economic decline.

The latter may affect several industrial countries (among which are Canada and Belgium), while only the United States experiences the loss of industrial leadership. The decline of U.S. hegemony can be measured by the loss of technological leadership in key industries such as steel, automobiles, mass transportation, and machine-tools, where the United States no longer has the technological edge, and is not even the most important national industry (in terms of value added or total production).

The Debates on the Decline

Neither Marxists nor non-Marxist academic economists seem able to agree about the economic decline of the United States. Several Marxists (for example, Jalée, Petras and Rhodes, and Andreff) argue that the economic supremacy of the United States remains unchallenged.[10] More numerous are those who maintain that the economic decline of the U.S. is evident (Varga, Mandel, Szymanski, and Magdoff and Sweezy).[11] However, the extent and characteristics, as well as the explanation of the decline, vary from one author to another. Magdoff, Sweezy, and Arrighi, for example, see only a monetary and financial decline, synonymous with the 1971 abandonment of the Bretton Woods post-war monetary arrangements. In fact, Magdoff explicitly rejects the idea of a widespread industrial or economic decline of the United States:

> The other scapegoat — the alleged declining competitiveness of the U.S. industry — also falls to the ground when exposed to a few basic facts. The argument clearly concerns exports of manufactures [but] U.S. manufacturers are not competing against foreign firms but against their own branches and affiliates located abroad.... *U.S. manufacturing firms located abroad are selling almost three times as much as is being exported from the United States.*[12]

According to Magdoff, the whole issue of U.S. industrial decline is an ideological screen designed to justify major cuts in industrial wages.

Against this position, Szymanski and Wallerstein argue that the U.S. decline is a long-term trend, fundamentally changing the structure of the capitalist world. Wallerstein maintains that the economic supremacy of the United States was a short-lived phenomenon, extending from 1945 to 1967. The reindustrialization of Europe and Japan, and the emergence of several NICs, have eroded the relative competitive advantage of U.S. industry. Comparing the U.S. decline with that of Great Britain after 1873 and the Netherlands after 1672 after short periods of world hegemony, Wallerstein argues that hegemony has always been brief and always followed catastrophic military defeats of rival powers. A hegemonic world structure has not been a frequent occurrence in the history of world capitalism. Hegemony gives rise to a free trade policy by the victorious power. It is followed by decline: the hegemonic power cannot prevent the international diffusion of its technology because of its own liberal policies; its labour costs grow rapidly during its world economic monopoly and they are detrimental to the country's competitiveness when the rival powers are reestablished; the hegemonic power engages in enormous military expenses to insure world peace. In short, a hegemonic international structure is essentially unstable, and it gives way to a multipolar structure with several rival, competing powers. Wallerstein adds that hegemonic decline comes in three stages: first agro-industrial, then commercial, and finally financial.

To complete this review, it should be mentioned that a small number of Marxist economists argue that industrial decline affects equally all the advanced capitalist countries.[13] The industrialization of the Third World, and especially the emergence of the NICs, is one of the most important factors in the relative decline of the developed countries.

The same cleavage exists among non-Marxists. For the product cycle theoreticians, the United States is and will remain in the foreseeable future, the leading economic power in the capitalist world due to its large internal market and to internal federal support for high technology.[14] Other authors argue that the increasing trade deficit has no particular meaning; on the one hand, it is less important when services and factor payments are taken into account, and on the other, the industrial composition of U.S. exports has changed in favour of high technology products and capital goods.[15] As for the growing foreign direct investment in the United States, and declining U.S. investment abroad, Balassa considers that the dollar devaluation of the 1970s was the cause of the reversal in old trends and predicts that the revaluation of the dollar since 1979 will bring the situation back to more familiar patterns of investment. Another economist argues that the elements for a recovery of U.S. hegemony are already in place: industrial wages are stagnant or even declining, and price increases for energy and natural resources favour the U.S. and penalize Europe and Japan, which are import-dependent in both cases.[16] Robert Lawrence posits that industrial employment and output have grown regularly in absolute terms in the United States for the last thirty years; according to him, only the overvalued dollar and an insufficient demand due to high interest rates have squeezed U.S. industry from 1981 to 1983.[17]

Among those who consider that the U.S. economy is declining, the analyses are very different. Neo-classical economists have blamed either an overvalued dollar during the entire post-war period, or government deficits and excessive regulation.[18] Others have argued that the technological catching up by Europe and Japan explains the relative American decline.[19] Low capital formation ratios in the United States are another common explanation while foreign direct investment by U.S. industrial firms has been blamed by both liberals like Gilpin and radicals like Bluestone and Harrison.[20] In management schools the poor quality of administration in large corporations is seen as a major factor in the decline: U.S. enterprises are managed by an increasing proportion of lawyers and business graduates, while engineers and other technical innovators are running Japanese, German, and French competitors.[21]

Bureaucracy and red tape have replaced quality control, product improvement, and innovation. Management adapted to mass markets no longer suits high technology production.

The role of governments in industrial policy is mentioned as the crucial factor by several authors.[22] In high technology industry, the influence of government policies is argued to be critical in public financing of research and development, technical education, foreign technology absorption, labour force retraining, and the capitalization of sunrise industries. Instead of protecting old manufacturing activities in which the United States cannot regain its competitiveness, the federal government should, according to these authors, help dynamic new firms to invest in new, high technology industries following the Japanese, the German, or the French examples.

A small number of authors argue that industrial decline is affecting all advanced capitalist countries.[23] High labour costs compared to those of the NICs, the depletion of natural resources in industrial countries, and the global diffusion of technology are pushing many manufacturing activities towards semi-industrial, developing countries. The same trend should be bringing about corresponding industrial decline in the United States, Western Europe, and Japan.

As for Canada, the question of economic decline has, quite understandably, never been equated with a concern for the economic hegemony of the western world. Canada has always been cognizant of the weakness of its industrial base. The accommodation which had been fashioned in the late nineteenth century by the National Policy, giving a secondary but still sufficient economic role to industrial capitalists within the staples-led growth model, was finally undermined in the mid-1960s with the multilateral negotiation of tariff reductions on manufactured goods. The prospect of trade-induced deindustrialization became real, and the economic weakness of branch-plant manufacturing was exposed.[24]

In the early 1970s the debate centred on the consequences of foreign ownership, and most of all on Canada's technological dependence on U.S. multinationals.[25] The possibility of industrial decline was only raised recently in relation to the economic crisis and its observed effects on the advanced capitalist countries. In addition to the weaknesses associated with import-substitution industrialization, Canada is now plagued with the same symptoms that affect U.S. industry.[26]

Low productivity and rising costs, high wages and excessive government regulations are all involved. An additional factor in the case of Canada is the limited size of its domestic market that prevents the full realization of economies of scale.[27]

The debate on industrial decline runs on two parallel paths. One stresses the increasing difficulty experienced by Canadian manufacturing production not only to be competitive internationally but also to maintain its share of the domestic market. This is not only true for so-called traditional sectors such as clothing and shoes but applies also to the core of the industrial base, the automobile industry, which has been freed through the Auto Pact from the limitations of a restricted domestic market.[28] The other path encompasses a broader view. It argues that since the Canadian economy is the result of the exercise of political will over market forces, the current difficulties of industry call into question the responsibility of the state to maintain economic expansion, protection, and renewal, and ultimately the social pact of which this country is the expression.

For some economists, and especially those that are ideologically close to the current Conservative administration, industrial decline is not a relevant issue. There is no necessity for an economy to develop its own industrial base and they see no reason why Canada should not be able to pay for its consumption of manufactured goods with the revenues obtained from the export of its primary products.

In fact, industrial decline is accepted as a normal outcome of trade liberalization. The specialization process in an open economy implies precisely that a limited number of export products will compensate for the import of goods that used to be produced locally. Why should we consider the "smoke-stack economy" a model, they ask, why not look towards the service-oriented society as a positive alternative? While the federal government was struggling internally over the industrial policy issue, this position was strongly argued by the Economic Council of Canada and echoed on the related free trade issue by the Senate Committee on Foreign Affairs.[29]

The North American Economic Decline

The U.S. Economic Decline: Theories and Facts

It is impossible to test so many different approaches and theses within this text, and, in fact, most of the neo-classical explanations of the decline have been omitted from this discussion. The existing literature provides good arguments and solid factual evidence arguing against that perspective.[30]

It seems more useful here to verify whether there is economic decline (industrial, financial, or commercial), deindustrialization, and/or loss of hegemonic position in the United States. The discussion concentrates on several factors, namely military expenditures, the multinationalization of production, and high labour costs. Wallerstein's three-stage theory, in which a hegemonic power loses its competitive edge first in production, then in commerce, and finally in finance, is also examined.

This choice is not fortuitous. The economic decline of the United States seems to be a real and long-term phenomenon, with structural and not simply conjunctural (for example, monetary) causes and consequences. This discussion aims to explore, and if possible, refine, both the explanations of the decline and the stages that decline should follow.

Tables 1 and 2 allow us to refute the thesis of an absolute industrial decline in the U.S. economy. Industrial employment (and especially manufacturing employment) shows positive changes during the post-war period. Following the employment definition, only the United Kingdom was "deindustrialized" during the last twenty-five years, losing 25 per cent of its labour force between 1961 and 1981. West Germany, France, and the Netherlands have lost some

Table 1

Civilian Labour Force
Principal Industrial Countries
1961-81 (thousands)*

		1961	1971	1981	Average Annual Changes 1961/71 %	1971/81 %
USA	All industries	21564	26092	30190	1.9	1.5
	Manufacturing	—	19066	21817	—	1.1
Canada	All industries	1979	2470	3094	2.2	2.3
	Manufacturing	1452	1766	2120	2.1	1.8
UK	All industries	11190	11104	8503	-0.7	-2.7
	Manufacturing	9215	8754	—	-0.8	—
W. Germany	All industries	12932	12741	11123	-0.1	-1.4
	Manufacturing	—	9835	8601	—	1.3
Italy	All industries	7646	7617	7728	0.0	0.1
	Manufacturing	5485	—	5388	—	—
France	All industries	7132	8113	7391	1.2	-0.9
	Manufacturing	—	5726	5269	—	-0.8
Netherlands	All industries	1666	1670	1486	0.0	-1.2
	Manufacturing	1185	1118	1039	0.1	-0.7
Japan	All industries	13460	18450	19700	3.2	0.7
	Manufacturing	10110	13830	13850	3.2	0.0

*"All industries" include resource extraction, manufacturing, public utilities, and building.

Source: OECD: *Labour Force Statistics* (Paris, several issues).

industrial jobs while Canada, the United States, Japan, and Italy actually gained some industrial jobs. Nor has there been any absolute industrial decline in U.S. production, according to table 2. The United States and Canada show slower industrial growth than other advanced competitors, apart from the United Kingdom.

Relative industrial decline is, however, evident from table 3, while relative economic decline can be seen in table 4. In 1980, the U.S. GDP was only

Table 2

Industrial Production
Index Numbers, 1967=100
Principal Industrial Countries

	USA	France	West Germany	Italy	Netherlands	UK	Japan	Canada	*
1970	108	120	131	118	137	111	152	115	130
1977	138	152	152	145	176	123	190	152	158
1978	146	154	154	148	178	127	201	158	163
1979	153	161	162	158	183	132	215	167	175
1980	147	160	162	167	183	124	225	165	176
1981	151	157	160	163	179	119	228	167	175
1982	139	156	156	159	175	119	228	149	173

*Average of France, West Germany, Italy, Netherlands, UK, Japan, and Canada.

Source: U.S. Dept. of Commerce: *International Economic Indicators* (Washington, D.C., several issues).

Table 3

U.S. Share of World Manufacturing Value Added, 1948-79

Year	Current Prices %	Constant Prices %
1948	56.7	
1953	55.3	
1958	34.2	
1963	37.6	29.7
1970		24.3
1975		21.3
1979		21.7

Source: R. Ballance et al., *Collapse and Survival* (1983), p. 16.

Table 4
GDP in Major OECD Countries 1960-80 (%)

Year	USA %	Japan %	West Germany %	France %	UK %	Canada %	Total OECD (billions U.S.$)
1960	53	5	8	6	8	4	944
1965	50	7	8	7	7	4	1388
1970	47	10	9	7	6	4	1927
1975	38	12	10	8	6	4	4081
1980	34	14	11	9	7	3	7544

Source: OECD: *National Accounts* (Paris, several issues).

one-third that of the OECD, compared with more than 50 per cent in 1960. Slow growth rates account for this decline.

Contemporaneous with this relative economic and industrial decline, is found what was defined earlier as commercial decline (see tables 5, 6, and 7). It should be noted that rival trade powers do not follow the same path: the EEC and Canada increased their share of world exports until the beginning of the 1960s. Only Japan steadily increased its share of world trade throughout the period. However, table 6 shows that the United States is the only country in which the growth rates of exports were consistently below the world average from 1950 to 1981. Table 7 shows that the U.S. share of the capitalist world's manufacturing exports fell from 22.3 per cent in 1960 to 14.9 per cent in 1981.

Financial decline is also evident from table 8. During the first twenty years of the post-war period, U.S. banks received large amounts of foreign deposits and made corresponding loans. However, their share of world financing rapidly diminished during the 1960s. In 1966, British banks regained first place in terms of foreign assets, and in 1970, in terms of foreign liabilities. The U.S. banks were not the only ones to decline: the banks of all developed countries saw their share of foreign assets and liabilities of deposit in the capitalist world diminish, while several Arab and NIC banks increased their share correspondingly.

These data refute the thesis that the United States has maintained its economic supremacy in the western world.[31] At the beginning of the 1980s the U.S. was only one industrial power among others, certainly the largest market economy but not a hegemonic power. These data also refute the three-stages pattern of decline suggested by the Wallerstein theory: industrial, commercial, and financial decline occurred at the same time in the U.S. case. Later in the text an explanation for this particular pattern is proposed.

The argument which seeks to explain U.S. deindustrialization as a result of direct investment abroad has similarities to the explanation which attributes it to the transfer of manufacturing production abroad.[32] Both hypotheses are partially confirmed by the data in table 9, which show that U.S. corporations are undertaking an increasing proportion of their industrial production abroad in order to capture foreign markets. These figures, however, have to be considered in light of the following remarks: U.S. corporations have not been alone in multinational expansion; other countries' large firms have not only adopted the same strategy, but the rate of increase of their overseas investment has been faster (see tables 10 and 11).

Table 5

World Exports by Value* 1950-81

	1950 %	1955 %	1960 %	1965 %	1970 %	1975 %	1980 %	1981 %
USA	16.7	16.4	15.9	14.5	13.7	12.3	11.0	11.8
EEC	26.8	30.4	32.6	34.4	35.6	34.0	32.9	30.5
Japan	1.4	2.1	3.2	4.5	6.1	6.4	6.5	7.7
Canada	4.8	4.7	4.3	4.3	5.1	3.7	3.2	3.5
Socialist bloc	8.1	—	11.7	—	10.6	—	—	9.2

*Calculated on f.o.b. exports, current dollars.

Source: UNCTAD: *Handbook of International Trade and Development Statistics* (Geneva, several issues).

Table 6

Average Annual Growth Rate of World Exports 1950-81*

	1950/60 %	1960/70 %	1970/80 %	1950/81 %
World	6.4	9.3	20.4	11.7
USA	5.1	7.8	18.2	9.7
EEC	8.5	10.1	19.4	12.4
Canada	5.3	11.8	14.9	10.6
Japan	15.9	17.5	20.8	18.1

*Calculated on f.o.b. exports, current dollars.

Source: UNCTAD: *Handbook of International Trade and Development Statistics* (Geneva, several issues).

Table 7

World Shares of Exports of Manufactured Products*

	1960 %	1965 %	1970 %	1975 %	1980 %	1981 %
USA	22.3	19.1	16.1	15.1	13.8	14.9
EEC	55.7	55.9	49.4	49.6	48.0	43.2
Japan	6.2	8.6	9.9	11.2	11.9	14.1
Canada	4.3	4.2	5.3	3.5	3.3	3.6

*Capitalist world only. No data before 1958.

Source: UN: *Monthly Bulletin of Statistics* (New York, several issues).

Not only is the U.S. economy itself being invaded by European, Japanese, and Canadian multinational corporations which are carving increasingly important places for themselves in U.S. industry, but many studies show the displacement of U.S. goods by other countries' exports in many foreign markets.[33] In short, the multinational expansion of U.S. manufacturing firms seems to be only a phase in the U.S. decline. Multinationalization is not a cause of decline, but a means of slowing down the decline, sheltering U.S. firms behind the protectionist barriers of client countries against European and Japanese competition. Nevertheless, U.S. overseas investment grows more and more slowly. In 1982, for the first time since World War II, it fell in absolute terms by nearly $6 billion. U.S. multinationals are not immune to the crisis, as Andreff argues;[34] and the revaluation of the dollar has not increased U.S. overseas investment, contrary to Balassa's prediction.

Other explanations of the U.S. economic decline fit the facts better. The explanation which emphasizes the burden of military expenditures is strongly confirmed both by the proportion military expenses account for of total expenses of each developed country, and by public financing of research and development.

In 1981 only 2.5 per cent of publicly financed research and development in the United States went into agriculture and industry, while in Japan and Canada, the equivalent figures amounted to approximately 33 per cent. At the same time, two-thirds of public funds committed to R&D went towards military activities in the United States, compared with 55 per cent in Britain, but only 17 per cent in Japan, 13 per cent in West Germany, and 12 per cent in Italy (see table 13). Moreover, military expenditures represented a larger proportion of total government expenditures in the United States than in any other industrial country; 44 per cent of all U.S. federal expenses went to defence between 1961 and 1970. Although that figure fell to 25 per cent between 1971 and 1980, it remained substantially higher there than in other countries. Once again, Japan is the least militarily burdened advanced country, while the United States is the most encumbered.

As to labour costs, U.S. production workers in manufacturing received compensation substantially higher than their European or Japanese counterparts from 1945 to 1970. For the last ten years (1973 to 1983) this is no longer

Table 8

Deposit Banks: Foreign Assets (% and U.S. billions)

	1963 %	1967 %	1972 %	1977 %	1982 %
USA	26.5	36.2	7.1	10.2	18.3
Canada	10.1	3.7	3.2	2.1	1.7
Japan	8.2	6.4	3.5	2.5	4.0
France	—	—	7.8	8.4	6.4
RFA	9.7	4.0	6.0	6.7	3.6
Belgium	3.0	3.7	3.2	3.3	2.9
Luxembourg	1.1	0.7	8.4	5.9	4.6
Switzerland	—	—	13.2	8.2	7.2
United Kingdom	19.3	22.2	23.4	19.4	20.4
Sub-Total	77.9	76.9	75.8	66.7	69.1
Industrialized countries	89.9	95.8	86.5	76.1	76.9
All countries (%)	100.0	100.0	100.0	100.0	100.0
(US$)	26.7	64.5	255.0	867.4	2267.9

Source: International Monetary Fund., *International Financial Statistics* (Annual Issue, New York 1983).

Table 9

USA: Manufacturing Exports and Foreign Sales of U.S. Firms 1960-77 (U.S. $ billions, current dollars)

Year	Manufacturing Exports[1]	Sales by Foreign Affiliates of U.S. Firms[2]	2 / 1
1960	12.3	23.6	1.9
1965	17.2	42.4	2.5
1970	29.1	78.3	2.7
1977	77.7	246.3	3.2

Sources: UNCTAD: *Handbook of International Trade and Development Statistics* (Geneva, several issues); U.S. Dept. of Commerce: *Survey of Current Business* (Washington, D.C., several issues).

Table 10

Assets Corresponding to Foreign Direct Investments 1967-81

	1967 %	1971 %	1976 %	1981 %
United States	53.8	52.3	47.6	41.0
Western Europe	37.5	37.6	37.0	42.0
Japan	1.4	2.8	6.7	9.0
Canada	3.5	4.1	3.9	5.0
Other countries	3.8	3.2	4.8	3.0
Totals	100.0	100.0	100.0	100.0

Sources: UN, C.T.C.: *Transnational Corporations in World Development* (New York, 1978), p. 262 (for 1967 to 1976); and U.S. Dept. of Commerce: *Business America* (Washington, D.C.).

true; compensation grew much more rapidly in Western Europe and Japan than in the United States, and wages are now equivalent to U.S. rates in most developed countries.[35] The NICs, of course, maintain a comprehensive advantage in many labour-intensive goods (see chart 1).

Canadian Industrial Decline: The Facts

Unlike Great Britain, which is experiencing a real process of deindustrialization, in Canada, as in most OECD countries, the contribution of the manufacturing sector to GDP has declined only slightly. Since the Canadian economy has grown at a rate inferior to that of most European nations during the last decade, Canada's industrial production index of 149 in 1982 was significantly below the mean index for the major industrial countries (see table 2). These data also show the extent of the damage wreaked upon industrial production by the recent recession.

Industrial decline is not a recent phenomenon in Canada. Manufacturing ceased to be the predominant activity leading Canada's economic growth in 1974. This becomes clear when the growth rate of GDP is compared to that of industrial production. The recession of 1981 led to a widening of the gap between these rates of national growth.[36] This decline is confirmed in a much more worrisome manner when the national data on productivity, employment, and trade are examined.

Declines in labour productivity, unknown in the 1960s, occurred four times in the 1970s. The average annual rate of growth in output per person employed in Canada between 1973 and 1980 was marginally negative (minus

Table 11

Foreign Direct Investment Flows, Principal Industrial Countries 1961-79

Country	1961-67 %	1968-73 %	1974-79 %
United States	61.1	45.8	29.3
Canada	2.3	4.5	6.2
Japan	2.4	6.7	13.0
Australia	0.7	1.4	1.6[1]
Belgium	0.3	1.4	2.5[2]
France	6.9	5.2	7.8
F.R.G.	7.2	12.5	17.0
Italy	3.6	3.3	2.0
Netherlands	4.4	6.8	9.6[3]
Sweden	2.0	2.4	3.7[4]
United Kingdom	8.7	9.1	9.2

[1] from 1974 to 1976.
[2] from 1965 on.
[3] from 1974 to 1978.
[4] from 1974 to 1977.

Source: OECD: *International Investment and Multinational Enterprise: Recent Trends in Foreign Direct Investment* (Paris, 1981), 43.

Table 12

Military Expenditure as % Public Expenditure Principal Industrial Countries, 1961-80

	1961-70 %	1971-80 %
USA	44.0	25.0
United Kingdom	17.0	14.0
France	19.0	8.0
West Germany	16.0	11.0
Japan	6.0	5.0

Source: UN: Statistical Yearbook, (New York, several issues).

Table 13

Public Financing of R & D, 1981
Principal OECD countries (%)

	USA %	West Germany %	France %	UK %	Japan* %	Italy %	Canada %
Defence and space	65.7	12.9	41.4	54.9	16.8	12.3	6.6
Energy, infrastructure	14.4	22.0	13.9	8.0	32.4	27.8	25.0
Agriculture, industry	2.5	12.8	12.7	11.6	35.6	21.6	33.2
Health, welfare	13.6	10.0	6.7	3.3	11.2	5.9	14.0
Promotion of knowledge	3.8	42.3	24.6	22.4	4.1	32.4	21.3
Total %	100.0	100.0	100.0	100.0	100.0	100.0	100.0
Total (U.S. billions)	(35.5)	(7.3)	(7.0)	(6.3)	(5.5)	(2.9)	(1.4)

*DATA 1980

Source: OECD: Informations no. 7, (Paris, 1983).

0.2 per cent), compared to positive rates in West Germany (plus 2.9 per cent), Italy (plus 2.1 per cent), and Japan (plus 4.1 per cent). A more accurate measure of labour productivity is the average growth in output per person-hour worked. For the latter, the average annual rate in Canadian manufacturing between 1975 and 1982 was only 1 per cent.[37]

Employment is certainly a major variable in evaluating the scale of industrial decline. Although total employment in Canada has increased significantly since 1970 (plus 34 per cent until 1982), absolute employment in the manufacturing sector has remained stable and is now responsible for a lesser share (minus 4 per cent) of total employment than fifteen years ago. The sector most affected by the decline in employment is the sector producing durable goods. The employment index for the latter, which reached an all-time high of 149 in 1974 (1961=100), had dropped to 122 in 1982, the fall having taken place essentially during the 1981 recession.[38]

The steady increase in unemployment should also be noted. The data show that not only has unemployment risen absolutely, but that it has been increasing faster than the economically active population. The unemployment rate, around 5 per cent in the 1960s, reached 6 per cent in the 1970s, passed the 8 per cent mark in the late 1970s, and has been well above 10 per cent since 1982. This increase indicates that a larger proportion of those willing to work cannot find employment. Even allowing for the growing number of those looking for work, we are faced with an absolute decline in the availability of jobs in the manufacturing sector. It should be stressed for those enamoured of the arrival of the service economy that the cost associated with the job dislocation process may prove to be socially very expensive. For society, all jobs were not created equal. When a worker in the auto industry loses his or her job and goes to work in a fast-food restaurant, society is losing a high productivity, high value added job in return for a low productivity, low value added one. A transition to a service economy is no panacea to Canada's decline.

Only two dimensions of the complex issue of Canadian trade patterns will be considered here. On a global scale, Canada was responsible in 1970 for 6 per cent of world trade; ten years later Canada was down to 3.7 per cent.[39] When exchange rate differences and fluctuations in prices are also taken into account, this represents a very sharp drop. Canada now depends on trade for more than 29 per cent of its GDP, a much higher proportion than for most developed countries with the exception of the Netherlands, Belgium, and Luxembourg. This dependence on trade is even greater for manufactured goods. We export over 30 per cent of the manufactured goods produced in Canada, and we import almost 32 per cent of goods consumed. In 1966 these percentages were respectively 18.8 per cent and 21 per cent. Given the instability of foreign markets and the very important fluctuations in currency exchange rates, and because two-thirds of Canadian trade is with the United States (25 per cent of this total is intra-firm trade), Canada is today much more dependent than in the past on cyclical changes in the U.S. economy and on fiscal and monetary policy decisions made in Washington.

The composition of Canadian exports is of major concern. Of the goods that Canada exports, only 32 per cent are finished goods, and automobiles usually represent 20 per cent of this total. Canada has a positive trade balance for manufactured wood products, pulp and paper, metals, and petroleum, all of which involve raw materials in the early stages of transformation with little value added. The final product trade balance is by itself responsible for a huge deficit of more than $20 billion. The Economic Council of Canada claims that this is not a cause for concern since Canada's export/import ratio for final products has increased significantly over the years: from 30 per cent in the mid-1960s to between 50 to 60 per cent for the period since 1968.[40] However, it must be noted that this ratio reached an all-time high of 64.4 per cent in 1970 and has been declining since then, while the overall trade deficit has reached enormous proportions. In 1964, when the export/import ratio was still 30 per cent, the trade deficit amounted to $2.6 billion; in 1981 a 55 per cent ratio corresponded to a $21 billion deficit. Unlike the Economic Council, we certainly don't see any reason for comfort in this rising ratio.

A complete picture of the full extent of Canadian industrial decline would require an examination of research and development expenditures, uneven regional development, and the evolution of specific manufacturing sectors, the so-called sunset and sunrise industries. However, it is sufficient to note that such analyses would only confirm this analysis of the weaknesses and inadequacies in the Canadian economy.

Chart 1. U.S. productivity and labor costs relative to 10 competitor countries, 1970-81 (1970 = 100)

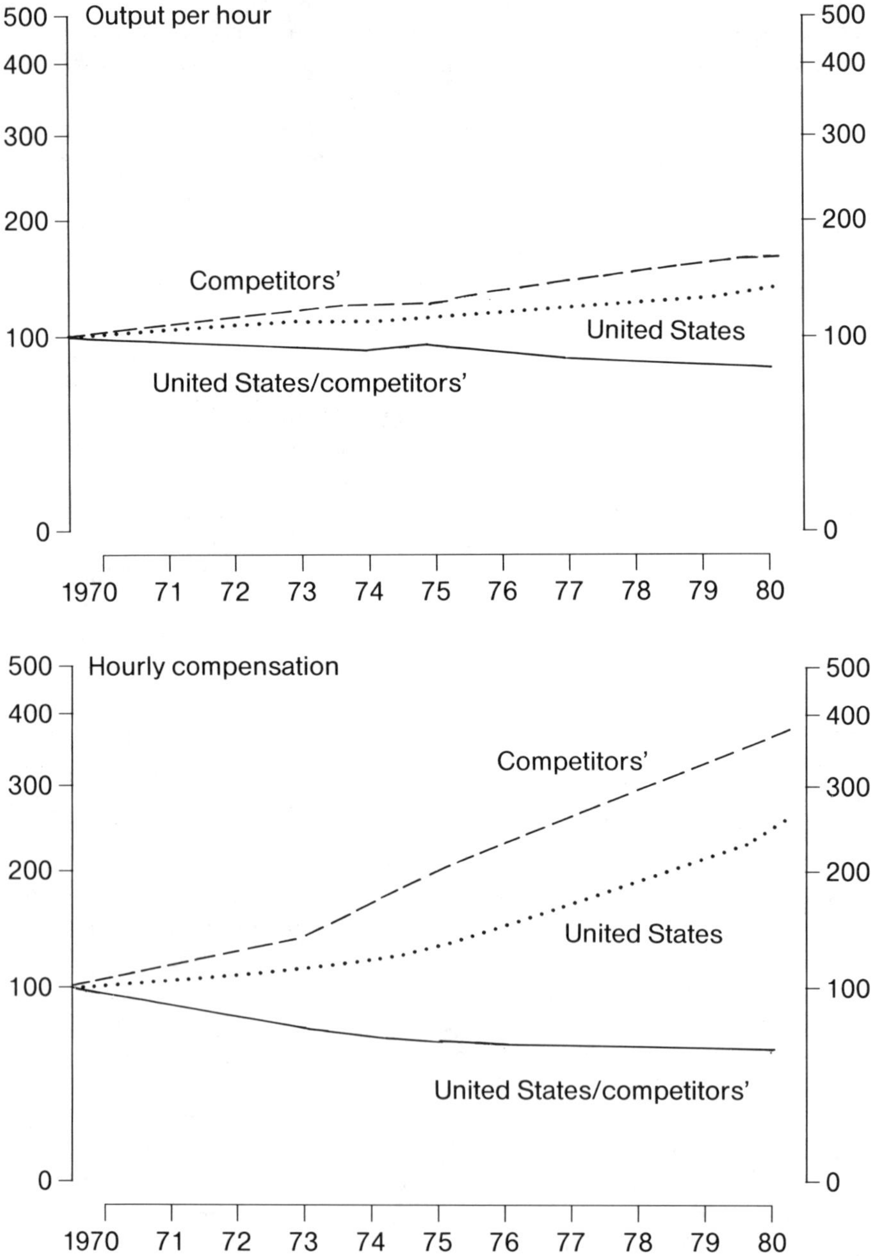

N.B.: Competitors are Canada, Japan, France, West Germany, Italy, Belgium, Netherlands, Denmark, Sweden and Switzerland.

Chart 1. (continued)

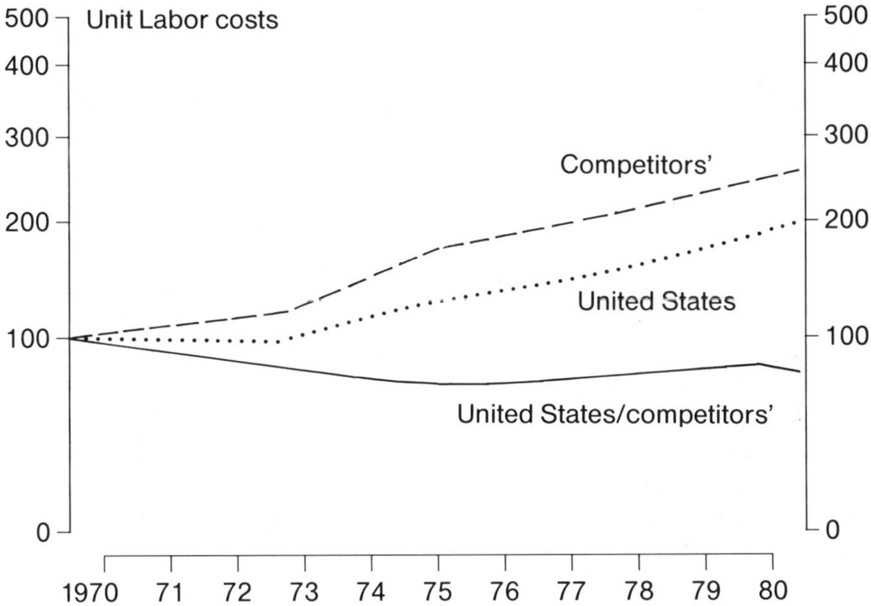

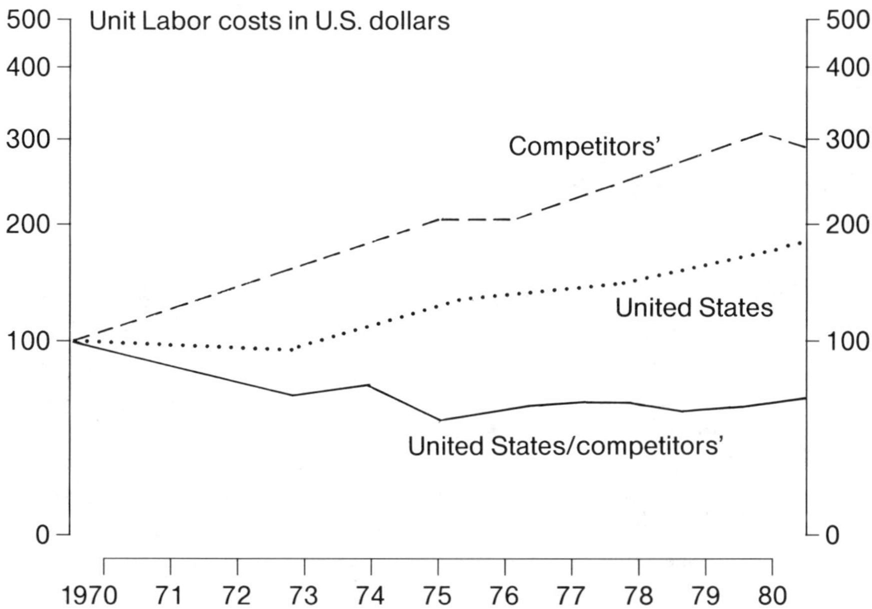

Source: U.S. Dept. of Labor: *Monthly Labor Review*, Dec. 1982, p. 11.

Conclusion

During the post-war period, the United States and Canada have not been deindustrializing, if this term is defined as an absolute loss of industrial jobs and/or an absolute fall in industrial production. Nevertheless, they have both suffered a relative decline in their position within the world economy, not only in manufacturing but also in commerce, and, for the United States, in finance. This decline is partially due to the rising competitiveness of Japan, Western Europe, and several newly industrialized countries, which have captured large shares of foreign and domestic markets previously served by North American products. In the United States, the decline is also due to the military effort; this is evident both in the use of public R&D funds, and in the share of total expenditures that defence spending accounts for. Continental Europe and Japan are much more centred on civilian R&D, while the United States and the United Kingdom use the most public funds for military research, which has decreasing spin-offs on civilian industry. For Canada, increasing foreign competition combined with the substantial liberalization of trade in the post-war period have made more explicit the structural shortcomings of our branch-plant industry. Being linked to a declining giant has the inconvenience that we share its weaknesses but dare not necessarily allow ourselves to take advantage of its remaining strengths.

Notes

1 See, for example, J. Cornwall, "Modern Capitalism and the Trend Towards Deindustrialization," *Journal of Economic Issues*, 14, 2 (1980).

2 B. Bluestone, and B. Harrison, *The Deindustrialization of America* (New York: Basic Books, 1982), 6.

3 S. Bowles, *et al.*, *Beyond the Waste Land* (New York: Anchor Press/Doubleday, 1983).

4 A.P. Thirlwall, "Deindustrialization in the United Kingdom," *Lloyd's Bank Review*, 144 (1982), 22.

5 Thirlwall, "Deindustrialization"; M. Khavisse, and D. Aspiazu, *La estructura de los mercados y la desindustrialización en la Argentina* (Buenos Aires: Centro de economía transnacional, 1983).

6 I.C. Magaziner, and R. Reich, *Minding America's Business* (New York: Random House, 1983); and R.B. Reich, *The Next American Frontier* (New York: Times Books, 1983).

7 G. Gilder, "A Supply-side Economics of the Left," in *The Public Interest*, 72 (1983).

8 H. Magdoff, and P. Sweezy, "The End of U.S. Hegemony," *Monthly Review*, 24 (1971).

9 I. Wallerstein, "The Three Instances of Hegemony in the History of the Capitalist World-Economy," in *The Politics of the World-Economy* (London: Cambridge University Press, 1984).

10 P. Jalée, *L'Imperialisme en 1970* (Paris: Maspéro, 1969); J. Petras, and R. Rhodes, "The Reconsolidation of the U.S. Hegemony," *New Left Review*, 97 (1976); and W. Andreff, *Les Multinationales hors la crise* (Paris: Le Sycomore, 1982).

11 E. Varga, *Essais sur l'économie politique du capitalisme* (Moscow: Ed. du Progress, 1967); E. Mandel, *Europe vs America* (New York: Monthly Review Press, 1979); A. Szymanski, "Is U.S. Imperialism Resurgent? A Critique to Petras and Rhodes," *New Left Review*, 101-102 (1977); A. Szymanski, *The Logic of Imperialism* (New York: Praeger, 1981); and Magdoff and Sweezy, "End of U.S. Hegemony."

12 H. Magdoff, "The U.S. Dollar, Petrodollars and Imperialism," *Monthly Review*, 30 (8) (1979), 11.

13 B. Warren, *Imperialism, Pioneer of Capitalism* (London: New Left Books, 1978); and F. Frobel, *et al.*, *The New International Division of Labour* (London: Cambridge University Press, 1981).

14 R. Vernon, *Storm over the Multinationals* (Cambridge, MA: Harvard University Press, 1977), 48-49.

15 B. Balassa, "Les États-unis dans l'économie mondiale," in *Économie prospective internationale*, No. 9, (Paris: 1982).

16 M. Fouet, *Les États-unis: Une économie dominante dans une période de transition* (Paris: La Documentation française, 1980).

17 R.Z. Lawrence, *Can America Compete?* (Washington, DC: Brookings Institution, 1984).

18 R. Cooper, *The Economics of Interdependence* (New York: McGraw-Hill, 1968); R. Solomon, *The International Monetary System 1945-1976* (New York: Harper & Row, 1977); and W. Simon, *A Time for Action* (New York: McGraw-Hill, 1980).

19 S. Hymer, and B. Rowthorn, "Multinational Corporations and International Oligopoly: The Non-American Challenge," in C.P. Kinderberger, ed., *The International Corporation* (Cambridge, MA: MIT Press, 1970); W. Branson, *Trends in U.S. International Trade and Investment Since World War II* (New York: National Bureau of Economic Research, 1980).

20 R.W. Kopcke, "Potential Growth, Productivity and Capital Accumulation," *New England Economic Review*, (May-June 1980); R. Gilpin, *U.S. Power and the Multinational Corporation* (New York: Basic Books, 1975); Bluestone and Harrison, *Deindustrialization*.

21 Magaziner and Reich, *Minding America's Business*; Reich, *Next American Frontier*; R.M. Kanter, *Change Masters: Innovation and Entrepreneurship in the American Corporation* (New York: Simon and Schuster, 1984).

22 J. Botkin, *et al.*, *Global Stakes: The Future of High Technology in America* (Cambridge, MA: Ballinger, 1982); Magaziner and Reich, *Minding America's Business*.

23 R. Ballance, *et al.*, *Collapse and Survival: Industry Strategies in a Changing World* (London: Allen & Unwin, 1983).

24 R. Mahon, *The Politics of Industrial Restructuring: Canadian Textiles* (Toronto: University of Toronto Press, 1984), 17.

25 I. Lumsden, ed., *Close the 49th Parallel* (Toronto: University of Toronto Press, 1970); R. Laxer, ed., *Canada, Ltd.: The Political Economy of Dependency* (Toronto: McClelland & Stewart, 1973); P. Bourgault, *L'innovation et la structure de l'industrie canadienne* (Ottawa: Conseil des sciences, 1972); J.H.N. Britton, and J.M. Gilmour, *The Weakest Link: A Technological Perspective on Canadian Industrial Underdevelopment* (Ottawa: Science Council of Canada, 1978).

26 G. Williams, *Not for Export* (Toronto: McClelland & Stewart, 1983).

27 R. Starks, *Industry in Decline* (Toronto: Lorimer, 1978), 34-56.

28 R. Perry, *The Future of Canada's Auto Industry* (Toronto: Lorimer, 1982).

29 R. French, *How Ottawa Decides: Planning and Industrial Policy Making 1969-1980* (Toronto: Lorimer, 1980).

30 Magaziner and Reich, *Minding America's Business*; Bowles, *Beyond the Waste Land.*

31 Jalée, *L'Imperialisme en 1970*; Petras and Rhodes, "Reconsolidation;" Fouet, *Les États-unis*; Balassa, "Les États-unis."

32 Bluestone and Harris, *Deindustrialization*; Magdoff, "The U.S. Dollar."

33 See, for example, J. Baranson, *Japanese Challenge to U.S. Industry* (Lexington, MA: Lexington Books, 1981).

34 Andreff, *Les Multinationales.*

35 OECD, *Labour Force Statistics* (Paris: OECD, 1983).

36 Statistics Canada, Cat. 61-005, annual (Ottawa: Statistics Canada).

37 Economic Council of Canada, *The Bottom Line* (Ottawa: Economic Council, 1983), 9.

38 OECD, Labour Force Statistics.

39 United States, Department of Commerce, *International Economic Indicators* (Washington, DC: USGPO).

40 Economic Council of Canada, *The Bottom Line*, 101.

Chapter 4

The United States' Federal Industrial Policy in a Multipolar World

Bertrand Bellon

WHILE IT IS BY NOW generally understood that the economic supremacy of the United States was eroded severely in the 1970s, this erosion actually began in the 1950s as the nations of Europe, and then Japan, began to rebuild their war-ravaged economies. In part, post-war reconstruction provided these countries with a unique opportunity to modernize their manufacturing sectors. The resulting influx of investment, coupled with strong domestic consumer demand, allowed these nations to achieve rates of economic growth during the 1950s and 1960s that were well above those observed more recently and, more importantly, well above those of the United States over the same period. In addition, the late 1960s saw the emergence of the newly industrialized countries or NICs (South Korea, Hong Kong, Taiwan, Singapore, Brazil, Mexico, Spain, and Yugoslavia) as full competitors in the world market. For the most part, the NICs followed explicit export-led growth strategies that concentrated production in a narrow range of manufactured goods; they also had the advantage of poorly paid labour.

The expansion of world trade between 1950 and 1970 benefitted all nations and throughout these two decades the United States led the cause for free trade through the General Agreement on Tariffs and Trade (GATT). The United States was supported in this effort by the Europeans and the period saw significant decreases in the level of tariffs and other barriers to the free and international movement of goods. While beneficial, the expansion of trade also necessitated a global restructuring of industries. The growing competitiveness of the European nations and Japan in such capital-intensive industries as steel and transportation meant a reduction in the U.S. market share of such products. More recently, the increased competitiveness of the NICs in such traditionally labour-intensive sectors as clothing and footwear has meant a further reduction in the U.S. share of the total world market. There is ample evidence of the erosion of the U.S market power in manufactured goods:

- The United States built 97 per cent of all cars and trucks in the world in 1946 — it built only 19 per cent in 1982, while Japan built 29 per cent.
- The U.S. share of international trade in manufactured goods fell from 22 per cent to 15 per cent between 1960 and 1981.
- Between 1970 and 1982, U.S. imports grew from 4 per cent to 8 per cent of GNP, while exports grew only from 4.3 per cent to 6.9 per cent.
- The U.S. had a balance-of-trade deficit of $70 billion in 1983 and more than $100 billion in 1984. At that rate, the total debt may reach $1 trillion by the turn of the century.
- International capital movements have, likewise, been turned upside down. Canadians, Europeans and Japanese now buy and establish plants in the United States. Today, DuPont De Nemours is controlled by Canadian capital, National Steel by Japanese, and American Motors by French.

The effects on the United States of two decades of increasing competition became acute in the 1970s. In part, an attempt by other countries to sustain the rates of economic growth achieved in the 1960s led nations to adopt policies and programs aimed at securing a greater share of the market in their respective lines of specialization. As all competitors, aided by their respective national policies, attempted to capture an increasing share of a particular market, the competition also changed, becoming one of competition among governments and their policies, rather than among companies.

The emergence of "Industrial Policies" in countries other than the United States occurred at the same time the erosion of U.S. market dominance became most visible. This led U.S. businesses and the U.S. government to first attribute the decline of U.S. dominance to the anti-competitive effects of other nations' policies. The U.S. response was, therefore, to consider the use of their own industrial policies; and thus, the primary justification for considering an explicit industrial policy in the United States was as a defence against the policies of competitor nations.

A record U.S trade deficit and a significant number of plant closings marked the year 1982 as a threshold for serious debate over the nature and scope of a U.S. industrial policy. In spite of appearances, the debate does not question whether there currently is or is not a U.S. industrial policy. The central question is whether any U.S. industrial policy should be explicitly recognized and, if so, what form such a policy should take in order to most efficiently restructure and restore the international competitiveness of U.S. industries.

The debate is probably as important for the future of the United States as were the famous Chicago meetings about the trusts in 1899 and 1907, the 1912 electoral campaign, or the Roosevelt New Deal in 1932. One thing is certain — U.S. industrial structure and strategies were well suited for the second industrial revolution spawned by the steel, automobile, and chemical industries: mass production, economies of scale, large demand for uniform manufactured goods, and access to lower cost raw materials and energy. These advantages, however, are not sufficient to insure success in the third industrial revolution, in which flexibility of production must also include more planning due to the uncertainty associated with high technology industries. New questions arise concerning the relations between business and public power, especially in a federal state such as the United States (only federal industrial policy will be considered here).

First, one can ask if there is any relationship between the amount of government support for business and its effectiveness. Business in the United States receives more governmental support than does business in any other country in the capitalist world. Support comes in a variety of forms and represents hundreds of billions of dollars. The most important support is contained in federal expenditures on military research and equipment, which represents 66 per cent of all federal equipment expenditures. The size of military expenditures could contribute to a general economic decline if the technical and financial rewards of such expenditures were not diffused within the economy. The nature of industrial policy could thus constitute a specific cause of economic decline.

Another element contributing to the ineffectiveness or inefficiency of government expenditure is that federal measures towards industry are entirely ad hoc; furthermore, there is rarely any coordination between the fifty-one state governments. Not only do the state governments never consult each other, they actually compete with each other. A third element is that current U.S. industrial policy responds primarily to immediate questions, and only in rare instances does it anticipate problems. Moreover, it does not address the issue of the growth and increasing competitive advantage of foreign countries.

Finally, given the preceding elements, it is appropriate to ask to what extent an industrial policy which is global in scope can be formulated at the federal level in a decentralized country whose population is double that of Japan and whose area is seventeen times that of France?

If there can be a federal industrial policy, what would be the best policy to respond to the new rules of international competition and to restore the United States to a position of world economic leadership? In particular, how should the U.S. government promote a new policy that corresponds to the new competitive rules and addresses the changing balance between social classes? With respect to the latter, the past decade has seen a dramatic weakening of the situation of working people and consumers, as well as their organizations; a renewal of competition between small business and big corporations; and a new balance of power between national and multinational corporations. In general, U.S. society believes the federal government responds primarily to the interests of major lobbies, and for many individuals, suspicion of the government leads them to hold the position that "government is not the solution to our problems. Government is the problem."

This essay addresses these issues and questions. First, the size of federal support of business, including legal and administrative intervention as well as any kind of financial transfer, is examined. The points of view of the principal social groupings are then analyzed. The new balance of financial powers leads to a distinction between big business, small business, and the unions, each of which are represented at the various political government levels.

The Size of Federal Support of Business

A 1984 study by the Congressional Budget Office on Federal support of U.S. business stated: "The Federal government extends financial aid to business as part of its constitutional duty to promote Industry and Commerce."[1] This study found the size of such aid to be at least $400 billion a year and noted its "significant identifiable commercial effects". Among the recipients of such funds was the Department of Defense, which received a total of $140 billion. Of this, $35 billion was spent for research and development programs not directly linked to industry, and about $100 billion went towards direct industrial supports. This second amount primarily comprises tax expenditure programs (almost 80 per cent of the total), most of which are tax incentives to promote investment.

Other forms of aid include direct spending programs ($13.7 billion in 1984 for direct subsidies, not including military expenses) and credit programs, costing a net amount of $8.8 billion in 1984 in terms of direct loan obligations and loan guarantees. Although aid in the form of tax cuts gives the U.S. industrial policy the appearance of being non-interventionist compared to the subsidies dispensed by the Japanese, the relative financial burden of tax expenditures is much heavier than that of subsidies.

Federal aid covers many actitivies: transportation, information networks, energy, research and development, labour skills, foreign trade, banking and credit; competition prevails. Most industries receive assistance of one form or another.

Three major types of federal aid can be distinguished:

- General measures to improve investment, and research and development. Theoretically, these incentives are not targetted towards specific firms, but in practice they benefit a small number of big corporations.
- Selective ad hoc measures which deal with a problem after it has occurred. These measures are not planned, and are usually decided on very quickly.
- Selected and planned measures are much less frequent. They are considered by officials as "industrial policy" and are undertaken only in response to the so-called European and Japanese interventionism and protectionism.

In spite of their common scale, no direct comparison can be made between European and U.S. industrial policy, mainly because the United States has a decentralized political system and the channels through which aid is distributed are varied and often contradictory.[2] For example, individual states, cities, and other kinds of public entities are all active in applying industrial policy. At the federal level, the largest provider of aid is the Department of Commerce. However, several other agencies also provide complementary or sometimes competing programs. These include the Departments of Labor, Housing, and Energy. In addition, the Antitrust Division of the Justice Department, the Federal Trade Agency, and the many commissions regularly established and dissolved by one of the three main powers (that is, Executive Branch, Senate, or Congress) also provide industrial aid. For example, a state may develop a complete recovery plan for an industry, but no complementary plan will be undertaken by the federal government. In other cases, the competition between different states or federal services leads to multiple subsidies for the same activity.

The question of a workable U.S. industrial policy must first address the efficiency with which a large amount of money is shared among the strongest competitors without any kind of coordination.

Regulation and Deregulation

Discussion of industrial policy is normally reserved for the last chapter of industrial organization textbooks or essays.[3] It is generally accepted that government responsibility towards business is to guarantee or to reestablish competition. Thus, apart from a few unprofitable activities (most school or hospital systems are considered as profitable as any other industry), the only microeconomic roles attributed to the government are anti-trust and regulatory systems. The effect of these systems, however, has been contested recently.

The anti-trust laws arose from litigation against railroad monopolies, and financial and industrial power in the 1870s. The Sherman Antitrust Act was passed in 1880, and had its day of glory with the break-up of the Rockefeller oil empire before World War I. The Act has become a central part of the business landscape and almost every trust has had some trouble with this legislation (for example, the recent dissolution of AT&T and the IBM case).

The anti-trust system is one of the most efficient pieces of legislation the federal bureaucracy has ever devised. It has also been the object of increasing criticism by different interest groups, especially big business, which argues that to compete with foreign companies (which supposedly receive greater subsidies than those available in the United States), the trusts must have more freedom to merge or to settle joint ventures. Different plans to restructure the anti-trust law are underway; one of the main contests concerns the Glass Steagle Act on banking partitioning.

The Regulation System is comprised of thousands of laws accumulated over the years. Certain laws address specific business problems while others are intended to protect consumers, savers, the environment, and elderly or disabled people.[4] These laws are administered by numerous agencies (there were fifty-seven in 1980). At the end of the 1970s these agencies controlled about 24 per cent of GNP and employed 88,000 people at an annual cost of $3.2 billion.

The efficacy of the regulatory system is not easy to measure and the data provided differ widely. Some conclude it is fully effective; others merely consider it necessary.[5] The Reagan administration, however, views deregulation as one of the cornerstones of its economic program. Deregulation concerns almost all institutions today; it is supposed to increase competition, lower prices, and remove bureaucratic obstacles. It has had some dramatic effects in industries such as air transportation but does not always result in lower prices.

One of the central arguments made in favour of regulation is not addressed by the advocates of deregulation, namely that the less quantifiable aspects of production (quality, pollution, or social safety) can hardly be measured by market indices alone.

Federal Industrial Policy Expenditures

The main characteristics of federal expenditures are their *amount*, their *stability*, and their *selectivity*.

It has already been mentioned that the total amount of these expenditures in the United States is significant. U.S. government purchases of military equipment, as well as direct industrial incentives, are larger than the whole annual state budget of France; total research and development expenditures exceed those of Japan and France combined, and 55 per cent of this sum is paid out by the federal government, more than half representing military-related research.

Financial transfers from public to private sectors are very stable. In spite of the relative capability to create and dissolve ad hoc governmental committees, the stability and the relative concentration of aid must be underlined.

The Federal Administration Buy American Program: an old law from the Roosevelt administration (the Buy American Act, 1933) requires the governmental agencies to buy U.S. products as long as their price is "reasonable". Reasonable is defined to mean that the U.S. price does not exceed by 50 per cent the foreign price in the case of purchases made by the Defense Department, 12 per cent for goods purchased by small businesses, and 6 per cent for other goods. Moreover, for certain departments (forestry, marine, energy, transportation) and in the case of military goods, buying U.S. products is mandatory. For many industries the federal government is the only, or the most important, purchaser. Today, military purchases alone represent 57 per cent of the aeronautical market, 54 per cent of national shipyard output, 33 per cent of radio and television equipment goods, and 26 per cent of the market for scientific instruments.

Federal Support for Research and Development: although expenditures on R&D have remained relatively unchanged (in constant dollars) for twenty years while private expenditures have increased regularly, the former still represent half of all U.S. R&D expenditures ($38.7 billion in 1983 not including $2.4 billion in tax cuts).

Since 1980 budget and administrative practices have changed to benefit the defence-related research and development budget. At the same time, the administration has reoriented its direct spending towards basic research in private business. Cuts have been deepest in the departments of energy, commerce, and the interior as well as in the Environmental Protection Agency. The federal R&D budget is concentrated in only a few industries: aerospace, telecommunications, nuclear energy, electronics, and agriculture.

The International Trade Incentives are very similar to those of the European countries, in that the U.S. government provides administrative and technical support. With respect to foreign markets, they also provide financial help to both export producers and buyers, thereby guaranteeing a demand for U.S. goods. The Eximbank or the "DISC Program" represented $4.5 billion of expenditures in 1984, to which must be added $9 billion of new loan guarantees as well as $4.3 billion of international loans conditioned by U.S. goods purchases. Here too, the industrial concentration of aid is very high: 80 per cent of Eximbank benefits went to the ten largest exporters in 1983.

Non-Tariff Barriers. In spite of the impression that the United States is less protectionist than its trading partners, U.S. non-tariff barriers have increased steadily as tariffs have been reduced under the GATT. In particular, the United States has renewed a policy of bilateral negotiations based upon the principle of reciprocity, which could represent the end of the "most favoured nation" principle. To a certain extent, the U.S. considers the GATT a tool which cannot be improved upon, one which, in fact, presents itself mainly as a constraint. New U.S. policy will therefore be composed of an unsettled mixture of tariff barriers, quotas, and bilateral negotiations, as well as other adjustment arrangements such as "orderly marketing agreements".

Recent history reveals that a large number of restrictive measures (the most visible being voluntary restrictions on exports to the U.S.), have been imposed in the paper, automobile, and steel industries. The events that give rise to this type of restriction occur in a consistent fashion: first, increasing demand for imports results in a loss of national market share. Then U.S. business, backed by unions, requests governmental protection. When such protection is insufficient to reduce imports, taxes as well as diplomatic negotiations with the competitor country lead to self-limitations. More often than not, the latter are obtained; in which case, anti-trust pursuits are abandoned and direct help to domestic industry is eased off. The appearance of a free market is thus safeguarded.

These forms of protectionism are far from the Frederick List theories on protection of new industries and are in fact concerned primarily with declining industries. They are also considered to be a public contribution to economic survival, rather than a possible means of restructuring investment.

There are also more complex "adjustment assistance" plans, such as the Footwear Industry Revitalization Program. Such programs combine subsidies, federal loan guarantees, interest subsidies, technical or trade assistance, and some tariff and non-tariff barriers. The most complete plan is probably the Steel Trigger Price Mechanism which has acted to limit imports from the EEC (4.1 million tons in 1982 compared to 5.6 million tons in 1980). Today, approximately 20 per cent of U.S. industry is protected by non-tariff barriers, and two more major industries (machine-tools and semi-conductors) are expected to obtain a similar type of aid in the near future.

In summary, while the U.S. has a much less overt system of legal and bureaucratic support of business than do the European countries and Japan, the amount of money transferred from the federal government to U.S. businesses is far greater. The sums involved (between $100 and $400 billion, according to the definition) represent permanent supports for certain industries or corporations, and are greater than those which are the outcome of planned industrial policies in many other countries.

The Partners' Point of View

New Balance of Power

The industrial dynamism of the United States is closely related to its principles of liberalism and individual responsibility, and it is felt that collective welfare and interest follow automatically from individual liberty and laisser faire public policy. Rhetorical commitment to a collective industrial responsibility becomes meaningless when set against the defence of specific group interests. For that reason it is hard to find any place to begin a discussion, to reach consensus, or to make decisions from a national point of view free from the influence of lobbies.

Many peoplè think that the U.S. social structure makes it impossible to have any kind of industrial policy, and they consequently ask for general government disengagement from business. The economic ideology of the "Chicago School" has had an increasing influence on politicians and business owners. According to this view, laisser faire has to be generalized and will provide a natural selection of winning corporations, and eventually, a renewal of U.S. industrial competitiveness. This view condemns any kind of industrial policy, and views the present anti-trust system as harmful.

Two major economic disruptions, however, have served as arguments to refute this Darwinian view. This first has been the complete destabilization of regions whose wealth was tied to smokestack industries. Plants have closed and not been replaced by any kind of new activity; unemployment has risen and collective standards of living deteriorated as major cities verge on bankruptcy; even several regional banks have failed. In such cases, the individual decisions of a firm have been translated into social problems and responsibilities at the local, regional, or national level.

The second disruption has been a change in the structure of industrial activity. Power inside the corporation has shifted, as the position of technician-manager has progressively given way to that of finance-manager.[6] At the same time, the relative power of different industries has changed. Electronic and high technology machine-tool industries have supplanted steel, chemical, and automobile production as leading industries. This transformation has meant that business is concerned more with financial production (profits, earnings) than with the production of real goods. This focus has had the effect of depressing the economy, with subsequent effects on the rate of growth, investment, employment, and profits.

The data in table 1 show the relative decline of manufacturing business. At the same time, internationalized big business (petroleum, automobile, computers...) have merged. As a result, there are expanding areas of common interest between these two sectors of U.S. business. More than half of the assets of U.S. Steel are now invested overseas, and in fact exceed those assets invested in steel production. On the opposite side, petroleum companies are more diversified and hold assets in a variety of domestic industries. The conflict between "smokestack" and "high tech" activities still lies ahead, the important difference being that the same corporations today ask for more protection for the former and more liberalism for the latter.

This explains the strong sectoral support policies which exist in the steel, textile, and automobile industries. In the computer products industry, the absence of explicitly protectionist policies is replaced by guarantees of domestic military purchases. These guarantees form the basis for a strong initiative devoted to closing the technology gap with Japan. The machine-tool industry is not covered by any federal adjustment assistance plan — possibly because it is a small business sector with insufficient influence in Washington.

The 500

The opinions of big business on the question of the appropriateness of an industrial policy vary depending on whether the question is considered in the abstract or on a practical level, directed specifically to the concrete difficulties of individual industries.[7]

At an abstract level, most managers vigorously oppose any federal interference in the business decision-making process, even if they are the first and (sometimes sole) beneficiary of public purchases. Arguments against an explicit industrial policy include:

- The U.S. is not facing any real deindustrialization.

Table 1

Profits by Principal Economic Sector, U.S. and Rest of the World, 1960-83 (In billions of current dollars)

	1960	1970	1980	1983	Variation 83/60
U.S.					
Petroleum and coal	2.5	3.5	28.2	21.2	x8.5
Trade	4.9	9.5	23.6	34.2	x7.0
Financial activities*	7.2	12.1	26.9	31.4	x4.4
Aluminum and chemical products	9.5	13.0	24.3	30.4	x3.2
Durable goods	11.6	10.2	20.4	17.8	x1.5
Transportation and public utilities	7.4	8.2	17.1	20.6	x2.8
Others	3.6	5.9	21.3	17.8	x4.9
Rest of the World	3.0	6.5	29.9	22.0	x7.3
Total	49.7	68.9	191.7	195.4	x3.9

*Consist of the following industries: banking, other credit agencies, security industry, insurance and real estate investment funds.

Source: Department of Commerce, Bureau of Economic Analysis.

- The industrial policies of other nations are not, in fact, successful (for example, Japanese successes are attributed to managerial practices and not to state assistance coordinated by MITI).
- The U.S. government has no technical capacity to choose between those industries or enterprises to be helped. It is already less competent than the market to choose between winners and losers.[8]
- Finally, any federal institution involved with industrial policy responsibilities would undoubtedly be subject to pressures from financial lobbies as well as from their electorate.

This debate, however, never addresses the public effect of research and development incentives and federal capital goods purchases. These expenditures are considered part of a normal, benevolent state attitude towards business.

At a practical level, this liberalism is tempered as soon as it becomes necessary to deal with the increasing difficulties faced by declining industries.[9] The increasing penetration of domestic markets by foreign capital has led managers to adopt a "tit for tat" attitude to any infraction of the GATT rules by other countries. They assume that the size of the U.S. market (often considered to include Canada) allows the country simultaneously to promote an independent policy and to vary its policy of discriminatory protectionism according to the specific country or industry in question. This tendency would explain the increase in both protectionist and liberal measures over the last two decades.

The "smokestack" industries have completely abandoned the principles of economic liberalism. The most structured manifestation of this tendency is the Labor-Industries Coalition for International Trade, formed in 1980 by eight corporations (Bethlehem Steel and corporations in the textile, glass, mining, and electrical equipment sectors) and eleven unions affiliated to the AFL-CIO.[10]

Other financiers, mainly connected with industries in the northeast, have suggested new organizational and financial "tools" to help restructure corporate activities (for example, Edward Jefferson and Irving Shapiro from Dupont de Nemours, or Felix Rohatyn from Lazard Frères).[11]

Despite this, the frequent rejection of an explicit industrial policy is linked to big business' capacity to "play the game" profitably even in the event of political change:

- Big business already has enough negotiating experience at different political and administrative levels to be sure that the collectivity will take care of industrial social costs as well as new equipment investments and the cost of subsequent redundancies.
- Big business knows how to deal with plants in predominantly rural states, while individual states compete to attract new activities.

- Big business makes no secret that it is ready to fight for its interests in the event of the establishment of explicit industrial policies. The different lobbies would be forced to act upon the major (or minor) implications of any financial decisions. Every election would thus represent a potential financial threat in that expenditures made in accordance with previously established industrial policies could be obsolete and thus require change — and *new* capital expenditures.

Small Business

The increasing convergence of interests between large international and national businesses has widened the gap between these and small businesses in the United States. However, as is the case in other highly industrial countries, the industrial network is composed of thousands of small independent enterprises that are constantly moving, creating, restructuring, taking risks, and contributing more than any other sector to economic dynamism. Today, mid-sized enterprises (100 to 500 employees) account for more employment and spend more for research and development than all other firms. Enterprises with less than 500 employees account for 58 per cent of employment but receive less than 20 per cent of federal aid for investment and, despite their importance, are declining because of increasing corporate concentration and a steady decline in their share of sales, capital, or profits.[12]

The only permanent claim from small business for industrial policy is that it should facilitate wider access to financial capital. It is, in fact, still more difficult to borrow small amounts of high risk capital than it is to cover large national or international corporate loans. A recent proposal for a new Reconstruction Finance Corporation (RFC) to be created in the image of the one formed in 1932 by President Hoover, is backed by different representatives of small business as well as north-east bankers and unions.[13] The RCF would be supervised by a board composed of representatives of business, unions, and public administration. The capital would be provided equally by the public and private sectors and help would be granted to any corporation, regardless of size.

The proposed RFC would promote and encourage small business participation and would seek to avoid the natural credit concentration which benefits big corporations. However, such an administration would find it hard to adjust itself to those specific local business environments within which small businesses operate. Moreover, what organization will lend money without disproportionate a priori control?

Despite the efficiency of the Small Business Administration, small business managers remain reluctant in their support for industrial policy initiatives. They give much more support to individual state investment funds, the promotion of industrial parks, direct subsidies, and increasing links with university research at the local or individual state level.

The Unions

From a European point of view, U.S. unionism appears to have very specific features; it is highly concentrated in certain industries (those representative of the division of labour specific to the second industrial revolution) and is completely absent in others. It is involved with the defence of the economic interests of union members (collective agreements) to the exclusion of those who are not unionized as well as of more "political" issues (consumerism, ecology, peace and war, socialism, and so forth). Moreover, unionism is represented by only one major federation (the AFL-CIO claims to represent 77 per cent of unionized workers) and for fifteen years has been in permanent trouble, with decreasing affiliation and no success in organizing workers in the new high tech industries.

But the AFL-CIO is deeply involved in industrial policy, starting with a protectionist program. The union federation has consistently opposed the multinational tendency towards foreign investment and exportation of jobs. On the other hand, unions have for years been relatively restrictive concerning technical industrial progress. Finally, the AFL-CIO has asked the federal government to protect vulnerable industries such as steel, glass, and automobiles.[14] Recently the unions have participated in coalitions with corporations in traditional sectors.[15]

In October 1983, the AFL-CIO convention adopted its broadest, most comprehensive, white paper on industrial policy to date:

> Lopsided growth and weakness in America's goods-producing industries are accelerating the economy's movement toward a two-tier workforce. New patterns of technology and international trade combine with unbalanced industrial growth to reduce the number of well-paid blue-collar jobs while inflating the ranks of low-paid workers performing relatively simple, low-skill, routine jobs in poor working environments. The layer of managers, scientists, engineers, and professionals at the top has been strengthened, but only slightly.
>
> When the millions of unemployed, discouraged workers, and involuntary part-time workers are considered, America faces not just a two-tier workforce but the emergence of a two-tier society. Needed job openings with a decent future are evaporating, with disastrous consequences for displaced communities and for women, minorities and the young.

A more recent study describes a wider approach to those selective measures which would have to be adopted in any acceptable industrial competition act.[16] But the original proposals are more concerned with the structure of U.S. society.

- They aim at building consensus by bringing together industry, labour, and government (federal, state, and local), to develop an agreed-upon analysis of industry's problems and potential.
- They ask for the establishment of a "Council on Industrial Competitiveness" to coordinate private and government actions affecting industry.

The measures presented will not be adopted by the Reagan administration but were integrated into the electoral program of Walter Mondale in his 1984 presidential campaign. They reflect a dramatic change in the feelings of an increasing percentage of the U.S. population concerning the appropriate role of the state in enhancing industrial competitiveness.

Conclusion

This discussion of the debate surrounding the question of industrial policy emphasizes recent events and is specific to the United States. A central issue is that current U.S. policy is a patchwork composed of a number of de facto industrial policy programs masquerading behind other names. The amounts of money which these programs receive, their permanency, and their selectivity mean that these measures exercise considerable influence over industrial development.

This form of "industrial policy" is, initially, horizontal and intended to insure an equilibrium between corporations (anti-trust system) as well as to favour research and development, investments, exports, or information circulation. These measures, except a few focussed on small business, favour the largest corporations (but not necessarily the most exposed or disadvantaged) and create a kind of protectionism within a generally competitive system. These measures represent a part of the U.S. industrial structure and are as rigid as similar measures in European countries. They appear to present very few opportunities to abet industrial restructuring without a high degree of protectionism.

These measures are very selective. They are concentrated on a few industries (defence-related, aerospace research-related, etc.) and are more attractive to those companies which are already profitable (since they use tax cuts instead of subsidies). Nevertheless, these policies, except for natural monopolies regulation, are under an ideological blockade. No specific clarification is made of the economic effects of federal intervention such as diplomatic steps to obtain voluntary export restraint programs from U.S. trading partners, compensation and safety clauses, military-related expenses, and rapidly increasing assistance to save enterprises and banks from bankruptcy.

The last aspect of the decentralized U.S industrial policy is its size. The size of the domestic market, the structure of the federal political system, the regionalization at the state level of many industries and, in particular, of the banking system, as well as the diversity of employment skills needed, gives to the individual states a distinct responsibility and rationale for promoting industrial development and dynamism.

The structural crisis besetting U.S. industry raises the question of whether coordinated economic relations between public and private interests are needed. The size, richness, and profitability of the natural resource-based industries in the U.S. have buoyed its economy, and allowed this question to remain unanswered, for too long. This dependence on primary industries, combined with the move offshore of U.S.-based multinational capital has, in a very real way, contributed to the relative decline of U.S. industry.

Notes

1 U.S. Congress, *Federal Support of U.S. Business*, by P. Webre, (1984), ix.

2 I.C. Magaziner and R.B. Reich, *Minding America's Business: The Decline and Rise of the American Economy* (New York: Random House, 1983); A. Etzioni, *An Immodest Agenda: Rebuilding America Before the 21st Century* (New York: McGraw-Hill, 1983).

3 P. Asch, *Industrial Organization and Antitrust Policy* (New York: Wiley, 1983); K.W. Clarkson and R. LeRoy Miller, *Industrial Organization, Theory, Evidence and Public Policy* (New York: McGraw-Hill, 1982).

4 L.J. White, *Reforming Regulation, Processes and Problems* (Englewood Cliffs: Prentice-Hall, 1981); and M. Schinter, *Contemporary Government and Business Relations* (Boston: Houghton Mifflin, 1983).

5 Clarkson and LeRoy Miller, *Industrial Organization*; and S. Tolchin and M. Tolchin, *Dismantling America — The Rush to Deregulate* (Boston: Houghton Mifflin, 1983).

6 S. McMelman, *Profit Without Production* (New York: Knopf, 1983).

7 H. Brown, *The Reaction of Business to Industrial Policy*, Annual Meeting of ASSA, San Francisco, December 1983, (New York: Anchor Press/Doubleday, 1983).

8 P.W. McCracken, "Industrial Policy — The Grin Without a Cat," *Across the Board* (January 1984).

9 J.L. Goldstein and S.D. Krasner, "Unfair Trade Practices: The Case for Differential Response," Annual Meeting of the American Economic Association, San Francisco, 1983.

10 LICIT (Labor-Industry Coalition for International Trade), *The Erosion of America's Competitive Edge* (Washington: 1982); and LICIT, *International Trade, Industrial Policies and the Future of American Industry* (Washington: 1983).

11 F.G. Rohatyn, *The Twenty-Year Century. Essays on Economics and Public Finance* (New York: Random House, 1983).

12 White, *Reforming Regulation.*

13 Rohatyn, *The Twenty-Year Century.*

14 W. Adams, *The Structure of American Industry* (New York: Macmillan, 1982).

15 LICIT, *The Erosion of America,* and *International Trade.*

16 AFL-CIO, *Deindustrialization and the Two-tier Society* (Washington: 1984).

Chapter 5

The Crisis of Fordism and the Restructuring of the Canadian Auto Industry

John Holmes

> The current crisis in the North American automotive industry is much more than just a temporary downturn in an industry noted for its cyclical nature ... at the heart of the current crisis lie fundamental changes in the nature of world markets and in the basis of competition for these markets.[1]

THE GOAL OF THIS essay is to provide an analysis and interpretation of the causes of, and forms taken by, industrial restructuring and reorganization in the "Canadian" automobile industry in the period since 1960.[2] This restructuring has occurred in two phases. The first was in the mid-1960s in response to a sectoral crisis confined largely to the Canadian auto industry. The second phase began in the late 1970s and is part of the general economic crisis which has enveloped the world economy over the past decade, leading to widespread and large-scale restructuring of industrial production throughout the economies of the OECD.

The outcome of the first phase of restructuring influenced the forms taken in the second period of restructuring in the Canadian industry. Since the mid-1960s, the Canadian automotive products industry has been an essential part of an integrated North American automobile production system. Its fortunes have therefore been linked intimately to developments taking place in the U.S. automotive industry. However, it is misleading to assume that developments in the "Canadian" portion of the North American auto industry simply mirror those in the "U.S." industry. For example, the industry in Canada has experienced a strong recovery from the deep recession of 1979-82 and the slowdown which continues to plague the U.S. auto industry appears to be over in Canada. Employment in the Canadian industry is now close to the previous peak levels achieved in 1979; few, if any, Canadian auto workers remain on permanent layoff; and, in sharp contrast to the large trade deficits of the late 1970s, over the last three years Canada has accumulated a $12 billion trade surplus on its automotive trade with the U.S., with a further $6 billion expected to be added to it during 1985. However, this apparent recovery of the Canadian auto industry is extremely fragile and masks fundamental problems which still remain within the North American automotive industry as a whole. The apparent strength of the industry in Canada relative to the U.S. reflects the uneven development of the industry *within* North America in response to geographically differentiated conditions of production.

While there seems to be general agreement regarding the existence of a crisis in the North American auto industry in the late 1970s and early 1980s, interpretations of its causes and possible resolutions differ widely. A recent influential report on the U.S. auto industry identified three major schools of interpretation.[3] The first argues that while serious, the current crisis is temporary, the result of changing consumer preferences and the initial lack of production capacity in North America to manufacture small cars; given sufficient time and money, the auto-makers will realign their product lines and the crisis will be solved. A second interpretation is based on product cycle theory. The crisis in the auto industry is seen as one example of a long-term trend towards the removal of manufacturing production in "mature" industries to lower cost production sites outside North America. The third group of interpretations assess the crisis as a reflection of the need for fundamental structural change in the auto industry and expect potential resolutions to the crisis to be found in rapid product and process innovation.

The interpretation arrived at here clearly falls into this last category. However, it goes further than those analyses which view the need for structural change solely within the context of the automotive industry itself, arguing that the crisis in this sector represents only one instance of a more general restructuring crisis which currently confronts many sectors of industrial production in North America. This restructuring crisis stems from the disintegration of the particular phase or model of capitalist accumulation which underlay the long post-war economic boom (labelled Fordism or the "regime of intensive accumulation" by writers of the French "regulation school").[4] An understanding of the mode of regulation which has underpinned Fordism also provides the key to understanding the first phase of restructuring in the Canadian auto industry.

This essay is divided into two main sections. The first makes some brief and general observations regarding the interrelationships between economic crises, industrial restructuring, and changes in the locational structure of production. It is mainly concerned with providing an interpretation of the development and characteristics of the restructuring crisis which has enveloped many sectors of industrial production in both the U.S. and Canada over the last decade and a half. This interpretation provides an essential context for understanding the forms taken by restructuring in the Canadian automotive products industry in the period after 1960. The second major section of the essay analyzes these forms in detail.

This analysis stresses the historically and geographically specific nature of industrial change. The precise forms restructuring takes will vary between individual industrial sectors. At the general level, investment and restructuring decisions within particular sectors and firms can be related to phases of accumulation which affect the general structure of economic relations within which all sectors or firms operate. At a more concrete level, the general structure is seen to be highly differentiated, and it is essential to consider the particular structure of competition and operating conditions facing the specific firm or sector in question.[5] It is therefore both difficult and dangerous to generalize about the nature of restructuring across a range of different sectors. To avoid this pitfall, the concrete analysis is restricted here to restructuring in only one industrial sector: the Canadian automotive products sector.

The Contemporary Restructuring Crisis in the Canadian Economy

> ...in the last decade, Canada has encountered ferocious economic problems. Unemployment has soared to levels unprecedented since the Great Depression. Inflation has leapt to heights never before experienced outside of wartime. And productivity growth has sunk to a rate so low that it has no historical parallel at all.[6]

Economic Crises, Industrial Restructuring, and Locational Change

The empirical evidence clearly demonstrates that the relatively stable postwar period of accumulation had come to an end in Canada by the mid-1970s, as it had throughout most of the advanced capitalist world. Since then, the manufacturing sector in Canada has displayed many of the symptoms characteristic of the crisis confronting the economies of virtually all of the OECD countries: a drastic slowdown in productivity growth, declining industrial employment, stagnating industrial output, and sharply rising unit labour costs.[7]

During the 1970s realized profit rates fell, and along with intensifying international competition, this forced many industrial sectors and individual firms to restructure and reorganize production on a very large scale. There is now general agreement that both the scale and nature of the restructuring underway during this period has been qualitatively different from normal capitalist processes of reorganization.[8]

Periods of extensive restructuring and reorganization within and across industrial sectors are precipitated by major crises in accumulation and occur in an attempt to reestablish or create conditions under which profitable accumulation is possible. Thus, as O'Connor notes:

> ...[crises] compel capital to reorganize itself to prepare for new rounds of capital accumulation...capital accumulates through crises which become the cauldrons in which capital qualitatively reorganizes itself for future economic expansion.[9]

Restructuring crises become a "veritable hothouse" for the development of the forces and relations of production. They often result in profound changes in the organization of labour processes, labour markets, and production systems as the search for new production technologies and the accompanying conflict between workers and management intensifies.[10]

Clearly, changes in the organization of production and labour processes associated with industrial restructuring have an impact on the geography of industry. But geography is not simply a reflection of restructuring, it is often an active ingredient of the restructuring process itself.[11] In reality, the geographical (spatial) and non-geographical (aspatial) aspects of restructuring and reorganization are inseparable. Simple existence of geographical unevenness in the conditions and factors of production, in addition to qualitative differences in the nature of this unevenness, will have an "effect" on the aspatial processes of reorganization and restructuring. In turn, one outcome of the latter will be to change the existing form of uneven spatial development and influence the future course taken by accumulation. As Massey notes:

> The nature of capital's response to spatial unevenness is itself a product of the interaction between the existing characteristics of spatial differentiation and the requirements at any time of the dominant process of production. This interaction is important — not only does production shape geography; the historically evolved geographical configuration (both the fact of spatial differentiation and its particular nature) has its influence on the course taken by accumulation.[12]

Thus, within any industry there exists a spatial division of labour which is subject to change over time.[13] Such changes may result either from a change in regional characteristics which influence the subsequent orientation of the accumulation process, or through changes in the production and labour processes as a result of restructuring which may change the locational requirements of firms in the industry.

The Nature of the Current Restructuring Crisis

To understand the character of the economic relations within which restructuring in the automotive products sector has taken place over the last two decades, it is necessary first to understand the nature and characteristics of the crisis which marked the end of the post-war boom and triggered the current period of restructuring. This crisis has affected not only the automotive sector but a wide range of other manufacturing industries as well.

There is a growing body of evidence and opinion which suggests that in the late 1960s the world economy entered the third "long swing" crisis of the past hundred years and that the restructuring now underway is an attempt to find a "solution" which would herald the emergence of a new and qualitatively distinct phase of capitalist accumulation.[14] Although writers differ in the specifics of their analyses, they have reached general agreement with respect to the approximate timing of the development of the crisis and the need to situate it in the context of the post-war boom. They also agree that this restructuring crisis is of profound significance, since it represents a major point of rupture within the history of capitalist development and involves major qualitative changes in economic and social institutions.[15]

This essay adopts the general interpretation of the post-war boom and subsequent crisis which was developed by the French regulation school,[16] emphasizing those aspects which are particularly pertinent to an analysis of the auto industry. Central to the regulation school's analysis of the post-war period is the development and subsequent crisis of the intensive regime of accumulation which they call "Fordism".

In the inter-war period, the application of the principles of work study and scientific management developed by Taylor, and of the assembly line system for organizing industrial production pioneered by Ford, laid the groundwork for a dramatic and sustained rise in labour productivity in the consumption goods sectors. The emphasis was on the production of goods capable of being produced in long production runs which would yield considerable economies of scale and a progressive reduction of the unit costs of production. However, the full development of intensive accumulation based on Taylorism and Fordist techniques of production organization was blocked during the inter-war period by insufficient purchasing power on the part of the working class. This led in turn to the massive and unprecedented crisis of overproduction in the early 1930s. The extensive restructuring which occurred in the late 1930s and early 1940s in the wake of that crisis ushered in a new mode of regulation by transforming the spheres of consumption and reproduction. To be successful, mass production "required" as a corollary the development of mass consumption. The latter was achieved in the post-war period by means of radical changes in the spheres of consumption and reproduction, which not only created outlets for new types of consumer goods but also enabled the satisfactory reproduction of workers suited to the new forms of work associated with Fordism.

In sum, the combination of the increasing specialization of the technical division of labour, the progressive generalization of Fordist techniques of production, and the continued expansion of mass consumption led to steady economic growth and rising levels of productivity in the period from 1945 to the late 1960s.[17] Two points should be emphasized: First, the crucial significance of the link between rising rates of productivity and the growth in real wages; and second, the fact that among the advanced capitalist societies Fordism developed as a regime of accumulation whose regulation was essentially internal to each national economy. It was predicated on the internal transformation of industrial production processes and on the growth of their internal domestic market through the development of mass consumption and rising real wages linked to productivity growth.

The onset in the late 1960s and early 1970s of the current economic crisis was the result of the breakdown of the mode of regulation upon which this regime of intensive accumulation was based. Two factors in particular are crucial to understanding the crisis of Fordism: the slowdown in productivity growth and the intensification of international competition.

The slowdown in productivity growth is particularly critical when considering the Canadian auto industry. In Canada, as in all the OECD countries, the rate of increase in labour productivity (measured in terms of output per person-hour) in the manufacturing sector slowed significantly after 1974, after showing strong growth throughout the late 1940s, 1950s, 1960s, and early 1970s (see table 1). The contrast between the last decade and the previous two is truly startling. For example, in the manufacturing sector as a whole, the average annual rate of growth in labour productivity in the period from 1961-62 to 1972-73 was 4.7 per cent but this fell to 1.2 per cent for the period from 1973-74 to 1981-82.[18] At a more disaggregated level, while there were variations in labour productivity between industrial subsectors, there is consensus that the productivity slowdown in Canada was widespread.[19] One consequence of this slowdown in productivity growth was a rapid increase in unit labour costs after 1973 (see table 1).

A number of factors are considered to have contributed to this dramatic slowdown in productivity growth. However, regardless of the causes of the slowdown, it resulted in a crisis of profitability as the labour cost per unit of output continued to rise and as further increases in the technical composition of capital (investment in new technology) failed to be offset by corresponding increases in productivity. For example, in the case of Canadian manufacturing, Zohar notes that in the period after 1973, while labour productivity growth slowed considerably, the degree of capital intensity accelerated. This was in

Table 1

Annual Percentage Changes of Labour Productivity and Unit Labour Costs in Canadian Manufacturing, 1961-83

Period	Output	Person Hours	Labour Compensation	Output per Person Hour	Unit Labour Cost
1961-84	3.9	0.6	10.1	3.3	5.9
1961-68	7.3	2.8	8.4	4.4	1.0
1968-73	6.0	0.9	9.1	5.0	2.9
1973-78	2.2	- 0.1	12.5	2.1	10.3
1978-82	- 1.8	- 2.0	9.8	0.1	12.0
1982-83	6.0	- 0.4	6.3	6.4	0.3
1983-84	8.3	4.2	5.8	4.0	- 2.3

Source: Statistics Canada: Aggregate Productivity Measures, cat. 14-201. Statistics Canada Daily, March 25, 1985.

sharp contrast to 1946-1973, a period when the rate of growth in capital intensity was roughly matched by that in labour productivity.[20]

The intensification of international competition resulted in large measure from the very success of Fordism in the 1950s and 1960s and the consequent development of an inherent tendency towards overcapacity. We noted earlier that Fordism emphasized the production of goods which were capable of being produced in long production runs. In order for individual firms to remain competitive there was pressure for them to strive constantly to increase productivity and concurrently to reduce unit costs. The drive to raise productivity levels led above all to the mechanization of production. This increased investment in fixed capital usually increased capacity and made it essential for firms to achieve very long production runs in order to gain the full benefits of increased productivity and to achieve lower operating costs per unit of output. Longer production runs resulted in increased volumes of production and the need to increase market penetration which, in turn, intensified competition among competitors. By the mid-1970s this competitive pressure to increase the scale of production within individual plants, coupled with a levelling off in demand as markets became saturated, led to considerable overcapacity in such sectors as auto, steel, and textiles.

During the immediate post-war period the mode of regulation of Fordism was essentially internal to each of the major capitalist economies. Throughout the 1950s and early 1960s, the rapid growth in domestic output in the consumption goods sectors was generally absorbed by growing internal domestic markets. However, this tendency towards ever-expanded production, in turn requiring ever-expanding markets, spilled over national borders so that competition among the major capitalist economies for each other's markets intensified. The markets on which the achievement of scale economies depended were to be found precisely in those advanced capitalist countries in which the conditions of production and consumption had been transformed most profoundly by Fordism. The existence of surplus capacity on a world scale and of substantial variations in unit costs of production between different national producers again had adverse effects upon the profitability of production in those countries with the higher unit costs of production.

In North America therefore, the combined effect of the slowdown in productivity growth and the intensification of international competition in the early 1970s was an increased downward pressure on rates of profit. The response of industry throughout the advanced capitalist world to this crisis of profitability has been to instigate a process of restructuring and relocation with the aim of restoring profitable accumulation. Two tendencies seem to have emerged as important features of this contemporary restructuring process: the further internationalization of production, and an attempt to increase productivity through the development of new process technologies and new forms of labour process organization.

Initially, the internationalization of production took place on a continental scale with the movement of plants from the traditional manufacturing regions of North America and Western Europe to new areas with cheaper and more pliant labour forces in the southern United States, and Southern and Eastern Europe. By the late 1970s, this movement had extended on a global scale to the relocation of certain segments of the production process (usually, but not always, the labour-intensive segments) in the newly industrializing countries of Southeast Asia and Latin America, and particularly in the free trade zones located in those regions. This relocation of production in the Third World for re-export to the advanced capitalist countries led to the emergence of what has been labelled the new international division of labour (NIDL).[21]

It should be noted that much of the literature on the NIDL has tended to exaggerate the significance of the industrial relocation seeking to take advantage of cheap labour, to the exclusion of other factors which have also contributed to the internationalization of production. Other factors include attempts to reduce the value of constant capital by gaining access to cheap sources of energy and raw materials, attempts to expand into new markets still partially protected by tariffs or non-tariff quotas, and attempts to socialize the fixed capital costs of production through state subsidies on new investment.[22]

Moreover, as Lipietz has pointed out, while the relocation of production strategy has served to increase the average rate of surplus value by reducing the cost of variable capital, it has not brought about a significant expansion in markets or an increase in productivity.[23] Consequently, it has not resolved the fundamental crisis of Fordism and the problem of how to give a new impetus to productivity and to consumption on a world-wide scale.

The continued escalation of unit labour costs has renewed the pressure to invest in technical research and new labour- and capital-saving technology. The introduction of robotics and other microprocessor-based process control and information-processing systems has created the potential for a radical restructuring of the labour process in both the manufacturing and the service sectors that may result in significantly higher levels of potential and actual productivity. In addition to changes in "hard" process technology, there have also been changes (particularly in the car industry) in so-called "soft" technology, involving the broader technical and social organization and management of the manufacturing process. These "soft" technologies include Just-in-Time Manufacturing and Flexible Manufacturing Systems. The recent tendency towards the production of a larger variety of products in smaller batches calls not only for more flexible, general purpose machine-tools but also for a work force that can adjust rapidly to new patterns of work organization. This contrasts sharply with the special purpose machines and unskilled workers which characterized Fordist production.

The Restructuring of the Canadian Automotive Industry, 1960-83

The automotive products sector occupies a position of primary importance within the industrial structure of Canada. It is the largest manufacturing sector, employing over 100,000 people directly, and approximately one in seven Canadian manufacturing jobs depend on the continued viability of the automotive industry. It is the single largest purchaser of a number of processed raw materials and fabricated products (for example, 17 per cent of iron and steel production, 17 per cent of rubber products, and 14 per cent of processed aluminum). The automotive industry is also a major contributor to Canada's export trade: over the last ten years automotive exports have contributed about 20 per cent of Canada's total merchandise exports and almost 60 per cent of Canadian exports of manufactured end products. As well, the very label "Fordism" underscores the fact that historically the automotive sector has been a "leading" sector in terms of the development of new process technologies and forms of labour process organization. Today it is one of the leading sectors in the application of microelectronic technology in production and process engineering. The development of the Canadian automotive sector in the post-war period serves to demonstrate both the nature of, and limits to, Fordism as a mode of regulation, in concrete terms.

The automotive industry consists of two major subsectors which have significantly different organizational structures: the automobile assembly sector and the automotive parts and components sector. The former is characterized by marked concentration and centralization of production. In Canada there are essentially four major producers (GM, Ford, Chrysler, and AMC-Renault — commonly referred to as the Big Four) with no more than seven assembly plants operating at any time since the late 1950s. These plants are very large, with a highly unionized labour force. All the firms in this sector are subsidiaries of foreign-based producers. The parts and components sector, on the other hand, is characterized by a large number of firms of varying size. In 1981 it was estimated that approximately 41 per cent of parts produced in Canada were made in "in-house" plants by the Big Four, 21 per cent in plants owned by twelve major U.S.-based multinational parts producers, and the remaining 38 per cent by over 450 other firms (approximately 60 per cent of these were Canadian-owned). The parts firms range in size from small workshops employing less than 10 workers to large plants of over 700 employees. At the peak of employment in 1979 there were approximately 110,000 workers employed in the Canadian automotive industry and these were split almost equally between the assembly and parts sectors.

Two other features of the Canadian automotive industry are worth noting. First, the industry is predominantly owned and controlled by a small number of U.S.-based firms. For example, the Big Four accounted for 73.4 per cent of all value added in the industry during the period 1966-79. Second, the industry is highly concentrated geographically in southern Ontario (85 per cent of employment) and part of southern Quebec (10 per cent of employment), and in many communities accounts for a significant proportion of local manufacturing employment.

Table 2 and figures 1 and 2 show, for the period 1955-83, the general trends in output, employment, and productivity for the Canadian auto assembly and automotive parts sectors. These data reveal that there have been, in fact, two crises and associated periods of restructuring and reorganization within the Canadian automotive products industry during the last thirty years. The first was a sectoral crisis in accumulation, confined to the Canadian automotive products industry, which developed in the late 1950s and early 1960s and interrupted the long post-war boom.[24] This crisis was a result of the limits to Fordism being reached in the Canadian automotive sector. The "balancing" of production and consumption in the consumption goods sector was purely internal to the Canadian economy, and total Canadian consumption of automobiles was simply not large enough to allow companies to achieve the potential economies of scale and gains in productivity that were technically possible with already installed production technology. The crisis was resolved by the negotiation of a conditional free trade agreement — the Auto Pact — between Canada and the United States, which enabled the reorganization and rationalization of automotive production in Canada and its integration with production in the United States. This agreement allowed the formation of one integrated North American production system in which production and consumption were "regulated" at the level of the combined U.S. and Canadian economies. Subsequently, the period 1962-70 saw renewed expansion and

Table 2

Canadian Automotive Industry: Employment, Production, and Labour Productivity; 1956-83

	Motor Vehicle Assembly Sector (SIC 323)			Motor Vehicle Parts and Accessories Sector (SIC 325)	
Year	Employment	Production (000's units)	Labour Productivity ($/hour)	Employment	Labour Productivity[1] ($/hour)
1956	35099	375	5.97	21471	5.10
1957	32547	340	5.73	17651	5.16
1958	25711	297	6.48	15446	5.43
1959	27852	301	7.82	15754	5.84
1960	27081	326	7.73	15531	5.99
1961	25183	324	8.21	20820	5.58
1962	27001	425	9.56	22203	5.89
1963	31727	532	10.40	25441	6.31
1964	36026	560	9.25	29442	6.00
1965	42432	707	9.65	31982	6.27
1966	42507	702	9.90	34759	6.90
1967	40861	721	12.71	34858	7.27
1968	39113	901	13.95	39454	7.81
1969	41916	1036	14.85	41541	8.64
1970[2]	38145	940	12.46	38866	8.57
1971	42334	1095	13.58	43810	9.63
1972	44042	1155	12.89	46189	10.29
1973	46831	1227	13.62	52831	10.13
1974	49402	1188	16.21	49642	10.15
1975	45256	1058	14.92	42639	10.26
1976	49079	1146	14.34	47331	11.64
1977	52473	1167	15.56	49755	12.06
1978	51103	1143	16.53	56600	11.87
1979	51914	988	16.33	54955	11.55
1980	44870	847	13.81	46326	10.09
1981	44267	796	13.70	49300	10.59
1982	42168	851	14.76	48050	11.34
1983[3]	47639	1000	17.48	49630	14.38

1. Productivity figures are calculated from real value added in production (expressed in constant 1971 dollars) divided by total production worker hours.
2. A major strike against GM during 1970 had a significant impact on production and employment figures.
3. Preliminary figures

Sources: Statistics Canada Catalogue 42-210 various years
Statistics Canada Catalogue 42-209 various years
Statistics Canada Catalogue 62-543 Industry Selling Price Indexes 1956-76
Statistics Canada Catalogue 62-011 Industry Selling Price Indexes various years

growth in the Canadian automotive industry, and the development of a clear spatial division of labour within the North American auto industry in which Canadian plants were "allocated" those parts of the production process which had a high labour content.

The second crisis developed in the late 1970s. It forms part of the general crisis of Fordism which marks the end of a particular period of capitalist development which began in the 1930s, and which reached its zenith in the long post-war boom of the 1950s and 1960s. The principal causes/symptoms of this later crisis have been a dramatic slowdown in the rate of productivity growth and intensified international competition. The ensuing restructuring of the North American auto industry has involved both the further internationalization of production and the beginnings of what promises to be a radical transformation of process technology.

(1) The Restructuring of the Canadian Automotive Industry, Phase 1, 1963-70: Crisis, the Auto Pact, and the Continentalization of Fordism

The post-war period until 1973 saw continued growth in the world-wide demand for cars. This growth was particularly strong in the OECD countries, where it was a result of rising incomes and the spread of mass consumption from North America to Europe and Japan; for example, during the 1960s the average annual rate of increase in the demand for cars in the OECD was 6.1 per cent.[25]

In the late 1950s and early 1960s, however, when most of the world's auto industry was still in the midst of the growth and expansion associated with the post-war boom, the Canadian automotive industry was faced with a deepening crisis. As Littler and Salaman note "Taylorism and Fordism as forms of work organization are constrained by certain economic and technical limits and...in particular they are set within a certain pattern of product markets and intercapitalist competition."[26] In order to understand both the crisis that developed in the Canadian auto industry in the early 1960s, and the crisis of the North American auto industry as a whole that developed in the late 1970s, it is necessary to understand the nature of these limits and to stress the strong interrelationships that existed between the nature of the product market, the competitive context within which auto-makers operated, the nature of the labour process, and the broader industrial organization of production in the industry during the "golden age" of Fordism.

Prior to the middle to late 1960s, production within the international automotive industry was organized essentially on a national basis. Most of the advanced industrial countries had a protected domestic market supplied by locally based producers. For example, in 1955 less than 2 per cent of all new vehicle sales in the world's seven largest markets (the United States, Japan, West Germany, France, Italy, the United Kingdom, and Canada) were imports. Among the major auto-producing nations, tariff rates of 30 per cent or more

Figure 1

Canada Motor Vehicle Manufacturing (SIC 323) Employment, Output, and Productivity (1977 = 100)

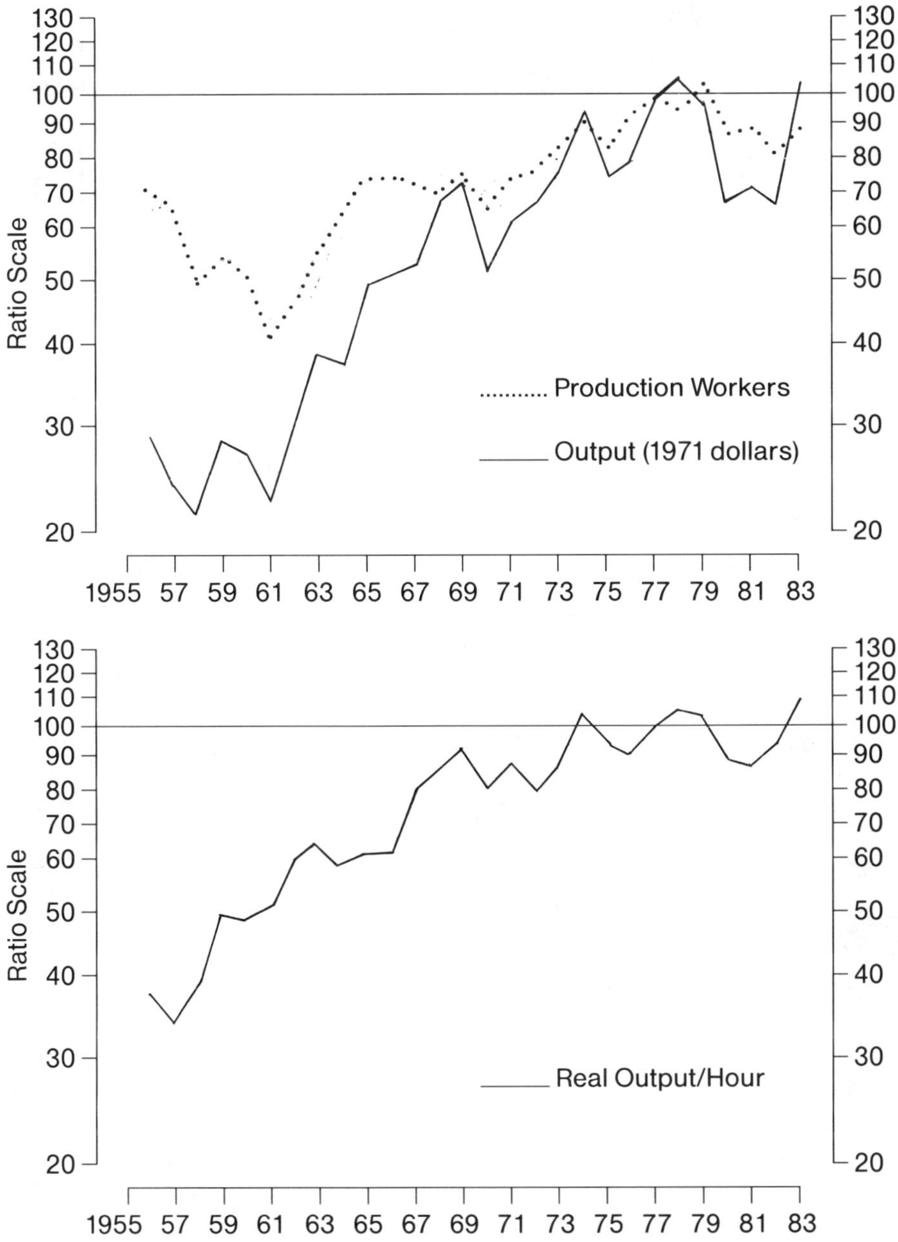

Source: As Table 2.

Figure 2

Canada Motor Vehicle Manufacturing (SIC 325)
Employment, Output, and Productivity (1977 = 100)

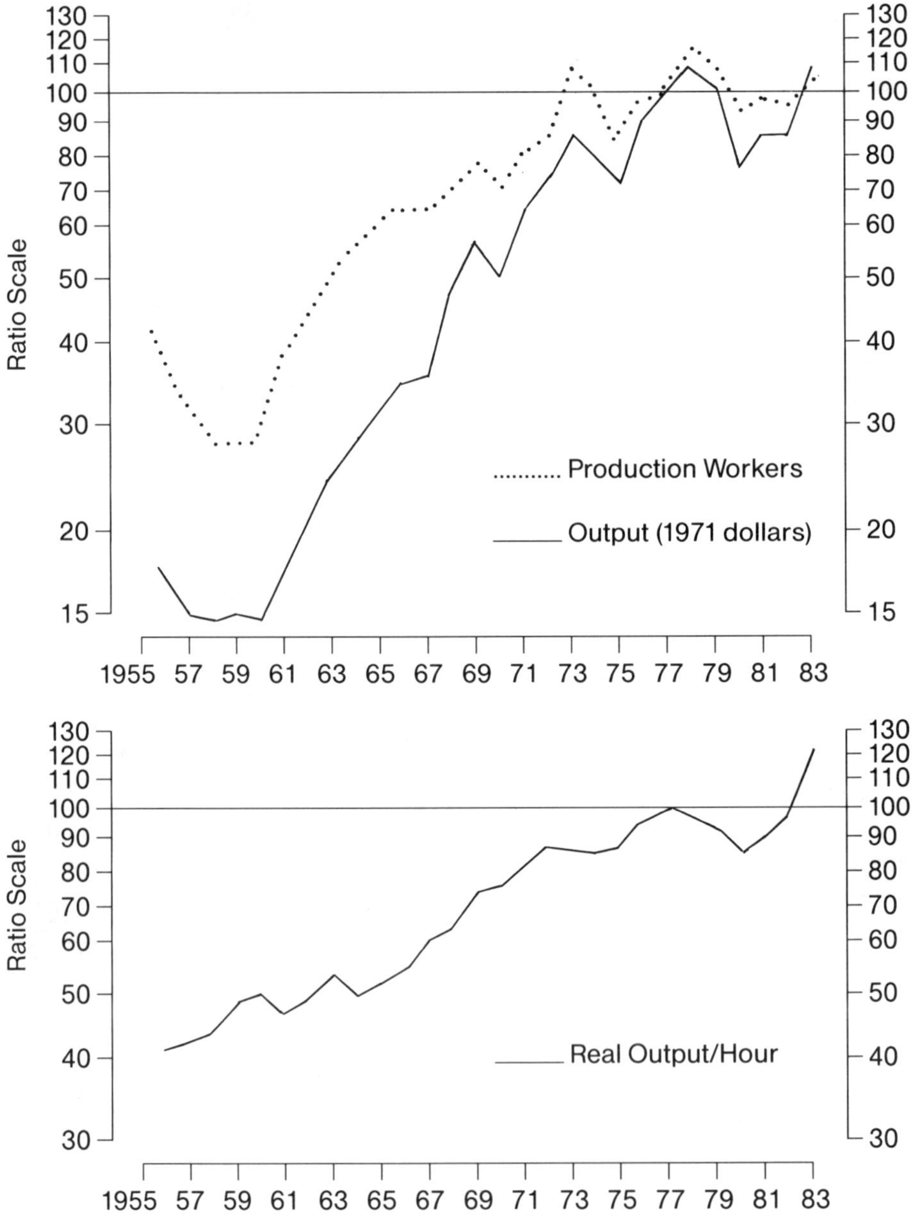

Source: As Table 2.

were still common as late as 1960.[27] Product designs within national markets were relatively stable and producers in each country concentrated on designs and sizes suited to their primary national markets. Thus, even the progressive dismantling of tariff barriers to automotive trade between most of the OECD countries in the 1960s was not perceived as a threat to any individual national auto industry because the types of vehicles demanded in the mass consumption markets of each country were markedly different. In fact, up until the late 1970s, cars produced for the North American mass market were essentially different products from those produced by European and Japanese car makers, and the response of North American producers to import competition was to differentiate their product as much as possible from cars produced elsewhere in the world and to concede the bottom end of the market (that is, small cars) to foreign producers.

Product technology, particularly with respect to major components such as engines, transmissions, and suspension systems, also remained stable within the North American auto industry with annual changes occurring only in body styling. One consequence of these stable product technologies was that competitive strategies between auto-makers within the Canadian and U.S. markets focussed on marketing and price competition. Production systems were therefore able to use higher and higher levels of mechanization for the production of components such as engines and transmissions. In contrast, the final assembly line, although designed along Fordist principles to produce large volumes of vehicles, remained relatively labour-intensive in order to provide some flexibility with respect to more frequent changes in body design.[28] The competitive pressure to reduce unit labour costs coupled with the trend towards greater integration of the production process had the effect of emphasizing the importance of scale of production as the ratio of constant to variable capital continued to rise. This competitive strategy had direct implications for the organization of the labour process for, as Abernathy stresses, "... production processes designed for efficiency, offer higher levels of productivity but they also become mechanistic, rigid, less reliant on skilled workers and more dependent on elaborate and specialized equipment."[29]

Thus, throughout the 1950s and the 1960s the use of Fordist production methods pushed minimum efficient operating scales in the car industry ever higher. During this period:

> ... most of the productivity growth in the automotive industry, which was substantial in that era, was due to the design and construction of ever more productive facilities with specialized tooling and automation to achieve maximum economies of scale. As each new plant came on stream, that particular firm's productivity would increase, but it was a temporary advantage that lasted only until companies built ever more productive facilities. A sustainable advantage in manufacturing costs could only come from achieving higher market penetration and hence greater production volumes.[30]

A related tendency was towards increased specialization and rationalization of production between plants. Firms needed to achieve economies of scale and higher productivity through increases in the length of production runs. Since different stages of the automobile production and assembly process have different minimum efficient scales, there were marked cost advantages to segmenting the production process and integrating production between geographically separate plants so that each component and assembly plant could achieve the full benefits of economies of scale at its stage of the manufacturing process.

It was in the context of these general tendencies within an automotive industry organized along Fordist principles that the crisis developed in the Canadian industry in the late 1950s and early 1960s. On the North American continent the auto industries of Canada and the United States, even though they were dominated by the same three giant auto corporations, were organized essentially as separate operations prior to 1963. The existence of significant tariffs on automobiles and automobile parts moving between the two countries had resulted in the development of a small replica of the U.S. industry within Canada. Each of the major auto-makers produced in its Canadian plants a broad range of models for domestic consumption within Canada and there was only limited trade in finished autos across the border. Auto parts manufacturers produced almost exclusively for the domestic assembly firms.[31]

By the end of the 1950s the major problem for the Canadian industry was that the Canadian domestic market was simply too small to take full advantage of the potential increases in productivity to be gained from using the latest production technology. The Canadian industry thus found its competitive position in relation to other auto-producing countries, and particularly in comparison with the United States, being seriously eroded. Even though Canadian per capita consumption of automobiles was roughly equivalent to that of the United States, total Canadian consumption was not large enough to allow companies to achieve the potential economies of scale and gains in productivity that were technically possible with existing installed production technology. Short production runs limited productivity in Canada to 70 per cent of productivity levels in the United States. For example, in the early 1960s, Ford was producing sixty variations of six different models at its Oakville assembly plant, compared to only two or three models at any one of its U.S. assembly plants. The volumes required to produce competitively such items as transmissions and large body stampings were far in excess of total Canadian requirements for such parts; automatic transmissions, for example, required production runs of 500,000 in order to be competitive, but that was more than the total number of cars built in Canada in 1960. Since wage bargaining was tied to productivity increases, wages in the Canadian automotive industry were also approximately 30 per cent lower than levels in the U.S. industry.

The "blockage" to further productivity growth was therefore not due to the technical limitations of the labour process in Canadian plants, but instead was caused by the limited size of the market. The crisis was manifested in declining competitiveness and profitability, falling output and employment, increased import penetration from the United States, and a growing trade deficit. However, it was rooted in the fact that within the Canadian automotive sector, in which the mode of regulation with respect to the "balancing" of production and consumption was internal to the Canadian economy, the point had been reached at which productivity increases, while technically possible, were fettered by market size.[32]

A royal commission appointed in the face of mounting economic and political pressure clearly identified the basic problem to be the Canadian industry's inability to remain competitive by increasing its productivity because of the limited size of the Canadian market. It went on to argue that the solution to the crisis confronting the Canadian automotive industry in 1961 lay in the rationalization and integration of assembly and parts production in the United States and Canada. Such integration was facilitated between 1962 and 1965 through a sequence of adjustments to the tariff structure which initially allowed duty remission on selected parts, but which eventually was widened into the Canada-U.S. Automotive Products Trade Agreement (the Auto Pact) to allow conditional free trade in assembled cars and original equipment parts. The real thrust of the Auto Pact was not free trade, the politically visible part of the agreement, but rather a series of restrictions and commitments that bore on the automobile manufacturers. Although the details of these commitments are complicated, their effect was to guarantee a minimum level of automotive production in Canada as a proportion of Canadian consumption. The explicit Canadian goal of the Auto Pact was to increase productivity in the Canadian assembly and parts industries by creating a larger market for automotive products within which the full benefits of specialization and large-scale production could be achieved. The aim was clearly to force the rationalization of the Canadian industry through the integration of production on a continent-wide basis — in effect, to achieve the continentalization of Fordism within the auto industry.

In the wake of these changes in tariff structure the anticipated reorganization and rationalization of production and restructuring of capital did take place, principally in the period from late 1963 until the end of 1969. The following points describe the impacts of this restructuring on the auto industry in Canada.

- There was considerable expansion of production in the Canadian assembly sector for export to the United States. The fact that employment in the assembly sector remained relatively constant between 1965 and 1970 while production expanded rapidly indicates that substantial increases in productivity were achieved during this period (see table 2). By 1969 it was estimated that productivity in Canada was 10 per cent higher than in the United States. In general, these gains in productivity stemmed from the full and efficient use of existing assembly plants rather than from investment in new capital equipment.

- In the period from 1964 to 1969, new capital invested in parts production exceeded $500 million, over 230 new plants were established, employment increased from 29,000 to 42,000, and productivity rose by over 50 per cent (see table 2). The bulk of the new investment in parts production in Canada was by large multinational parts producers. The location of the new plants caused a noticeable change in the overall locational structure of the industry with many firms locating in the smaller towns of southwestern Ontario and the south Georgian Bay area, and on the Niagara Peninsula. Another striking feature of the new parts plants which opened during this period was their concentration on the production of low- to medium-value parts or subassemblies with a relatively high direct labour content. Consequently many of the jobs provided by these plants were low skilled.
- Thus, the large auto-makers assigned to their Canadian plants a disproportionately large share of final assembly and labour-intensive subassembly work, while most of the "in-house" production of high value parts such as engines and transmissions remained in the United States. This contributed to the development of a clear spatial division of labour in the automotive industry between Canada and the U.S., the former having a lower proportion of skilled jobs. At the time that the Auto Pact was signed, wage rates in the Canadian automotive industry were approximately 30 per cent lower than they were in the United States. Thus, in the rationalization and integration of production which occurred in the wake of the pact, there was a tendency to locate those parts of the production process which had a high labour content in Canada. The lower wage rate coupled with the possibility of large and rapid productivity increases as a result of rationalization contributed to the higher rates of profit in Canadian compared to U.S. plants during the latter half of the 1960s and the early 1970s. This spatial division of labour also led to a trade pattern in which Canada since 1965 has continually run large trade surpluses in finished cars and large trade deficits in parts and components.

The period between 1963 and 1970 was one of considerable expansion for the Canadian auto industry, with significant increases in investment and employment in both the assembly and parts sectors. Furthermore, in the short run at least, Canada appeared to benefit considerably from this period of restructuring. The crisis which had confronted the industry in the late 1950s had been successfully overcome and profitable accumulation had been restored in the Canadian industry. The new continental spatial division of labour which emerged from this first phase of restructuring is crucial to an understanding of the second phase of restructuring, presently occurring in response to the more general crisis of Fordism which affected the whole of the North American auto industry in the late 1970s. In particular, it helps to explain the uneven development of, and the uneven response to, the crisis in Canada and the United States.

(2) The Postwar Restructuring of the Canadian Automotive Industry, Phase II, 1979-83: The Crisis of Fordism and the Struggle to Establish a New Model of Accumulation

> [In 1979] the world economy was entering the worst economic downturn since the Great Depression and the auto industry was among the hardest hit sectors.[33]

The late 1970s and early 1980s was a period of major crisis for the North American auto industry, which came under tremendous pressure to increase productivity and reduce costs in the face of intensified international competition and rapidly escalating unit labour costs resulting from the slowdown in productivity growth. The crisis represents a breakdown of the Fordist model of accumulation which had been at the root of the prolonged growth and expansion from 1945 to 1973. In fact, a number of tendencies which precipitated this crisis can be traced back to the late 1960s and are rooted in the very success of the Fordist model during the post-war boom. The current crisis also underscores the limitations of Fordism in which "regulation," in general, was achieved only at the level of individual national economies.

The sharp "recessions" which occurred in the North American auto industry in 1979-80 and 1981-82 were simply the most pronounced moments in a decade of increasing uncertainty and deepening economic crisis. However, when viewing industrial change in the North American auto industry within the context of the world industry as a whole, it is important to distinguish between the early to mid-1970s and the late 1970s-early 1980s. In the first period, although there were marked cyclical fluctuations in employment and output within national auto industries, including those of Canada and the United States, employment and market shares between the major auto-producing countries remained remarkably stable. However, in contrast the late 1970s-early 1980s saw the end of this stability as international competition intensified and certain countries (including Canada and the U.S.) faced serious competitive challenges from offshore producers, particularly Japan.[34]

For the Canadian auto industry the data on employment and output (see table 2, figures 1 and 2) show strong growth in both areas from the early 1960s through to 1973 (the data for 1970 are distorted because a major strike occurred that year) and a strong recovery in 1976-78 in the wake of the sharp, but apparently temporary, 1974-75 downturn associated with the first of the OPEC oil price increases. The extent of the downturn which occurred in

1979-83 was remarkable — output fell by over 30 per cent and employment by over 20 per cent. It is important to note, however, that the downturn experienced by the U.S. auto industry during this period was even deeper, and that the recovery in 1983-84 much slower than was the case in Canada (see figure 3). The slowdown in productivity growth in the early 1970s, documented for the Canadian manufacturing sector as a whole earlier, is also very evident in the automotive sector (see table 3).

Concurrent with this major downturn in output and employment, the auto-makers have embarked on a round of massive new capital investments (see table 4). Between 1980 and 1982, the Big Three invested $3.2 billion in new plant and tooling for their Canadian operations. As a recent government report points out, "...although this investment is necessary if they are to remain competitive it has taken a significant toll on the financial strength of companies. The net funds generated by the Big 4 in 1980-82 were $19.5 billion while the requirements for new plant and tooling were $40 billion...the companies made up this shortfall by depleting working capital and significantly expanding long term debt and other liabilities."[35] This provides further evidence of the scale and significance of this restructuring crisis, which clearly represents a major rupture within capitalist accumulation.

What then were some of the tendencies inherent in the Fordist model of accumulation which contributed to the development of the crisis? First and foremost was the continuation and accentuation of the drive to achieve lower unit costs through the pursuit of ever-increasing scales of production, one of

Table 3

Labour Productivity, Canadian Automotive Industry, 1956-83 Annual Average Rate of Increase

	Average Annual Percentage Increase in Real Output/Production Worker Hour	
Period	Motor Vehicle Assembly Sector	Motor Vehicle Parts Sector
1956-1983	5.0%	4.2%
1956-1961	7.0%	2.0%
1961-1966	4.2%	4.5%
1966-1971	7.5%	7.0%
1971-1976	1.5%	4.0%
1976-1981	1.5%	-1.7%
1981-1983	13.1%	17.0%

Source: Same as Table 2

Figure 3
Auto Industry Production Workers, Canada and U.S.A., 1972-84

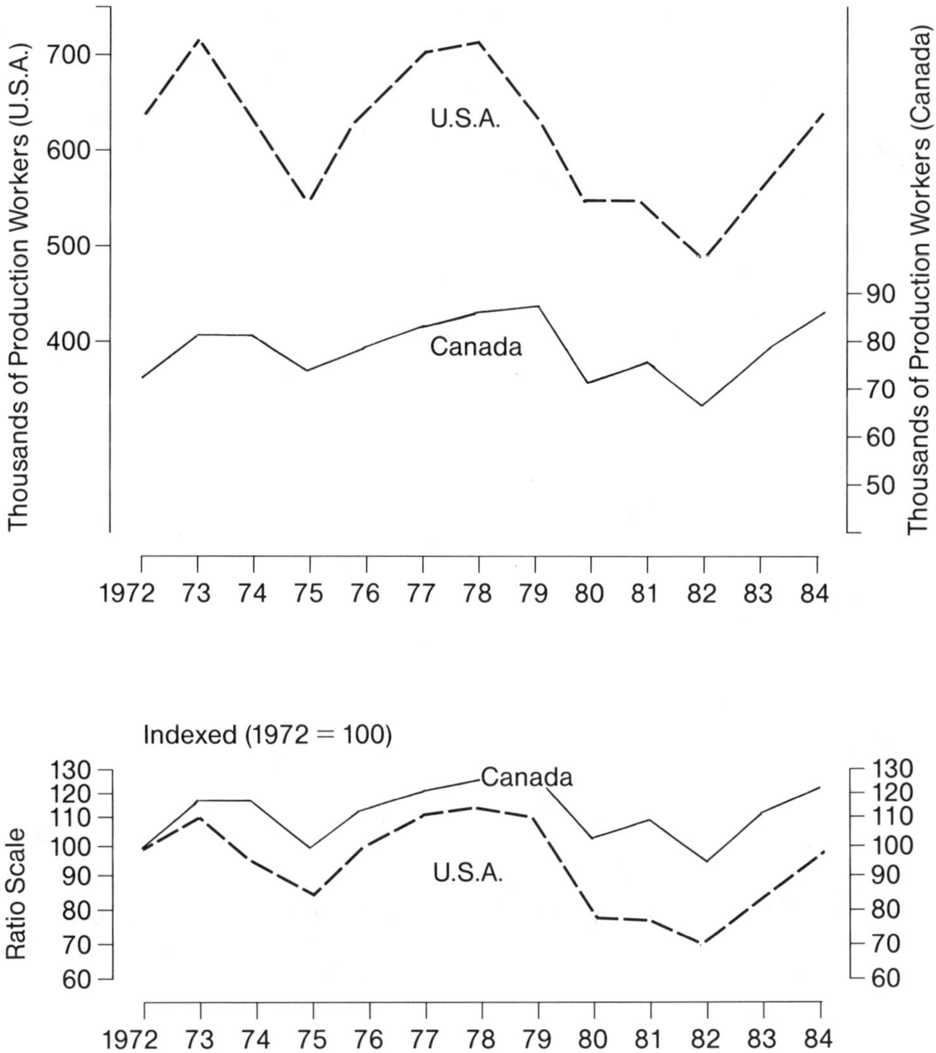

Source: U.S. Bureau of Labor Statistics, Employment, Earnings, and Hours, various years.
Statistics Canada Catalogue 72-002, various years.

the hallmarks of production under Fordism. This process, coupled with a levelling off in the world demand for cars (insufficient demand in developing countries and market saturation within the OECD countries), led to substantial overcapacity in the industry by the mid-1970s. This in turn led to an intensification of competition at the international level among auto-makers, both for the markets of the OECD and for markets in those developing countries which were perceived to offer the greatest potential growth in demand for mass consumption products. Thus, in the 1970s the annual growth rate in demand for autos in the OECD fell to 1.6 per cent (from over 6 per cent in the previous decade) and the percentage of new vehicle sales of imports in the seven largest national markets increased from 2 per cent in 1955, to 14 per cent in 1970, to 24 per cent in 1981. Between 1978 and 1982, world demand for cars declined by 13 per cent, but world trade in automobiles increased by over 30 per cent.[36]

Other strategies which emerged in the 1970s as firms sought to eke out the maximum potential productivity from what remained essentially Fordist production techniques included a reduction in the number of separate parts

Table 4

New Capital Expenditures, Canadian Automotive Industry, 1972-83.

Year	Motor Vehicle Assembly Sector (SIC 323)	Motor Vehicle Parts and Accessories Sector (SIC 325)	Total
	New Capital Expenditures ($Can millions)		
1972	45.9	55.9	101.8
1973	60.8	78.7	139.5
1974	104.7	119.9	224.6
1975	79.5	81.2	160.7
1976	82.9	62.5	145.4
1977	176.6	109.6	286.2
1978	99.0	203.9	302.9
1979	153.1	330.9	484.0
1980	183.6	780.9	964.5
1981	305.1	666.5	971.6
1982	236.7	188.5	425.2
1983	487.7	164.0	651.7

Source: Statistics Canada: Catalogue 61-214
Capital and Repair Expenditures
Manufacturing Sub-Industries.

used in the production of a particular vehicle with the aim of further simplifying and automating the labour process on the final assembly line in order to gain increases in productivity; design coordination and joint ventures between companies (becoming increasingly more formalized and more important, particularly between North America and Japanese producers) were used to increase the number of interchangeable parts between different models and even between models assembled by different companies; and firms moved to rationalize their model ranges to one basic model per size class. Such developments helped attain longer production runs of particular parts and higher productivity levels. Standardized production also encouraged assembly firms to develop price oriented "arm's length" relationships with suppliers, in which only the price of the components and assured supply were important. Thus, competitive bidding by suppliers for orders and multisourcing of parts were used to increase competitive pressure on suppliers to reduce unit costs and prevent production disruptions in the assembly plant.

By the late 1960s (even by the late 1950s in Canada) the minimum efficient scales both for vehicle assembly and for the production of a number of major parts and components began to exceed the levels of demand for those items within an increasing number of individual national domestic markets. Pressure to rationalize and integrate the production process at an international level so that all plants could operate at near optimum operating levels increased. The growing internationalization of production led to a significant increase in the flow across national boundaries of parts, components, and assembled automobiles between members of the OECD. This occurred first in the late 1960s and early 1970s on a continental scale (a result of the Auto Pact in North America, and the integration of production within Western Europe by Ford), and then later on a global scale.[37] In fact, the "World Car" concept represents Fordism taken to its logical conclusion within the world automotive industry — a single standardized design to be produced at the cheapest possible cost, on a global scale.[38]

Fordism was also characterized by particular forms of labour-management relations. Standardized production systems resulted in a division of labour within the factory which was inflexible, hierarchical, and characterized by increasing automation, routinization, and mechanization of production tasks. Under this system, "...it was assumed that the assembly workers would not report problems, would not repair their own machines and would take no initiative in spotting or correcting faults. It seemed to follow that large inventories of parts would be needed as buffers."[39] The pattern for post-war labour contracts in the North American auto industry was largely set by the 1948 contract between the UAW and GM. Under this type of contract, annual increases in base wage rates became virtually automatic, but in return production-related matters such as line speeds, work standards, and the design of jobs remained the sole prerogative of management. There is general agreement that this system of labour-management relations:

> seems to have provided a workable approach to workforce management throughout the twenty year period from 1945 to 1965. At the plant level, the primary competitive objective was production, an objective well suited to methods of control based on machine pacing, supervision and work standards... as conditions and people changed in the late 1960s, it became increasingly unprofitable. In retrospect it is clear that while the traditional employment relationship gave the worker a limited voice in setting conditions of work and while it paid well it did not secure loyalty. Nor was it intended to... production objectives required people to operate the equipment, but as long as minimum standards were met (and supervisors ensured they were) loyalty or commitment were not essential.[40]

Throughout the 1950s and 1960s the annual increases in base wage rates were financed out of the sustained increases in labour productivity. The slowdown in labour productivity growth which occurred in the early 1970s, coupled with continued annual increases in wage rates, was a major factor contributing to the decline in profitability.

The coalescence and mutual reinforcement of these tendencies in conjunction with other factors, such as the rapid rise in gasoline prices through the 1970s, and the slump in demand associated with the adoption of monetarist policies in North America and Western Europe, resulted by 1979 in a collapse of the Fordist model of accumulation in the automotive sector. As Altshuler notes:

> ...after 1979 all this [the market and competitive conditions associated with Fordism] changed. The types of automobile demanded across the developed world converged dramatically... suddenly every world manufacturer was a threat to every other manufacturer in a largely integrated world market... some national industries (notably Japan and parts of Europe) were able to produce cars of unchallenged quality or at substantially lower cost, or both, and so a dramatic export surge developed as the less competitive national industries reeled under a flood of imports in addition to a deep slump in the overall market.[41]

This situation raised the possibility of dramatic shifts in the location of employment within the international auto industry, since national auto industries were very differently positioned to deal with these new competitive conditions.

The issue that has overidden all others for the North American automotive industry in the early 1980s is the productivity and cost differentials that exist between it and the Japanese automotive industry. Perry summarized the competitive position of the Japanese automotive industry relative to North America in mid-1981 as follows:

> ...total hourly compensation in the Japanese automotive industry was estimated to be 62 per cent of that in Canada and 46 per cent of that in the U.S.... labour

> productivity in the Japanese auto industry accelerated dramatically in 1979 and 80 as a result of both a significant expansion in production and a coincident decline in labour inputs. Conversely labour productivity in the Canadian and U.S. automotive industries deteriorated from 1978 to 1980.... In the period from 1978 to 1979 Japanese producers required an average of 80.3 man hours per vehicle while U.S. producers required 144 man hours.[42]

In 1979 it was estimated that the combination of lower hourly compensation and the superior productivity achieved by both direct and indirect labour yielded a landed cost advantage to the Japanese producers of $U.S. 1,650 per vehicle. A similar calculation by Perry for Canada in 1981 yielded an estimated differential in direct unit labour costs of $Can. 1,882 per vehicle in Japan's favour.[43]

Earlier, two general tendencies were mentioned that seem to be emerging as a response to the crisis of Fordism: the further internationalization of production, and concerted efforts to increase productivity through the development of new process technologies and new forms of labour process organization. Each of these tendencies may be detected in certain recent developments in the automobile industry and each will likely lead to particular consequences for the future organization and structure of the industry in Canada.

The International Division of Labour in the Automobile Industry

It is important to stress that the increasing internationalization of the auto industry is different from that process in industries such as clothing, where production has simply "moved south" to take advantage of lower wages. Although there has been some shift of automotive production to the semi-industrialized countries (the SICs, which accounted for virtually 0 per cent of world auto production in 1950, have progressively increased their share to 2.4 per cent in 1960, 5.3 per cent in 1970, and 9.5 per cent in 1980; the chief producers in this new group include Brazil, Mexico, Spain, India, South Korea, and Argentina), in 1979 they still accounted for only 2.7 per cent of car imports and 2.8 per cent of parts and components imports to the OECD. The lack of the necessary infrastructure, particularly parts suppliers, and the problem of scale (in countries whose domestic markets are small) have worked against relocating automobile assembly outside of the industrialized countries (other than in kit form — so-called completely knocked down or "c.k.d." assembly). Instead, internationalization has taken the form of integration within and among the industrialized countries and the development of world-wide sourcing of some parts and subassemblies (for example, engines, transmissions, and wheels).[44] Given the relatively high capital intensity of the automotive industry (with the important exception of auto assembly activities) the wage differentials that exist between the less developed countries and the more industrialized countries appear to be relatively unimportant. Such factors as the ability to gain access to markets still partially protected by tariff and non-tariff barriers, or to obtain state subsidies to socialize the costs of fixed capital, have been much more important in shaping the internationalization of production in the automotive industry.[45]

There has been a geographical shift of production within the major auto-producing regions. In order to counter rising costs and increased levels of labour militancy and production disruption in the traditional auto-making centres, there was a tendency in the 1970s to move assembly and other labour-intensive parts of the production process to "peripheral" regions of the advanced capitalist countries, where labour was cheaper and labour organization was relatively weak (for example, to Southern Europe or the sunbelt of the United States).[46] An effort was also made to develop multisourcing of parts.

What are the consequences of this internationalization process for the auto industry in Canada? One feature of the newly emerging spatial division of labour at the international level is the sourcing of parts in Canada which have a high energy content, for example, parts made from aluminum or plastics. There has been considerable investment in aluminum diecasting for engines by Ford and Chrysler in Ontario; the first major investment in Canada by a Japanese producer involved the production of aluminum wheels by Toyota in British Columbia for export for assembly in Japan; Volkswagen is also planning to produce aluminum wheels at Barrie, Ontario to supply assembly plants in both the United States and Germany; and Magna, in association with a French company, is building a new plant in the Toronto area to manufacture aluminum radiators for Renault.

The fact that the final assembly of cars is likely to remain highly concentrated within existing auto-producing regions of the OECD has important implications for Canada when viewed in the context of the continental spatial division of labour which developed in North America in the late 1960s and early 1970s in the wake of the Auto Pact. In part, it also helps to explain the relatively milder impact of the 1979-82 downturn on the auto industry in Canada compared to the United States, and the fact that in the early 1980s the Canadian industry apparently staged a remarkable recovery. Assembly plants are working at close to full capacity (although there has been a more modest recovery in employment) and Canada has registered record surpluses in automotive trade with the United States under the Auto Pact. This was due to strength in the U.S. auto market and the temporary respite afforded to North American producers by the voluntary export restraint program of the Japanese. One consequence of the continental integration of the industry under the Auto Pact was that it locked Canada into a trade dependency with the United States because of the large difference in the sizes of their respective domestic markets. Canadian assembly plants producing a limited range of models are extremely vulnerable to shifts in demand by U.S. customers for those particular models. In the past ten years this has worked at different times both against and to the advantage of Canadian plants. It also means that Canadian production is no longer "regulated" by Canadian consumption. The implications of this shift from "regulation" at a national level to "regulation" on a continental scale need to be fully assessed, particularly in the context of recent discussions about creating more sectoral free trade agreements between Canada and the United States.

The other factor which affects levels of automotive production in Canada is the currency exchange rate with the United States. While there has been nominal wage parity between Canadian and U.S. auto workers since the early 1970s, the exchange rate currently gives Canada a significant labour cost advantage over the United States. For example, at the time of the GM labour contract negotiations in 1984 it was acknowledged that there was a labour cost differential of $Can 7.50 *an hour* (the hourly wage rate under the previous contract had been slightly over $13 for a regular assembly line worker) in Canada's favour, due to the exchange rate and differences in medical plan premiums and other fringe benefits. Therefore, it is not just coincidence that Canadian assembly plants have been working flat out while assembly plants in the U.S. have been closed or operate below capacity.[47] This suggests that in any new spatial division of labour that might emerge from this current round of restructuring it is likely that Canada will retain the more labour-intensive segments of the industry, particularly assembly.

Changes in the Technical and Social Organization of Automobile Production

Faced with the need to cut costs in order to remain competitive with offshore producers, and with the wholesale movement of production, especially final assembly, to low wage areas offshore precluded for the reasons stated above, North American producers have sought to develop new product and process technologies. The emphases have been on cutting production costs by increasing labour productivity and engaging in other cost cutting measures, on improving quality control and, perhaps most importantly, on increasing the flexibility of production systems so that product differentiation and quality can become important competitive strategies along with price. Although there has been considerable debate among industry analysts concerning the "source" of the present Japanese productivity and production cost advantage, there seems to be a growing consensus that the advantage lies primarily in the "social organization and management of the production process" which results in higher process yields[48] and, hence, higher labour productivity; and, secondly, in lower wage rates: and that it is *not* due to greater capital investment or more sophisticated "hard" process technologies.[49] Thus, the Japanese manufacturers have established a new standard of best practice for the world automotive industry by demonstrating that dramatic productivity growth and cost savings can be obtained in ways other than the relentless pursuit of economies of scale. Consequently, "the social organization of the production process, long thought to be fully perfected and 'rationalized' along classical Ford and Sloan lines is now in dramatic flux."[50] In other words, the technical and social organization of production which characterized Fordism is being fundamentally transformed.[51]

The main elements of this new standard of best practice in the automobile industry include:

- The introduction of microprocessor controlled robotics and other computer numerically controlled machine-tools which result in better quality control through stricter adherence to specifications and manufacturing tolerances. These machines have dramatically increased the flexibility of the manufacturing system by reducing the minimum efficient scale for individual product lines. Their flexibility also permits rapid adjustments in product mix as market demand shifts, and will speed up the introduction of new models.
- Improved quality control is being achieved primarily through the introduction of "quality circles" on the shopfloor within the plants and the use of statistical quality control techniques among suppliers, with the aim of reducing defective parts to an absolute minimum. The latter increases process yield and reduces the size of the required inventory buffers which were formerly required to achieve high process yield. The old adage that quality entails increased production costs has been stood on its head.
- The restructuring of relationships with component suppliers, including an increase in the outsourcing of parts by the auto assemblers, the elimination of multisourcing of parts, a reduction in the number of suppliers, and longer term contracts with suppliers, all designed to improve productivity among suppliers; and the use of computer-based inventory control to cut the costs of circulating capital in the form of parts inventory, imitating the Japanese "just-in-time" or "kanban" system which was pioneered by Toyota.[52] In North America most assembly plants are placing a maximum limit on how far their major subcontractors can be located from the parent plant. There is therefore a very strong tendency towards the geographic reconcentration of production. The impact on the locational structure of the Canadian industry probably will be to eliminate suppliers in more peripheral areas and to concentrate production in areas with well-developed networks of suppliers.

- More flexible production systems require more flexible work practices and greater worker commitment to quality control and maintenance. There has been considerable pressure to change traditional ("Fordist") patterns of shopfloor labour relations. Hence, we are seeing a recomposition of skill taking place at the level of the shopfloor, an attempt to move to broader and more flexible job classifications, and the introduction of techniques such as "quality circles". However, at the same time management practices must also change. An early management response to the crisis was to attempt to increase the rate of exploitation by rolling back wages, reducing the number of paid holidays, revising work practices and, importantly, breaking the pattern of annual increases in base wage rates which, since the late 1940s, had been a standard feature of the employment relation under Fordism. It has even been suggested that one reason why U.S. auto firms have made only modest investments in low wage offshore countries is that: "...U.S. car makers are well aware that substantial savings in labour costs could be realized without moving offshore. They hope that the gap between hourly wages in the car industry and the manufacturing sector as a whole can be eroded."[53]

The latter point raises an interesting and crucially important question. Given the other tendencies noted above, and despite the fact that there have been some new investments in "greenfield" sites in the United States (mainly by offshore producers), the industry is likely to remain geographically concentrated in the traditional auto-producing regions. This means that shopfloor labour relations will have to be remade where they are.[54] It must be emphasized that the transformation of production which is underway is not simply a technical process but is one that also involves the social reorganization of production within the plant. A plan for reorganizing cannot simply be implemented by managerial fiat.

In the early 1980s, it appeared to be much more difficult for management to implement some of these strategies in Canadian than in U.S. plants. On at least three occasions — union resistance in Canada to worker concessions as part of the Chrysler rescue, the 1982 strike against Chrysler Canada to restore wage increases, and the 1984 strike against GM Canada which aimed to preserve the traditional post-war Fordist model of annual base wage rate increases and to reduce working time — Canadian auto workers have shown that they are prepared to adopt a more resistant and militant stance than their counterparts in the United States.[55] In large measure the different posture taken by the UAW in the two countries can be explained by the specific forms taken by uneven development within the North American automotive industry. The extent and depth of the crisis in the United States has considerably undermined and weakened the bargaining strength of the UAW and has made issues such as job security and extended unemployment and retraining benefits of the upmost importance to UAW members in recent contract negotiations. In contrast, the relatively strong position of the Canadian industry and the significant production cost differential in Canada's favour has enabled Canadian members of the UAW to fight to maintain or enhance the share of value added going to workers, and to try to protect jobs in the face of the significant gains in productivity which are being made through the application of new process technologies, by pressing for a reduced work week with no loss of real income (a progressive demand similar to that made by the IG Metall, the German metal workers union, in the historic strike of 1984).

Conclusion

It is still too early to discern precisely the impact of the most recent period of restructuring on the Canadian auto industry. In the mid-1980s, in the midst of a strong, but increasingly fragile, recovery in the North American economy, it is tempting to assume that the crisis in the auto industry has been resolved. The North American auto-makers are recording record profits, sales have increased in comparison with the lows of 1982, and there have been significant gains in labour productivity. However, the relative competitive imbalances between national production systems have not changed in any fundamental way, and the temporary trade barriers raised after 1979 to protect the North American market during the "transition" have now crumbled, opening the way for a new onslaught on the North American market by Japanese and Korean producers.

In the early phases of the crisis most studies of the international auto industry were based on the conviction that an increasing degree of product standardization was inevitable, and that the key competitive strategy for automakers would remain one of lowering unit production costs through increased automation and economies of scale. Thus, the need to cut costs indicated a shift of production to low wage locations and the development of the "world car". The uncritical acceptance of this scenario has led several recent writers to predict an extremely bleak future for the Canadian auto industry.[56] However, the "world car" strategy, widely touted in the late 1970s as the solution to the crisis of Fordism on a continental scale, is now rejected by most industry analysts as the most likely future scenario for the world auto industry. Instead they argue that

> ...the new production technologies mean that the shift to low wage locations will not occur on the scale once expected. The markets of the developed countries are demanding precise, high quality production. Flexible manufacturing in

> combination with the redesign of products to gain its full benefits can provide this while sharply increasing labour productivity. These innovations have shifted the focus of thought about the future geography of production location from the less developed countries to the concentrated production of most components near the point of final assembly in the developed countries.[57]

If this tendency proves to be more enduring than was the trend towards the "world car", then the short- and medium-term prospects for the survival of a significant auto industry in Canada are much enhanced.

This latest restructuring crisis in the world economy, by no means confined to the auto industry, resulted from the breakdown of the mode of regulation which underpinned Fordism. To use O'Connor's analogy, everything is now back in the cauldron and in a state of flux: technology, shopfloor labour relations, patterns and norms of consumption, labour market structure, wage determination, and political relations. The restructuring still occurring is an attempt to "construct" a new mode of regulation which can sustain a renewed period of expanded accumulation. Although the precise contours of any new mode of regulation are still far from clear, one thing that is certain (and that this essay has sought to emphasize) is that there is no going back to the "golden age" of Fordism.

Notes

1 Canada, Federal Task Force, *An Automotive Strategy for Canada* (Ottawa: Supply and Services, 1983), 45.

2 In this chapter, the terms "automobile industry" and "automotive industry or sector" are used interchangeably and include both final assembly of passenger vehicles and the manufacture of parts and components which go into the final assembly of passenger vehicles.

3 National Academy of Science, *The Competitive Status of the U.S. Auto Industry* (Washington: National Academy Press, 1982).

4 M. Aglietta, *A Theory of Capitalist Regulation: The U.S. Experience* (London: New Left Books, 1979); A. Lipietz, *The World Crisis: The Globalization of the General Crisis of Fordism.* Studies in National and International Development, Occasional Paper 84-203, (Kingston: Queen's University, 1984).

5 A. Sayer, "Explanation in Economic Geography," *Progress in Human Geography*, 6, (1982), 68-88.

6 Economic Council of Canada, *The Bottom Line* (Ottawa: Economic Council, 1983), 3.

7 P. Armstrong, A. Glyn, and J. Harrison, *Capitalism Since World War II* (London: Fontana, 1984).

8 Of course, to some extent industrial restructuring and reorganization are always present within capitalist economies. Any industrial sector is subject to almost continuous minor changes in ownership, product, and process technology, labour process organization within individual firms, and changes in the geographical organization of production. However, this restructuring and reorganization is much more diffuse and incremental and related to the internal dynamics of relatively stable periods of accumulation, such as the operation of "normal" business cycles, than the substantial changes that are currently underway in response to a major rupture in accumulation. In fact, one notable feature of the normal functioning of the business cycle is to restore conditions for rapid accumulation.

9 J. O'Connor, "The Meaning of Crisis," *International Journal of Urban and Regional Research*, 5, 3 (1982), 301-29, esp. 312.

10 K. Morgan, and A. Sayer, *A Modern Industry in a Mature Region: Electrical Engineering in South Wales*, Urban and Regional Studies Working Paper No. 39 (University of Sussex, 1984), 4.

11 Elsewhere I have discussed a general analytical framework for analyzing the interrelationships which exist between changes in locational structure and industrial restructuring: J. Holmes, "Industrial Reorganization, Capital Restructuring and Locational Change: An Analysis of the Canadian Automobile Industry in the 1960s," *Economic Geography*, 59,3 (1983), 251-71.

12 D. Massey, "Regionalism: Some Current Issues," *Capital and Class*, 6, (1978), 106-25, esp. 114.

13 The term "spatial division of labour" is taken from Massey and refers to "... the way in which economic activity responds to geographical inequalities in the conditions of accumulation — the particular kind of use made by capital of such inequality." Massey, "Regionalism," 14.

14 E. Mandel, *Long Waves of Capitalist Development* (Cambridge: Cambridge University Press, 1980); Aglietta, *Theory of Capitalist Regulation;* M. De Vroey, "A Regulation Approach Interpretation of the Contemporary Crisis," *Capital and Class*, 23 (1984), 45-66; Lipietz, *The World Crisis;* D.M. Gordon, R.C. Edwards, and M. Reich, *Segmented Work, Divided Workers: The Historical Transformation of Labour in the U.S.* (Cambridge: Cambridge University Press, 1982).

15 Given the view that the economic slowdown has profound social and political roots, then the resolution of the restructuring crisis requires not only changes in production but also broader social and political change: see D. Evans and R. Kaplinsky, "Slowdown or Crisis?" editorial introduction, *IDS Bulletin*, 16, 1 (1985), 1-8, esp. 6. Therefore, equally important and clearly interlinked with the process of industrial restructuring is the need to transform virtually every aspect of what the French regulation school refers to as a "regime of accumulation" (Aglietta, *Theory of Capitalist Regulation*) and what Gordon, *et al.* refer to as a "social structure of accumulation" (Gordon, *et al., Segmented Work*), that is, patterns and norms of consumption, labour relations, the labour market, wage determination, the monetary system, etc. While there is accumulating evidence of fundamental changes underway in these spheres in Canada in the mid-1980s, space precludes discussion and analysis of them here. However, I would like to stress their importance for achieving a full understanding of the current restructuring crisis. Also, see M. Davis, "The Political Economy of Late Imperial America," *New Left Review*, 143 (1984), 6-38; and M. Davis, "Reaganomics' Magical Mystery Tour," *New Left Review*, 149 (1985), 45-65, for an insightful analysis of such changes in the United States.

16 Aglietta, *Theories of Capitalist Regulation*; De Vroey, "A Regulation Approach"; and Lipietz, *The World Crisis.*

17 Of course the "mode of regulation" entailed many "functional" forms other than those mentioned here, for example, the welfare state, the development of administered pricing by large oligopolistic firms, the development of credit money, etc.

18 The data in table 1 also raise the interesting and crucial question of whether or not the crisis is now over. From the preliminary data released for 1983 and 1984 it appears that we may be starting to see the first hard evidence that a qualitative transformation of production is underway, resulting in sharp increases in labour productivity and declines in the rate of growth in unit labour costs (note that 1984 saw the first absolute decline in unit labour costs in Canadian manufacturing since 1964). The evidence on labour productivity and labour costs for the U.S. show a similar trend. See L.J. Fulco, "Strong Post-Recession Growth in Productivity Contributes to Slow Growth in Labor Costs," *Monthly Labour Review* (December 1984), 3-10.

19 Economic Council of Canada, *The Bottom Line*. U. Zohar, *Canadian Manufacturing: A Study in Productivity and Technological Change* (Toronto: James Lorimer, 1982).

20 Zohar, *Canadian Manufacturing*, 31.

21 F. Frobel, J. Heinrichs and D. Kreye, *The New International Division of Labour* (Cambridge: Cambridge University Press, 1979); and F. Frobel, "The Current Development of the World Economy: Reproduction of Labour and Accumulation of Capital on a World Scale," *Review*, 5 (1982), 507-55. Note that this global reorganization of production would not have been feasible even as recently as twenty-five years ago. The vastly increased "locational capability" of capital today has depended critically both upon the sophisticated development of Taylorism in the manufacturing labour process, which has led to the decomposition of production processes into elementary units and the deskilling of many tasks, and upon the development of advanced electronic communications and data processing technologies and associated developments in managerial practices which enable the exercise of centralized managerial control over a globally organized production system. See M. Storper and R. Walker, "The Spatial Division of Labor: Labor and the Location of Industries," in W. Tabb and L. Sawers, eds., *Sunbelt Snowbelt* (New York: Oxford University Press, 1983).

22 R. Jenkins, "Divisions Over the International Division of Labour," *Capital and Class*, 22 (1984), 28-58.

23 Lipietz, *The World Crisis*.

24 Holmes, "Industrial Reorganization."

25 OECD, *Long Term Outlook for the World Automobile Industry* (Paris: OECD, 1983), 14.

26 C.R. Littler and G. Salaman, *Class at Work: The Design, Allocation and Control of Jobs* (London: Batsford Academic, 1984), 90.

27 A. Altshuler, *et al.*, *The Future of the Automobile: The Report of MIT's International Automobile Program* (Cambridge MA: MIT Press, 1984), 220.

28 W. Abernathy, *The Productivity Dilemma: Roadblock to Innovation in the Automobile Industry* (Baltimore: Johns Hopkins Press, 1978).

29 *Ibid.*, 4.

30 Canada, Federal Task Force, *Automotive Strategy*, 51.

31 Holmes, "Industrial Reorganization," 259.

32 For a detailed analysis of this period see Holmes, *ibid.*

33 Altshuler, *The Future of the Automobile*, vii.

34 *Ibid.*, 200.

35 Canada, Federal Task Force, *Automotive Strategy*, 42.

36 Department of Regional Industrial Expansion (DRIE), Canada, *1981 Report on the Canadian Auto Industry*, (Ottawa: DRIE, 1984), 38.

37 G. Bloomfield, "The Changing Spatial Organization of Multinational Corporations in the World Automotive Industry," in F.E.I. Hamilton and G. Linge, eds., *Spatial Analysis, Industry and the Industrial Environment*, (London: Wiley, 1981).

38 D. Friedman, "Beyond the Age of Ford: The Strategic Basis of the Japanese Success in Automobiles," in J. Zysman and L. Tyson, eds., *American Industry in International Competition* (Ithaca: Cornell University Press, 1983), 367.

39 Altshuler, *The Future of the Automobile*, 137.

40 National Academy of Science, *Competitive Status*, 115.

41 Altshuler, *The Future of the Automobile*, 7.

42 R. Perry, *The Future of Canada's Auto Industry* (Toronto: James Lorimer, 1982), 31.

43 Some caution should be exercised with respect to the accuracy of these figures. For a good discussion of the difficulties involved in estimating productivity and cost differentials between North American and Japanese auto producers, see National Academy of Science, *Competitive Status*; W. Norsworthy, and D.H. Malmquist, "Input Measurement and Productivity Growth in Japanese and U.S. Manufacturing," *American Economic Review*, 73 ((1983), 947-67; and R.E. Cole and T. Yakushiji, *The American and Japanese Auto Industries in Transition* (Ann Arbor, MI: Center for Japanese Studies, University of Michigan, 1984). Nevertheless, despite disputes over the correct magnitude of the absolute figures there is agreement that the differentials are substantial and favour Japanese producers.

44 W. Johnston, *Issues in the Multinational Sourcing of Production*, Working Paper US-B-82-6, (Cambridge MA: MIT Future of the Automobile Program, 1982); B. Dankbaar, "Maturity and Relocation in the Car Industry," *Development and Change*, 15, 2 (1984), 223-50; and R.B. Cohen, "The New Spatial Organization of the European and American Automotive Industries," in F. Moulaert and P.W. Salinas, eds., *Regional Analysis and the New International Division of Labour* (Boston: Kluwer-Nijhoff Publishing, 1983), 135-44.

45 Jenkins, "Divisions Over."

46 Cohen, "New Spatial Organization"; and A. Amin, *Industrial Restructuring, State Intervention and Regional Growth: the Example of Alfa Sud in Southern Italy*, Reading Geographical Papers, 77.

47 It can be argued that the lesser impact of the recession on auto production in Canada is due, in part, to the protection afforded Canada by the Auto Pact. For example, the fact that the Big Four each have only one or two assembly plants in Canada would make it impossible for them to close an assembly plant and still meet the commitments made under their letters of agreement.

48 The process yield of a given labour process is determined not only by line speed but also by the number of defective parts produced and by the percentage of nonproductive "downtime."

49 Altshuler, *The Future of the Automobile*; Canada, Federal Task Force, *Automotive Strategy*, and National Academy of Science, *Competitive Status*.

50 Altshuler, *The Future of the Automobile,* 183.

51 This transformation goes significantly beyond the changes in production methods which occurred in the mid-1970s and which were labelled "neo-Fordist" by a number of French political economists. See C. Palloix, "The Labour Process From Fordism to Neo-Fordism," in *The Labour Process and Class Strategies,* (London: Stage 1, 1978), 46-64; and B. Coriot, "The Restructuring of the Assembly Line: A New Economy of Time and Control," *Capital and Class* 11(1980), 34-43. The latter were viewed simply as further refinements of Fordist techniques aimed at the further deskilling of workers and increasing managerial control over the labour process.

52 Y. Sugimori, *et al.,* "Toyota Production System and Kanban System: Materialization of Just-in-Time and Respect-for-Human System," *International Journal of Production Research,* 15, 6 (1977), 553-64; and P. Sheard, "Auto-production Systems in Japan: Organizational and Locational Features," *Australian Geographical Studies,* 21, 1 (1983), 49-68.

53 R.H. Ballance and S.W. Sinclair, *Collapse and Survival: Industry Strategies in a Changing World* (London: George Allen and Unwin, 1983), 99.

54 See H.C. Katz, "The U.S. Automobile Collective Bargaining System in Transition," *British Journal of Industrial Relations,* 22, 2 (1984), 205-17, for a full discussion of the post-war "paradigm" for contract bargaining and the current transformation of the employment relationship in the North American auto industry.

55 Ultimately this has led to the recent secession of the Canadian auto workers from the UAW to form their own autonomous Canadian union. It is ironic that this split in an international union — note that the U.S. UAW will no longer be able to call itself an international union — has occurred in the industry for which there is the strongest material basis for an international union: an integrated production system and common employers.

56 Perry, *Future of Canada's Auto Industry;* and M. Van Ameringen, "The Restructuring of the Canadian Automobile Industry," in D. Cameron and F. Houle, eds., *Canada and the New International Division of Labour* (Ottawa: University of Ottawa Press, 1985), 267-87.

57 Altshuler, *The Future of the Automobile,* 249.

Chapter 6

The Global Economic Crisis and Quebec's Peripheral Position in the Capitalist Economy

Alain G. Gagnon and Mary Beth Montcalm

THE CURRENT INTERNATIONAL economic crisis has had severe consequences in the developing countries. Equally significant, however, is the impact of the global crisis and the restructuring of capital in industrialized states as a whole and in peripheral regions of developed states. One clear example of the economic and political consequences of the international crisis in peripheral areas of developed countries is represented by the political scenario within Quebec. Macroeconomic trends have eroded the economic foundation of both the province's links with the Canadian state and the relative balance in economic and political relations within Quebec itself. The tenuous political relationship of Quebec to the Canadian state is illustrated by the fact that after 1976 the provincial government was formed by the Parti québécois (until its December 1985 defeat by the Liberal Party), a party committed to the independence of Quebec from Canada.[1] Political relations within the province also display a realignment of class relations which can be traced to economic trends.

In this essay, the pattern of alliances and conflicts within Quebec society is addressed. Current conflicts in Quebec can be traced to shifting class positions and alliances which are influenced by the restructuring occurring in domestic and international capitalist relations. To understand current alliances and conflicts within Quebec, one must situate them in an era of both high material aspirations and economic contraction. Of course, this environment of economic contraction and current class struggle is influenced by the global economic crisis and Quebec's continuing peripheralization within the Canadian, continental, and, indeed, world capitalist economic system.

This study begins with an examination of Quebec's position in the larger capitalist economy. It goes on to illustrate the relationship between Quebec's economic peripheralization within North American capitalism and the political consequences of state intervention aimed at alleviating this trend. Finally, the limitations on state capitalism's efforts at staving off economic peripheralization are examined, and the transformation of Quebec's class structure implied by these broad economic changes and current conflicts in Quebec politics is described. Throughout the essay, the shifting pattern of class alliances within the province is viewed as integrally related to the global crisis and to Quebec's peripheral position in the capitalist economy.

Until recently, much that was written about Quebec politics interpreted major changes there as the result of a transition from a traditional to a modern society. Quebec was implicitly viewed as having undergone a change in which the ascendancy of "modern" elements, and in particular the technocratic middle class (which was closely linked to the Liberal Party of Quebec in the 1960s and afterward to the Parti québécois) had become pervasive and assured.

Recent Quebec politics has manifested serious challenges to the often-assumed ascendancy of the technocratic new middle class. In recent years the apparently complacent relationship between Québécois and "péquistes", and indeed among those ostensibly committed to the independence option, turned acrimonious. The increasing political difficulties of the Parti québécois are illustrated by a series of twenty-two consecutive by-election defeats and the resounding provincial election victory for the Liberals on December 2, 1985. Moreover, the Parti québécois' fractious relations with the major public service unions contributed to a near Liberal sweep of the Quebec City region with the defeat of sixteen out of seventeen PQ candidates.[2]

The rupturing of alliances within the Parti québécois itself came to a head at a party congress held January 19-20, 1985, when a decision not to hold the forthcoming election on the issue of independence was ratified. This decision shook the Parti québécois to its roots and brought about the defection of prominent members of both the caucus and the cabinet (seven ministers in total), numerous presidents of riding associations, and no less than four of the fifteen members of the national executive.

By 1986, PQ leader Pierre Marc Johnson told the three hundred National Council members who met February 22-23 to assess the party's situation that the party's program, including the goal of independence and the concept of sovereignty, needed to be redefined.[3] While future political alignments cannot be predicted with any certainty, the status of the Parti québécois undoubtedly will be complicated by the decision of the "hard-liners" to form a new political movement, the RDI (Railliement démocratique pour l'indépendance) and, as well, by increased activity on the part of the Progressive Conservatives, the New Democrats, and the Union nationale.[4]

While the numerous defections from the party and the dilution of the Parti québécois' commitment to the sovereignty option signalled the declining popularity of the party (see table 1), results of the recent provincial election, in which the Liberals received 56 per cent of the popular vote against 39 per cent for the Parti québécois, unambiguously confirmed this trend. These developments indicate that major realignments of political forces are underway in Quebec. Moreover, such shifting alliances are no surprise, since the popularity of the independence option, and indeed the apparent ascendancy of the technocratic new middle class, have evidently been circumscribed by Quebec's economic fortunes.[5]

Quebec in the Capitalist Economy

Since World War II, western economies have become increasingly integrated. While a full discussion of the effects of international economic integration is beyond the scope of this essay, three dimensions with repercussions for Quebec are noteworthy. These are continental economic integration, geographic shifts within the Canadian economy, and the growth of state capitalism.

Economic internationalization has involved increasing integration of the

Table 1

Quebec Provincial Party Preference (%)

Question: If provincial elections were held today, which one of the following parties would you vote for? Perhaps you have not yet made up your mind: Is there nevertheless a party you might be presently inclined to support?

Parti libéral du Québec	44	34	46	53	59
Parti québécois	40	52	31	21	19
Union nationale	7	—	9	9	6
Other*	10	16	15	17	16
Survey Report	09/80	09/81	09/82	09/83	03/84
Total Sample	567	584	581	576	588

*Other: includes other parties, not planning to vote, don't know, and refuse to answer.

Source: CROP (Le Centre de recherches sur l'opinion publique) Poll surveys, 1980-84.

Canadian and U.S. economies and an overall restructuring within North American capitalism. Despite the prominent role of Canada's financial bourgeoisie in international capitalism, it is widely acknowledged that the Canadian economy fulfills a modest role within the North American context and that continental economic integration has involved substantial presence of U.S. multinationals in Canada.

Less remarked is the degree to which the restructuring of capital has involved its concentration within Canada and expansion of Canadian firms into the United States. Canadian enterprises experienced a series of major mergers in the finance, resource, and commercial sectors during the 1970s and early 1980s. Between 1977 and 1981 the average number of mergers in Canada was over 430 per year. This compares with an annual average of 378 in the period from 1970 to 1974 and 192 in the period from 1960 to 1964. Moreover, a major portion of the takeovers was generated by eight large conglomerates, seven of them controlled by a single family.[6] Examples of this pattern of growing concentration include consolidation of the National Bank, and Noranda; major mergers of trust companies (such as National, Victoria and Grey) in order to enhance their competitive position with Canada's major banks; and the strengthening of the Thomson family, which took control of the Hudson's Bay Company (already in control of Zellers and Simpsons).[7] In 1982, the Canadian deputy minister of consumer and corporate affairs acknowledged that one hundred companies controlled over half the assets of all Canadian corporations. The aggregate level of concentration in Canada is now substantially higher than it is in the United States, and in many industries it is also higher than in European countries.[8]

The major restructuring in the finance, resource, and commercial sectors was accompanied by expansion of Canadian firms (such as Bombardier) in the U.S. market. In fact, the expansion of Canadian direct investment in the United States from 1975 to 1980 was unprecedented. The major Canadian banks substantially expanded their foreign operations and the largest Canadian producer of telecommunications equipment, Northern Electric, became a multinational under the name Northern Telecom, and expanded into the U.S. market.[9]

The structural changes within North American capitalism have also involved the expansion of Quebec-based firms into the U.S. market. Lavalin (engineering), Domtar (resource sector), and the National Bank (financial sector) are among the firms experiencing the greatest success in the conquest of foreign markets. Niosi suggests one plausible reason for the expansion of Quebec-based firms into the United States:

> While the conquest of the Quebec market seems a precondition for foreign expansion, it is evident that francophone corporations choose most often to

> grow in the United States and Europe rather than fight for a piece of the English-Canadian market. The English-Canadian economy may be too concentrated, too sparsely populated, or (probably) not sufficiently receptive to French-Canadian enterprise.[10]

As well as growing patterns of concentration in Canada and expansion of Canadian firms into the U.S. market, North American economic integration has involved the gradual elimination of tariffs "protecting" the Canadian market from U.S. economic hegemony. As trade liberalization proceeds (under the tariff cuts negotiated during the GATT Tokyo Round), a number of consequences will likely ensue. Among the probable consequences will be the closing of U.S. branch plants in the Canadian market. In order to benefit from economies of scale, U.S.-based multinationals are likely to concentrate in the United States and export to Canada. Moreover, this pattern is liable to be intensified by U.S. policies encouraging the concentration of corporate activity in the United States.[11]

A second aspect of economic internationalization (and one which can be linked to the trend towards continental economic integration) is a geographic shift in economic activity in Canada. In recent decades, the centre of economic dynamism within Canada has shifted westward, heightening the level of economic activity in provinces such as Alberta, and firmly establishing Toronto rather than Montreal as Canada's major economic centre. Although there has been some reversal in the westward trend most recently, this reversal seems to be to the benefit of Ontario more than Quebec.[12] A corollary to both the shift westward and recent difficulties in that region has been a decline in the economic role of Montreal within the Canadian economy and the economic peripheralization of Quebec within continental capitalism. Of course, this has exacerbated the effects of the overall economic contraction and heightened political struggle between classes in Quebec.

Finally, along with most other "industrial" states, Canada and the province of Quebec have undergone a period of economic adjustment in the face of the international restructuring of capital. This readjustment has involved among other things greater state intervention in the economy (or the growth of state capitalism) aimed at maintaining high levels of employment in spite of Canada's declining attractiveness to labour-intensive industries. There are indications that the federal government wants to become more involved at the level of economic planning and support for accumulation while restricting the expansion of its social development envelope.[13] What is particularly noteworthy is that greater state capitalism has not only accentuated conflictual relations between the Quebec and Canadian governments but it has enmeshed the Quebec state apparatus in the changing class configuration within Quebec.

Quebec's Economic Peripheralization

The implications of changes such as the growth of state capitalism, economic continentalization, the westward shift of economic activity, and Quebec's economic peripheralization have been subjects of considerable discussion by students of Canada's political economy.[14] Their effects clearly have been compounded in Quebec, and have led to the current scenario of struggle to obtain ever-diminishing economic resources.

Since World War II (and, indeed, even prior to it) capitalist trends have had negative implications for the Quebec economy: head offices gradually relocated outside Quebec, the once-powerful Montreal anglophone bourgeoisie has been gradually leaving the province, and the overall level of economic activity within the formerly central Montreal business community has shown a consistent decline.[15] The relative decline of the Quebec economy within the Canadian and the continental economic market is illustrated by almost any economic indicator one chooses.

By the end of the war, the Montreal stock exchange had lost its supremacy to the Toronto stock exchange (see table 2). As well, whereas in 1952 Montreal had 124 company headquarters for each 100 in Toronto, as early as 1972 this ratio had declined to 62 per 100 and recent studies show this to be a continuing trend.[16] In the 1976 to 1982 period, investment in Quebec declined

Table 2

$ Value of Transactions: Montreal Stock Exchange, Toronto Stock Exchange and M.S.E./T.S.E. %. (Selected years, 1945-80)

	T.S.E. $	M.S.E. $	M.S.E./T.S.E. %
1945	617,817,836	284,347,970	46.0
1950	902,461,781	662,199,363	73.4
1955	2,699,008,896	1,161,746,903	43.0
1960	1,223,330,494	671,992,634	54.9
1965	3,199,062,626	1,251,960,639	39.1
1970	3,653,783,248	1,205,025,476	33.0
1975	4,089,020,234	1,384,724,314	33.9
1980	29,514,529,845	3,856,810,125	13.1

Sources: Toronto Stock Exchange data provided by T.S.E. statistical services, *Montreal Stock Exchange and Montreal Curb Market, Monthly Review*, various years; *Montreal Stock Exchange and Canadian Stock Exchange, Monthly Review*, various years; *Bourse de Montréal /Montreal Stock Exchange, Monthly Review*, various years.

approximately 3 per cent annually whereas in Canada as a whole it increased approximately 2.5 per cent annually.[17] Until very recently, trends in the manufacturing sector similarly indicated a continued decline of Quebec relative to provinces such as Ontario, Alberta, and British Columbia (see tables 3 and 4). Interprovincial migration data show that in the 1961-83 period, Quebec experienced heavy losses of population while Alberta and British Columbia made substantial gains (see table 6).[18]

It is important to note, however, that this decline of the Montreal and Quebec economies relative to Toronto and other parts of Canada has been rooted in long-term economic trends rather than in particular policy decisions adopted by Quebec governments. Despite frequent assertions that nationalist legislation has frightened business investment away from Quebec, historical data suggests that the restructuring of capital within the North American setting has simply involved the gradual peripheralization of Quebec in the continental economy.

The early effect of this peripheralization by market forces was camouflaged by massive growth of the state apparatus in the 1960s and 1970s as the Quebec government undertook increasing public commitments aimed at shoring up the Quebec economy. From 1960 to 1980, Quebec provincial expenditures grew at a faster rate than in other provinces. The government of Canada has also kept its expenses at a high level (see table 6). The rapid expansion of the Quebec state is indicated in table 7, which shows the evolution of the public sector work force and expenditures during the 1960s and 1970s. State capitalism in Quebec, and the extensive state apparatus it implied, not only postponed evidence of Quebec's economic peripheralization but enhanced

Table 3

Employment Patterns in Manufacturing Industries (in thousands)

Year	Quebec	Ontario	Alberta	British Columbia	Canada
1975	586	877	71	153	1871
1976	589	909	76	167	1921
1977	560	906	79	170	1888
1978	571	940	79	176	1956
1979	605	1007	85	178	2071
1980	619	1009	102	178	2111
1981	593	1036	106	184	2122
1982	542	951	95	159	1930
1983	533	935	86	151	1886

Source: Statistics Canada, *Labour Force Annual Averages, 1975-83*, Catalogue no. 71-529 (annual).

Table 4

Employment Patterns in Manufacturing Industries (in thousands)

Month/Year	Quebec	Ontario	Alberta	British Columbia	Canada
January 1984	614	1035	107	184	2125
February 1984	635	1036	102	181	2147
March 1984	640	1034	101	180	2151
April 1984	630	1042	106	177	2159
May 1984	641	1069	109	177	2126
June 1984	666	1085	108	174	2264
February 1985	604	1104	90	167	2166

Source: Statistics Canada, *The Labour Force,* Catalogue 71-001 (monthly).

Table 5

Interprovincial Migration Trends in Canada, 1977-83 (number of persons)
Net Migration Flows

Region	1976-81	1981-82	1982-83*
Newfoundland	-18983	-5693	1665
Prince Edward Island	-829	-856	209
Nova Scotia	-7140	-1936	1428
New Brunswick	-10351	-2842	2491
Quebec	-156496	-25790	-22568
Ontario	-57826	-5665	15112
Manitoba	-42218	-2625	389
Saskatchewan	-9716	-323	2660
Alberta	186364	36562	-3344
British Columbia	122625	8705	3632
Yukon	-933	81	-1903
Northwest Territories	-4497	382	229

*Statistics Canada, *Postcensal Annual Estimates of Population by Marital Status, Age, Sex, and Components of Growth for Canada and the Provinces, June 1, 1982 and 1983,* November, 1984, Catalogue no. 91-210.

Sources: Statistics Canada, *Quarterly and Annual Net Interprovincial Migration by Province, 1976-83,* Catalogue no. 91-208 (July, 1984).

the power of the technocratic new middle class located primarily in Quebec's state structures. The new middle class came to dominate Quebec's politics. Nevertheless, the limits to state capitalism became apparent in the late 1970s and early 1980s and, as current struggles in Quebec illustrate, these limits have engendered a new struggle for ascendancy in the province.

Changing Class Structure and Current Conflicts

In the post-war era, most western states readily resorted to state intervention to counteract the negative impact of economic internationalization. Although in recent years there has been a slowing (if not a reversal) of this trend, state capitalism has resulted in the growth of public sectors and in a more prominent role by the states in capitalist economies.

In the 1940s and 1950s, Quebec politics was dominated by the traditional middle class (although the power of this class was always circumscribed by the capitalist mode of production and the powerful position Quebec's anglophone bourgeoisie held within that mode of production), and marked by increasing challenges on the part of the industrial working class and the rising technocratic middle class in Quebec's urban centres.

With the Liberal government's assumption of power in 1960, it appeared that "modern" elements of Quebec society had taken over the helm in the province. The links between the new middle class and the Liberal Party of Quebec in the 1960s and, subsequently, the Parti québécois are unmistakable. These governments disproportionately derived their electoral support from this class and adopted policies beneficial to it.[19] The substantial increase in the size of the public sector and its activities in the 1960s and 1970s suited the interests of the new middle class.

The forms which interventionism took in Quebec, most of which served to enhance the power of the technocratic new middle class, were as varied as they were widespread. The Quebec government made extensive use of *sociétés d'états* (provincial crown corporations) to stimulate economic growth and to restructure regional economic activity in order to improve the province's position in the Canadian context. The reestablishment of the Conseil d'orientation économique du Québec (COEQ) in 1961 reflected, among other things, a desire both to modernize Quebec's economic and social structure and to secure Quebec's links with broader market forces. The formulation of the development plan for the eastern Quebec region (1963-66) by the Bureau d'aménagement de l'est du Québec (BAEQ) had similar objectives. Other notable interventions by the Quebec government included the establishment of Caisse de dépôt et de placement, the Société générale de financement, Sidbec, and the nationalization of Hydro-Québec. In essence, these initiatives aimed to utilize Quebec's natural resource wealth to build a viable and employment-producing secondary sector, and to allow Quebec to compete on the international economic scene. Furthermore, these undertakings were clearly part of an overall approach to economic planning in which the powerful state apparatus would be the major initiator and player.

Although these interventions were meant to stop Quebec's peripheralization, they at no time posed a fundamental challenge to the capitalist economy but simply maintained the economic structure and sought to protect Quebec's position and to replace English Canadian and U.S. capital with Quebec capital. In addition to expanding the state sector, this policy approach fostered an indigenous Quebec bourgeoisie (which increasingly occupied the position of the departing big bourgeoisie). It failed, however, to reverse the process of Quebec's peripheralization. Moreover, since the economic structure remained capitalist, the state eventually had less and less means to intervene

Table 6

Evolution of Public Expenditures as a Percentage of Gross Provincial Product, Gross National Product (all levels of government)

	1961	1980
Alberta	29.6	25.7
Ontario	27.5	37.2
Quebec	26.7	48.2
Canada	30.4	40.3

Source: Statistics Canada. *Provincial Economic Accounts,* Catalogue no. 13-213.

Table 7

Evolution of Budgetary Expenditures and Permanent Employees of the Quebec Government, 1960-80

	Expenditures ($thousands-constant)	Index (1971=100)	Employees
1960-61	1,455,508	59.1	29,298
1964-65	2,108,087	68.2	32,779
1969-70	3,163,359	94.2	53,791
1974-75	4,626,835	155.8	47,882
1979-80	—	—	62,542

Source: L. Quesnel-Ouellet, "L'Appareil gouvernemental et législatif," in G. Bergeron and R. Pelletier, eds., *L'État du Québec en devenir* (Montreal: Boréal Express, 1980), 108.

in the process of accumulation and to insure that market forces would work to Quebec's advantage.

While the dramatic growth in Quebec's state apparatus delayed the impact of Quebec's economic peripheralization and forged a bond between the *étatiste* Parti québécois and its major supporters (the technocratic new middle class), by the early 1980s the economic contraction imposed by the overall economic crisis, compounded by the process of Quebec's economic peripheralization, could no longer be evaded. It became increasingly apparent that Quebec could not continue to support a massive state apparatus within a capitalist economic context experiencing serious economic dislocation.

As a response to this new reality, the Parti québécois government, which had become identified with a statist approach to economic activity, apparently converted to the idea that the marketplace provided the most effective allocator of economic resources. An examination of traditional positions adopted by the Parti québécois, such as its 1975 electoral platform, shows that economic planning had been a pillar in its economic development strategy. Since the Parti québécois never fully challenged the capitalist system itself, however, the lifespan of such an approach was limited from the start. The gradual shift of the PQ away from a state-led approach towards a reliance on the market is evident in policy statements such as *Challenges for Quebec*[20] and more recently in *The Technology Conversion*, in which it addressed problems related to adjustment of existing manufacturers to market conditions, new industrial development opportunities, and the need to improve the efficiency of resource industries. This policy statement made clear the government's intention to base its hopes for a reversal of economic dislocation on private enterprise initiatives. The document states in part:

> The responsibility of ensuring sufficient, sustained development lies first of all with the private sector, since most enterprises are in this sector. The government of Quebec has, as one of its prime objectives, to create and maintain conditions favourable to the development and dynamism of private initiatives, and feels that the best system of effectively allocating resources remains the market economy.[21]

This document also maintained that provincial crown corporations should assume that the rationale of the marketplace is the primary criterion for making decisions. It states:

> All industrial and commercial government corporations are now subject to rules of competition and profitability, and the performance of each is assessed according to the same standards as are used in the private sector.[22]

Paradoxically, the Quebec government, which had put into place in the 1960s and 1970s widely diverse instruments geared to implementing a well-integrated development strategy, increasingly appeared willing to rely on private enterprise and the vagaries of the marketplace in order to undertake the badly-needed structural transformation of its economy. The acceptance of a capitalist context inevitably limited what was possible through state intervention, and the ultimate power of market demand reasserted itself in the 1980s.

Notably, affirmation of the Parti québécois government's faith in private enterprise as the motor of economic growth was accompanied by increasing divergence between the interests of the long-allied péquistes and the technocratic new middle class. The latter, based in the public sector and represented by organizations such as the public sector unions, continued to demand artificially high salaries and to seek insulation from the impact of economic dislocations inherent in the recession. The Parti québécois, as a result of the limits on state capitalism, could not continually acquiesce to the demands of the new middle class. It became increasingly apparent that the Quebec government, like its counterparts in other jurisdictions, was going to have to impose constraints on the public sector if Quebec was to respond to current capitalist needs for less public sector spending and borrowing. The widening gap between the interests of the technocratic middle class and those of the governing Parti québécois was, in fact, simply one dimension of a new era of conflict, controversy, and struggle for ascendancy within Quebec.

The recent election of the Quebec Liberal party does not signal a major departure from the PQ government's policy in this sphere. In fact, as he unveiled contract offers to the 300,000 government employees, Treasury Board President Paul Gobeil indicated that they should not expect more than a 3.5 per cent wage increase for the next year. The minister also stressed that the cost-of-living index was no longer the reference point for salary hikes in the public sector.[23]

In the 1980s, other classes have asserted themselves and are challenging the position of the technocratic new middle class. Quebec is now the scene of deep political ferment and the tensions obvious there indicate the crumbling of alliances that dominated Quebec politics throughout the 1960s and 1970s and a realignment of class forces. Richard French captures this development in an article published in *Le Devoir*:

> Social leadership, held for a decade by an intellectual bourgeoisie and those in the field of communication, is rapidly shifting to the business or economic bourgeoisie . . . . It remains to be seen which of these will have power in Quebec: those who define political discourse with the government and whose ultimate objective is independence or those whose preoccupations are economic and thus are oriented towards investment and expansion of the Quebec market.[24]

As a consequence of the less prominent role played in Quebec by the once-dominant anglophone bourgeoisie and also as a result of state efforts to foster francophone business, the strength of a francophone bourgeoisie had gradually increased. Eventually this indigenous bourgeoisie demanded both restrictions on the new middle class in the public sector and increased acquiescence to its interests in government policy. The satisfaction of these demands is illustrated by events during recent economic summits held by the PQ government. In fact, these reveal a turn towards the interests of various levels of the private sector. Brian Tanguay observes:

> On the whole, business and the private-sector unions (represented by the FTQ and the CSD) have been quite satisfied with the functioning of concerted action in Quebec: business, because of the increased amount and variety of state largesse promised to it at the various summits; the private-sector unions, because of the specific "concessions" they have secured from the government. Among these concessions the FTQ and the CSD would undoubtedly number Corvée Habitation, the anti-scab provisions in the Labour Code, and (to the FTQ at any rate) the government's support for the Fonds de solidarité, an investment fund financed by worker contributions to provide venture capital for Quebec industries.[25]

Increasing tension between the governing Parti québécois and its traditional ally (the technocratic new middle class lodged in Quebec's public sector) is evident in the labour tensions that arose between the PQ government and the public sector unions. In response to the present economic conjuncture, the PQ government passed in 1982-83 a series of laws which reduced government employees' pension benefits, dictated bargaining conditions and salaries, arbitrarily determined conditions of work for the following three years of public employees' contracts, and put an end to the CEGEP and public school teachers' strike and imposed retroactive pay reductions in the public sector (Bills 68, 70, 105, and 111). Clearly, these laws had a devastating effect on the level of support available from its former staunch ally.

It would nevertheless be incorrect to infer that relations between the PQ government and all unions were ruptured entirely. One aspect of the major realignment underway within Quebec society has involved, as noted earlier, a greater rapprochement between the PQ and the business sector and, as well, with private sector unions. The choice made by the Parti québécois government increasingly to restrict governmental activities and to foster instead private sector initiatives naturally led to greater conflict with public sector unions and greater accord with various elements of the private sector.

Economic peripheralization involved a considerably reduced role for the formerly powerful anglophone bourgeoisie (in part this is due to relocation of elements of this class outside Quebec). State capitalism in Quebec during the 1960s and 1970s not only enhanced the position of the technocratic new middle class, it also had the effect of strengthening the position of Quebec's indigenous francophone bourgeoisie. In short, the new middle class increased in size and made important gains but the benefits accruing to a francophone bourgeoisie were no less real, although they were initially less evident. Despite the obvious shift of power from the traditional middle class, state capitalism in the 1960s and 1970s not only aided the technocratic new middle class but also gave considerable assistance to a previously fragile francophone bourgeoisie.

Class relations have been further complicated by the persistence of petty producers in Quebec's rural areas. The subsistence mode of production has proven resilient in the face of capitalist forces. (A more advanced version of this mode of production, one establishing stronger links with the capitalist mode itself, is embodied in community enterprises and co-ops in Quebec's rural areas.) As links between the Quebec economy and the broader market dynamic became increasingly tenuous, classes linked to the petty producers' mode of production reasserted themselves politically. This reassertion has become a major element in the competition between social classes in Quebec and illustrates the continuing importance of local and regional power bases within Quebec's class constellation. The political tensions involved in the PQ's increasing reliance on the private sector and the problematic relationship between the government and the large public sector unions were added to by the growing reassertion of regional political forces (notables) that seemed to have disappeared from the province's political landscape in the 1960s and 1970s. A study of popular movements in Quebec by Alain Gagnon, based on a review of developments in eastern Quebec, illustrates that a major realignment of power has taken place at the rural level over the past fifteen years:

> During the 1960s, "organic intellectuals" (technocrats) appropriated for themselves specific powers to the detriment of "traditional intellectuals" (community leaders, priests). The 1970s saw a political will to reverse this trend and reassert the role of parliamentarians. In this campaign, both politicians and technocrats sought to amass the support of local populations.... In this respect the organismes de développement communautaire (ODCs), by calling into question certain unpopular government policies like relocation [that is, community resettlement] acquired some important support from the rural population. Thus, it is no mystery that politicians and bureaucrats have given these people so much attention in the past few years. Everyone wants them as allies.[26]

Today, it must be recognized that regional power groups, especially in the form of popular groups in Quebec's rural areas, have reemerged and pose a growing challenge to the present Quebec government's plans for Quebec society through the 1980s. Particularly indicative has been the resistance of popular groups to the spatial restructuring and the rationalization of economic activities in the peripheral regions of the province.

While it is difficult to predict the success of popular forces' efforts to put regional issues on the political agenda in the 1980s, it appears that further confrontation is likely. This is suggested not only by the reorganization currently underway at the regional level through the establishment of Municipalités régionales de comté (MRCs), but by the current scenario of state power in Quebec. For example, the policy statement produced by the Quebec Ministry of State for Planning and Development, *Le Choix des régions*, indicates an awareness by the provincial authorities of a need for broad social consensus regarding future developments within Quebec.[27] However, the policy proposal fails to address the fundamental problem which has confronted Quebec's peripheral regions since the beginning of industrialization. By calling on the regions to pursue self-development, the statement fails to confront the relationship between the structural weaknesses evident in the peripheral regions and the uneven development in the province implied by current capitalist needs.

In short, Quebec is currently the scene of conflict and shifting alliances involving not only the government party, the technocratic middle class, and the working class, but also a revitalized francophone bourgeoisie and the renewed importance of notables who were such a dominant element of Quebec's power structure prior to the ascendance of the technocratic new middle class and its political expression in the Quebec Liberal Party during the 1960s and the Parti québécois in the 1970s. Indeed, Quebec society gives every indication of undergoing a major realignment in its power structure that is equal to, if not greater than, the much discussed shifts epitomized in the Quiet Revolution.

Conclusion

The shifting alliances manifest in Quebec today have undermined the position of the Parti québécois and threaten the interests of the new middle class which became powerful in the 1960s and 1970s.

Transformation in the world economy and the restructuring of capitalist relations with its requirement of a new international division of labour circumscribe the shifting class alliances and the current struggle within Quebec society. The initial stages of Quebec's economic peripheralization and the Quebec state's response to this (in the form of increasing state intervention) facilitated the increased political power of the technocratic middle class. It is now evident that the capacity of the Quebec state to intervene, as it did in the 1960s and even the 1970s, has weakened considerably. It is also clear that the Parti québécois can no longer remain closely tied to the interests of the technocratic new middle class. It has to reckon now with the reassertion of power in Quebec's peripheral regions, a francophone bourgeoisie renewed and strengthened by many state initiatives taken in the 1960s and 1970s, and with workers located in the private sector. While it is difficult to predict whether the current Quebec government will be able to ride the tide of shifting class structures in Quebec, it does appear that the next few years will continue to manifest political upheavals which can be linked to the impact of macroeconomic trends on Quebec society.

Notes

1 For a discussion of the impact of macroeconomic changes on Quebec-Canada relations, see Alain G. Gagnon and Mary Beth Montcalm, "Economic Peripheralization and Quebec Unrest," *Journal of Canadian Studies*, 17, 2 (1982), 32-42.

2 Daniel Drolet, "Civil Servants' Revenge: 16 Liberals Win in Capital," *The Gazette*, Montreal, December 3, 1985, C-3; Pierre Vincent, "Les Employés de l'État ont pris leur revanche sur le gouvernement du P.Q.," *La Presse*, Montreal, December 3, 1985, A-5

3 François Shalom, "Johnson Urges a Major Overhaul of P.Q. Party Program After Defeat," *The Globe and Mail*, Toronto, February 24, 1986, A-21.

4 Lawrence Martin, "Voters Facing Crowded Field in Quebec's Political Arena," *The Globe and Mail*, March 9, 1985, A-8; Sarah Scott, "Hardline Separatists Cheer Fall of Party They Once Called Home," *The Gazette*, December 3, 1985, C-7.

5 See,for example, Maurice Pinard and Richard Hamilton, "The Independence Issue and the Polarization of the Electorate: The 1973 Quebec Election," *Canadian Journal of Political Science*, 10, 2, 215-60.

6 W.T. Stanbury and Susan Burns, "Consumer and Corporate Affairs: Portrait of a Regulatory Department," in G. Bruce Doern, ed., *How Ottawa Spends Your Tax Dollars, 1982* (Toronto: James Lorimer, 1982), 190-91.

7 One recent discussion of the degree to which corporate concentration is evident in Canada is "Big Chunk of Business in Hands of a Few," *The Globe and Mail, Report on Business*, Toronto, August 25, 1984.

8 Paul K. Gorecki and W.T. Stanbury, *The Objectives of Canadian Competition Policy, 1888-1983* (Montreal: The Institute for Research on Public Policy, 1984), 135.

9 Yves Bélanger and Pierre Beaulne, "Bourgeoisie et constitution au Canada," *Au-delà du parti québécois* (Montreal: Centre de formation populaire, Nouvelle Optique, 1982).

10 Jorge Niosi, "The Rise of French-Canadian Capitalism," in Alain G. Gagnon, ed., *Quebec: State and Society* (Toronto: Methuen, 1984), 196.

11 Stephen Clarkson, *Canada and the Reagan Challenge* (Toronto: James Lorimer, 1982), 114-24.

12 See Duncan McMonagle, "Ontario Growing While Population Shrinks in West," *The Globe and Mail*, March 20, 1985.

13 Cy Gonick, "The New Supply Side Economics," *Canadian Dimension*, 15, (1981), 17-21.

14 Garth Stevenson, "Canadian Regionalism in Continental Perspective," *Journal of Canadian Studies*, 15, (1980), 16-28.

15 J.H. Chung, "La Nature du déclin économique de la région de Montréal," *L'Actualité Economique*, (July-September, 1974), 41; Fernand Martin, *Montreal: An Economic Perspective* (Montreal: C.D. Howe Institute, 1979).

16 Chung, "La Nature"; Government of Quebec, *Les Sièges sociaux et l'emploi au Québec* (Quebec: Office de planification et de développement, 1978).

17 Yves Rabeau, *Major Investments in Quebec 1983 to 1995* (Calgary: Canada West Foundation, 1983).

18 Most recent trends, however, suggest a decline in Alberta's population undoubtedly as a consequence of the economic downturn in the Alberta economy. See McMonagle, "Ontario Growing."

19 Kenneth McRoberts and Dale Posgate, *Quebec: Social Change and Political Crisis* (Toronto: McClelland and Stewart, 1980) revised edition, 138; Maurice Pinard and Richard Hamilton, "The Parti Québécois Comes to Power," *Canadian Journal of Political Science*, 11 (1978); Albert Breton, "The Economics of Nationalism," *Journal of Political Economy*, 72 (1964).

20 Government of Quebec, *Challenges for Quebec* (Quebec: Développement économique, 1979).

21 Government of Quebec, *The Technology Conversion* (Quebec: Développement économique, 1982), 20.

22 Quebec, *The Technology Conversion*, 21.

23 Canadian Press, "Quebec P S Unions Offered 3.5% Wage-Package Increase," *The Citizen*, Ottawa, February 20, 1986, A-12.

24 Richard French, "Plus qu'un Débat entre Québec et Ottawa, une polarisation entre deux bourgeoisies," *Le Devoir*, December 16, 1982, 7.

25 Brian Tanguay, "Concerted Action in Quebec," in Gagnon, ed., *Quebec*, 381.

26 Alain G. Gagnon, *Développement régional: État et groupes populaires* (Hull: Les Éditions Asticou, 1985); "The Evolution of Political Forces in Quebec," in Gagnon, ed, *Quebec*, 262.

27 Government of Quebec, *Le Choix des régions* (Quebec: Aménagement et développement régional, 1983).

Chapter 7

The United States and Canada: State Policy and Strategic Perspectives on Capital in Central America

James F. Petras and Morris H. Morley

The United States and Central America: The Military Dimension

One of the most striking features of U.S. policy towards Central America is the continuity that has been maintained by different administrations. From a regional perspective, it has made little difference whether there have been Democrats or Republicans, or liberals or conservatives in the White House. U.S. policy-makers (with brief exceptional interludes) have relied on their military options and alliances with the area's armed forces to maintain Central America within Washington's orbit. The fundamental continuity in policy reflects the shared strategic position of both major political parties that U.S. domination is an unalterable goal.

At particular moments, U.S. liberal administrations have appeared to promote a social democratic option in Central America, but the policies and priorities pursued by Washington have undermined the possibility of sustaining a reformist option — for the simple reason that social and economic changes have always been subordinated to the strategic goal of defeating revolution.

Essentially, U.S. liberals propose to carry out changes that improve the standard of living of the masses at the cost of local élites and without adversely affecting the multinationals, their local economic partners, or the institutional position of the military and police forces. U.S. conservatives, on the other hand, seek to unify all sectors of the local ruling class and downplay reforms in favour of an exclusively military approach. While the liberals try to forge an alliance between the middle class and the military, the conservatives promote a power bloc in which the traditional oligarchical-military right is dominant. The liberals also support violent measures against radical class-based organizations but hope to exclude Christian democratic and other centre-based groups from the wave of terror. The conservatives usually do not draw these fine distinctions. Instead they support each and every effort by military-controlled governments to stamp out independent organized forces in society.

While these distinctions between liberals and conservatives have surfaced in U.S. public debate, one major factor has produced a unity, which results in similar policy consequences: the ultimate reliance on the military and police forces to establish dominance in the target country. In the case of Guatemala, for example, the policies of all administrations from Eisenhower to Reagan, whatever their initial intentions, have consolidated the repressive forces in society and, in so doing, strengthened precisely the most significant obstacles to any serious and sustained program of socio-economic change. During the Kennedy and Carter presidencies, the White House launched major efforts to promote a social democratic option in Guatemala. Neither proved capable of bringing about reforms or modifying the pattern of state-authored mass repression. The unwillingness of either Kennedy or Carter to break with the Guatemalan military, which had destroyed the very social movements capable of instituting such changes (despite criticism of the armed forces' "excesses"), indicated that their priorities dictated the defeat of radical social movements before looking towards social and economic reforms. In supporting the destruction of these movements, U.S. liberals strengthened the very groups opposed not only to the social democratic option but to all changes — effectively undermining the "centrist" position as well. In sum, the differences between U.S. liberals and conservatives, while important in a specific conjunctural context, do not lead to different outcomes.

The Militarization of Civil Society

Since the 1950s, the United States has played a paramount role in financing, training, and equipping the armed forces and police constabularies of Central America. These coercive forces have, in turn, acted as powerful institutional collaborators in the pursuit of the imperial state's economic, strategic, and political goals in the region. The Alliance for Progress included a significant expansion of Washington's military program as part of the Kennedy administration's determination to prevent "another Cuba" in the hemisphere. During the late 1960s and early 1970s, large-scale U.S. military assistance strengthened military missions, and the active participation of the Green Berets provided much of the wherewithal for the Guatemalan armed forces' brutal campaign to "pacify" insurgent movements in the countryside. The Somoza National Guard, a creature of the Pentagon from its inception to its demise, received millions of dollars worth of U.S. weapons from the Ford and Carter administrations, enabling it to wage war against a growing mass-based, urban-rural, multi-class opposition in Nicaragua. Since 1981, an additional factor has reinforced the growing U.S. military presence in the region: the Reagan administration's need to achieve a military victory in order to justify the vast armaments program that forms the core of the "New Cold War". El Salvador, in particular, has become the theatre in which Reagan hopes to demonstrate that force, not negotiation, works — thus intertwining regional with global politics. Central America as a whole has become the arena where the United States hopes to recapture its worldwide supremacy through military confrontation and military victory.

The Nicaraguan revolution of July 1979 and the developing revolutionary processes in El Salvador and Guatemala initially caused the Carter government to pressure the Guatemalan generals, through military aid cutbacks, to be more selective in their repressive policies, and to forge an alliance between reformist civilian and rightist military officials in El Salvador. During 1979 and 1980, however, more conservative forces in the State Department and the National Security Council, proponents of the notion that the Central American crisis was essentially part of a bipolar global conflict, emerged as the dominant voices within the foreign policy bureaucracy. Responding to the combined impact of this shift and the failure of the "reformist" option, Washington escalated its military aid program to El Salvador and began to expand the U.S. military commitment to Honduras. The relative decline in arms sales to the region which occurred under Carter was reversed before the end of his presidency, and this trend has been dramatically accelerated by the Reagan administration as it seeks to overthrow established governments and to defeat popular movements seeking state power.

The military build-up in Central America orchestrated by Reagan's government has been concentrated in El Salvador and Honduras. Between 1981 and 1984, El Salvador received over $950 million in U.S. security assistance, approximately $400 million of this amount in the form of congressionally authorized military aid.[1] During this period, at least 15,000 Salvadoran soldiers and officers benefitted from Pentagon training expertise. (As of 1983, almost a hundred Pentagon officials were stationed in El Salvador, the majority attached to the U.S. Military Assistance Advisory Group [MAAG].)[2] The Reagan administration's $483.4 million joint economic-military aid package for El Salvador in 1985 assumed that most of these requested funds would be used to support military activities.[3] The public White House-State Department rationale for massive military involvement in El Salvador has been presented as the desire to prevent "other Cubas" and to defend Central America from a Cuban-Soviet "take-over". Reagan has even described such aid as crucial to maintaining the "strategic balance of the world."[4]

The U.S. military presence in Honduras is equally comprehensive. U.S. military assistance increased dramatically from a combined $6.2 million in 1979 and 1980 to $58.3 million in 1983 alone.[5] Authorized congressional appropriations, however, do not provide a complete picture of the Pentagon's role in Honduras. A classified 1983 report of the House Armed Services Military Construction Subcommittee noted the construction of airstrips, houses, radar facilities, ocean piers, roads, an eleven-mile-long tank trap, and other facilities which all point to a "significant additional U.S. military presence in Honduras *for an indefinite period*."[6] Under Reagan, the number of U.S. military personnel permanently stationed in Honduras has risen to approximately 1,300, and the country has been the site of continuing large-scale U.S. military exercises involving thousands of U.S. military personnel (for example, the 1983 and 1984 "Big Pine I & II" exercises, and the April-May 1985 manoeuvres). The cost of the exercises has been estimated at well in excess of $100 million, not including the funds provided by the White House for housing, radar stations, building or improving eight airfields, and establishing a regional military training centre — all necessary accompaniments of these U.S. military exercises. U.S. armed forces personnel in Honduras have also provided combat support and training for the Salvadoran army, trained thousands of local soldiers and officers, and launched aerial surveillance missions over El Salvador and Nicaragua from bases inside the country.[7] A key aspect of Honduras' interlocking military relation with Washington has been its complicity in the U.S. war against the Sandinista regime in Nicaragua, to the extent that its territory is being used as the centre of operations and the most important staging area for the U.S.-financed and trained counterrevolutionary forces seeking to overthrow the elected revolutionary government in Managua. Efforts made by the Honduran military leadership in 1984-85 to redefine the terms of its relations with the United States are not indicative of any disposition to restructure the basic relationship with Washington or to shift its commitment away from Reagan's policy objectives in the area.[8]

The 1986 foreign aid request submitted to Congress by Reagan's administration reflected its determination to further increase U.S. military involvement in Central America. Even though the total request for El Salvador ($483.4 million) represented only a slight increase over 1985, it was heavily weighted towards military assistance, and senior executive branch officials made it clear that supplementary military requests were on the White House agenda, especially if the course of the military struggle began to shift in favour of the guerrilla forces. The Honduran aid package for 1986 was similarly biased towards military spending, while the administration was also asking Congress for a major increase in military assistance to the repressive military junta in Guatemala — from a mere $300,000 in 1984 to $35.5 million in 1985.[9]

The single most important objective behind this massive expansion of U.S. military assistance to Central America, apart from a desire to prop up client regimes and allies, has been "to step up the pressure" on the Nicaraguan government to make political and economic concessions.[10] One official privy to the White House-National Security Council-Pentagon-CIA discussions towards the end of 1983 summarized the policy consensus: "The Sandinistas are on the ropes — keep the pressure on."[11] Total U.S. government security assistance to the three countries that border Nicaragua (El Salvador, Honduras, and Costa Rica) skyrocketed from $89.3 million in 1981 to $287.2 million in 1982 to $476.2 million in 1983 to $784.6 million in 1984.[12] Meanwhile, officially authorized CIA funding of the contras between early 1982 and the end of 1984, amounting to $150 million, significantly understates actual expenditures which have been bolstered by withdrawals from executive branch secret contingency funds, the transfer of equipment and facilities to the contras under cover of U.S. military manoeuvres in Honduras, the use of third party surrogates to provide expertise and weapons (for example, Israel and Argentina), and White House encouragement of efforts by private organizations to raise aid for the CIA-backed forces.[13] The administration also tried unsuccessfully to induce Congress to release $14 million in covert action funds blocked in the spring of 1984. Congress members' objections were due less to the contra program of economic "harassment" — mining of harbours, sabotage missions directed against communications and public utilities, and so on — than to continuing documented reports of contra atrocities, including indiscriminate killings of unarmed Nicaraguan civilians. The administration, however, continued to seek release of the funds, in part because its ultimate objective had by now become explicit: to exert pressure to extract concessions leading to a change of government in Managua. Destabilization and the removal of the Sandinistas has become the openly declared goal of Washington policy-makers. In February 1985, President Reagan stated that the aim of the White House was to "remove" the "present structure" of the Nicaraguan government.[14] In June 1985, following Nicaraguan President Ortega's visit to Moscow and the U.S.S.R.'s commitment of $200 million in aid, Congress hurriedly agreed to sanction renewed aid to the contras "for humanitarian purposes."

Under Reagan, U.S. policy in Central America has subordinated immediate economic interests to the logic of war: military build-ups, the mining of harbours, and arming opponents of established regimes in violation of international law has replaced economic logic to such a degree that Washington now links its global policy to a successful military resolution of the regional conflict. The prospect of a military defeat for the collaborator regime in El Salvador will almost certainly provoke direct U.S. military intervention. Senior officials of the Reagan imperial state have acknowledged the existence of contingency plans for possible use of U.S. combat troops in El Salvador if the current regional militarization strategy fails.[15] While the strategic-military emphasis is divorced from immediate economic interests, however, it must be placed within the specific historical context of a larger effort to reconstitute the ideology of imperialism and the imperial state in the post-Vietnam era. Washington views the build-up of military power in Central America as the critical element in recreating economic opportunities on a world scale. El Salvador has been defined as the favoured country in which to reassert U.S. power, to gain a military victory which would not only legitimize Reagan's regional policy but also the whole thrust of the administration's New Cold War definition of international politics.

The United States and Central America: The Economic Dimension

Although the internal politics of the Central American region have been fraught with instability, diverse sectors of U.S. capital have had no difficulty adjusting their interests to changing circumstances. While the types, scope, and direction of capital flows have varied — beginning with direct investment in agro-mineral areas followed by manufacturing, financial loan capital, state and international bank capital — there has been no significant rupture or division among U.S. capitalist sectors regarding Washington's policy, or in their relations with dictatorial regimes. Essentially the process of adding new capital to old has been an additive-accommodative one. The absence of any rupture between the various forms of capital reflects the complementary role which each type performs, the interlocking interests they share, and their narrow socio-political bases of support in a region which requires strategic alliances with local repressive élites and dependence on the U.S. imperial state.*

*The emergence and consolidation of the United States as an imperial state since 1945 has been the central factor enabling the massive growth of U.S. capital overseas. The U.S. imperial state can be defined as those executive bodies or agencies charged with promoting and protecting the expansion of capital across state boundaries by the multinational corporations. It exercises interrelated economic, coercive, and ideological functions which facilitate capital accumulation and reproduction on a worldwide scale. The economic apparatus includes both agencies serving particular forms of capital (for example, Department of Agriculture) and agencies performing specific tasks that cut across the different forms of capital (for example, Treasury and Commerce departments) promoting investments, loans, and trade. The Department of the Treasury also pursues the larger objective in the multilateral development banks (for example, World Bank, Inter-American Development Bank, Inter-

Forms of U.S. Capital Expansion

During the post-World War I period, the United States displaced Britain as the dominant economic power in Central America. Between 1919 and 1929, the U.S. investment stake more than doubled, to $251 million, and was distributed in every important sector of the Central American economies: railroads, banking, public utilities, industries, mining, and banana and rubber plantations. From the Great Depression to the Alliance for Progress years, the pattern of metropolitan capital flows served to consolidate and deepen the area's monoculture economy and agro-export dependence. Between 1950 and 1959, for instance, almost $100 million in new U.S. investments were made in El Salvador, Honduras, Guatemala, and Nicaragua — most of it in public utilities, minerals, agro-exports, and the highly profitable food and raw material producing sectors.[16]

The tripling of U.S. direct investments in Central America between 1960 and 1980 was parallelled by an increasing concentration of new capital in manufacturing at the expense of agro-mining investments. In 1960, only $12 million out of a total $342 million was industrial investment; by 1980, approximately 40 per cent of total U.S. investment ($417 million out of $1,033 million) was in the manufacturing sector, especially in textiles, chemicals, food products, and pharmaceuticals.[17] Even in Nicaragua where the Somoza family-dominated economy limited the growth of an internal market and placed major constraints on large-scale foreign capital flows into areas of profitable investment, there was no dearth of U.S. multinationals operating in the industrial sectors on the eve of the Sandinista victory. The diminished proportion of new regional investments flowing into non-manufacturing activities, on the

---

national Monetary Fund) through its responsibility for the appointment of U.S. representatives to these "international" institutions. The coercive apparatus serves to promote the legitimacy of imperial activities directly through the U.S. Information Agency and the related propaganda arms of the state or through subcontracted activities related to the practices of unofficial groups. The elaboration and coordination of U.S. imperial state policy is largely confined to the White House, National Security Council, and the State Department. The State Department, as well as Treasury, Defense, Commerce, Agriculture, and the Central Intelligence Agency, also plays an important role in "operationalizing" the general policy positions and in devising strategies to realize imperial objectives. This distinction between goals and tactics makes it possible to observe the continuities and common purposes in policy-making on the one hand and the differing institutional interests and bureaucratic conflicts that are consequential within the larger agreed upon consensus over goals on the other.

other hand, did not imply the erosion of the agro-mining export-based economy. Despite the changing investment pattern, all Central American economies still remain largely wedded to this type of development strategy based on growth "from above and outside."

Finance capital, particularly the largest U.S. private multinational banks (Bank of America, Citicorp, Chase Manhattan, Wells Fargo), began to play an increasingly important role in Central America during the 1970s as the governments sought to cope with the twin problems of spiralling oil import costs and declining export markets. Between 1970 and 1981, financial capital assumed a commanding role in most countries: gross inflows of medium- and long-term loans to Honduras increased from $29 million to $254 million, to Guatemala from $37 million to $144 million, to El Salvador from $8 million to $182 million, and to Nicaragua from $44 million to $398 million.[18] This accelerated dependence on external sources of financing was accompanied by massive growth in these countries' external debt over this same period: from $90 million to over $1.2 billion in Honduras, from $88 million to $664 million in El Salvador, from $106 million to $684 million in Guatemala, and from $155 million to almost $2 billion in Nicaragua.[19] By 1981, private U.S. banks had $3.3 billion in loans outstanding to the Central American public and private sectors.[20]

U.S. banking capital moved into the region's private sector on a significant scale during the 1970s. By 1979, U.S. banks had investments in twenty-nine of the forty-one private multinational banks doing business in Central America and in numerous non-financial enterprises such as breweries, sugar mills, and textile mills.[21] Moreover, they assumed positions of great importance within the agro-export production sectors. In Guatemala, according to a senior U.S. executive, the Bank of America is "*the* agricultural bank," second only to the government as a source of capital for those industries (coffee, sugar, cotton, beef) which account for over 80 per cent of the country's export earnings.[22]

The Central American dictatorships have been the recipients of a vast program of bilateral and multilateral aid from the U.S. since the Alliance for Progress. Between 1962 and 1978, Washington and the so-called international banks provided the ruling classes of El Salvador, the Guatemalan oligarchy, the military-dominated regimes in Honduras, and the Somoza clan in Nicaragua with combined economic assistance totalling almost $2.4 billion.[23] Following the demise of the human rights lobby within the Carter administration in 1979, the selective temporary closure of access by the right-wing military or military-controlled regimes in Honduras, El Salvador, and Guatemala to large-scale economic assistance from these traditional sources began to be reversed. The shift in Washington's overall regional policy begun under Carter was cemented by the Reagan government, and was reflected in the further loosening of loan spigots by the United States and the "international" banks to favoured regimes in Central America. During 1979 and 1980, Honduras and Guatemala received a combined total of almost $110 million in economic assistance from the United States; over the three-year period from 1981 to 1983, the figure rose to $347 million. In the case of El Salvador, the Reagan imperial state has channelled economic aid to sustain a repressive state at an even greater rate (and at the cost of massive loss of civilian lives): approximately $1 billion dollars during the first four-year term of the Reagan presidency compared with just under $61 million for the 1979 and 1980 period. In the case of the "international" banks, El Salvador again represents the most striking instance of renewed economic largesse: from $105 million in 1980 to $306 million during 1981 to 1982, levelling off slightly to total a still significant $474 million for the duration of the first Reagan administration.[24]

In its efforts to mobilize support for its political objectives in Central America within the "international" banks, the Reagan administration has pursued a two-pronged strategy: exerting maximum pressure to secure passage of loan requests by collaborator governments in El Salvador and Guatemala, and sustaining implacable opposition to all development aid to the revolutionary government in Nicaragua, which it defines as hostile to U.S. political and economic interests in the region. The White House has forced loan requests by El Salvador through the Inter-American Development Bank (BID) without consideration of serious operational problems or human rights violations perpetrated by the armed forces, security and police forces, and the death squads. It has also secured International Monetary Fund (IMF) assistance for the regime over the objections of the fund's technical staff — most notably in the case of a $35 million loan submission in July 1981. A subsequent Salvadoran loan request to the fund in July 1982 for $85 million was the prelude to heavy U.S. pressure on the IMF's technical staff to secure a favourable recommendation to the IMF board.[25]

While El Salvador has been the major beneficiary of Reagan's total rejection of human rights factors as a consideration shaping U.S. voting decisions in the "international" banks, White House efforts to mobilize support within these institutions for renewed aid to the Guatemalan military rulers also has reflected this new general line and has achieved some success in promoting it. Because U.S. representatives in the BID were required by a 1976 law either to vote against or to abstain from voting on loans to major human rights violators — with the exception of loans defined as serving "basic human needs" — the Reagan administration was constrained in pursuing its goal. For example, it reluctantly abstained from voting on a $45 million BID loan for a hydroelectric dam project approved by the bank in late 1981. It did, however, decide to support two later Guatemalan loan submissions to the BID, and another before the IMF, on the grounds that they served "basic human needs". Congress did not oppose the executive branch position on these three loans, but it did caution against a positive U.S. vote for a proposed $18 million BID loan for a telephone project in rural Guatemala announced in December 1981. State and Treasury department officials failed to convince a sceptical House Banking Committee to support the loan and, under the threat of a legislative vote against the total foreign aid bill, managed to convince the Guatemalan regime temporarily to withdraw its request. Following a military coup that deposed General Lucas Garcia in March 1982, the loan was resubmitted for BID consideration and on this occasion the State Department argued that since there had been a change of government, Guatemala could no longer be categorized as a major human rights offender. Finally, in October, the administration simply announced that it would not be bound by human rights considerations in deciding whether to support Guatemalan loan requests in the "international" banks.[26] BID loans to Guatemala almost quadrupled between 1981 and 1982, rising from $25.5 million to $112.5 million.[27]

The Reagan administration's unremitting hostility towards the Sandinista government in Nicaragua has also been strikingly reflected in its behaviour within the "international" banks. Between July 1979 and January 1981, in spite of the Carter government's growing dissatisfaction with the policies of the Sandinista government, loans to Nicaragua from the World Bank and the BID totalled $175 million.[28] During the transition from Carter to Reagan, a more vigorous U.S. opposition to "international" bank loans to Managua was immediately put into practice, based on what a Treasury Department official termed the new administration's "overall political problem with the direction [of the Nicaraguan regime]."[29] In mid-1981, the U.S. government "adopted a position of opposing all development projects, both in formal votes and with delaying techniques during the preparation of projects by the technical staff [of the Banks]." This policy was successful in forcing a suspension of World Bank loans to Nicaragua and "in slowing down a number of projects in the other [international banks]."[30] In the case of the IMF, executive branch policymakers indicated a readiness to work against any improvement in the already cool relationship between the Sandinistas and the fund, which had its roots in an IMF decision to make available a loan to the Somoza dictatorship only weeks before its overthrow.

Nowhere has the Reagan administration more actively pursued its efforts to deny Nicaragua long-term development credits than in the Inter-American Development Bank. In November 1981, it forced Managua to withdraw a fishing sector loan request; in March 1982, Washington prevailed upon the BID board to rebuff efforts to resubmit this loan. In mid-1983, the administration vetoed a $2.2 million road-building disbursal partly on the grounds that insufficient encouragement was given by the Sandinistas to private enterprise within their development program. Between January 1982 and September 1983, the U.S. executive director cast negative votes on seven loan requests by Nicaragua involving a total of $84.4 million, all on the grounds of "inappropriate macroeconomic policies."[31] In early 1985, American Secretary of State George

Shultz personally intervened with the BID president to block a vote on a $58 million loan to Nicaragua to provide financial credits for small- and medium-sized farmers, which had been under consideration by the BID for more than two years. Shultz expressed strong opposition to the loan on the grounds that the Managua regime was "not creditworthy" and he raised the threat that approval of the loan might endanger or, as he put it, make "even more difficult" U.S. efforts to provide new financial contributions to the BID.[32] One highly placed Nicaraguan government official has estimated that these U.S. actions between 1981 and 1984 cost Nicaragua hundreds of millions of dollars in terms of credits and loans denied by these so-called international banks.[33]

U.S. Policy and Capitalist Class Interests in Central America

Historically, U.S. capitalist interests operating in Central America have worked closely with the U.S. imperial state and its repressive clients. In periods of crisis, particularly during those moments when the imperial state has lost the capacity to impose its will, capitalist interests develop a variety of positions relative to the regime in question ranging from outright opposition to accommodation. The clearest case in point has been the accommodating style of behaviour displayed by the private banks and the multinationals operating in Nicaragua, behaviour which contradicts the confrontationist posture adopted by Washington. The two faces of imperialism, business collaboration and military confrontation, reflect different estimates of a given regime's durability and different sets of strategic priorities. For Washington, this regional conflict is embedded in its global strategy, and the ideological and symbolic significance of "defeating Marxism" therefore becomes paramount. For bankers and multinationals, the strategic issue is to prevent the repudiation of the debt and the disintegration of the private sector in which they have a stake.

Thus, the historical convergence of policy between the state and capital is not always incompatible with apparent divergences at a particular conjuncture. Investment capital's flexibility is indicative of a belief that the imperatives of underdevelopment force revolutionaries to come to terms with the multinationals. The prudent counterrevolutionary policy adopted by business reflects a desire to support the destabilization of the regime, provided there are good chances that the policy will succeed. On the other hand, these capitalists are opposed to hardline policies if they provide few prospects for success, since the eventual outcome would be to radicalize the regime. Divergences between capital and the state therefore reflect a pragmatic or opportunist position on the part of capital which, however, may succumb to a state with strong ideological-strategic concerns — a consequence which apparently is unfolding in Nicaragua.

Investment Capital and the Regional Crisis

The U.S. multinational investment and banking community in Central America has not projected a completely uniform response to the socio-political conflicts in the area, either as representatives of state policy or as individual companies and financial institutions with their own economic stakes in the area.

Organizations such as the American Association of Chambers of Commerce in Latin America were vociferous critics of Carter administration policy in Central America and welcomed the Reagan presidency as the harbinger of a new approach which would reverse what it viewed as Carter's "abdication of responsibility and traditional leadership in the region."[34] The American Chamber of Commerce in Guatemala decried the "doctrinaire adherence to slogans" and the adverse impact this tenacity had on the local investment climate: "U.S. foreign investment has stopped and U.S. banks and companies are reluctant to finance trade with Guatemala." The Chamber of Commerce expressed the hope that the Reagan White House would be "moved by pragmatic considerations of U.S. interests" leading to closer political and military relations between Washington and Guatemala's ruling generals.[35] But most U.S. companies and banks continued to take a "wait and see" attitude before making new financial commitments in the region.

The strategies formulated by multinational corporations with operations in Central America have been dictated by a number of factors, including the type and amount of investment, size and profitability in relation to other subsidiaries around the world, internal market dynamics, and so forth. Companies with large fixed investments, for instance, have endeavoured to ride out the changes in countries like Nicaragua and to adapt to the new operating environment. Since 1979 there has nevertheless been a notable absence of significant new foreign investment in all countries of the region. One involved U.S. company official said in April 1982: "We operate on a day-to-day basis in the region."[36] At the time, another U.S. firm with region-wide investments had gone so far as to prepare to absorb the loss of one of its subsidiaries as the cost of continuing to do business in Central America.[37] Still, a number of U.S. enterprises, taking advantage of declining competition and a high demand for consumer products, have continued to reap high profits despite the persistence of operating problems such as restrictions on payments for imports. In some cases, the subsidiaries of U.S. multinationals in Central America earn profits in excess of profits earned in other parts of Latin America.[38]

In El Salvador, U.S. direct investment declined from $150 million in 1979 to approximately $100 million in 1980, parallelling a major expansion of the civil war and important gains achieved by the guerrilla forces.[39] Even so, a U.S. embassy survey made in February 1981 found that eighty-two affiliates of U.S. corporations were still in business there, and taking advantage of severely weakened labour organizations and very low labour costs.[40] According to the American Chamber of Commerce in El Salvador, only twelve firms pulled up stakes between 1979 and late 1981.[41] The majority of factories still operating are engaged in assembly production for export, which requires limited capital, and they are managed primarily by Salvadoran employees. U.S. companies surveyed in March 1982 exhibited a lack of enthusiasm for making new investments but most still looked forward to maintaining operations — whatever the outcome of the internal social conflict.[42]

The main concern of U.S. investors in El Salvador at that time was the shortage of foreign exchange and the prolonged post-1978 economic recession which was accompanied by a substantial decline in industrial and agricultural production (coffee, cotton, sugar), massive unemployment, the flight of capital, and negative foreign reserves. By early 1984, however, a number of U.S.-owned textile factories that had ceased operations for an extended period were reopening; many U.S. executives in El Salvador were declaring that the economic downturn had reached its limit and the worst was over. The manager of Citibank's branch operation projected plans for expansion after the March elections: "We are here to stay; it's a matter of adjusting to circumstances."[43] Scarce foreign exchange required for the import of machinery or goods and long delays in obtaining the Central Bank letters of credit needed to assure U.S. suppliers of payment were not obstacles to many subsidiaries making what *Business Latin America* described at the time as "healthy profits for their operations in [El Salvador]".[44] Renewed confidence was reinforced by a growing belief among most executives of U.S. companies doing business in the region that Washington's policies in Central America had forestalled any major political upheaval in El Salvador or Honduras, thereby providing the basis for more stable and durable political orders.

In Nicaragua, most international companies surveyed by *Business Latin America* at the end of the Reagan administration's first year in office described their relations with the Sandinista government as "good or at least reasonable."[45] A number of U.S. corporations had resumed operations after July 1979 in a context in which the new government confined its nationalization policy to properties owned by the Somoza family. The inevitable delays in obtaining foreign exchange for raw material imports and replacement parts, complaints over the inability to remit dividends, and other operating problems were offset by the "pragmatic" behaviour of Ministry of Economy officials and the absence of any serious capital-labour conflicts. Although the number of U.S. businesses in Nicaragua declined by about half (from twenty or twenty-five to approximately twelve)[46] during the first four years of Sandinista rule, interviews conducted in 1981 (and again in 1983) with executives of multinationals which maintained operations in the country reveal general agreement that relations with the government were "pretty much business as usual."[47] Representatives of many foreign companies which sold to the domestic market or to the state acknowledged the provision of "ample" or "fair" pricing margins and some projected future new investments ("The market is still sizeable") unless the government "decided to take over everything."[48] At the same time, not even profitable existing investments have eliminated apprehension over the ultimate political-economic direction of the Sandinistas, a concern which has been reflected in the continuing absence of significant new flows of investment capital into any sector of the economy. Still, there is a growing belief among U.S. corporate and banking interests with holdings or financial exposure in Nicaragua that the Sandinista regime is permanent and that if the private sector is not abolished economic realities will ultimately lead to a less statist-oriented economy.

While multinational executives were predicting moderation in Nicaragua's domestic policies once economic realities "hit more directly,"[49] by mid-1983 they were expressing growing unease with the apparent direction of the Reagan administration's policy. Economic sanctions against Nicaragua appear to some to be opposed to the interests of foreign capital (for example, the virtual elimination of Nicaragua's sugar quota, the drying up of public economic assistance, and the vetoes of loan proposals in the multilateral development banks): "... there is a feeling that what Reagan is doing is not good for business, and that economic aid is needed down there," a corporate industry specialist on the Nicaraguan economy reported. "Businessmen are worried they will end up bearing the brunt of an invasion."[50] Washington's policy had already produced an unprofitable consequence for U.S. multinationals: increased commercial relations between Nicaragua and competing capitalist and socialist bloc countries at the expense of U.S. traders.

Banking Capital and the Regional Crisis

The reaction of the U.S. private banking community to the political and social conflicts in Central America has been threefold: to emphasize short-term lines of credit which can be easily increased or reduced in dealings with Honduras and Guatemala; to halt virtually all cash-collaterized exposure in El Salvador; and to defer consideration of new loans to Nicaragua prior to the renegotiation of all outstanding debts.[51] Overall, there has been a greater reluctance on the part of U.S. banks to finance the Central American private sector since the late 1970s. Between 1979 and 1982, for example, commercial bank and commodity trader lines of credit to the Guatemalan private sector fell by an estimated $760 million.[52]

The evolution of the relationship between the private U.S. multinational banking community and the Sandinista government in Nicaragua offers a number of insights into how banks behave with regard to their own investments when bank interests and imperial-state policy converge. The debt renegotiation meetings between Sandinista officials and the country's major financial creditors during 1980 were instrumental in shaping U.S. bankers' views of the Nicaraguan regime.[53]

The Somoza dictatorship had bequeathed to the Sandinistas a $1.5 billion foreign debt owed to approximately 120 North American, Western European, and Japanese banks. Approximately 50 per cent of the debt was held by 13 banks including Citibank (the largest claimant), Bank of America, the Royal Bank of Canada, and the First National Bank of Chicago. Representatives of these 13 banks constituted the steering committee that negotiated with Nicaraguan officials. Within this committee, there were initially two sharply divergent positions on how to proceed: some banks expressed concern over a possible Nicaraguan walkout if negotiations were strung out and "would have been willing to sign anything"; others, such as Citibank (which at one point argued for debt service payments equivalent to one-third of Nicaragua's 1980 export revenue), were adamant that the renegotiation process remain subject to standard commercial terms. In October 1980, an agreement was reached to reschedule $600 million (approximately 80 per cent owed to U.S. banks) of Nicaragua's total debt over a two-year period. The development of consensus within the steering committee that produced this result grew out of shifting perceptions of the Nicaraguan government's authority and intentions over the course of the negotiations. Ultimately, it became clear to these bankers that Managua was determined to negotiate a settlement; that it was prepared to deal pragmatically with the U.S. financial community and to consider concessions in pursuit of its objective; that the Sandinistas were firmly in control of political-state power and, therefore, in a position to make necessary concessions; and that the enormous scope of economic devastation combined with the broad-based, cross-class opposition to the Somoza dynasty made the Nicaraguan case a unique one.

The successful restructuring of Nicaragua's foreign debt did not, however, lay the groundwork for the extension of new lines of credit to the country. The same private foreign banks that had authorized credit lines exceeding $150 million annually to the Somoza regime during its final years provided the current government with a paltry $11 million in new loans between July 1979 and July 1983. Meanwhile, over the same four-year period, Nicaragua made interest payments on its outstanding debt to these banks totalling $160 million.[54] Nicaraguan Central Bank President Luis Enrique Figueroa was informed by a number of U.S. bankers that they had been pressured by the State Department to withhold loans to the Sandinista regime.[55] In late 1982, a consortium of twelve banks, including the Bank of America, provided a $25-$30 million loan to Managua — but only in order to allow the financially strapped government to meet a $40 million interest payment on its foreign debt.[56] Some commercial banks, including Citibank, have made short-term credit available; others have refused to do so. One U.S. banker who turned down a Nicaraguan request for trade credits in January 1983 explained his decision with reference to the confrontationist policies of the Reagan White House: "We think the U.S. government is going to push Nicaragua into a default whether it's by backing exile invasions or cutting off their access to credit."[57]

U.S. bankers have continued to assess the Nicaraguan regime's approach to its financial problems as "pragmatic", noting that until it missed a $4 million payment in March 1983, every previous foreign debt interest payment had been made on time. With the exception of some guaranteed, pre-export credit deals made in 1982, Nicaragua has received virtually no new bank loans since mid-1979 — a fact which is related to the way in which U.S. policy has influenced and limited the options available to banks. Officials of these private banks contend that Washington has not applied direct pressure to stop credits to Managua. But as one analyst pointedly noted, "given the relative small size of Nicaragua's debt, its economic prospects and the country's refusal to go to the International Monetary Fund for assistance, no pressure has been required."[58] Furthermore, the Sandinista regime's ability to meet its foreign debt obligations has been directly affected by actions taken by the Reagan White House, for example, the approximately 90 per cent reduction in the Nicaraguan sugar quota, which has traditionally accounted for between $45 and $60 million in foreign exchange earnings, in May 1983. Also in May 1983, Nicaraguan finance officials informed U.S. commercial bank lenders in New York that they could not meet a $45 million payment deadline in July due to the combined impact of flood damage totalling approximately $400 million, losses resulting from a severe drought affecting the cotton and sugar industries, and the costs (almost $60 million) incurred as a result of economic sabotage and other activities wrought by the U.S.-financed counterrevolutionary invasions in the first half of the year. They requested a suspension until July 1984.[59]

The increasingly military orientation of Washington's relations with the Sandinista regime means that state-to-state relations take precedence and multinational-Sandinista relations take second place in imperial-state priorities. Concretely this means that "private" economic enterprises and interests become tools wielded by the imperial state; they essentially promote the policies of that state even when such policies adversely affect their own private economic interests. The continuing subordination of private to imperial-state interests increasingly defines a period of preparation for "total warfare" — an open break in relations and unrelenting efforts to subvert the revolutionary regime.

Canada and Central America: The Economic Dimension

Neither the Canadian state nor Canadian capital has the long-term deep structural ties with the Central American ruling classes that their U.S. counterparts have developed. Canadian linkages are primarily commercial, relatively recent, and largely independent of client-state patronage. The nature of the Canadian commitment is essential to an understanding of the Canadian government's capacity to disassociate itself from the most heinous regimes or policies in the region, on the one hand, and its willingness to trade with human rights violators (for example, with Guatemala) allied with the U.S. imperial state on the other. The economic-trade emphasis in Canada's relations with Central America, as opposed to a political-military emphasis, also explains why it is easier for Ottawa to diverge from Washington's policy when the latter attempts to impose an economic blockade on a regime such as that in Nicaragua. Trading with revolutionary states and U.S. clients reflects the primarily commercial considerations that shape Canadian foreign policy in the region.

The other facet of Canadian policy is its accommodation to U.S. policy in Central America, reflecting the opposition of Canadian capital to social revolution and the recognition that the U.S. imperial state provides an umbrella under which to operate. Insofar as Canadian capital depends on the same type of social and political conditions to reproduce itself, it benefits from this U.S. umbrella and hence is reluctant to criticize its benefactor. Insofar as U.S. linkages with local power structures lead to monopoly advantages for U.S. capital, however, they stimulate Canadian opposition. Moreover, Canadian capital, having no vested interest in any particular set of rules, can be more flexible in adapting to change, particularly if the alternatives do not threaten Canadian interests. The dilemma of Canadian policy revolves around its opposition to U.S. hegemonic aspirations that may exclude Canadian economic interests as well as to local revolutionary movements that may expropriate Canadian and other foreign capitals. Canadian policy is formulated between these two parameters: one side threatening displacement, the other expropriation. Canadian capital, as the capital of a "follower nation", seeks to limit intervention without facilitating revolution, carving out political and economic space for itself.

The formulation of Canadian policy also reflects the centrality of state-to-state relations: the paramount importance which Canadian capital ascribes to its relations with the United States. The margins of independence are in the first instance restricted to symbolic utterances which invoke democratic principles, while the substantive policy of accommodation reflects the imperatives of the bilateral tie which is the cornerstone of Canadian foreign economic policy.

Canadian Capital and State Policy

The Canadian economic presence in Central America has grown steadily over the last decade and a half. In 1980, approximately 17 per cent (27 out of 152) of Canadian corporations with Latin American operations were active in Central America. Investments totalling approximately $300 million were distributed among various economic sectors: consulting services, engineering, food and food products (Guatemala); chemicals and paper products (El Salvador); and mining and petroleum (Guatemala and Honduras).[60] Guatemala appears to have been the most favoured location of Canadian finance capital. In June 1981, for instance, the Bank of Nova Scotia participated in a $54 million loan to the country's Central Bank and loaned $5 million towards completion of a major hydroelectric project; some months later it reportedly participated with the Toronto Dominion Bank, the Royal Bank of Canada, and the Canadian Imperial Bank of Commerce in a $180 million syndicated loan to finance a multi-year Guatemalan government road construction program.*[61] The concentration of Canadian investment capital in both extractive and manufacturing sectors, although not indicative of any clear-cut pattern, does suggest activities that parallel *and* compete with U.S. investors in the area. To the extent that trade was assigned greater importance than investment or banking capital by the Trudeau government, the movement of Canadian finance capital into countries such as Guatemala, that have emerged as important markets for Canadian exporters, may reflect the interests of state policy-makers seeking to promote such trade.

In the early 1970s, Ottawa enunciated its "third option" strategy, a plan largely intended to break Canada's trade dependence on the United States. Since then, it has aggressively promoted expanded trade ties with South and Central America and the Caribbean. This objective was facilitated by the establishment of two state agencies: a Canadian International Development Agency (CIDA) which administers the government's bilateral aid program for the hemisphere, and an Export Development Corporation (EDC) which provides subsidies and other supports for Canadian traders. Although the largest trade gains during the 1970s were recorded in Latin America and the Commonwealth Caribbean, the value of Canadian exports to Central America more than quadrupled, from $25.7 million in 1970 to $140.3 million in 1980.[62]

In spite of official Canadian government statements decrying human rights violations in Central American countries, the commitment to trade expansion appears to have taken precedence in determining the actions of Ottawa policy-makers. The EDC, for example, insured and guaranteed almost $9 million in exports to El Salvador and Guatemala during 1982. EDC loans influenced the Guatemalan military regime to award a $14 million contract to supply locomotives and parts to Guatemala's national railways to Bombardier Inc. of Montreal, a contract which led to Canada's first trade surplus with Guatemala in several years.[63] Ottawa's ambiguous position on human rights violations with respect to Guatemala surfaced again in March 1983 when the Trudeau government co-sponsored a United Nations resolution condemning human rights violations by the country's military rulers at the same

---

*The program was subsequently cancelled in 1982 by the new military junta.

time Canadian embassy officials were negotiating with Guatemalan air force representatives over a sale of De Havilland Aircraft planes. Although Canadian bilateral aid for new development projects in El Salvador and Guatemala was formally suspended in 1981, Ottawa continued to disburse previously approved assistance for projects such as a $10.3 million hydroelectric transmission line in El Salvador and a $5.5 million potable water project in Guatemala.[64]

The Trudeau government's bilateral aid program in Central America and its voting behaviour within the "international" banks also mirrored some of the contradictory qualities of official policy statements. Instances in which Canada collaborated with the Carter and Reagan administrations over U.S. objectives interacted with decisions that reflected independently developed Canadian positions. The military regime in Honduras and the revolutionary government of Nicaragua have been the largest recipients of Canadian bilateral assistance since 1980. Designated a "country focus" by CIDA, Honduras, a centre of U.S. military activities in Central America and counter-revolutionary operations against the Sandinista regime, received $44 million or 43.4 per cent of total disbursed Canadian government aid to Central America between 1980 and 1984.[62] Efforts to promote military sales suffered a set-back in late April 1983 when Ottawa was forced to cancel the sale by financially depressed De Havilland of STOL aircraft worth approximately $30 million because of gross human rights violations in Honduras and pressures exerted by other hemispheric states.[66] In the case of Nicaragua, Ottawa sought simultaneously to promote trade through aid but at a level that would not unduly antagonize Washington. While official CIDA statistics show Nicaragua receiving more Canadian government assistance than Honduras during the 1980-84 period, a significant proportion of the CIDA total included aid channelled to non-governmental and business organizations, which concentrated their activities in projects eligible for matching CIDA funds. In actuality, disbursed bilateral aid to Nicaragua totalled $24 million or 23.4 per cent of all economic assistance to the region, less than half the CIDA dollars that found their way to Managua as a result of undertakings by private Canadian enterprises.[67]

The sharpest area of disagreement between the United States and Canada within the "international" banks revolved around the question of economic assistance to the Sandinista government in Nicaragua — especially in the Inter-American Development Bank (BID) where Reagan White House efforts to halt all aid to Managua were opposed by a majority of the membership, including Canada. One of the more notable clashes between Washington and Ottawa concerned a $2.2 million Nicaraguan loan disbursal request in June 1983 to complete a road building project in a coffee farming area. The initial project loan had been approved by the BID board in 1976 and construction began in 1978, but the project was delayed in 1979 due to the combined impact of the civil war and widespread flooding in that part of the country.

With the passage of time, a new vote was required to extend the remaining $2.2 million of an original $18.4 million voted in 1976. Every member country except the United States supported the extension, which the U.S. executive director ultimately vetoed on "macroeconomic" grounds. At the June meeting of the board, Canadian representative Henry Hodder argued that there was no economic basis for rejecting the proposal and he noted that the bank staff had found the loan request perfectly acceptable. "Whatever the macroeconomic policies of Nicaragua may be," he declared, "it seems to us that in this particular case the benefits of completion of the road project are certainly commensurate with the cost and the macroeconomic policies of the country would seem to bear little relation to the completion of the project."[68]

Between 1980 and 1982 the Canadian government also abstained on three BID loan submissions by El Salvador which were all vigorously supported by the United States. The loans for agricultural and road construction projects totalled $86.4 million. Ottawa's abstentions were justified primarily in terms of the problems associated with implementing these kinds of projects in a situation of extreme political instability and civil war. Yet Canadian policy was inconsistent on this point. Its executive director in the BID was directed to approve another 1982 loan request by El Salvador for $79 million to complete a dam project in the Rio Lempa region even though this was a major zone of military combat.[69] In the International Monetary Fund (IMF), Canadian actions have been similarly erratic. The Trudeau government supported a July 1981 request by El Salvador for a $36 million loan from the fund's compensatory financing facility. Under enormous U.S. pressure, the loan was eventually approved, even though, as one Western European executive director pointed out, some of the basic conditions attaching to this type of funding were absent: "It does not establish the existence, let alone the size of the (balance of payments) shortfall, and it does not contain a staff proposal to the board."[70] While Canada aligned itself with Washington to support the first loan ever sanctioned by the IMF over the objections of its technical staff, it diverged over another loan request by El Salvador later that same year. In September, Canada opposed a $120 million fund "standby" loan on the grounds of technical feasibility and operational problems likely to be encountered in a country engulfed by political and military conflict.

Since the election of the Reagan government, Ottawa's verbal expressions of concern over human rights violations by the Central American armed forces and its paramilitary allies do not appear to have played a significant role in shaping Canadian voting patterns within the "international" banks. In the case of the two principal human rights violators in the region, El Salvador and Guatemala — which received a favourable Canadian vote for a $45 million BID loan to complete a hydroelectric project in late 1981 — loans have been approved or opposed largely without reference to the issue of state-authored violence and repression. In August 1983, a correspondent for *The Globe and Mail,* discussing a Trudeau cabinet disagreement over whether human rights criteria should be an important factor in determining Canadian positions within the "international" banks, concluded that the absence of any consistent policy suggests that "Canada is tailoring its actions at the IMF to continue conforming to U.S. foreign policy interests."[71]

Canada and Central America: The Political Dimension

While Canadian policy towards Central America displays relative independence from the United States, the Trudeau government's behaviour nonetheless suggests that the capacity or willingness of Ottawa to develop a consequential position differing from Washington's is sharply limited. There are several basic constraints on Canadian actions which account for practical accommodations with White House policy. First are the bilateral relations which govern foreign economic ties for Canada. Second, there is the dependence of Canadian capital on the U.S. imperial state to counter revolutionary developments in the area. Third are the interests and activities shared by U.S. subsidiaries in Canada operating in Central America and U.S. multinationals. Fourth, there are the joint banking efforts or consortiums that divide up the loan and interest market in the region.

Within these constraints, however, divergences in the trade sphere persist. Canada has developed an increasingly important stake in overseas trade: it is interested in breaking into new markets independently of the ideological texture of the regime. In Central America, not only do politically tied or client governments closely linked with U.S. corporate interests provide limited opportunities for such expansion but the political conflict engendered by overt U.S. military intrusions also clashes with the essentially market-oriented policies of the Canadian government. At the same time, these trade policies allow Canadian exporters to displace their U.S. counterparts when the latter abandon markets for political reasons. The relatively greater importance of market concerns and non-dependence on client political regimes allows Ottawa to adopt a more flexible approach within the parameters of its ties with the United States. The question of how far Canadian governments will pursue these differences is a function of how salient the Central American issue becomes for the Reagan White House. As Washington's commitment to a military confrontation increases, and as more and more resources and personnel are allocated, it becomes more likely that Canadian policy will conflict less directly with the United States, hiding behind the commonplace rhetoric of accommodation to "great power" hegemony in the region.

Conflict and Collaboration with U.S. Policy

Canadian policy towards Central America under Trudeau was a contradictory mix of public criticism of and practical cooperation with U.S. actions. This reflected a determination on Ottawa's part not to allow differences over this particular issue to provoke a fundamental rupture in relations between the two countries.

The public statements of senior Canadian foreign policy officials during the Trudeau period were often at sharp variance with Reagan administration objectives in Central America: the origins of the crisis were ascribed to internal economic and social factors rather than to Soviet-Cuban subversion; a cluster of ideologically diverse regimes was preferred by Canada over a region dominated by repressive and autocratic pro-U.S. regimes; and political negotiations, not the militarization of civil society, were seen by Ottawa as the only realistic solution to the area-wide conflict. These themes were expressed in numerous speeches and statements by Trudeau and senior cabinet ministers after Reagan moved into the White House. In March 1982, Secretary of State for External Affairs Mark MacGuigan, in a major policy statement almost identical to one given by the prime minister in February 1983, declared:

> Instability in Central America . . . is not a product of east-west rivalry. It is a product of poverty, the unfair distribution of wealth and social injustice. . . . So when we look at Central America today, we cannot view this region exclusively through the prism of east-west rivalries because they are not at the root of the problem. . . . I believe that the states in the region have the right to choose to follow whatever ideological path their people decide. I don't believe that when a country chooses a socialist or even marxist path it necessarily buys a "package" which automatically injects it into the Soviet orbit. This, I think, is where our views and those of the U.S.A. diverge. The internal systems adopted by countries of Latin America and the Caribbean, whatever these systems may be, do not in themselves pose a security threat to this hemisphere.[72]

Trudeau directly addressed the issue of U.S.-Canadian differences over Central America at a press conference in late April 1983: "There are major divergences, beginning with the fact that we object to the interference in the internal affairs of other countries by any major power, even if that power is our friend. We certainly said that to the (United) States before."[73] Opposition to big power involvement in the region's internal social struggles, and to the notion that Central America constitutes an arena of U.S.-Soviet global confrontation, was accompanied by repeated expressions of support for political dialogue as the only alternative to an endless military operation. The Canadian government expressed its official concern at the highest levels in Washington over reports that the White House had authorized a multi-million dollar covert action program to finance and train anti-Sandinista forces in Honduras. A Central American specialist in the Department of External Affairs emphasized Canadian opposition to this type of initiative, noting Trudeau's support for Mexican and Venezuelan efforts to promote negotiations between Nicaragua and Honduras.[74] In mid-1983, the new secretary of state for external affairs (and deputy prime minister), Allan J. MacEachen, restated the basic Canadian policy in a speech at the University of Ottawa:

> The process of social change and economic progress in both El Salvador and Nicaragua cannot achieve success in a military confrontation. Canada, therefore, fully endorses the regional peace initiative sponsored by the Contadora Group.... We also think that at an appropriate stage these talks should be supplemented by direct dialogue between the United States and Nicaragua, between the United States and Cuba, and between Nicaragua and Costa Rica.[75]

The Canadian ambassador to the United States, Allan Gotlieb, articulated Ottawa's concern over escalating U.S. military assistance to Central America and the apparent downgrading of the search for a diplomatic solution to the regional conflicts in a series of meetings with Reagan administration officials in August 1983. He emphasized the importance of a "political approach" in resolving differences with Nicaragua (also partly reflected in Canada's refusal to align itself with Washington in opposing Sandinista loan requests to the "international" banks), arguing that accelerated military pressure on Managua was a "two-edged sword" which could just as easily make the revolutionary regime more intransigent rather than force them to the negotiating table. He also told State Department officials that the multi-dimensional U.S. military presence in Honduras threatened to erode even further the already limited authority of the civilian regime, which could only increase the power of the armed forces and its leader, General Gustavo Alvarez.[76]

Canada-United States differences over Central America again became prominent in April 1984 when External Affairs Minister MacEachen resisted strong pressure from U.S. Secretary of State George Shultz to include El Salvador in a scheduled tour of Nicaragua, Costa Rica, Colombia, and Honduras. The White House was particularly displeased over the inclusion of Nicaragua on the minister's itinerary. In statements made prior to his trip, MacEachen reiterated Canadian support for Contadora efforts to "demilitarize the area," expressed his government's opposition to "third party intervention by anyone," and responded to Reagan's description of the forthcoming Nicaraguan elections as merely "rubber stamping" Sandinista control with the comment that any evaluation of the elections should "not [be] blinded by ideological blinders." Discussing Nicaragua, he also stated that "improvements have taken place" since the overthrow of Somoza and that Canada was "attempting to understand the social transformation" that was occurring.[77]

On his return, MacEachen again criticized U.S. military involvement in the region. "We have differences," he said. "They've become even clearer on this mining [of Nicaragua's harbours] question."[78]

The transition from Liberal to Conservative Party rule in late 1984 was not, at least initially, accompanied by any major shift in Canadian policy towards Central America. Addressing the United Nations in September, the new government's external affairs minister, Joe Clark, declared that "Canada regrets the extension to Central America of East/West confrontation and the related militarization of the area," expressed Ottawa's continued support for the Contadora peace process, and advocated direct negotiations between Washington and Managua.[79] The commitment to Contadora and a political solution was again mentioned by Clark in the course of a general review of U.S.-Canadian relations with U.S. Secretary of State Shultz in mid-October. Announcing a sweeping review of Canadian foreign policy in February 1985, the external affairs minister conceded that Washington's "unsettling" policies in Central America remained a source of disagreement between the two western allies.[80]

Despite Canada's differences with the United States over Central America, Ottawa's unease has been conveyed primarily through "quiet diplomacy"[81] and has coexisted with instances of both public and private alignment with White House policy. The way in which "quiet diplomacy" served to mask a good deal of practical collaboration with U.S. policy in the region is well illustrated in the case of El Salvador.

In mid-1980, the Canadian secretary of state for external affairs, Mark MacGuigan, rationalized the Carter administration's decision to supply "nonlethal" military equipment to the Salvadoran junta on the grounds that the "so-called American aid is purely of a defensive nature."[82] Soon after Reagan's election, MacGuigan conferred with the new U.S. secretary of state, Alexander Haig, at which time he was made privy to materials that subsequently formed the substance of the first Reagan white paper on El Salvador. These documents so "impressed" MacGuigan that, combined with his discussions with Haig, they had given him "reason to pause" over continued Canadian opposition to U.S. involvement in El Salvador.[83] Eventually, the external affairs minister announced that Washington "can at least count on our quiet acquiescence" if it decides to provide "offensive arms" to the Salvadoran regime.[84] During Reagan's 1981 visit, MacGuigan reaffirmed this position and sought to downplay Canada's role by contending that the region was not "an area of traditional Canadian interest."[85] According to MacGuigan, the meeting between the two heads of state produced a convergence of views on Central America: "There was no difference between the positions of our two governments."[86]

The same month, however, MacGuigan described U.S. military assistance to El Salvador as "neither desirable or necessary" and termed it a major "difference" between Ottawa and Washington. Nonetheless, he continued to give credence to the unproven and unsubstantiated assertions contained in the white paper, expressing opposition to "the import of huge quantities of arms from Cuba and other Communist countries through Nicaragua to El Salvador."[87] Throughout 1982 and 1983, Canadian statements critical of the "escalating military confrontation" in Central America were accompanied by declarations of support for the U.S. military build-up in El Salvador which officials justified by ascribing legitimacy to the existing government and exhibiting concern over recent guerrilla gains. In mid-1983, External Affairs Minister MacEachen outlined Canada's position: "We know that the guerrilla forces are obtaining support from abroad and we accept that the government of El Salvador has the right to seek support from other countries, such as the United States, to defend itself."[88]

Following a Trudeau-Reagan conference in April 1983, White House aides described the Canadian leader as basically sympathetic to U.S. imperial designs in Central America: "The Prime Minister said he appreciated the reasons behind the President's policy and generally supported it."[89] Less than two months later, Trudeau told the House of Commons that he saw no reason for the United States to end its military activities in the region as long as other external forces were similarly involved.[90] His implied acceptance of Washington's contention that Central America was an arena of U.S.-Soviet "testing of wills" was again suggested when he declared before Parliament "that what the United States does in Latin America is its own business because the Spanish-speaking world is one of its spheres of influence."[91] The Canadian government, according to External Affairs Minister MacEachen, "fully appreciate[s] the dilemma that is facing the United States as it seeks to respond to these explosive events in a region of strategic importance to U.S. interests."[92] Periodic assertions of Canadian unease over the "escalating military confrontation" in the area were increasingly accompanied by criticisms of the guerrilla movement in El Salvador and statements of "dismay" over "the increasing tendency toward authoritarianism" in Nicaragua.[93] In April 1984, MacEachen informed Secretary of State Shultz that while he would not include El Salvador or exclude Nicaragua from his forthcoming Central American tour, he had recently asked the Nicaraguan foreign minister to tone down his government's criticisms of the United States.[94]

Canadian policy towards Central America since 1980 has thus evolved independently of the United States — but only to a limited degree. Ottawa's refusal to lend itself to military adventures, its consistent support for a political solution to the regional crisis, its more eclectic choice of economic partners (Guatemala *and* Nicaragua, for example), and its refusal to collaborate with Washington in opposing "international" bank loans to the Sandinista regime all reflect an independent stance. More recently, however, a gradual shift appears to have taken place in the direction of conceding the primacy of

U.S. interests in the region, parallelled by official criticism of the internal policies of the Nicaraguan government and of the guerrilla movement in El Salvador. This developing convergence with U.S. policy is shaped largely by a concern not to allow Central America to become the occasion for a serious rift in bilateral relations. Ironically, neither an accommodative nor a conflictive Canadian policy has achieved an outcome compatible with Ottawa's objectives. From neither stance has Canadian policy influenced the course of U.S. actions. Moreover, although Canada remains critical of the United States' emphasis on military solutions in Central America, both countries share a common global purpose and ultimately Canada depends on the "umbrella" provided by the U.S. imperial state that maintains the imperial system of which they are both a part.

Notes

1 See U.S. Agency for International Development, *U.S. Overseas Loans and Grants and Assistance from International Organizations, July 1, 1945-September 30, 1982*, 47; Steven R. Weisman, "Reagan Denies Aim is Bigger Presence In Latin Countries," *New York Times*, July 27, 1983, 1, 11; Hedrick Smith, "Reagan Seeks a Fourfold Increase In Arms Aid for Salvador Regime," *New York Times*, February 18, 1984, 4; MLC-032, 98th Congress, Issue 8, in Congressional Research Service, The Library of Congress, *Major Legislation of the 98th Congress*, December 1984 (Summary Issue); "U.S.-Nicaraguan Tension Grows As Congressional Deadline Nears," *Central America Bulletin* (U.S.), 4, 2 (December 1984), 5; "U.S. Policy Towards El Salvador: Surface Successes Conceal Present and Potential Troubles," *Central America Bulletin*, 4, 111 (January 1985), 4.

2 See *ibid.*, 4; Lydia Chavez, "More Americans Sent to Salvador," *New York Times*, February 27, 1984, 4.

3 See John M. Goshko, "Big Boost Proposed in Latin Aid," *Washington Post*, February 5, 1985, A1, A4.

4 Quoted in Francis X. Clines, "Reagan Criticizes the Latin Debate," *New York Times*, April 18, 1984, 13.

5 See U.S. Agency for International Development, *U.S. Overseas Loans*, 51; Weisman, "Reagan Denies Aim," 1, 11.

6 Quoted in Fred Hiatt and Joanne Omang, "U.S. Buildup in Honduras Described," *Washington Post*, February 1, 1984, A1 (emphasis added). Also see Joel Brinkley, "Senate Study Questions a Buildup by Pentagon in Honduras," *New York Times*, February 2, 1984, 10.

7 See Hiatt and Omang, "U.S. Buildup," A8; Robert J. McCartney, "U.S. is Dotting Honduras Countryside With Military Facilities," *Washington Post*, February 17, 1984, A25; Richard Halloran, "G.I.'s Will Train in Honduras Again," *New York Times*, February 24, 1984, 4; Fred Hiatt, "Buildup: U.S. Has Steadily Amassed Troops, Counterrevolutionaries in Latin America,"

Washington Post, April 15, 1984, A1, A28; Joanne Omang and Edward Cody, "Honduras Wary of U.S. Policy," *Washington Post*, February 24, 1985, A1, A24; James LeMoyne, "U.S. to Hold More War Games in Honduras," *New York Times*, March 27, 1985, 4.

8 See, for example, "Honduras: Strains in U.S. Strategy," *Central America Bulletin*, 4, 4 (February 1985), 1, 2, 7.

9 See Goshko, "Big Boost," A1, A4.

10 Quoted in Hedrick Smith, "Ambiguities on Goals," *New York Times*, April 11, 1984, 8.

11 Quoted in Hedrick Smith, "U.S. Policy on Nicaragua: Keep the Pressure On," *New York Times*, December 1, 1983, 15. Also see Lou Cannon and Don Oberdorfer, "President Approved 'Harassment' Plan," *Washington Post*, July 13, 1984, A1, A14.

12 See "U.S.-Nicaragua Tension Grows," 5.

13 See "U.S. Hitmen: the Nicaraguan Contras," *Central America Bulletin*, 4, 1 (November 1984), 11-12.

14 Quoted in John Goshko, "Nicaraguans Fight on the Hill," *Washington Post*, February 26, 1985, A12. Also see John Lantigua, "Reagan Seeks More Anti-Rebel Funds Sandinistas Say," *Washington Post*, February 23, 1985, A13.

15 See Richard Halloran, "U.S. Said to Draw Latin Troops Plan," *New York Times*, April 8, 1984, 1, 12; Doyle McManus, "U.S. Draws Contingency Plans," *Washington Post*, July 13, 1984, A27.

16 Walter LaFeber, *Inevitable Revolutions: The United States in Central America* (New York: W.W. Norton, 1983), 60-62, 127-28, and *passim*.

17 See U.S. Department of Commerce, Bureau of Economic Analysis, *Selected Data on U.S. Direct Investment Abroad, 1950-76* (February 1982), 1-27; U.S. Department of Commerce, *Survey of Current Business*, 61, 8 (August 1981), 31, 32; U.S. Department of Commerce, *Survey of Current Business*, 63, 8 (1983), 23, 24.

18 The World Bank, *World Development Report 1983* (New York: Oxford University Press, 1983), 176.

19 *Ibid.*, 178.

20 Tom Barry, Beth Wood and Deb Preusch, *Dollars and Dictatorship: A Guide to Central America* (New York: Grove Press, 1983), 9.

21 *Ibid.*, 60.

22 Quoted in Allan Nairn, "Bank of America Asked to Explain its Support for the Guatemalan Death Squads," *Multinational Monitor*, 3, 3 (March 1982), 15.

23 See U.S. Agency for International Development, *U.S. Overseas Loans*, 47-48, 51-52, 54, 202-05.

24 See *ibid.*, 47; Weisman, "Reagan Denies Aim," 1, 11; Smith, "Reagan Seeks a Fourfold Increase in Arms Aid," 4; James Morrell and William Jesse Biddle, *Central America: The Financial War* (Washington, D.C.: Center for International Policy, March 1983), 8; "U.S. Policy Towards El Salvador: Surface Successes Conceal Present and Potential Troubles," 6.

25 These two loans are discussed in Morrell and Biddle, *Central America*, 2-4.

26 See *ibid.*, 6-7.

27 *Ibid.*, 8.

28 *Ibid.*, 7.

29 Quoted in *ibid.*, 7.

30 Caleb Rossiter, *The Financial Hit List* (Washington, D.C.: Center for International Policy, February 1984), 4.

31 See Morrell and Biddle, *Central America*, 7, 10; "How the U.S. Uses its Lending Vote," *Latin America Regional Reports: Mexico & Central America*, RM-84-01, January 31, 1984, 2.

32 Quoted in Karen De Young, "Shultz Intervenes On Loan," *Washington Post*, March 8, 1985, A1, A17.

33 See "Growing Loss Column for Nicaragua," *Latin America Regional Reports: Mexico & Central America*, RM-84-10, November 30, 1984, 4.

34 Statement of R. Bruce Cuthbertson, regional vice president for Central America, Association of American Chambers of Commerce in Latin America, in U.S. Congress, House, Hearings, Committee on Foreign Affairs, Subcommittee on Inter-American Affairs, *Business Perspectives on Latin America*, 97th Congress, 1st Session, April 28, 1981 (Washington: U.S. Government Printing Office, 1981), 15.

35 Statement submitted by the American Chamber of Commerce in Guatemala, in U.S. Congress, *Business Perspectives*, 46, 48.

36 Quoted in "Central American Elections Signal Little Improvement in MNC Working Conditions," *Business Latin America*, April 14, 1982, 114.

37 See *ibid.*, 114.

38 See "Despite Political Woes, Central American Markets Offer Business Incentives," *Business Latin America*, March 14, 1984, 83, 87.

39 On U.S. investment in El Salvador, see "El Salvador: U.S. Plants Hum Along Despite the Turmoil," *Business Week*, April 13, 1981, 60.

40 See "Dozens of MNCs Brace El Salvador's Civil War to Keep Foot in Door," *Business Latin America*, August 26, 1981, 270.

41 See "MNCs Successfully Adapt to Hardships of Business in War-Torn El Salvador," *Business Latin America*, March 17, 1982, 83.

42 See *ibid.*, 83-84.

43 Quoted in Fred R. Bleakley, "Americans in Business in El Salvador: Juggling Risk, Fear and Returns," *New York Times*, March 25, 1984, 6F.

44 "MNCs Maintain Presence, Show Some Profits in War-Torn El Salvador," *Business Latin America*, March 30, 1983, 99, 104.

45 Quoted in "Survey Finds Most MNC's Receive Fair Treatment From Sandinistas," *Business Latin America*, August 12, 1981, 249-251.

46 See Joanne Kenen, "U.S. Is Still Nicaragua's Top Trading Partner," *Journal of Commerce*, May 11, 1983, 5A.

47 Kenneth N. Gilpin, "Nicaragua Outlook Worries Executives," *New York Times*, August 15, 1983, D1.

48 Quoted in "Survey Finds Most MNC's Receive Fair Treatment From Sandinistas," 249-51.

49 Quoted in "U.S. Executives Express Optimism Over Latin America Investment Climate," *Business Latin America*, October 5, 1983, 315.

50 Gilpin, "Nicaragua Outlook," D7.

51 See John F.H. Purcell, "The Perception and Interests of U.S. Business in Relation to the Political Crisis in Central America," in Richard E. Feinberg, ed., *Central America: International Dimensions of the Crisis* (New York: Holmes and Meier Publishers, 1982), 115.

52 Barry, Wood and Preusch, *Dollars and Dictatorship*, 58.

53 The discussion of the debt negotiations draws on Purcell, "Perceptions and Interests of U.S. Business," 107-08, 110-11. On the amount of the Nicaraguan debt and the proportion owed to U.S. banks, see "Nicaragua: Foreign Debt Talks Run Aground," *Latin America Regional Reports: Mexico & Central America*, RM-80-07, August 15, 1980, 5; Terri Shaw, "Cuba's Debt Mistakes: A Lesson for Nicaragua," *Washington Post*, October 5, 1980, G1, G7.

54 See Central American Historical Institute (Georgetown University), *Update*, No. 8, November 5, 1982; "U.S. Pressure on Lenders Blamed for Liquidity Crisis," *Latin American Markets* (Financial Times), No. 63, August 1, 1983, 12.

55 See interview in Central American Historical Institute, *Update*.

56 Barry, Wood and Preusch, *Dollars and Dictatorship*, 237.

57 Quoted in "Nicaragua: A Warmer Welcome for U.S. Businessmen," *Business Week*, January 10, 1983, 43.

58 Gilpin, "Nicaragua Outlook," D7.

59 See *ibid.*, D7.

60 See Tim Draimin, "Canadian Foreign Policy and El Salvador," in Liisa North, *Bitter Grounds: Roots of Revolt in El Salvador* (Toronto: Between the Lines, 1981), 100; "Canadian Investment, Trade and Aid in Latin America," *LAWG Letter*, 1/2 (May-August 1981), 15-17.

61 See the Taskforce on the Churches and Corporate Responsibility, *Canadian Economic Relations with Countries that Violate Human Rights*, A Brief to the Sub-Committee on Latin America and the Caribbean of the Standing Committee on External Affairs and National Defence, June 1, 1982, 13-14.

62 See "Canadian Policy Review Suggests Greater Role in Regional Affairs," *Business Latin America*, January 5, 1983, 4. Also see D.R. Murray, "The Bilateral Road: Canada and Latin America in the 1980's," *International Journal*, 37, 1 (Winter 1981-82), 119-20.

63 See Canadian International Development Agency, *Canadians in the Third World: Statistical Annex*, CIDA's Year in Review 1981-82 (Ottawa, 1983). Figures supplied by CIDA to Canada-Caribbean-Central American Policy Alternatives, Toronto, Ontario, published in an *AID Memo*, September 10, 1983.

64 See letter of Allan J. MacEachen, External Affairs Minister, March 1, 1983, quoted in *ibid.*

65 "Canada and Central America: Turner Takes Charge," *Central America Update*, 4, 1 (July-August 1984), 9.

66 "Canadian Policy: Variations on the U.S. Themes," *Central America Update*, 6, 6 (June 1983), 34.

67 "Canada and Central America: Turner Takes Charge," 2, 9.

68 Quoted in Caleb Rossiter, *Financial Hit List*, 4. Also see "Political Veto Scuttles Loan," *The Globe and Mail*, Toronto, October 3, 1983, B3.

69 See Michael McDowell, "El Salvador Aid 'Squandered' Analyst Reports," *The Globe and Mail*, March 24, 1983, 15; Morrell and Biddle, *Central America*, 4. Also see Suzanne Fournier and Arthur Moses, "Canadians Back Opposing Sides in Tropical Wars," *The Globe and Mail*, January 18, 1983, 14.

70 Quoted in Olivia Ward, "IMF Accused of Breaking Own Rules to Lend $85 Million to El Salvador," *Toronto Star*, September 12, 1982, A17.

71 Martin Mittelstaedt, "Federal IMF Policy Called Inconsistent," *The Globe and Mail*, August 20, 1983, B14.

72 Quoted in R.V. Gorhan, assistant under-secretary, Bureau of Latin America and Caribbean Affairs, Department of External Affairs, Ottawa, *Canadian Policy Toward Latin America, Central America and the Caribbean*, speech to Council on Hemispheric Affairs, New York, May 2, 1982, 10-12. Also see a speech by Secretary MacGuigan, March 31, 1981, University of Toronto, quoted in Canadian Embassy, Public Affairs Division, *Central America and Canadian Foreign Policy*, April 5, 1982. Trudeau's restatement is included in remarks delivered at a conference of heads of state of Caribbean Commonwealth countries in February 1983. See Darryl Dean, "Canada 'Committed' to Caribbean Aid," *Miami Herald*, February 23, 1983, 7A; Charlotte Montgomery, "Canada a Friend 'For All Season', Trudeau promises," *The Globe and Mail*, February 21, 1983, 12.

73 Quoted in John Gray, "Trudeau Accuses U.S. of Interference in Central America," *The Globe and Mail*, April 23, 1983, 1.

74 "The Government has made very clear to the Government of the United States at the most senior levels its opposition to foreign interventions in Central America, including Nicaragua," letter from Secretary of State for External Affairs Allan J. MacEachen to Mr. John M. Kirk, Department of Spanish, Dalhousie University, Halifax, Nova Scotia, May 27, 1983. Prime Minister Trudeau expressed opposition to U.S. financing and training of the contras in House of Commons, *Debates*, May 2, 1983, 2506.

75 *Statement Discourse*, notes for a speech by the Hon. Allan J. MacEachen, deputy prime minister and secretary of state for external affairs, University of Ottawa, June 3, 1983.

76 See Michael Valpy, "In the U.S. Ear," *The Globe and Mail*, August 9, 1983, 6.

77 Quoted in Patrick Martin, "Canada Spurns Appeal by U.S. on El Salvador," *The Globe and Mail*, April 3, 1984 (on telex, Canadian Embassy, Washington, D.C.).

78 Quoted in Patrick Martin, "U.S. Taking Wrong Road: MacEachen," *The Globe and Mail*, April 17, 1984 (on telex, Canadian Embassy, Washington, D.C.).

79 "Canada & Central America: Clark Promises Moderating Role," *Central America Update*, 6, 2 (September-October 1984), 14.

80 Quoted in *The Globe and Mail*, February 10, 1985 (on telex, Canadian Consulate, Sydney, Australia).

81 See, for example, Michael McDowell, "Canada Will Coax, Won't Push the U.S. on Central America," *The Globe and Mail*, May 28, 1983, 15.

82 Quoted in Tim Draimin, *Bitter Grounds*, 102.

83 Quoted in "Less Canadian Opposition Seen to U.S. Aid for Salvador Junta," *The Globe and Mail*, February 5, 1981, 14.

84 Quoted in Tim Draimin, *Bitter Grounds*, 103.

85 Quoted in *ibid.*, 104.

86 Quoted in *ibid.*, 104.

87 Speech by Secretary of State MacGuigan, March 9, 1981, quoted in R.V. Gorhan, *Canadian Policy*, 12-13.

88 *Statement Discourse*.

89 Quoted in Bruce Ward, "PM's Central American Policy Rapped," *Toronto Star*, May 3, 1983, A8.

90 See "U.S. Needn't Withdraw Latin Aid, Trudeau Says," *The Globe and Mail*, June 9, 1983, 14.

91 Quoted in Susan Riley, "Canada's Uneasy Stand on a Tricky Issue," *Maclean's*, August 8, 1983, 22.

92 Quoted in "Canada Moves Closer to U.S. on Central America," *Christian Science Monitor*, July 18, 1983, 5.

93 Quoted in *ibid.*, 5.

94 Quoted in Patrick Martin, "U.S. Taking Wrong Road."

Chapter 8

The Grenadian Crisis and the Caribbean Left

Clive Y. Thomas

THE GRENADIAN REVOLUTION was widely hailed as the most important achievement of the left in the English-speaking Caribbean. Regionally, its importance is dwarfed only by the Cuban revolution and the Sandinistas' struggles in Nicaragua. It is therefore of great importance to analyze the impact its collapse in October 1983 had on the "popular forces" of the English-speaking Caribbean. "Popular forces" here refers to the broad group of people opposed: to colonization and neo-colonial forms of metropolitan domination of the region; to regional involvement in international rivalries; to the perpetuation of poverty and vast domestic inequalities in the distribution of income, wealth, jobs, and power; and to the systematic violation of human rights and the effective exclusion of the broad masses of the region's population from a major say in their own government. Some of this constituency is organized into left-wing political parties, but by no means all of it is, and these general tenets are compatible with a multiplicity of party organizations.

To evaluate the events in Grenada, it is useful to distinguish between the execution and assassination of Bishop, his allies in the government, and others, and the invasion by the Organization of the Eastern Caribbean States (OECS) and the United States. While these two aspects are closely linked, the former set of events is unique in the region's historical experience, whereas U.S. invasion (albeit this time in alliance with the OECS states) is commonplace. It is said that U.S. administrations have ordered the invasion of other countries more than a hundred times in the past hundred years, and in the western hemisphere alone it has done so more than sixty times this century. Given the frequency of these invasions, they should perhaps be expected, if not accepted. What we certainly have not come to expect, and hopefully will never accept, is that the execution of Bishop and his colleagues belongs to any tradition of any section of the popular forces of the region. Had the invasion not occurred, the Grenadian revolution — with all its positive gains — would have self-destructed with the execution of Bishop, and because of this would have had no continued legitimacy among the broad mass of the Caribbean peoples. In a perverse way, because the invasion took place after the revolution had already destroyed itself, it resulted in breathing new life into the corpse.

The Paralysis of Regional Integration

It is useful to begin by noting the main lines of development of the regional integration movement just prior to these events, using them as an index of regional political consciousness.

(1) Following a long period in which the highest decision-making authority of the regional integration movement, the Caribbean Community (CARICOM) Heads of Government Conference, could not be convened, two Heads of Government Conferences were held within a period of eight months: in November 1982 and June 1983. Following these meetings, the pronouncements made by the various governments were very optimistic about the future of the regional movement. These included Grenada, whose full incorporation into the CARICOM fold then seemed beyond question.

(2) The concerns of the smaller CARICOM states, which had always plagued the integration movement, were placed high on the regional agenda, and the assimilation of the grouping into the OECS in 1981 marked a major advance in addressing the plight of the small states. Grenada had played a leading part in this development, a further confirmation of the increasing acceptance of its revolutionary process into the regional outlook.

(3) National and international developments were taking a severe toll on the economic arrangements of CARICOM in several areas at a regional level (for example, causing the collapse of the regional currency settlement and clearing facility [the CARICOM Multilateral Clearing Facility], the rise in protectionism, and a growing tendency towards intra-regional trade and exchange rate conflicts). Nevertheless, there was increasing adherence to strategies promising greater local and regional control over resources, increased decision-making power in economic affairs, and technology and skills development. This shift was accompanied by many public pronouncements of an anti-imperialist nature by governments, trade

unions, churches, and human rights and social organizations. These statements included pointedly sceptical remarks about, and criticisms of, the Caribbean Basin Initiative (CBI), and its hidden designs aimed at "recolonization of the region"; strongly critical statements about the European Economic Community and its handling of the EEC-ACP (European Economic Community-Africa Caribbean Pacific) economic arrangements; and forceful support in international forums for a new international economic order (NIEO), along with calls for greater South-South cooperation to counter balance domination by the North. These attitudes were also reflected in a more favourable disposition by all the major institutions of the popular forces towards the non-alignment movement.

(4) In the international relations arena, the idea that the Caribbean should be declared a "zone of peace" gained wider acceptance. While the Caribbean Conference of Churches had played a leading role in the development of this idea, many other non-governmental organizations and some governments and ruling parties had also declared their support for it. With escalated U.S. warfare in the region and the Reagan administration's aggressive re-assertion of a "right" to dictate the political complexions of governments "in its own backyard," this marked the development of an important anti-imperialist consensus.

(5) Within the region generally, and particularly in government, there was a concerted move towards an acceptance of "political pluralism" as a feature of the integration movement. While important sections of the popular forces wanted this linked to an insistence on minimal standards of political culture, such as representative governments, and a positive environment for the development of human rights, both Forbes Burnham's brand of dictatorship in Guyana and the Grenadian revolutionary process were accepted as being the "internal concerns" of the countries themselves, and not issues to be deliberated upon by a regional intergovernmental organization. (This also represented a reversal of the initial refusal of the heads of government to accept the 1979 overthrow of Eric Gairy in Guyana. This refusal was one of the factors that had prevented the convening of the Heads of Government Conference.)

While these trends were unevenly developing among and within the territories concerned, there can be little doubt that a progressive, liberal, anti-imperialist, and nationalist consciousness had come to constitute the hegemonic tendency in regional opinion. This was not arrived at overnight, of course. It was the end of a long series of conflicts between the popular forces and the colonial consciousness which had evolved within the region through the centuries of colonial domination; and later, after World War II, between the ideas of the popular forces and the hysterical anti-communist, anti-socialist, and anti-Cuban opinion emanating especially from the ruling circles of the United States, a set of ideas which the dominant classes in the Caribbean hoped would supersede the colonial outlook. Naturally, the success of the nationalist-progressive ideas depended upon, and in turn supported, the increasingly favourable national, regional, and international context of working-class and peasant struggles after World War II, and the growth of locally educated classes which followed the establishment of a national and regional higher education system.

The trauma of the Grenadian executions, which were used as a means to settle political issues on the left, shattered the esteem in which the body of opinion, theories, and ideas which support the interests of the popular forces in the Caribbean was held. This blow was critical, since without the growth and consolidation of the hegemonic position of progressive/liberal/nationalist opinion in the region, the organizational and ideological growth of the left must always remain stunted. Without this regional consciousness, the mass of the population is easily swayed by the appeal of the baser aspects of the ruling classes' ideology (given the social, cultural, communication, and other forms of metropolitan domination of the area). This destruction of the hegemony of the ideology of the popular forces was not due to the invasion but to the imploding of the revolutionary process. Indeed, one has only to envisage an invasion in another context (with Bishop alive) to be able to imagine how different the effects on the status of the popular forces' ideas would have been (it is some measure of this that despite threats, no invasion was attempted before Bishop's death). Several pieces of evidence can be assembled in support of this judgement.

(1) The growing acceptance of the notion of political pluralism referred to earlier has been replaced by a polarization of ideologies in the region: pro-colonial sentiments have become more pronounced and now dominate the media. Many advocates of pro-colonial views, previously silenced by the weight of prevailing regional opinion, have emerged, emboldened by the atrocities of the Grenadian left and public outrage against them. Examples include the summary expulsion of Ricky Singh, editor of *Caribbean Contact* — easily the most important and widely circulated publication in the region — from Barbados. Published by the Caribbean Conference of Churches, the paper condemned the Grenadian executions outright, but had also convincingly opposed the invasion by the United States and the OECS, exposing in its reportage much of the misinformation spread by the invaders at the time. There is also Jamaican Prime Minister Edward Seaga's call for the exclusion of Guyana (which had opposed the invasion) from CARICOM on human rights grounds, while at the same time suggesting the incorporation of Haiti and the Dominican Republic into a CARICOM II. The move by the government of St. Christopher-

Nevis in the aftermath of the invasion to give citizenship to "substantial investors" in that country, whether or not the persons concerned had ever lived in or visited the territory, can also be cited.

(2) The "zone of peace" concept, which had gained widespread acceptance, was replaced by Cold War exchanges, a shift which reinforced the polarization of ideological positions and weakened acceptance of the principle of political pluralism in the regional system. The invaders claimed that they had thereby "eliminated the Marxist-Leninist axis of conspiracy and violence in the region." In turn, this provoked calls for the left to "stop being naive" and to forge close links to the "presumed axis" since without these no progressive, nationalist development within the region would be possible. The invaders backed up their statements with moves aimed at increasing their military capabilities substantially under U.S. guidance, using their special connections with the U.S. government openly after the invasion as a basis for "stabilizing" the existing order in the region. That their position was a popular one cannot be denied, since the wave of snap elections in OECS states in the wake of the invasion led to the return of the incumbent administrations with enlarged majorities.*

(3) Instead of the increasing assertion of national consciousness and opposition to metropolitan domination, those who presumably hold political power have reduced the region, and CARICOM in particular, to a position where the major axis revolves around the positions taken on the invasion. In some quarters, in Trinidad-Tobago for example (which opposed the invasion and whose government justifiably felt that it was deceived and manipulated over it), this has bred a certain "inwardness" in attitudes at all levels of the society — a factor that had proved instrumental in the earlier demise of the West Indies Federation.

(4) Finally, it is clear that the United States has effectively filled whatever power vacuum had existed in the region. Despite the propaganda of conservatives, neither Cuba nor the Soviet Union, nor any of their alleged proxies, had come anywhere near to filling the power vacuum which was created by the removal of Britain as the colonial power. The final seal was put on U.S. ascendancy at the Commonwealth Heads of Government Conference held in India in November 1983, where the conference communiqué for the Caribbean declared that "the emphasis should now be on reconstruction, not recrimination." This formulation clearly put the U.S. action

---

*In the case of Jamaica's Seaga, who has strongly identified his administration with Reagan's ideology, the snap election produced a "one-party state"; Michael Manley's PNP boycotted the elections because known irregularities in the voters' list had not been corrected, despite the existence of an agreement with the government that they would be before any elections were held.

"above the law," since even governments opposed to the invasion thus effectively abjured their responsibility to protest the violation of international law involved. The emphasis was only on "repairing the damage": such a development would not have been possible if the invasion had not taken place in the context of a revolutionary process which had already destroyed itself.

The Abandonment of Constitutionality

The self-destruction of the revolutionary process in Grenada also bears directly on the organization and future development of popular political formations in the region. The events which led up to the execution of Maurice Bishop and others clearly indicate the importance which must be attached to constitutionality, legality, and due process in the legitimation of political action within the region. The success of the New Jewel Movement and the Maurice Bishop government in gathering support to overthrow the Gairy regime, and subsequently in winning the support of most West Indians for the Grenadian revolutionary process, rested largely on systematic exposure, when in opposition, of Gairy's methods of dictatorial rule and his gross violations of regionally accepted norms of constitutionality, legality, and due process. Conversely, their own subsequent failure to hold free and fair elections tarnished their reputation in the eyes of large sections of the popular forces. This was especially noticeable because immediately after the successful overthrow of Gairy, a pledge was made to hold "free and fair elections, and elections free from fear," to uphold due process, and to protect the human rights which Gairy had so grossly violated. The hands of critics were stayed by fear of splitting ranks in the face of threats of imminent invasion by the United States, as well as by what appeared — to sympathetic outsiders, at least — to be serious efforts on the part of the New Jewel Movement to develop alternative forms of so-called direct democracy.

The betrayal of trust implicit in the murderous way in which the political struggles in the New Jewel Movement finally resolved themselves in October 1983 has been particularly traumatic for those sections of the popular forces which had refrained from open criticism in the interest of solidarity. The immediate consequence of this is that no regime, no matter how popular it may be initially, will be able to sustain the support of the popular forces of the region if its political rule is not grounded in constitutionality, legality, and due legal process. This lesson can be a lasting gain for the West Indian peoples. One can only regret that the price paid for learning it was so high.

After Grenada, no social project carried out in the name of the masses of the Caribbean peoples, whether by government or opposition, will receive widespread popular support unless it clearly follows principles of political democracy as its guide for political conduct. Whatever difficulties may exist in interpreting this general proposition, it must mean (i) that legal and/or administrative discrimination on the grounds of race, religion, tribe, property/income, political party affiliation, or any discrimination which might affect the free expression of political opinion, either directly or through elected representatives be absent; (ii) that there be no restrictions on the eligibility of a person to vote, apart from age; (iii) that equal legal status for all political parties be ensured, in order that contests between organized political groups are real, representing real alternatives; (iv) that principles of majority rule in the election of representatives and in the legislative process be upheld — with the proviso that this does not limit the minority's freedom to become a legal and constitutional majority; (v) and that due process be adhered to within the legal system, to ensure that the above rights are enforceable.

The denial of these rights in Grenada was the more damaging given certain elements in the region's history. In the English-speaking Caribbean, the struggles against slavery, indentured servitude, and colonial bondage had more frequently than not taken a legal and constitutional form. The struggle against servitude was often expressed as a struggle for the right to personal liberty, guaranteed and protected by law. Similarly, the struggles against colonial bondage and the forms of economic domination associated with it were often expressed as a struggle for such principles as one person-one vote and the right to self-determination, independent trade unionism, and so forth. A deeply embedded tradition which views constitutional and socio-economic issues as inseparable has therefore evolved. This is not simply the product of "colonial propaganda about the virtues of Westminster parliamentarianism," as some would glibly dismiss it. It reflects a deep recognition on the part of the popular forces that the current levels of constitutionality, representative government, legality, and due process are the product of successful struggles which were waged under colonialism and since independence, and which are not simply "gifts" of the colonial or post-colonial authorities. In addition, the prevailing norms of political behaviour directly affect the institutional forms and organizational procedures adopted by the popular forces, and these will always bear directly on their struggles for social advances. To ignore these truths is to imperil the mass movement in the region, and thus the long-term project of creating an egalitarian, democratic, and socialist society.

An observation common to various analyses of the independence settlements made after World War II is that the transfer of power from the colonizer to colonized was based on the exclusion of the masses, in particular working-class organizations, from state power, except where these were preceded by "wars of national liberation" which resulted in an effective "smashing of the colonial state structures." Within the Caribbean region the truth of this observation can be seen most clearly in the successful exclusion of the

Peoples Progressive Party (PPP) from effective state power in Guyana from 1953 onwards. In 1953, the PPP was probably the most advanced working-class political organization in the region, if not in the British Empire. It held the distinction of being the first freely elected Marxist government in that empire (and indeed in this hemisphere). The controlling classes to whom the colonizing power instead handed over state power have sought to perpetuate, through whatever means possible, the systematic exclusion of the masses from holding authentic power.

It is this negation of their democratic rights which determines much of the popular forces' opposition to the existing political order. Any political process which reproduces this exclusion cannot enjoy popular respect, and the naive vanguardism and "left-wing" authoritarianism of the New Jewel Movement prior to Bishop's overthrow opened the way to a renewed depoliticization of the peoples of the region.

In this situation there existed a political party of less than a hundred members (including candidate members and applicant members) discussing the future of Grenadian society (which despite its small size was exceedingly complex) as if the important decisions to be made were their sole prerogative. Worse still, effective power lay in the hands of the "majority" in the much smaller political bureau, regardless of where the debates took place in the party. When the masses reacted against Bishop's detention and freed him, the same vanguardism inexorably led this "majority" to execute summarily the head of the government, leader of the revolutionary process, and commander-in-chief without any pretence whatsoever of due process. In retrospect, it appears that this development might well have been a foregone conclusion from the moment that Bishop was put under house arrest on the basis of a "decision" made by a political bureau acting as if its decisions automatically became law. Is it any wonder that many rightly asked: if the party could treat its own in such a manner, what then was the position of all those who did not belong to the "chosen" hundred? The savagery and contempt for life displayed in these actions will be remembered and pointed to time and again in the region as the "lunacy of the left." The distrust which these events have generated will for a long time limit the incorporation of socialist ideology into the struggles of the popular forces throughout the region.

The Responsibility of the Intellectuals

The "organic intellectuals" of the Caribbean contributed to the undermining of the prevailing homogeneity of colonial and metropolitan ideas in the region. Many of these progressive intellectuals (like some of their counterparts in Western Europe and North America) have been demonstrably uncritical of political processes initiated in the name of the "left," operating as "cheerleaders" rather than constructive and creative critics. While this is seen as "giving solidarity," in reality it indicates an important weakness.

The weakness lies in a failure to grasp the distinction between recognizing progressive social development and politically supporting the class or group which controls state power at the time this takes place. Marx faced this issue squarely when he acknowledged the objective progress the bourgeois class had made in breaking the fetters of feudal domination. This did not, however, lead him to support the bourgeoisie politically. He perceived the bourgeois political project to be the substitution of one form of domination for another.

In contrast to Marx, intellectuals in the Third World and elsewhere are able to identify social advances — for example, the spread of political independence, the subsequent nationalization of natural resources, and so on — but then accept these improvements as sufficient grounds for devoting uncritical political support to the political groups controlling state power at the time these developments are achieved. Loyalty to the regime in power is substituted for a constructively critical attitude. In making this substitution, the intellectuals as a group negate their single most important social attribute: the capacity for creativity and the exercise of independent critical power. One can understand the temptations which give rise to this attitude: fear of giving ammunition to the imperialist enemy; the need to maintain morale among revolutionary leaders; the fear of creating doubts about one's own revolutionary credentials. Succumbing to these temptations, however, as was the case in Grenada, does not serve the long-term project of social transformation aimed at ending all forms of exploitation. Those who hold state power sense this tendency, which adds to the corruptibility inherent in all situations where too much power is concentrated in too few hands.

In retrospect, events in Grenada show there is an urgent need for a serious process of self-criticism among intellectuals aligned with the popular forces. Many examples showing such a need can be found in the failure to respond to major issues generated by the Grenadian revolutionary process. For instance, did the geo-political realities of a micro-state located in the strategic backyard of the United States permit the playing of a leading rhetorical role in the global ideological struggles between imperialism and socialism? To what extent does such rhetoric unnecessarily raise the profile of the micro-state? In doing so, is the danger increased of directly embroiling it in the heightened overt and covert hostilities of the two major military blocs? Do the same considerations arise when the small state is under conservative political control, as in the case of Jamaica, where Seaga plays a leading role in the global ideological debates between imperialism and socialism? Or is it simply, as some argue (after Grenada), that there is no political or national "space" available to a small state in the highly polarized international arena of today, which will allow it to operate independently, when it is bent on a process of radical transformation? To what extent must such issues affect the search for consensus among the popular forces?

Similar fundamental issues not being faced by intellectuals on the left include the question of what problems are created when political rhetoric, and strong foreign policy positions on matters of global significance to the major powers, outstrip the internal economic transformation of the country; whether the power vacuum created by the departure of the British could have been filled in ways which did not require the ascendancy of one of the two major military blocs in the region; or whether the Grenadian experiments with direct democracy could have constituted an authentic alternative to representative democracy.

Issues such as these had to be confronted daily while the Grenadian revolutionary movement existed. Yet, apart from the last item (about which disputes occurred in whispered tones and the issues were in any event only raised obliquely) little real debate took place and creative solutions were not evident. It is therefore not surprising that those at the centre of political events easily accepted the profoundly anti-democratic theses advanced during the inner-party disputes which immediately preceded the tragedy of October 1983. No one challenged the implicit assumption of the protagonists in the dispute that if the majority of the party's leadership moved to a "scientific" embrace of Marxist-Leninist ideology, the time was *ipso facto* ripe for a Leninist or Soviet-type model of social transformation. The rich regional history of inner-party struggles, such as those experienced by the People's National Party of Jamaica, or the PPP of Guyana during the 1940s and 1950s, was never once referred to in the course of these developments. Instead, there occurred the arrogant assumption of the truth of one political theory overriding the wishes of the masses.

Conclusion

Subsequent events confirm several of the major points made here. Since the invasion, the U.S. government has moved to fill the power vacuum in this region with brutal swiftness. Prior to the overthrow of Gairy's regime, U.S. military aid to the region was virtually non-existent except for some small grants, loans, and training facilities provided to Jamaica. Most of the military aid has come after 1979. When total U.S. military aid received by the invading OECS states and Jamaica up to the end of 1983 is computed, 85 per cent of it was received between 1981 and 1983. In 1984, the allocation of military aid to these countries grew by nearly 250 per cent.

This development has been paralleled by increased aggression against Nicaragua by the U.S. government and its allies in the region, despite congressional reverses and considerable public opposition in the United States.

In the late 1980s, a U.S. commitment of large-scale ground forces to the war against Nicaragua, if not a direct invasion of that country, remains a distinct possibility. If this occurs, it would lead to a hemispheric conflagration of unprecedented dimensions. But while this scenario unfolds there is no collective governmental response in the region, reflecting the sad fact that the movement in support of the Caribbean as a "zone of peace" has been all but extinguished by the continuing aftermath of Grenada.

Accompanying the increasing militarization of the region has been the leverage exercised by the Reagan administration in favour of the "privatization" of the region's economy as a necessary step in bringing about its adjustment to the prevailing internal and external economic crises. This is seen as a means of halting the development of statist tendencies in the region, which had grown in all the territories since their independence, and until quite recently, largely irrespective of the ideological line of any particular government. Thus "cooperative socialism" in Guyana and "pragmatic capitalism" in Trinidad-Tobago have both produced large-scale state control of economic processes. Privatization is also seen by the U.S. administration as a way of bolstering the business sector's claims to play the leading social, political, and economic roles in the region. Consequently, USAID and the Caribbean Basin Initiative (CBI), along with bilateral and multilateral credits (mainly through the Inter-American Development Bank, the World Bank, and the IMF) have been used as both "carrot and stick" to bring the various administrations within the region into line.

To facilitate this process the Reagan administration has placed increasing reliance on bilateral aid arrangements. This aspect of the CBI package is central to the exercise of its leverage. This approach contrasts with earlier support for the policy of "regional cooperation" as one way of dealing with the multitude of mini-states in the Caribbean. It promotes the reversal of the regionalist tendencies which had grown significantly prior to the invasion. It is also worth noting that the conception underlying the CBI is primarily strategic. This can be seen in the fusion of the Caribbean and Central America to the point where states which do not even touch the Caribbean Sea are involved in it, as well as in the leading roles assigned in this initiative to the United States' closest allies and/or its proxy regimes.

Not unexpectedly, a number of new business associations and agencies have either been created or resuscitated in an effort to promote the privatization process. In the U.S. the main agency is the Caribbean/Central American Action (CCAA) which developed out of the former Committee for the Caribbean headed by Robert West, chairman of Tesoro Petroleum. In the Caribbean its main counterpart has been the revitalized Caribbean Association of Industry and Commerce (CAIC).

It is important also to note that the drive to "privatize" the region's economy has been advocated not merely as a solution to the present crisis, but as the only long-term sustainable solution to the region's underdevelopment and its attendant social ills. It has been elevated to the status of an ideology in itself and, moreover, one which directly contradicts the claims of socialism. It thus complements the stepped-up drive to assert U.S. cultural hegemony over the region.

A vital element in this strategy was the early holding of "free and fair elections in Grenada." Despite the presence of the occupying forces of the U.S. and OECS states, strenuous efforts were made to promote a political formation which would win "a free and fair election" in Grenada. This was designed in order to achieve three things: to continue the process of delegitimation of the Bishop era; to legitimize the invasion; and to legitimize the political formation which came out of the invasion. This interpretation is supported by the hostile denunciation by the Reagan administration of the process of free and fair elections in Nicaragua. Nevertheless, the widespread judgement that the Nicaraguan elections were remarkably free and fair, despite all the attendant circumstances, has done much to legitimize Sandinista rule both within and outside of Nicaragua, and largely blunted U.S. propaganda which had consistently referred to the Sandinista government as a dictatorship. As time passed and the immense upheaval which led to the defeat of Somoza receded into the background, the effect of the U.S. propaganda would have grown. But the Sandinistas, through their commitment to democracy, were able to call the U.S. administration's bluff.

In Grenada, the post-invasion elections cannot be separated from the invasion and the events which preceded it. If they were, we would fail to appreciate the deeper significance of the fact that the invaders, who throughout Central America have violated every norm of democracy, constitutionality, and sovereignty, have been forced by the circumstances of Grenada to seal their victory by a political process of legitimation in which free and fair elections played a crucial role. To dismiss the elections *entirely*, on the grounds that they were an invader's subterfuge and ploy (which they were), is to miss the deeper significance of the fact that popular consciousness in Grenada, beaten and battered as it was, helped to forge a process in which political democracy had to be paid more than lip service. In the long run, this may well hold the key to the resurgence of the Grenadian masses, situated as they are in the United States' backyard.

Chapter 9

Democracy and Social Transformation in Jamaica

Michael Kaufman

YEARS AFTER THE 1980 defeat of the Manley government in Jamaica, there remains something dramatic and intellectually challenging about its story. But then, an experiment in radical social change on a small island could hardly fail to be so. It seemed at one and the same time to be remote from the rest of the world, yet immensely vulnerable. The richness of the tropical setting stood in stark contrast to economic austerity and political constraint, and the dilemmas of political and economic direction were as sharp as the outline of the mountains looking down on the streets of Kingston.

From the viewpoint of political theory and practice, no dilemma was greater than the issues connected with the place of democracy and democratic institutions within a process of radical socio-economic transformation. The People's National Party (PNP) experiment faltered not only due to structural economic constraints, external and internal opposition, and a myriad of mistakes, large and small. It was also unable to transcend the limitations of the existing structures of the Jamaican state so that it could develop new structures and institutions of grassroots political, economic, and social power. Such new structures were essential in order to infuse fresh meaning and new weight into the liberal democratic traditions of Jamaican politics. And new institutions were a critical element in the transformation of the population from political consumer to producer of its own political destiny. Such a process of political empowerment would be the key to the transformation of social, economic, and political relations, and to mobilizing the dormant energies of the population. It would also be crucial in the positive polarization of political discourse, in contrast to the tribalism of Jamaica's paternalistic party system.

The attempts to create new institutions and relations of social, economic, and political power were at best suggestive — sometimes innovative, yet all too often stillborn. If we can assume that the many obstacles to change were givens — the internal and external forces of opposition, the structural economic legacy of the island, the world economic crisis — then it was the failure to create these new institutions that proved to be the main variable in the failure of the democratic socialist experiment of the 1970s in Jamaica.

This essay summarizes the experience of the PNP in office, focusses on a few of the projects which tried to create political alternatives, examines some relevant issues of liberal democracy and democratic socialism, and concludes with an analysis of the relationship of mobilization, new structures of political power, and the prospects for success of future democratic socialist experiments.

The PNP in Office

One of the most interesting tendencies of the PNP in office was its overall evolution in a leftward direction, unlike most electorally-oriented parties of the left. The tremendous expectations generated by the lengthy process of constitutional decolonization had provided Jamaica's political momentum for twenty-five years. But the hopes created by independence in 1962 did not materialize. In the 1960s unemployment hovered at 15 to 20 per cent; mass emigration to the United States and Canada remained a major escape valve and an avenue for personal promotion; the slums of Kingston were seething zones of squalor swollen by young migrants from the countryside searching for a better life. The black man and woman remained at the bottom of a national hierarchy in which there remained a strong correlation between colour and class.

In the 1960s it was on this ground that black power sentiments were kindled and Rastafarianism triumphed among ghetto youth. There was an understanding among young, often educated, blacks that political independence had affected neither the economic status quo nor the international political and economic domination of Jamaica. The ghetto triumph of Rastafarianism, the campus success of black power, the links between these two, the slowly percolating nationalism of the middle and upper class, and the diffusion into the crevices of Jamaican society of black pride, all had an impact on the PNP. By the time Michael Manley and the PNP were chosen to form a government in 1972, there had been an integration of young militants into the party and a wide impact of diffuse black power sentiments. All these factors, plus new developments in the first two years of office, led to the leftward evolution of the political program of the PNP.

The eight and a half years in which the PNP held office can be divided into four periods:[1]

(1) 1972-73. The election of the PNP in 1972 was the election of a populist, reform-oriented party. The heated debates over socialism that would inflame the 1976 and 1980 elections were not a feature of the 1972 election; good government and popular reforms were. During its first two years, the new government rode on its initial multi-class popularity and introduced a number of programs that lessened income disparities (subsidies for essential food items, public works programs, equal pay for equal work, the prohibition of various luxury imports) and added to Jamaica's reservoir of skills, agricultural productivity, and access to land (for example, a program that leased idle land to peasants, a literacy program, training programs, and educational reforms).

(2) 1974 to early 1977. Under the surface the ruling party was moving to the left. Both international and internal developments played a role. Internationally, there was the progress of the oil producers' cartel, the agitation for a new international economic order, and the growing political isolation of the post-Vietnam/Watergate United States. Internally, the young militants who had entered the party in recent years were beginning to play a key organizational role and were helping set the political agenda of the party and government. But most importantly, the PNP was discovering, with every problem it began to address, that radical measures were needed to address structural social, economic, and political problems that dated back for centuries.[2]

This political evolution became evident in 1974 with three events. First was a dramatic new approach to the country's major export industry, bauxite-alumina. The government announced plans to buy all bauxite lands and to buy into bauxite and alumina operations. Most dramatic was the declaration of a levy on all bauxite and alumina production, a move that increased government revenue almost eightfold in one year and earned the wrath of the multinational aluminum producers.

Second was a new set of international policies that placed tiny Jamaica in the leadership of the non-aligned movement and which sought closer relations with Jamaica's closest neighbour, Cuba.

Third was the program of democratic socialism adopted in 1974 and elaborated in the following years. Formally a social-democratic party almost since its inception in 1938, the PNP had jettisoned socialist language in the early 1950s due to the Cold War and the party's electoral ambitions. In a single step the proclamation of democratic socialism stepped beyond traditional social democratic policies of bringing mild reforms to the status quo. Democratic socialism, a term that was always somewhat ambiguous,was now defined as:

> a political and economic theory under which the means of production, distribution and exchange are owned and/or controlled by the people. It is a system in which political power is used to ensure that exploitation is abolished, that the opportunities of society are equally available to all and that the wealth of the community is fairly distributed. A process rather than a rigid dogma, its application must depend on the particular conditions which obtain from time to time in each country. It emphasises co-operation rather than competition; and service rather than self-interest as the basic motive forces for personal, group and communal action. Its ultimate objective is the building of a classless society by removing the element of entrenched economic privilege which is the basis of class divisions. As distinct from scientific socialism, its method is based on the alliance of classes around clear objectives.[3]

As an economic philosophy, democratic socialism rejected "capitalism as the system upon which to base the future of Jamaica" but affirmed "the right of every Jamaican to own private property." It maintained that "Jamaica will flourish best under a mixed economy in which there is a clear and honourable role for the responsible private business working in partnership with the public sector of the economy."[4]

According to the program, the negative effects of private ownership and control of important parts of the means of production would be tempered by an appeal to " the national interest". "Under socialism the private businessman is expected to work within the bounds of [the] National interest and the rights of the people."[5] The program spoke of national control, a term which referred to either public or private ownership. The question of control was presented as a matter of conformity to a set of social goals that superseded individual profit-making.

The weaknesses of this program, that is, an economic strategy that required the support of capital while shifting social power and the economic surplus to what the PNP called " the sufferers," would soon be evident.

The most far-reaching political aspect of the democratic socialist program was the idea of developing community councils and workers' participation to supplement the basic parliamentary institutions of Jamaica. "We believe that Parliament is the foundation of democracy but we recognise that parliamentary democracy is only a beginning to the democratic process."[6] "The achievement of democratic socialism requires bringing decision-making to the broad mass of the people."[7] This would take place through strengthening local government, the launching of community councils, developing a system of workers' participation, responsive and democratic school boards, and so forth.

The enunciation of these new programs — democratic socialism, the bauxite policies, and new international policies — launched a period of class-based political polarization that culminated in the reelection of the PNP in December 1976. This time the election platform of the party was explicit: "Forward to Democratic Socialism." The PNP's majority was even greater than it had been in 1972, but polls indicated that it had already lost most of its support from capitalists and high-income professionals, and its support from white-collar workers had fallen dramatically.[8] All of these were groups whose standard of living had been threatened by the stagnation of the economy and the restrictions on luxury imports, who were terrified by the spectre of violence as the opposition Jamaica Labour Party mounted a well-organized campaign of terror, and who were ideologically susceptible to anti-communist propaganda. Support for the PNP increased among blue-collar workers, farm labourers, the unskilled, and the unemployed. These were groups who had experienced an improvement in their standard of living or at least had a strong belief that a new Jamaica was in the making. There had been over the preceding few years a rise in real wages, legislation that introduced the first national minimum wage, rent controls and rent reductions, automatic recognition of trade unions, a modest drop in unemployment, and a program that set up workers' cooperatives on the sugar estates.

The first three months of 1977 were the fulcrum of the democratic socialist experiment. The big win of December further shifted the balance of power to the PNP's left wing and appeared to convince Michael Manley at the party centre that the electoral result was a mandate to proceed rapidly with the party's economic program. An Emergency Production Plan was drafted that stressed political mobilization as the basis for an economic program based on self-reliance, making use of local materials, production of food crops, and new employment opportunities.[9] But by the spring, friendly overtures from the new Carter administration in Washington and a worsening economic situation at home convinced the Cabinet — which was dominated by the party centre and right — to turn to the International Monetary Fund for balance-of-payments support. Although the initial IMF program was very moderate by IMF standards, its adoption signalled the political defeat of the PNP left and effectively demobilized the energy created by the 1976 election.

(3) **1977-79.** These years saw the steady deterioration of the Jamaican economy, the imposition of ever harsher IMF austerity programs, the flight of capital, and what appear to have been systematic campaigns of propaganda and political terror to discredit the government. As might be expected, it was a time of decreasing support for the PNP.

Ironically, this was also the period when some of the most politically innovative programs of the PNP were being introduced. The contradiction between the radical nature of these programs and the middle-of-the-road temper of the government, and the general atmosphere of disillusionment, meant that these programs failed to get off the ground.

(4) **1980.** At the end of 1979 the obvious failure of the IMF path and the crisis of political leadership led to a new leftward shift of the PNP leadership, particularly at the rhetorical level. But so great was the economic crisis, so unrelenting the political violence, and so discredited the PNP among a majority of the population, that it was too late to save its fortunes. At the end of October 1980, Michael Manley was defeated by the right-of-centre Jamaica Labour Party led by Edward Seaga.

The Institutions of Alternative Power

Although born out of the mass mobilizations of the 1938 labour rebellion, the PNP in its early years was a middle-class party with links to the Fabian movement in Britain.[10] One of the political legacies of the party was a stress on injustices in the mode of distribution and a belief that these injustices could be reduced through the actions of the existing state apparatus. This belief in the potential effectiveness of the existing state if it had an enlightened, technocratic leadership became a cornerstone of the thought and practice of the People's National Party. It was the link between an electoralist orientation and a commitment to social reform.[11]

One of the shakiest foundations of mainstream social democracy is its notion that a government can direct fundamental change in a society where the basic structures of domination have been left intact. Such a belief ignores the realities of economic power. It also ignores many of the realities of political power. Political power is viewed as if isolated from economic power. This reproduces the division of economic and political power inherent in a bourgeois democratic polity, and shifts attention away from production and towards distribution. Just as working people are seem primarily as consumers on the market (and not as the producers of society's wealth) the capitalist democracies hold out the possibility that working people can act as consumers of the political products of various parties, representatives, and functionaries, but not as producers and shapers of their own political and social destinies.

The ability of the mass of the population to conceptualize an alternative to the status quo, to believe that this alternative is realistic, and to be able to organize in and out of the existing institutions to struggle for such changes, depends on incorporation of these ideas into practical action directed towards change. It entails a shift in role from one of political consumer to one of political producer. The changes of mass consciousness that are both the prerequisite and the result of this process of change are tied into social polarization and mobilization. The desire by the PNP — in its early years and even in the

1970s — effectively to restrict the actions of the majority to supporting what the government would do for the people undermined its ability to harness the nascent energies of the masses. This made people prone to eventual cynicism and vulnerable to victimization at the hands of the political and economic opposition. Because the PNP maintained a belief that "government" had the answers, the real questions were rarely asked. The real questions had to do with how to discover, release, and direct the potential of a population which, for example, was not feeding itself adequately although one-third of the population was unemployed and hundreds of thousands of acres were left idle. By maintaining the mystique of a paternal governmental power, the PNP not only tended to block the resolution of Jamaica's problems but created a situation in which any failures and setbacks, regardless of the real culprits, would be blamed on the PNP itself.

Like most political parties, the PNP was a party of internal conflicts and contradictions: conflicts based in class, on political ideology, and on an attempt to reconcile opposing interests in the party and in Jamaica; and contradictions born of an attempt to radicalize the island's polity without an adequate commitment to a fundamental transformation of the basic political structures. Within the PNP there were forces who clearly saw the need to develop new institutions of political, economic, and social power. Manley himself dismissed "as self-evident nonsense the notion that a society is democratic merely because people vote every five years and are free to exercise that vote in a choice between different political parties or different individual candidates."[12] Yet his position was one in which he was trying to reconcile and hold together a diverse party — a party which at one extreme counted votes on the basis of its ability to dispense jobs and handouts to constituents while, at the other extreme, taking the first tentative steps to overcoming the fragmented legacy of Jamaican clientelist politics and taking the rhetoric of democratic socialism at its word.

Those forces both within and outside the PNP interested in attempting to shift the basis of economic and political power helped create a number of new institutions, institutions that were embryonic structures of people's power. Although many barely got off the ground and none was an unqualified success, the experiments were rich and showed promise.

The Community Councils and Community Economic Organizations

The most innovative attempt to mobilize human and material resources at the local level for economic, political, and social change involved the Community Councils and Community Economic Organizations.

Part of the Jamaican landscape since the late 1930s, Community Councils had been coordinating bodies of service and welfare organizations, particularly in villages and rural areas. In 1976, at the height of the democratic socialist enthusiasm, proposals were developed within the government to transform these councils into representative bodies of various community organizations, trade unions, and affiliates of all political parties. By 1978 the idea evolved towards the establishment of mass membership bodies at the community level, organized around a neighbourhood in the case of the cities, or a string of villages in the case of rural areas.

According to the draft legislation regarding the councils, they would have five functions: taking initiatives for new plans for economic and social development; mobilizing local participation; helping coordinate the efforts of central government programs at the local level; developing channels of local communications; and representing the community on all relevant government bodies making decisions that affected the community.[13]

Council activists often went farther. At their two national conferences in 1978 and 1979 resolutions were adopted that proposed that councils should distribute government benefits within the community, should be "the main instrument of coordination within the community," should take a role in monitoring rents and prices with "powers of prosecution of hoarding [and] overcharging," and should have the right to recall members of Parliament and parish councillors.[14]

By the end of 1980, there were 534 registered councils with a membership of 25,000.[15] (Some councils were much more active than others and the accuracy of these membership figures is difficult to assess.) Where they were more active they helped build community centres, brought people together for monthly meetings, provided new lines of communication, brought supporters of rival parties into common projects, and gave people a taste of self-organization.

But it would be an exaggeration to suggest that the councils had a substantial impact on political developments. The government dragged its feet on passing the legislation that would legalize the councils and give them the power that was promised. This inaction reflected the opposition to the councils by many MPs and parish councillors, who felt threatened by any challenge to their political power or their ability to dispense government largess. It also reflected the indifference of civil servants and many elected officials who could not see beyond the bureaucratic/parliamentary system established by the British. There was little coordination between the various branches of the state with responsibilities at the local level, and no concerted effort to develop the councils. Even among the supporters of the councils, energies, priorities, and attention were divided by the depth of the economic and political crisis in the late 1970s. The councils simply did not get adequate attention. They were a focus neither for mobilizing the population nor for challenging the partisan political affiliations that divided working people, the peasantry, and the unemployed.

Related to the councils was a proposal, first aired by George Beckford, to launch Community Economic Organizations. Conceived in 1977 (in the Emergency Production Plan) as the economic arm of the Community Councils, the CEOs were to become the means of developing community initiative, control, and self-reliance in meeting basic needs. They were seen as an economic mechanism "higher" in socialist development than cooperatives, because they would be based on collective, community control. In the two long years it took for the government mechanisms to be set up, however, three things happened: the economy had fallen into such terrible shape that the state was unable to provide more than token financial support for their establishment; enthusiasm and support for government programs were waning; and the stress had shifted from enterprises set up by Community Councils to small but viable business establishments. In the end only a handful of CEOs were established — some as genuine community efforts, others as private businesses.

Sugar Cooperatives

Following an intense process of worker agitation on the sugar estates, the main sugar producing estates (but not the sugar factories) were reorganized as worker "co-ops" in 1976. It was a major victory of self-organization, but numerous problems plagued the co-ops: the estates were run down to start with, they carried over an oppressive labour process and work hierarchy that dated almost back to slavery, and they suffered from inadequate start-up funding, inadequate education, and strong traditions of labour militancy that were inconsistent with a co-op structure. In spite of grave problems, on the farms where intense educational campaigns were conducted in the late 1970s there was a marked economic turnaround accompanied by visible changes in social relations and actual rank-and-file control.[16]

Voluntary Price Inspectors

The use of Voluntary Price Inspectors got off the ground in 1980 after intense pressure on the government from the women's movement. It was a time of hoarding by distributors and manufacturers, and shortages of basic necessities. The VPIs were empowered to search warehouses and storerooms, and to order the immediate distribution of goods that were not on the shelves. But the government dragged its feet first on training and then on sending the VPIs into the field, probably for fear of alienating shopkeepers. There were many dramatic stories of VPI activities, but the VPIs barely scratched the surface of the food problem.

Home Guards

Set up in the mid-1970s in response to the rising problem of urban violence, the Home Guard was a voluntary corps of civilians who patrolled their neighbourhoods. They quickly came under police control. (By the middle of the PNP's second term, most of the police force supported the opposition JLP.) Far more effective was the spontaneous community self-defence organized in many of the ghettos.

Workers' Control

The three or four workplaces where workers' councils were set up were government offices or the media where the PNP left wing or the Moscow-oriented Workers Party of Jamaica had considerable support. The trade unions were fairly hostile to worker participation schemes, not so much because of the possibility of corporatism, but because workers' councils had the potential of eroding the traditional field of trade union rights and responsibilities.

All these new institutions and initiatives showed there was a potential within the Jamaican context for home-grown structures that would begin to transfer economic and political power to the grassroots level. But the limited development of each of them indicates that without a concerted and systematic approach, new institutions cannot be expected to succeed.

Liberalism, Social Democracy, and Democratic Socialism

One of the reasons for the somewhat slippery character of the PNP's notion of democratic socialism was that the party's strongest political roots were in mainstream social democracy. Inherited from the Fabians of the British Labour Party (which provided both inspiration for many of the founders of the PNP and ongoing support after the party's formation) was a belief in the capacity to achieve substantial social reform through the existing institutions of parliamentary democracy. In the 1930s the ideological power of British liberalism within the Jamaican intelligentsia was so pervasive that even before the vast majority of Jamaicans were able to vote, the leaders of the PNP fervently affirmed — in actions and beliefs — a faith in the essential justice and reformative capacities of the Westminster system. These beliefs were nurtured by the British during the 1940s and 1950s through their carefully orchestrated policies of orderly decolonization culminating in political independence in 1962.

The political doctrines of the PNP were complemented on the economic front by the rapid growth of the Jamaican economy during the 1950s and early

1960s under the impact of foreign investment, particularly in the bauxite industry. The changes of these years — universal suffrage, the growth of a strong trade union movement, the development of the PNP as a multi-class party and its election in the mid-1950s, political independence, and the prospect of continued economic growth and the consequent modernization promised by development economists — only heightened the moderate trends within the party. These moderate trends would only be disrupted by the rise of the black power movement in the late 1960s and the evolution of the PNP once in office. But in the meantime the political foundations of the party had been carefully laid.

These foundations reflected the ideological, economic, and political conditions that form the basis of contemporary social democratic theory, particularly in the advanced capitalist countries:[17]

(1) First has been the rise of Stalinism and mass rejection of the repugnant model of bureaucratic socialism. The Gulags, forced collectivization, lack of basic personal and political liberties, and economic follies in the practice of socialism in one country (in spite of gains realized by state ownership) tarnished the image of socialism in the eyes of the majority of working-class voters in the West. The presentation of the Stalinist nightmare by the mainstream media, governments, and many academics made the images more frightening, perhaps, but they cannot be credited with inventing the nightmare itself.

(2) Meanwhile capitalism in its wartime and post-war boom was showing it could deliver the goods in the advanced capitalist countries. Massive trade union drives before and after the war, economic growth, and the adoption of Keynesianism meant that the standard of living of the population as a whole was rapidly improving. The immiserated proletariat, which had nothing to lose but its chains, was hard to recognize with its homes, cars, colour TVs, matching appliances, and summer vacations. That all workers in the advanced capitalist countries did not taste such fortunes did not fully matter: the possibility of consumer acquisitions and a steady job seemed real. In many different ways mid-twentieth century capitalism in the advanced capitalist countries was not the capitalism of the era in which the socialist movements were born. Important changes were there to see in the living standards of workers, improved working conditions, gains in political and trade union rights, the growth of a large white-collar and technical fraction of the working class, and the integration of working people and working-class parties into the state structures.

(3) The liberal ideals of individual and group freedoms and the possibility of realizing one's own capabilities had become powerful beliefs among working-class and middle-class supporters of social democratic parties. There was an identification of these beliefs with modern capitalism. The

"fact that liberal values grew up in capitalist market societies"[18] and the fact that capitalism appeared to be the means to realize these ideals helped preserve the identification of liberal ideals with modern capitalism.

One of the unfortunate traditions of Marxist political thought, common to both Stalinist and many non-Stalinist varieties, has been the dismissal of liberalism as bourgeois and therefore irrelevant to working people. This bias, traceable in part to the political conditions in Europe at the time of the birth of Marxism and later in Russia at the time of the first revolutionary socialist experiment, ignores the important tradition of working-class and peasant struggles to secure the rights associated with a liberal, democratic polity. These struggles — for universal male and female suffrage, for the right to form trade unions, for the rights of free speech and assembly — have been struggles to secure rights that the bourgeoisie itself has often shown a reluctance to extend to the population as a whole.

Opposed to this tradition has been one that clearly embeds democratic goals within the socialist project. This approach has not only been advanced by thinkers such as Luxemburg and Gramsci but can also be found within the original political writings of Marx and Engels. This approach was advanced very forcefully by C.B. Macpherson in the 1960s and 1970s in his attempts to reclaim liberal democratic values for socialists. "Is liberal democracy nearly finished?" he asks rhetorically at the beginning of *The Life and Times of Liberal Democracy:*

> "Yes," if liberal democracy is taken to mean, as it still very generally is, the democracy of a capitalist market society (no matter how modified that society appears to be by the rise of the welfare state); but "not necessarily" if liberal democracy is taken to mean... a society striving to ensure that all its members are equally free to realize their capabilities. For "liberal" can mean freedom of the stronger to do down the weaker by following market rules; or it can mean equal effective freedom of all to use and develop their capacities. The latter freedom is inconsistent with the former... It may be argued that... the appetite for individual freedom has outgrown its capitalist market envelope and can now live as well or better without it, just as man's productive powers, which grew so enormously with competitive capitalism, are not lost when capitalism abandons free competition or is replaced by some form of socialism.[19]

This thesis is of the utmost importance for understanding the failure of the PNP in the 1970s. That is, without freeing the dormant intellectual, productive, and creative capacities of the Jamaican masses, the country would be unable to effect a fundamental socio-economic transformation against such daunting odds.

Jamaica and the Limits of the Social Democratic Vision

In Jamaica the integration of liberal democratic thought within a socialist strategy is one important reason for the mass credibility of Jamaican social democracy. After all, the original struggles of the Jamaican masses were against slavery — a social system based on the complete denial of individual liberties. Traditions of freedom of speech, religion, and association, trade union freedoms, and the right to multi-party organization were fought for by generations of Jamaican working people. Their attainment represents victories won by popular sectors under capitalism, even though these victories have often been overruled in practice by governments, courts, and the police. Social democrats know this as a matter of "common sense", but do not give it the serious attention it deserves: that is, the need to go beyond a version of liberal democracy that is only compatible with capitalism and to develop an approach that is consistent with — and in fact essential for — socialism. A key aspect of a new approach is to integrate an understanding of political democracy with an understanding of basic economic rights — the right to a job, proper food, clothing, and shelter, and so forth.

In other words, a major flaw of the mainstream social democratic thought inherited by the PNP was not — as the left of the PNP and the WPJ tended to assert — respect for the liberal democratic tradition, but reliance on the institutions of the existing state apparatus as the almost exclusive arena of struggle for political change, and the tendency to separate these rights from issues of economic justice instead of intimately linking them.

The State, Politics, and the Struggle for Socialism

Michael Manley's fundamental orientation was one of social engineering for socialist goals. "We feel we must use social engineering to eliminate the errors of private enterprise," he said.[20] In other words, political management had a moral end. This separated Manley from the majority of Third World leaders for whom political management was a means to facilitate accumulation for themselves and other state functionaries.[21]

At the same time, this approach assumed that the primary vehicle for change would be an enlightened leadership directing the existent Jamaican state in a somewhat modified form. This approach ascribes to the state a rule over "sectional" interests, over working people and capitalists alike. It is not an outlook relying directly on the organizational and political strength — that is, on the active participation and control — of those who stand to benefit from the redistribution of social wealth and new relations of political and economic power. And it ignores the realities of state power as these have developed under the capitalist version of liberal democracy.[22]

As a parliamentary democracy, the Jamaican state must secure popular consent for governments and government actions. The existence of basic democratic rights and this need for popular consent provides a certain space for the expression of oppositional views and organizations around the goals of working people and the poor. There are severe constraints on this space, but the existence of a parliamentary democracy, instead of a dictatorship, represents a real gain for the masses and is an indication of their capacity to struggle.

On the other hand, the Jamaican state is also based on the separation of the masses from the means of political power. This separation is based on both the existing relations of political power and economic power. Politics are controlled by representatives elected for four or five years by cross-class constituencies; there is the administration and influence of civil servants and technocrats; and there is the power of the legal system, the standing army, and the police force.

Economic structures also exclude the masses from political power. First there is the massive direct political influence of capital, due to personal, social, and educational ties and due to what Hamza Alavi calls "the structural imperative" of the capitalist state. The leading actors within the government and bureaucracy operate according to the structural imperative of capitalism. This is not an imperative in the sense that it "predetermines *actions* of . . . the capitalist state. Rather, its imperative character lies in the fact that it determines the *consequences* of all such actions."[23] It did not take more than one term for the PNP government to discover these consequences.

Second, in a society based on gross inequalities and inequities, the majority of the population does not have the educational, ideological, or economic resources or the psychological orientation to intervene directly and consciously in the political affairs of state on an ongoing basis. The simple struggle for survival within what appears to be an inevitably unjust society further reduces the ability of the population to engage in political struggle.

These factors constitute the means by which effective political power is kept out of the hands of the majority. The exercise of political power by the state apparatus mirrors the separation of the masses from the means of economic power.

The role of the state is also the outcome of structures of patriarchal power. Patriarchal structures are not only the system of male domination and female subjugation — that is, unequal relations between the sexes in the economic, social, and political spheres. Patriarchal structures also reflect larger organizing principles for the structured power relations among humans, between the sexes, between different age groups, in our relationship with nature, in our systems of religious beliefs, perhaps even in our systems of scientific doctrine — above all, the idea that "power" is something exercised over certain groups, over society, over the economy, over nature, over other individuals. Power is the means to dominate.[24]

The combination of class and patriarchal structures of power systematically takes power away from specific social groups and classes who together constitute the vast majority of the population. In a sense, power ultimately is taken away from all individuals. Inasmuch as structures come to dominate society and dominate us as social actors, we all lose our ability to reshape and remodel the world of social relations in accordance with basic human needs. Marx said about the capitalist, "As a capitalist, he is only capital personified. His soul is the soul of capital."[25] What is true for a capitalist — a person with comparatively large social and economic power — is doubly true for the worker who is the mere muscle of capital, let alone for the unemployed person who is its waste product.

This takes us back to social democracy, liberalism, and radical social change. One of the acquisitions of social democracy is some sort of recognition of one of the basic goals of liberalism: the full development of the capabilities of the individual human being. One of the great failings of social democracy, though, is the implicit belief that this liberal ideal can be met in a semi-capitalist market society, that it can be achieved without totally different principles of economic and social organization. But on the other hand, where revolutionary socialists speak of a society geared to meeting human needs, too little attention is given to a transformation of the institutions through which we exercise political and social power; to the organization, and not simply the ownership, of production, and to our insertion into the natural environment.

Any understanding of the process of radical social transformation must focus on the dialectic between active political mobilization and consolidation of new socio-economic and political structures. One major factor is the process of popular mobilization and the radical shifts in consciousness that are both the result and the stimulant of mobilization. This is the one time when broad groups and classes simultaneously reevaluate the world in which they live and, by fits and starts, seek to reshape it. Individual interests are subordinated to the needs of the many, and yet at the same time, within this process, individual capacities are greatly expanded. Because the society which created and constantly nurtures an individual's psychology and motivations is interrupted, the psychology of "normalcy" and adjustment to an inhuman reality is also broken. The individual and collective power normally denied to the oppressed and the exploited is rediscovered and reasserted on the social and individual levels. This explosive coming together of individual and social change has been a theme in all social upheavals: it is Lenin's notion of revolution as a festival of the oppressed.

Because such a process does not happen smoothly, completely, or evenly, leadership is necessary to help ensure that the process of collective and individual self-discovery and self-activity continues to take place and achieves collective ends. It only takes place as the lived reality is shifted. Key to this is a shift in the exercise of political power.

Jamaican politics in particular, and West Indian politics in general, cannot be understood without acknowledging the role of a succession of strong, charismatic, male leaders. This is an especially important factor in patriarchal societies rooted in slavery. The legacy of colonialism (in which the governor was ultimately the government) lives on in the role of the strong individual leader. It lives on in the personification of the state. But at the same time there is a relation between the role of a strong, gifted leader in *this* tradition and the sort of technocratic and patriarchal view expressed in Manley's conception that the PNP and the Jamaican state would engineer a new society for the sufferers. Power would be exercised for the people, not by the people.[26]

There thus existed a constant tension between the ultimate goal of the democratic socialist project and the strategy for its attainment. The goal — sincerely believed in by the centre and left of the PNP — was a society of self-reliance and social justice. But the strategy failed to build new organizations of popular power or to bring about substantial reforms in the existing organs of the state. There was no attempt to reform the organization and operation of Parliament, parish councils, the electoral process, or the judiciary. The only attempt to change control of the police and army was the formation of the ineffectual Home Guards. There was much talk of political mobilization, but the so-called mobilization was often merely an exercise in developing support among the people for what the government was doing for them. The alternative — creating new programs and institutions to place power in the hands of the common people plus reforming existing institutions — was present in an embryonic fashion but was undermined either by the party right and the state bureaucracy, or by neglect.

The most heated debates within the PNP in its second term of office, between 1977 and 1980, were over economic policy, in particular over what relationship there should be with the International Monetary Fund. There was also a political dilemma, although it was rarely stated: how to preserve the hard-won gains of freedom of organization, speech, and fair elections, and at the same time displace the ideological and economic dominance of capital and promote the capture of political and economic power by working people and peasants.

Given the extremes of income distribution and economic power, given the scarcity of material resources (which precludes a rapid and massive assault on poverty and the many other inherited evils of colonialism and semi-colonialism), and given the legacy of political patronage and what Jamaicans call party "tribalism", is it necessary to institute a highly centralized and oppressive bureaucratic "socialism"? Are the hardships and acute tensions of economic development and the need to extract sacrifices not only from the rich but from working people and the poor in order to realize a real and lasting socio-economic transformation, incompatible with democracy and democratic rights? The answer given by Manley (and, from a somewhat different perspective, my answer as well) is no, they are not incompatible.

But in the end the PNP remained trapped within Westminsterism. A commitment to democratic rights and the extension of democracy was a vital and positive part of the PNP experiment and Manley's "Third Path" between capitalism and bureaucratic state socialism. This commitment was accompanied with an unflagging support not simply for the strengths but inadvertently for the limitations of the Westminster system. The inadequate backing given to institutions that would have in part supplemented and in part replaced the existing, insufficient democratic system blocked the possibilities of mobilization and self-reliance within the process of change.

The problem was compounded because the government remained committed to the institutions, norms, rules, and values of western parliamentary democracy even when all of these had been completely ridiculed, subverted, and made inoperative by the opposition. The commitment was demonstrated most clearly by the PNP's willingness to continue to abide by the polite rules of parliamentary life when the JLP was bringing in vehicles and weapons that were being used to kill hundreds of ghetto dwellers.

Dealing with a political opposition of this sort is one of the most vexing problems possible for any party that wants to retain political pluralism. Although it requires a much fuller discussion, a few observations seem in order here. It is the right of those struggling for a democratic and socialist society to circumscribe political liberties when the opposition steps beyond the practice of criticism, propaganda, and demonstration and begins arming itself and its supporters in order to bring down the system. But even then it is a matter of the balance of political forces and the government's capacity to enforce its will. The important point is to prevent the balance of forces from shifting in the opposition's favour to the point where it can mount such a campaign of terror with impunity. Preventing this requires, as argued above, the active political mobilization of the population in the process of change. Such a mobilization brings the population into the struggle for a new society as key actors rather than as passive recipients of government actions.

One of the most contentious issues in Jamaica and among the Caribbean left is the attitude to be adopted towards the press. In Jamaica in the late 1970s, the *Daily Gleaner* played a major role in disseminating misinformation and helping to promote a climate of fear, particularly among white-collar workers and the middle class. It has even been suggested that its techniques were learned from CIA media specialists. Comparisons with changes in papers such as *El mercurio* in Chile and *La Prensa* in Nicaragua seem to substantiate this charge. As a consequence, many of those on the PNP left and in the Workers' Party of Jamaica have subsequently talked of the need to close down such a paper; but such a policy would be an error on many counts.

First of all it would, in a single blow, turn the opinion of the world media against the experiment of change. A revolutionary socialist project can ill afford enemies among those who might otherwise be neutral or even sympathetic. Second, because of the murky ground that divides virulent criticism from libel and support for counterrevolutionary terrorism, it would set a precedent that limits free expression. The right of full and open debate in a society in transition is an indispensible requirement for the free flow of ideas that will allow the society to most fully confront its problems and openly discuss its options.

Does this mean that the media should be allowed to become an instrument not of opposition but of counterrevolution? There are a few key points. First the government must enforce laws against libel and malicious reporting. Second, the government needs to develop its own media. For this project to be successful, efforts must be made to avoid the self-proclamatory and heavily rhetorical coverage and language that leaves a population cynical and mistrustful. There is every reason for government-owned media to allow space for oppositional groups to present their ideas. Third, workers in the privately-owned media can be encouraged to fight at least for editorial control over (if not outright ownership of) the paper, TV, or radio station. Fourth, in situations of civil war, the government should reserve the right to censor reportage that directly and immediately relates to the war and war-related production. Because of the danger of abuse, such censorship must be exercised only as an emergency measure of last resort. Overall, however, the battle for ideas will not be won by censoring oppositional voices, but through education about, and mobilization for, the process of change.

Conclusion

The extension of political democracy is not only an essential part of a socialist vision but is a key strategy for attaining socialist transformation. The extension of political power to the population as a whole is inseparable from the overall process of active political mobilization. Such an extension requires the preservation or extension of liberal democratic rights; the development of new institutions of direct political power at the grassroots level; the creative reform of parliamentary institutions (where they actually exist) to make use of the advantages of a representative system based on political pluralism in combination with the new institutions of direct democracy; and, at the base of all this, economic changes that are necessary for meaningful political and social participation by the masses. Faced with the challenge of qualitatively transforming the realm of social, economic, and political power, the new society will be more than a socialist economy plus a pluralistic, liberal political system. The problems of socialist development will surely open up new concepts of political power, transcending not only the unequal power of different social classes within capitalism, but also the unequal power of worker and bureaucrat in the present-day post-capitalist societies of Europe and Asia.

Notes

1 See Michael Kaufman, *Jamaica Under Manley: Dilemmas of Socialism and Democracy* (Toronto: Between the Lines; London: Zed Books, 1985), chapters 4-9.

2 See Kaufman, *Jamaica Under Manley,* chaps. 1-3 for an analysis of Jamaican socio-economic and political structures.

3 People's National Party, "Principles and Objectives," September 1978, 65-66. A number of useful sources on democratic socialism are to be found in Michael Manley, *The Search for Solutions*, John Hearne, ed. (Oshawa: Maple House Publishing, 1976).

4 Michael Manley, "Democratic Socialism: The Jamaican Model," November 1974, in Manley, *Search for Solutions*, 156-57.

5 *Ibid*, 160.

6 Michael Manley, "Address to the National Executive Council of the PNP," September 28, 1975, in Manley, *Search for Solutions*, 70.

7 *Ibid.*

8 Carl Stone, "Jamaica's 1980 Elections," *Caribbean Review* 10, 2 (Spring 1981), 40.

9 The draft Emergency Production Plan — consisting of thirty-five mimeographed documents — has never been published and few copies still exist. For an examination of the draft EPP, see Kaufman, *Jamaica Under Manley*, 133-39.

10 The most important accounts of the birth and early evolution of the PNP are the two mammoth works by Ken Post, *Arise Ye Starvelings. The Jamaica Labour Rebellion and its Aftermath* (The Hague: Martinus Nijhoff, 1978), and *Strike the Iron: A Colony at War — Jamaica, 1939-1945* (New Jersey: Humanities Press, 1981).

11 This and the following two paragraphs closely follow Kaufman, *Jamaica Under Manley,* 59-62.

12 Michael Manley, *Jamaica: Struggle in the Periphery* (London: Third World Media/Writers and Readers Publishing Cooperative, 1982), 52.

13 Jamaica, Social Development Commission, "Guidelines on the Structure and Role of Community Councils," April 1979 (mimeographed), 12; and see Kaufman, *Jamaica Under Manley,* 154-157.

14 Jamaica, Social Development Commission, "Report on Regional Workshops in Preparation for the National Conference of Community Councils," February 1978, and "Report of the National Community Councils Conference," November 1979.

15 Jamaica, *Economic and Social Survey 1980*, Section 19, 14.

16 See Kaufman, *Jamaica Under Manley,* 100-04, 167-73.

17 The following three paragraphs closely follow Kaufman, *Jamaica Under Manley*, 167-73.

18 C.B. Macpherson, *The Life and Times of Liberal Democracy* (London: Oxford University Press, 1977), 2.

19 *Ibid.*

20 Michael Manley, *New York Times*, July 25, 1976.

21 For an examination of this tendency see the discussion in Clive Thomas' excellent volume, *The Rise of the Authoritarian State in Peripheral Societies* (New York: Monthly Review Press, 1984), 61-63, and *passim.*

22 Various parts of this section are based on Kaufman, *Jamaica Under Manley*, chapter 11.

23 Hamza Alavi, "State and Class Under Peripheral Capitalism," in *Introduction to the Sociology of 'Developing' Societies*, Hamza Alavi and Teodor Shanin, eds. (New York: Monthly Review Press, 1982), 294. Emphases in the original.

24 This is a much broader and more descriptive use of the term patriarchy than that advanced by Michele Barrett, for example, in her book, *Women's Oppression Today* (London: Verso Books, 1980).

25 Karl Marx, Capital, Volume I, Ben Fowkes, trans. (New York: Vintage Books, 1977), 342.

26 Although Manley represented these paternalistic politics it is important to note that as an individual he was one of the few men in the PNP during the 1970s with a strong personal commitment to women's liberation, a personal commitment he took right into his home.

Chapter 10

Capitalist Crisis, Imperialist Crisis, and the Response of the Nicaraguan Sandinista Revolution

Fred Judson

"STRUGGLE" IS SOMETHING most of us know as a concept rather than as a flesh and blood reality: in Nicaragua the revolutionaries speak of the radicalization the daily experience of the 1980s has brought, and they refer specifically to "feeling in your own flesh" the reality of imperialism and aggression when fighting the CIA-directed mercenaries, the contras. One political officer said that to see a comrade-in-arms fall in battle was "to feel in your own flesh just what imperialism is and what the Revolution is worth."[1] Francisco Gonzalez, then secretary of international relations of the Sandinista Trade Union Center, also referred to the effect of such an experience on one's political consciousness: "Every time a comrade falls, the people are more ready to take up a weapon."[2] Yet such individuals would be the first to declare that concepts and ideas are also weapons wielded in a struggle and indeed are a realm of struggle themselves.

Most students of the area would agree that the main focus of struggle in contemporary Central America is the Sandinista revolution in Nicaragua.[3] Two very broad questions about this struggle place it in the context of declining U.S. hegemony in the region. The first is "what is the general context of this struggle?"; that is, what is the situation facing the Central American revolution today? And second, "what is the response to that general context and situation?"

On the broadest conceptual level, the Central American revolution, in particular its manifestation as state power in Nicaragua, faces a crisis of capitalism compounded by a crisis of imperialism. The dimensions of that dual crisis and the literature dealing with it have become relatively familiar to specialists, but certain broad outlines merit repetition here.

The Crisis of Capitalism in Central America

The crisis in the capitalist economy is more severe in Central America than it is in North America or Western Europe. It has exacerbated the uneven development and underdevelopment of the dependent capitalism that characterizes the economies of the region. Distortions in the dependent economies have been more severe. All the figures for unemployment, underemployment, inflation, foreign debt, shortages of foreign exchange and basic consumer goods, as well as of capital, are far more severe than they are in North America.

Using a wide range of statistical sources, the Instituto de Investigaciones Económicas y Sociales (INIES) in Managua has produced a summary of economic indicators for the Central American economies.[4] Most of them speak for themselves; but INIES has drawn conclusions in its analysis of the figures. It points out that the regional GNP performance is only equal to the level reached fifteen years ago, and only Nicaragua had a GNP in 1984 higher than it was in 1980.[5] The fall in industrial production is an even sharper measure of what has happened to the Central American common market. The figures for consumption are roughly parallel; people are consuming 15 per cent less than they did five years ago. INIES points out that reduced consumption is not due to increased investment, but to reduced production. In 1980, investment rates as a proportion of GNP were nearly twice the rates in 1984-85.

The first set of figures is specifically a regional and national measure of the crisis in the capitalist economies, while in the figures for exports, foreign debt, and terms of trade, the impact of the crisis in the capitalist world economy can be measured. As a result of the overall 25 per cent deterioration in the terms of trade, for example, "in effect, our region has lost $4.5 billion."[6] It is not so much a drop in production of export products; rather, the prices available on the world market have dropped, while the prices of imported goods have increased. To this must be added two kinds of capital flight. The first is a flight of national capital, seeking more profitable investment opportunities abroad. The second is capital that leaves the regional economies as payments, debt servicing, and increased interest on new and old loans. INIES calculates that Central America has "helped to finance the deficits of the developed countries with some $40 billion in the five years, double what the UN Economic Commission on Latin America calculated would be necessary to finance regional development in the decade 1980-90."[7]

Table 1

Central America In Figures, 1980-84

GNP ($U.S. millions)	1980	1981	1982	1983	1984
Costa Rica	3410	3332	3087	3160	3254
El Salvador	3342	3065	2893	2893	2937
Guatemala	8455	8514	8216	8027	8027
Honduras	2420	2449	2405	2393	2441
Nicaragua	2219	2337	2309	2401	2368
GNP % Change					
Costa Rica	0.8	−2.3	−7.3	2.3	3.0
El Salvador	−9.0	−8.3	−5.6	0	1.5
Guatemala	3.7	0.7	−3.5	−2.7	0
Honduras	2.8	1.2	−1.8	−0.5	2.0
Nicaragua	10.0	5.3	−1.2	4.0	−1.4
GNP per Capita (1980=100)					
Costa Rica	100	95	86	85	86
El Salvador	100	89	82	79	78
Guatemala	100	98	94	87	85
Honduras	100	98	95	89	88
Nicaragua	100	102	97	98	94
GNP — Industrial (% Change)					
Costa Rica	0.8	−0.5	−14.9	−1.8	4.0
El Salvador	−15.5	−15.8	−8.4	−4.3	0
Guatemala	6.3	−2.5	−5.8	−2.1	0
Honduras	7.8	1.7	−1.3	0.6	2.0
Nicaragua	11.8	2.9	−1.7	4.6	0.2
Consumption per Capita (1980=100)					
Costa Rica	100	95	87	88	90
El Salvador	100	91	83	81	80
Guatemala	100	101	96	96	95
Honduras	100	98	98	95	94
Nicaragua	100	98	91	91	90

Table 1 (continued)

Exports ($U.S. Millions)	1980	1981	1982	1983	1984
Costa Rica	1001	1002	871	851	960
El Salvador	1075	798	704	732	780
Guatemala	1520	1299	1200	1092	1150
Honduras	850	784	677	695	740
Nicaragua	451	500	406	429	382
Terms of Trade (1979=100)					
Costa Rica	96.3	82.4	74.1	70.4	71.8
El Salvador	85.2	74.4	75.5	70.1	70.4
Guatemala	85.0	74.8	70.1	59.2	58.8
Honduras	101.9	87.6	87.1	86.3	85.6
Nicaragua	98.0	92.6	83.8	72.9	77.6
Foreign Debt ($U.S. Millions)					
Costa Rica	3183	3360	3497	3848	4050
El Salvador	1176	1471	1683	2000	2300
Guatemala	1053	1409	1504	1776	2420
Honduras	1510	1708	1800	2079	2250
Nicaragua	1579	2163	2797	3838	4529
Foreign Debt as % of GNP					
Costa Rica	71.0	121.3	144.0	126.8	133.5
El Salvador	33.0	42.5	47.2	70.0	80.0
Guatemala	13.4	16.4	17.2	19.6	26.7
Honduras	62.4	69.7	74.8	86.9	92.1
Nicaragua	72.1	83.9	94.2	107.3	119.1
Debt Service as % of Exports					
Costa Rica	47.6	50.6	35.9	80.7	79.0
El Salvador	12.8	20.0	30.8	30.0	27.0
Guatemala	7.9	13.7	15.7	22.4	24.8
Honduras	25.2	33.3	40.9	34.4	36.2
Nicaragua	13.3	34.2	48.3	40.0	57.2

Table 1 (continued)

Consumer Price Index (% Change)

	1980	1981	1982	1983	1984
Costa Rica	17.8	65.1	90.0	33.0	17.0
El Salvador	18.6	11.6	13.8	15.5	15.0
Guatemala	9.1	8.7	2.5	15.4	7.0
Honduras	15.0	9.2	9.5	10.2	12.5
Nicaragua	24.8	23.2	24.8	37.3	60.0

Unemployment (% of Economically Active Population)

Costa Rica	8.1	9.7	14.4	10.9	12.0
El Salvador	16.2	25.0	30.0	30.0	35.0
Guatemala	31.2	34.2	38.8	41.7	42.9
Honduras	15.0	19.3	20.4	21.2	25.0
Nicaragua	18.3	15.9	18.5	17.5	21.1

Source: *Data Bank INIES/CRIES* (Managua 1985).

The combination of deteriorating terms of trade and the increased costs of capital has caused a precipitous rise in the foreign debt. The regional external debt doubled between 1980 and 1984 to some $16 billion, while the proportion of export earnings devoted to debt servicing also doubled, and in the case of Nicaragua, nearly quadrupled. The story was even more dramatic in the case of the proportion of export earnings consumed by interest payments. At the national economic level, these increases were parallelled by tax increases and national budget deficits. The latter rose from 5 per cent of GNP in 1980 to 10 per cent in 1984, with Nicaragua "breaking records with a deficit of nearly 25 per cent of GNP in 1984."[8] In addition, such deficit spending does not indicate productive investment since, particularly in the case of Nicaragua, spending has been increasingly directed to defence needs.

Inflation, of course, is an indicator of economic crisis in Central America, but other figures speak more directly of the human suffering caused by the crisis. Unemployment, for example, is a direct measure, and it has risen at the regional level from 15 per cent in 1980 to approximately 25 per cent in 1984. As INIES puts it, some "three million Central Americans able to work cannot, while underemployment has risen from approximately 25 per cent to some 50 per cent...this means that three-fourths of the economically active population either has no work or work that is insufficient to earn a living."[9] Such a reality is reflected in an increased rate of urban in-migration from rural areas. Managua, for example, is currently estimated to have nearly one million people, sharply up from the 600,000-700,000 at the time of the popular insurrection in 1979. In addition, the informal sector is absorbing more and more of the work force, as workers either cannot find jobs in the formal sector or opt for the statistically better chances of informal sector incomes keeping pace with inflation.

INIES' survey of statistics from a wide variety of sources also concludes that there has been an overall decline in nutritional and health standards in the region during the last five years. Consequently, with the notable exception of Nicaragua, caloric intake and protein consumption have fallen, while infant mortality has risen. In the case of Nicaragua, the advances in public health and the social wage subsidies of the basic food basket have kept the figures from worsening. Yet Nicaragua has had to cut back on public expenditures on health since 1983. The primary reason this has not had such an adverse effect is that much of the improvement in health standards in Nicaragua after 1979 was the result of popular mobilizations, for example, in vaccination and hygiene campaigns.

Two other reasons account for the regional deterioration in living standards. First, income distribution, with the exception of Nicaragua, has become more unequal in the last five years.[10] Second, the human rights situation has been abysmal in Central America since 1980: "no less than 200,000 people have died by force of arms since 1980, while one million have been displaced from their residences."[11]

To say the least, the impact on Central America of the capitalist crisis is dramatic. Just considering the deteriorating terms of trade, the figures are stunning. In 1977, for example, Central American coffee producers could purchase a particular tractor with the earnings from 77 bags of coffee. In 1981, they had to produce 224 bags to purchase the same tractor.[12] Nicaragua's Ministry of Foreign Trade informed U.S. delegations in the summer of 1983, again regarding the purchasing power of coffee, that while in 1972 one bag of coffee could purchase thirteen barrels of oil, by 1981 only three barrels could be purchased with the same amount of coffee. Even in the case of cotton, which has not had such a vertiginous drop in value, the terms of trade have deteriorated. In 1972, 319 bags of cotton could purchase a certain tractor, but in 1981 it took 461.[13] And the terms of trade have deteriorated further since 1981.

One of the reasons why the capitalist crisis has struck Central America with such an impact is that it came after two decades of sustained economic growth. Thus, as Petras and Morley point out in this volume, what Central America experienced in the 1960s and 1970s was not the underdevelopment of stagnation and non-growth. Rather, economic growth, according to the United Nations Economic Commission on Latin America, averaged a 5.3 per cent annual increase in GNP in Central America from 1950 to 1978.[14] But after 1978, the area registered a growth rate for four years of minus 1.3 per cent, even below the average of minus 0.3 per cent for Latin America as a whole, and well below that for the world of plus 2.6 per cent for 1978-82.[15]

The post-war period of growth in Central America, as Walter LaFeber's book shows in a readable and non-technical way, gave the present economic crisis of capitalism in the region its character.[16] It was very rapid growth, with two central distortions. First, it was agro-export-led growth; coffee, cotton, beef, and sugar export production took up more and more of the best lands. Second, industrial expansion followed the import substitution pattern: expensive consumer items directed to a limited market were produced by branches of multinational corporations while secondary finishing and assembly industries fulfilled a role in the global plans of some of the same multinationals. Industrialization was neither national nor rational, and the nature and consequences of that growth provide the material basis for the political crisis of the local ruling classes and their ally and mentor at the international level, the United States imperial state. The politicization of increasing numbers of landless peasants in the region has to be seen in this light, as has the increased propensity of the urban population for political organization.[17]

Economic contradictions accumulated on three levels in the Central American economies. National economies suffered the strains of dependent capitalist development. The regional economy was distorted by parallel production of the same agro-export commodities and by the industrial advantage enjoyed by Guatemala and El Salvador in the Central American Common Market. At the same time, the insertion of the Central American economies into a world capitalist economy exhibiting the strains of a general crisis of capitalist accumulation had its price.[18] In fact, the Central American economies have been economies of permanent crisis for decades, notwithstanding the statistical growth (as opposed to "development") registered in the post-war period.

Dimensions of the Crisis of Imperialism

Compounding what amounts, then, to a double capitalist crisis in Central America, which not only the Nicaraguan Revolution but all Central America must face, is the crisis of imperialism. Essentially the crisis of U.S. imperialism is the decline of empire, economically, politically, and ideologically. Although Marxists and others with an analysis rooted in the vocabulary of political economy may speak of hegemonic decline, while the U.S. "New Right" speaks of the "Vietnam syndrome", both are referring to the underlying fact that U.S. capitalism is not as powerful, in relative terms, as it was during the twenty-odd years following World War II. European and Japanese competition have challenged the United States' economy in the areas of marketing, productivity, control of resources, and technological development. The basic industrial plant of the United States has deteriorated while other economies have modernized. Some Third World economies have come to challenge the formerly strong, if not dominant, position of selected smokestack industries, textiles, even pharmaceuticals. Actually existing socialist economies have grown steadily and have become more numerous, restricting the prospects for capitalist expansion as well as competing in certain commodity markets.

The position of the dollar, however strong it may seem from time to time, has been steadily eroded since the massive deficit spending of the Vietnam War was married to the "Great Society" social spending of the 1960s. The militaristic budget overruns of the Carter and Reagan administrations have continued the erosion process. The looming and continuing Third World debt crisis combines with this objectively to weaken the dollar, while the policy of high interest rates appears to be a desperate attempt to maintain the dominant position of United States finance capital.[19] Sooner or later, though, the dollar's worth will depend on productive investment and productivity, not massive capital transfers from the Third World and the artificial health of armaments industries.

In the United States, the crisis of imperialism has been felt mostly as an economic crisis, in the dimensions of production, competitiveness, and currency strength. The existence of large numbers of marginalized workers is witness to this, as are the "chronically depressed" regions. This is to some extent a reflection of the unevenness of capitalist development, shown for example in the phenomenon of runaway industries, the exhaustion of natural resources, and the operation of commodity cycles. Currently, the restructuring of capitalist production at the international and national levels appears to be imposing on capital the strategy of enlarging the reserve army of labour. Capital is attacking the existing division of surplus value, claiming more for itself as a way to resolve the crisis of accumulation. This strategy, when added to certain political and ideological strategies of capital within the United States, amounts to what Marlene Dixon and Susanne Jonas have called the "implosion of empire."[20]

Until recently, the centre of the empire, or at least large numbers within the centre, enjoyed bourgeois democracy. Repression and direct rule by capital, unhampered by populism, characterized the empire's holdings in the Third World. Dictatorship was for "them" and the ideological apparatus in the centre convinced the majority of the centre that empire had nothing to do with Third World poverty, repression, and dictatorship. Now, as Dixon and Jonas write, "it is the very beginning of an era in which the people of the United States will begin to see the democratic veils stripped away from the face of American power; they will begin to experience what has been the fate of the colony."[21] Unemployment, which has become less intermittent and more chronic for larger numbers, deteriorating social services, growing numbers of the homeless, increasing evidence of illiteracy, malnutrition, and restricted access to medical care are one dimension of the implosion: immiseration. Attacks on civil rights legislation, affirmative action programs, and reproductive rights are another. Such attacks constitute an attempt to reinstitute a higher degree of racism and sexism which have historically characterized the United States.

Along the political dimension, the political right in power has launched attacks on the freedom-of-information legislation and loosened the Watergate-Vietnam era fetters on the domestic police and intelligence agencies. Stricter loyalty oaths and penalties for government employees with access to national security information have parallelled measures against draft resisters, Central American solidarity organizations, anti-apartheid activists, and anti-nuclear and anti-militarist movements. Ideologically, an offensive has been launched to isolate dissent through an appeal to anti-communism and the trusted myths of capitalism: free enterprise as God's will, the citizens of the United States as the chosen people, the United States as the defender of the free world, the marketplace as the proper distributor of goods and values, wealth as virtue, poverty as punishment for sins, and capital as the creator of value and jobs.

The implosion of empire, however, is not enough to resolve the crisis of U.S. capitalism or the crisis of empire, and the capitalist class is not united around a single strategy for imperial recovery. Some strong transnational capitalist elements and particularly finance capital (with tremendous loans outstanding in the Third World) are not certain that revived militarism in the economy and interventionism abroad provide solutions to the crisis of accumulation; in the meantime, they cannot come up with a coherent plan for solutions or for domestic political hegemony. So what Petras and Morley identify as statism, however ideologically reactionary and militaristic, proceeds with deficit military production and protectionism buttressed by high interest rates to attract foreign capital. It is as though the trilateralism of the Carter administration has remained politically neutralized by the ideological offensive of the right, while the right itself is unable to present an alternative imperial vision.

The Santa Fe document[22] discloses the core elements of the ideological offensive of the right in response to the decline of imperial hegemony, and in particular to the Somoza, Shah, and Gairy "shocks". With the Reagan administration's foreign policy, the empire returned with a vengeance to interventionism, to force as the preferred policy. The ideological repertoire of this renewed interventionism includes anti-communism and containment from the Cold War, "anti-terrorism" to bring it in line with the 1970s and 1980s, and an appeal to 1950s chauvinism: "America is back." Underlying the renewal of interventionism in this epoch of imperial decline is not so much a response to the more recent "shocks" as a deeper and more psychological imperial reaction to the defeat in Indochina. The experience of the Indochina wars provides both the ideological rationale and the strategic thinking for the present wave of interventionism. Nonetheless, imperialism would see itself obliged to resort more and more to direct intervention, whether hegemonic decline had been accompanied by the Indochina defeats or not. The fact is that the economic crisis of imperialism puts client regimes at risk, while the political crisis of imperialism compounds the economic problems. As the client regimes[23] face revolution, political and economic decline, and the waning enthusiasm of regional gendarmes and alliance structures, imperialism resorts more and more to the political, economic, and military support of repressive and isolated regimes, supported by a clear threat of direct intervention. The paradox is that such regimes are necessarily regimes of superexploitation and virulently anti-popular, which puts them even more at risk and forces imperialism seriously to entertain the possibility of direct intervention, with its unknown risks.

What the crisis of imperialism amounts to in Central America is one of those world-historical dialectical processes that are the delight of materialists. The crisis of capitalist accumulation, both in the long term (the role of the region in the world capitalist division of labour) and the short term (rapid and uneven growth since 1950; the current stresses) set the material conditions for what LaFeber terms the "inevitable revolutions" of the region. The crisis of imperialism, manifested in ever more repressive military regimes and massive U.S. intervention in the region, accelerates polarization and radicalization there, while simultaneously diverting resources from the U.S. economy and contributing to the implosion of empire within the United States.

The reality of this dialectic is a tragedy in human lives. Thus all the military manoeuvres and training of local military forces, the massive economic and military aid advocated in the report of the Kissinger Commission, the invasion of Grenada, the blockade and embargo of the Nicaraguan economy and the CIA-contra attacks on the people of Nicaragua, the U.S.-directed, funded, and supported war against the Salvadoran population — all amount to the pain of superexploitation and the suffering of aggression. Thus the struggle returns from the conceptual realm to that of flesh and blood. The Nicaraguan Revolution must struggle in both realms.

The Nicaraguan Response, A Sandinista Response

Nicaragua is the one country of the region which has so far achieved national liberation from the dictatorships and oligarchies that have characterized the whole region, except for Costa Rica. It can be argued, therefore, that Nicaragua has the best political base from which to respond to the crisis. It takes state power to respond to the crisis effectively, and revolutionary state power has considerably more space in which to operate.

One of the first questions to be addressed in considering the Nicaraguan revolution's response to the crisis of capitalism and imperialism in Central America is that of its political character. To what degree is the Sandinista revolution a socialist revolution and in what way is Nicaraguan socialism unique in theory and practice? This is not an easy question to answer, but in general the ideology of the Sandinista National Liberation Front (FSLN) denotes socialism as the goal of the revolution. Though Cesar Augusto Sandino, from whom the FSLN takes its inspiration, was not himself a Marxist, the most important contemporary interpreter of Sandinismo, Carlos Fonseca Amador, was.[24] Fonseca, commented Tomas Borge, said that the Sandinistas were revolutionaries more "from feelings of disgrace and dignity than from consciousness," more in practice than in theory.[25]

The writings and speeches of the members of the FSLN National Directorate can be called essentially Marxist in vocabulary and methodology.[26] The FSLN newspaper *Barricada* is too, particularly in the language it uses in its editorials and in the section called "Lunes Socio-Económico." The Sandinistas call their basic political principle the "logic of the majority" and declare that they act in the name of the poor and the working majority of Nicaraguans. In his May 1, 1982 speech, for example, Commandant Tomas Borge, minister of the interior and the sole surviving founder of the FSLN, used the following language to discuss the character of the Nicaraguan revolutionary process:

> This revolution was made, not to reaffirm the old society, but to create a new society. This struggle, which is fundamentally a task of the working class, has special characteristics stemming from the economic, historical and cultural conditions of Nicaragua.... Our economy...developed as a dependent economy. This forced our people to struggle for their national liberation, and this struggle took on a specific form, which is nationalism.... That is why the struggle of our people took the form of a struggle against the *Somocista* dictatorship, which was, in its essence, a struggle against imperialism. And through this dialectical link between national liberation and the anti-Somoza struggle victory was reached, a victory that took the *form* of the overthrow of the *Somocista* tyranny, but whose *content* was a victory of national liberation.[27]

Borge sees the role of the FSLN within this struggle as that of the vanguard party, in classical Marxist terms, which he prefers to call the "theory of revolution":

> It was the FSLN, it was *sandinismo* that knew how to apply the theory of revolution to the concrete reality of Nicaragua. Therefore, the FSLN was the living instrument for the conquest of power by the workers, and the living instrument for the consolidation of the power of the workers. What does this mean? Just like the human body needs vitamins and protein to nourish itself and develop, the Sandinista front needs to draw its sustenance from the working class. The vitamins and protein of the Sandinista front are the Nicaraguan workers and peasants. The intellectuals, professionals and other sectors of society who want to identify with the Sandinista people's revolution, must identify with the interests of the workers and peasants.[28]

Sandinismo is perhaps a more pragmatic socialism than some academics and activists of the left would prefer. In ideological terms the revolution is committed to political pluralism, a mixed economy, non-alignment and anti-imperialism. Private property remains the majority sector in the economy, though not in political life: "there will be a mixed economy but political power is in the hands of the working people."[29] Tomas Borge has often pointed out that a mixed economy in a country where there has been a revolution must be distinguished from one where there has not. Mexico and Venezuela, for example, both have mixed economies, but there the concessions are made to the working class by the bourgeoisie and the state. In Nicaragua it is the working class and the state which grant concessions to the bourgeoisie.[30] Jaime Wheelock Roman spells out the pragmatic approach of *sandinismo* as a body of revolutionary thought and practice:

> We are not just working with objective or material conditions, but political ones, too. The popular Sandinista Revolution triumphed as a product of a series of very peculiar factors which the vanguard took advantage of to produce the revolution in 1979. To make the revolution we had to force history a bit and base ourselves in a series of factors in the society, some of which were mature, others of which were not, but they all determined that we would be able to overthrow the dictatorship. More than developing the struggle between capitalism and socialism we had to develop a struggle of the whole people against the dictatorship for national liberation...we find that it was not always the advanced or organized sectors of the industrial working class that sustained, in a stubborn, stable and massive way the banners of the revolution. It was the peasant base and the urban poor and the students.[31]

Perhaps revolutionary Nicaragua is more properly termed a transitional social formation moving towards socialism; it contains a socialism in struggle in a different sense than that in which Cuban socialism is a socialism in struggle:

> What Reagan and his administration fear the most is that here we are developing an authentically national model — national, Latin American, and in addition a continuation of the work of Bolivar, Marti, and Sandino.... The appeal and attractiveness of a revolution like this — humanist, generous, anti-dictatorial, participationist, popular, involving social transformations, with economic successes, with great support worldwide — is a defeat for imperialism much greater than the defeat we handed them in battle. It is something bigger than Nicaragua, something more important than a local revolution. This revolution shattered a general model of imperialist power, and for that reason some of the imperialists think that the end is near, that this is the beginning of the end for imperialism.[32]

Response to the Economic Crisis

In the economic sphere, the Nicaraguan revolution confronts four realities: the legacy of underdevelopment and the form it took under the Somoza dictatorship,[33] the exceptional destruction wrought during the war of liberation (see table 2), the impact of the regional and global capitalist crisis, and the costs of the ongoing United States/contra war and United States economic blockade/embargo.

The first reality is summed up by the Ministry of Foreign Trade:

> During the period of Somoza's rule, Nicaragua's economy was fundamentally one that fit into the international division of labour by means of its exported goods — chiefly cotton, coffee, bananas, and such minerals as gold and silver. In the case of the mineral products, the transnational corporations were directly involved, basically those representing North American capital. The Somoza group, having political hegemony, also took advantage of the country's natural wealth, appropriating for itself the profits from those exports.[34]

The basic policy of the Sandinistas for dealing with this inherited agro-export economy is twofold. First, because the need for foreign exchange is so pressing, in order to pay debt-service charges and to purchase needed food, medicines, arms, raw materials, capital goods, and spare parts, the agro-export economy must be maintained and expanded. Thus coffee, sugar, cotton, and beef production have proceeded and investments have been devoted to their expansion. Second, adjustments have been made to compensate for overemphasis, for example, with the reduction in the amount of cotton hectares. Plans have been made for the eventual development of agro-industrial capacity:

> Nicaragua should base its development on the industrial transformation of its own natural resources, taking as a base the agro-pecurian sector. Agro-industry

Table 2
Economic Costs of the War of Liberation

Categories	Millions of Dollars	Percentage
Physical Destruction	481	21
Decapitalization and Theft	518	23
Economic Inactivity	1,246	56
Total	2,245	100

From: Jaime Wheelock Roman, *Entre La Crisis y La Agresión: La Reforma Agraria Sandinista* (Managua: Editorial Nueva Nicaragua, 1985), 116. Sources: *UN Economic Commission on Latin America*; Nicaraguan Ministry of National Planning.

should be the axis of such an industrial transformation, which should include forest resources, fishing and mining. With that development it will be possible to overcome dependency and advance in the struggle against backwardness and underdevelopment.[35]

There are several hitches: economic sabotage of the agro-export economy by the contras and the CIA, the U.S. embargo on trade with Nicaragua, the need to increase food production for national consumption, diversion of some of the formerly available rural landless labourers to full-time employment, reduced productivity levels due to war damage and the reduction of working hours for the formerly superexploited rural labourers, decapitalization, and uneven cooperation from the capitalist agro-export sector. The revolution has responded with a variety of policies: generous credits to private producers, cancellation of most small farmers' debts in July 1983, change of the academic year to permit students to participate as volunteers in the crucial harvest months of November to February, provisions in land reform to enable some of the landless to become agro-export producers, expropriation of decapitalized, abandoned, or willfully misused large estates, and diversification of markets.[36] The rationale, as explored by Collins, is that private property per se will not be expropriated, but the product will be socialized. Private property has a social mortgage on it, a moral responsibility to produce, and marketing as well as exports are controlled by the revolutionary state.

The second economic reality is one around which reconstruction programs have centred. To begin to cover the losses shown in Table 2, the foreign debt has increased exponentially. Besides that, writes Wheelock, "we had to pay resettlement costs, social security pensions, back wages, all in the midst of falling prices for our products."[37] The first three years of the revolution were years of massive infrastructure investments, social spending, and purchases of productive inputs for agriculture and industry. In addition, large sums were spent on consumer goods. Job creation, one of the commitments of the revolution, "represented a significant degree of indebtedness, but as revolutionaries, after so many years of struggle we were anxious for the people's welfare."[38] "Besides," he adds, "we had commitments for health, education and later subsidies for basic goods."[39]

The third reality, the capitalist crisis, is just the same as the first, but many of the policies directed to the first include policies directed to the third set of problems. Again, the logic of the majority dictates the fundamental policies, those of feeding the population and restructuring the economy. Food self-sufficiency is the goal, first in the provision of basic foods such as corn, beans, and rice, and then progressively increasing production of meat, poultry, fish, eggs, cooking oil, soya, sesame, etc. In 1982, for example, "we've grown — compared to what there was under Somoza — 10 per cent more corn, 45 per cent more beans, 89 per cent more sorghum, and 100 per cent more rice."[40] The 1982 figures for cooking oil, egg, pork, fish, and chicken production were even more impressive.

The long-term agricultural policy combines an agro-industrial strategy with food self-sufficiency:

> Exploit the Pacific zone through overcoming the prolonged dry season with irrigation, which will permit cultivation all year long of successive crops — sorghum, corn, beans, cotton, etc. — the best soils of the country for intensive annual agriculture; use the climatic conditions, i.e. the rainfall, that the north central zone has, for cattle and coffee; and finally, rationally exploit the vast humid tropical plain of the Atlantic region for perennial cultivation — African palm, coconut, rubber, cocoa, spices, bananas, tubers.[41]

As the United States/contra war endures, problems in the daily food supply have arisen. These problems are based in the following conditions.

> The phenomenon of shortages is related to two distinct problems. On the one hand, there is the question of the efficiency of the food production system and the flow of inputs and outputs throughout the food production chain. Several problems converge here which prevent food from reaching consumers on a regular basis, or in sufficient quantity or at prices that are within their reach. On the other hand, shortages must be understood as a symptom of the revolutionary transformation of income and consumption structures. The development of more equitable structures generates a higher level of demand and consumption, which places pressure upon supplies and creates conditions tending towards shortages.[42]

In response, the Sandinistas have sought to rationalize the economy, both to deal with the capitalist crisis and to manage the costs of the United States/contra war.[43] Spending on social services has been curtailed, land reform has accelerated, systems to guarantee the supplies of basic food goods through subsidies and rational distribution have been developed. As *Envio* says, "on the short-term level, there are no real solutions. Since the lack of foreign exchange is the major limitation, it is difficult to foresee a period in the near future when Nicaragua will be able to resolve completely the food shortage problem."[44] One short-term solution has been to solicit donations and foreign aid, as well as loans and lines of credit with which to purchase food and agricultural inputs. In 1985, considerable success was achieved using this strategy. As Foreign Minister D'Escoto said July 6, 1985 to the Central American Historical Institute: "the embargo was something like a blessing in disguise, because it won us considerable solidarity in Europe."[45] Both the visit of President Daniel Ortega and the aid mission of Vice-President Sergio Ramirez to Europe in 1985 were successful.

But with high interest rates and reduced world purchases of tropical products (both among the effects created by the global capitalist crisis), there are no short-term solutions to the problems of the agro-export economy in Nicaragua. With the structural legacy of underdevelopment and the impact of the crisis (limiting regional and world markets, and lowering prices), diversification of production and marketing has its limits. U.S. aggression compounds the problems of the three economic realities. Not surprisingly, Sandinista policies developed to confront these realities converge. Agro-industrial development — that is, food processing, a textile industry based on cotton, diversification of production and markets, investments in infrastructure and transport which will coordinate and more closely unify the national economy — provides the long-term structural solution. Land use changes which both follow the logic of the majority and further the overall development of the economy are also being planned: the application of advanced technology to basic food production, irrigation projects, incentives for diversification.

In the Collins and Wheelock volumes, the political element in the Sandinista response to the three economic realities emerges clearly. The FSLN intends to foster cooperatives rather than state farms as the priority, yet the emphasis of land reform speeches and ceremonies around the time of the sixth anniversary of the revolution in June and July 1985 was on land for the small peasant and landless producer.[46] The Sandinistas have remained flexible and committed to a mixed economy in agriculture: private enterprise is generously assisted by the state and can garner a healthy profit, but workers must be respected and the new laws on labour rights, minimum wages, and working conditions must also be respected.[47] Large productive units belonging to *Somocistas* and decapitalized or idle estates have, for the most part, become state farms. The FSLN has sought to strike a balance between social justice, the need to produce, the commitment to pluralism and a mixed economy, the socialist and cooperative principles of *Sandinismo*, and the peasant desire for land.

The fourth economic reality which faces the Nicaraguan revolution is the most immediate: the impact of the United States/contras. Comandante Daniel Ortega summed up this impact in May 1984: "the attacks on economic objectives have been costly and damaging, resulting in the necessity of reorienting material resources and labor power to defense of the homeland."[48] The war, which began in earnest in 1981, has had an increasing human and material cost. In 1981, damages were assessed at $220,000, but in 1982 they had risen to $23 million, in 1983 to $128 million, and in 1984, to $206 million by November.[49] The total costs, counting lost production, diversion of resources, and suspended projects, amounts to some $3 billion dollars: "$679 million in physical damages, $427 million in lost production, $364 million in suspended projects, etc."[50]

There is no area of the national economy which remains unaffected by the state terrorism the United States is waging against Nicaragua. The damage extends from the well-known mining of Nicaragua's harbours to cattle rustling by the mercenary bands, from attacks on peasant cooperatives to destruction of hydroelectric projects and road-building equipment.[51] Economic warfare at the international level (actions taken by the United States to block loans) have resulted in a drop in the participation of multilateral loan agencies in Nicaragua's external financing from 32.3 per cent in 1980 to 15.6 per cent in 1983.[52]

Social programs have suffered since schools, popular food distribution centres, clinics, and adult education collectives have been contra targets. As the CIA manual "Psychological Operations in Guerrilla Warfare," reportedly being used by the contras in the fall of 1984, demonstrates, health workers, artists, agronomists, teachers, and community organizers are specific targets of the terrorist groups organized and directed by the CIA. Some 135 volunteer adult education teachers had been killed up to May 1984.[53] Programs to extend electric power, clean water, and improve housing and roads to rural areas had been severely disrupted and some 200,000 people had been relocated from the border areas.

The costs of confronting this reality have been very high. Up to half the national budget is now dedicated to defence and austerity affects every sector of national life: "in short, the standard of living of all Nicaraguans has, to a greater or lesser degree, been affected in multiple ways by the U.S. administration's policy of state terrorism."[54] The human costs are also very high. There have been over 8,000 victims among the killed, wounded, and kidnapped, with the numbers drastically increasing in 1984.

The economic response of the revolution has been considerable: budget austerity, hard currency controls, new taxes, reductions in subsidies, increased control of basic goods distribution, concentration of efforts in food and export crop production, self-defence cooperatives, and military units in the export crop harvests.[55]

Dimensions of the Crisis of Imperialism in Central America

There are three broad areas in the crisis of imperialism and a number of corresponding measures the empire has taken to restructure itself in Central America. First, there are revolutionary movements in the area, in Guatemala, El Salvador, and Nicaragua, and in Nicaragua one has come to power. As Walter LaFeber has shown, this was inevitable. Revolution, though, brings counterrevolution; this corollary is considered by the Sandinistas to be a natural phenomenon, a law of history.[56] Second, Central America, under the impact of revolutionary movements and the crisis of capitalism, has lost its former condition of being the secure "backyard" of imperialism. Because of this, the imperial centre itself appears beleaguered; national security is at stake. As the tongue-in-cheek title of Stan Persky's book puts it, the crisis of imperialism in Central America makes "America the last domino."[57] Third, the ideological apparatus of imperialism in Central America has been crumbling. The language and symbolism of imperialism is no longer sufficient, either in Central America or in the United States, to justify dictatorships, death squads, superexploitation, and unequal exchange.

The first response of imperialism has been a military restructuring in Central America. As the American Friends Service Committee report of June 1985 ("Invasion: Guide to the U.S. Military Presence in Central America") shows, military programs in the area increased from $10 million in 1980 to $254 million in fiscal year 1986.[58] In El Salvador, the United States has spent nearly half a billion dollars building up the government forces and has become increasingly involved itself in the war against the civilian population and the revolutionary forces of the FMLN.[59] The United States has sought to make Honduras a new regional gendarme to replace Somoza's Nicaragua and to create as well a base for direct intervention against Nicaragua, and the revolutionary movements in El Salvador and Guatemala.[60] Costa Rica is also the subject of militarization: U.S. military aid, which amounted to $350,000 in 1981 and between one and two million dollars in 1982 and 1983, "during 1984 and the first two months of 1985, climbed to almost 18 million dollars," according to the Costa Rican vice-minister of public security.[61] The publications of the International Institute for Strategic Studies in London report that while there were 5,000 armed soldiers in 1981, the Costa Rican forces now number nearly 15,000.[62] U.S. military advisors have established programs in Costa Rica, and military road and base construction near the Nicaraguan border started in 1985.

The United States has also mounted a series of massive land, sea, and air manoeuvres, mostly centred in Honduras, over the last five years. One of these exercises became reality in October of 1983, with the invasion of Grenada. Permanent naval, air, and land forces have been stationed in Honduras, El Salvador, and off the Nicaraguan coasts. The attacks on Nicaraguan ports from CIA mother ships and by fast boats are well known. They resulted in the International Court of Justice case in The Hague.[63]

But the core of the military response to the crisis of imperialism has been the organization, funding, and direction of the contra forces based in Honduras and Costa Rica. Long familiar to the public, the use of these contra forces constitutes state terrorism by the U.S. government, and their activities are combined with CIA operations designed to provoke confrontations between

Nicaragua and its neighbours, to create domestic opposition and to establish an ideological climate in the U.S. which would permit direct intervention.[64] Recent press reports on foreign mercenaries in Costa Rica have raised serious questions about Costa Rican neutrality and the complicity of the Monge government with the contra forces, while the direct cooperation of the Honduran army and political authorities with the CIA and the contras has been public knowledge in the United States for over three years.

The third response of imperialism has been a combination of diplomacy to isolate the Nicaraguan revolution, political moves in the United States to achieve the same end, and a series of economic pressures against Nicaragua. Pressure was brought to bear on Western European allies and Latin American countries with some success around the time of the Nicaraguan elections in the fall of 1984. In the spring of 1985 the embargo against Nicaragua was declared, in addition to major cuts in purchases of Nicaraguan products, the cessation of aid and loans, and the economic sabotage by the CIA and the contras. In Congress, after a series of battles over aid to the contras, the Reagan administration won renewed aid in the spring of 1985. This was followed by the Folley Amendment to the military appropriations bill for 1986, which would permit the president to use military force against Nicaragua in relatively flexible circumstances.

In the area of ideological restructuring, imperialism has pursued several tactics. It has revived anti-communism and Cold War language of an East-West contest in Central America. It has labelled Nicaragua as "totalitarian" and the contras as "democratic" forces. At its most extreme, it has called the contras "freedom fighters" and the "moral equivalent" of the "founding fathers." It has also resorted to outright lies about the character and policies of the Sandinista government. Last, but not least, it has sought to use religion and religious sentiments in Central America to drive a wedge between the revolutionaries and the population. As the Santa Fe document made very clear, liberation theology and the trends in the Catholic Church over the last two decades have been seen by imperialism as a subversive force. Thus the contras have sought to identify themselves with the figures of Christ, the Pope, and Cardinal Miguel Obando y Bravo, and to create a corresponding image of the Sandinistas as godless and anti-religious.

Nicaraguan Responses to the Crisis of Imperialism

The first response of the Nicaraguan revolutionaries to the crisis of imperialism, as in fact is the case with all their responses, has itself contributed to the crisis: it was to take power. As Tomas Borge has pointed out in numerous speeches since 1979, revolutionary state power is the guarantor of the revolution. The repressive apparatus of the dictatorship was destroyed and the revolution has created a new apparatus of armed power and state security.

In the military realm, the response has had several aspects. The Sandinista Popular Army has been consolidated and arms procured for national defence. On July 13, 1985 Minister of Defense Humberto Ortega announced that some 200,000 light arms had been distributed among the armed forces and the popular militias and reserves.[65] He sketched the mobilization of 1985 and the preparations to meet the threat of direct U.S. invasion.

Since 1983 there has been military conscription in Nicaragua, called Patriotic Military Service. It has been supplemented by civilian revolutionary vigilance organized by the Sandinista Defense Committees and mass organizations affiliated with the FSLN. Popular defence was stressed in 1985, particularly after the vote on aid to the contras in the United States was held and Reagan designated Nicaragua a "terrorist state." Tomas Borge described this spirit of popular resistance to invasion on July 15, 1985.

> We are preparing the conditions so that the enemy will never be secure here. From any street corner, from a bush, from a window, in an intersection, the mortal shot will come or a mine will explode . . . hundreds of thousands of men and women will make life unbearable. Their powerful weapons are useless against a people armed. Our people armed will be nowhere and everywhere, like a birdsong in the mountains, a schoolgirl with an angelic face in the street, an old man seated in his doorway; they will never know from where and when death's justice will find them.[66]

Defence efforts have been oriented towards defeating the contras militarily and preparing to defend the country against a direct invasion. In 1984-85 there have been some results against the contras and for some time U.S. military officials and CIA leaks have confirmed that the contras are no military threat to Nicaragua.

In the intelligence and state security area, too, the agencies have been largely successful in preventing acts of terrorism in the cities, breaking up assassination plots, infiltrating the CIA's "internal front" and combatting the ideological offensive of the reaction.[67] The amnesty offered to peasants who have joined the contras has been increasingly effective, and some contra military leaders, such as Efren Mondragon, have come forward.[68] Mondragon's testimony has been particularly damaging, since it gave details on links with the CIA, the U.S. embassy in Tegucigalpa, contra-Honduran army cooperation, the concerted policies of terror, torture, rape, and murder employed, and the connections of the contras with sectors of the domestic opposition in Nicaragua.

In the area of the economy, the responses have been directed most recently at alleviating the effects of the U.S. embargo. Vice-Minister of Foreign Commerce Alejandro Martinez Cuenca declared on 19 July 1985 that though the embargo has had its effects, Nicaragua has managed to "muffle" them. Only 17 per cent of Nicaragua's trade was with the United States in 1984, well down from the 60 per cent level maintained during the Somoza dictatorship. Trade diversification has been the policy since 1979, with socialist countries accounting for 20 per cent, 22 per cent with Latin America, a total of 60 per cent divided between Western Europe, Japan, Canada, and the United States in 1984, and the rest with other Third World countries.[69] Products sold in the United States before the embargo have found other markets, mostly in Western Europe, while aid missions secured nearly $400 million dollars in the first six months of 1985, evenly divided between the socialist countries and Western Europe.[70]

On the diplomatic front, then, the embargo has not been a great problem for Nicaragua. But talks with the United States in Manzanillo were cut off by the U.S., which has also had some success in neutralizing the Contadora process. Nonetheless, Nicaragua registered a diplomatic victory, which was increasingly felt in 1985 in Latin America, by being the only country to accept and sign the Contadora draft treaty in 1984. Further, the Organization of American States Commission investigating the incident of May 31, 1985 in which two Costa Rican civil guards were killed concluded that there was no evidence for the Costa Rican charge that the Sandinista army had been responsible. On the contrary, it concluded that "irregular forces" (read the contras) had been in the area and had considerable liberty of operation in Costa Rica.[71] The OAS itself defeated a motion of condemnation brought by Costa Rica against Nicaragua. Latin American countries gave a generally positive reception to the proposal by Nicaraguan President Daniel Ortega that he and Costa Rican President Luis Alberto Monge hold talks on the border situation and that an internationally-patrolled demilitarized zone between the two countries be established.

The Latin American Parliament, a body of representatives from the national legislatures, and the Latin American Association of Political Parties, both gave Nicaragua a vote of confidence on its November 1984 elections. Nicaragua was readmitted to the first and was elected to the vice-presidency of the second in 1985. The European Parliament, which has informal ties to its Latin American counterpart, noted the consolidation and institutionalization in Nicaragua.

The U.S. embarrassment at the International Court of Justice in The Hague over its state terrorism in the mining of Nicaraguan ports also contributed to the rising diplomatic prestige of Nicaragua in the past two years. Nicaragua had already enjoyed considerable esteem in the Third World, as the Non-Aligned Movement held a conference in Managua in 1983, and it had been elected to the UN Security Council.

In the face of claims by some of the western press and in Washington that popular support for the Sandinistas has been eroding and that they have been unable to consolidate their political hegemony, the evidence seems to indicate the contrary. Particularly since 1983, political institutionalization has proceeded apace. In that year the Council of State passed legislation on political parties and elections. In 1984 the registration of voters reached over 85 per cent of the eligible voters (aged sixteen and over), some 1.4 million Nicaraguans.[72] In the elections of November 1984, the FSLN took 67 per cent of the vote, with another 13 per cent going to allied parties. Both the FSLN and the Latin American parliamentary association consider the turnout and the result of the November election as proof that political pluralism is alive and well in Nicaragua.[73] Both President Daniel Ortega and Vice-President Sergio Ramirez have been activist office-holders, while the proportionally elected National Assembly, with seven political parties represented, was charged with preparing a constitution during 1985. Thus, the period 1979-84 was that of the first transitional revolutionary regime and the laying of the groundwork for institutionalization; the period 1985-90 ought to be one of consolidation, with the more or less final institutional forms in place by the end of the decade.

One of the most important aspects of the political response to the crisis of imperialism inside Nicaragua is the Sandinista commitment to political pluralism, political rights, and human rights. Three reports in July 1985 gave a rough measure of the situation in this area. First, the *Nuevo Diario* published interviews of assessments by leaders of opposition parties on the occasion of the sixth anniversary of the 1979 victory over the dictatorship.[74] The character of their remarks varied broadly, ranging from charges that private enterprise was being discouraged to accusations that the revolution was selling out to imperialism. Charges of corruption in government were made and too heavy a blame for Nicaragua's present economic difficulty on the United States/contra aggression was also ascribed. This open criticism of the government was parallelled in the opposition newspaper *La Prensa*, even with the continuing state of emergency and mild censorship, and in the numerous non-Sandinista radio stations.

Second, the assessment made by an AFL-CIO delegation visiting Nicaragua in July 1985 was very positive regarding pluralism and civil liberties.[75] It singled out the situation of non-Sandinista labour unions as one in which "the unions have offices, hold meetings, have publications, hold training workshops and collect funds. They are active members of the political opposition." The report concluded, "Although the Nicaraguan government has imposed some restriction on the democratic process, it is not a repressive and totalitarian regime, as the Reagan administration has claimed." Further, the delegation found "no social base of support in the country for the counter-revolution."

Third, the human rights organization Americas Watch, based in Washington, gave Nicaragua another positive judgement on the situation with respect to political and human rights in 1985.[76] The report, entitled "Human Rights in Nicaragua: Reagan, Rhetoric and Reality," was based on several visits to Nicaragua, and to Honduras and Costa Rica, where Nicaraguan ex-patriates were interviewed. The report concluded that in Nicaragua there is no policy of torture, murder, or disappearances, as charged by the Reagan administration, nor is there anti-Semitism, persecution of Catholics or Protestants, or a policy against Miskito Indians, though problems in the latter area are acknowledged. Regarding the 1984 elections, the report concluded that they compared favourably not only with those in El Salvador and Guatemala that year, but also with those held in Honduras, Mexico, and Panama: "There was no prohibition of the participation of any political party and those that participated could attack the Sandinista party freely and use free radio and television time." Americas Watch and other human rights organizations maintain offices in Nicaragua and freely distribute their reports on a monthly basis. Criticisms included the occasional censoring of *La Prensa*, jailings in the past of some union leaders, and an ongoing prohibition against street demonstrations by opposition parties.* The violations of human rights, nevertheless, that are most violent, said the report, "have been committed by the contras, whom President Reagan calls our brothers, freedom fighters and the moral equivalent of the founding fathers."

Three other areas have evidenced the political consolidation of the revolution in Nicaragua, despite efforts of the contras and the propaganda offensive of imperialism. In 1985 serious efforts at giving regional autonomy to the Atlantic coast went forward; a national commission on autonomy produced a resolution, the National Assembly will include autonomy in the constitution, and the FSLN named Tomas Borge to head a national task force to address the problems of the coast area. In 1985, talks with various sectors of the Miskito population, including those living in exile in Honduras and those who have taken up arms, were proceeding, while the return of Miskito communities to the banks of the River Coco had been initiated.

The second and third areas were those of popular consultation on the constitution and the advancing agrarian reform. The FSLN is committed to

---

**La Prensa* was closed by the government in July 1986 because of the paper's apparent support for the Reagan administration, immediately following the latter's success in securing congressional approval for its $100 million program of aid to the contras.

full popular discussions of constitutional proposals at the grassroots level and in the mass organizations, not just among the political parties and inside the assembly. The agrarian reform has now affected half the peasant families in the country and is increasingly dealing with the landless and the small family private plot, shifting the emphasis from cooperatives. This is seen as fulfilling a historical commitment and is also a response to the growing pressures and organization of the landless and small peasantry.

The ideological response to the crisis of imperialism and its offensive has been varied. It has been both spontaneous and concerted, directed and dispersed.[77] In what is called *trabajo político* — "political work" — the Sandinistas have undertaken the political education of the whole nation, and in particular the working class and the personnel of the state and its organs. In the cultural area, popular education, the literacy campaign, and the productions under the auspices of the Ministry of Culture have had broadly political themes at their core. Nicaraguan social science and philosophy have also experienced a revolutionary reorientation.[78]

Two specific fronts where ideological struggle against imperialism has taken place have been the concept of "terrorism" and the idea of the "destiny and continuity" of the people of Nicaragua and their struggles. During 1985, with the United States' designation of Nicaragua as a "terrorist state" and its threats of invasion or other military action (the U.S. diplomatic note of July 17, 1985 was a particularly harsh example of this ideological offensive of imperialism), the revolutionary leadership has concentrated on the concept of terrorism. Examples are the July 19 speech of President Daniel Ortega,[79] the content of Vice-President Sergio Ramirez's dialogues with Latin American governments during visits in June and July 1985,[80] the speech of Tomas Borge about the threat of invasion in July of 1985,[81] and the interview with Foreign Minister Miguel D'Escoto as he was beginning his fast in July 1985.[82] They ask if carrying out economic sabotage, mining ports, bombing oil storage facilities, creating hunger, kidnapping peasants, raping peasant women, publishing the CIA manual on assassination, and other actions such as these are not terrorism; they ask "who is the terrorist?"

The FSLN claim, with considerable moral weight, to be the inheritors of the great figures in national history — Nicarao, Diriangen, Dario, Zelaya, Zeledon, and Sandino. They identify the Nicaraguan people with Sandino and with resistance to imperialism and dictatorship, while the contras are identified with Somoza, with national disgrace in the past, and with the imperialist aggressors. The FSLN is seen as the continuation of the best nationalist traditions, the defender of sovereignty and dignity.[83] In addition, the FSLN has considerable claim to theoretical and practical innovations within the world revolutionary tradition. The participation of Christians,[84] which is a continuing phenomenon, and the collective nature of the revolutionary leadership, have been combined with a policy and theoretical flexibility that has confounded the efforts of imperialism to apply simple labels.

The Nicaraguan response to the crises of capitalism and imperialism provides a classic illustration of the principle of a dialectic between history and human affairs. Each term of the contradiction conditions the actions of the other, yet each term has its own development and dynamic. The remarkable aspect of this contradiction is its pervasiveness in Nicaragua's current national experience and the impact of the overall Nicaraguan response to the crises of imperialism. Few examples come to mind of such a small centre of resistance to such a large empire having such great historical significance.

Notes

1 Interview with a Nicaraguan Foreign Ministry official who had served as a political officer in 1982-83. July 1983, Managua.

2 "Interview with Nicaraguan Labour Leader," *Labour /Le Travailleur* 12 (1983), 137-143. Gomalez died in a plane crash in 1985.

3 See, for example, Walter LaFeber, *Inevitable Revolutions: The U.S. in Central America* (New York: Norton, 1983); Stan Persky, *America, The Last Domino* (Vancouver: New Star, 1984).

4 *Pensamiento Propio*, 21 (March 1985).

5 *Ibid.*, 27.

6 *Ibid.*

7 *Ibid.*, 27-28.

8 *Ibid.*, 28.

9 *Ibid.*, 29.

10 *Ibid.*, 30.

11 *Ibid.*

12 Centro de Investigaciones y Estudios de la Reforma Agraria and Barricada, *Lunes Socio-Económico de Barricada 1983-84*, primera edición (Managua: MIDINRA, 1984), 24.

13 MINCOMEX briefing, June 1983, in *Contemporary Marxism*, 8 (Spring 1984), 27-33; see also Jaime Wheelock Roman, *Entre La Crisis y La Agresión: La Reforma Agraria Sandinista* (Managua: Editorial Nueva Nicaragua, 1985), 74, 105.

14 *Lunes Socio-Económico*, 23.

15 *Ibid.*, 19.

16 See also George Black, *Triumph of the People* (London: Zed Press, 1982); Tommie Sue Montgomery, *Revolution in El Salvador* (Boulder: Westview, 1982); George Black, *Garrison Guatemala* (New York: Monthly Review Press, 1984); Jim Handy, *Gift of the Devil: A History of Guatemala* (Toronto: Between the Lines, 1984).

17 As described eloquently by Montgomery, Black, and Penny Lernoux, in her *Cry of the People* (New York: Penguin, 1982).

18 Ernest Mandel develops the notion of a general crisis of capitalist accumulation after 1967 in his *Late Capitalism* (London: New Left Books, 1974); Alain Lipietz updates the argument and offers a novel theoretical approach in the present volume.

19 See Fidel Castro, *How Latin America's and the Third World's Debt Can and Should be Cancelled and the Pressing Need for the New International Economic Order* (Havana: Editora Politica, 1985).

20 See Marlene Dixon and Susanne Jonas, eds., introduction to *Revolution and Intervention in Central America* (San Francisco: Synthesis Publications, 1983), i-ii.

21 *Ibid.* See Bertram Gross, *Friendly Fascism* (Montreal: Black Rose, 1980) for an extended discussion of the potential for a totalitarian political formation in the United States; and John S. Saloma, *Ominous Politics: The New Conservative Labyrinth* (New York: Hill and Wang, 1984) for an introduction to the ideology of the new right.

22 Committee of Santa Fe, "A New Inter-American Policy for the Eighties," (Santa Fe: May 1980).

23 Characterized as "a network of subfascist client states" by Noam Chomsky and Edward Herman in their *Political Economy of Human Rights*, 2 vols. (Montreal: Black Rose, 1978).

24 See Carlos Fonseca Amador, *Obras* (Managua: Editorial Nueva Nicaragua, 1983); and Sergio Ramirez, "The Relevance of Sandino's Thought," in *Nicaragua: The Sandinista People's Revolution: Speeches by Sandinista Leaders* (New York: Pathfinder Press, 1985), 332-39.

25 Tomas Borge, "Clausura del II Coloquio Nacional de Filosofia 6 Julio 1985, Universidad CentroAmericana," (Archives of Dept. of Public Relations, Ministry of the Interior, Managua), 3.

26 See *Nicaragua: The Sandinista People's Revolution*; Jaime Wheelock Roman, *El Gran Desafio* (Managua: Editorial Nueva Nicaragua, 1983); *Sandinistas Speak* (Berkeley: Solidarity Publications, 1982).

27 Tomas Borge, "This Revolution Was Made To Create a New Society," 1 May 1982, in *Nicaragua: The Sandinista People's Revolution*, 27.

28 *Ibid.*, 29.

29 Tomas Borge, "Interview with Victoria Furio, of Mutuality in Mission," (Archives of Public Relations, Ministry of Interior, Managua), 8.

30 Tomas Borge, "Conferencia de Prensa, 19 Oct. 1982," (Archives of Public Relations, Ministry of Interior, Managua), 17.

31 Wheelock Roman, *Entre La Crisis y La Agresión*, 23-24; and further: "Here what has to be posed theoretically is whether it is possible that the bourgoisie simply produce, without power, that they limit themselves as a class to a productive role. That is, that they limit themselves to

exploiting their means of production and use these means of production to live, not as instruments of power, of imposition;" from "The Great Challenge," in *Nicaragua: The Sandinista People's Revolution*, 134-35.

32 "The Great Challenge," 147.

33 See O. Nunez Soto, *El Somocismo y el modelo capitalista agro-exportado* (Managua: Universidad Nacional Autonoma de Nicaragua, 1978); J. Wheelock Roman, *Imperialismo y dictadura: crisis de una formacion social* (Mexico: Siglo XXI, 1979); Black, *Triumph of the People*.

34 Briefing of June 1983, *Contemporary Marxism*, 8, 1984.

35 Wheelock Roman, *Entre La Crisis y La Agresión*, 46.

36 See Wheelock Roman, and also Joseph Collins, *What Difference Would A Revolution Make?* (San Francisco: Institute for Food and Development Policy, 1982) for two of the most comprehensive accounts of these policies. See also the very thorough interview with Daniel Nunez of October 9, 1984, "If The Peasantry Did Not Trust the Revolution, We Would Be Through," in *Nicaragua: The Sandinista People's Revolution*, 367-74.

37 Wheelock Roman, *Entre La Crisis y La Agresión*, 27.

38 *Ibid.*, 31.

39 *Ibid.*

40 Wheelock Roman, *Imperialismo y dictadura*, 83-85.

41 Wheelock Roman, *Entre La Crisis y La Agresión*, 56-57.

42 "Food Supply: Nicaragua's Daily Challenge," *Envio*, September 1983 (Managua: Central American Historical Institute); see also the discussion on production and scarcity in Wheelock Roman, *Entre La Crisis y La Agresión*, 87-96.

43 See the FSLN electoral platform of 4 November 1984, in particular, "The New Economy," in *Nicaragua: The Sandinista People's Revolution*, 313-27 and the speech by Daniel Ortega, "A Dirty War is Being Carried Out Against Nicaragua," 4 May 1984, in *ibid.*, 290-99.

44 *Envio*, September 1983.

45 Interview printed in *Nuevo Diario*, July 7, 1985.

46 See, for example, the interview with Cdte. Jaime Wheelock Roman in *Barricada*, July 8, 1985, and his report of July 17, 1985 in *Nuevo Diario*.

47 See the interview with Cdte. Lenin Cerna, Chief of State Security, *Soberanía*, July 1985, 45.

48 Ortega, "A Dirty War," in *Nicaragua: The Sandinista People's Revolution*, 290.

49 *Ibid.*, 291; and the interview with Cdte. Lenin Cerna, Chief of State Security, *Soberanía*, July 1985, 45.

50 Wheelock Roman, *Entre La Crisis y La Agresión*, 31.

51 See Ortega, "A Dirty War," in *Nicaragua: The Sandinista People's Revolution*.

52 *Ibid.*, 293.

53 *Ibid.*, 296.

54 *Ibid.*, 297.

55 *Ibid.*, 297-98; Wheelock Roman, *Entre La Crisis y La Agresión*, 99-110; *Barricada Internacional*, July 11, 1985.

56 Cdte. Borge remarked on this even before the July 19, 1979 victory, speaking in Leon July 15, "Toma de la hacienda La Maquina," (Archives of Dept. of Public Relations, MINT).

57 Persky, *The Last Domino*.

58 Cited in *Soberanía*, 15, July 1985, 5.

59 See Persky, *The Last Domino*, for a review of militarization in El Salvador between 1980 and 1984; see also *Pensamiento Propio*, 21, March 1985, the interview with General Edgardo Mercado Jarrin, director of Peru's Instituto de Estudios Geopolíticos y Estratégicos: "Centroamérica: A New Geopolitical Role."

60 See Persky, *The Last Domino*; Stella Calloni, "Honduras: One Step Away From War," *Soberanía*, July 1985, 6-12.

61 Cited in Gregorio Selser, "Costa Rica: More Soldiers than Teachers?" *Soberanía*, July 1985, 19-21.

62 *Ibid.*, 21.

63 See the account in Persky, *The Last Domino*, 236-41.

64 See the interview with Lenin Cerna, *Nuevo Diario*, 15-16, July 1985.

65 *Barricada*, 14 July 1985.

66 Cdte. Tomas Borge, "Conmemoración de la muerte de Julio Buitrago," July 15, 1985 (Archives of Public Relations, MINT).

67 See the interview with Lenin Cerna.

68 See the interview with Mondragon in *Soberanía*, "The CIA Wanted to Turn Me Into a Criminal," July 1985, 13-18.

69 *Nuevo Diario*, July 17, 1985.

70 Interview with Foreign Minister Miguel D'Escoto, *Barricada*, July 8, 1985.

71 *Barricada*, July 12, 1985.

72 See *Envío* and *Pensamiento Propio* for the fall of 1984.

73 Cdte. Bayardo Arce, of the Sandinista Directorate, summed up the political accomplishments of the revolution in an interview in *Barricada*, July 16, 1985.

74 *Nuevo Diario*, July 15, 1985.

75 See *Nuevo Diario*, July 12, 1985, "AFL-CIO: Libertades Plenas en Nicaragua."

76 *Nuevo Diario*, July 16, 1985, "Americas Watch Devela las insidias de Reagan."

77 For a theoretical discussion of ideology, political education and consciousness, see Fred Judson, *Cuba and the Revolutionary Myth* (Boulder: Westview, 1984), and "Revolutionary Morale in the Sandinista Armed Forces," (Managua, Archives of Public Relations, MINT, 1985).

78 See, for example, Borge's address to the Second National Colloquium on Philosophy, 6 July 1985, reprinted as "El quehacer filosófico en la Revolución," *Nuevo Diario*, 13 July 1985.

79 See *Barricada*, July 20, 1985.

80 See *Barricada* and *Nuevo Diario* accounts for this period; also *Barricada International*, July 4, July 11, 1985.

81 "En conmemoración de Julio Buitrago," July 15, 1985 (Archives of Public Relations, MINT).

82 *Barricada*, July 8, 1985, "Mi ayuno es para que oigan este clamor que pide paz."

83 See the interview with Tomas Borge, "El FSLN es la síntesis de Sandino y de Carlos," *Barricada*, July 15, 1985.

84 See, for example, Teofilo Cabestrero, *Ministros de Dios, Ministros del pueblo* (Bilbao: Editorial Desdee de Brouwer, 1983); Tomas Borge, *La Revolución Combate Contra La Teología de la Muerte* (Managua: 1984); Margaret Randall, *Christians in the Nicaraguan Revolution* (Vancouver: New Star, 1983).

Contributors

Bertrand Bellon, Centre de Recherche en Economie Industrielle, Université de Paris-Nord, Paris, France and Department of International Business, New York University, New York, U.S.A.

Philippe Faucher, Department of Political Science, Université de Montréal, Montréal, Quebec

Alain Gagnon, Department of Political Science, Carleton University, Ottawa, Ontario

John Holmes, Department of Geography, Queen's University, Kingston, Ontario

Fred Judson, Department of Political Science, University of Alberta, Edmonton, Alberta

Michael Kaufman, Department of Political Science, York University, Downsview, Ontario

Colin Leys, Department of Political Studies, Queen's University, Kingston, Ontario

Alain Lipietz, Centre d'Etudes Prospectives et Mathématiques Appliqués à la Planification, Paris, France

Mary Beth Montcalm, Department of Political Studies, University of Manitoba, Winnipeg, Manitoba

Morris Morley, Department of Politics, Macquarie University, New South Wales, Australia

Jorge Niosi, Department of Sociology, Université du Quebec à Montréal, Montreal, Quebec

James Petras, Department of Sociology, State University of New York, Binghampton, New York, U.S.A.

Clive Thomas, Institute of Development Studies, University of Guyana, Georgetown, Guyana

Other Titles on the Third World

Gift of the Devil
A History of Guatemala
by Jim Handy

Jamaica Under Manley
Dilemmas of Socialism and Democracy
by Michael Kaufman

Children of the Volcano
by Alison Acker

Quiet Complicity
Canadian Involvement in the Vietnam War
by Victor Levant

Mirrors of War
Literature and Revolution in El Salvador
Translated and with an introduction by Keith Ellis

South African Women on the Move
by the Vukani Makhosikazi Collective

Perceptions of Apartheid
The Churches and Political Change in South Africa
by Ernie Regehr

between the lines

ആശ്രമം

2

ashramam
novel

•

vaikom chandrasekharan nair

•

first chintha edition
february 2015

•

second edition
march 2019

•

typesetting
star communications, thiruvananthapuram

•

published
chintha publishers, thiruvananthapuram

•

printed
repro india ltd, mumbai

•

cover
midas

•

price
rupees two hundred and fifteen only

വിതരണം

ദേശാഭിമാനി ബുക്ക് ഹൗസ്
H O തിരുവനന്തപുരം–695 035
phone: 0471-2303026, 6063026
www.chinthapublishers.com
chinthapublishers@gmail.com

ബ്രാഞ്ചുകൾ

ഹെഡ്ഡാഫീസ് ബ്രാഞ്ച് കുന്നുകുഴി • സ്റ്റാച്യു തിരുവനന്തപുരം • കെ എസ് ആർ ടി സി ബസ് സ്റ്റേഷൻ ആലപ്പുഴ • കെ എസ് ആർ ടി സി ബസ് സ്റ്റേഷൻ എറണാകുളം • ഐ ജി റോഡ് കോഴിക്കോട് • മാവൂർ റോഡ് കോഴിക്കോട് • എൻ ജി ഒ യൂണിയൻ ബിൽഡിങ് കണ്ണൂർ • സെൻട്രൽ ബസ് ടെർമിനൽ കോംപ്ലക്സ് താവക്കര കണ്ണൂർ

CR - 2070 / 4961
ISBN - 978-93-85018-10-7

ആശ്രമം
(നോവൽ)

വൈക്കം ചന്ദ്രശേഖരൻ നായർ

ചിന്ത പബ്ലിഷേഴ്സ്
തിരുവനന്തപുരം-695 035
വില : ₹215

വൈക്കം ചന്ദ്രശേഖരൻനായർ (1928-2005)

കോട്ടയം ജില്ലയിലെ വൈക്കത്ത് ജനിച്ചു. നോവലിസ്റ്റ്, നാടകകൃത്ത്, മാധ്യമപ്രവർത്തകൻ, പ്രഭാഷകൻ എന്നീ നിലകളിൽ വ്യക്തിമുദ്ര പതിപ്പിച്ചു. കോട്ടയം സി എം എസ് കോളേജിൽ പഠിക്കുമ്പോൾ രാഷ്ട്രീയ പ്രവർത്തകനായി. സാമ്പത്തികക്ലേശം നിമിത്തം പഠനം തുടരാനായില്ല. *കേരളഭൂഷണം, മലയാളമനോരമ, പൗരപ്രഭ, കേരളം* എന്നീ പത്രങ്ങളിൽ പ്രവർത്തിച്ചു. കമ്യൂണിസ്റ്റ് പ്രസ്ഥാനത്തിലും അതിന്റെ സാഹിത്യ-സാംസ്കാരിക വിഭാഗത്തിലും സജീവ പ്രവർത്തകനായി. പാർട്ടി മുഖപത്രമായ *ജനയുഗ*ത്തിന്റെ സ്ഥാപക പത്രാധിപന്മാരിൽ ഒരാൾ. പിന്നീട് *കുങ്കുമം, ചിത്രകാർത്തിക* എന്നീ വാരികകളുടെ പത്രാധിപരായി. പത്രാധിപത്യം വഹിച്ചിരുന്ന പ്രസിദ്ധീകരണങ്ങളിൽ ചിത്രങ്ങളും വരച്ചിരുന്നു. നാടകങ്ങളിലും സിനിമകളിലും അഭിനയിക്കുകയും ചെയ്തിട്ടുണ്ട്.

ഗോത്രദാഹം, സ്മൃതികാവ്യം, കയീന്റെ വംശം, ഒരു മൃദുസ്പർശം, നഖങ്ങൾ, മാധവിക്കുട്ടി, പാമ്പുകളുടെ മാളം, നീലക്കടമ്പ്, ഉദ്ഘാടനം, ദാഹിക്കുന്നവരുടെ വഴി തുടങ്ങിയവയാണ് പ്രധാന നോവലുകൾ. *പഞ്ചവൻകാട്, സ്വാതിതിരുനാൾ, മാമാങ്കരാത്രി, വേണാട്ടമ്മ, തെക്കംകൂർ, അടിയാത്തി, നീലക്കടൽ* തുടങ്ങി നിരവധി ചരിത്രാഖ്യായികകളും രചിച്ചു. *അനുഭവങ്ങളേ നന്ദി എന്ന ആത്മകഥയും,* 'ബൈബിളിലേക്ക് ഒരു സഞ്ചാരം,' 'മഹാഭാരതത്തിലൂടെ,' 'പ്രാചീന നാടകത്തിലൂടെ ഒരു പര്യടനം' എന്നീ പഠനങ്ങളും *ഡോക്ടർ, തണ്ണീർപ്പന്തൽ, കുറ്റവും ശിക്ഷയും, കടന്നൽക്കൂട്, ഉദ്യോഗപർവം, ജാതൂഗൃഹം, കാലൊച്ചകൾ, സ്വീറ്റ്സെവന്റി, വെളിച്ചം കിഴക്കുതന്നെ* തുടങ്ങി നിരവധി നാടകങ്ങളും അദ്ദേഹത്തിന്റേതായുണ്ട്.

കേരള സാഹിത്യ അക്കാദമി അവാർഡ്, കേരള സംസ്ഥാനചലച്ചിത്ര അവാർഡ്, എന്നിവയ്ക്ക് പുറമേ നാടകരംഗത്തെ മികച്ച സംഭാവനകൾക്കുള്ള പുരസ്കാരം നൽകി സംസ്ഥാന സർക്കാർ ആദരിച്ചു (1994). 2000 ൽ കേരള സാഹിത്യ അക്കാദമി മലയാളഭാഷയ്ക്കും സാഹിത്യത്തിനും നൽകിയ സമഗ്ര സംഭാവനയ്ക്കുള്ള പുരസ്കാരം നൽകി ആദരിച്ചു. 1978-81 കാലയളവിൽ കേരള സംഗീത നാടക അക്കാദമി അധ്യക്ഷനായിരുന്നു. 2005 ഏപ്രിൽ 13 ന് തിരുവനന്തപുരത്ത് അന്തരിച്ചു.

ഒന്ന്

ഉഷസ്സ് പൊട്ടിവിരിഞ്ഞ് സൂര്യതേജസിന്റെ ചുവന്ന പൂക്കൾ തൂവി വീഴുന്ന വഴിത്താരയിൽക്കൂടി ഭാനുമതി നടന്നു. സദനത്തിലേക്ക് ഇനി ഒരു ഫർലോങ് കൂടിയുണ്ട്. പുൽക്കൊടികളിലെ മഞ്ഞുതിർന്ന് പാദങ്ങളിൽ പറ്റുമ്പോൾ സുഖമുള്ള തണുപ്പ് അനുഭവപ്പെട്ടു. തണുത്ത കാറ്റ് കൈതപ്പൂമണം ചാലിച്ചു കൊണ്ടുവരുന്നു. ശിരസിലിട്ട സാരിത്തലപ്പ് മഞ്ഞുതുള്ളികൾ വീണ് നനഞ്ഞിരിക്കുന്നു. ഇരുപുറത്തും വീട്ടുമുറ്റങ്ങളിൽ ഒരു പുതിയ പ്രഭാതത്തിന്റെ തിരക്കിട്ട ശബ്ദങ്ങളും ചലനങ്ങളും ആരംഭിച്ചിരിക്കുന്നു.

തലേന്നുരാത്രിയിലെ സഞ്ചാരത്തിന്റെ ക്ഷീണം ഭാനുമതിയുടെ മുഖത്തുണ്ട്. തീർഥാടകരുടെ വാനിലാണ് യാത്ര ചെയ്തത്. അവർ രാത്രി മുഴുവൻ പാടിയ സ്തോത്രങ്ങളും ഗീതങ്ങളും മനസിൽ മുഴങ്ങിക്കൊണ്ടിരുന്നു. അതിലൊന്നിന്റെ വരികൾ വിടാതെ നിൽക്കുന്നു. 'ജന്മാന്തര കൃതപുണ്യം തായേ, ഇനിയും ജായാപദപൂജകളും മാനസിവസിക്കുക ദേവീ..' അത് മൂളാൻ തോന്നി. എന്തുകൊണ്ടോ ചെറുപ്പത്തിൽ പാട്ടു പഠിച്ചതും അന്നത്തെ അധ്യാപകൻ സ്ഥലം മാറി പോയപ്പോൾ പാട്ടു പഠിത്തം നിർത്തിയതും എല്ലാം ഓർമിച്ചു.

രണ്ടു കാളകളെ തെളിച്ചുകൊണ്ട് ഒരു ഉഴവുകാരൻ എതിരെ വന്നു. വഴി ഒഴിഞ്ഞുകൊടുത്തു. കാളകളും കാളക്കാരനും കടന്നുപോയി. അപ്പോൾ തന്റെയും കാളകളുടെയും കാളക്കാരന്റെയും നിഴൽ നിലത്തിൽ വീഴുന്നത് ശ്രദ്ധിച്ചു.

സാരിത്തലപ്പിനിടയിൽക്കൂടിയും പാറിക്കിടന്ന മുടി ഒന്നൊതുക്കി വച്ചു. മുൻപ് ഒരിക്കൽമാത്രമേ സദനത്തിൽ വന്നിട്ടുള്ളൂ. അത് ഒരുവർഷം മുൻപാണ്. അന്നുണ്ടായിരുന്ന ചിലർ ഓരോ സ്ഥലങ്ങളിലേക്ക് പോയതായി അറിവുണ്ട്. പ്രധാനപ്പെട്ട അംഗങ്ങളെല്ലാം ഇപ്പോഴും ഇവിടെത്ത

ന്നെയുണ്ട്. യോഗമയീദേവി സ്ഥലത്തുള്ള സമയമാണെങ്കിൽ സംഗതിക്ക് എളുപ്പം നടത്തിപ്പുണ്ടാകുമെന്നാണ് വാസവമേനോൻ പറഞ്ഞിരിക്കുന്നത്. അവർ ആണ്ടിൽ രണ്ടോ മൂന്നോ തവണ മാത്രമേ വരാറുള്ളൂ. വന്നാൽ ഒരുമാസത്തിലധികം താമസിക്കാറില്ല. പിന്നെ പോകും. എങ്ങോട്ടാണ് പോകുന്നതെന്നു പറയാറില്ല. ഇപ്പോൾ അവർ ഉണ്ടായിരിക്കാൻ സാധ്യതയുണ്ടെന്ന് മേനോൻ പറഞ്ഞു.

എന്തിനാണ് മേനോൻ തന്നെ അയച്ചിരിക്കുന്നത്. അത് അറിയില്ല. അറിയേണ്ടെന്നാണ് പറഞ്ഞത്. ഒരു കത്ത് കൊടുത്തയച്ചിട്ടുണ്ട്. അത് ഒട്ടിച്ച കവറാണ്. തുറന്നുനോക്കുന്ന പ്രശ്നമേയില്ല. അതുംകൊണ്ട് നടന്നിട്ട് എന്ത് ആപത്ത് വന്നാലും നേരിടുകയല്ലാതെ മറ്റൊന്നുമില്ല. മേനോൻ സദനത്തിനും അതിന്റെ രാജ്യത്തിന്റെ അനുയായികൾക്കും അങ്ങനെ ഒരാളാണ്. അദ്ദേഹത്തിന്റെ കൽപ്പനകളെ ശിരസാവഹിക്കുക മാത്രമാണ് അനുയായികളുടെ കർത്തവ്യം.

സദനത്തോട് അടുത്തു കഴിഞ്ഞു. പഴയ ഒരു വണ്ടിപ്പേട്ടയുണ്ട്. അത് കഴിഞ്ഞാൽ പിന്നെ പത്തു ചുവടേയുള്ളൂ. വണ്ടിപ്പേട്ടയായി. ഭാനുമതി ധൃതിയിൽ നടന്നു.

സദനത്തിന്റെ ഗേറ്റ് തുറന്നിട്ടിരുന്നു. അവൾ നേരെ മുറ്റത്തേക്ക് ചെന്നു. അകത്ത് ആരുടെയോ ശബ്ദം കേൾക്കുന്നുണ്ട്. അവൾ സാവധാനം തിണ്ണയിലേക്ക് കയറി അൽപ്പം തുറന്നുകിടന്ന വാതിലിൽക്കൂടി അകത്തേക്ക് നോക്കി. അപ്പോൾ മങ്ങിയ വെളിച്ചത്തിൽക്കൂടി ഒരാൾ നടന്നുവരുന്നു. ശ്രദ്ധിച്ചുനോക്കി, അൻപതു വയസിലധികം തോന്നിക്കുന്ന, മുടിയാകെ വെള്ളചൂടിയ, ആ സ്ത്രീ യോഗമയീദേവി തന്നെയാണെന്നു മനസിൽ കരുതി. പണ്ടെന്നോ അവരുടെ ഒരു ചിത്രം കണ്ട ഓർമ ഉണർന്നു. വെളുത്ത പുടവ ഇരുവശത്തുനിന്ന് വലിച്ച് കഴുത്തിലൂടെ പിന്നിലേക്ക് ഏത്താപ്പു ചുറ്റിയിരിക്കുകയാണ്. അതിനു മീതെ രുദ്രാക്ഷമാല കിടപ്പുണ്ട്.

വരാന്തയിൽ നിൽക്കുന്ന യുവതിയെ അവർ സൂക്ഷിച്ചു നോക്കിക്കൊണ്ട്, അടുത്തുവന്നു.

“ആരാ കുട്ടി? എവിടുന്നുവരുന്നു?” ശാന്തമായ സ്വരം.

“ഭാനുമതി എന്നാണ് പേര്. തൃത്താലയിൽനിന്ന് വരുന്നു. വാസവമേനോൻസാറ് അവിടെ ഉണ്ട്. ഒരു കത്ത് തന്നയച്ചു.”

ആ സ്ത്രീ ഭാനുമതിയെ അടിമുടി നോക്കി. പുഞ്ചിരിച്ചു. “വനിതാസമാജത്തിന്റെ സെക്രട്ടറി അല്ലേ?”

“അതെ.”

“ആ സന്ധ്യാദേവി പറഞ്ഞറിയാം. ആർക്കാണ് കത്ത്?”

“സന്ധ്യാദേവിക്ക്.”

“അവർ കൊടുങ്ങല്ലൂർക്ക് പോയിരിക്കുന്നു. നമ്മുടെ അരവിന്ദനെ അറിയുകയില്ലേ? കവി? അദ്ദേഹം ക്ഷണിച്ചിട്ടു പോയതാണ്. അവിടെ ഒരു വനിതാ സമ്മേളനം നടന്നു. അരവിന്ദൻ അതിന്റെ സംഘാടകനാണ്. ഇന്നു വൈകിട്ട് വരും. ഇന്നലെയായിരുന്നു സമ്മേളനം.”

ഭാനുമതിയെ അവർ അകത്തേക്ക് ക്ഷണിച്ചു. കുളിക്കാനും ആഹാരം കഴിക്കാനുമുള്ള ഏർപ്പാടുകൾ ചെയ്തു. സദനത്തിലെ പ്രവർത്തകരെല്ലാം ആ അതിഥിയുടെ ചുറ്റും കൂടി. ഭാനുമതിയെപ്പറ്റി അവർക്കെല്ലാം അറിയാം. കഴിഞ്ഞവർഷം അവർ ഇവിടെ വന്നപ്പോൾ കണ്ടവർ പരിചയം പുതുക്കിക്കൊണ്ട് കുശലങ്ങളന്വേഷിച്ചു. തൃത്താല എങ്ങനെയിരിക്കുന്നു? സമാജം എങ്ങനെയിരിക്കുന്നു? ഭാനുമതി ഉറങ്ങാറുണ്ടോ? സമയത്ത് ഉണ്ണാറുണ്ടോ? കല്യാണം കഴിച്ചോ?

എല്ലാറ്റിനും മറുപടി പറഞ്ഞ് ഒന്നിനൊഴിച്ച്: കല്യാണം!

ഊണുവരെ വിശ്രമിച്ചു. സദനത്തിലെ ഓരോരുത്തരെയും മനസിൽ വരച്ചുവയ്ക്കാൻ ശ്രമിച്ചു. ഉഷാമേനോൻ— മെലിഞ്ഞു നീണ്ട പെൺകുട്ടി. സാരി ഉടുത്ത് തുടങ്ങിയതേയുള്ളൂ. ഉഷയെ കണ്ടാൽ മറ്റെല്ലാം മറക്കും; ആ വലിയ കണ്ണുകൾമാത്രം ഉള്ളിൽ പതിയും. അംബികത്തമ്പുരാട്ടി — ചന്ദനക്കുറിയിട്ട് മുടി നീട്ടിക്കെട്ടിയിട്ട്, ഒന്നരയും മുണ്ടുമുടുത്ത ആ സ്ത്രീക്ക് ക്ഷത്രിയലക്ഷണം തികഞ്ഞു നിൽക്കുന്നു. റീന— എപ്പോഴും പുഞ്ചിരിക്കും. എപ്പോഴും പൂക്കൾ വിടരുന്ന ചെടിപോലെ, സൗന്ദര്യമല്ല, ഓമനത്തമാണ്. പാർവതി–കുലീനത എഴുതിവച്ചിരിക്കുന്ന മുഖം. സ്നേഹത്തിന്റെ നിറകുടമാണ്. അത് എല്ലാവർക്കുമറിയാം. കീർത്തി – എപ്പോഴും തമാശ പറയുന്ന ചെറുപ്പക്കാരി. ശബ്ദമുണ്ടാക്കുന്ന പെണ്ണ്. കളിയാക്കാൻ എന്ത് വിരുത്! വാസവമേനോനെപ്പറ്റി കീർത്തി അന്വേഷിച്ചതുതന്നെ ഇങ്ങനെയാണ്. "സ്ത്രീവിരോധിക്കു സുഖമാണോ?"

ഊണു കഴിഞ്ഞു വീണ്ടും കിടന്നു. അപ്പോൾ കീർത്തി അടുത്തുകൂടി. അവൾ അങ്ങനെയാണ്. ഒട്ടിക്കൂടും. ലോകത്തിൽ ആരെ കണ്ടുമുട്ടിയാലും അവൾക്ക് ഒരുപാടു കാര്യങ്ങൾ അറിയണം.

അടുത്ത കട്ടിലിൽ കിടന്നു.

"തൃത്താലയിൽ വലിയ ക്ഷേത്രമുണ്ടോ?" അവൾ തുടങ്ങി.

"ഉണ്ട്. ദേവീക്ഷേത്രം."

"ചേച്ചി ദിവസവും തൊഴാൻ പോകാറുണ്ടോ?"

"ഉണ്ട്."

"അപ്പോൾ ആണുങ്ങൾ കമന്റടിക്കുമോ?"

ഭാനുമതി ചിരിച്ചു.

"ഇല്ല."

"ഇവിടെയൊക്കെ അതില്ലാത്തതുകൊണ്ട് കീർത്തിക്കു സങ്കടമാണോ?"

കീർത്തി ചിരിച്ചു.

"ചേച്ചി എന്തിനാ വന്നത്? വാസവമേനോൻ സാറ് എന്തിനാ കത്ത് തന്നയച്ചിരിക്കുന്നത്?"

"എനിക്ക് ഒന്നുമറിഞ്ഞുകൂടാ കീർത്തി."

"ചേച്ചിക്ക് അമ്മയും അച്ഛനും ഒക്കെയുണ്ടോ?"

ഒരുനിമിഷം മൗനം.

"എനിക്ക് ആരുമില്ല. കീർത്തി – അച്ഛനും അമ്മയും സഹോദരങ്ങളും ആരും."

കീർത്തി മിണ്ടാതെ കിടന്നു. പിന്നെ പറഞ്ഞു.

"ചേച്ചി ഇനി ഇവിടെനിന്നു പോകണ്ട. ഇവിടെ താമസിച്ചാൽ മതി."

ഭാനുമതി ആലോചനയിൽ നിന്നുണർന്നു.

"അയ്യോ, അതെങ്ങനെ നടക്കും കീർത്തി?"

രണ്ടുപേരും മയക്കത്തിൽനിന്ന് ഉണർന്നപ്പോൾ വൈകി. സന്ധ്യാദേവി വന്നിട്ടില്ല. എന്താണ് ഇത്ര വൈകുന്നത്? എല്ലാവരും ആലോചിച്ചു, ചോദിച്ചു.

ചായ കുടിച്ചു. അപ്പോൾ കീർത്തിക്ക് ഒരഭിപ്രായം.

"നമുക്ക് ഭാനുമതിച്ചേച്ചിയെയും കൊണ്ട് ക്ഷേത്രത്തിൽ പോകാം."

പാർവതിയും അംബികത്തമ്പുരാട്ടിയും സമ്മതിച്ചു.

യോഗമയീദേവി കടന്നുവന്നു.

"ഇന്ന് കൽക്കത്തയിൽനിന്ന് വിനായക് ചാറ്റർജി വന്നിട്ടുണ്ട്. ടൗൺ ഹാളിൽ അദ്ദേഹം പ്രസംഗിക്കുന്നുണ്ട്. നിങ്ങൾ ക്ഷേത്രത്തിൽ പോയിട്ട് അതിലേ വരണം. ഞാൻ നേരത്തേ പോകാം. ഏഴുമണിക്കാണ് പ്രസംഗം."

സമ്മതിച്ചു.

ക്ഷേത്രമൈതാനത്ത് ചെറുപ്പക്കാർ പല സംഘങ്ങളായി വട്ടമിട്ടിരിക്കുന്നു. ഭാനുമതിയും കൂട്ടുകാരും കടന്നുപോകുമ്പോൾ ഒരുത്തൻ പറഞ്ഞു.

"ഇന്ന് പുതിയ ഒരു സാധനം കൂടിയുണ്ടെടാ."

അവർ നാലമ്പലം ചുറ്റി പ്രദിക്ഷണംവച്ച്, നടയ്ക്കൽ നിന്നു തൊഴുതു. ദീപാരാധനയ്ക്കു നടതുറന്നപ്പോൾ വീണ്ടും തൊഴുതു പ്രസാദം വാങ്ങി പുറത്തിറങ്ങി.

സന്ധ്യ മയങ്ങിത്തുടങ്ങിയതേയുള്ളൂ.

ചെറുപ്പക്കാർ അവിടെത്തന്നെ ഇരിക്കുന്നു. കടന്നു പോയപ്പോൾ കീർത്തി കൂടെയുള്ളവരോട് പറഞ്ഞു. "ഒന്ന് നിൽക്കൂ."

അവർ നിന്നു. അവൾ കമന്റടിച്ച ചെറുപ്പക്കാരനെ വിളിച്ചു.

"ചേട്ടാ ഒന്നിങ്ങ് വരൂ."

അയാൾ സംശയിച്ച്, എഴുന്നേറ്റ് വന്നു.

"ഈ പുതിയ സാധനത്തിന്റെ പേര് ഭാനുമതി എന്നാണ്. കണ്ടോളൂ. നാളെ കാണാൻ പറ്റില്ല. അവർ അവരുടെ നാട്ടിലേക്ക് പോകും."

അയാൾ സ്തംഭിച്ചുനിന്നു.

അവൾ തിരിഞ്ഞു നടന്നു. മറ്റുള്ളവരും.

തന്റേടമുള്ള കീർത്തി ഇത് ചെയ്യാറുണ്ട്. ആരുപറഞ്ഞാലും ഇടയ്ക്ക് അവളിത് പ്രയോഗിക്കും.

"എന്താ കീർത്തീ ഇത്?" ഭാനുമതിക്ക് അത് പുതിയ കാര്യമാണ്.

"ഇടയ്ക്ക് വേണം ചേച്ചീ. ഇതുങ്ങള്. ഈ ചെറുപ്പക്കാര്, സത്യത്തിൽ പാവങ്ങളാണ്. കൂട്ടുചേരുമ്പോഴുള്ള രസമാ. വല്ലപ്പോഴും ഇങ്ങനെയൊന്നു കൊടുത്താൽ കുറച്ചുനാളത്തേക്ക് സമാധാനമുണ്ട്."

ടൗൺഹാളിന്റെ മുൻപിലെത്തി. വിനായക് ചാറ്റർജിയുടെ പ്രസംഗം ആരംഭിച്ചതേയുള്ളൂ. ഇംഗ്ലീഷിലാണ്.

"What do they give us? Abuse, humiliations, guns and human crisis... what do they take? All our resources and manpower away to their aggrandisement."

ഒരു ഘട്ടത്തിൽ അദ്ദേഹം പറഞ്ഞു:

"Imperialism is blood Imperialism is fire. Imperialism is the souliness theory and practice of inhuman materialism. Stirke it, fight it, bury it deep in the sands of time..."

ആറടി ഉയരം, കഷണ്ടി, കറുത്ത ഫ്രെയിമുള്ള കണ്ണട, പുതുപ്പ്, സുഭാഷ് ചന്ദ്രബോസിനെ അനുസ്മരിപ്പിക്കുന്ന രൂപം. വിനായക് ചാറ്റർജിയുടെ ശബ്ദം. സദസിന്റെ മനസിൽ അനേകം സ്ഥായികളിൽക്കൂടി സഞ്ചരിക്കുന്നതായി അനുഭവപ്പെട്ടു.

ഭാനുമതിയും കൂട്ടരും യോഗം കഴിഞ്ഞ് വിനായക് ചാറ്റർജിയെ അടുത്തുകണ്ടു. അദ്ദേഹം സൗമ്യമായി അവരോടെല്ലാം സംസാരിച്ചു. മലയാളികളെ അദ്ദേഹത്തിന് പ്രത്യേകിച്ചും ഇഷ്ടമാണെന്ന് പറഞ്ഞു. അദ്ദേഹം പിറ്റേന്നുരാവിലെ തിരുവനന്തപുരത്തേക്ക് പോകുന്നു. ഒരു പക്ഷേ തലസ്ഥാനനഗരിയിൽ പ്രസംഗിക്കാൻ അധികാരികൾ അദ്ദേഹത്തെ അനുവദിച്ചില്ലെന്നുവരും.

എട്ടുമണി കഴിഞ്ഞപ്പോഴാണ് അവർ സദനത്തിലെത്തിയത്. അവിടെ അരവിന്ദൻ ഇരിക്കുന്നുണ്ട്. സന്ധ്യാദേവിയും അരവിന്ദനും ഒരുമിച്ചു പോന്നു.

യോഗമയീദേവി പരിചയപ്പെടുത്തി.

"ഇത് അരവിന്ദൻ"

"കേട്ടിട്ടുണ്ട്." ഭാനുമതി പറഞ്ഞു.

"ഇത് ഭാനുമതി തൃത്താല വനിതാസമാജം സെക്രട്ടറിയാണ്."

അവർ പരസ്പരം തൊഴുതു.

അകത്തേ മുറിയിൽ വച്ചാണ് ഭാനുമതി സന്ധ്യാദേവിയെ കണ്ടത്. ആദ്യമായി കാണുകയാണ്. ഭാനുമതി രണ്ടുനിമിഷനേരം നോക്കിനിന്നു. ആ രൂപം അവൾക്ക് കണ്ടുകൊണ്ടു നിൽക്കാൻ തോന്നി. ഒരു സ്ത്രീക്ക് ഇത്ര അഴകുണ്ടാകുമോ?

ലയിച്ചു നിന്നുപോയി.

"ഭാനുമതിയല്ലേ? ഉണ്ടെന്ന് ഇവിടെ പറഞ്ഞു. കത്തെവിടെ?" ഇരിക്കാൻ ക്ഷണിച്ചുകൊണ്ട് സന്ധ്യാദേവി ചോദിച്ചു.

ഭാനുമതി അവരുടെ വശീകരിക്കുന്ന സ്വരത്തിൽ അലിഞ്ഞ്, ഒരു നിമിഷം കൂടി നിന്നു. പിന്നെ ബാഗിൽനിന്ന് കത്തെടുത്തു കൊടുത്തു.

കവർ പൊട്ടിച്ച് സന്ധ്യാദേവി അതു വായിച്ചു. കുറച്ചു സമയം അതിൽത്തന്നെ നോക്കിയിരുന്നു. കത്തിൽ നിന്ന് മിഴികൾ ക്ലേശിച്ചു പിൻവലിക്കുന്നതുപോലെ തോന്നി.

“ഭാനുമതി മുറിയിലേക്കു പൊയ്ക്കൊള്ളൂ. എനിക്കു കുറച്ചുജോലിയുണ്ട്. അൽപ്പം കഴിഞ്ഞ് ഞാൻ അങ്ങോട്ട് വരാം.”

നിരാശ തോന്നി. കുറച്ചുകൂടി അവരുടെ മുൻപിലിരിക്കാൻ ആഗ്രഹിച്ചു. മടിച്ച് എഴുന്നേറ്റു. പിന്നെയും കാണാമല്ലോ എന്നു സമാധാനിച്ചു. മുറിയിൽനിന്നും ഇറങ്ങി നടന്നു.

സന്ധ്യാദേവി കത്ത് വീണ്ടും വായിച്ചു.

“പ്രിയമിത്രമേ, ഭാനുമതിയെ അങ്ങോട്ടയയ്ക്കുന്നു. അവളെ അറിയാമല്ലോ? അവൾക്ക് ഭൂമിയിൽ ആരുമില്ല. ഞാൻ കുറച്ചു നാളായി ആലോചിക്കുന്ന ഒരു കാര്യം നടപ്പാക്കണമെന്ന് ആഗ്രഹിക്കുന്നു. അവളുടെ വിവാഹം, നമ്മുടെ അരവിന്ദനെയാണ് ഞാൻ മനസിൽ കണ്ടിരിക്കുന്നത്. എന്താ നല്ലതല്ലേ? അരവിന്ദന് തർക്കമുണ്ടാവില്ല എന്നാണ് എന്റെ വിശ്വാസം. ഞാൻ നേരിട്ട് സംസാരിക്കാത്തതെന്തെന്ന് മനസിലാകുമല്ലോ? അയാളോടെന്നല്ല, ആരോടും ഈ ഒരു കാര്യം മാത്രം ഞാൻ സംസാരിക്കുകയില്ല. എനിക്ക് അതിനർഹതയില്ല. സ്ത്രീയുടെയും പുരുഷന്റെയും ഈ വിഷയത്തിലുള്ള മനസ്സ് എനിക്കറിയില്ല. സംഭാഷണം ചെയ്ത് അറിയാനും ഒരു കടവിലടുപ്പിക്കാനും എനിക്ക് കെൽപ്പില്ല. ഭാനുമതിയെ വിവാഹം കഴിപ്പിക്കണം. അത് ആവശ്യമാണ്. നമ്മുടെ കടമയാണ്. ഇക്കാര്യത്തിൽ ഇടപെടാൻ സന്ധ്യാദേവിയാണ് വേണ്ടത്. അതാണു നല്ലതും. ഈ കത്തിലെ വിവരങ്ങൾ അവൾക്കറിയില്ല. ഇത് അരവിന്ദനോടു സംസാരിക്കണം. എന്റെ ആഗ്രഹവും നിശ്ചയവുമാണെന്നു പറയണം. ഒരു തീരുമാനമെടുത്ത് എന്നെ അറിയിക്കണം. ഒട്ടും താമസിപ്പിക്കരുത്. എന്ന് ക്ഷേമാന്വേഷണങ്ങളോടെ, വാസവമേനോൻ.”

ദീർഘമായ ഒരു നിശ്വാസത്തോടെ സന്ധ്യാദേവി എഴുന്നേറ്റു. ആലോചന. പിന്നെ ഇരുന്നു.

“അരവിന്ദേട്ടൻ വിളിക്കുന്നു.” സമാജത്തിലെ ജോലിക്കാരി സുമതി വാതിൽക്കൽ നിന്നു പറഞ്ഞു.

ഉടനെ എഴുന്നേൽക്കാതെ കത്ത് മേശവലിപ്പിനുള്ളിൽ വച്ചു. തലയിണ ഉയർത്തിവച്ച് കട്ടിലിൽ ചാരിക്കിടന്നു. അവരുടെ ഇരുണ്ട മുടി ഇരുഭാഗത്തും വിതറി വീണു.

ആ കത്തിന്റെ ഉള്ളടക്കത്തെപ്പറ്റി ആലോചിക്കുകയായിരുന്നു. പ്രതീക്ഷിക്കാത്ത ഒരു പരീക്ഷണം അതിനെ എങ്ങനെ നേരിടും? മേനോൻ സാറിന്റെ കത്താണ്. അതനുസരിക്കുകയല്ലാതെ മാർഗമില്ല. പക്ഷേ അരവിന്ദനോട് താൻ എങ്ങനെ ഇതുപറയും? കൊടുങ്ങല്ലൂരു നിന്ന് ഇങ്ങോട്ട് സഞ്ചരിക്കുമ്പോൾ അയാൾ പറഞ്ഞ കാര്യങ്ങൾ... ഇല്ല, പറഞ്ഞില്ല, സൂചിപ്പിക്കുകയായിരുന്നു. ആ സൂചനാവാക്കുകളിൽ, വാചാലമായ മനസ്സ് അന്തർഭവിച്ചിരുന്നു. താൻ മിണ്ടാതിരുന്നു. ഒന്നും അങ്ങോട്ട് മറുപടി പറഞ്ഞില്ല. പറയാത്തതും അറിയിക്കാൻ കാര്യമില്ലാഞ്ഞല്ല. തന്റേടം തോന്നിയില്ല. ചില വിചാരങ്ങളായിരുന്നു. അരവിന്ദൻ ഹൃദയശാലിയാണ്. വലിയവനാണ്. ആ കവിതകൾ ജനഹൃദയങ്ങളെ ഹരം പിടിപ്പിക്കു

ന്നതും തുള്ളിച്ചാടിക്കുന്നതും നേരിട്ട് കണ്ടിട്ടുണ്ട്. എറണാകുളത്തെ രാജേന്ദ്രമൈതാനത്ത് അയാൾ സ്വന്തം കവിത വായിക്കുന്നത് നേരിട്ടുകേട്ടു. ആയിരക്കണക്കിനാളുകൾ തിങ്ങിക്കൂടിയിരുന്നു. ഓരോ ഈരടിയും ചൊല്ലിത്തീരുമ്പോൾ മനുഷ്യർ ആവേശം കൊണ്ട് ആർത്തുവിളിച്ചു. മാസ്മരശക്തിയുള്ള തൂലിക! ലോകമെല്ലാം ബഹുമതിനേടിയ ആ മനുഷ്യനോട് പലപ്പോഴും സംസാരിക്കാൻ തന്നെ ആദരപൂർവമായ ഭയം തോന്നാറുണ്ട്. അങ്ങനെ പലതുംകൊണ്ടാണ് യാത്രയ്ക്കിടയിൽ മൗനം ദീക്ഷിച്ചത്. മനഃപൂർവം മിണ്ടാതിരുന്നതാണെന്ന് അയാൾ മനസിലാക്കിയാൽ മതിയായിരുന്നു...

യോഗമയീദേവിയെക്കൊണ്ട് ഇക്കാര്യം പറയിച്ചാലോ?

പോരാ അപ്പോൾ, താൻ വാസവമേനോന്റെ കത്തനുസരിച്ച് പ്രവർത്തിച്ചില്ലെന്ന് വരില്ലേ?

ആലോചിച്ചു. ഒരിടത്തും എത്തിയില്ല.

കുറച്ചുനേരം തളർന്ന് കിടന്നു. കീർത്തി ഓടിക്കയറി വന്നു.

"യാത്ര ചെയ്ത് ക്ഷീണിച്ചതല്ലേ, ചേച്ചീ, അത്താഴം കഴിക്കാം, ചേച്ചിക്ക് നേരത്തെകിടക്കാമല്ലോ." അവൾ നിറുത്തി പെട്ടെന്ന് പറഞ്ഞു: "ഓ അല്ല. അരവിന്ദേട്ടൻ കവിത വായിക്കാമെന്നു പറഞ്ഞു. അപ്പോൾ അതിന് ഒരു മണിക്കൂറ്. ഏതായാലും ചേച്ചി വരൂ."

സന്ധ്യാദേവി എഴുന്നേറ്റു. അൽപ്പം നേരത്തെ ഭക്ഷണം വിളമ്പി. കാരണമുണ്ട്. അരവിന്ദൻ പുതിയ കവിത എഴുതുമ്പോൾ സദനത്തിലുള്ളവരെയെല്ലാം വായിച്ചു കേൾപ്പിക്കാറുണ്ട്. ഇന്ന് ഒരു കവിത വായിക്കാൻ പോകുന്നു. എല്ലാവരും മേശയ്ക്കരികിൽ ഇരുന്ന് ഭക്ഷണം കഴിക്കുമ്പോൾ കീർത്തി ചോദിച്ചു:

"കവിത എത്രവരിയുണ്ട്, അരവിന്ദേട്ടാ?"

"ലക്ഷങ്ങൾ" അരവിന്ദൻ ഗൗരവത്തോടെ മറുപടി പറഞ്ഞു.

കീർത്തിയുടെ മിഴികൾ വിടർന്നു നിന്നു.

"ലക്ഷങ്ങൾ?"

"അതെ. പക്ഷേ, എഴുതിയിരിക്കുന്നത് അത്രയുമില്ല. അനേകലക്ഷം വരികളിൽ ചൊല്ലിയാലും തീരാത്ത ഒന്നിനെപ്പറ്റിയാണ് കവിത."

"അതെന്തോന്നാ?"

വായിക്കുമ്പോൾ മനസിലാക്കിയാൽ മതി.

"അതെന്തോന്നാ ചേച്ചീ?" അടുത്തിരുന്ന ഭാനുമതിയോട് അവൾ പതുക്കെ ചോദിച്ചു.

"എനിക്കറിയില്ല കീർത്തി" ഭാനുമതി ചിരിച്ചു.

അത്താഴം കഴിഞ്ഞ് എല്ലാവരും ഒരുമിച്ചു കൂടിയിരുന്നു. അരവിന്ദൻ കവിത വായിച്ചു.

എത്ര വാസരപുഷ്പം കൊഴിഞ്ഞു
എത്രമേഘങ്ങൾ തൂവിയൊഴിഞ്ഞു
എന്റെ ദേവത കണ്ണുതുറന്നി–

ലെന്തിനീ പൂജ; മൂകമാം പൂജ?
ചൈത്രമാസരജനികൾ മായാ–
ചിത്രജാലം വരയ്ക്കും നിലാവിൽ
മാലതിപ്പൂക്കൾ ലോലമിഴിയാൾ
മാരപൂജ നടത്തുന്ന കാവിൽ
വന്നു നിന്നു ലതാഗൃഹവാതിൽ
തന്നിൽ നീ, മോഹവിഗ്രഹം പോലെ!
സ്വീകരിച്ചൂ മധുരവികാര–
ചാരുചന്ദ്രികാകംബളം നീർത്തി,
രാഗരോമാഞ്ചധൂളികയാലെ
രാമണിയകതൽപ്പം വിരിച്ചു.
നീയിരുന്നൂ, മനോഹരീ, ചാരെ,
ദേവലോക നിശാഗന്ധി പോലെ!
അക്ഷരങ്ങൾ വരികളായി, ഓരോ
മുഗ്ധകാവ്യാർഥതീർഥങ്ങളായി,
ധാന്യകീർത്തനധാരകൾ നാനാ
ഭാവരാഗതടിനികളായി,
നിന്റെ പുഷ്പാധരം ചലിക്കാനായ്
നിന്നു ഞാൻ, തപസ്വിയെപ്പോലെ!
ദേവി, നിർല്ലീനമാനസയായി
നീയിരിക്കുന്നു നിർമുക്തഭാവം
കാലമെത്രകഴിഞ്ഞുപോയിന്നും
ഞാനുപാസനദുഃഖിയായ് നിൽപ്പൂ!
എത്രവാസരപുഷ്പം കൊഴിഞ്ഞൂ!
എത്ര മേഘങ്ങൾ തൂവിയൊഴിഞ്ഞു
എന്റെ ദേവത കണ്ണുതുറന്നി–
ല്ലെന്തിനീപൂജ; മൂകമാം പൂജ?

ആരും മിണ്ടിയില്ല. ഒരു ലഹരിയിൽപ്പെട്ട് ഇരുന്നു. വിളക്കിനു ചുറ്റും പറന്ന വെളുത്ത ശലഭങ്ങൾ മുറിയിലാകെ ഓടിക്കളിക്കുന്ന നിഴലുകൾ സൃഷ്ടിച്ചു.

"എന്താ ഇതിന്റെ അർഥം?" പതിവുപോലെ കീർത്തി പെട്ടെന്ന് മനസിലുദിച്ചത് ചോദിച്ചു പോയി.

എല്ലാവരും ചിരിച്ചു. അടക്കിപ്പിടിച്ച ചിരി.

അരവിന്ദൻ പുഞ്ചിരിയോടെ കീർത്തിയെ നോക്കി.

"കീർത്തി, ഈ കവിതയ്ക്ക് ഓരോരുത്തർക്കും, തോന്നുന്ന അർഥമേയുള്ളൂ."

അവളുടെ മുഖത്ത് പെട്ടെന്നു തെളിഞ്ഞുവന്ന ജാള്യത എല്ലാവരും ശ്രദ്ധിച്ചു. സന്ധ്യാദേവി മുഖം കുനിച്ചു. നിമിഷങ്ങൾക്കുശേഷം അവർ എഴുന്നേറ്റ് അകത്തേക്കു നടന്നു.

ഓരോരുത്തരും എഴുന്നേറ്റ് ഒന്നും മിണ്ടാതെ അകത്തേക്കു പോയി. അരവിന്ദൻ ഒറ്റയ്ക്കിരുന്നു.

രണ്ട്

ഒരു വിപ്ലവകാരിക്ക് ശ്രദ്ധവേണം. ശ്രദ്ധ എന്ന വാക്ക് ഞാൻ ആയിരം തവണ പറയുന്നു, അരവിന്ദൻ നിങ്ങൾക്ക് അതിന്റെ അർഥം മനസിലായോ? പണ്ടൊരുകാലത്ത്, നചികേതസ്സ് എന്ന ആ കൊച്ചന് ശ്രദ്ധയുണ്ടായി. രാജാവ് മഹായാഗം നടത്തിയപ്പോൾ മകന്റെ മനസിൽ സംശയങ്ങളും നിശ്ചയങ്ങളും ഉദയം ചെയ്തു. ജീവിതത്തിലെ പലതും തനിക്കു ചെയ്യാൻ കഴിയും. പക്ഷേ, മരണത്തിന്റെ സത്യമെന്ത്? നചികേതസ്സ് ആലോചിച്ചു. ആ ചോദ്യത്തിനു മറുപടി എവിടെ കിട്ടും? മരണത്തിന്റെ മുഖത്തുനിന്നു, അവിടെ നിന്നു മാത്രം. ആ കൊച്ചൻ അങ്ങോട്ടു നടന്നുചെന്നു. മരണത്തോട് നേരിട്ടു സംസാരിക്കാൻ...

'ധീരത അതാണ്. അന്വേഷിക്കാനും കണ്ടെത്താനും സാക്ഷാൽക്കരിക്കാനുമുള്ളത്. ഏത് അഗ്നിപരീക്ഷണത്തിന്റെ ആലയത്തിലിരുന്നാലും... അങ്ങോട്ടു കടന്നു ചെല്ലുക, യഥാർഥ സത്യാന്വേഷി ദീപത്തിനരികിലേക്ക് എത്തുന്ന നിശാശലഭങ്ങളെപ്പോലെയാണ്. ശലഭങ്ങൾ ഇരുട്ടിലേക്കു തിരിച്ചുപോകുകയില്ല. പലപ്പോഴും വിളക്കിന്റെ തീക്ഷ്ണമായ താപത്തിൽ ഹോമിക്കപ്പെട്ടുപോകും. സത്യത്തെ തേടിയിറങ്ങുന്നവർക്കും ഈ അനുഭവം ഉണ്ടായെന്നു വരാം. വിപ്ലവകാരിയുടെ വഴിയും, സാക്ഷാൽക്കാരവും അങ്ങനെയാവാറുണ്ട്...

അൽപ്പം വളർന്ന കറുത്ത താടിയിൽ തടവിക്കൊണ്ട് വാസവമേനോൻ ഇരുന്നു. ആറ് ശാന്തമായിക്കിടക്കുന്നു. പ്രഭാതത്തിന് ഇനി അൽപ്പസമയമേയുള്ളൂ. ജലപ്പരപ്പിൽ വീഴുന്ന നിലാവിൽ കൊച്ചോളങ്ങൾ രചിച്ചുകൊണ്ട് ഇടയ്ക്കിടെ തോണികൾ കടന്നുപോകുന്നുണ്ട്. ഈ കൊച്ചു വീടിന്റെ മുളന്തണ്ടുകൊണ്ട് പഴകിയ അഴികളിൽക്കൂടി തണുപ്പ് അരിച്ചു കയറിക്കൊണ്ടിരിക്കുന്നു. പുക പിടിച്ച റാന്തവിളക്ക് അവർക്കിടയിൽ മങ്ങിക്കത്തുന്നു. ആറ്റിലെ തോണിക്കാർ സംസാരിക്കുന്ന ശബ്ദം, ഏതോ വിദൂരലോകത്തിൽനിന്നു വരുന്നുവെന്നു തോന്നും.

രാത്രി മുഴുവനും അദ്ദേഹം അങ്ങനെ സംസാരിക്കുകയാണ്. വേദാന്തം, വിപ്ലവം, ഭീകരപ്രവർത്തനം, അനാസക്തി, ഭക്തി... അരവിന്ദൻ അതു കേട്ടുകൊണ്ടിരിക്കുന്നു. അവർ കണ്ടുമുട്ടിയാൽ അങ്ങനെയാണ്. അഗാധമായ അറിവും വിപുലമായ ജീവിതപരിചയവുമുള്ള മേനോൻ പലനേരവും മനസിലാക്കാൻ കഴിയാത്ത ഒരു മനുഷ്യനായി മാറുമെന്ന് അരവിന്ദനു തോന്നിയിട്ടുണ്ട്. ഈ രാത്രി അങ്ങനെയായിരുന്നു. മടിച്ചു മടിച്ചാണ് താൻ അദ്ദേഹത്തിന്റെ ഈ ഏകാന്തമന്ദിരത്തിലേക്കു കടന്നുവന്നത്. വ്യഥയുണ്ടാക്കുന്ന ഒരു വിഷയത്തെപ്പറ്റി പറയുവാനാണ്. പക്ഷേ ഇതുവരെ അതു നടന്നില്ല.

ഒരു കത്തയച്ചിരുന്നു. അതുകൊണ്ട് തൃപ്തിയായില്ല. നേരിട്ട് വന്നു കണ്ട്, തന്റെ മനസ്സ് അസ്പഷ്ടരൂപത്തിലെങ്കിലും കാട്ടിക്കൊടുക്കണം. തുറന്നുപറയാൻ പ്രയാസമുള്ള എന്തോ ഉണ്ടെന്ന് വളരെവേഗം മനസിലാക്കാൻ വാസവമേനോന് കഴിയും. 'എനിക്ക് മനുഷ്യനെ മനസിലാവുകയില്ല' എന്നദ്ദേഹം ആവർത്തിച്ചു പറയാറുണ്ട്. അതിസ്നേഹപൂർവം മറ്റുള്ളവരെ പരിഹസിക്കാനാണെന്ന് തോന്നാറുണ്ട്. ഇപ്പോൾ പ്രശ്നം മറ്റൊന്നാണ്. പറയാൻ എന്ന വിഷയത്തിലേക്ക് ഒന്നെത്തിനോക്കാൻ പോലും അദ്ദേഹം സമ്മതിച്ചിട്ടില്ല.

അത് മനഃപൂർവമാണോ?

"പറവകൾ ഉണർന്ന് പുറത്തിറങ്ങുന്നു. അരവിന്ദൻ, ഇനി നമുക്ക് വേദാന്തത്തിൽനിന്നും പോകാം. സൂര്യപ്രകാശത്തെ നേരിടാനായി" അദ്ദേഹം കണ്ണട എടുത്ത് താഴെ വച്ചു. എന്നിട്ട് ചോദിച്ചു: "അരവിന്ദന് രാവിലെ പോകണം, ഇല്ലേ? പത്രമാഫീസിൽ വൈകുന്നേരമെങ്കിലും എത്തണ്ടേ?"

"അതെ."

അടുത്തകാലത്ത് അരവിന്ദൻ 'മുക്തി' എന്ന പ്രസിദ്ധീകരണത്തിന്റെ പത്രാധിപത്യം ഏറ്റെടുത്തിരിക്കുകയാണ്.

അപ്പോഴും ആ വിവാഹക്കാര്യത്തെക്കുറിച്ചു ഒന്ന് സൂചിപ്പിക്കാൻ കഴിഞ്ഞില്ല. അരവിന്ദൻ മടങ്ങിപ്പോകാനൊരുങ്ങി. വാസവമേനോൻ അടുക്കളയിലേക്ക് പോയി. അൽപ്പസമയത്തിനുള്ളിൽ കാപ്പിയുമായി വന്നു. അതൊക്കെ അദ്ദേഹം സ്വന്തമായി നിർമിക്കുന്നു. മറ്റാരുടേയും സഹായമാവശ്യമില്ല. രണ്ടുപേരും കാപ്പി കുടിച്ചു.

ഇപ്പോൾ ഒന്നും സംസാരിക്കേണ്ട എന്ന തീരുമാനത്തിലാണ് അരവിന്ദൻ. അയാൾ എഴുന്നേറ്റ് യാത്ര പറഞ്ഞു.

അപ്പോൾ വാസവമേനോൻ ചോദിക്കുന്നു.

"അരവിന്ദൻ നിങ്ങളുടെ കത്തിനെപ്പറ്റി ഞാൻ ഒന്നും പറഞ്ഞില്ല, അല്ലേ?"

വൈഷമ്യത്തോടെ മറുപടി നൽകി:

"ഇല്ല, ഞാൻ വന്നത്...."

"അതെ, വന്നത് അതിനാണെന്ന് മനസിലായി. വേദാന്തത്തിന് ഇങ്ങനെ ഒരുദൂഷ്യമുണ്ടല്ലോ. അപ്പോൾ വേണ്ടത് മറന്നുപോകും. ഇന്നലെ രാത്രി അങ്ങനെയൊരു വിഷയമായിപ്പോയി. എന്നാൽ ഞാൻ പറയട്ടെ; കത്തുകിട്ടി ഉള്ളടക്കം മനസിലാക്കി. ഒരാഴ്ചക്കാലമായിട്ടും ഞാൻ മറുപടി എഴുതാതിരുന്നത്, മറ്റൊരു സംഗതി കൊണ്ടാണ്. ഭാനുവിന് ഞാൻ വേറൊരാളെ തേടിപ്പിടിച്ചിരിക്കുന്നു. അയാൾ ഇന്നു വരും. ഇനി നടത്തിപ്പു കാര്യം മാത്രം ഒന്ന് നിശ്ചയിച്ചാൽ മതി. ഇന്നോ നാളെയോ ഇത് അറിയിക്കാമെന്ന് വിചാരിച്ചാണ് മൗനം ദീക്ഷിച്ചത്."

ആശ്വാസമായി, ഒരു പ്രതിസന്ധി തരണം ചെയ്തിരിക്കുന്നു.

"ആജ്ഞ കൈക്കൊള്ളാൻ കഴിയാത്ത ശിഷ്യന്റെ പരുങ്ങലോടെ

യാണ് ഞാൻ കടന്നുവന്നത്." അരവിന്ദൻ പറഞ്ഞു.

വാസവമേനോൻ പുഞ്ചിരിച്ചു.

"വേദാന്തം പറയുമ്പോഴെല്ലാം ഞാനത് കണ്ടുകൊണ്ടാണിരുന്നത്."

അരവിന്ദനും മേനോനും കടവിലേക്ക് നടന്നു. അദ്ദേഹത്തിന്റെ പതിവാണത്. ആരു വന്നാലും യാത്രയയക്കാൻ കടവുവരെ ചെല്ലും. അതിന് ഒരു ന്യായം പറയും.

"ജലം കാണുംവരെ ചെല്ലണം എന്ന ചൊല്ലിനെ ആദരിച്ചിട്ടല്ല, അത്രയും കൂടി ആക്രമിച്ചുവിടാനുള്ള വാസന കൊണ്ടാണ് ഞാൻ കടവുവരെ ആളുകളെ യാത്രയാക്കുന്നത്."

അരവിന്ദൻ വള്ളത്തിൽ കയറി. അത് നീങ്ങി. അലസമായി ഇരുന്നെങ്കിലും മേനോന്റെ രൂപം കാണുകയായിരുന്നു. ആ മെലിഞ്ഞ ശരീരവും നരവീണ മുടിയും കറുത്ത താടിയും ഏതോ ക്ലാസിൽ പെയിന്റിങ്ങിൽ കണ്ടിട്ടുള്ള മികച്ച രൂപം പോലിരിക്കുന്നു. അദ്ദേഹം പറയും. 'എനിക്ക് അറിവും അറിവുകേടുമുണ്ട്. തലമുടി അറിവിന്റെയും താടി അറിവുകേടിന്റെയും ചിഹ്നങ്ങളാണ്.' ഇപ്പോൾ സൂര്യോദയത്തിന്റെ വെളിച്ചത്തിൽ അദ്ദേഹം നിൽക്കുന്നു. ചുവപ്പു ചേർത്തെഴുതിയ മനുഷ്യ ചിത്രം.

അന്നു വൈകിട്ട് വാസവമേനോൻ കടവിൽ ഇരുന്നു. അദ്ദേഹം മറ്റൊരു സന്ദർശകനെ പ്രതീക്ഷിക്കുന്നു, ദിവാകരനെ. ദൂരെ നിന്ന് വള്ളം വന്നപ്പോൾ അയാൾ വരുന്നുവെന്നു കണ്ടു.

ഭാനുമതിയുടെ വിവാഹം നിശ്ചയിക്കാൻ കഴിഞ്ഞത് യാദൃച്ഛികമായിട്ടാണ്. ദിവാകരൻ സന്തോഷപൂർവം അതു സമ്മതിച്ചു. അയാളെയും കൂട്ടിക്കൊണ്ട് അവളുടെ താമസസ്ഥലത്തുപോയി. അവളെ കണ്ടു. രണ്ടുപേർക്കും സമ്മതം. ദിവാകരന്റെ രണ്ടാം കല്യാണമാണ്. ഭാനുമതിക്ക് അതിൽ അപ്രിയമൊന്നുമില്ല. ദിവാകരന്റെ ഭാര്യ മരിച്ചിട്ട് ഒരു വർഷം കഴിഞ്ഞു. അയാൾക്ക് സാമാന്യം സൗകര്യമുണ്ട്. നല്ല വീട്. ഒരുകാറ്. കുറച്ച് എസ്റ്റേറ്റ്. അയാൾ സുമുഖനാണ്. സുന്ദരിയായ ഭാനുമതിക്ക് അയാൾ ചേരും.

അന്ന് വളരെ വൈകുംവരെ അവർ സംസാരിച്ചിരുന്നു. ദിവാകരൻ അന്നു മടങ്ങിപ്പോകേണ്ടെന്നു നിശ്ചയിച്ചു. കടത്തു വള്ളക്കാരൻ വീട്ടിൽപ്പോയി. വിളിച്ചാൽ വരും. എന്നാലും വേണ്ട.

കിടന്നുകഴിഞ്ഞ് വാസവമേനോൻ പറഞ്ഞു.

"വനിതാ സമാജത്തിന്റെ ഹാളിൽ വച്ചു നടത്താം."

"അതുമതി" ദിവാകരനു തർക്കമില്ല.

"അവൾക്കു ബന്ധുക്കളാരുമില്ല. എല്ലാം സമാജക്കാർ തന്നെ. പിന്നെ സദനത്തിലെ ആൾക്കാരേയും വിളിക്കാം."

"അങ്ങനെയാവട്ടെ."

അർധരാത്രി ദിവാകരൻ എഴുന്നേറ്റു. അയാൾ ഉറങ്ങിയില്ല. മെല്ലെ കതകു തുറന്നു പുറത്തേക്കിറങ്ങി. ആറ്റിനരികിലേക്കു നടന്നു. കടത്തു കടവിൽ മരത്തിൽ ചാരി ഇരുന്ന് അയാൾ തേങ്ങിക്കരയുകയായിരുന്നു.

കടന്നുപോകുന്ന ഒരു വള്ളക്കാരൻ പറയുന്നു.

"വടക്കേ പടിഞ്ഞാറ് കോളുവച്ചിട്ടൊണ്ട്. മഴ വരുമെന്നാ തോന്നുന്നത്."

വള്ളം കടന്നുപോയി. ദിവാകരൻ ഒരിക്കൽ മുഖം തുടച്ചു. പക്ഷേ, വീണ്ടും അയാളുടെ സമനില തെറ്റി. അടക്കാൻ വയ്യാത്ത ഓർമകൾ മനസിന്റെ ഭിത്തികളിൽ വീണ്ടും ആഞ്ഞടിച്ചു ശബ്ദമുണ്ടാക്കുംപോലെ.

അയാൾ മലർന്നുകിടന്നു.

വെളുപ്പാൻകാലത്ത് ജോലിക്കാർ കടത്തുകടവിലേക്കു വരുന്ന കാൽപ്പെരുമാറ്റം കേട്ടപ്പോഴാണ് അയാൾ എഴുന്നേറ്റു വീട്ടിലേക്കു നടന്നത്. വാസവമേനോൻ എഴുന്നേറ്റു. അകത്തു കയറി, കാപ്പിയുണ്ടാക്കി ദിവാകരനു കൊടുത്തു. താനും കുടിച്ചു.

"ഇവിടെ പാമ്പിന്റെ ശല്യമൊന്നുമില്ല." കാപ്പി ഊതിക്കുടിക്കുന്നതിനിടയ്ക്ക് മേനോൻ പറഞ്ഞു.

ദിവാകരൻ നോക്കി.

"അല്ല, നിങ്ങൾകടവിൽ പോയി ഇരിക്കുമ്പോൾ ഞാൻ ഉണർന്നു കിടക്കുകയായിരുന്നു. പാമ്പിന്റെ ശല്യമുണ്ടായിരുന്നെങ്കിൽ, അവിടെയിരിക്കാൻ ഞാൻ സമ്മതിക്കുകയില്ലായിരുന്നു."

ദിവാകരന്റെ മുഖം അസ്വസ്ഥമായി.

ഭാര്യ മരിച്ച് ഒരു വർഷം കഴിഞ്ഞതേയുള്ളൂ. മറ്റൊരു പെണ്ണിനെ കൂട്ടിന് കൊണ്ടുവരാൻ പോകുന്നു. ദുഃഖം തോന്നുക സ്വാഭാവികമാണ്. മേനോൻ പിന്നെ ഒന്നും പറഞ്ഞില്ല.

ദിവാകരൻ യാത്ര പറഞ്ഞുപോയപ്പോൾ മേനോൻ മനസാ വിചാരിച്ചു.

"ആ പെൺകുട്ടി രക്ഷപ്പെട്ടു."

അരവിന്ദനെക്കുറിച്ച് ആലോചിച്ചു. പുരുഷന്റെയും സ്ത്രീയുടെയും മനസ്സ് തനിക്കറിയില്ല. എന്തൊരു തോൽവിയാണത്! അരവിന്ദൻ ഒരിക്കലും തന്റെ വാക്കുകൾ തള്ളിക്കളഞ്ഞിട്ടില്ല. ഇപ്പോൾ തന്റെ അഭിമതം സ്വീകരിക്കാൻ കഴിഞ്ഞില്ല. അതിൽ അയാൾക്കു ദുഃഖമുണ്ട്. അതാണ്, നേരിട്ടുവന്നത്. എന്നിട്ടും പറഞ്ഞൊപ്പിക്കാൻ പ്രയാസമായിരുന്നു. അയാളുടെ ഉള്ളിൽ മറ്റേതോ പെൺകുട്ടി സ്ഥാനം പിടിച്ചിട്ടുണ്ടെന്നു തോന്നുന്നു. ആരായിരിക്കും അത്?

പിന്നീട് അതറിയാൻ കഴിയും.

ദിവാകരൻ മഴച്ചാറ്റലിൽക്കൂടിയാണ് അക്കരെയിട്ടിരുന്ന കാറിലേക്ക് ചെന്നു കയറിയത്. അപ്പോൾ തലേന്നു രാത്രിയിൽ വള്ളക്കാരൻ നടത്തിയ പ്രവചനത്തെപ്പറ്റി ഓർമിച്ചു; മഴ പെയ്യും. കാറു വിട്ടു. അരവിന്ദനെ കാണണം. പരിചയമില്ലാ, ഒരിക്കൽപ്പോലും കണ്ടിട്ടില്ല. സ്വയം പരിചയപ്പെടുത്താം.

അരവിന്ദൻ പത്രമാഫീസിലിരിക്കുന്നു. ദിവാകരൻ കടന്നു വന്നു. അയാൾ ഇരുന്ന്, താനാരെന്ന് അറിയിച്ചു. അൽപ്പസമയം കൊണ്ട്, പരിചയത്തിന്റെ പരിധി വികസിപ്പിച്ചെടുത്തു. കാരണം, ദിവാകരന് കൊടുങ്ങല്ലൂര് ബന്ധുക്കളുണ്ട്. അവരെ അരവിന്ദന് അറിയാം. അവരിൽ പലരും സുഹൃത്തുക്കൾ. അങ്ങിനെ പരിചയം പൂർത്തിയായി.

ദിവാകരൻ തന്റെ വരവിന്റെ ലക്ഷ്യം സൂചിപ്പിച്ചു. സ്വകാര്യമായി

ഒന്ന് സംസാരിക്കണം.

ആ മുറി അതിന് പറ്റിയതാണെന്ന് അരവിന്ദൻ അറിയിച്ചു. ആരും അങ്ങോട്ടുവരില്ല. സഹപ്രവർത്തകർ ഇനി രാത്രിയിലേ മടങ്ങി വരൂ.

അൽപ്പനേരം ഒരുങ്ങി രഹസ്യത്തിന്റെ അന്തരീക്ഷം ഉണ്ടാക്കി പിന്നെയാണ് ദിവാകരൻ സംസാരിച്ചത്. അയാൾ ചോദിച്ചു:

"മിസ്റ്റർ അരവിന്ദൻ മറ്റൊന്നും വിചാരിക്കരുത്. ഒരു സംഗതി അറിയാനാണ് അതെ, ഒരു കാര്യം ഒന്നറിയാൻ, ഭാനുമതിയെ താങ്കൾക്ക് പരിചയമുണ്ടോ?"

കരുതലോടെ അയാൾ നോക്കി ഇരുന്നു. ഒന്നാലോചിച്ച് അരവിന്ദൻ പറഞ്ഞു:

"ഉണ്ട്, നാലഞ്ചു ദിവസത്തെ പരിചയം"

"നാലഞ്ചു ദിവസത്തെ?" ദിവാകരൻ അത്ഭുതം കാട്ടി.

"അതെ... എന്താണ്?"

"ഞാൻ.. ഞാൻ ആ പെൺകുട്ടിയെ വിവാഹം കഴിക്കാൻ പോവുകയാണ്." ദിവാകരൻ പൊടുന്നനെ പറഞ്ഞു.

"അറിഞ്ഞു, നല്ലത്" അരവിന്ദൻ പുഞ്ചിരിച്ചു. "പക്ഷേ, എന്താണ് പരിചയത്തെപ്പറ്റി അന്വേഷിച്ചത്?"

"ഇല്ല ഒന്നുമില്ല. വാസവമേനോനാണ് ഈ പ്രപ്പോസൽ കൊണ്ടുവന്നത്. ആ പെൺകുട്ടിയെ കണ്ടിട്ടു എനിക്ക് തൃപ്തിയായിത്തോന്നി. ഞാൻ സമ്മതിച്ചു. അവരെ സംബന്ധിച്ച വിവരങ്ങൾ പരിചയമുള്ളവരോട്...."

അയാൾ നിർത്തി, പെട്ടെന്ന് തുടർന്നു:

"അല്ല, അത് ഭംഗിയല്ലെന്ന് എനിക്കറിയാം. പക്ഷേ മിസ്റ്റർ അരവിന്ദനെപ്പോലെയുള്ളവർക്ക് അറിവും കാര്യവിവരവുമുണ്ടല്ലോ. ഒന്നു നേരിട്ടു കണ്ട്, അന്വേഷിച്ചുകളയാമെന്ന് വിചാരിച്ചു. അത്രേയുള്ളൂ."

"നിങ്ങൾക്ക് അവരെപ്പറ്റി മേനോൻ മാസ്റ്ററോട് ചോദിക്കാമായിരുന്നില്ലേ?" അരവിന്ദന്റെ ആ വാക്കുകൾ അയാളെ അസ്വസ്ഥനാക്കിയതുപോലുണ്ട്.

"ഇല്ല മിസ്റ്റർ അരവിന്ദൻ, അങ്ങനെയൊന്നുമില്ല. അങ്ങനെയൊരു ഗവേഷണത്തിന്റെയൊന്നും ആവശ്യമില്ല. അതിനല്ല ഞാൻ വന്നതും. ബുദ്ധിമുട്ടിച്ചെങ്കിൽ ക്ഷമിക്കണം."

"നിങ്ങൾക്ക് ഒരു വഴി ഞാൻ പറഞ്ഞുതരാം. ഇവിടെ ഒരു സദനമുണ്ട്. അവിടെച്ചെല്ലുക, അവിടത്തെ അധികാരി ഒരു സന്ധ്യാദേവിയാണ്. അവർക്ക് ഭാനുമതിയെപ്പറ്റി എല്ലാ വിവരങ്ങളും അറിയാം."

"വളരെ നന്ദി?"

ദിവാകരൻ എഴുന്നേറ്റു തൊഴുതു. അരവിന്ദൻ അയാളെ യാത്രയാക്കി.

അരവിന്ദൻ ഓർമിക്കാൻ ശ്രമിച്ചു. ഈ മനുഷ്യനെ എവിടെ വെച്ചാണ് കണ്ടത്? കണ്ടിട്ടുണ്ട്. ഇപ്പോൾ പിടികിട്ടുന്നില്ല. മനസ്സ് പല സ്ഥലങ്ങളിലും സഞ്ചരിച്ചു. പല സന്ദർഭങ്ങളും എടുത്തുവച്ചു നോക്കി. എവിടെ? എവിടെവച്ച്?

ഒരു മിന്നൽപോലെ ഓർമ വീശുന്നു, മൂന്നാലു വർഷം മുൻപ് മലബാറിന്റെ അതിർത്തിയിൽ വച്ച് ഒരു സംഘം രാഷ്ട്രീയ പ്രവർത്തകരെ പോലീസിന് ഒറ്റിക്കൊടുത്തത് ഇയാളാണ്. അന്ന് അവിടെയെങ്ങോ വനത്തിലെ തടിവെട്ടിയിറക്കുന്ന പണിയായിരുന്നു ഇയാൾക്ക്. പിന്നെ അയാൾ കൊടുങ്ങല്ലൂര് വന്നു. ഈ മനുഷ്യനെ മനസിലാക്കിയ അവിടത്തെ പ്രവർത്തകർ ഇയാളെ ഒളിച്ചിരുന്ന് കൊല്ലാൻ നിശ്ചയിച്ചു. എങ്ങനെയോ അത് മണത്തറിഞ്ഞ്, ഇയാൾ സ്ഥലം വിട്ടു.

അതേ, ഇയാൾ തന്നെ, അരവിന്ദൻ അന്ന് കണ്ടിട്ടുണ്ട്. ഇപ്പോൾ ശരീരം കുറച്ചുകൂടി തടിച്ചിരിക്കുന്നു.

വാസവമേനോന് ഇതറിഞ്ഞുകൂടെ? അറിയില്ലായിരിക്കും.

മേശ വലിച്ചു തുറന്ന് കടലാസുകൾക്കിടയിൽ പരതി. മറ്റൊരു വലിപ്പിൽ തപ്പി. ഒരു കടലാസ് ഓർമയിലേക്ക് വന്നു. അതാണ് നോക്കുന്നത്. അലമാര, ട്രേ ഇല്ല. എവിടേക്കാണ് അത് എറിഞ്ഞുകളഞ്ഞത്? വീണ്ടും നോക്കിയപ്പോൾ ട്രേയുടെ കീഴിൽ അതിരിക്കുന്നു. ദിവസങ്ങൾക്ക് മുമ്പ് പ്രത്യേകം എടുത്തുവച്ചതാണ്. അത് നിവർത്തി വായിച്ചു. സംശയം തീർന്നു. ദിവാകരൻ എന്ന മനുഷ്യന്റെ കഥ എഴുതി വന്നതാണ്. ചുരുക്കമായി ഇത്രയും മാത്രം: ഒരു സഹകരണ സംഘത്തിന്റെ തിരഞ്ഞെടുപ്പിൽ അയാളെ എതിർത്ത മൂന്നുപേരെ, ഒരാഴ്ചക്കാലം എവിടെയോ കൊണ്ടുപോയി അടച്ചിട്ടിരുന്നു. ചെറിയ കാര്യം. പക്ഷേ, അയാൾ പഴയ ശീലം തുടർന്നുവരുന്നു.

ഭാനുമതി എന്ന സാധുപെൺകുട്ടിയെ രക്ഷിക്കാൻ കഴിയുമോ? ഒന്നും മിണ്ടാൻ തനിക്ക് അർഹതയില്ല. അവളെ തിരസ്കരിച്ചവനാണ്. അവൾക്ക് മറ്റൊരു വിവാഹം ഉറപ്പിച്ചപ്പോൾ അതും തടസപ്പെടുത്താൻ ചെന്നിരിക്കുന്നു എന്ന് തോന്നും. സന്ധ്യാദേവിക്ക് എന്തെങ്കിലും ചെയ്യാൻ കഴിയുമോ? അല്ലെങ്കിൽ യോഗീമയിക്ക്? അല്ലെങ്കിൽ സദനത്തിലെ ആർക്കെങ്കിലും? തനിക്ക് ഇക്കാര്യത്തിൽ മേനോൻ മാസ്റ്ററെ അഭിമുഖീകരിക്കാൻ പ്രയാസമുണ്ട്.

ഭാനുമതി സദനത്തിൽനിന്ന് മടങ്ങിപ്പോകുമ്പോൾ അരവിന്ദൻ അവിടെയുണ്ടായിരുന്നു. അവൾ അപ്പോൾ പോകുന്നുവെന്ന് അറിഞ്ഞില്ല. അറിഞ്ഞിരുന്നെങ്കിൽ, അവിടെ വരില്ല. മേനോന്റെ കത്തുമായി വരുമ്പോൾ അതിലെ ഉള്ളടക്കം അവൾ ധരിച്ചിട്ടില്ല. പിന്നെ അത് മനസിലായി. ആ കഥയിലെ അധീരനായ നായകൻ താനാണ്. കീർത്തിയും പാർവതിയുമൊത്ത് മുൻവശത്തേക്ക് വന്നു. പുറകേ യോഗമയീദേവിയും അരവിന്ദൻ പ്രതിമ കണക്കിരുന്നു. അവൾ ഒന്നു തടഞ്ഞുനിന്നു. കാലുകൾ നിശ്ചലമായതുപോലെ.

ആരും മിണ്ടാത്ത നിമിഷങ്ങൾ

ഭാനുമതി ധൈര്യം കാട്ടി.

“ഞാൻ പോകുന്നു, അരവിന്ദേട്ടാ.”

അരവിന്ദൻ എഴുന്നേറ്റു.

"ശരി."

കീർത്തി മുഖം താഴ്ത്തിനിന്നു.

അവൾ പടിയിറങ്ങിപ്പോകുമ്പോൾ അരവിന്ദന്റെ മുഖം താണു. ഒരു ദുഃഖിതയുടെ ചിത്രമല്ല അവളിൽ കണ്ടത്. പരാജിതയുടെ രൂപം പോലെ അയാൾക്കു തോന്നി. നിരസിക്കപ്പെട്ടവൾ. അവൾ തന്നെ കൈയൊഴിഞ്ഞ ചെറുപ്പക്കാരന്റെ മുൻപിൽ യാത്ര പറഞ്ഞു പോകുന്നു.

കീർത്തിയും പാർവതിയും യോഗീമയിയും അകത്തേക്ക് പോയി.

ഉയർന്ന മതിലുകളുള്ള വീട്ടിലാണ് പിറന്നത്. നാട്ടിൽ ആഢ്യത്വം കൽപ്പിച്ചുകിട്ടിയിരുന്ന കുടുംബം. ആ ഉയർന്ന മതിലുകൾക്കും വലിയ പടിപ്പുരയ്ക്കും അർഥമുണ്ടായിരുന്നു. അത് ഒരു ലോകമാണ്. ആചാരങ്ങൾ ആ വീടിന്റെ മുറ്റത്തും പറമ്പിലും അകത്തളത്തിലും കുടുമ്മയും കുറിയുമായി ഇരുന്നരുളുന്നുണ്ടായിരുന്നു. പൂർവവിധികൾ അവിടെ ശബ്ദങ്ങളെയും ചലനങ്ങളെയും നിയന്ത്രിച്ചുനിർത്തിയിരുന്നു. നാഴികകൾ തോറും ആജ്ഞകൾ വരികയും അവ വരവണ്ണം തെറ്റാതെ നടപ്പാക്കപ്പെടുകയും ചെയ്തിരുന്നു. അവിടെയാണ് അരവിന്ദൻ എന്ന കുട്ടി ജനിച്ചുവീണത്. അവൻ വളർന്നത് പണ്ട് പുരാതനകാലം മുതൽക്കുള്ള ആ മുറകളുടെ എല്ലാ വരികളും പാലിച്ചുകൊണ്ടാണ്. അവൻ വളർന്ന് പടിക്ക് പുറത്തേക്ക് സഞ്ചരിക്കുവാൻ തുടങ്ങിയപ്പോഴും കുടുംബത്തിലെ ശിക്ഷണവിധികളുടെ ഓരോ അക്ഷരവും കാത്തുകൊണ്ടിരുന്നു. വളരെക്കാലം അതിൽനിന്നും വ്യതിചലിച്ചില്ല.

പിന്നെ വിശാലമായ ലോകം അവനെ ഗ്രസിക്കുകയോ കരവലയങ്ങളിലേക്ക് ഏറ്റെടുക്കുകയോ ചെയ്തു. എന്നിട്ടും പഴയതെല്ലാം മനസിൽ കിടന്നു. ഒരു പെൺകുട്ടിയെ തിരിഞ്ഞുനോക്കാതെ ഭൂമിയിൽക്കൂടി നടന്നു. ചെന്നു കയറിയത് കർശന നിബന്ധനകളുള്ള രാഷ്ട്രീയ പ്രസ്ഥാനത്തിലാണ്. നാലുകെട്ടിനുള്ളിലെ പിരിമുറുക്കിവച്ച ക്രമങ്ങൾ എത്രയോ സൗമ്യം. ഇവിടെ അച്ചടക്കമെന്ന വാള് നിറുകയുടെ മീതെ കെട്ടിത്തൂക്കിയിട്ടിരിക്കുന്നു. ആവശ്യമില്ലാത്ത കാൽപ്പെരുമാറ്റംപോലും ഉണ്ടാവാതെ, സംഘത്തിൽ ഒരാളായി നടന്നു. ഇവിടെ യോഗ്യതയുടെ സീമ കടക്കുന്ന മൃദുലമായ ഒന്നുമില്ല. തീസിസ്സുകളുടെ ശൈലിയിലല്ലാതെ വിചാരങ്ങൾപോലുമില്ല. പിറന്നപ്പോൾ മുതൽക്കു ഒതുക്കം പഠിച്ച അരവിന്ദാക്ഷന്, പ്രത്യേകിച്ചൊരു ഭാരം തോന്നിയില്ല.

കവിതയെഴുതി. അപ്പോൾ, പുതിയ മുഖങ്ങൾ തന്നെ സ്നേഹപൂർവം നോക്കുന്നത് അരവിന്ദൻ കണ്ടു. പ്രസ്ഥാനത്തിനപ്പുറത്തുള്ളവർ അടുത്തുവന്നു തോളിൽതൊട്ടു. അവരുടെ കൂടെ അൽപ്പദൂരമൊക്കെ നടക്കേണ്ടിവന്നു. ആത്മാവിൽ നിന്നുതിർന്ന കവിതയുടെ ഈണം പ്രതിധ്വനിയോടെ തിരിച്ചുവന്ന് മനസിനെ തൊട്ടുണർത്തിയ മുഹൂർത്തങ്ങളുണ്ടായി. എന്നാലും അതും പ്രസ്ഥാനത്തിന്റെ വികാരത്തിൽനിന്നും വന്ന ഈണങ്ങളാണ്. അക്ഷരങ്ങളിലും വാക്കുകളിലും കൂടി പകർന്നത്. യുദ്ധത്തിന്റെ ഹൃദയ സൗന്ദര്യമാണ്... ചോരയണിഞ്ഞു പൊടിപുരണ്ട,

വലിഞ്ഞു നിൽക്കുന്ന മാംസപേശികളുള്ള, സൗന്ദര്യം...

അപ്പോൾ, ദാ, ഒരു നിമിഷം ഒരുവളെയും കൊണ്ടു കടന്നു വന്നു. ഭൂമിയിലെ സൗന്ദര്യങ്ങൾക്കുള്ളിലുള്ള എന്തോ ഒന്ന് അവളിൽ കണ്ടു. ഒരു പുതിയതരം കവിത ആത്മാവിൽ ജനിക്കുകയായിരുന്നു. അവളുടെ ഓരോ ചലനവും ഭാവനയിൽ ഓരോ ചാതുരകൾ തുന്നിച്ചേർത്തു. അവൾ ഓർമയായി, വികാരമായി, അസ്വസ്ഥതയായി ഒരു പുരുഷന് ഒരു സ്ത്രീ വേണമെന്ന പ്രകൃതിസത്യം ഇവിടെ സാക്ഷാൽക്കരിക്കപ്പെടുന്നുവെന്ന് അയാൾക്ക് തോന്നി. അവൾക്കും അതു തോന്നിയെന്ന് അവളുടെ കണ്ണുകൾ പറഞ്ഞു.

മിണ്ടാതെ, അവർ ആശയങ്ങൾ പരസ്പരം ഊതിയുണർത്തി. അവർ അടുക്കുകയാണെന്ന് ഓരോ നിമിഷവും മനസിലായി....

സന്ധ്യാദേവി പുറത്തേക്കുവന്നു. അരവിന്ദനെ കണ്ടു. അവരുടെ കണ്ണുകൾ കലങ്ങിയിരുന്നു.

മൂന്ന്

സദനത്തിലെ വരാന്തയിൽ ഇരുന്നപ്പോൾ അകത്തുനിന്ന് കീർത്തിയുടെ പാട്ടുകേട്ടു.

ചൈത്രമാസരജനികൾ മായാ-
ചിത്രജാലം വരയ്ക്കും നിലാവിൽ
മാലതിപ്പൂക്കൾ ലോലമിഴിയാൽ
മാരപൂജ നടത്തുന്ന കാവിൽ,
വന്നു നിന്നു ലതാഗൃഹവാതിൽ
തന്നിൽ നീ, മോഹവിഗ്രഹംപോലെ.

അരവിന്ദൻ ശ്രദ്ധിച്ചു. കീർത്തി ഇത്ര നന്നായി പാടുമോ? അതു പുതിയ അറിവാണ്. അവൾ ആ കവിത മനഃപാഠമാക്കിയിരിക്കുന്നു. അന്ന് അവൾ ചോദിച്ചു. “എന്താ ഇതിനർഥം?”

കീർത്തി വെളിയിലേക്കു വന്നു. അരവിന്ദനെ കണ്ടു. അവൾ നാണിച്ചുപോയി. മുഖം പൊത്തി: “അയ്യോ, അരവിന്ദേട്ടൻ ഉണ്ടായിരുന്നോ?”

“ഇങ്ങു വരൂ.” അകത്തേക്കോടിയ അവളെ വിളിച്ചു. അവൾ വന്ന് മറഞ്ഞുനിന്നു.

“സന്ധ്യാദേവി എവിടെ?”

“ഇവിടെ ആരുമില്ല.”

“എവിടെപ്പോയി?”

“യൂസഫിന്റെ വീട്ടിൽ കല്യാണത്തിന്.”

“കീർത്തി എന്തേ പോകാഞ്ഞത്?”

അവൾ മുന്നോട്ടു വന്നു.

“എനിക്കു സുഖമില്ലായിരുന്നു. സുമതിയും ഞാനും ഇവിടെ ഇരിക്കാമെന്നു പറഞ്ഞു.”

“എനിക്കും ഇങ്ങനെയാണ്. സുഖമില്ലാത്തപ്പോൾ പാടാൻ തോന്നും.”

അവൾ ചിരിച്ചു.

"ഞാൻ പോകട്ടെ?"

"ഇരിക്കൂ അരവിന്ദേട്ടാ."

അവൾ അകത്തേക്കു പോയി, ചായ കൊണ്ടു വന്നു. അയാൾ കുടിക്കുമ്പോൾ പറഞ്ഞു.

"ആ കവിത ഒന്നു പാടൂ. കേൾക്കട്ടെ."

വിസമ്മതം കാട്ടി. നിർബന്ധിച്ചു. ഒടുവിൽ മാറിനിന്ന് അവൾ അതു പാടി. വാതിൽപ്പാടിൽ തെല്ലു മറഞ്ഞിരുന്ന മുഖത്തേക്ക് ഉറ്റുനോക്കിയിരുന്ന അയാൾ, അവളുടെ കണ്ണുകൾ നിറഞ്ഞൊഴുകുന്നെന്നുകണ്ട് വല്ലാതായി. എന്തിന് അവൾ കരഞ്ഞു? എപ്പോഴും പൊട്ടിച്ചിരിച്ച്, കളി പറഞ്ഞു നടക്കുന്ന അവൾ?

"കീർത്തി."

"എന്താ?"

"നീ കരഞ്ഞോ?"

"ഇല്ല.. ഇല്ല. ഏട്ടാ."

"എനിക്ക് നിന്റെ മുഖം കാണാം."

അവൾ വാതിലിൽ മറഞ്ഞു.

"എന്തിനാണു കരഞ്ഞത്?"

വൈകി മറുപടി വന്നു.

"എനിക്കറിയില്ല."

സാവധാനം ചോദിച്ചു:

"ആ കവിതയുടെ അർഥം മനസിലായോ?"

മറുപടിയില്ല.

"പറയൂ."

"മനസിലായില്ല."

"കള്ളംപറയരുത്."

താഴ്ന്ന സ്വരം

"മനസിലായി."

നിമിഷങ്ങൾ ഒഴുകിപ്പോയി രണ്ടുപേരും മനഃപൂർവം ശ്വാസമടക്കിക്കഴിയുന്നതുപോലെ. ഉറക്കെ ശ്വസിച്ചാൽ അതിൽനിന്ന് ആയിരം ശബ്ദങ്ങൾ വന്നു പോകുമെന്നു ഭയപ്പെട്ടതുപോലെ അരവിന്ദൻ എഴുന്നേറ്റു.

"ഞാൻ പോകുന്നു. കീർത്തി."

അവൾ മിണ്ടാതെ നിന്നു. അയാൾ ഇറങ്ങി നടന്നു. പടികടന്നു പോകുമ്പോൾ കീർത്തിയുടെ മിഴികൾ അയാളെ പിന്തുടർന്നു.

ലോഡ്ജിലെ മുറിയിലിരുന്നുകൊണ്ട്, നിരത്തിലേക്കു നോക്കി. എതിർവശത്ത് സിനിമാ തീയേറ്ററാണ്. അവിടെ വലിയ തിരക്ക്. എന്താണ് ഇന്നത്തെ സിനിമ *ദേവദാസ്* ശരച്ചന്ദ്ര ചാറ്റർജിയുടെ ആ മനോഹരമായ പ്രേമകഥ. കൽക്കട്ടാ ന്യൂതിയേറ്റേഴ്സിന്റെ ഉജ്വലകലാശിൽപ്പം. സൈഗാളിന്റെ ഒരു ഗാനമാണ് തിയേറ്ററിനു പുറത്തേക്കു വച്ചിരിക്കുന്നത്. ആ

കണ്ഠത്തിന്റെ മാസ്മരശക്തി അനുഭവപ്പെടുന്നു. അത് വേദനയുടെ സ്വര മാണ്. ആ അത്ഭുതാത്മാവ് മനുഷ്യരെ പാടി വേദനിപ്പിക്കുന്നു. അദ്ദേഹ ത്തിന്റെ മനസ്സു നിറയെ ദുഃഖമാണോ? അതുകൊണ്ടല്ലേ ആ ശബ്ദത്തിന് ഇത്ര ശക്തിയുണ്ടായത്?

സ്വന്തം മനസിലേക്കു അയാൾ ആഴ്ന്നിറങ്ങി. അവിടെ നിറയെ ചൂടുള്ള പ്രവാഹമാണ്. ഞരമ്പുകൾ അത് വഹിച്ചുകൊണ്ട് ബോധ ത്തിന്റെ കേന്ദ്രത്തിലേക്ക് വരുന്നു. ഇതുവരെയുള്ളതെല്ലാം ദുഃഖത്തിന്റെ രൂപത്തിൽ ഉണർത്തപ്പെടുന്നു.

കൊടുങ്ങല്ലൂരുനിന്ന് ഉള്ളിലേക്ക് മാറിയുള്ള ആ തറവാട്. അപ്പൂപ്പൻ മരിച്ചതുകണ്ടു. അമ്മൂമ്മ മരിച്ചതു കണ്ടു. രണ്ടു സഹോദരിമാർ വിവാ ഹിതരായി വീട്ടിൽ നിന്ന് ഇറങ്ങിപ്പോയപ്പോൾ എല്ലാവരും ആശ്വസിച്ചു. പിന്നെ അച്ഛൻ മരിച്ചതുകണ്ടു നിന്നു. തലമുറകളെയും കൊണ്ട് നൂറ്റാ ണ്ടുകൾ താണ്ടിയ തറവാടിന്റെ ചുമരുകൾ തകർന്നു വീഴുന്ന ശബ്ദം കേട്ടുകൊണ്ടിരുന്നു. പറമ്പിൽ അസ്ഥിമാടങ്ങൾ അവശേഷിക്കുന്നു. പുല്ലു പിടിച്ച മുറ്റത്ത് അമ്മ മാത്രം പ്രാഞ്ചിക്കിതച്ചു നടന്നു. വാർധക്യത്തിന്റെ ഭാരംചുമന്ന്, ഈ ഭൂമിയോട് അവർ നിത്യവും യാത്ര ചോദിക്കുന്നത്, ഉമ്മറത്ത് നോക്കിയിരുന്നു. പൂർത്തിയാക്കാത്ത വിദ്യാഭ്യാസവുമായി അങ്ങ നെയിരുന്നപ്പോഴാണ് അമ്പലമൈതാനത്ത്, വിപ്ലവകാരികളുടെ ശബ്ദം കേട്ടത്. അവരുടെ കൂടെ നടന്നു.

ആദ്യം കവിതയെഴുതിയത് തലമുറകളുടെ കുഴിമാടങ്ങൾ മാത്രം അവശേഷിച്ച തറവാടിനെപ്പറ്റിത്തന്നെയാണ്. അമ്പലവിളക്കുകളുടെ പിന്നിൽ ഒന്നരയും മുണ്ടുമുടുത്ത് വന്നുനിന്ന പെൺകുട്ടികളെപ്പറ്റിയും എഴുതി. സ്വപ്നങ്ങളും സത്യങ്ങളും ഉള്ളിലിളക്കിവിട്ട നിഴലും വെളിച്ച വുമെല്ലാം ഈരടികളിൽ പകർന്നുവെച്ചു. ബങ്കിംചന്ദ്രന്റെ 'വന്ദേമാതരം' ആദ്യം കേട്ടപ്പോൾ ഹരംപിടിച്ചു തുള്ളിച്ചാടി. പിന്നെ ടാഗോറിന്റെയും നസ്റുൾ ഇസ്ലാമിന്റെയും ഗീതങ്ങൾ...

മനസ്സ് പുതിയ തീയും പുകയും കൊണ്ട് അസ്വസ്ഥമായി. പുതിയ സൗന്ദര്യബോധം കവിതയ്ക്ക് പുതിയ ശബ്ദമുണ്ടായി...

എന്നാലും എല്ലാറ്റിലും ദുഃഖത്തിന്റെ ഒരു താളം കിടപ്പുണ്ട്; അതിൽനിന്ന് രക്ഷപ്പെടുക സാധ്യമല്ല. മരണം മധുരമാണെന്നു തോന്നിയ നിമിഷങ്ങളുണ്ട്. പക്ഷേ, ജീവിതം വളയിട്ട്, പൂ ചൂടി, പുഞ്ചിരിച്ച്, നൃത്തം വച്ച്, പാട്ടുകൾ പാടി മുൻപിൽ വന്നുനിൽക്കുന്നതും അനുഭവപ്പെടാറുണ്ട്. ജീവിതം മഹത്തായ ഒരുചൈതന്യപ്രവാഹമായി പലപ്പോഴും കാണാറു ണ്ട്. അപ്പോൾ പ്രസാദം നിറഞ്ഞ ആത്മാവോടെ അതിനെപ്പറ്റി പാടുന്നു.....

ഇവിടെവരെ നടന്നെത്തി.ഇനിയോ? ഓരോ ദിവസവും ജീവിത ത്തിന്റെ വെളിച്ചം തെളിഞ്ഞുവരികയാണ്. ആത്മാവ്, അതിനെപ്പറ്റി ഉച്ച ത്തിൽ പാടാൻ പ്രേരിപ്പിക്കുന്നു.

സന്ധ്യാദേവിയെക്കുറിച്ചും അരവിന്ദൻ ആലോചിച്ചു. അങ്ങനെ ഒരു സ്ത്രീയെ കാണാൻ പ്രയാസമാണ്. ആ സൗന്ദര്യം അസാധാരണമാണ്.

ആ മനസ്സ് അത്ഭുതകരവും! അവരെപ്പറ്റി കവിതയെഴുതാൻ തോന്നിയിട്ടുണ്ട്. എഴുതിയില്ല. അത് താണതരം വികാരമായിപ്പോകുന്നു. കുളിച്ച് വെള്ളവസ്ത്രമണിഞ്ഞ് മുടി റിബൺ കൊണ്ട് നീട്ടിക്കെട്ടിയിട്ട് അവർ വന്നു മുൻപിൽ നിൽക്കുമ്പോൾ അതിലും വലിയ കവിതയില്ലെന്നു തോന്നും. ഇരുപത്തിയാറു വയസുള്ള ഒരാൾക്ക് ഇത്രയും പാകത വരുമോ? ചിലപ്പോൾ കൊച്ചുകുട്ടിയുടെ മുഖമാണത്. അതുപോലെയുള്ള സംസാരവും, ചിലപ്പോൾ എല്ലാ ഗൗരവവും സടകുടഞ്ഞ് എഴുന്നേറ്റു നിൽക്കുംപോലെ.

തന്റെ മുമ്പിൽ അവൾ ദുർബലയാണ്. താനും അങ്ങനെയായിരിക്കുന്നു. ഇത് എവിടെച്ചെന്നെത്തും?

അരവിന്ദൻ ചിന്തയിൽ മുഴുകി, മയങ്ങിപ്പോയി.

കീർത്തി ഉറങ്ങാതെ കിടന്നു. കല്യാണത്തിനു പോയവർ സന്ധ്യ കഴിഞ്ഞപ്പോൾ വന്നു. അപ്പോൾ അവൾ കിടക്കുകയാണ്. അത്താഴം കഴിച്ചില്ല. ഒരു പാത്രം കാപ്പി കുടിച്ചു. ക്ലോക്ക് ശബ്ദിക്കുന്നത് ശ്രദ്ധിച്ചു കൊണ്ടിരുന്നു. ജനാലയ്ക്കരികിലാണ് കിടക്കുന്നത്. മുറ്റത്ത് നിലാവ് പെയ്തുവീഴുന്നത് കാണാം. മണി എത്രയായെന്ന് നിശ്ചയമില്ല. പുറത്തെവിടെയോ ആരോ അടക്കി സംസാരിക്കുന്നതായി തോന്നി. എഴുന്നേറ്റു നോക്കി, രാജമല്ലി മരച്ചുവട്ടിൽ രണ്ടുപേർ നിൽക്കുന്നു. സൂക്ഷിച്ചു നോക്കി.

സന്ധ്യാദേവിയും ഒരു പുരുഷനും...

മിഴിച്ചിരുന്നുപോയി. വിശ്വസിക്കാൻ മനസുവരുന്നില്ല. അപ്പോൾ ക്ലോക്ക് ശബ്ദിക്കുന്നു. പന്ത്രണ്ട്. ഒരിക്കലും പ്രതീക്ഷിക്കാത്തതാണ് കാണുന്നത്. ആ മനുഷ്യൻ ആരാണെന്ന് മനസിലായില്ല. ഉണർന്നു കിടക്കുകയായിരുന്നു. മുൻവശത്ത് ആരും വന്നു വിളിക്കുന്നത് കേട്ടില്ല. വാതിൽ തുറക്കുന്നതുപോലും കേട്ടില്ല. രഹസ്യമായി നടക്കുന്ന കൂടിക്കാഴ്ച എന്നർഥം. കഷ്ടം ഇതു പാടില്ലായിരുന്നു. ഇത് വേണ്ടായിരുന്നു. സന്ധ്യാദേവി എത്ര വലിയവളാണ്.

പുലർച്ചക്കോഴി വിളിച്ച് ഉണർത്തിയപ്പോൾ, ആദ്യമോർമിച്ചത് രാത്രിയിലെ സംഭവമാണ്. രാവിലെ എട്ടു മണിക്കാണ്, കാപ്പി കുടിക്കുമ്പോൾ, സന്ധ്യാദേവിയെക്കണ്ടത്. അവരുടെ കണ്ണുകൾ തളർന്നിരിക്കുന്നു. മുടി പാറി കിടന്നു പതിവില്ലാത്ത ഒരു ക്ഷീണം അവരുടെ മുഖത്തുണ്ട്. അവരെ അങ്ങനെ നോക്കിയിരിക്കാൻ കഴിഞ്ഞില്ല. സദനത്തിലെ മറ്റു വല്ലവരും കൂടി അത് കണ്ടിട്ടുണ്ടോ? രാവിലെ ആരും അന്യോന്യം മിണ്ടുന്നില്ല. എന്നത്തേയും ബഹളം ഇന്നില്ല.

പത്തുമണിയായിട്ടില്ല. അപ്പോൾ ദിവാകരൻ വന്നു. അരവിന്ദൻ കുറേ ദിവസങ്ങൾക്കുശേഷമാണ് സദനത്തിൽ വന്നത്. അതുകൊണ്ടു ദിവാകരനെക്കുറിച്ച് പറയാൻ കഴിഞ്ഞില്ല. അയാൾസ്വയം പരിചയപ്പെടുത്തി. സന്ധ്യാദേവി അയാളെ മാന്യമായി സ്വീകരിച്ചു. ഭാനുമതിയോടുള്ള സ്നേഹം മുഴുവനും അവളെ വിവാഹം കഴിക്കുന്ന മനുഷ്യനോടുള്ള പെരുമാറ്റത്തിൽ കണ്ടു. അവർ സംസാരിച്ചു. അയാൾ പലതും ചോദിച്ചു.

സാധാരണ ചോദ്യങ്ങൾ. സന്ധ്യാദേവി അറിയാവുന്നതെല്ലാം പറഞ്ഞു.

ദിവാകരൻ ഒടുവിൽ ഒരുകാര്യം പറഞ്ഞു:

"ഒരു സംഗതി അറിയാൻ വേണ്ടിയാണ് ഞാൻ ഇതെല്ലാം ചോദിച്ചത്. എന്റെ ജീവിതത്തിലെ ഏകാന്തത അവസാനിപ്പിക്കാൻ സഹായിച്ചതിൽ എനിക്ക് മേനോൻ മാസ്റ്ററോട് നന്ദിയുണ്ട്. നിങ്ങളുടെയൊക്കെ സ്നേഹമാർജിച്ച ഒരു പെൺകുട്ടിയായത്, കൂടുതൽ സന്തോഷകരവുമാണ്. പക്ഷേ, ഞാൻ... ഒന്നും തോന്നരുത്... ഞാൻ രണ്ടാം വിവാഹം നടത്തുകയാണ്. എന്റെ ഭാര്യ മരിച്ചു. രണ്ടാമതുവരുന്ന പെൺകുട്ടി ഭയമുള്ളവളാണെങ്കിൽ, അവൾ ആ വിചാരവും കൊണ്ട് കഴിഞ്ഞുകൂടുകയാണെങ്കിൽ....

സന്ധ്യാദേവി ഉടനെ പറഞ്ഞു:

"അങ്ങനെയൊന്നുമില്ല. ഭാനുമതി തന്റേടമുള്ള പെൺകുട്ടിയാണ്. ധീരയാണെന്നുതന്നെ പറയാം. അവളെപ്പറ്റി ഞങ്ങൾക്കെല്ലാം എന്തു മതിപ്പാണെന്നോ."

"അതല്ല" അയാൾ പറയാൻ തുടങ്ങി. പറഞ്ഞില്ല.

"പിന്നെ."

"ഞാൻ ഉദ്ദേശിക്കുന്നത്...... ഉദ്ദേശിക്കുന്നത്" ആശയം പ്രകടമാക്കാൻ അയാൾ വാക്കുകൾക്കുവേണ്ടി തിരയുകയാണെന്നു തോന്നി. ഒരു വിധം അതു വ്യക്തമാക്കി. "ഞാൻ അന്ധവിശ്വാസിയാണ്."

"എനിക്ക് മനസിലാവുന്നില്ല. മിസ്റ്റർ ദിവാകരൻ" സന്ധ്യാദേവി അയാളെ ഉറ്റുനോക്കി.

അയാൾ ചിരിച്ചു. അയാളുടെ ചുണ്ടുകൾ വികൃതമായി കാണപ്പെട്ടു.

"ഞാൻ പറയാം." ഒരു ഞെരുക്കത്തിൽപ്പെട്ടതുകണക്ക് അയാളുടെ ആശയം പുറത്തുവന്നു. "എന്റെ ഭാര്യ – അവൾ ചീത്തയായിരുന്നു."

സന്ധ്യാദേവിയുടെ ദൃഷ്ടികൾ അയാളിൽ തങ്ങിനിന്നു എന്താണ് അയാളിങ്ങനെ പറഞ്ഞത്?

തിടുക്കത്തിൽ ദിവാകരൻ തുടർന്നു.

"പറയാം. എന്നെ തെറ്റിദ്ധരിക്കേണ്ടാ. എല്ലാ മനുഷ്യരും, ദുർബലരാണ്. എല്ലാവർക്കും ആശങ്കകൾ ഉണ്ട്. ഞാൻ രണ്ടാമത് വിവാഹം കഴിച്ചാൽ... കഴിച്ചാൽ... എന്റെ മരിച്ച ഭാര്യയുടെ പ്രേതം പുതിയ എന്റെ ഭാര്യയെ ആക്രമിക്കുമോ എന്നു ഞാൻ ഭയപ്പെടുന്നു. ഇതു മനസിന്റെ ഒരു വിചാരമാണ്. വെറും തോന്നൽ. അതെനിക്കറിയാം. എവിടെ പ്രേതം? എന്തു പിശാച്? ഇതൊക്കെ അറിയാമെങ്കിലും, ഇടയ്ക്കിടയ്ക്ക് അങ്ങനെയൊക്കെ തോന്നും. വരുന്ന പെൺകുട്ടി ധൈര്യശാലിയായിരുന്നാൽ എനിക്കു സമാധാനമായി. അവൾ എനിക്കു കൂടി ധൈര്യം തരണം. ഒരു പെൺകുട്ടിയെ വിവാഹം കഴിക്കുമ്പോൾ അവൾക്ക് ധൈര്യമുണ്ടോ എന്ന് ആരെങ്കിലും അന്വേഷിക്കാറുണ്ടോ? ആർക്കെങ്കിലും അങ്ങനെ ചോദിക്കാൻ കഴിയുമോ? പക്ഷേ, എന്റെ കാര്യത്തിൽ അൽപ്പം അങ്ങനെ വേണ്ടി വന്നിരിക്കുന്നു. അതുകൊണ്ടാണ് നിങ്ങളെ വന്നു കണ്ടത്. ഞാൻ ബുദ്ധിമുട്ടിച്ചെങ്കിൽ ക്ഷമിക്കണം."

"ഓ അങ്ങനെയൊന്നുമില്ല. നിങ്ങളെ കണ്ടതിൽ ഞങ്ങൾക്ക് സന്തോഷമേ ഉള്ളൂ." സന്ധ്യാദേവി പറഞ്ഞു.

കാപ്പി കുടിച്ച് യാത്ര പറഞ്ഞ് ദിവാകരൻ പോയി.

സന്ധ്യാദേവി തിടുക്കത്തിൽ ഒരുങ്ങി. അവൾ വീട്ടിലേക്കു പോകുന്നു എല്ലാവരും മുൻവശത്തേക്കു വന്നു.

"കീർത്തി എവിടെ?" സന്ധ്യാദേവി ചോദിച്ചു:

"അകത്തുണ്ട്."

ഉഷാമേനോൻ അകത്തുചെന്ന് അവളെ വിളിച്ചു.

"കീർത്തി ഞാൻ നാട്ടിലേക്ക് ഒന്നു പോകുന്നു. എന്റെ അമ്മ മരിച്ചു. അതു കഴിഞ്ഞിട്ട് ദിവസങ്ങളായി. അവർ എന്നെ അറിയിച്ചില്ല. അതങ്ങനെയാണ്. ഇന്നലെ രാത്രിയിൽ അവിടെ നിന്ന് ആൾ വന്നു. അതും അവര് പറഞ്ഞയച്ചതല്ല. നീ മരുന്നു കഴിക്കണം, കേട്ടോ."

കീർത്തി നിശ്ശബ്ദയായി നോക്കി നിന്നു. സന്ധ്യാദേവി പുറത്തേക്ക് നടന്നു.

കൊടുങ്ങല്ലൂരുനിന്ന് വന്ന കത്ത്. അരവിന്ദൻ ഒരാഴ്ചയായി അവിടെ സുഖമില്ലാതെ കിടക്കുന്നു. സന്ധ്യാദേവി കത്തു വായിച്ചു നോക്കി.

"ബഹുമാനമുള്ള സന്ധ്യാദേവി?"

ഒരാഴ്ചയായി ഞാൻ ഇവിടെ വന്നിട്ട്. സുഖമില്ല. പനിയായിരുന്നു. ഇപ്പോൾ കുറവുണ്ട്. ഒരു കത്തെഴുതണമെന്ന് ഈ ദിവസമത്രയും വിചാരിച്ചു. ഇന്ന് എഴുതുന്നു. ഒരു കവിയുടെ വികാരംകൊണ്ട് ഈ വരികൾ എഴുതുകയാണെന്ന് കരുതുകയില്ലെന്ന് വിശ്വസിക്കുന്നു. ഒരു മനുഷ്യന്റെ മനഃപ്രയാസം കുറിക്കുന്നു എന്ന് ധരിക്കണം. ഭാനുമതിയുടെ കാര്യമാണ്. ഞാൻ നേരിട്ട് ചോദിക്കട്ടെ. അവളുടെ വിവാഹത്തെപ്പറ്റി എനിക്ക് ആശങ്കയുണ്ട്. ആ വിവാഹത്തിന്റെ ഫലത്തെപ്പറ്റി. അയാളെ എനിക്കറിയാം. നമ്മുടെ ഭാഷയിൽ അയാൾ സാമൂഹ്യവിരുദ്ധനാണ്. അയാളെ ആ പെൺകുട്ടി വിവാഹം കഴിക്കേണ്ടിവന്നതിന് കാരണക്കാരൻ ഞാനല്ലേ? അല്ലെങ്കിൽ എന്നോട് ക്ഷമിക്കണം നമ്മൾ രണ്ടുപേരുമല്ലേ? വാസവമേനോന്റെ കത്തുമായി ആ കുട്ടിവന്നപ്പോൾ അതിലെ ഉള്ളടക്കം എന്നെ ധരിപ്പിക്കാൻ മടിച്ചു. ഇല്ലേ? കീർത്തിയുടെ കൈയിൽ ആ കത്ത് കൊടുത്തയച്ചിട്ട്, അകത്തുകിടന്നു കരയുകയായിരുന്നില്ലേ? ഞാൻ മനഃപൂർവം ആ ജനാലയ്ക്കരികിൽ വന്നു. ആരും കാണാതെ അകത്തേക്കു നോക്കി അപ്പോൾ രണ്ടു കവിളുകളിലും കൂടി ഒഴുകുന്ന കണ്ണുനീർ ഞാൻ കണ്ടു. അത് കണ്ടുകൊണ്ട്, ഞാൻ ആ വിവാഹത്തിന് സമ്മതിക്കണമോ? എനിക്ക് വയ്യായിരുന്നു. ഞാൻ അതിൽ നിന്നു ഒഴിഞ്ഞുമാറിയപ്പോൾ സന്ധ്യാദേവിയുടെ മനസിൽ സന്തോഷം തോന്നിയില്ലേ? മേനോൻ മാസ്റ്ററുടെ ഒരു വാക്കും ഞാൻ നിരസിച്ചിട്ടില്ല. അദ്ദേഹത്തെ അഭിമുഖീകരിക്കാൻ എനിക്ക് ധൈര്യമില്ലായിരുന്നു. എന്നിട്ടും മുൻപിൽ ചെന്നുനിന്നു. എന്റെ അഭിപ്രായം പറഞ്ഞു. അദ്ദേഹം എന്നോട് ഭംഗ്യന്തരേണ ഒരു ചോദ്യം ചോദിച്ചു. അരവിന്ദന്റെ മനസ്സ് കണ്ടുപിടിക്കുന്നതിൽ ഞാൻ

തോറ്റു, ഇല്ലേ? യഥാർഥത്തിൽ എന്റെ മനസ്സ് മനസിലാക്കിയിട്ടല്ലേ അദ്ദേഹം അങ്ങനെ പറഞ്ഞത്? ഒന്നും അവകാശപ്പെടാത്ത, ഒരു വലിപ്പവും ഭാവിക്കാത്ത, മഹാശയനാണ് ആ മനുഷ്യൻ. ആ നല്ല മനുഷ്യന്റെ മുൻപിൽ സത്യം പറഞ്ഞാലോ എന്ന് ഞാൻ ആലോചിച്ചു. രണ്ടു കാര്യങ്ങളാണ് എന്നെ തടസപ്പെടുത്തിയത്. സന്ധ്യാദേവിക്ക് അത് ഇഷ്ടപ്പെടാതെ വന്നാലോ? പിന്നെ ഇതുവരെ പരസ്പരം ഒന്നും പറഞ്ഞിട്ടില്ലാത്ത ഒരു സംഗതിയെക്കുറിച്ച് എങ്ങനെ പറയും? ഏതായാലും ഞാൻ ഒരു വിധത്തിൽ അദ്ദേഹത്തിന്റെ മുന്നിൽ നിന്ന് പിൻവാങ്ങി.

എന്റെ മനസ്സ് കുറ്റബോധംകൊണ്ട് നിറഞ്ഞിരിക്കുന്നു. വേദനിപ്പിക്കാനല്ല ഇത് എഴുതുന്നത്. ഭാനുമതിയുടെ വിവാഹത്തെ എന്തിന്റെ പേരിലായാലും തടയാൻ നമുക്ക് രണ്ടുപേർക്കും ധാർമികമായി അവകാശമില്ല. അധികാരമില്ല. ആ വിവാഹത്തിന് ചെല്ലണമെന്ന്. ഭാനുമതിയുടെ വ്യക്തിപരമായ ഒരു കത്ത് ഇന്നെനിക്ക് കിട്ടി. ഞാൻ പോകുകയില്ല. സന്ധ്യാദേവി പൊയ്ക്കൊള്ളൂ. എനിക്കും കൂടി വേണ്ടി പോകൂ.

ഞാൻ ഒന്നു പറഞ്ഞോട്ടെ; ഈ അവസ്ഥ എന്റെ ദിനരാത്രങ്ങളെ അലട്ടുന്നു,

എന്നോട് ക്ഷമിക്കുക,

സ്നേഹപുരസ്സരം അരവിന്ദൻ.

നെടുവീർപ്പുകളിൽ മുങ്ങിപ്പോകുമെന്ന് തോന്നി. ഈ കത്തിൽ സ്നേഹമാണോ പാരുഷ്യമാണോ അടങ്ങിയിരിക്കുന്നത്? അരവിന്ദനെ ആദ്യം കണ്ടത് സന്ധ്യാദേവി ഓർമിച്ചു. കോളേജിൽ ഒരുമിച്ച് പ്രസംഗിക്കാൻ ചെന്നു. യോഗം കഴിഞ്ഞ് ഒരു കാറിൽ തിരിച്ച് യാത്ര ചെയ്തു. കവിതയെപ്പറ്റി അനേകം അഭിനന്ദനങ്ങൾ പറഞ്ഞു. അത് ആത്മാർഥമായിരുന്നു. അതെല്ലാം കേട്ട്, ഒന്നും മിണ്ടാതിരുന്നു. ധാരാളം ഇങ്ങോട്ട് സംസാരിച്ചെങ്കിൽ, എന്നാഗ്രഹിച്ചു. 'എന്താ ഒന്നും മിണ്ടാത്തത്?' എന്ന് രണ്ടു മൂന്നു തവണ ചോദിച്ചു. 'എന്റെ സ്വഭാവം അങ്ങനെയാണ്' എന്ന് ഒടുവിൽ സമാധാനം പറഞ്ഞു. ഇറങ്ങാൻ നേരത്ത് കൈയിലിരുന്ന റോസാപ്പൂ കൊടുത്തു. അത് വിനയപൂർവം വാങ്ങി. 'സദനത്തിലേക്ക് ഒരിക്കൽ വരണം, അഭ്യർഥിച്ചു. 'കേട്ടിട്ടുണ്ട് വരാൻ ആഗ്രഹമുണ്ട്, വരാം, മറുപടി പറഞ്ഞു. തൊഴുതു പിരിഞ്ഞു.

ഒരു മാസം കഴിഞ്ഞ് സദനത്തിൽ വന്നു. തുടർച്ചയായി മൂന്നുനാലു തവണ. അപ്പോഴെല്ലാം മിതമായേ സംസാരിക്കൂ. ഒരിക്കൽ മനഃപൂർവം ചോദിച്ചു.

"ഒന്നു മിണ്ടരുതോ?"

അയാൾ ചിരിച്ചു പോയി.

എങ്കിലും പിന്നീട് കുറച്ചുകൂടി സംസാരിക്കാൻ തുടങ്ങി. ഒരു ദിവസം ഒരു കുസൃതിത്തരം പറഞ്ഞു:

"സംസാരിപ്പിക്കാൻ പഠിപ്പിച്ചത് ഞാനാണ്. ആ ഓർമ വേണം."

അയാൾ ഉറ്റുനോക്കിയിരുന്നു.

അന്നാണ്, ആ നിമിഷത്തിലാണ് മനസുകൾ യഥാർഥത്തിൽ സന്ധിച്ചത്. അവിടെ തമ്മിൽപ്പിരിയാനുള്ള പ്രയാസം രണ്ടുപേർക്കും അനുഭവപ്പെട്ടു. മറ്റൊരു രീതിയിലാണ് അയാൾ അത് പ്രകടിപ്പിച്ചത്. ഇങ്ങനെ പറഞ്ഞു.

"സമ്മതിച്ചു എന്ന് ഞാൻ പറഞ്ഞില്ല അല്ലേ? പറഞ്ഞിരിക്കുന്നു. പറയാൻ പോലും മറന്നുപോയി."

നിശ്ശബ്ദമായിട്ടാണ് ആ അടുപ്പം വളർന്നത്. തന്നിൽ നിന്ന് ആരും അത് പ്രതീക്ഷിക്കുന്നില്ല. ഒരു വിവാഹം കഴിക്കാൻ തീരുമാനിച്ചാൽ, അവർക്ക് ഒന്നും തോന്നുകയില്ലായിരിക്കാം. പക്ഷേ, പ്രേമം... തനിക്ക് അത് പറ്റിയതല്ല. ഒരു ചലനം കൊണ്ടുപോലും മറ്റുള്ളവർക്ക് സംശയമുണ്ടായിട്ടില്ല. വാസവമേനോന്റെ കത്തുമായി ഭാനുമതി വന്ന ദിവസം തന്റെ അസ്വസ്ഥത മറ്റുള്ളവർ മനസിലാക്കിയോ എന്ന് ആശങ്കിച്ചു. ഇല്ല ഇന്നും അരവിന്ദനോട് സംസാരിക്കുമ്പോൾ ഭയമുണ്ട്. അറിവുള്ള വലിയ ചെറുപ്പക്കാരൻ.

ഇപ്പോൾ വന്ന കത്ത്, സന്ധ്യാദേവിയെ യഥാർഥത്തിൽ വേദനിപ്പിച്ചു. അതിലെ ഓരോ അക്ഷരവും സത്യമാണ്. ഒടുവിലെഴുതിയിരിക്കുന്ന വാചകം അവരുടെ അന്തഃകരണത്തെ സ്പർശിച്ചു. ഈ അവസ്ഥ എന്റെ ദിനരാത്രങ്ങളെ അലട്ടുന്നു... എന്താണതിനർഥം. അരവിന്ദന്റെ ശ്രദ്ധയെ ആകർഷിച്ചത് താനാണ് എങ്ങനെ അത് നിഷേധിക്കാൻ കഴിയും? കണ്ടുമുട്ടിയപ്പോഴെല്ലാം അങ്ങോട്ടു കാട്ടിയ ബഹുമാനമെല്ലാം ഹൃദയത്തിന്റെ ആഴങ്ങളിൽ സ്പർശിക്കുന്ന മൂകനിവേദനങ്ങളായിരുന്നു. അങ്ങനെ ആയത് എന്തുകൊണ്ടാണ്? തന്റെ ഉള്ളിൽ തടഞ്ഞു പിടിക്കാൻ നിവൃത്തിയില്ലാത്ത മമത വളർന്നുകൊണ്ടിരുന്നു. അതിന്റെ തെറ്റും ശരിയും അറിയില്ല. ജീവിതത്തിൽ ഒരിക്കലും സ്വസ്ഥതയുണ്ടായിട്ടില്ല. സുഖം എന്ന വാക്കിന്റെ അർഥം അറിഞ്ഞിട്ടില്ല. ഈ സദനം സ്ഥാപിച്ചതോടെ, മറ്റെല്ലാം മറന്ന് ഇതിലേക്കു ഒതുങ്ങിക്കൂടുകയായിരുന്നു. ധാരാളം മനുഷ്യരുമായുള്ള ഇടപെടൽ, സമ്മേളനങ്ങൾ, ചർക്കാസംഘത്തിന്റെ പ്രവർത്തനം ഇവിടെത്തന്നെ പരസ്പരം സ്നേഹിക്കുന്ന നല്ല കുറച്ച് സഹപ്രവർത്തകരുമായുള്ള ബന്ധം. എല്ലാംകൂടി ഒരുവിധം സമാധാനത്തോടെ കഴിയുന്നു. അരവിന്ദൻ മനസിലേക്ക് കടന്നുവന്ന ഒരത്ഭുത ശക്തിയാണ്. ശക്തമായ ആ കവി ഹൃദയത്തെ അപഹരിച്ചത് താൻപോലും അറിഞ്ഞില്ല. ഒരിക്കലും അങ്ങനെയൊരു അഭിനിവേശമുണ്ടാകുമെന്ന് സ്വപ്നത്തിൽപ്പോലും വിചാരിച്ചതല്ല. അജ്ഞാതമായ ഒരുപ്രേരണയിൽക്കൂടി, മനഃപൂർവം എന്നു പറയാൻ വയ്യാത്ത ഒരാഗ്രഹത്തിൽക്കൂടി ഒഴുകിയൊഴുകി ആ മനുഷ്യനിലേക്ക് ലയിച്ചുചേർന്നുപോയി.

എന്തുചെയ്യണം? ഇതു സുഖകരമായ പാതയല്ല. സ്വയം നിർമിച്ചു വച്ച വിലക്കുകൾ പലതുണ്ട്. ഈ സദനം ജീവനർപ്പിച്ചു വളർത്തിയ സങ്കേതമാണ്. ഇവിടത്തെ അന്തേവാസികളായ കുട്ടികളെ മിക്കവരെയും അങ്ങോട്ടുച്ചെന്നു പ്രേരിപ്പിച്ചുകൊണ്ടുവന്നതാണ്. വന്നപ്പോൾ അവർ ഇതിന്റെ ഭാഗമായിത്തീർന്നിരിക്കുന്നു. അവരെ വിട്ടിട്ട്, സ്വന്തം സുഖ

ത്തിന്റെ അന്തഃപുരത്തിലേക്കു മടങ്ങിപ്പോകാൻ കഴിയുമോ? അങ്ങനെ പോയില്ലെങ്കിൽപ്പോലും വിവാഹം കഴിച്ച താൻ സ്വകാര്യ താൽപ്പര്യങ്ങളെ മറ്റൊരു സ്ത്രീയായിട്ടു മാറുകയല്ലേ ചെയ്യുക?

അരവിന്ദനോടു താൻ തെറ്റുചെയ്തുകൊണ്ടിരിക്കുന്നു.

യോഗമയീദേവി തൊട്ടുനോക്കി ശരീരം തണുത്തുവെറുങ്ങലിച്ചിരിക്കുന്നു. അവർ അംബികത്തമ്പുരാട്ടിയെ വിളിച്ചു. അവർ വന്നു. സന്ധ്യാദേവി ബോധരഹിതയായി കിടക്കുന്നു. വെള്ളം കൊണ്ടുവന്നു. ഉഷയും റീനയും പാർവതിയും കീർത്തിയും സുമതിയും എല്ലാവരും ഓടിവന്നു. യോഗമയി ആ കത്ത് മേശയ്ക്കകത്തേക്ക് എടുത്തുവച്ചു. അവർ സന്ധ്യാദേവിയെ പലവുരു വിളിച്ചു. ഡോക്ടറെ വിളിച്ചാലോ എന്ന് അവർ ആലോചിച്ചു.

കീർത്തിയുടെ കണ്ണുകൾ നിറഞ്ഞു. അവൾ പൊട്ടിക്കരഞ്ഞുപോയി. അംബികത്തമ്പുരാട്ടി അവളെ സമാധാനിപ്പിച്ചു.

ഒരു നാഴിക കഴിഞ്ഞപ്പോൾ സന്ധ്യാദേവി കണ്ണുതുറന്നു ചുറ്റും നോക്കി. ഒരു ഉറക്കം കഴിഞ്ഞ് ഉണർന്നതുപോലെയേ തോന്നിയുള്ളൂ.

"ഒന്നുമില്ല. എനിക്ക് എന്തോ ഒരു വല്ലായ്മവന്നു. അത് പോയി." സന്ധ്യാദേവി സാവധാനം പറഞ്ഞു.

അന്നു രാത്രിയിൽ എല്ലാവരും ആ മുറിയിൽ കിടന്നു. കീർത്തി ഉറങ്ങിയില്ല. അവൾ സന്ധ്യാദേവിയുടെ തലയ്ക്കരികിലേക്ക് ശിരസർപ്പിച്ച് കട്ടിലിനരികിലിരുന്നു.

രണ്ടുമൂന്നു ദിവസങ്ങൾ. സന്ധ്യാദേവിയുടെ ക്ഷീണമെല്ലാം മാറി. സദനം പഴയതുപോലെ ഉത്സാഹപൂർണമായി. യോഗമയി-സന്ധ്യാദേവിയെ ഉപദേശിച്ചു. "ഉറക്കമിളയ്ക്കരുത്. ഓരോ കാര്യങ്ങൾ അധികമാലോചിച്ച് മനസിനെ അലട്ടരുത്. എവിടെപ്പോയാലും സമയത്ത് വല്ലതും കഴിക്കണം. എന്റെ മകളെ ഞങ്ങൾക്കു വേണം. നാട്ടിനുവേണം..."

കീർത്തിയുടെ പെരുമാറ്റത്തിൽ വലിയ മാറ്റം വന്നു. അത് എല്ലാവരും ശ്രദ്ധിക്കുകയും ചെയ്തു. അവൾ സന്ധ്യാദേവിയുടെ അരികിലാണ് എപ്പോഴും. അവർ വായിക്കുകയോ എഴുതുകയോ ചെയ്യുമ്പോൾ, നൂൽ നൂൽക്കുമ്പോൾ, എന്തെങ്കിലും മറ്റു ജോലികൾ ചെയ്യുമ്പോൾ കീർത്തി അടുത്തുച്ചെന്നിരിക്കും; ഒന്നും മിണ്ടുകയില്ല. ഒരുവിധത്തിലും ശല്യം ചെയ്യുകയില്ല. ഇപ്പോൾ, അവർക്ക് വെള്ളമെടുത്തു കൊടുക്കുന്നത്, കാപ്പിയും പലഹാരവും വിളമ്പുന്നത്, കിടക്ക വിരിച്ചുകൊടുക്കുന്നത് എല്ലാം അവളാണ്. അന്നു രാത്രിയിൽ സന്ധ്യാദേവിയെ തെറ്റിദ്ധരിച്ചതോർമിച്ച് അവൾ പലതവണ കരഞ്ഞു. അവർക്ക് ആലസ്യം വന്നപ്പോൾ അവളുടെ നെഞ്ചു തകർന്നുപോയി. തനിക്ക് അവരോട് ഇത്ര സ്നേഹമുണ്ടെന്ന് അപ്പോഴാണ് അവളറിഞ്ഞത്. അവരുടെ രൂപം കാണാതിരിക്കാൻ അവൾക്കു കഴിയില്ല. ഒരു ദിവസം രണ്ടുപേരും ഒറ്റയ്ക്കായപ്പോൾ സന്ധ്യാദേവി ചോദിച്ചുപോയി: "കീർത്തി, നിന്റെ സ്നേഹം കണ്ടിട്ട് ഞാൻ പലപ്പോഴും ദുർബലയായിപ്പോകുന്നു. ഞാൻ എങ്ങനെ ഇതു തിരിച്ചു തരും?" അവൾ മറുപടിയൊന്നും പറഞ്ഞില്ല.

അവൾ അവർ കിടക്കുന്ന കട്ടിലിനരികിൽ നിലത്തുകിടക്കും. അവർ രാത്രിയിൽ തിരിഞ്ഞും മറിഞ്ഞും കിടന്നാൽ, എഴുന്നേറ്റിരുന്ന് സാവധാനം ഉണർത്താതെ, കാലുകൾ തലോടും.

അവരുടെ ഉടുവസ്ത്രങ്ങൾ അവൾ കഴുകിയിടും. അതിന് സന്ധ്യാദേവി അവളെ കർശനമായി വഴക്കു പറഞ്ഞു. എന്നാലും അവളതു ചെയ്യും.

അപരിചിതനായ ഒരു മനുഷ്യൻ ഒരു ദിവസം രാവിലെ കയറി വന്നു. അയാൾ സന്ധ്യാദേവിയെ ചോദിച്ചു. അവർ ചെന്ന് അയാളെ സ്വീകരിച്ചിരുത്തി. തടിച്ച ശരീരവും ചെറിയ മീശയും പതിഞ്ഞ ശബ്ദവുമുള്ള അയാൾ പേരുപറഞ്ഞു: "രാഘവൻനായർ." എന്തുകൊണ്ടോ അതു ശരിയല്ലെന്ന് സന്ധ്യാദേവിക്ക് തോന്നി. സ്ത്രീകളുടെ സദനമാണ്. അങ്ങനെ ചിലർ വിനോദത്തിനുവേണ്ടി വരാറുണ്ട്; കാഴ്ച കാണാൻ. അവരോട് മര്യാദയ്ക്കു പെരുമാറണമെന്ന് അവർ നിഷ്കർഷിച്ചിട്ടുണ്ട്. അതുപോലെ ഇപ്പോഴും പെരുമാറി. രാഘവൻനായർ തന്നെപ്പറ്റി കൂടുതൽ കാര്യങ്ങൾ പറഞ്ഞു.

"ഞാൻ കണ്ണൂരാണ് താമസിക്കുക. ദേശീയ പ്രസ്ഥാനവുമായിട്ട് കുറേ അടുപ്പമുണ്ട്. നാലഞ്ചുവർഷക്കാലം വാർധായിലായിരുന്നു. മഹാത്മാഗാന്ധിയുടെ അന്തേവാസിയായിക്കഴിയാനും ഭാഗ്യം കിട്ടിയിട്ടുണ്ട്. പിന്നെ മലബാറിലേക്ക് പോന്നു. അവിടെ പ്രവർത്തനം നടത്തുന്നു. ഇടയ്ക്ക് മദിരാശിയിലും പോകും. തിരുവിതാംകൂർ പ്രദേശത്തെ കാര്യങ്ങൾ ഒന്നു കണ്ടുപഠിച്ചു പോകാമെന്ന് കരുതി വന്നു. വാസവമേനോനെ അറിയാം. അദ്ദേഹവും വാർധയിലുണ്ടായിരുന്നല്ലോ. ഇപ്പോൾ കുറെക്കാലമായി കണ്ടിട്ട്. ഈ സദനത്തെപ്പറ്റി കേട്ടിട്ടുണ്ട്. ഒന്ന് സന്ദർശിച്ചുകളയാമെന്ന് വിചാരിച്ചു."

"വളരെ സന്തോഷം." സന്ധ്യാദേവി പറഞ്ഞു.

കാപ്പി വന്നു. അത് കുടിക്കുമ്പോൾ അയാൾ ചോദ്യങ്ങൾ ചോദിച്ചു തുടങ്ങി.

"എത്രകാലമായി ഇത് സ്ഥാപിച്ചിട്ട്?'

"നാലഞ്ചു വർഷങ്ങളായി."

"സന്ധ്യാദേവിയുടെ മുൻകൈയാണ്, അല്ലേ?"

"അങ്ങനെ പറഞ്ഞുകൂടാ, ഞാൻ ആദ്യം മുതൽക്ക് ഇതിന്റെ പ്രവർത്തകയാണ്. പക്ഷേ, ഇതിന്റെ ആരംഭം കുറിച്ചത് വാസവമേനോനും യോഗമയീദേവിയുമാണെന്ന് എല്ലാവർക്കുമറിയാം. അന്ന് മേനോൻ മാസ്റ്റർ ശാന്തിനികേതനത്തിൽ പ്രൊഫസറായിരുന്നു. യോഗമയീദേവി ബനാറീസ് സർവകലാശാലയിലെ പ്രൊഫസറും. അവർ ഇവിടെ വന്ന് എന്നെക്കാണാനിടയായി. ഈ സദനം സ്ഥാപിച്ച് എന്നെ അതിന്റെ ചുമതലയേൽപ്പിച്ചു."

"അതെയതെ, വാസവമേനോൻ ഇതിനൊക്കെ സമർഥനാണല്ലോ. ഒന്നാന്തരം സംഘാടകൻ. ഇപ്പോൾ എവിടെയാ മൂപ്പര്?"

"അറിയില്ല. അദ്ദേഹം ലോകസഞ്ചാരിയാണല്ലോ." മനഃപൂർവമാണ് സന്ധ്യാദേവി അങ്ങനെ പറഞ്ഞത്. മേനോന്റെ അതതുകാലത്തെ താവ

ളങ്ങൾ ആരെയും അറിയിക്കാറില്ല.

"യോഗമയിയമ്മയെ ഞാൻ കണ്ടിട്ടില്ല."

സന്ധ്യാദേവി വാതിൽക്കലേക്ക് ചെന്നു. യോഗമയിയെ വിളിച്ചു. അവർ വന്നു. രാഘവൻനായർ ഭവ്യതയോടെ അവരെ തൊഴുതു. പരിചയപ്പെടുത്തി. അവർ അവിടെ നിൽക്കാതെ അകത്തേക്ക് പോയി.

അയാൾ വീണ്ടും ഇരുന്നു.

"ഇപ്പോൾ ഇവിടെ അന്തേവാസികളായി എത്രപേരുണ്ടാവും?"

"ആറേഴുപേരുണ്ട്."

"വാസവമേനോൻ മാസ്റ്റർ വരാറുണ്ടോ?"

"ഇല്ല."

"നമ്മുടെ ഒരു കവിയുണ്ടല്ലോ... അതെ, അരവിന്ദൻ.. ഞങ്ങൾ ഒരിക്കൽ കണ്ടിട്ടുണ്ട്. അദ്ദേഹം ഇപ്പോൾ എവിടെയാണ്?"

ആ ചോദ്യം സംശയത്തിനു വിത്തുപാകി. അരവിന്ദനെ ഒരിക്കൽ കണ്ടിട്ടുള്ള ഇയാൾ, ആ മനുഷ്യനെപ്പറ്റി ഇവിടെ അന്വേഷിക്കുന്നതിലർഥമെന്ത്? അരവിന്ദന് ഈ സദനവുമായി ബന്ധമുണ്ടെന്ന് ഇയാൾ എങ്ങനെ നിശ്ചയിച്ചു?

സന്ധ്യാദേവി പിന്നെ കുറച്ചുകൂടി കരുതലോടെ മറുപടികൾ പറഞ്ഞു.

"അരവിന്ദൻ എവിടെയാണെന്ന് അറിയില്ല."

"നല്ല കവിയാണ്. മിടുക്കൻ. നമ്മുടെ ദേശീയപ്രസ്ഥാനത്തിൽ ആ കവിതകൾ ഒരു മുതൽക്കൂട്ടാണ്. ആകട്ടെ, ഞങ്ങൾ അവിടെ ചർക്കാസംഘത്തിനും മറ്റും പണമുണ്ടാക്കാൻ വളരെ പ്രയാസപ്പെടുന്നുണ്ട്. ഇവിടെ ഇതുപോലൊരു സ്ഥാപനം നടത്തിക്കൊണ്ടുപോകാൻ എത്ര ബുദ്ധിമുട്ടുണ്ടാവും! എങ്ങനെയാ പണമൊക്കെ സാധിക്കുന്നത്?."

"ഓ, ഇവിടെ വലിയ പണച്ചെലവൊന്നുമില്ല. ഞങ്ങളുടെ ആഹാരച്ചെലവാണ് പ്രധാനം. അത് മിക്കവാറും ഞങ്ങളുടെ വീടുകളിൽനിന്നു തന്നെയാണ് കൊണ്ടുവരിക."

"ഓഹോ, അവിടെ രഹസ്യമായി ചില പണക്കാരൊക്കെ സഹായിക്കും. ഇവിടെയും അങ്ങനെ വല്ലവരെയുമൊക്കെ സമീപിക്കണം. ഇല്ലാതെ എങ്ങനെ നടത്താനാണ്? വീടുകളിൽനിന്ന് എത്രകാലം കൊണ്ടുവരും? ഇവിടെ വല്ലവരെയും അങ്ങനെ സമീപിച്ചിട്ടുണ്ടോ?"

"ഇല്ല."

സന്ധ്യാദേവിയുടെ ക്ഷമ നശിച്ചുതുടങ്ങി. അവർ തിടുക്കം കാട്ടി. ഒടുവിൽ അയാൾ എഴുന്നേറ്റു. അയാൾ ആളുമാറി സംസാരിക്കുകയാണെന്നു ശക്തിയായ വിശ്വാസം തോന്നി. ഉള്ളിൽ ക്ഷോഭം പതഞ്ഞു പൊങ്ങി.

"നിങ്ങൾക്ക് ഇനി വല്ലതും അറിയണോ?" സന്ധ്യാദേവി പൊടുന്നനെ ചോദിച്ചു. അവരുടെ സ്വരം പരുഷമായി.

അയാൾ പെട്ടെന്നു വല്ലാതായി. അവരെ നോക്കി. "എന്താ അങ്ങ

നെയൊരു ഭാവം?"

"മനസിലായില്ലേ?"

"തെറ്റിദ്ധരിക്കേണ്ട."

"ശരിയായിത്തന്നെ ധരിച്ചു. നിങ്ങൾ മിനക്കെടാതെ പോകൂ." അയാൾ ഗേറ്റിലേക്ക് നടന്നു. അയാളുടെ ഡയറിയിൽ അശ്രദ്ധമായി വച്ച ഒരു കടലാസിൽ സർക്കാരിന്റെ മുദ്ര സന്ധ്യാദേവി കണ്ടു.

നാല്

സദനത്തിന്റെ വാർഷികം കൊണ്ടാടി. പതിവിലും ആർഭാടപൂർവമാണ് അതു നടന്നത്. അങ്ങനെയാകാൻ കാരണമുണ്ട്. ഉഷാമേനോന്റെ അച്ഛൻ കൽക്കത്തയിലാണ്. അവിടെ നല്ല ഒരു ബിസിനസ് നടത്തുന്നു. അദ്ദേഹം നാട്ടിൽ വന്നപ്പോൾ വാർഷികത്തിന്റെ കാര്യം സന്ധ്യാദേവി പറഞ്ഞു. അദ്ദേഹം അതിന്റെ ചിലവു മുഴുവൻ ഏറ്റെടുത്തു. നല്ല പ്രസംഗകരെ കൊണ്ടുവരണം. തൊഴിലാളികളുടെയും കൃഷിക്കാരുടെയും ഇടയിൽ നിന്നുള്ള കലാകാരന്മാരെ പങ്കെടുപ്പിച്ച് പാട്ടും നൃത്തവും നടത്തണം. സദനത്തിലുള്ളവർ ഒരു നാടകം അവതരിപ്പിക്കണം. അതൊക്കെ അദ്ദേഹത്തിന്റെ പദ്ധതികളായിരുന്നു. എല്ലാറ്റിനും അദ്ദേഹം തന്നെ നേരിട്ടു ബന്ധപ്പെട്ടു. കൽക്കത്തയിൽ നടക്കുന്നത് അദ്ദേഹം പറഞ്ഞു കേൾപ്പിച്ചു. അവിടെ പുരോഗമനവാദികൾ അങ്ങനെയാണ് സംഗതികൾ നടത്തുന്നത്. ഇവിടെയും അതുപോലെവേണം.

പ്രസംഗങ്ങൾ പ്രശസ്തരായ രണ്ടുമൂന്നു രാഷ്ട്രീയനേതാക്കൾ. രണ്ടുമൂന്നു സാഹിത്യകാരന്മാർ. കയർ ഫാക്ടറികളിലെ തൊഴിലാളികളുടെ ഒരു കലാസംഘമാണ് പാട്ടും നൃത്തവും അവതരിപ്പിച്ചത്. അതു കാണികളെ ആകർഷിച്ചു. നൂറ്റാണ്ടുകളായി അടിമകളായിക്കിടന്ന കൃഷിക്കാർ ചങ്ങല പൊട്ടിച്ച് സ്വാതന്ത്ര്യം നേടിയത് നൃത്തത്തിൽക്കൂടി കണ്ടപ്പോൾ, സദസ്സ് മുദ്രാവാക്യങ്ങൾ വിളിച്ചു. ഭാരതത്തിന്റെ സ്വാതന്ത്ര്യഭേരി മുഴക്കുന്ന പടപ്പാട്ടുകൾ ഉയർന്നപ്പോൾ അവർ എഴുന്നേറ്റുനിന്ന് കൂടെപ്പാടി.

ഹൃദയസ്പർശിയായ ഒരു നാടകമായിരുന്നു അത്. സദനത്തിലെ എല്ലാവരും അതിൽ പങ്കെടുത്തു. കൂടാതെ അരവിന്ദനും വാസവമേനോനും വേഷം കെട്ടി. സന്ധ്യാദേവി നായികയായിരുന്നു. അരവിന്ദൻ പ്രധാന കഥാപാത്രവും. ജീവിതത്തിന്റെ അർഥമന്വേഷിച്ചിറങ്ങിയ ഒരു തീർഥാടകന്റെ കഥ. ഒരു ഗ്രാമത്തിലെ കൃഷിക്കാരിപ്പെണ്ണിന്റെ ജീവിതത്തിൽ അയാൾ ചെന്നെത്തുന്നു. അവിടെനിന്ന് മനുഷ്യാധ്വാനത്തിന്റെ മഹനീയമൂല്യം ഗ്രഹിച്ച് അയാൾ തന്റെ അന്വേഷണലക്ഷ്യം സാക്ഷാൽക്കരിക്കുന്നു.

പല നേതാക്കളും പ്രസംഗിച്ചെങ്കിലും വാസവമേനോന്റെ ചെറിയ ഭാഷണം, ആ വാർഷികത്തിലെ മറക്കാൻ വയ്യാത്ത നിമിഷങ്ങളായി നിന്നു. അത് എല്ലാവർക്കും അനുഭവപ്പെട്ടു. താണസ്വരത്തിൽ ഓരോ

പൂക്കളെടുത്തർപ്പിക്കും പോലെ വാക്കുകൾ വിന്യസിച്ച്, വശീകരിക്കുന്ന നേരിയ പുഞ്ചിരിയോടെ അദ്ദേഹം പറഞ്ഞു:

"ജീവിക്കണം മരിക്കരുത് — ഈ രണ്ടാഗ്രഹങ്ങൾ നമുക്കുണ്ട്." രണ്ടും ഒന്നാണ്. ഒരാഗ്രഹമാണ്. വെറുതെ ജീവിച്ചാൽ മതിയോ? പോരാ. ജീവിതത്തിന് ഒരർഥം കണ്ടുപിടിക്കണം. എന്നിട്ട് ആ അർഥം സാക്ഷാൽക്കരിക്കാൻവേണ്ടി ജീവിക്കണം. ഇത് ശ്രമകരമാണ്. ഭാരതീയാചാര്യന്മാർ ഇതാണ് ചെയ്തത്. എന്നിട്ട്, അവർ അത് പരമ്പരകളോട് പറഞ്ഞു. അങ്ങനെയാണ് നമുക്ക് ഉപനിഷത്തുക്കളും മറ്റും കിട്ടിയത്. ശങ്കരാചാര്യരെപ്പോലുള്ള ഗുരുക്കന്മാർ ഋഷിപ്രോക്തങ്ങളായ സത്യങ്ങൾക്ക് വ്യാഖ്യാനം നൽകി, നമ്മെ കൂടുതൽ പഠിപ്പിക്കാൻ ശ്രമിച്ചിരിക്കുന്നു. വിവേകാനന്ദനും റാം മോഹൻറോയിയും മറ്റും ആ അറിവുകളെ വീണ്ടും ലളിതമാക്കി നമ്മെ വെളിച്ചത്തിലേക്ക് കൂട്ടിക്കൊണ്ടുപോകുന്നു.

ചെറിയ മനുഷ്യരായ നമ്മൾ, ആ വലിയ കാര്യങ്ങൾ മനസിലാക്കേണ്ടിയിരിക്കുന്നു. അത് സാധ്യമാണോ? സാധ്യമാണ്. എല്ലാ അറിവിന്റെയും പരമമായ ലക്ഷ്യം കർമമാണ്. കർമം ചെയ്യുന്നവർ ജീവിക്കുന്നു. എന്തു കർമം? വിശക്കുമ്പോൾ ആഹാരം കഴിക്കണമെന്ന് നമുക്കറിയാം. ആഹാരം കഴിക്കണമെങ്കിൽ, അത് ഉൽപ്പാദിപ്പിക്കണമെന്ന്. അല്ലെങ്കിൽ സമ്പാദിക്കണമെന്ന് പ്രത്യേകം പറയണോ? എല്ലാ കർമങ്ങളും ജീവിതത്തെ നിലനിർത്താനും വളർത്താനുമുള്ളതാണ്. താൻ ചെയ്യേണ്ട കർമം കണ്ടുപിടിക്കുക. ജീവിതത്തിന്റെ അർഥം കണ്ടുപിടിക്കൽ തന്നെയാണ്.

അത്രയുമെങ്കിലും നാം അറിഞ്ഞിരുന്നാൽ മതി. ഓരോ ഘട്ടത്തിലും ജീവിതത്തിനാവശ്യമായ കർമം വിശദാംശങ്ങളിൽ വ്യത്യസ്തമായിരിക്കും. ഇപ്പോൾ നമുക്കാവശ്യം സ്വാതന്ത്ര്യമാണ്. ഭാരതത്തിന്റെ സ്വാതന്ത്ര്യം. അത് കൈവന്നാലേ നമുക്കു ജീവിക്കാനാവൂ. അതുകൊണ്ട് അത് നേടാനുള്ള പ്രവൃത്തിയാണ് ഇപ്പോൾ ആവശ്യം. എല്ലാ പ്രവർത്തിക്കും അതിന്റേതായ ക്ലേശങ്ങളുണ്ട്. ഇതിനുമുണ്ട്. നമ്മുടെ നാട് ജീവിക്കാൻ, അത് മരിക്കാതിരിക്കാൻ; നിങ്ങൾ കർമം ചെയ്യുക."

എല്ലാ പരിപാടികളും കഴിഞ്ഞപ്പോൾ രാത്രി പതിനൊന്നു മണിയായി. ആളുകൾ പിരിഞ്ഞു. വാസവമേനോനും അരവിന്ദനും സദനത്തിൽ ഇരുന്നു. ഒട്ടുനാൾ കൂടിയിട്ടാണ് മേനോൻ വരുന്നത്. വെളുപ്പിനെ പോകണം. അതുകൊണ്ട് രാത്രിയിൽ ആരും ഉറങ്ങിയില്ല. അദ്ദേഹവുമായി സംസാരിച്ചുകൊണ്ടിരുന്നു.

സന്ധ്യാദേവി ഇടയ്ക്ക് പറഞ്ഞു:

"മേനോൻമാസ്റ്ററെ എപ്പോഴും കളിയാക്കുന്ന ഒരാൾ ഇവിടെയുണ്ട്."

"ആരാണത്?" മേനോൻ രസമുള്ള ഏതു കാര്യത്തിലും കടന്നുപിടിക്കും.

"ഇവൾ – കീർത്തി" സന്ധ്യ ചൂണ്ടിക്കാട്ടി.

കീർത്തി ചൂളിപ്പോയി.

"ഏട്ടത്തി വെറുതെ പറയുകയാണ് മാസ്റ്ററെ." അവൾ ആരോപണം നിഷേധിച്ചു.

"അല്ല മാസ്റ്ററെ, അവൾ അങ്ങയെ സ്ത്രീവിരോധി എന്ന് ദിവസവും മൂന്നുതവണ വിളിക്കും!"

"അയ്യോ ഈ ഏട്ടത്തി."

"കീർത്തി സത്യമല്ലേ പറഞ്ഞത്." മേനോൻ ചിരിച്ചുകൊണ്ട് പറഞ്ഞു. പക്ഷേ, ഒരു തിരുത്ത്. "വിരോധിയല്ല. അജ്ഞാനി! അതിനൊപ്പിച്ച് ഒരു വാക്ക് ഉണ്ടാക്കിക്കൊള്ളൂ കീർത്തി. സ്ത്രീയെപ്പറ്റി അജ്ഞാനി. അറിഞ്ഞുകൂടാത്തതിനെ കൂടെ ചേർക്കരുത്. അതുകൊണ്ടാണ് ഞാൻ ഇങ്ങനെ ഒറ്റയ്ക്ക് നടക്കുന്നത്!"

എല്ലാവരും ചിരിച്ചു.

മേനോൻ നിർത്തിയില്ല.

"ദാ, മറ്റൊരു വിരോധി. അല്ല അജ്ഞാനി ഇരിക്കുന്നു!" അദ്ദേഹം അരവിന്ദനെ ചൂണ്ടിക്കാട്ടി.

വീണ്ടും ചിരി. സന്ധ്യാദേവിയും അക്കൂട്ടത്തിൽ കൂടി. അരവിന്ദൻ വല്ലാതായി. മാസ്റ്ററോട് എന്തു പറയും? എങ്കിലും സന്ദർഭം അതായതുകൊണ്ട് പറഞ്ഞു.

"ഗുരുവിന്റെ ഗുണമല്ലേ ശിഷ്യനും കിട്ടുക?"

എല്ലാവരും പൊട്ടിച്ചിരിച്ചുപോയി.

"തോറ്റു. അരവിന്ദൻ തോറ്റു!" മേനോൻ ആ മറുപടിയിൽ രസിച്ചു.

പുറത്ത് ആരോ ഒന്ന് ചുമച്ചു. സന്ധ്യാദേവിയും മറ്റും ശ്രദ്ധിച്ചു. അവർ വാതിൽ തുറന്നുനോക്കി. വരാന്തയിൽ ഒരു ചെറുപ്പക്കാരി നിൽക്കുന്നു. ആളെ മനസിലായില്ല.

"നിങ്ങൾ ആരാണ്?" സന്ധ്യാദേവി ചോദിച്ചു.

"ഇങ്ങോട്ടു വന്നതാണ്. ചേച്ചിയോടു ചില കാര്യങ്ങൾ പറയാനുണ്ട്." അവൾ അറിയിച്ചു.

സന്ധ്യാദേവി അവളുടെ അടുക്കലേക്കു ചെന്നു.

"എന്താണു കാര്യം പറയൂ."

"ഞാൻ ഈ വാർഷികത്തിനു വന്നതാണ്. ചേച്ചിയെ കാണാൻ വേണ്ടി കാത്തുനിൽക്കുകയായിരുന്നു. നിങ്ങളെല്ലാം അകത്തുകയറി വാതിലടച്ചതുകൊണ്ട് ഞാൻ ഇവിടെയിരുന്നു. എന്റെ വീട് കുറച്ച് അകലെയാണ്. മനോരമ എന്നാണ് പേര്. വീട്ടിൽ അച്ഛനും അമ്മയും ഇല്ല. ഒരു അമ്മാവനാണ് ഉള്ളത്. അങ്ങേരുടെ മക്കളും. എനിക്ക് അവിടെ പൊറുക്കാൻ വയ്യ. എന്നെ ഇവിടെ സ്വീകരിക്കണം. ഞാൻ കുറെ പഠിച്ചിട്ടുമുണ്ട്. അത് അന്വേഷിച്ചാൽ ചേച്ചിക്ക് അറിയാൻ കഴിയും. ജീവിതത്തിൽ എന്നെ രക്ഷിക്കാൻ നിങ്ങൾക്കേ കഴിയൂ."

അസാധാരണമായിത്തോന്നി. പക്ഷേ ഇതു സംഭവിക്കാവുന്നതാണ്. പീഡനമനുഭവിക്കുന്ന പെൺകുട്ടികൾ ധാരാളമില്ലേ? ഇവൾ പൊതുപ്രവർത്തനവുമായി ബന്ധപ്പെട്ടിട്ടുള്ളതുകൊണ്ട് ഈ ധൈര്യം കാട്ടിയതാവും.

"നിൽക്ക്" സന്ധ്യാദേവി പറഞ്ഞു. അവർ അകത്ത് മേനോനോട് വിവരം പറഞ്ഞു. മനോരമയെ അകത്തേക്ക് വിളിച്ച് അദ്ദേഹം സംസാരി

ച്ചു. പിന്നെ നിർദേശിച്ചു.

"ഇവരെ സ്വീകരിക്കുന്നതിൽ തെറ്റില്ല. പക്ഷേ, നിങ്ങൾ ഇവരുടെ വീട്ടുകാരെ വിവരം അറിയിക്കണം. ഒരു സമയത്ത് അവർ കലാപത്തിനു വരാൻ ഇടയാവരുത്. അതുപോലെ ഇവർ അവിടെ പ്രവർത്തിച്ചിട്ടുണ്ടെങ്കിൽ പരിചയക്കാരുടെ പേരുചോദിച്ച് അവരോടും ഒന്ന് അഭിപ്രായമാരായണം."

അത്താഴം കഴിക്കാതെ വിശന്നിരുന്ന മനോരമയ്ക്ക് ആഹാരം കൊടുത്തു. കീർത്തിയാണു അടുക്കളയിൽപ്പോയത്. പിന്നെ ഒരു മുറിയിൽ കിടക്കാൻ ഒരുക്കം ചെയ്തുകൊടുത്തു.

"മടങ്ങിച്ചെന്നാലുടനെ ഞാൻ മധുരയിലേക്കു പോകും. ഭാനുമതിയുടെ വിവാഹത്തോടടുപ്പിച്ചേ വരൂ. മധുരയിലെ തുണിമില്ലുകളിൽ ഒരു പണിമുടക്ക് സംഘടിപ്പിക്കുന്നുണ്ട്. അതിനാണ് പോകുന്നത്. നിങ്ങൾ എല്ലാവരും വിവാഹത്തിന് പോകണം. അരവിന്ദനും പോകാൻ മടിക്കേണ്ടതില്ല. കേട്ടോ."

വെളുപ്പാൻകാലത്ത് മേനോൻ യാത്രയായി. അതുവരെ ആരും ഉറങ്ങിയില്ല. അദ്ദേഹവുമായി കഴിച്ചുകൂട്ടാൻ കഴിയുന്ന അപൂർവസന്ദർഭങ്ങൾ ആരും നഷ്ടപ്പെടുത്തുകയില്ല. മേനോൻ ഒരുമിച്ചുകൂടുമ്പോൾ ഒരു തത്വവും പറയാറില്ല. ഒരു കാരണവരെപ്പോലെ ജ്യേഷ്ഠനെപ്പോലെ ചിലപ്പോൾ അറിവില്ലാത്ത കുട്ടിയെപ്പോലെ ഭാവിച്ചു സംസാരിച്ചുകൊണ്ടിരിക്കും. ഈ രാത്രിയിൽത്തന്നെ അങ്ങനെയൊക്കെയാണ് കഴിച്ചുകൂട്ടിയത്. ഒരു ഘട്ടത്തിൽ കീർത്തിയോട് ചോദിച്ചു.

"ഏറ്റവും ഇഷ്ടമുള്ള പക്ഷി ഏതാ?"

"കീർത്തി മിഴിച്ചുനോക്കി. ഏതാണ്?" അവൾക്കു തന്നെ അറിഞ്ഞുകൂടാ.

"നീർക്കുതിര." അരവിന്ദൻ പറഞ്ഞു. "അല്ലേ കീർത്തി!"

അവൾ ചൊടിച്ചു. "കളിയാക്കാതെ ഏട്ടാ. എനിക്കിഷ്ടം ...... ഇഷ്ടം .... മയിലിനെയാണ്."

"എന്തുകൊണ്ട്?" മേനോൻ ചോദിച്ചു. അവൾ ആലോചിച്ചു.

"അതിന് നല്ല ഭംഗിയുണ്ട്."

"കഷ്ടമായിപ്പോയി. ഞാൻ ഒരു മയിലായിട്ടു ജനിച്ചിരുന്നെങ്കിൽ കീർത്തി എന്നെ ഇഷ്ടപ്പെട്ടേനെ. സ്ത്രീ വിരോധി എന്നു വിളിക്കില്ലായിരുന്നു." അദ്ദേഹം തുടർന്നു. "പക്ഷേ വേണ്ട കീർത്തി എന്നെ കൂട്ടിലടച്ച് ഭംഗി കാണുമായിരുന്നു. എന്റെ സ്വാതന്ത്ര്യം നഷ്ടപ്പെട്ടേനെ. അങ്ങനെ സംഭവിക്കാത്തതുകൊണ്ട് എനിക്കിപ്പോൾ നാട്ടിൽ നടന്ന് സ്വാതന്ത്ര്യത്തിനുവേണ്ടി പ്രവർത്തിക്കാൻ കഴിയുന്നു. വേണ്ട എനിക്ക് മയിലാകേണ്ട!"

കീർത്തി എന്തോ രഹസ്യം പറഞ്ഞു. അടുത്തിരുന്ന ഉഷ കേട്ടു. അതെന്തെന്ന് മേനോൻ ചോദിച്ചു. ഉഷ പറഞ്ഞു.

"അടുത്ത ജന്മം മേനോൻ മാസ്റ്റർ മയിലായിട്ട് ജനിക്കുമെന്ന്!"

"അന്ന് കീർത്തി വാസവമേനോനായിട്ട് ജനിക്കും."

കുറെക്കഴിഞ്ഞ് അദ്ദേഹം ചോദിച്ചു.

"കീർത്തി ഉച്ചയ്ക്കു മുൻപ് നാലുകാലിൽ, ഉച്ചയ്ക്ക് രണ്ട് കാലിൽ വൈകുന്നേരം മൂന്നു കാലിൽ. ഇത് ഏതു ജീവിയാണ്?"

അവൾ ഒരിക്കൽക്കൂടി അത് ചോദിച്ചു. അദ്ദേഹം ആവർത്തിച്ചു പറഞ്ഞു. അവൾ തല പുകഞ്ഞ് ആലോചിച്ചു.

"ഇത് പറഞ്ഞാൽ, ഒരു സമ്മാനമുണ്ട്." മേനോൻ വാക്കുകൊടത്തു.

ആലോചന. കടുത്ത ആലോചന. ഒടുവിൽ അവൾ വിളിച്ചു പറഞ്ഞു.

"മനുഷ്യൻ!"

"അതെങ്ങനെ?"

"ശിശുവായിരിക്കുമ്പോൾ നീന്തി നടക്കുന്നു, പ്രായമാകുമ്പോൾ രണ്ടു കാലിൽ നടക്കുന്നു. വാർധക്യകാലത്ത് വടി കുത്തിപ്പിടിച്ചു നടക്കുന്നു!"

മേനോൻ പോക്കറ്റിൽ നിന്നും തന്റെ പേനയെടുത്ത് കീർത്തിക്കു കൊടുത്തു.

"വേണ്ട മാസ്റ്ററേ!"

"ഇത് എന്റെ സമ്മാനമാണ് വച്ചോളൂ."

അവൾ സന്തോഷപൂർവം അതു സ്വീകരിച്ചു.

മേനോൻ എഴുന്നേറ്റു, സുമതി കടുംകാപ്പി കൊണ്ടുവന്നു. അതു കുടിച്ചിട്ട് അദ്ദേഹം പറഞ്ഞു.

"ഞാൻ പ്രത്യേകം ഓർമിപ്പിക്കേണ്ടാത്ത ഒരു കാര്യം ഒന്നുപറയട്ടെ. ഇത് ഒരുകുടുംബമാണ്. ഈ സദനം. നിങ്ങളുടെ പരസ്പര സ്നേഹംകൊണ്ട് എന്റെ മനസ്സ് തുള്ളിച്ചാടുന്നുണ്ട്. ഒരിക്കലും ഇതിനു ഭംഗം വരരുത്."

മൗനത്തിൽക്കൂടി ആ വാക്കുകൾ സ്വീകരിച്ചു.

വണ്ടിയാപ്പീസിലേക്ക് മേനോനും അരവിന്ദനും ഒരുമിച്ചു നടന്നു. മഞ്ഞു പെയ്യുന്നുണ്ട്. ചായക്കടകൾ തുറന്നുകൊണ്ടിരിക്കുന്നു. പയ്യന്മാർ അന്നത്തെ പത്ര വിൽപ്പന ആരംഭിച്ചിരിക്കുന്നു. മേനോൻ ഒന്നും മിണ്ടാതെ നടന്നു. ആലോചനയിലാണ്. അപ്പോൾ എന്തെങ്കിലും പറഞ്ഞ് അദ്ദേഹത്തെ ശല്യപ്പെടുത്താറില്ല. തന്റെ കഥ ഒന്നു സൂചിപ്പിക്കണമെന്ന് അരവിന്ദൻ ആഗ്രഹിച്ചതാണ്, ആ രാത്രിയിൽ. പലവുരു ഒരുങ്ങി, പറയാൻ തോന്നിയില്ല. ആ കത്തയച്ചതിനുശേഷം സന്ധ്യാദേവിയുമായി ഒറ്റയ്ക്കു സംസാരിക്കാൻ കഴിഞ്ഞിട്ടില്ല. ഒരിക്കലെങ്കിലും അവരുമായി ഒന്നിരുന്നു കാര്യങ്ങൾ പറയണം. ആ കത്ത് അവരെ നോവിച്ചിരിക്കും. പക്ഷേ, കണ്ടുമുട്ടിയപ്പോൾ അതൊന്നും പ്രകടിപ്പിച്ചില്ല. മറ്റാളുകളുടെ മുമ്പിൽ അവർ കഴിയുന്നത്ര ഒതുങ്ങിക്കളയും.

വണ്ടി വന്നു നിന്നു. മേനോൻ എന്തോ പറയാൻ തുടങ്ങുന്നുവെന്ന് അരവിന്ദന് മനസിലായി.

"അരവിന്ദൻ"

"എന്താ..."

"ഞാൻ ഒരുകാര്യം അറിയാൻ ആഗ്രഹിക്കുന്നു. നിങ്ങൾ സ്നേഹിക്കുന്നത് സന്ധ്യയെയാണ്. അല്ലേ?"

അരവിന്ദൻ നിമിഷനേരത്തേക്ക് അങ്ങനെ നിന്നു. പിന്നെ മറുപടി

പറഞ്ഞു.

"അതെ. പക്ഷേ, ഞങ്ങൾ അതൊന്നും സംസാരിച്ചിട്ടില്ല. മാസ്റ്റർ."

"ശരി. അതിൽ അപാകതയൊന്നുമില്ല. ഞാൻ മടങ്ങിവരുമ്പോൾ നമുക്ക് കൂടുതൽ സംസാരിക്കാം."

"ആകട്ടെ മാസ്റ്റർ."

അദ്ദേഹം വണ്ടിയിൽ കയറി, അത് സ്റ്റാന്റിൽ നിന്നിറങ്ങി. വടക്കോട്ടുള്ള വഴിയേ പോയി.

അഞ്ച്

ജീവിതത്തിന്റെ പിന്നിലെ വഴിത്താരകളിലേക്കു ഭാനുമതിയുടെ മനസ്സ് ഒരു നിമിഷം താനറിയാതെ ഓടിച്ചെന്നു. മങ്ങിയതും തെളിഞ്ഞതുമായ ചിത്രങ്ങൾ. വ്യക്തവും അവ്യക്തവുമായ ശബ്ദങ്ങൾ. അവയെല്ലാം കാലം സൃഷ്ടിച്ച മരുപ്പച്ചകളായിരുന്നു. വളർത്തിയവരുടെ പ്രോത്സാഹിപ്പിച്ചവരുടെ ഒരുമിച്ചു കഴിഞ്ഞുകൂടിയവരുടെ രൂപങ്ങൾ, സ്വരങ്ങൾ. ദിവാകരൻ അവളുടെ കഴുത്തിലേക്ക് താലി കെട്ടിക്കൊടുത്തു. ആർപ്പുംകുരവയുമില്ലാതെ, ആശീർവാദങ്ങളർപ്പിക്കുന്ന കണ്ണുകളുടെ മുമ്പിൽ ആ ചടങ്ങ് നടന്നു.

ഓർമവച്ചപ്പോൾ തുടങ്ങി മനസ്സ് എന്തിനെയോ പ്രദക്ഷിണം വയ്ക്കുകയായിരുന്നു. താൻ അനാഥയാണെന്ന വിചാരംകൊണ്ട് ആരേയും ശല്യം ചെയ്യാതെ ജീവിച്ചു മരിക്കാനുള്ള തപസായിരുന്നു അത്. ഒന്നും മോഹിച്ചില്ല. ഒരു ആകർഷണത്തിലേക്കും മനസിനെ വിട്ടില്ല. താൻ പ്രദക്ഷിണം വച്ചത് സർവശക്തയായ ദേവിയെയായിരുന്നോ? അതെ. അവിടെയാണ് എല്ലാം സമർപ്പിച്ചത്. ആ പ്രാർഥനകൾ അഭിനിവേശങ്ങളല്ലാത്ത വഴിത്താരകൾ, ദാ ഇവിടെ കൊണ്ടുവന്നെത്തിച്ചിരിക്കുന്നു.

ചടങ്ങുകൾ കഴിഞ്ഞ്, കൂട്ടുകാരികളുടെ ഇടയിലേക്കു ചെന്നപ്പോൾ, അതൊരു വേർപാടാണെന്ന് ഭാനുമതിക്കു തോന്നി. അങ്ങനെയാണ്, ഒരുമിച്ചു കഴിഞ്ഞുകൂടിയവരുടെ ഇടയിൽ നിന്ന് താൻ പിരിഞ്ഞുപോകുന്നു.

ദിവാകരൻ ഭാനുമതിയുടെ കഴുത്തിൽ താലികെട്ടുമ്പോൾ, അരവിന്ദൻ പിന്നിൽ മാറിനിന്നിരുന്നു. ദിവസങ്ങളായി പല വിചാരങ്ങളും മനസിനെ അലട്ടി. തെറ്റുകാരനല്ലെങ്കിലും ഒരു കുറ്റബോധത്തിന്റെ നിമിഷങ്ങൾ ഇടയ്ക്കിടയ്ക്കു കടന്നുവന്നു. പിന്നെ, സമാധാനിച്ചു. ഒരു ദിവസം വാസവമേനോനെ കണ്ടു, സംസാരിച്ചു. ദിവാകരനെപ്പറ്റിയുള്ള തന്റെ അഭിപ്രായങ്ങൾ അറിയിച്ചു. മേനോൻ അതെല്ലാം കേട്ടിരുന്ന് ചോദിച്ചു.

"അരവിന്ദൻ, ഭാനുവിന് എന്തായാലും ഒരു വിവാഹം ആവശ്യമല്ലേ?"

"അതെ." അരവിന്ദൻ സമ്മതിച്ചു.

"അവളെ മാനമായി ജീവിപ്പിക്കാൻ കഴിവുള്ള ഒരാൾ വേണ്ടെ അവളെ കല്യാണം കഴിക്കാൻ?"

"വേണം."

"രാഷ്ട്രീയാഭിപ്രായവും സ്വന്തം കാര്യത്തിലുള്ള അൽപ്പം അമിതമായ താൽപ്പര്യവുമൊഴിച്ചാൽ, ദിവാകരനും മറ്റ് കുറ്റമൊന്നുമില്ലല്ലോ?"

"ഇല്ല."

"അയാളുടെ രണ്ടാം വിവാഹമാണെന്നത് വലിയ പോരായ്മയായി തോന്നുന്നുണ്ടോ?"

"ഇല്ല, മാസ്റ്റർ.."

"പിന്നെന്താണ്?"

അരവിന്ദൻ ആലോചിച്ചിരുന്നിട്ടു പറഞ്ഞു:

"ഒരുപക്ഷേ, ഇക്കാര്യത്തിൽ എന്റെ വിചാരഗതി ശരിയല്ലായിരിക്കാം. അവരെപ്പോലെ ഒരു സ്ത്രീക്ക് നമ്മുടെ ചിന്താരീതിയുള്ള ഒരു ഭർത്താവുതന്നെ വേണമെന്ന് ഞാൻ ആഗ്രഹിച്ചു. അത്രയേ ഉള്ളൂ. മാസ്റ്റർ.."

"ഞാനത് മനസിലാക്കുന്നു." മേനോൻ പറഞ്ഞു. "പക്ഷേ, വിവാഹം കഴിഞ്ഞ് ഒരാളുടെ മനസ്സ് പിന്തിരിപ്പാനായിക്കൂടെ? അങ്ങനെ സംഭവിച്ചിട്ടുള്ളത് നമുക്കനുഭവമില്ലേ അരവിന്ദൻ?"

പിന്നെ ആ സംഭാഷണം നീണ്ടില്ല. ഒരു വാചകം മാത്രം മേനോൻ കൂട്ടിച്ചേർത്തു.

"നിങ്ങൾ തീർച്ചയായും കല്യാണത്തിനു വരണം."

വനിതാസമാജത്തിന്റെ വാടകക്കെട്ടിടത്തിൽ വച്ചാണ് വിവാഹം നടന്നത്. വലിയ ഒരു ജനക്കൂട്ടമായിരുന്നു. ഭാനുമതിയോട് നാട്ടുകാർക്ക് മതിപ്പും സ്നേഹവും അവിടെ കണ്ടു. ദിവാകരൻ ഒറ്റയ്ക്കു വന്നു. ബന്ധുക്കൾ ആരുമില്ല. പലരും അതിൽ പല വ്യാഖ്യാനങ്ങൾ കണ്ടെത്തി. ആരെയും അറിയിക്കാഞ്ഞതാവാം. രണ്ടാം വിവാഹമല്ലേ അതിന് ആരെ ക്ഷണിക്കാനാണ്? വൈകുന്നേരം സ്വീകരണമുണ്ടായിരുന്നു. അതിനു ശേഷം അതിഥികൾ യാത്ര പറഞ്ഞു.

ഭാനുമതിയും ദിവാകരനും കാറിൽ കയറിയപ്പോൾ വാസവമേനോനും അരവിന്ദനും സന്ധ്യാദേവിയും സദനത്തിലേയും സമാജത്തിലേയും അംഗങ്ങളും കൂടിനിന്ന് അവർക്ക് വീണ്ടും ഭാവുകങ്ങൾ നേർന്നു. കാറ് മെല്ലെ നീങ്ങി.

നാൽപ്പതു മൈൽ ദൂരത്തെ യാത്രയുണ്ട്. അതിനിടയ്ക്ക് ഒന്നു രണ്ടു വാക്കുകൾ മാത്രമേ അവർ തമ്മിൽ സംസാരിച്ചുള്ളൂ. ദിവാകരൻ സീറ്റിലേക്കു ചാരിക്കിടന്നു മയങ്ങി. തണുത്ത കാറ്റ് ഭാനുമതിക്കു സുഖം തോന്നി. വഴിവിളക്കുകളും കടകമ്പോളങ്ങളും കടന്നുപോകുന്നു. ചെമ്മീനിന്റെ ഗന്ധമുള്ള തെരുവുകൾ അന്നത്തെ ജോലി കഴിഞ്ഞു മടങ്ങുന്ന തൊഴിൽക്കാർ, കാളവണ്ടികൾ, വേഗത്തിൽ പോകുന്ന ബസുകൾ, കാറുകൾ അത്രയും കാലം ജീവിച്ച അന്തരീക്ഷത്തിൽ നിന്ന്, മറ്റൊരു ലോകത്തിലേക്കു പോവുകയാണ്. തിരിച്ചു വരാം. എന്നാലും ഇനി ജീവിതം അവിടെയാണ്.

രണ്ടു മണിക്കൂർ പട്ടണത്തിലെ വിളക്കുകൾ കണ്ടു. നിരത്തിൽ ആളുകളുടെ തിരക്ക്. വേഗം കുറച്ചു കാറു നീങ്ങി. ഇടത്തോട്ടു തിരിഞ്ഞു

ഒരു ചെറിയ വഴിയിൽക്കൂടി രണ്ടു ഫർലാങ്ങോളം പോയി. ഒരു വലിയ ഗേറ്റിനു മുൻപിൽ അതു നിന്നു ഹോണടിച്ചു. ഗേറ്റുതുറക്കപ്പെട്ടു. ദിവാകരൻ ഉണർന്നു പുറത്തിറങ്ങി.

"വരൂ."

ഭാനുമതിയും ഇറങ്ങി.

വലിയ വീട്. ഇരുനില. ഏറ്റവും ആധുനികമാണ്. വിശാലമായ മുറികൾ. നീലാകാശത്തിന്റെ കീറുകൾ പലരൂപത്തിൽ അടുക്കിവച്ചതുപോലെ. വൈദ്യുത വിളക്കിന്റെ മങ്ങിയ പ്രഭ അങ്ങനെയൊരു ലോകം ചമയ്ക്കുന്നു. സ്വീകരിക്കാൻ നിന്ന ജോലിക്കാരെ കണ്ടു. അവർ എത്ര പേരുണ്ട്. നാല്, അഞ്ച്, ആറ്, അതേ നാലു പുരുഷന്മാർ, രണ്ടു സ്ത്രീകൾ അവർ പുതിയ വീട്ടമ്മയെ കാണുകയാണ്. അവളുടെ കൂടെ ദിവാകരനുമുണ്ട്. മുകളിലത്തെ നിലയിലേക്കു കയറി. അവിടെയും ആർഭാടങ്ങൾ. അതും കണ്ടു.

ചുമരുകളിലെല്ലാം വലിയ ചിത്രങ്ങൾ. ശകുന്തളയും അരയന്നവും, സാവിത്രിയും സത്യവാനും, ഹരിശ്ചന്ദ്രന്റെ ശ്മശാനജീവിതം, ഗജേന്ദ്രമോക്ഷം, ഭക്തമീരയുടെ ധ്യാനനിർവൃതി...

താഴേക്കു വന്നു. ബെഡ്റൂമിലേക്ക് നടന്നു. അതിന്റെ വാതിൽക്കൽ നിന്ന് ദിവാകരൻ ചോദിച്ചു.

"വീടൊക്കെ ഇഷ്ടപ്പെട്ടോ?"

"ഇഷ്ടപ്പെട്ടു..." അവൾ ചോദിച്ചതുകൊണ്ട് മറുപടി പറഞ്ഞുവെന്നേയുള്ളൂ. കാരണം, ആ ചോദ്യം തന്നെ ആവശ്യമില്ലായിരുന്നു.

രണ്ടുപേരും ബെഡ്റൂമിൽ കയറി.

"യാത്ര ചെയ്തതല്ലേ? കുളിച്ചോളൂ."

അവൾ സമ്മതിച്ചു.

അയാൾ കട്ടിലിൽ കിടന്നു. അവൾ കുളിമുറിയിലേക്കു പോയി. മാർബിൾ നിരത്തിയ കുളിമുറി. നിന്നു കുളിക്കാൻ നാണം തോന്നിക്കുന്ന വലിയ കണ്ണാടി.

ഒരുവിചാരം, ഇവിടെ വരുമ്പോൾ ഭർത്താവിന്റെ സുഹൃത്തുക്കൾ ആരെങ്കിലും ഉണ്ടാവുമെന്ന് കരുതി. ബന്ധുക്കൾ ആരുമില്ല. എന്തായിരിക്കും അത്? രഹസ്യമായി ഇത് നടത്തിയെന്ന് വിചാരിക്കാൻ നിവൃത്തിയില്ല. ആരും വരേണ്ടെന്ന് ശട്ടംകെട്ടിയതാവുമോ?

കുളിച്ചു വന്നപ്പോൾ അയാൾ അവിടെയില്ല. അവൾ വസ്ത്രങ്ങൾ മാറി. മുടി ചീകി. പൊട്ടുതൊട്ടു. കട്ടിലിൽ ഇരുന്നു. തന്റെ ജീവിതത്തെപ്പറ്റിയാണ് അപ്പോൾ ഓർമ വന്നത്. പ്രതീക്ഷിക്കാത്ത, താനൊരിക്കലും ചേരാത്ത, ഒരിടത്തു വന്നിരിക്കുന്നു. ഒരു അനാഥപെണ്ണ്. ഇങ്ങനെയൊരിടത്ത് വന്നെത്തുക. കഥകളിൽമാത്രം വായിച്ചിട്ടുള്ള കാര്യമാണ്. മനസിൽ ഒരു ഭയം. കാര്യമില്ലാത്ത ഭയമാണ്. നിരൂപിക്കാത്ത കാര്യങ്ങൾ കൈവരുമ്പോൾ, മനുഷ്യൻ അങ്ങനെ ഭയപ്പെടും.

അപ്പുറത്ത് സംസാരം കേൾക്കുന്നു. ആ മനുഷ്യന്റെ ശബ്ദമാണ്.

അത് വലിയ മുറികൾ കടന്ന്, ഒരു മുഴക്കത്തോടെ ഇങ്ങെത്തുന്ന ആ മുറിയാകെ കണ്ണോടിച്ചു. നിലത്തോ, ഭിത്തിയിലോ ഒരഴുക്കിന്റെ പാടു പോലും പറ്റിയിട്ടില്ല. ഡബിൽകോട്ടിൽ സൂര്യപടംപോലുള്ള വിരിപ്പ്. കൊതി തോന്നിക്കുന്ന തലയിണകൾ. ഇതിന് നാലുമുറികളുടെ വലിപ്പ മുണ്ട്. മേശ, കസേര, അലമാര എല്ലാം പുതിയ ഫാഷനിലുള്ളത്.

വാതിൽക്കൽ നിന്ന് ഒരു സ്ത്രീ ശബ്ദം.

"കൊച്ചമ്മേ കുടിക്കാൻ എന്തുകൊണ്ടുവരണം?"

"ഇങ്ങുവരൂ." അവൾ വിളിച്ചു.

ആ സ്ത്രീ മടിച്ച് കയറിവന്നു. മധ്യവയസ്കയാണ്. യോഗ്യതയുള്ള സ്ത്രീ.

"എന്താണ് പേര്?"

"രാജമ്മ."

"ഇവിടെത്തന്നെയാണോ വീട്?"

"ഇത്തിരി ദൂരെയാ."

"ഞാൻ അങ്ങോട്ടു വരാം."

അവൾ എഴുന്നേറ്റു നടന്നു. ഒരു മുറിയും ഇടനാഴിയും കടന്ന് അടുക്കളയിലെത്തി. അവിടെ മറ്റേ ജോലിക്കാരി പാചകം ചെയ്തു കൊണ്ടു നിൽക്കുന്നു.

ഭാനുമതി അങ്ങോട്ടു ചെന്നു.

"നിങ്ങളുടെ പേര്?"

"അന്നയെന്നാ കൊച്ചമ്മാ."

അവർ ക്രിസ്ത്യാനിയാണെന്നറിയാം. ഞൊറിയിട്ടുടുത്തിരിക്കുന്നു. നാൽപ്പത്തഞ്ചുവയസെങ്കിലും പ്രായംകാണും.

"ഒരു ഗ്ലാസ് പച്ചവെള്ളം തരൂ."

രാജമ്മ ഐസിട്ട വെള്ളം കൊണ്ടുവന്നു. അതു കുടിച്ചു.

മീനിന്റെയും ഇറച്ചിയുടെയും രുചിയുള്ള ഗന്ധം.

"എന്നും ഇതെല്ലാംവേണമെന്ന് അദ്ദേഹത്തിന് നിർബന്ധമുണ്ടോ?"

രാജമ്മ മെല്ലെ ഒന്നു ചിരിച്ചു. എന്നിട്ട് ഒതുക്കത്തോടെ പറഞ്ഞു:

"ഇതു രണ്ടും വേണം. ഇല്ലെങ്കിൽ ഒന്നും കഴിക്കത്തില്ല."

"അത് ഞാൻ തന്നെ ഉണ്ടാക്കിക്കൊടുക്കണം. അതാ ഇഷ്ടം." അന്ന അവകാശവാദം പുറപ്പെടുവിച്ചു.

ഭാനുമതി ലോഹ്യം പറഞ്ഞിട്ട് അടുക്കളയ്ക്കു പിന്നിലേക്കിറങ്ങി ഒരു ഭാഗത്ത് കിണറ്. കോഴി തുടങ്ങിയവയെ വളർത്താനുള്ള കൂട്. രണ്ടു പശുക്കൾ നിൽക്കുന്നു.

"പുറകിൽ ഒരു, കുന്നാണ് കൊച്ചമ്മേ. അത് ഈ പറമ്പിനോട് ചേർന്നുകെടക്കുവാ, അതും ഇവിടത്തെ വകയാ. അവിടെ ഒരു വീടൊണ്ട്." രാജമ്മ അറിയിച്ചു.

"പക്ഷേങ്കില്, അവിടെ ചോദിക്കാതെ രാത്രീല് അങ്ങോട്ട് പോകണ്ട."

ഇരുട്ടിലേക്ക് നോക്കി. കുന്നിന്റെ ചരിവ് അവ്യക്തമായി കാണാം.

വീട്ടിന്റെ വെളുത്ത നിറവും. അതിനു മീതെ ആകാശവും അഞ്ചാറ് നക്ഷത്രങ്ങളും.

ഭാനുമതി അകത്തേക്ക് നടന്നു ബെഡ്റൂമിലെത്തി. അപ്പോൾ, അയാൾ അകത്ത് കുളിച്ചുകൊണ്ടിരിക്കുന്നു. അവൾ ഇരുന്നു. കുളിച്ചു വന്ന് ഒരു കൈലിയുടുത്തിട്ട് അയാൾ കസേരയിലിരുന്നു. ഒന്ന് ചിരിച്ചു കൊണ്ട് അയാൾ സംസാരിച്ചു.

"ഭാനു..."

"എന്താ.."

"എനിക്ക് ഒരു ചെറിയ ദുശ്ശീലമുണ്ട്. അത് നേരത്തേ പറഞ്ഞേക്കാം. എന്താണെന്ന് ഊഹിക്കാമോ?"

അവൾ ഉറ്റുനോക്കി പുഞ്ചിരിച്ചു.

"പറഞ്ഞുതരൂ."

"ഞാൻ അൽപ്പം മദ്യം കഴിക്കും."

"കഴിച്ചോളൂ." അവൾ പൊടുന്നനെ പറഞ്ഞു.

"അപ്പോൾ നമുക്ക് മട്ടുപ്പാവിലേക്ക് പോകാം. അവിടമാണ് അതിനുള്ള സ്ഥലം."

രണ്ടാം നിലയ്ക്കു മുകളിൽ മട്ടുപ്പാവിൽ ചെന്നപ്പോൾ അവിടെ മേശയും രണ്ടു കസേരകളും മേശപ്പുറത്ത് കുപ്പിയും ഗ്ലാസുകളും ഒരുക്കിവച്ചിരിക്കുന്നു.

അവർ ഇരുന്നു.

"ദാ, ഭാനുമതിക്ക് ഓറഞ്ച് ജ്യൂസ്. എനിക്ക് ഇതും." അയാൾ എടുത്തു കൊടുത്തു.

മദ്യം പകർന്ന് ഒന്നു ചുണ്ടിൽ തൊടുവിച്ച്, താഴെ വച്ചു.

"ബിസിനസിൽ പ്രവേശിച്ച കാലത്തു കിട്ടിയ ശീലമാണ്. തടി കോൺട്രാക്റ്റിന്റെ ആദ്യകാലത്ത്, കാട്ടിലും മലയിലും തണുപ്പത്തു കിടക്കണം. അപ്പോൾ ഇതായിരുന്നു ഒരു സഹായി. പിന്നെ നാട്ടിലായപ്പോഴും തുടർന്നു. മര്യാദയ്ക്കേ കുടിക്കാറുള്ളൂ കേട്ടോ."

ജോലിക്കാർ പ്ലേറ്റിൽ ഇറച്ചി കൊണ്ടുവന്നു വച്ചിട്ടു പോയി.

"ഇറച്ചിയും മീനും നിർബന്ധമാണ്. അല്ലേ." അവൾ ചോദിച്ചു.

"ആരു പറഞ്ഞു?"

"അതൊക്കെ ഞാൻ മനസിലാക്കി."

"ങാ അടുക്കളയിൽ അന്ന പറഞ്ഞുകാണും. ആ എനിക്ക് വലിയ ഇഷ്ടമാ."

ഒരു മണിക്കൂർ നേരം അവിടെയിരുന്നു. അയാൾ മൂന്നു നാലു തവണ മദ്യംകഴിച്ചു. മാറ്റം വല്ലതുമുണ്ടോ എന്നു ഭാനുമതി ശ്രദ്ധിച്ചു. വലിയ മാറ്റമില്ല.

ഡൈനിങ് ഹാളിൽ അത്താഴം ഒരുക്കിയിരുന്നു. അവിടെയും ഒരു ഗ്ലാസ് മദ്യം കൂടി കഴിച്ചു. ആഹാരം കഴിച്ച് അവർ കിടപ്പുമുറിയിലേക്കു പോയി.

രാത്രി വളരെ വൈകുംവരെ അവർ മുഖത്തോടുമുഖം നോക്കിയി

രുന്നു സംസാരിച്ചു. അയാളാണ് എല്ലാം പറഞ്ഞത്. അവൾ കേട്ടുകൊണ്ടിരുന്നു. "നിന്റെ കഥ എനിക്കറിയാം. അതിൽ പ്രത്യേകിച്ചൊന്നുമില്ല. എന്റെ കഥ നിനക്കറിഞ്ഞുകൂടല്ലോ." എന്നുള്ള മുഖവുരയോടെയാണ് അയാൾ സംസാരിച്ചത്. പല ഭാഗങ്ങളും അവൾക്ക് പിടികിട്ടിയില്ല. പക്ഷേ ചില ഭാഗങ്ങൾ അവൾക്ക് അസ്വസ്ഥത ഉണ്ടാക്കി. അയാളുടെ ജീവിതം ഒരു സാഹസികന്റേതാണെന്നു തോന്നത്തക്ക സംഭവങ്ങൾ.

ഒരാഴ്ച കഴിഞ്ഞു. ദിവാകരൻ സ്ഥലത്തില്ല. കോഴിക്കോട്ടു ബിസിനസു കാര്യങ്ങൾക്കായി പോകുന്നു എന്നാണ് പറഞ്ഞത്. ഭാനുമതി വാസവമേനോന് സമാജത്തിലേക്കും സദനത്തിലേക്കും കത്തുകളയച്ചു. അവരോടെല്ലാം ഉള്ള ഹൃദയപൂർവമായ സ്നേഹവും നന്ദിയും അറിയിച്ചു. ഏകാന്തത അനുഭവപ്പെടുന്നു എന്നും ചങ്ങാതിമാരുടെ നടുവിൽ കഴിഞ്ഞതാണ്. ഇപ്പോൾ വലിയ വീട്ടിൽ ഒറ്റയ്ക്കു കഴിയുന്നു. രാജമ്മയും അന്നയും അടുത്തുവന്നിരുന്നു സംസാരിക്കും. പക്ഷേ, രണ്ടു മൂന്നു ദിവസങ്ങളായപ്പോൾ, അതും വല്ലപ്പോഴുമായി. രണ്ടുപേരും വായാടികളല്ല, അവർ തനിക്കുവേണ്ടി സംസാരിക്കുകയാണ്. അതവൾക്ക് തോന്നി.

ഇത്രയും ദിവസങ്ങൾ കടന്നുപോയിട്ടും, പ്രത്യേകിച്ചാരും അവിടെ വന്നില്ല. ഒരു പുതിയ സ്ത്രീ അവിടെ വന്നിരിക്കുന്നു. അവരുടെ കൗതുകത്തിനു വേണ്ടിയെങ്കിലും അയൽവക്കത്തു നിന്ന് ആരെങ്കിലും വരേണ്ടതല്ലേ? ഈ വീട് ആരും കയറാത്ത ദ്വീപാണോ? ദിവാകരന് ചുറ്റുപാടുകളോട് ബന്ധങ്ങളില്ലേ?

ഒന്നും മനസിലായില്ല.

രാത്രിയാണ്. രാജമ്മ മുറിയുടെ വാതിൽക്കൽ വന്നു. അവരെ അകത്തു വിളിച്ചിരുത്തി. ഈ വീട്ടിൽ വന്നപ്പോൾ മുതൽക്ക് ഒരു സംഗതി ഉള്ളിൽ കിടക്കുന്നു. അത്, ഇന്ന് ചോദിക്കണം ദിവാകരന്റെ മരിച്ചുപോയ ഭാര്യ...

"അദ്ദേഹത്തിന്റെ ഭാര്യയുടെ പേരെന്തായിരുന്നു. രാജമ്മേ.." ഭാനുമതി ചോദിച്ചു.

"രത്നമ്മ."

"അവർ മരിച്ചിട്ട് എത്ര നാളായി?"

"ഒരു വർഷം കഴിഞ്ഞു."

"അവർ എങ്ങനെയുള്ള സ്ത്രീയായിരുന്നു."

"കൊച്ചമ്മയ്ക്ക് ഒന്നും തോന്നരുത്." രാജമ്മ പതുങ്ങുന്നു.

"എന്താ?" ഭാനുമതി നിവർന്നിരുന്നു. "എന്താ അങ്ങനെ പറഞ്ഞത്? അവർ ചീത്തസ്ത്രീയായിരുന്നോ?"

"അല്ല കൊച്ചമ്മേ. രാജമ്മയുടെ മുഖത്ത് വിഷാദം പരന്നു. നല്ല സ്ത്രീയായിരുന്നു. തങ്കപ്പെട്ട സ്വഭാവമായിരുന്നു. അവർ മരിച്ചെന്നറിഞ്ഞപ്പം ഈ നാട്ടുകാരു മുഴുവൻ കരഞ്ഞുപോയി."

"ഓഹോ! അവർ നല്ലവരാണെന്ന് പറഞ്ഞാൽ എനിക്ക് മുഷിച്ചിലു തോന്നുമെന്ന് രാജമ്മ വിചാരിച്ച് അല്ലേ? ഞാൻ അങ്ങനെയുള്ളവളല്ല

രാജമ്മേ, എന്റെ കഥ ഞാൻ പറഞ്ഞില്ലേ? ഒരിക്കലും ഓർമിച്ചിരിക്കാതെ, ഞാനിവിടെ വന്നുചേർന്നു. ഞാൻ കണ്ടിട്ടില്ലെങ്കിലും, ആ നല്ല സ്ത്രീയുടെ ആത്മാവിനു വേണ്ടി ഞാൻ പ്രാർഥിക്കുന്നു."

നിശ്ശബ്ദത. പിന്നെ ചോദിച്ചു.

"അവരുടെ ഫോട്ടോയൊന്നും ഇവിടില്ലേ?" ഒന്നും കണ്ടില്ല.

രാജമ്മ പുറത്തു ആരെങ്കിലുമുണ്ടോ എന്ന് എത്തിവലിഞ്ഞു നോക്കി. എന്നിട്ടു പറഞ്ഞു.

"ഇവിടെയില്ല. എന്റെ കയ്യില് ഞാൻ ഒരെണ്ണം സൂക്ഷിച്ചുവച്ചിട്ടുണ്ട്. ഞാൻ കാണിച്ചുതരാം."

രാജമ്മ എഴുന്നേറ്റ് പുറത്തേക്ക് പോയി. ഭാനുമതി ആലോചിച്ചു കിടന്നു. വൈകിയില്ല. അവർ വന്നു. ഏതോ രഹസ്യവസ്തുപോലെ മേൽമുണ്ടിനിടയിൽ നിന്നും ഫോട്ടോ എടുത്തുകൊടുത്തു.

ഭാനുമതി നോക്കി. അവളുടെ മിഴികൾ വിടർന്നു നിന്നു. മുഖത്ത് ഏതോ സംഭ്രമം ബാധിച്ചതുപോലെ. ആ ഫോട്ടോയിൽ നിന്നു ദൃഷ്ടികൾവിട്ടുപോരുന്നില്ല. അതിൽ തറച്ചുനിൽക്കുന്നു. ചലനമില്ലാതിരിക്കുന്ന കൊച്ചമ്മയുടെ രൂപത്തിലേക്ക് ഉറ്റുനോക്കി, രാജമ്മ നിന്നു. ഭാനുമതിയുടെ കണ്ണുകൾ പിന്നെയും ആ പടത്തിലേക്ക് ആഴ്ന്നിറങ്ങുന്നു. ശ്വാസം പിടിച്ച്, ഇമചിമ്മാതെ, അതു കാണുകയാണ്. താൻ സ്വപ്നം– കാണുകയാണെന്ന് അവൾക്കു തോന്നി. സ്വപ്നം ഒരു മാസത്തിലധികമായി ആരംഭിച്ച സ്വപ്നം. ഈ വീട്ടിലും ഈ ചിത്രങ്ങളിലും കൊണ്ടു ചെന്നെത്തിച്ചിരിക്കുന്നു.

രത്നമ്മയുടെ ഫോട്ടോ.

രത്നമ്മയെ ഭാനുമതിക്കറിയാം. വർഷങ്ങൾക്കുമുമ്പ് അവളുടെ കൂട്ടുകാരി. തൃത്താലയിൽ വന്നെത്തുന്നതിന് വളരെ മുമ്പ്. നാട്ടിൽ സ്വന്തമായി ആരുമില്ലാത്തതുകൊണ്ട് ഒരു വീട്ടിൽ ജോലിക്കുപോയി. ആ വീട്ടുകാർ നല്ല മനസുള്ളവരായിരുന്നു. അവരുടെ സ്വന്തം മക്കളെപ്പോലെ കരുതി. രത്നമ്മ ആ വീട്ടിലെ കുട്ടിയായിരുന്നു. ഒരുമിച്ചു വളർന്നു. ഒരമ്മയുടെ വയറ്റിൽ പിറന്നതുപോലെ അവൾ സ്കൂൾ ഫൈനൽ ക്ലാസിൽ ജയിച്ച് കോളേജിൽ പോയി. അന്നാണ് ആ സംഭവം നടന്നത്. ഒരുദിവസം അവൾ തിരിച്ചുവന്നില്ല. ആരോ തട്ടിക്കൊണ്ടുപോയെന്നാണ് അറിവായത്. നാട്ടുകാരും പോലീസുകാരും ഒരുപാട് തിരഞ്ഞു. ഒരു തുമ്പും കിട്ടിയില്ല.

കാലംപോയി. അവൾ ഒരിടത്തുണ്ടെന്ന് അറിവുകിട്ടി. അന്നേക്ക് അവളുടെ അച്ഛനും അമ്മയും മരിച്ചുകഴിഞ്ഞിരുന്നു. മൂത്ത സഹോദരൻ അവളെ കാണാൻ ചെന്നു. അവൾ ഒരാളുടെ ഭാര്യയായി, സുഖമായിട്ടു കഴിയുന്നു. സഹോദരനു സന്തോഷമായി. മടങ്ങിപ്പോന്നു.

ഒരു വർഷം മുമ്പ് അവൾ മരിച്ചെന്നുകേട്ടു. ഇക്കാലമത്രയും അവളെ കാണാൻ ആഗ്രഹിച്ചിരുന്നു. അവളെ കാണാതായപ്പോൾ തുടങ്ങി അവൾക്കുവേണ്ടി ദുഃഖിച്ചു. കഴിയുകയായിരുന്നു. അപ്പോഴാണ് അവൾ മരിച്ചെന്നുകേട്ടത്. ഒന്നു കാണാൻ കഴിയാതെ അവൾ പിരിഞ്ഞുപോയി.

കഥകളോർമിച്ച് ഭാനുമതി അതേപടി ഇരുന്നു. പെട്ടെന്ന് ഒരു ഞെട്ടൽ.

എന്താണ് പിന്നെ കേട്ടത്? ആ വാർത്ത ശരിയായിരുന്നോ? അങ്ങനെ സംഭവിച്ചിരിക്കുമോ? രത്നമ്മയെ അവളുടെ ഭർത്താവുകൊന്നതാണെന്ന്, ഒരിക്കൽ ഒരാൾ വന്നു പറഞ്ഞു. വിശ്വസനീയനായ ഒരാൾ. ആ ഭർത്താവ് പണക്കാരനാണ്. അതുകൊണ്ട്, ഒരിക്കലും അത് പുറത്തുവരാൻ പോകുന്നില്ലെന്ന്.

ഭാനുമതി മെല്ലെ തലയിണയിലേക്ക് ചാരിയിരുന്നു. അവളുടെ ഭാവഭേദം കണ്ടുനിന്ന രാജമ്മ ചോദിച്ചു.

"എന്താ കൊച്ചമ്മേ?"

അവൾ മിണ്ടിയില്ല.

ഇടയ്ക്കിടയ്ക്ക് ആ ഫോട്ടോ നോക്കിക്കൊണ്ട് കുറച്ചു സമയംകൂടി കിടന്നു. പിന്നെ രാജമ്മയോടു പറഞ്ഞു:

"നിങ്ങൾ പോയി അത്താഴം കഴിച്ചോളൂ."

"കൊച്ചമ്മ ഒന്നും കഴിച്ചില്ല." രാജമ്മ ഏതോ വിചാരത്തിൽ മുഴുകിയിരിക്കുന്നു.

"എനിക്കു വേണ്ട. രാജമ്മേ."

"വിശന്നുകിടക്കരുത്. കൊച്ചമ്മേ."

"എനിക്ക് വിശപ്പില്ല."

നിർബന്ധിച്ചു. എന്നിട്ടും ഭാനുമതി പോയില്ല. രാജമ്മ അപ്പുറത്തേക്കു നടന്നു.

കണ്ണുകൾ നിറഞ്ഞൊഴുകി. അത് തുടച്ചു. ആ വേലക്കാരി മടങ്ങിവരും. അവർ ആ മുറിയുടെ വാതിൽക്കലാണ് കിടക്കുന്നത്. എന്തിന് അവർ കാണണം?

ജീവിതത്തിൽ എന്തെല്ലാം സംഭവിക്കുന്നു! എവിടെയാണ് വന്നെത്തിയിരിക്കുന്നത്? ആ മുറിയാകെ നോക്കി. അവിടെ മരണത്തിന്റെ ഗന്ധം നിറയുന്നതുപോലെ. ആ ശൂന്യമായ ചുമരുകൾക്കുള്ളിൽ നിന്ന് ശബ്ദം കേൾക്കുന്നുണ്ടോ? മരണത്തിന്റെ ശബ്ദം? ആ ആഡംബരവസ്തുക്കളെല്ലാം ഏതോ ഭീകരതയുടെ ആവരണമാണെന്ന് തോന്നിപ്പോകുന്നു.

രത്നമ്മയെ കൊന്നതാണെന്ന് പറഞ്ഞത് വിശ്വസ്തനായ ആളാണ്. ഒരു സമാജം പ്രവർത്തകയുടെ ഭർത്താവ്.

വാസവമേനോന് ഇതൊന്നും അറിഞ്ഞുകൂടായിരുന്നോ? ഇല്ല. അറിയില്ല. തീർച്ച. അച്ഛനെപ്പോലെ ഒരാൾ തനിക്ക് ഭൂമിയിലുള്ളത്, അദ്ദേഹമാണ്. മകളെ കെട്ടിച്ചയയ്ക്കുന്ന സന്തോഷമായിരുന്നു അദ്ദേഹത്തിന്. നിർദോഷിയായ ആ വലിയ മനുഷ്യൻ.

ഈ കിടക്കയിൽ, ഈ വിലപിടിപ്പുള്ള സൂര്യപടമെത്തയിൽ, ഒരിക്കൽ രത്നമ്മ കിടന്നിരുന്നു. ഇതിൽ അവളുടെ കണ്ണുനീർ ധാരാളം വീണിട്ടുണ്ട്.

അവളുടെ പിറകേ താൻ ഇവിടെ വന്നു കിടക്കുന്നു. അവൾ കിടന്ന സ്ഥലത്ത് ഒരുകാലത്തും താൻ കിടക്കരുതായിരുന്നു. വിധി ഇത്ര കണ്ണില്ലാതെ പെരുമാറാൻ താനെന്ത് തെറ്റുചെയ്തു.

രാജമ്മ പുറത്ത് പായ് വിരിക്കുന്നു. അവർ അകത്തേക്ക് വന്നു പറഞ്ഞു.

"കൊച്ചമ്മേ, ആ ഫോട്ടോ ഇങ്ങ് തന്നേക്ക്. അതെങ്ങാനും ഇവിടെ കണ്ടാല്. എന്നെ വച്ചേക്കത്തില്ല."

ഭാനുമതി പിടഞ്ഞെഴുന്നേറ്റു.

"എന്താ? ഈ ഫോട്ടോ കാണുന്നത് അദ്ദേഹത്തിന് ഭയമാണോ?" ഉള്ളിലെ ക്ഷോഭം അങ്ങനെ ഒരുചോദ്യമായി പുറത്തു ചാടിപ്പോയി.

രാജമ്മ വിറങ്ങലിച്ചു നിൽക്കുന്നു. അവരുടെ മുഖത്ത് ഭയമുണ്ട്. മറുപടി പറയാൻ കഴിയാതെ നിൽക്കുന്നു.

കൂടുതൽ ചോദിക്കാൻ പാടില്ല. സമചിത്തത വീണ്ടെടുക്കാൻ ശ്രമിച്ചു. എന്തും വരട്ടെ. പുതിയ ഒരാത്മധൈര്യം പെട്ടെന്ന് ഞരമ്പുകളിൽക്കൂടി പൊന്തിവന്നതുപോലെ, നിമിഷങ്ങൾ. അവൾ ആ ഫോട്ടോ നീട്ടി. രാജമ്മ അതു വാങ്ങി പുറത്തേക്കു നടന്നു.

കണ്ണുമടച്ചു കിടന്നു. വെളുപ്പാൻകാലത്താണ് ഒന്നു മയങ്ങിയത്. പുലർന്നപ്പോൾ എഴുന്നേറ്റു. എല്ലാ ക്ഷീണങ്ങളും കുടഞ്ഞു മാറ്റി ദിനകൃത്യങ്ങൾ ചെയ്തു, അടുക്കളയിൽപ്പോയി. മുറികളിൽക്കൂടി നടന്നു. വീടിന്റെ മുൻവശത്ത് ചെന്നിരുന്നു. എതിർവശത്ത് ഒരു മാളികക്കെട്ടിടം. അതിന്റെ രണ്ടാംനിലയിലെ വരാന്തയിൽ നിന്നുകൊണ്ട് ഒരു കുട്ടി സൂക്ഷിച്ചുനോക്കുന്നു. ചിരിക്കുന്നു, ഭാനുമതി അതിന്റെ നേർക്ക് കൈകാട്ടി. അതും കൈനീട്ടി അഭിവാദനം ചെയ്തു. അതിന്റെ അമ്മയാണെന്നു തോന്നുന്നു. പുറത്തേക്കു വന്നു. അവർ കുറച്ചുനേരം ഭാനുമതിയെ നോക്കിനിന്നു. പിന്നെ, കുട്ടിയേയും കൊണ്ട് അകത്തേക്കു പോയി.

അപ്പോൾ, പുറത്ത് കാറു വന്നു നിൽക്കുന്നു. ഒന്നല്ല, രണ്ട്. ഉറക്കെ വർത്തമാനം. പൊട്ടിച്ചിരികൾ, അവർ ഗേറ്റ് തുറന്ന് ഇരച്ചുകയറുന്നു. ഒരു സംഘം ചെറുപ്പക്കാരികൾ. ചെറുപ്പക്കാർ പുറകെ, ദിവാകരനുമുണ്ട്.

പെൺകുട്ടികൾ ആർത്തുകൊണ്ട് കയറിവന്നു.

"ഹലോ! ഗുഡ്മോർണിങ്! ഗുഡ്മോർണിങ് മിസിസ് ദിവാകരൻ.." പലരും ഒരുമിച്ച് പറയുന്നു.

തൊഴുതു ഉത്സാഹം നടിച്ചു ദിവകാരൻ അങ്ങോട്ടു വന്നു.

"ഭാനു ഭയപ്പെടേണ്ട. എന്റെ സുഹൃത്തുക്കളും അവരുടെ ഭാര്യമാരുമാണ്. എല്ലാം വികൃതികളാണെന്നുമാത്രം!"

"അങ്ങയുടെ സുഹൃത്തുക്കളല്ലേ! പിന്നെങ്ങനെ വികൃതികളാകാതിരിക്കും?" ഇംഗ്ലീഷ് രീതിയിൽ മലയാളം പറയുന്ന ഒരുത്തി ദിവാകനെ നോക്കി ഫലിതം പറഞ്ഞു. മറ്റെല്ലാവരും ചിരിച്ചു.

എല്ലാവരും സ്വീകരണമുറിയിൽ ഇരുന്നു. ചായ വന്നു. ഭാനുമതിക്ക് എല്ലാവരെയും ഒരുത്തി പരിചയപ്പെടുത്തി. "സോഫിയ, അവളുടെ കെട്ടിയവൻ തോമസ്, രാധിക അവളുടെ ഭർത്താവ് മന്മഥൻ, രേണു, അവളുടെ പ്രിയപ്പെട്ട നായര് രാഘവൻ കർത്താവ്, പിന്നെ വിലാസിനി എന്ന ഞാൻ എന്റെ ആനക്കാരൻ മി. രഘുനാഥൻ, ആ നിൽക്കുന്ന ആളെ അറിയാമല്ലോ ദിവാകരൻ മിസ്റ്റർ ഭാനുമതി!"

എല്ലാവരുടെയും കൂട്ടച്ചിരി. അവൾ ഇരുന്നു.

അന്ന് വൈകുന്നേരംവരെ ആ വീട്ടിൽ ബഹളമായിരുന്നു. ആ ദിവസങ്ങളിലെല്ലാം ശബ്ദമില്ലാതിരുന്ന, പ്രത്യേകിച്ചു ചലനമൊന്നുമില്ലാതിരുന്ന അവിടം, ഉറക്കെയുള്ള വർത്തമാനം കൊണ്ടും പൊട്ടിച്ചിരികൊണ്ടും കാടിളകിയതു കണക്കാക്കി. ഭാനുമതി എല്ലാത്തിനും ഒത്തു നിന്നു. ഏറ്റവും ഭംഗിയായി പെരുമാറി. അതിഥികൾക്ക് സന്തോഷമുണ്ടാകത്തക്കവിധം സംസാരിച്ചു. ദിവാകരൻ അത് ശ്രദ്ധിച്ചു. അവളുടെ രീതികൾ അയാളെ ആഹ്ലാദിപ്പിച്ചത് വ്യക്തമായി കാണാമായിരുന്നു.

എല്ലാവരും പുറത്തിറങ്ങി, കുറെ നടന്നു തിരിച്ചുവന്നു കാറിൽ കയറി സിനിമയ്ക്കു പോയി തിരിച്ചുവന്ന്, മട്ടുപ്പാവിൽ കൂട്ടംകൂടി. ദിവാകരൻ അവർക്ക് മദ്യം പകർന്നുകൊടുത്തു. ചെറുപ്പക്കാരും ചെറുപ്പക്കാരികളും അത് കഴിച്ചു. ചിലർ നിലവിട്ടു സംസാരിച്ചു. ഭാനുമതി അവർക്ക് ഇറച്ചിയും മീനും മറ്റുപലതരം വിഭവങ്ങളും വിളമ്പിക്കൊടുത്തു. അവൾ അവരുടെ താളത്തിനൊത്ത് നല്ല വാക്കുകൾ പറഞ്ഞു. ഒരുത്തി നിർബന്ധിച്ചു.

"മിസിസ് ദിവാകരൻ, കഴിക്കൂന്നേ. ഒരു പെഗ് വിസ്കി കഴിക്കൂ."

അവൾ അതിനു രസകരമായി മറുപടി പറഞ്ഞു.

"ഇതുമായി ഒന്നു പരിചയിക്കട്ടെ. എന്നിട്ട് നമുക്കൊരുമിച്ചു കഴിക്കാം."

ലഹരി പിടിച്ചവർ, അതു സമ്മതിച്ചു.

ലഹരിയുമായി അവർ രാത്രിയുടെ ആഴത്തിലേക്കു സഞ്ചരിച്ചു. രണ്ടുമണിക്ക് ചിലർ അവിടെയിരുന്ന് ഉറങ്ങി. മറ്റു ചിലർ പലയിടത്തെത്തി കിടന്നു.

വെളുപ്പിനുതന്നെ ആ സംഘം പോയി. അവർ ഒട്ടേറെ സമ്മാനങ്ങൾ കൊണ്ടുവന്നിരുന്നു. അതെല്ലാം നോക്കി ട്രാൻസിസ്റ്റർ, പാവകൾ, സാരികൾ മാല, ടീസെറ്റ്...

അയാൾ കുളിക്കാൻ പോയി, ഭാനുമതി മേശപ്പുറത്തു വച്ചിരുന്ന ഒരു കവർ കണ്ടു. സന്ധ്യാദേവിയുടെ മേൽവിലാസത്തിലുള്ള കവറാണ്. ഒട്ടിച്ചിരുന്നില്ല. അത് തുറന്നുനോക്കി. സദനത്തിന് രണ്ടായിരത്തൊന്നുരൂപയുടെ ഒരുചെക്ക്! സംഭാവനയാണ്. അത് കൂടെയുള്ള കത്തിൽ എഴുതിയിരുന്നു. പെട്ടെന്ന് ഉള്ളിൽ ക്ഷോഭം തോന്നി. അടുത്ത നിമിഷം അതടക്കി. പാടില്ല അതൊന്നും ഇപ്പോൾ കാട്ടരുത്.

കുളിച്ചുവന്ന ദിവാകരൻ പറഞ്ഞു:

"ആ കവറ് തുറന്നുനോക്കൂ."

"ഞാൻ കണ്ടു..." അവൾ പറഞ്ഞു.

"എന്താ നല്ല കാര്യമല്ലേ?"

"അതെ."

അവൾ അയാളെ ഡൈനിങ് ഹാളിലേക്കു കൂട്ടിക്കൊണ്ടുപോയി.

ആറ്

സന്ധ്യാദേവി അവരുടെ വീട്ടിൽ പോയിരിക്കുന്നു. കീർത്തി ഏകാ

കിനിയെപ്പോലെ അങ്ങുമിങ്ങും ചെന്നു കുത്തിയിരിക്കുന്നു. എല്ലാവരും ഓരോന്നുപറഞ്ഞ് അവളെ കളിയാക്കി. അധികം സംസാരിക്കാത്ത അംബിക തമ്പുരാട്ടി പറഞ്ഞു. "അയ്യോ, കുഞ്ഞിന്റമ്മ പോയി ഇല്ലേ വേഗം മടങ്ങിവരും മോളേ" റീന അടുത്തുവന്നിരുന്ന് ഒരുകഥ പറഞ്ഞു തുടങ്ങി. "ഒരിടത്ത് ഒരാട്ടിൻകുട്ടി ഉണ്ടായിരുന്നു അത് ഒരിക്കലും അതിന്റെ തള്ളയെ പിരിഞ്ഞിരിക്കാറില്ല.... കീർത്തി ചൊടിച്ചു. "പോടീ കളിയാക്കാതെ" ഒടുവിൽ തമാശ പറയാത്ത യോഗമയീദേവി കീർത്തിയുടെ മുൻപിൽ വന്നുനിന്നു. "ഞാൻ പറഞ്ഞതാ, ഇതിനെക്കൂടി കൊണ്ടുപൊയ്ക്കൊള്ളാൻ. അപ്പോൾ സന്ധ്യയെ വല്ലവരും കെട്ടിക്കൊണ്ടുപോയാൽ എന്തുചെയ്യും?" റീന വിട്ടില്ല. പിന്നിൽ നിന്നു പറഞ്ഞു. "കൂടെപ്പോകും!"

പക്ഷേ, ഈ ദിവസങ്ങളിൽ കീർത്തിക്ക് ഒരു ചെറിയ സമാധാനം കിട്ടി, മനോരമ പുതിയ ആളാണ്. അവർ കീർത്തിയുടെ അടുത്തുവന്നിരിക്കും. അവൾക്ക് പുതിയ കാര്യങ്ങൾ പറയാനുണ്ട്. മനോരമയെക്കുറിച്ച് സന്ധ്യാദേവി അന്വേഷണങ്ങൾ നടത്തി. അവൾ താമസിച്ചിരുന്ന ബന്ധുവീട്ടിൽ അവളെപ്പറ്റി നല്ല അഭിപ്രായമല്ല. അവർ ഒന്നും തുറന്നു പറഞ്ഞില്ല. എങ്കിലും അവിടുത്തെ കാരണവർ ഇങ്ങനെ പറഞ്ഞു: "ആ അവള് അവിടെയെങ്കിലും നിന്ന് നന്നാവട്ടെ. സന്ധ്യാദേവിയും അംബിക തമ്പുരാട്ടിയും കൂടിയാണ് പോയിരുന്നത്. കാരണവർ നടത്തിയ ആത്മഗതത്തിന്റെ അർഥം അവർക്ക് പിടികിട്ടിയില്ല. അവൾ ചർക്കസംഘത്തിൽ പ്രവർത്തിച്ചിരുന്നതായി കാരണവരും സമ്മതിച്ചു. അവൾ സദനത്തിൽ നിൽക്കുന്നതിൽ അവർക്ക് എതിർപ്പൊന്നുമില്ല.

സന്ധ്യാദേവി മടങ്ങിവന്ന് മനോരമയെ വിളിച്ചു. പലതും ചോദിച്ചു. അവളുടെ ജീവിതത്തിൽ അവൾ മറച്ചുവയ്ക്കുന്ന എന്തോ ഒക്കെ ഉണ്ട്. അത് തോന്നി. ആ പുറങ്ങൾ ഉടനെ അവൾ വായിച്ചുകേൾപ്പിക്കുകയില്ല. ഇവിടെ ഒരു പുതിയ ജീവിതം തുടങ്ങട്ടെ. സന്ധ്യാദേവി ചില ഉപദേശങ്ങൾ നൽകി. ഈ സദനം ഉന്നതമായ ലക്ഷ്യങ്ങൾക്കുവേണ്ടി പ്രവർത്തിക്കുന്ന ഒരു സങ്കേതമാണ്. ഇവിടെ അച്ചടക്കവും സ്നേഹവും ശുദ്ധിയും വേണം. അത് എപ്പോഴും ഓർമയിലിരിക്കണം. അവൾ അത് ഏറ്റുപറഞ്ഞു.

ഒരു രാത്രിയിൽ അരികത്തു കിടന്നുകൊണ്ട് മനോരമ കീർത്തിയോടു മന്ത്രിച്ചു:

"ഞാൻ ഒരാളെ സ്നേഹിച്ചിരുന്നു, കീർത്തി. അയാൾ എന്നെ വഞ്ചിച്ചു. ഞാൻ ആത്മഹത്യചെയ്യാൻ പോയതാണ്. പിന്നെ, ജീവിക്കാൻ തീരുമാനിച്ചു. ഇനി ഞാൻ ഒരുത്തനേയും സ്നേഹിക്കുകയില്ല."

"ആരാണ് ചേച്ചിയെ വഞ്ചിച്ചത്?" കീർത്തി ചോദിച്ചു.

മറുപടിയില്ല. പിന്നെ അവൾ ചോദിച്ചുമില്ല.

കീർത്തിക്ക് അനുകമ്പ തോന്നി. പുരുഷൻ അങ്ങനെ വഞ്ചിച്ചാൽ പെണ്ണ് എന്തുചെയ്യും? അവളുടെ മനസ്സ് തകർന്നുപോവുകയല്ലാതെ എന്തുചെയ്യും?

പേരുമാത്രം അറിയിക്കാതെ, പല ദിവസങ്ങളിൽക്കൂടി, ആ മോഹ

ത്തിന്റെ കഥയിലെ നുറുങ്ങുകൾ മനോരമ കീർത്തിയുടെ കാതുകളിലേക്ക് മന്ത്രിച്ചുകൊണ്ടിരുന്നു. ഒരു ദുഃഖകവിതയിലെ നായികയായി മാറി അവൾ. മറ്റാരോടും അവൾ ഇത് തുറന്നു സംസാരിച്ചിട്ടില്ല. എന്തിന് സംസാരിക്കണം? സ്വന്തം കദനത്തിന്റെ കഥ ഉള്ളിലൊതുക്കിപ്പിടിച്ചു നടന്നാൽ മതി.

ഒരിക്കൽമാത്രം മനോരമ രഹസ്യമായി തന്റെ മനസ്സ് വെളിപ്പെടുത്തി.

"എനിക്ക് ജീവിക്കണം. അന്തസ്സായി ജീവിക്കണം. ആരേയും ആശ്രയിക്കാതെ കഴിയണം. പണമുള്ളവനാണെങ്കിൽ, ഏതു കെളവനേയും ഞാൻ കെട്ടാൻ സമ്മതിക്കും. കെളവന്മാരാ നല്ലത്."

കീർത്തിക്ക് വല്ലായ്മ തോന്നി. എന്തൊരു വർത്തമാനമാണത്! ഒരു പക്ഷേ, ജീവിതത്തിലെ അനുഭവങ്ങൾമൂലം പലവിചാരങ്ങൾ വരുന്നതാവാം. മനുഷ്യന് വൈരാഗ്യം എന്നൊന്നുണ്ടല്ലോ. എന്നാലും ആ പ്രസ്താവനയിൽ എന്തോ ഒരു അസുഖകരമായ അംശമുണ്ട്.

പിന്നീട് സന്ദർഭം വന്നപ്പോൾ കീർത്തി അതുചോദിച്ചു. അപ്പോൾ മനോരമ അലസമായി മറുപടി പറഞ്ഞു.

"ഓ ഞാൻ ചുമ്മാ പറഞ്ഞതാ."

സദനത്തിലുള്ളവർ ചില ദിവസങ്ങളിൽ ക്ഷേത്രത്തിൽ പോകാറുണ്ട്. ചിലപ്പോഴൊക്കെ ചെറുപ്പക്കാർ അഭിപ്രായങ്ങൾ പറയാറുണ്ട്. പക്ഷേ, ഇപ്പോൾ പരിചയം വർധിച്ചു അതുകൊണ്ട് രസമുള്ള കമന്റുകളേയുള്ളൂ. അവർക്കെല്ലാം കീർത്തി ഇഷ്ടപ്പെട്ട ഒരു തെറിച്ച പെണ്ണാണ്. "ഞങ്ങൾക്കു വേണ്ടിക്കൂടി പ്രാർഥിച്ചേക്കോ!" എന്നൊക്കെയാവും അവരുടെ കമന്റ്. അത് അസുഖകരമായി ആർക്കും അങ്ങനെ തോന്നാറുമില്ല. മനോരമ പുതിയ ആളായിട്ടും അവർ ശ്രദ്ധിച്ചിട്ടില്ലെന്നു തോന്നുന്നു. അഭിപ്രായങ്ങൾ വന്നില്ല.

തൊട്ടടുത്ത് പെൺകുട്ടികളുടെ സ്കൂളുണ്ട്. കീർത്തി അവിടെയാണ് പഠിച്ചത്. അവിടെ പുതിയ ഹാൾ പണിതിരിക്കുന്നു. അത് സംബന്ധിച്ച് ആഘോഷമുണ്ട്. സദനത്തിന്റെ സഹകരണം ഹെഡ്മിസ്ട്രസ്സ് അഭ്യർഥിച്ചു. സന്ധ്യാദേവി അത് സമ്മതിച്ചു. പൂർവ വിദ്യാർഥിനിയായ കീർത്തി അവരുടെ കലാപരിപാടികളിൽ പങ്കെടുക്കണം. താൻ സ്ഥലത്തുണ്ടാവില്ലെന്ന് സന്ധ്യാദേവി അറിയിച്ചു. കീർത്തിയെ അയക്കും. സദനത്തിലുള്ളവർ തീർച്ചയായും സഹകരിക്കും.

അന്ന് വൈകീട്ടുതന്നെ അവർ സ്കൂളിലേക്കുപോയി. മീറ്റിങ്ങും പ്രസംഗവും നടന്നു. എട്ടുമണിക്ക് കലാപരിപാടി ആരംഭിക്കുന്നു.

കീർത്തി ഭാരതമാതാവാണ്. അടിമച്ചങ്ങലയണിഞ്ഞ ഭാരതമാതാവ്. മക്കളുടെ വേദനയും കഷ്ടപ്പാടുംകണ്ട് ദുഃഖിക്കുന്ന അമ്മ.

നൃത്തംപഠിച്ച കീർത്തി, ഭാരതമാതാവിന്റെ വേഷത്തിൽ അരങ്ങത്തു വന്നു. ശംഖധ്വനികൾക്കിടയ്ക്ക് കത്തിച്ച വിളക്കുകൾക്ക് നടുവിൽ സുഗന്ധധൂമങ്ങളുടെ വലയത്തിനുള്ളിൽ, ആ അമ്മ പ്രത്യക്ഷപ്പെട്ടു. സദസ്സ് നിശ്ശബ്ദമായി ഇരുന്നുപോയി. അവളുടെ മുഖത്തെ ചൈതന്യം, അവളുടെ

ശരീരത്തിന്റെ രൂപസൗകുമാര്യം അവളുടെ ചലനങ്ങളിലെ ചാരുത, രോമ ഹർഷമണിയിക്കാൻ പര്യാപ്തമായിരുന്നു. ആ വിടർന്ന മിഴികൾ ദുഃഖ ത്തിന്റെയും തീവ്രമായ അഭിമാനവികാരത്തിന്റെയും രസങ്ങൾ ചുറ്റുപാടും വാരിവിതറി. ആ ചുണ്ടുകൾ മന്ദഹാസത്തിന്റെയും മക്കളെക്കുറിച്ചുള്ള വേദനകളുടെയും സൂക്ഷ്മഭാവങ്ങൾ മാറിമാറി പ്രകാശിപ്പിച്ചു.

വന്ദേമാതരം!

ആയിരങ്ങളെന്ന് തോന്നിക്കുംവിധം കനമുള്ള പുരുഷശബ്ദങ്ങളും നിർമലജലംപോലുള്ള സ്ത്രീശബ്ദങ്ങളും ഒരുമിച്ചു ചേർന്ന് സാവധാനം അത് പാടി.

സുഫലാം, സുജലാം,
സസ്യശ്യാമളാം...
മാതരം!
വന്ദേമാതരം!

ഹരം പിടിപ്പിക്കുന്ന നിമിഷങ്ങൾ... കീർത്തി ചലിച്ചു. പിന്നെ കുറെ മിനിട്ടുകളിലേക്ക് അവൾ ആ അരങ്ങിൽ നിറഞ്ഞുനിന്നു. ഭാരതമാതാവ്, ഭാരതത്തിലെ ജനങ്ങളുടെ ആത്മാവാണെന്ന് അവൾ കാട്ടി. തൊഴിലാ ളികൾ, കൃഷിക്കാർ, കച്ചവടക്കാർ, കലാകാരന്മാർ, വീട്ടമ്മമാർ, പട്ടാള ക്കാർ, പോലീസുകാർ, കീർത്തി പതിഞ്ഞും ഇളകിയും നൃത്തം ചെയ്ത് അതെല്ലാമായി. ഭാരതമെന്ന അമ്മയായി. കൈവിലങ്ങണിഞ്ഞ ആ അമ്മ, ആത്മദുഃഖത്തിന്റെ പ്രതീകംപോലെ തളർന്നിരുന്നു. പിന്നെ, മക്കളുടെ വരവാണ്. അവർ മർദിക്കപ്പെട്ടു. കൊലചെയ്യപ്പെട്ടു. ഒടുവിൽ ഉണർന്നെ ഴുന്നേറ്റ് പോരാടി അമ്മയെ മോചിപ്പിച്ചു. തന്നെ അപമാനിക്കാൻ വന്ന ബ്രിട്ടീഷ് അധികാരത്തിന്റെ നേർക്ക് ആ അമ്മയുടെ കണ്ണുകളിൽനിന്ന് തീപ്പൊരി പാറി. മക്കളെ മർദിച്ചപ്പോൾ, കൊന്നൊടുക്കിയപ്പോൾ അവ രുടെ ആത്മാവ് നൊന്തു. അവർ പടപൊരുതിയപ്പോൾ ആവേശത്തിന്റെ ഗദ്ഗദങ്ങൾ ഉതിർന്നു. സ്വതന്ത്രയായപ്പോൾ ആ മാതൃത്വത്തിന്റെ ഏറ്റവും വലിയ ധന്യസ്വരൂപമായി ആ അമ്മ നിലകൊണ്ടു.

നിറകണ്ണുകളോടെ മന്ദഹസിച്ചുനിന്ന ആ രൂപത്തിനു പിന്നിൽനിന്ന് ഈ ഗാനം കടന്നുവന്നു.

അനാദിയാണമ്മേ! അവിടു-
ന്നനാദിയാണമ്മേ!
ബ്രഹ്മതപസിൽ കൽപ്പയുഗങ്ങളിൽ
നിന്നുമുണർന്നൊരുഭൂമി
കണ്ണുതുറന്നൂ, കണ്ടു സനാതന
പുണ്യദേവത നിന്നെ-ഭാരത-
താംബികേ നിന്നെ!
ദേഹമഹസുകൾ മന്വന്തരവര-
വാണിയുണർത്തി നിന്നിൽ
സപ്തസൈന്ധവഹൃദയങ്ങളിൽ സ്വയ-

മെത്തി, ദേവമന്ത്രങ്ങൾ
ഹിമവൽഗിരിതടമിരുവിട്ടു
ഋഷിഗീതങ്ങൾ, കാവ്യങ്ങൾ
അരണ്യഗാഥകൾ സ്മൃതിയായ്,
ശ്രുതിയായ്,
അപൂർവരാഗങ്ങളായി.
കന്യാദേവി കനിഞ്ഞുപകർന്നൂ
സുന്ദരശാങ്കരഭാഷ്യങ്ങൾ
ഋതുദേവതമാരിറങ്ങിവന്നൂ
സുകൃതം ചാർത്തി നിന്നിൽ
അനാദിയാണമ്മേ അവിടു-
ന്നനാദിയാണമ്മേ!
യുഗസംക്രമമായ്, അമ്മേ, മോചന
യുദ്ധക്കളമൊരുങ്ങി,
വരുന്നു ചോരപ്പൂവുകൾ മനസി-
ലണിഞ്ഞ യോദ്ധാക്കൾ - ഞങ്ങൾ
മോചനയോദ്ധാക്കൾ
അടിമകളില്ലിനിയമ്മേ, നമ്മ-
ളടിമകളല്ലൊരുനാളും!
ആവേശം പൂണ്ട ഹസ്തഘോഷങ്ങൾ

യവനിക വീണു. സദസിനു ഭാരതമാതാവിനെ കാണണം. അവർ അതു വിളിച്ചു പറഞ്ഞു. തിരശ്ശീലയ്ക്കു പിന്നിൽനിന്ന് പത്തുമിനിട്ടുനേരത്തെ സാവകാശം അപേക്ഷിച്ചു. കാണികൾ നിശ്ശബ്ദരായിരുന്നു. പ്രതീക്ഷയുടെ നിശ്ശബ്ദത. വീണ്ടും അരങ്ങു തെളിഞ്ഞു. കർട്ടൻ ഉയരുന്നു. മുടി കെട്ടിവെച്ച് പച്ച ബ്ലൗസും കസവുനേര്യതും ധരിച്ച് ശാലീനയായ കീർത്തി രംഗത്തേക്കു വന്നു. അവൾ താണുതൊഴുതു. കൈയടികളും ഹൃദയപൂർവമായ അഭിനന്ദനശബ്ദങ്ങളും കൊണ്ട് അവിടം മുഖരിതമായി. എന്തുചെയ്യണമെന്നറിയാതെ അവൾ നിന്നു. പലവുരു സദസിനെ വന്ദിച്ചു. അവൾ തിരിഞ്ഞപ്പോൾ “പോകരുതേ” എന്ന് അവർ വിളിച്ചുപറഞ്ഞു. ധ്യാനത്തിൽ മുഴുകിയതു പോലെ അവൾ നിന്നു. കണ്ണുകൾ നിറഞ്ഞു. അവളുടെ കവിളുകൾ നനയുന്നത് സദസ്സ് കണ്ടു. നിശ്ശബ്ദത. കർട്ടൻ സാവധാനം താഴോട്ടു വീണു.

പിറ്റേന്നു രാവിലെ വൈകിയാണ് ഉണർന്നത്. സദനത്തിൽ എല്ലാവരുടേയും മനസിൽ അവളെപ്പറ്റി അഭിമാനപൂർവമായ വിചാരമാണ്. വായാടിപ്പെണ്ണ്. കുസൃതി. പെട്ടെന്നു വാടിപ്പോകുന്ന മനസുള്ള പെണ്ണ്. അരങ്ങത്ത് അത്രയും കാട്ടാൻ അവൾക്ക് കഴിഞ്ഞല്ലോ! റീന അതിനിടയ്ക്ക് ഒന്നു കളിയാക്കി. “ഓ, മുഖത്ത് കുറേ ചായംതേച്ച് വന്ന് കുറേ ആടിയെന്നും പറഞ്ഞ് പെണ്ണിന് എന്തൊരു ഭാവം!” കീർത്തി ഒരു നുള്ളു കൊടുത്തു. അപ്പോഴെല്ലാം അവൾക്ക് ഉള്ളിൽ ഒരു വ്യാകുലത തോന്നി

യിരുന്നു. തന്റെ അഭിനയം കാണാൻ അരവിന്ദേട്ടൻ വന്നില്ല...

അന്നു വൈകുന്നേരം മറ്റുള്ളവരുമൊത്ത് അമ്പലത്തിൽ പോയി അവൾ. ചെറുപ്പക്കാരിലൊരുത്തന്റെ കമന്റ്. "അമ്മേ, മാതാവേ രക്ഷിക്കണേ!"

"സാധ്യമല്ല, കുഞ്ഞ് നടയ്ക്കൽപ്പോയി പ്രാർഥിക്ക്. കീർത്തി ഉടനെ അതിനു മറുപടി നൽകി. ചെറുപ്പക്കാർ രസിച്ചു. അവൾ കൊഞ്ഞനംകുത്തിയിട്ടു നടന്നു.

അന്നു രാത്രിയിൽ ഒരനുഭവമുണ്ടായി. നല്ല ഉറക്കമാണ്. താൻ പൂക്കളുടെ ഒരു കൂമ്പാരത്തിനുള്ളിൽ കിടക്കുകയാണെന്നു തോന്നി. സുഗന്ധങ്ങൾ മൂടിയിരിക്കുന്നു. ആ ഗന്ധം ഞരമ്പുകളിൽ അരിച്ചുകയറുന്നു. അതിനിടയിൽക്കൂടി ആകാശം കാണാം. ചന്ദ്രനെ കാണാം. താൻ നഗ്നയാണെന്ന് ഒരു തോന്നൽ. പിന്നെ താൻ ഒരു പൂവാണെന്ന് തോന്നൽ. വിടരുന്നതിന്റെ ഒരു അസ്വസ്ഥത. ശരീരമാകെ വിറയ്ക്കുന്നു. കാറ്റത്ത് പൂവിതളുകൾ കമ്പിച്ചുനിൽക്കുംപോലെ കാറ്റ് വർധിച്ചു. ആകെ ഉലഞ്ഞു. ഉണർന്നുപോയി. ആരോ തന്നോട് ഒട്ടിക്കിടക്കുന്നു. ഭയന്നുപോയി. ഞെട്ടി എഴുന്നേൽക്കാൻ ഭാവിച്ചു. ആ ആൾ കട്ടിലിൽ നിന്നെഴുന്നേറ്റ് കീഴോട്ടു മാറി. കീർത്തി എഴുന്നേറ്റിരുന്നു ആലോചിച്ചു. ആരാണ് അടുത്തു കിടന്നത്? ഓർമ വന്നു. ആ മുറിയിൽ കിടക്കുന്നത്, മനോരമയാണ്.

വെറുപ്പു തോന്നി. ശരീരമാകെ വിയർത്തിട്ടുണ്ട്. ഇരുട്ടിൽ തപ്പിത്തടഞ്ഞ് അവൾ ഉടുത്തിരുന്ന സാരി മാറ്റി. അത് മൂലയിലേക്കെറിഞ്ഞു.

കിടന്നു. കുറേനേരം കഴിഞ്ഞ്, തളർന്നുറങ്ങി.

പിറ്റേന്ന് മനോരമയെ ശ്രദ്ധിച്ചു. അവൾക്ക് ഒരു ഭാവവ്യത്യാസവുമില്ല. പഴയതുപോലെ തുറന്ന്, സ്നേഹത്തോടെ പെരുമാറുന്നു. അത് ഒരു സ്വപ്നമായിരുന്നുവെന്ന് വിശ്വസിക്കാൻ കീർത്തി ശ്രമിച്ചു.

വൈകുന്നേരം ഒരു പയ്യൻ ഒരു കത്ത് കൊണ്ടുവന്നു. യോഗമയി ദേവി അത് വായിച്ചു. അരവിന്ദന്റെ കത്താണ്.

"ഇന്നലെ ഞാൻ സ്കൂളിൽ വന്നിരുന്നു. വൈകിയാണ് വന്നത്. പക്ഷേ, കീർത്തിയുടെ അഭിനയം കണ്ടു. എന്റെ അഭിനന്ദനങ്ങൾ അറിയിക്കുക. പത്രമാഫീസിൽ പിടിപ്പത് ജോലിയുണ്ടായിരുന്നതുകൊണ്ടാണ് ഉടനെതന്നെ പോയത്. ഇന്ന് മറ്റൊരിടത്ത് പോകുന്നു.

സ്നേഹപുരസ്സരം അരവിന്ദൻ."

കീർത്തിയുടെ മനസ്സ് ഉണർന്നു. അരവിന്ദേട്ടൻ അത് കണ്ടല്ലോ. ആ അഭിനന്ദനത്തിന് മതിക്കാൻ വയ്യാത്ത വിലയുണ്ട്.

സന്ധ്യാദേവിയുടെ കുടുംബത്തിൽ ചില പ്രശ്നങ്ങളുണ്ട്. അമ്മ മരിച്ചതോടെ തല പൊന്തിച്ച പ്രശ്നങ്ങൾ. രണ്ട് അനിയത്തിമാരുണ്ട്. ഒരനിയനും. അച്ഛൻ നേരത്തെ മരിച്ചു. അച്ഛന്റെ അനിയനാണ് കാര്യങ്ങൾ നോക്കുന്നത്. അദ്ദേഹത്തിന് സന്ധ്യാദേവിയെ ഇഷ്ടമല്ല. പൊതുപ്രവർത്തനത്തിന് ഇറങ്ങിയതാണ് കാരണം. അനിയനും അനിയത്തിമാർക്കും വിരോധമൊന്നുമില്ല. പക്ഷേ, അവർക്ക് താൽപ്പര്യവുമില്ല. തങ്ങളുടെ കാര്യങ്ങൾ നോ

ക്കേണ്ടത് മൂത്തചേച്ചിയാണെന്ന് അവർ കരുതുന്നു. കോളേജ് വിദ്യാഭ്യാസം കഴിച്ച്; ബി എ പാസായ ചേച്ചി അവർക്ക് ഒരു ജോലിക്കു പോയ്ക്കൂടായിരുന്നോ? എങ്കിൽ വീട്ടിൽ ബുദ്ധിമുട്ടുണ്ടാവുമായിരുന്നോ? സഹോദരങ്ങൾക്ക് കൂടുതൽ പഠിക്കാൻ കഴിയുമായിരുന്നില്ലേ? അനിയൻ ഒരിക്കൽ അത് ചോദിച്ചു. "ചേച്ചിക്ക് ഞങ്ങളെ വേണ്ടല്ലോ. വേണമെന്നു തോന്നിയിരുന്നെങ്കിൽ ഞങ്ങൾ രക്ഷപ്പെടുമായിരുന്നു. അച്ഛൻ എന്തിനാണ് ചേച്ചിയുടെവിദ്യാഭ്യാസത്തിനു വേണ്ടി പണം ചെലവഴിച്ചത്? ഞങ്ങൾക്കുംകൂടി കിട്ടേണ്ടപണം മുടക്കിയത്. ഞങ്ങൾ ഇങ്ങനെ കിടക്കാനാണോ?"

മറുപടിയൊന്നും പറഞ്ഞില്ല.

ഇപ്പോൾ ഭാഗം എഴുതിവയ്ക്കണം. അതിനാണു വിളിച്ചിരിക്കുന്നത്. സന്ധ്യാദേവി ഒരു തീരുമാനം ചെയ്തിട്ടാണു പുറപ്പെട്ടിട്ടുള്ളത്. തന്റെ വീതം മൂന്നു സഹോദരങ്ങൾക്കായിട്ട് കൊടുക്കണം.

പത്രമാഫീസിൽവന്ന്, നാട്ടിലേക്കു പോകുന്ന വിവരം അരവിന്ദനോടു പറഞ്ഞു. അവിടെനിന്നാണ് വണ്ടി ആഫീസിലേക്കു പോയത്.

അച്ഛന്റെ സഹോദരൻ തണുത്ത കണ്ണുകളുമായി ഇരുന്നു. ഭാഗപത്രം എഴുതുന്നയാൾ പഴയ കണ്ണാടിക്കുള്ളിൽക്കൂടി നോക്കി ദീർഘമായി എഴുതിക്കൊണ്ടിരുന്നു. അനിയൻ ഉമ്മറത്ത് ഭിത്തിയിൽ ചാരിയിരുന്നു. അനിയത്തിമാർ അകത്തിരുന്നു. ഉച്ചയായപ്പോൾ എഴുതിയത് വായിക്കാൻ തയാറായി. രണ്ടു ദിവസത്തെ എഴുത്താണ്. വായിച്ചു നീണ്ടുപോകുന്ന വാചകങ്ങളും മറിഞ്ഞുകൊണ്ടിരുന്ന പുറങ്ങളും സന്ധ്യാദേവി ശ്രദ്ധിച്ചില്ല! എല്ലാം നേരത്തേ ധാരണയിലെത്തിയതാണ്. തന്റെ ഇരുപത്തിമൂന്നു സെന്റ് സ്ഥലവും രണ്ടുപറ കണ്ടവും മറ്റുമൂന്നുപേരുടേതിലേക്കുവീതിച്ചു. ചേർത്ത് എഴുതാൻ പറഞ്ഞിട്ടുണ്ട്. പെരുമ്പാമ്പിഴയുന്നതുപോലുള്ള നീണ്ട വാചകങ്ങളിൽ ആധാരമെഴുത്തുകാരൻ അതിർത്തികളും എലുകളും സെന്റും പറമ്പും കണ്ടവും എല്ലാം മുറിച്ച് ഉണക്കി ഒപ്പിച്ച്, രൂപപ്പെടുത്തി.

ഒപ്പിടണം. രജിസ്ട്രാർ സ്ഥലത്തില്ല. രണ്ടു ദിവസത്തെ താമസം വരും. രണ്ടാഴ്ചത്തേക്ക് വരില്ലെന്നു പറഞ്ഞിട്ടാണ് സദനത്തിൽനിന്ന് പോന്നത്. ആവശ്യമുണ്ട്. മൂത്ത അനിയത്തിക്ക് പത്തൊൻപത് വയസായി. അവളുടെ കാര്യത്തിന് പഴയ ഒരുകൂട്ടുകാരിക്ക് എഴുതിയിരുന്നു. അവരെ കാണണം. ആലോചിക്കണം.

നാട്ടിൽ കുറേപ്പേർക്ക് തന്നോട് പുച്ഛമാണ്. പൊതുപ്രവർത്തകർക്കും മറ്റു കുറേപ്പേർക്കും സ്നേഹമാണ്. ഉച്ച തിരിഞ്ഞ് പുറത്തിറങ്ങി. പരിചയക്കാരെ കാണണം. സന്ധ്യക്ക് അമ്പലത്തിൽ പോയി ദീപാരാധന തൊഴണം. വാസവമേനോൻ തന്റെ നാട്ടുകാരനാണ്. മേനോന്റെ അമ്മയ്ക്ക് പത്തെൺപത് വയസുണ്ട്. അവർ ആരോഗ്യത്തോടെ ജീവിച്ചിരിക്കുന്നു. ഇവിടെ വന്നാൽ ആദ്യം അവരെയാണ് കാണാൻ പോവുക. ഇക്കുറി ഭാഗ്യവിചാരംകൊണ്ട് പോകാൻ സാധിച്ചില്ല. അങ്ങോട്ടാണ് നടന്നത്. അവിടെ മേനോന്റെ ഏകസഹോദരിയും താമസിക്കുന്നു. അവർക്ക് ഭർത്താവും കുട്ടികളുമുണ്ട്.

ഒരിക്കലും ഒരിടത്തും അടങ്ങിയിരിക്കാത്ത ആ അമ്മ ഉമ്മറം തൂത്തു കൊണ്ടിരുന്നു. കണ്ണിന് അൽപ്പം കാഴ്ചക്കുറവുണ്ട്. സന്ധ്യാദേവി അടുത്തു ചെന്നു.

"സന്ധ്യാദേവിയാണ് അമ്മേ."

പല്ലില്ലാത്ത ആ ചിരി. ചൂല് താഴെയിട്ടു സന്ധ്യാദേവിയുടെ കൈക്കു പിടിച്ച് അരത്തിണ്ണയിൽ ഇരുത്തി.

"എന്റെ മോളെ... കഴിഞ്ഞ തവണ മോളു വന്നേച്ചുപോയതിൽപ്പിന്നെ കെടപ്പിലായിരുന്നു പനി. ചത്തുപോകുമെന്നാ വിചാരിച്ചത്. വാസുക്കുട്ടൻ എവിടെയാണെന്ന് അറിഞ്ഞുകൂടാ. രണ്ടുമാസമായി അവൻ വന്നിട്ട്. പിന്നെ,. ഒത്തിരി മരുന്നു കഴിച്ചു. എഴുന്നേറ്റു. ഇപ്പാഴും ക്ഷീണമൊണ്ട്." അവർപറഞ്ഞു.

"അപ്പോൾ കമലമ്മയും കുഞ്ഞുങ്ങളും എവിടെ?" സന്ധ്യാദേവി മകളെപ്പറ്റി അന്വേഷിച്ചു.

"അവര് നാരായണമേനോന്റെ വീട്ടില് പോയിരിക്കുന്നു. അയാടെ അമ്മയ്ക്ക് അസുഖമായിട്ടു കെടപ്പാ. ഇന്നലെ പോയതാ. ചെലപ്പം വരാൻ ഇന്നു രാത്രിയോ നാളെയോ ആയേക്കും."

"അമ്മ ഒറ്റയ്ക്ക് എങ്ങനെ?"

"അത്, അങ്ങേതിലെ ആ പെണ്ണിനെ അറിഞ്ഞുകൂടേ? രാധ, അവളൊണ്ട്. അവള് ഊണും കഴിഞ്ഞ് ഇപ്പഴങ്ങ് പോയതേ ഉള്ളൂ. ഒടനേ വരും. പിന്നെ വല്ലതും മേടിച്ചുതരാൻ അവളുടെ ആങ്ങള ഗോപാലകൃഷ്ണനുമുണ്ട്."

സന്ധ്യാദേവി വീട്ടുകാര്യങ്ങളിൽ മുഴുകി, ബാക്കി തൂപ്പുനടത്തി. അതൊന്നും അമ്മയ്ക്കിഷ്ടമല്ല. മറ്റ് ആര് ചെയ്താലും തൃപ്തിയാവില്ല. പക്ഷേ, സന്ധ്യാദേവിയോടു കടുത്ത സ്നേഹവും വിശ്വാസവുമാണ്. അവർ എന്തു പറഞ്ഞാലും കേൾക്കും. തൂപ്പുകഴിഞ്ഞ് അടുക്കളയിൽ കയറി കാപ്പി തിളപ്പിച്ചു അമ്മയ്ക്ക് കൊടുത്തു. അപ്പോഴേക്കും രാധ വന്നു. ഗോപാലകൃഷ്ണൻ വന്നു. അവർക്കെല്ലാം സന്ധ്യാദേവിയെ അതിരു കവിഞ്ഞ ഇഷ്ടമാണ്.

"മോള് ഇന്ന് പോകണ്ട. ഗോപാലകൃഷ്ണനെ അയച്ച് ഞാൻ മോള്ടെ വീട്ടിൽ പറയിച്ചോളാം. ഇന്നിപ്പം അവിടെ ചെന്നിട്ട് അത്യാവശ്യമൊന്നുമില്ലല്ലോ." വൈകുന്നേരമായപ്പോൾ അമ്മ പറഞ്ഞു.

സന്ധ്യാദേവിക്ക് സന്തോഷമാണ്. അമ്മയ്ക്കു കൂട്ടുകിടക്കുന്നത് രസമാണ്. സമ്മതിച്ചു. അമ്മ ഗോപാലകൃഷ്ണനെ ആ വീട്ടിലേക്ക് പറഞ്ഞയച്ചു. അവർ അമ്പലത്തിൽപ്പോയി ദീപാരാധന തൊഴുത് മടങ്ങിവന്നു.

രാത്രി അത്താഴംകഴിഞ്ഞ് അമ്മയും സന്ധ്യാദേവിയും അകത്തേമുറിയിൽ സംസാരിച്ചുകൊണ്ടിരുന്നു. മുറ്റത്ത് കാൽപ്പെരുമാറ്റം കേട്ടു. രാധ അവളുടെ വീട്ടിൽ പോയി. ഗോപാലകൃഷ്ണൻ അപ്പുറത്തു കിടക്കുന്നു. സന്ധ്യാദേവി പുറത്തേക്കു ചെന്നു. അവർ അത്ഭുതപ്പെട്ടു. അരവിന്ദൻ വന്നിരിക്കുന്നു.

"എന്താ ഇപ്പോൾ വന്നത്?"

മേനോൻ മാസ്റ്ററുടെ കത്തുവന്നു, മധുരയിൽനിന്ന് ഇവിടെ വരണമെന്ന് ഭാഗസംബന്ധമായി ചില്ലറ തർക്കങ്ങളുണ്ടാവുമെന്ന് ശരിപ്പെടുത്തണമെന്നായിരുന്നു കത്തിലെ നിർദേശം. ഞാൻ വീട്ടിൽക്കയറി. അപ്പോൾ എഴുത്തൊക്കെ കഴിഞ്ഞെന്നറിഞ്ഞു. എന്നാൽ മോനോൻസാറ് ഒരു കാര്യം പറഞ്ഞിട്ടുണ്ട്. ആധാരം ഒപ്പിടാൻ കൊണ്ടുവരുമ്പോൾ അതിന്റെ ഉള്ളടക്കം അൽപ്പം മാറിയിരിക്കും. എവിടെയോവച്ച് കൊച്ചച്ഛനെ കണ്ടു. അപ്പോൾ ഇതേക്കുറിച്ചു സംസാരിച്ചു. വളരെ നാളായി നിങ്ങളുടെ കുടുംബകാര്യങ്ങൾ നോക്കുന്നത് ആ മനുഷ്യനാണ്. അതുമൂലം അദ്ദേഹത്തിന് കുറേ നഷ്ടം സംഭവിച്ചിട്ടുണ്ട്. അതിന് പരിഹാരം കാണണം. സന്ധ്യ അതു പറയുമോ എന്നറിഞ്ഞിട്ടുവേണം അങ്ങോട്ട് അതു പറയാൻ. അതാണ് കൊച്ചച്ഛൻ സംസാരിച്ചത്. കൊച്ചച്ഛൻ വല്ലതും പറഞ്ഞോ?"

"ഇല്ല."

"എന്നാൽ പറയും."

"പറയട്ടെ."

"പക്ഷേ, അനിയത്തിമാർക്കും അനിയനുമല്ലേ നഷ്ടം വരുന്നത്?"

"ഞാൻ അതിനു സമ്മതിക്കില്ല. എനിക്കു ഭാഗം വേണ്ടെന്ന് നിശ്ചയിച്ചു. അങ്ങനെയാണ് ആധാരമെഴുതിയിരിക്കുന്നത്. എന്റെ സഹോദരങ്ങളുടെ ഒരിഞ്ചു ഭൂമിയോ ഒരു പൈസയോ അവർക്ക് നഷ്ടപ്പെടാൻ അനുവദിക്കില്ല."

"കരുതി വേണ്ടത് ചെയ്യൂ."

അരവിന്ദൻ അമ്മയുടെ അടുക്കലേക്ക് ചെന്നു. കുശലങ്ങൾ പറഞ്ഞു. അരവിന്ദൻ ആഹാരം കഴിച്ചിട്ടാണ് വന്നത്. കാപ്പിതിളപ്പിച്ചത് ഇരിപ്പുണ്ട്. സന്ധ്യാദേവി കാപ്പി കൊണ്ടുവന്നു കൊടുത്തു.

"ഞാൻ പോകട്ടെ?" അയാൾ ചോദിച്ചു.

അവർ നോക്കി മെല്ലെ പറഞ്ഞു.

"വേണ്ട."

രാത്രിയിൽ വണ്ടിയില്ല. എങ്കിലും വണ്ടിയാപ്പീസിൽ കഴിഞ്ഞുകൂടാമെന്ന് വിചാരിച്ചു. അകത്തുനിന്ന് അമ്മ വിളിച്ചു പറഞ്ഞു.

"മോനേ ആ തെക്കേ മുറീല് കെടന്നോ."

അമ്മയ്ക്ക് അരവിന്ദൻ അന്ന് പോവുകയെന്ന പ്രശ്നമേയില്ല.

അയാൾ അരത്തിണ്ണയിൽ ഇരുന്നു. സന്ധ്യാദേവി തെക്കേമുറിയിൽ പായ് വിരിക്കാൻ പോയി.

അരവിന്ദൻ ആ വീടിനെപ്പറ്റി ആലോചിച്ചു. ദേശീയ നേതാക്കൾ പലരും വന്നിട്ടുണ്ട്. പലർക്കും അത് താവളമായിരുന്നിട്ടുണ്ട്. ആ അമ്മ എത്രയോ പൊതുപ്രവർത്തകർക്ക് വച്ചുവിളമ്പിക്കൊടുത്തിട്ടുണ്ട്. ഇന്നും അതു പലർക്കും ഒരഭയകേന്ദ്രമാണ്. ഐശ്വര്യമുള്ള അമ്മ. ഗുണവതിയായ സഹോദരി. അവർക്ക് ചേർന്ന ഭർത്താവ്, നാരായണമേനോൻ. മിടുക്കത്തിയും മിടുക്കനുമായ രണ്ടു കുട്ടികൾ. ആ അമ്മ യഥാർഥത്തിൽ

ഭാഗ്യവതിയാണ്.

സന്ധ്യാദേവി കിടപ്പിനുള്ള ഒരുക്കങ്ങൾ ചെയ്ത്, അമ്മയുടെ അടുക്കലേക്കുപോയി. അമ്മ കിടന്നുകഴിഞ്ഞു. അരവിന്ദനുമായി അൽപ്പസമയം സംസാരിച്ചിട്ട് വരാമെന്ന് പറഞ്ഞ് അവർ പുറത്തേക്കു വന്നു. അരവിന്ദൻ ആ മുറിയിലേക്ക് കയറി. കട്ടിലിൽ ഇരുന്നു. അയാൾ ഉറങ്ങാൻപോവുകയാണെന്ന് തോന്നി. എങ്കിൽ ഉപദ്രവിക്കേണ്ട.

പകുതി വാതിൽ ചാരിയിട്ടുണ്ട്. സന്ധ്യാദേവി അരത്തിണ്ണയിലിരുന്നു. കുറച്ചു സമയം പോയി. അരവിന്ദൻ കിടന്നിട്ടില്ല. നോക്കി. അയാൾ അതേപടി ഇരിക്കുന്നു. അങ്ങോട്ടു ചെന്നു വാതിൽക്കൽ നിന്നു.

"വരൂ." അയാൾ ക്ഷണിച്ചു. അയാളുടെ മുഖം ചുവന്നിരുന്നതും കണ്ണുകളിൽ ഉദ്വേഗം തെളിഞ്ഞിരുന്നതും അവർ കണ്ടു.

ഒട്ടും മടികാട്ടാതെ സന്ധ്യാദേവി അകത്തു കയറി കസാലയിലിരുന്നു.

രണ്ടുപേരും മിണ്ടിയില്ല. വിളക്കിലെ വെട്ടത്തിലേക്കാണ് രണ്ടുപേരും നോക്കിയിരുന്നത്. മുറ്റത്തെ തൈമാവിന്റെ ചില്ലകൾ ഇളകുന്നു. ഏതോ പക്ഷി അങ്ങോട്ടുമിങ്ങോട്ടും ചാടുന്നതു പോലെ.

"എന്താ ഒന്നും മിണ്ടാത്തത്?" സന്ധ്യാദേവി ചോദിച്ചു.

"ഒന്നുമില്ല." അയാളുടെ കണ്ഠം വിറയ്ക്കുന്നുണ്ടായിരുന്നോ?

പഴയ ഒരുകാര്യം ഓർമിപ്പിച്ചു.

"ഞാൻ സംസാരിക്കാൻ പഠിപ്പിച്ചതെല്ലാം മറന്നോ?"

"ഇല്ല."

നിർവികാരമായ മറുപടിപോലിരുന്നു.

നിമിഷങ്ങൾ കഴിഞ്ഞ് അയാൾ ചോദിച്ചു:

"എല്ലാം നടന്നുകഴിഞ്ഞു. എങ്കിലും എന്റെ ആ കത്ത് വേദനിപ്പിച്ചോ?"

"ഇല്ല." അവരും അതേ നിർവികാരമായ സ്വരത്തിൽ മറുപടി പറഞ്ഞു.

വീണ്ടും മൂകത.

"ഞാൻ അമ്മയോട് അറിയാതെ ഒരു കള്ളം പറഞ്ഞു." അവൾ മിണ്ടി.

"എന്താണത്?"

"അരവിന്ദനുമായിട്ട് സംസാരിച്ചിട്ടു വരാമെന്ന്. കുറച്ചു നേരം മിണ്ടാതിരുന്നിട്ട് വരാമെന്നു പറയേണ്ടതായിരുന്നു?"

"തിരിച്ചുച്ചെന്ന് സത്യംപറഞ്ഞാൽ മതി." അയാൾ സ്വയം ചിരിച്ചുപോയി.

ആ ഫലിതം അവരുടെ മനസിൽ പ്രവേശിച്ചില്ല. അത് മറ്റൊരുതരത്തിൽ അവിടെ സ്പർശിച്ചു. അയാളുമായി സംസാരിക്കാനുള്ള മോഹം, ഉള്ളിൽ വിങ്ങിനിൽക്കുകയായിരുന്നു. പെട്ടെന്ന് അവരുടെ കണ്ണുകൾ നിറഞ്ഞു. അവർ മുഖം കുനിച്ചു. കണ്ണുനീരിന്റെ തുള്ളികൾ മടിയിലേക്കു വീഴുന്നതു അരവിന്ദൻ കണ്ടു.

"ക്ഷമിക്കണം. ഞാൻ വെറുതെ പറഞ്ഞതാണ്."

അവർ മുഖം തുടച്ചു എഴുന്നേറ്റു ജനാലയ്ക്കരികിൽ പോയി നിന്നു. അയാളുടെ കണ്ണുകൾ അവരെ പിന്തുടർന്നു. റാന്തൽ വിളക്കിന്റെ വെളിച്ചത്തിൽ അവരുടെരൂപം നോക്കിയിരുന്നു. നീട്ടിക്കെട്ടിയ മുടി. അതിൽ തുളസിയിലയും തെറ്റിപ്പൂവും ചൂടിയിരിക്കുന്നു. വെളുത്ത ബ്ലൗസ്, വെളുത്ത സാരി, കനകം പോലുള്ള പുറവും കഴുത്തും. ആ നിറം സാരിക്കു പുറത്തേക്ക് കാണുന്നതുപോലെ. ഇതിലും വടിവൊത്ത രൂപം കണ്ടിട്ടില്ല. പാദത്തിന്റെ പിൻപുറം താമരയിതളുകൾപോലെ കാണുന്നു.

ഒരു രസം തോന്നി. പോക്കറ്റിൽ നിന്ന് പേനയെടുത്തു തുറന്നു. ഡയറി തലയിണയിൽ ഇരിക്കുന്നു. അത് തുറന്നു.

ചന്ദനലതയിൽ നിന്നു പണ്ടൊരു
സുന്ദരരൂപിണി വന്നു
മലയാനിലനിൽ, മഞ്ഞണിരാവിൽ,
മലർവാടിയിലവൾ വന്നു
ദേവമനോഹരി, മന്ദസ്മിതമധു
തൂവി വിമൂകം നിന്നു...

സന്ധ്യാദേവി തിരിഞ്ഞു. അയാൾ ഇരുന്നു കുറിക്കുന്നതു കണ്ടു. ഒന്നും ചിന്തിച്ചില്ല. ഡയറി പിടിച്ചു വാങ്ങി കസാലയിലിരുന്നു അത് വായിച്ചു. സാവധാനം അതു മടക്കി മടിയിൽ വച്ചു.

"പണ്ട് അങ്ങനെ എന്തെല്ലാം നടന്നിരിക്കുന്നു!" ആത്മഗതം പോലെ പറഞ്ഞു.

"പണ്ടല്ല. പണ്ടെന്ന് പറഞ്ഞത്, കാലം അൽപ്പം മാറ്റിപ്പറയാൻ കവി സ്വീകരിച്ച സ്വാതന്ത്ര്യമാണ്."

അരവിന്ദൻ നിവർന്നിരുന്നു

"കവികൾക്ക് സ്നേഹത്തെപ്പറ്റി എഴുതാനല്ലേ അറിയാവൂ? അത് എന്താണെന്നറിയാമോ?" അവർ ചോദിച്ചു.

"അറിയാത്ത ഒരു വസ്തുവിനെപ്പറ്റി എങ്ങനെ എഴുതും?"

"സങ്കൽപ്പിക്കാൻ കഴിയും."

"സങ്കൽപ്പവും സത്യവുമൊക്കെ ചർച്ച ചെയ്യാൻ എനിക്കിപ്പോൾ വയ്യ." അയാൾ പേന അടച്ചുവച്ചു.

"പിന്നെ എന്തുവേണം?" അവരുടെ മിഴികൾ അയാളുടെ കണ്ണുകളിലേക്കു ചെന്നെത്തി.

അയാൾ മറുപടി പറഞ്ഞില്ല.

"വല്ലതും പറയൂ." അവർതന്നെ വീണ്ടും സംസാരിച്ചു.

"ഞാനൊന്നു ചോദിക്കട്ടെ, നമ്മൾ എന്താണു ചെയ്യുന്നത്?" അയാൾ ചോദിച്ചു.

"ഇപ്പോഴോ? ഇപ്പോൾ ഒരു മുറിയിൽ ഏകാന്തതയിൽ ഒരുമിച്ചിരിക്കുന്നു."

"ഞാൻ വല്ല തെറ്റും ചെയ്തുപോയാലോ?"

പൊടുന്നനെ ആ ചോദ്യം പ്രതീക്ഷിച്ചില്ല. അവരുടെ കണ്ണുകൾ തുരു

തുരാ ചിമ്മി. അയാളെ ഉറ്റുനോക്കി.

"അരുതേ, എന്നു ഞാൻ അപേക്ഷിക്കും." അവരുടെ സ്വരത്തിൽ ആർദ്രത കലർന്നിരുന്നു.

"അതു കേട്ടില്ലെങ്കിലോ?"

"വീണ്ടും മൊഴി മുട്ടി."

"കാലുപിടിച്ച് കരഞ്ഞുനോക്കും."

"എന്നിട്ടും ഫലിച്ചില്ലെങ്കിലോ?"

അവർ ഡയറിയെടുത്ത് മുഖം മറച്ചുപിടിച്ചു.

"എന്നോട് അങ്ങനെ ചോദിക്കരുത്."

അയാൾ മൗനം ദീക്ഷിച്ചു പിന്നെപ്പറഞ്ഞു:

"മുഖം കാണട്ടെ."

അവർ ഡയറി വീണ്ടും മടിയിലേക്ക് വച്ചു ആ മിഴികളിൽ മനസിലെ ചഞ്ചലത തെളിഞ്ഞുനിന്നു.

"ആ കൈ ഇങ്ങോട്ട് നീട്ടൂ" അയാൾ പറഞ്ഞു.

താനറിയാതെന്നപോലെ അവരുടെ കൈ അയാളുടെ നേർക്കു നീട്ടി. അയാൾ അത് തന്റെ കൈപ്പത്തിയിൽവച്ചു മുഖം മുനിച്ചു. ആ നീണ്ട വിരലുകളിൽ ചുംബിച്ചു.

അവൾ കൈ വലിച്ചു. ആ വിരലുകളിൽ തീക്കനൽവന്നുതൊട്ടതുപോലെ. അവരുടെ നെഞ്ച് ഉറക്കെ തുടിക്കുന്നു.

"എന്നെക്കുറിച്ച് പുച്ഛം തോന്നുന്നുണ്ട്. അല്ലേ?" അയാൾ അസ്വസ്ഥനാണ്.

"ഇല്ല. ഒരിക്കലുമില്ല. ഞാൻ ഇതിന് അർഹയല്ലല്ലോ. എന്നോർമിച്ച് ഇരുന്നുപോയി. ഒരു വലിയ മനുഷ്യന്റെ മനസിലേക്കു കടന്നിരിക്കാൻ എനിക്കെന്തു യോഗ്യത?" അവളുടെ ഉള്ളു കിടന്നു തേങ്ങുന്നു.

അയാൾ എഴുന്നേറ്റ് അവരുടെ പിന്നിൽച്ചെന്നു നിന്നു. അവർ മുഖം കുനിച്ചിരുന്നു. അവരുടെ കൈകൾ വിറയ്ക്കുന്നുണ്ടായിരുന്നു.

അരവിന്ദൻ സന്ധ്യാദേവിയുടെ ഇടതൂർന്ന മുടിയിൽ തലോടിക്കൊണ്ടുനിന്നു. അവർ അനുസരണയുള്ള കുഞ്ഞിനെപ്പോലെ ഇരുന്നു.

മുഖം കുനിച്ച് അയാൾ പറഞ്ഞു:

"പോയി കിടന്നോളൂ."

അവർ അനങ്ങിയില്ല.

കാതിലേക്ക് മന്ത്രിച്ചു.

"കിടന്നോളൂ."

അവർ സാവധാനം മുഖം തിരിച്ചു അയാളുടെ മുഖത്തേക്ക് നോക്കി. അയാളുടെ ചുണ്ടുകൾ അവരുടെ മുടി പാറിവീണ നെറ്റിയിൽ തെല്ലു നേരം അമർന്നു. പിന്നെ, അയാൾ കട്ടിലിൽ ചെന്നിരുന്നു.

ഡയറി അരവിന്ദന്റെ കൈയിലേക്കു കൊടുത്ത് സന്ധ്യാദേവി എഴുന്നേറ്റു സ്നേഹം നിറഞ്ഞ മിഴികൾകൊണ്ട് അയാളെ നോക്കിയിട്ട് പുറത്തിറങ്ങി, വാതിൽ ചാരി.

ഏഴ്

കൊച്ചച്ഛനുമായി സന്ധ്യാദേവി ഭാഗം ഉടമ്പടിയെപ്പറ്റി സംസാരിച്ചു. അത് മനഃപൂർവമായിരുന്നു. ഇങ്ങോട്ട് എന്തെങ്കിലും പറയുമോ എന്നറിയണം. വളരെ നേരം അതുമിതും പറഞ്ഞിട്ട്, ആ മനുഷ്യൻ തന്റെ ഉദ്ദേശ്യം അവതരിപ്പിച്ചു.

"കൊച്ചച്ഛന് എന്താണു വേണ്ടത്?" സന്ധ്യാദേവി ചോദിച്ചു.

"എനിക്ക് വന്ന നഷ്ടം എന്റെ പിള്ളേരെ ബാധിക്കുകയില്ലേ? നിന്റെ കുടുംബത്തിനു വേണ്ടിയാണ് ഇതുവരെ എന്റെ സമയം മുഴുവനും ഞാൻ ചെലവഴിച്ചത്. നിങ്ങൾക്കാർക്കും അതൊന്നും കേൾക്കുകയും അറിയുകയും വേണ്ടല്ലോ. ഇനി എനിക്ക് ഒന്നു സ്വസ്ഥനാകണം. വന്നുപോയ നഷ്ടത്തിന് ഒരു പ്രതിവിധിയുണ്ടാവണം." അയാൾ വിശദീകരിച്ചു.

"കൃത്യമായി കാര്യം പറയണം." അവർ ആവശ്യപ്പെട്ടു.

"ആ കണ്ടത്തിന്റെ പകുതി എനിക്ക് വയ്ക്കണം."

ഒരു നിമിഷം മിണ്ടാതെ നിന്നു പിന്നെ ചോദിച്ചു.

"പിന്നെ, ഇന്നലെ ഉടമ്പടി വായിച്ചപ്പോൾ അത് പറയാതിരുന്നതെന്താ?"

"പറയേണ്ടത് ആരാ? ഞാനാണോ? ഔചിത്യമറിഞ്ഞു ചെയ്യേണ്ടത് നിങ്ങളാ ഞാനല്ല."

സന്ധ്യാദേവി ആലോചിച്ച് ഒരു ചോദ്യമുന്നയിച്ചു.

"എന്തിനാണ് ഇപ്പോൾ ഭാഗം വയ്ക്കുന്നത്?"

"അല്ലെങ്കിൽ പിള്ളേര് തമ്മിലടിച്ച് തലകീറും. നിനക്ക് അതൊന്നും കാണണ്ടല്ലോ." മറുപടി നേരത്തെ ഒരുക്കിവച്ചതുപോലെ ഉടനെ വന്നു.

"ഇല്ല അങ്ങനെവരാതെ ഞാൻ നോക്കിക്കൊള്ളാം."

"അതൊന്നും നടപ്പില്ല പെണ്ണേ."

"ഈ ഭാഗം ഇപ്പോൾ നടത്തേണ്ട.." ദൃഢസ്വരത്തിലാണ് അത് പറഞ്ഞത്.

കൊച്ചച്ഛൻ ക്ഷോഭിച്ചു. അത് പുറത്തു കാട്ടിയില്ല. പരുങ്ങുന്ന സ്വരത്തിൽ ചോദിച്ചു.

"അപ്പോ, ഞാനിങ്ങനെ ഇനിയും ഇവിടെ കാത്തുകെട്ടി കെടന്നോളണം അല്ലേ?"

"അങ്ങനെ വരട്ടെ." അവർ ശാന്തമായി പറഞ്ഞു: "കൊച്ചച്ഛന് ഒരു വീതംകിട്ടണം അത് ഉടനെ വേണംതാനും. അത് തുറന്നുപറഞ്ഞാൽ പോരെ? പക്ഷേ, എന്റെ കാര്യമിരിക്കട്ടെ. ഞങ്ങൾക്ക് അച്ഛനും അമ്മയുമില്ല. അൽപ്പം സ്വത്തുക്കൾ അവശേഷിച്ചിട്ടുണ്ട്. അത് മൂന്നു പിള്ളേർക്കായിട്ട് വീതിച്ച് കൊടുക്കാനുള്ള ചുമതല, കോടതിയെ ഏൽപ്പിക്കാൻ പോവുകയാണ്. കൊച്ചച്ഛന്റെ അവകാശത്തിനുവേണ്ടി അവിടെ വാദിച്ചുകൊണ്ടാൽ മതി."

അവർ എഴുന്നേറ്റ് മറുപുറത്തേക്കു പോയി.

കൊച്ചച്ഛൻ മുണ്ടുമാറി, തോർത്തെടുത്തിട്ട്, ദേഷ്യത്തിൽ പുറത്തേ

ക്കിറങ്ങി. മുറ്റത്തുനിന്നുകൊണ്ട് സന്ധ്യാദേവിയുടെ സഹോദരനെ വിളിച്ചു:

"എടാ സതീശാ!"

"എന്താ.." അവൻ പുറത്തേക്കുവന്നു.

"ഞാൻ ഇതിന് ഒരുപ്രതിവിധി കണ്ടിട്ടേ അടങ്ങൂന്ന് നിന്റെ ചേച്ചിയോട് പറഞ്ഞേക്ക്."

അയാൾ വിറയ്ക്കുന്നുണ്ടായിരുന്നു. അവൻ അന്തിച്ചു നിന്നു ആ മനുഷ്യൻ തിടുക്കത്തിൽ പടിയിറങ്ങിപ്പോയി.

മടങ്ങിപ്പോകാൻ നിശ്ചയിച്ചു. പക്ഷേ, അനിയത്തിമാരേയും അനിയനെയും മാത്രമാക്കിയിട്ടു എങ്ങനെ പോകും. കൊച്ചച്ഛൻ പിണങ്ങി. ഇനി ആ മനുഷ്യൻ എങ്ങനെ പെരുമാറുമെന്ന് അറിയില്ല. അരവിന്ദൻ പട്ടണത്തിലേക്കു പോയിരിക്കുകയാണ്. മടങ്ങിവരും. ചോദിച്ചിട്ടു വേണ്ടതു ചെയ്യാം.

ഉച്ചയൂണു കഴിഞ്ഞ്, കുട്ടികളെ വിളിച്ചു. അവർ ഇങ്ങോട്ടു സംസാരിച്ചു.

"ഭാഗം വയ്ക്കുന്നില്ലേ?" അനിയനാണു ചോദിച്ചത്.

"ഇപ്പോഴില്ല. ഇപ്പോൾ വേണ്ട."

"പിന്നെ."

"നിങ്ങളോട് ആരാണ് ഇപ്പോൾ ഈ ഭാഗക്കാര്യം പറഞ്ഞുതന്നത്? നിങ്ങൾ ഒരിടത്തും എത്തിയിട്ടില്ലാത്ത പിള്ളേരാണ്. ഭാഗംവച്ചിട്ട് നിങ്ങൾ എന്തു ചെയ്യാൻ പോകുന്നു?"

അനിയൻ ക്ഷോഭിച്ചതു പോലെ പറഞ്ഞു:

"ചേച്ചി ഇപ്പം പോകും. ഞങ്ങളുമാത്രാവും. കൊച്ചച്ഛൻ ഞങ്ങളെയിട്ടു വഴക്കുപറകയുകയും തല്ലുകയും ചെയ്യും. ഞങ്ങളെന്തു വേണം."

അത് മനസിൽ കൊണ്ടു. അവരുടെ നിസ്സഹായവസ്ഥയാണ് അവൻ പറഞ്ഞത്. കൂടുതൽ സംസാരിച്ചില്ല. കുട്ടികളുടെ മനോവിഷമം കാണാൻ വയ്യ. അവർക്ക് വേദനയുണ്ടാക്കാതെ, കാര്യങ്ങൾ നോക്കണം.

"ചേച്ചി എല്ലാം വേണ്ടതുപോലെ ചെയ്തോളാം. പൊയ്ക്കൊള്ളിൻ."

അവൻ അടുക്കളത്തളത്തിൽ പായ് നിവർത്തുകിടന്നു.

വൈകുന്നേരം അരവിന്ദൻ വന്നു. അയാൾ ഒരു വാർത്ത കൊണ്ടുവന്നിട്ടുണ്ട്. സന്ധ്യാദേവിയുടെ അച്ഛൻ, അദ്ദേഹത്തിന്റെ അനിയന് കണ്ടത്തിൽ പകുതി ഇഷ്ടദാനമായി എഴുതികൊടുത്തിട്ടുണ്ട്. ഭാഗം നടത്താനുള്ള അധികാരപത്രവും കൊടുത്തിട്ടുണ്ട്.

രണ്ടുവർഷം മുൻപാണ് അച്ഛൻ മരിച്ചത്. ഒരുപക്ഷേ അദ്ദേഹം രോഗശയ്യയിലായിരുന്നപ്പോൾ രഹസ്യമായി അദ്ദേഹത്തെ സ്വാധീനിച്ച് കാര്യം സാധിച്ചതാവണം. ഏതായാലും അങ്ങനെ ഒരു രേഖയുണ്ട്. അരവിന്ദനെ സന്ധ്യാദേവിയുടെ കൊച്ചച്ഛൻ അതു കാണിച്ചു. അൽപ്പം മുമ്പാണ് അവർ തമ്മിൽപ്പിരിഞ്ഞത്.

അതിന്റെ അർഥം ഭാഗം നടക്കുമെന്നും കണ്ടത്തിന്റെ പകുതി അദ്ദേഹത്തിന്റേതാകുമെന്നുമാണ്. മകളുടെ സമ്മതത്തോടെ അതു നടക്കുമെങ്കിൽ ആവട്ടെ എന്ന് അയാൾ വിചാരിച്ചിരിക്കണം. അതു നടക്കില്ലെന്നു കണ്ടപ്പോൾ അവരുടെ അഭ്യുദയകാംക്ഷിയായ അരവിന്ദേട്ടനോടു വിവരം

പറഞ്ഞതാണ്. അരവിന്ദൻ ഒറ്റയ്ക്കു കാണാൻ വേണ്ടി അയാളുടെ വീട്ടിൽ ചെന്നു. സ്നേഹപൂർവം സ്വീകരിച്ച് അയാൾ പറഞ്ഞതും കാട്ടിയതും അതാണ്.

ഒരു പരാജയം പറ്റിയതുപോലെ തോന്നി. സന്ധ്യാദേവി കുറച്ചുനേരം മൗനമായിരുന്നു. സ്വത്തിൽ കുറച്ചുഭാഗം പോയി എന്നുള്ളതല്ല സഹോദരങ്ങൾക്കു കിട്ടേണ്ടത് നഷ്ടപ്പെട്ടതിനു കാരണക്കാരി താനാണ്. അമ്മ ഒന്നുമറിഞ്ഞുകൂടാത്ത സാധുസ്ത്രീയായിരുന്നു. അച്ഛൻ ഉദാരതയ്ക്ക് കേഴ്വികേട്ട ആളാണ്. മറ്റുള്ളവരെ കഴിയുന്നത്ര സഹായിച്ചു ജീവിച്ചു. പ്രത്യേകമായി ഒന്നും സമ്പാദിച്ചില്ല. സ്വന്തം കുടുംബക്കാരോടു വലിയ സ്നേഹമായിരുന്നു. അവർ സ്നേഹിച്ചില്ല. അവരുടെ ആവശ്യങ്ങൾക്ക് അച്ഛനെ ഉപയോഗിച്ചു.

കാര്യവിവരമുള്ള ആരും ഇവിടെ ഉണ്ടായിരുന്നില്ല. ആ സന്ദർഭമാണ് കൊച്ചച്ഛൻ ഉപയോഗപ്പെടുത്തിയത്.

ഇനി എന്തുചെയ്യണം? ഒന്നും ചെയ്യാനില്ല. എതിർത്താൽ കോടയിലേക്കു പോകേണ്ടി വരും. അച്ഛൻ കൊടുത്ത രേഖ കൊച്ചച്ഛന്റെ കൈയിൽ ഉണ്ടെങ്കിൽ, കോടതിയിൽ പോയിട്ട് എന്തു പ്രയോജനം? തോൽക്കാൻ വേണ്ടി ആ തിണ്ണയിൽചെന്ന് പണം മുടക്കി തപസിരിക്കണോ?

"അരവിന്ദൻ, ഇവിടെ കുട്ടികളുടെ കാര്യത്തിന് എന്തെങ്കിലും ഏർപ്പാടുണ്ടാക്കാതെ ഞാൻ അങ്ങോട്ടു വരുന്നില്ല. അവരെ നോക്കാൻ ഇവിടെ വരുമെന്നു തോന്നുന്നില്ല. അങ്ങേര് സംസാരിച്ചതും അങ്ങനെ തന്നെ."

ഗാഢമായി ആലോചിച്ച് അരവിന്ദൻ പറഞ്ഞു.

"താൽക്കാലികമായ ഏർപ്പാടുമാത്രം പോരാ. സതീശനും സാവിത്രിയും വീട്ടിൽ നിൽക്കുകയാണ്. സരോജം സ്കൂളിൽ പോകുന്നു. അതുകൊണ്ട് എല്ലാംകൂടി വച്ചുകൊണ്ടുവേണം തീരുമാനം ചെയ്യുക. എനിക്ക് ഒരഭിപ്രായമുണ്ട്. ഭാഗം നടത്തേണ്ട കണ്ടത്തിൽ പകുതി കൊച്ചച്ഛന് കൊടുത്തേക്കു. ആ പ്രശ്നംതീരട്ടെ. സന്ധ്യാദേവിക്കു സദനം വിട്ടുപോരാൻ സാധ്യമല്ല. കുട്ടികളെ വാസവമേനോന്റെ വീട്ടിലാക്കുക. അവിടെ ധാരാളം സൗകര്യമുണ്ട്. നമ്മുടെ വീട് ഒന്നുകിൽ പൂട്ടിയിടുക. അല്ലെങ്കിൽ വാടകക്കാരെ കിട്ടുമെങ്കിൽ കൊടുക്കുക. ഉടനെ ചെയ്യേണ്ടത്, അവരെ അങ്ങോട്ടു മാറ്റുകയാണ്. മനസിന് സ്വസ്ഥത കിട്ടും. ഭാവിയിൽ എന്തു ചെയ്യണമെന്ന് സാവധാനം ആലോചിക്കാം."

വളരെനേരം സംസാരിച്ചു. ഒടുവിൽ ആ നിർദേശത്തിൽത്തന്നെയാണ് ചെന്നെത്തിയത്.

അരവിന്ദനു പോകണം. പത്രമാഫീസിൽ നിന്ന് രണ്ടു ദിവസത്തിൽ കൂടുതൽ മാറി നിൽക്കാൻ നിവൃത്തിയില്ല.

ഒരു ധാരണയിലെത്തിയപ്പോൾ, സന്ധ്യാദേവിയുടെ മനസിന് സമാധാനമായി. ഇപ്പോൾ അങ്ങനെയൊക്കെ നടക്കട്ടെ. പിന്നീട് സാവകാശമായി മറ്റ് ഏർപ്പാടുകൾ ഉണ്ടാക്കാം.

വൈകുന്നേരത്തെ വണ്ടിക്ക് അരവിന്ദൻ പോയി.

പിറ്റേന്ന് വാസവമേനോന്റെ വീട്ടിൽ ചെന്നു സംസാരിച്ചു.

അമ്മയ്ക്കും സഹോദരിക്കും ഭർത്താവിനും സന്തോഷമാണ്.

കൊച്ചച്ഛന്റെ മുമ്പിൽ മുഖം കറുപ്പിച്ചുകാണിച്ചില്ല. എന്താവശ്യം? അച്ഛൻ കൊടുത്ത രേഖ വായിച്ചു നോക്കി. അതിനുമേൽ തർക്കിച്ചിട്ട് കാര്യമില്ല. ഉടമ്പടി രജിസ്റ്റർ ചെയ്തു. കൊച്ചച്ഛന് തൃപ്തിയായി. അനിയത്തിമാരെയും അനിയനേയും കൂട്ടി മേനോന്റെ വീട്ടിലേക്ക് പോയി. പൂട്ടിയ വീട്ടിന്റെ താക്കോല് അവിടെ ഏൽപ്പിച്ചു.

എല്ലാം നാലഞ്ചു ദിവസങ്ങൾ കൊണ്ട് നിർവഹിച്ചു. ഒരു വലിയ ഭാരം താൽക്കാലികമായിട്ടെങ്കിലും ഇറക്കിവച്ചതായി അനുഭവപ്പെട്ടു.

* * * * * *

പുതിയ വീട്ടിലെ ജീവിതവുമായി ഭാനുമതി വളരെവേഗം ഇണങ്ങിച്ചേർന്നു. ഭർത്താവിന്റെ ശീലങ്ങളും ഇഷ്ടങ്ങളും മനസിലായി. ഒന്നിനും മുടക്കം വരാതെ സൂക്ഷിച്ചു. അസുഖകരമായ ഒരു നിമിഷം പോലും ഉണ്ടായിട്ടില്ല. ഉറച്ച തീരുമാനങ്ങളോടെ അവൾ ജീവിക്കാൻ തീരുമാനിച്ചു. താനറിഞ്ഞതൊന്നും ആരേയും അറിയിക്കേണ്ട. രാജമ്മ അധികം സംസാരിക്കാറില്ല. ആ രാത്രി കഴിഞ്ഞതിനുശേഷം അവൾ ഭയപ്പെട്ട് നടക്കുന്നതുപോലെയാണ്. അവരുടെ ഭീതി മാറാൻവേണ്ടി, ഭാനുമതി പലപ്പോഴും അങ്ങോട്ട് കയറി സംസാരിക്കും. അവർ ഒഴിഞ്ഞുമാറുംപോലെ.

അന്ന അടുക്കളയിൽത്തന്നെയാണ്. അവിടെനിന്ന് ഇറങ്ങാൻ ഇഷ്ടമില്ലെന്നു തോന്നും. ഭാനുമതി സഹായിക്കാൻ ചെന്നാൽ, കൊച്ചമ്മ അങ്ങോട്ടിരുന്നാട്ടെ എന്നുപറഞ്ഞ് സ്റ്റൂളു മാറ്റിയിട്ടുകൊടുക്കും. എന്നാലും, ഇടയ്ക്കു കയറി വല്ലതുമൊക്കെ സഹായിച്ചുകൊടുക്കും. അത് സന്തോഷവുമാണ്.

പല വിരുന്നുകൾക്കും പോയി, അവിടെ പണക്കാരുടെ ജീവിതം നേരിട്ടു കണ്ടു. എല്ലാം കുറെ ദൂരെയാണ്. അടുത്തെങ്ങും ഒരു ബന്ധവുമില്ല. അതിന്റെ അർഥം ഭാനുമതിക്ക് മനസിലാക്കാൻ കഴിഞ്ഞു. എല്ലാം ശ്രദ്ധിച്ചുനോക്കാനുള്ള കാണാനുള്ള, ഒരു വാസന വളർന്നിരിക്കുന്നു.

ഓരോ മനുഷ്യനും പണം എങ്ങനെ വാരി ചെലവു ചെയ്യുന്നു. ഓരോ സായാഹ്നവും ധൂർത്തിന്റെ ഘോഷയാത്രയിൽ കഴിയുന്നു. ഭൂമിയിൽ ചുരുക്കം ചിലർക്കു മാത്രം വിധിച്ചിട്ടുള്ള സുഖങ്ങൾ പുരുഷന്മാരുടെ ധൂർത്ത് മനസിലാവും. സ്ത്രീകൾ ആഡംബരത്തിൽ മുങ്ങി അഴിഞ്ഞാടുന്നതു കാണുമ്പോൾ വേദന തോന്നാറുണ്ട്. വനിതാ സമാജത്തിന്റെ പ്രവർത്തനത്തിനിടയിൽ കണ്ടുമുട്ടിയിട്ടുള്ളവർ അവരും സ്ത്രീകളാണ്. അവരും ഈ ഭൂമിയിൽ ജീവിക്കാൻ വിധിക്കപ്പെട്ടിട്ടുള്ളവരാണ്. രണ്ടു ബ്ലൗസും രണ്ടു സാരിയും കൊണ്ട് ഒരു സംവത്സരം കഴിച്ചുകൂട്ടുന്നവർ കുട്ടികളുടെ ആരോഗ്യം നിലനിർത്താൻ മാത്രം ആഹാരം കൊടുക്കാൻ കഴിവില്ലാത്തവർ അവിടെ നിന്ന് ഈ ലോകത്തിലേക്കു വന്നപ്പോൾ എന്തു മാറ്റം!

അന്നു വൈകിട്ട് ഒരു വിരുന്നിനുപോകണം. എവിടെയാണെന്നും ആരാണെന്നും പറഞ്ഞില്ല. പുറത്തുപോയിട്ട് നേരത്തെ വന്നു കുളിച്ച് ഒരുങ്ങി ഏറ്റവും നല്ല വസ്ത്രങ്ങൾ അണിയാൻ നിർബന്ധിച്ചു. കാരണം, ഏറ്റവും പ്രൗഢിയിൽ ജീവിക്കുന്നവരുടെ മുൻപിലേക്കാണ് പോകുന്നത്. അവിടെ ഒട്ടും കുറയാൻ പാടില്ല, പറഞ്ഞതുപോലെ ഒരുങ്ങി.

മൈലുകൾക്കപ്പുറത്ത്, ഒരു തോട്ടമെന്നു തോന്നുന്ന സ്ഥലത്തുകൂടി കാറുപോയി, സന്ധ്യയായപ്പോൾ ഒരു വലിയ ഗേറ്റ് കടന്നു. പിന്നെയും കാറ് നീങ്ങി ഇരുപുറത്തും ഉയർന്ന മരങ്ങൾ ചീവിടുകളുടെ നിരന്തരമായ ശബ്ദം. പക്ഷികൾ കരയുന്നു. സന്ധ്യവെളിച്ചത്തെ വൃക്ഷങ്ങൾ മറയ്ക്കുന്നു. നേരിയ നിലാവ് വീണു തുടങ്ങിയിരിക്കുന്നു. ഏതാനും മിനിറ്റുകൾക്കു ശേഷം കാറ് ഒരു ചെറിയ കയറ്റംകയറി മറ്റൊരു ഭംഗിയുള്ള ഗേറ്റു കടന്ന് ഒരു ബംഗ്ലാവിന്റെ മുന്നിൽ നിന്നു. മുറ്റത്ത് ജീപ്പുകളും കാറുകളും കിടക്കുന്നു.

രണ്ടുപേരും ഇറങ്ങിയപ്പോഴേക്കും മധ്യവയസ്കനായ ഒരാൾ പൂമുഖത്തേക്കുവന്നു. വഴികാട്ടാനെന്നപോലെ രണ്ടു ജോലിക്കാർ ഓടിയെത്തിക്കഴിഞ്ഞിരുന്നു.

"ഹലോ, മിസ്റ്റർ ദിവാകരൻ. ഹലോ മിസിസ് ദിവാകരൻ" ആ ആൾ അവരെ സ്വാഗതം ചെയ്തു. ദിവാകരൻ ഹസ്തദാനം ചെയ്തു. അയാൾ അവരെ അകത്തേക്ക് ആനയിച്ചു സ്വീകരണമുറി. അവിടെ നിന്ന് വലത്തേക്ക് ഇടനാഴിയിൽക്കൂടി നടന്നു. ഇടതുവശത്തെ ഒരു വാതിലിൽക്കൂടി പ്രവേശിച്ച വിശാലമായ ഒരു മുറി. അത് കടന്ന് മറ്റൊരു ഇടനാഴി. പിന്നെ ഒരുചെറിയ മുറി. അതിനപ്പുറത്ത് വിശാലമായ മറ്റൊരു മുറി. അവിടെ ഒരു സംഘം ആളുകൾ ഇരിക്കുന്നു. പുരുഷന്മാരും മൂന്നുനാലു സ്ത്രീകളും.

കടന്നുവന്ന മുറികളുടെ ആർഭാടങ്ങൾ ഭാനുമതിയുടെ മനസിൽ പതിഞ്ഞു. അവരെ കണ്ടയുടൻ എല്ലാവരും നിശ്ശബ്ദരായി എഴുന്നേറ്റു താഴ്ന്ന സ്വരത്തിൽ എല്ലാവരും "ഹലോ ഗുഡ് ഈവനിങ് എന്നു സ്വാഗതം ചെയ്തു." ദിവാകരനും ഭാര്യയും തൊഴുതു. അവർ പ്രതിവന്ദനം നടത്തി. അതിഥികൾ ഇരുന്നപ്പോൾ മറ്റുള്ളവരും ഇരുന്നു.

മദ്യക്കുപ്പികൾ ധാരാളമുണ്ട്. ധാരാളം തീൻവിഭവങ്ങളും. ജോലിക്കാർ രണ്ടുപേർ മദ്യം പകർന്നു. സ്ത്രീകൾക്കു ലൈംജൂസ്, ചിയേഴ്സ് എല്ലാവരും ഗ്ലാസുകൾ ചുണ്ടിൽ സ്പർശിച്ച് താഴെവച്ചു.

അടക്കിപ്പിടിച്ച സംസാരമായിരുന്നു ഓരോരുത്തരുടേതും. ഓരോ ആളും ഏറ്റവും നല്ല മര്യാദ കാട്ടാൻ ശ്രദ്ധിക്കുന്നതായിത്തോന്നി. മദ്യ ഗ്ലാസുകൾ ഒഴിഞ്ഞു. വീണ്ടും പകർന്നു. ചിലർ ആഹാരപദാർഥങ്ങളിൽ മെല്ലെ തൊട്ടു, വീണ്ടും ഗ്ലാസുകൾ ഒഴിയുന്നു. വീണ്ടും നിറയുന്നു.

രണ്ടു മൂന്നു തവണ ആയപ്പോൾ സ്ത്രീകൾ എഴുന്നേറ്റു അവർ ഭാനുമതിയെക്കൂട്ടി അകത്തേക്കുപോയി. ഒരു ബെഡ്റൂമിൽ പലയിടത്തായി ഇരുന്നു. ഭാനുമതിയുടെ പേരും നാടും എല്ലാം അവർക്കറിയാമെന്നു വ്യക്തമായി. അവൾ അങ്ങോട്ടു ചോദിച്ചു.

"എനിക്കു നിങ്ങളെ ആരെയും മനസിലായില്ലല്ലോ."

അവർ പരിചയപ്പെടുത്തി. ഗൃഹനായിക റോസിക്കുട്ടി. ഗൃഹനാഥൻ റോബർട്ട്. മറ്റ് സ്ത്രീകൾ, മേഴ്സി, ജോർജി, വിനോദിനി, സുകുമാരിയമ്മ, അവരുടെ ഭർത്താക്കന്മാർ ആ മുറിയിലുണ്ട്. ഇത് ഒരു എസ്റ്റേറ്റാണ്. ഗൃഹനാഥന്റെ വക എസ്റ്റേറ്റ്. ആ മുറിയിൽ വെളുത്ത പാന്റ്സും വെളുത്ത അരക്കൈയൻ ഷർട്ടുമിട്ട് ഇരിക്കുന്നത്, ഒരുവലിയ പൊലീസ് ഉദ്യോഗസ്ഥനാണ് ഹരീന്ദ്രൻനായർ. അദ്ദേഹം യാദൃച്ഛികമായി ഇന്നുവന്നതാണ്. ഈ സ്വീകരണം അറിഞ്ഞു വന്നതല്ല. അദ്ദേഹം ഗൃഹനാഥന്റെയും ദിവാകരന്റെയും മറ്റും സുഹൃത്താണ്.

പൊലീസ് ഉദ്യോഗസ്ഥൻ എന്നു കേട്ടപ്പോൾ ഭാനുമതി ഉള്ളിൽ ഒരു ചൂട് പതഞ്ഞു പൊന്തി. മുഖത്ത് വികാരഭേദം വരാതെ അവൾ സൂക്ഷിച്ചു. എങ്കിലും പിന്നീട് സംസാരിച്ചുക്കൊണ്ടിരുന്നപ്പോഴും ആ ചൂടിൽനിന്ന് മോചനം കിട്ടിയില്ല.

അവർ നാട്ടുവിശേഷങ്ങൾ പറഞ്ഞു. ഭാനുമതിക്ക് അറിഞ്ഞുകൂടാത്ത വിശേഷങ്ങൾ. ഒരു കാര്യം മനസിലായി. കുറച്ചു ദിവസങ്ങൾക്കുമുൻപ് എസ്റ്റേറ്റിൽ ഒരു തൊഴിലാളി തൂങ്ങി മരിച്ചു. ഒരു സൂപ്രണ്ടിന്റെ മകളും അയാളും തമ്മിൽ പ്രേമമായിരുന്നത്രെ. കേസൊന്നുമില്ല.

പതിവുപോലെ ഡിന്നർ നീണ്ടുപോയി. ഭാനുമതിക്ക് ഡൈനിങ് ഹാളിൽ ഭക്ഷണം വിളമ്പി. മറ്റുസ്ത്രീകളും കൂടെയിരുന്നു. അവരും സാവധാനമാണ് ആഹാരം കഴിച്ചത്. റോസിക്കുട്ടി പറഞ്ഞു

"നമുക്ക് മെല്ലെ ഇരുന്നാൽ മതി. അപ്പുറത്ത് പരിപാടി തീരുമ്പോൾ വെളുപ്പാൻ കാലമാകും."

അവർ സംസാരിച്ചുക്കൊണ്ടിരുന്നു. ഭാനുമതി അതെല്ലാം കേൾക്കുക മാത്രം ചെയ്തു. ഭക്ഷണം കഴിഞ്ഞ് കൈകഴുകി. ജോർജി നേരത്തെ എഴുന്നേറ്റു. അവൾ മുറിയിലേക്ക് നടന്നു.

"ജോർജി, ബാത്ത്റൂം അറിയാമല്ലോ അങ്ങേയറ്റത്ത്.." റോസിക്കുട്ടി വിളിച്ചു പറഞ്ഞു.

"അറിയാം." ജോർജിയുടെ മറുപടി.

മേഴ്സിയും വിനോദിനിയും സുകുമാരിയമ്മയും കൈകഴുകി. റോസിക്കുട്ടി ഒരു ഗ്ലാസ് പാലുമാത്രം കുടിച്ചതേയുള്ളൂ. അവർ നാലുപേരും അവിടെത്തന്നെ ഇരുന്നു. സംഭാഷണം തുടർന്നു. ജോലിക്കാരൻ മേശപ്പുറം വെടിപ്പാക്കി.

ഭാനുമതി ആ ബെഡ്റൂമിന്റെ നേർക്കു നടന്നു. അതിന്റെ വാതിൽക്കലെത്തിയപ്പോൾ ദൂരെ, ഇടനാഴിയുടെ അങ്ങേയറ്റത്ത് ജോർജി നിൽക്കുന്നു. അവിടെ നല്ല വെളിച്ചമുണ്ട്. ജോർജി തിടുക്കത്തിൽ ഭാനുമതിയുടെ നേർക്ക് കൈകാട്ടി വിളിച്ചു. സംശയിച്ചു നിന്നു. വീണ്ടും അവൾ വിളിക്കുന്നു. എന്തോ മനസിൽ ശങ്കതോന്നി. പെട്ടെന്ന് അതു മാറി. എന്തു ഭയപ്പെടാൻ അവൾ അങ്ങോട്ടു നടന്നു. ജോർജി തിടുക്കം കാട്ടുന്നു.

അടുത്ത് ചെന്നപ്പോൾ ജോർജി ധൃതിയിൽ അടക്കം പറഞ്ഞു.

"ആ പൊലീസ് ഉദ്യോഗസ്ഥനെ ഭാനുമതി അറിയുമോ?"

ഭാനുമതി ജോർജിയെ സൂക്ഷിച്ചുനോക്കി, മറുപടി നൽകി.

"ഇല്ല. എന്താണ് ചോദിച്ചത്?"

"ആ മനുഷ്യനെപ്പറ്റി ഞാൻ ചിലത് കേട്ടിട്ടുണ്ട്."

"എന്തു കേട്ടു?"

"ഇല്ല. ഞാൻ ഇപ്പോൾ ഒന്നും പറയുന്നില്ല."

"പറയൂ."

"അദ്ദേഹം ഭാനുമതിയെപ്പറ്റി എന്റെ ഭർത്താവിനോട് സംസാരിച്ചിട്ടുണ്ട്. അതൊക്കെ പിന്നെപ്പറയാം."

ജോർജി നിറുത്തി.

"വരൂ പോകാം." അവൾ തിടുക്കത്തിൽ നടന്നു. ഭാനുമതി പിറകേ നടന്നു. രണ്ടുപേരും ബെഡ്റൂമിൽ ഇരുന്നു.

അപ്പോഴും മറ്റ് സ്ത്രീകൾ ഡൈനിങ് ഹാളിലാണ്.

ഭാനുമതി പുറത്തേക്ക് ശ്രദ്ധിച്ചിട്ട് ചോദിച്ചു.

"കാര്യങ്ങളുടെ സൂചന പറയാമോ?"

"പാടില്ല. അവർക്ക് സംശയം തോന്നണ്ടല്ലോ."

കാൽപ്പെരുമാറ്റം കേട്ടു. പെട്ടെന്ന് അവൾ സംസാരം നിറുത്തി. റോസിക്കുട്ടി വന്നു.

"എന്താണോ ഇന്ന് ഡിന്നറ് നേരത്തെ നിറുത്തി. എനിക്ക് തോന്നുന്നത്. ഹരീന്ദ്രൻനായർ വന്നിട്ടാണെന്നാ. ആ പൊലീസുദ്യോഗസ്ഥൻ."

അരമണിക്കൂറിനുള്ളിൽ ആ വലിയ സദസ് എഴുന്നേറ്റു. സ്ത്രീകൾ അങ്ങോട്ടു ചെന്നു. ഓരോരുത്തർ യാത്രപറഞ്ഞു. മേഴ്സി, ജോർജി, വിനോദിനി, സുകുമാരിയമ്മ എന്നിവർ ഭാനുമതിയോട് യാത്ര ചോദിച്ച് ഇറങ്ങി. പൊലീസ് ഉദ്യോഗസ്ഥനും ദിവാകരനും ഭാനുമതിയും അവശേഷിച്ചു. അവരും റോബർട്ടിനോടും ഭാര്യയോടും വിടവാങ്ങാൻ ഭാവിച്ചു. ആദ്യം ഹരീന്ദ്രൻനായർ റോബർട്ടിനോട് പറഞ്ഞു.

"ഞാൻ വന്നത് നിങ്ങളുടെ കമ്പനിക്ക് അസൗകര്യമായോ?"

"നോ നോ.. യു വേർ ക്വയിറ്റ് വെൽക്കം. പിന്നെ വന്ന സ്ഥിതിക്ക് ഇതിൽ പങ്കുചേരാതെ പോകുന്നത് ശരിയാണോ?" റോബർട്ട് പറഞ്ഞു.

ഹരീന്ദ്രൻനായർ ആതിഥേയരെ തൊഴുതു. പിന്നെ ദിവാകരനെയും ഭാനുമതിയെയും തൊഴുതു. അദ്ദേഹം പുറത്തേക്കു പോയി. റോബർട്ട് ജീപ്പിനരികിലേക്കു ചെന്നു. ഹരീന്ദ്രൻനായർ ജീപ്പ് സ്റ്റാർട്ടു ചെയ്ത്, ഗേറ്റ് കടന്നുപോയി.

ദിവാകരനും ഭാനുമതിയും കാറിൽ കയറി.

"ഗുഡ് നൈറ്റ്!" റോബർട്ട് യാത്രാനുമതി നൽകി.

ഭാനുമതി റോസിക്കുട്ടിയോട് നന്ദി പറഞ്ഞു

ദിവാകരൻ അസ്വസ്ഥനായിരുന്നു. അത് ഭാനുമതിക്ക് കാണാൻ കഴിഞ്ഞു. ആ പൊലീസ് ഉദ്യോഗസ്ഥൻ അവളുടെ മനസിൽ ഭയത്തിന്റെ ഒരു നിഴൽ വിരിച്ചു. ഈ വിരുന്നു ദിവസവും അദ്ദേഹം വന്നതിൽ വല്ല അർഥവുമുണ്ടോ? യാദൃച്ഛികമായി വന്നു എന്ന് പറഞ്ഞത്, വെറുതെയല്ലേ?

അദ്ദേഹം ഇവരുടെയെല്ലാം സുഹൃത്താണത്രേ. ഇവരുടെയെല്ലാം ജീവിത രീതിക്ക് മറപിടിക്കുന്ന ഉദ്യോഗസ്ഥനെന്നല്ലേ അതിനർഥം? അദ്ദേഹം തന്റെ ഭർത്താവിന്റെ പരിചിതനോ സുഹൃത്തോ ആണെന്ന് തോന്നി. വന്നപ്പോഴും യാത്രപറഞ്ഞു പോയപ്പോഴും വെറും പരിചയമല്ലേ കാട്ടിയത്. അപ്പോൾ തന്റെ ഭർത്താവിന്റെ കഥകൾ അദ്ദേഹം അറിയാതിരിക്കുമോ?

അങ്ങനെ ആലോചിച്ചപ്പോൾ, താനറിയാതെ മനസിന് സമാധാനമുണ്ടായി. ഉപദ്രവിക്കാത്ത പൊലീസ് ഉദ്യോഗസ്ഥൻ...

പക്ഷേ, ജോർജി എന്ന ചെറുപ്പക്കാരി പറഞ്ഞ കാര്യം.. അതിൽ എന്തോ സംഗതിയില്ലേ? ഇത് രഹസ്യങ്ങളുടെ ലോകമാണോ? എന്തിന് അങ്ങനെയൊരു ലോകവുമായി തന്റെ ഭർത്താവ് ബന്ധപ്പെടുന്നു? അങ്ങനെയല്ലാത്ത എത്രയോ ബിസിനസുകാരില്ലേ?

എല്ലാ വിചാരവും കുറേ നേരത്തേക്ക് വലിച്ചെറിയാൻ തീരുമാനിച്ചു പിറകോട്ടുചാഞ്ഞു കിടന്നു. ദിവാകരൻ കണ്ണടച്ചുകിടക്കുകയാണ്.

കാറ് വീട്ടിൽ വന്നു നിന്നു. ഒന്നും മിണ്ടാതെ രണ്ടുപേരും ഇറങ്ങി ബെഡ്റൂമിലേക്ക് പോയി. അയാൾ വേഷംമാറി കിടന്നു അവളും. നിശ്ശബ്ദത ആ വീടിനെ പൊതിഞ്ഞു.

ദിവസങ്ങൾ ഇഴഞ്ഞുപൊയ്ക്കൊണ്ടിരുന്നു. ഭാനുമതി സുഖമില്ലാതെ കിടക്കുന്നു. മനഃപൂർവം കിടന്നതാണ്. ഇനിയും വിരുന്നുകൾക്ക് പോകാൻ കഴിയില്ല. ജോർജി എന്ന ചെറുപ്പക്കാരിയുടെ വാക്കുകൾക്ക് എന്തെങ്കിലും അർഥമുണ്ടെങ്കിൽ...

ഒരു ദിവസം മധ്യാഹ്നത്തിനുമുമ്പ് ജോലിക്കാരൻ വന്നു പറഞ്ഞു.

"കൊച്ചമ്മേ ഒരാൾ വന്നിരിക്കുന്നു."

"അദ്ദേഹം ഇല്ലെന്ന് പറയൂ."

"അല്ല, കൊച്ചമ്മയെ തിരക്കിയാണ് വന്നത്."

ഭാനുമതി എഴുന്നേറ്റ് മുൻവശത്തേക്കു വന്നു. ആളെ കണ്ടപ്പോൾ പകച്ചുനിന്നു...... ഹരീന്ദ്രൻനായർ.

"ഭയപ്പെടേണ്ട.... അഞ്ചുമിനിട്ട് സംസാരിച്ചിട്ട് പൊയ്ക്കൊള്ളാം." എഴുന്നേറ്റുതൊഴുതിട്ട് ചിരിച്ചുകൊണ്ട് ആ ഉദ്യോഗസ്ഥൻ പറഞ്ഞു. ഇരുന്നു. "ഇരിക്കൂ, അദ്ദേഹം അഭ്യർഥിച്ചു.

ഭാനുമതി അൽപ്പം മാറി ഇരുന്നു

"ഞാൻ വന്നത് ഒരു സംഗതി പറയാനാണ്." ഹരീന്ദ്രൻ നായർ സംസാരിച്ചു.

"പറയൂ." അവൾ ഹൃദയക്ഷോഭം അടക്കിപ്പിടിച്ചു. അകത്തേക്ക് കാപ്പിക്ക് പറഞ്ഞു.

"എനിക്ക് കാപ്പിയൊന്നും ഇപ്പോൾ വേണ്ട. വാസവമേനോൻ എന്നൊരാളെ പരിചയമില്ലേ?"

"ഉണ്ട്."

"അദ്ദേഹം ഒരു രാഷ്ട്രീയപ്രവർത്തകനാണെന്നറിയാമല്ലോ?"

"അറിയാം."

"മിസ്റ്റർ ദിവാകരന് പരിചയമുള്ള ആളാണ്. അതെനിക്കറിയാം. പക്ഷേ, മിസ്റ്റർ ദിവാകരൻ രാഷ്ട്രീയത്തിൽ അദ്ദേഹത്തിന്റെ എതിരാളിയാണ്. നിങ്ങളുടെ സ്ഥിതി അതല്ല. ആ വനിതാസമാജവും അദ്ദേഹവുമായി ബന്ധമുണ്ടെന്ന് അധികാരികൾക്ക് അറിവുണ്ട്. അതിന്റെ പ്രധാന പ്രവർത്തക നിങ്ങളുമാണ്. ഇപ്പോൾ നിങ്ങളെപ്പറ്റി അന്വേഷിക്കാൻ എഴുതി വന്നിരിക്കുന്നു. ഇതിനു കാരണമുണ്ട്. വാസവമേനോൻ നോട്ടപ്പുള്ളിയാണ്. പക്ഷേ, കർശന നടപടി ഒന്നും എടുത്തിരുന്നില്ല. മധുരയിൽ ഒരു പൊതുപണിമുടക്ക് ഉണ്ടാക്കിയിട്ട് ഇപ്പോൾ അദ്ദേഹം ഒരാഴ്ചയായി ഒളിവിൽപ്പോയിരിക്കുന്നു. നിങ്ങളുടെ പ്രദേശമൊക്കെ എന്റെ അധികാരപരിധിയിൽപ്പെട്ടതാണ്. വനിതാസമാജത്തിലെ രണ്ടുപേരെ അറസ്റ്റു ചെയ്തു ചോദ്യം ചെയ്യുന്നുണ്ട്. അതുപോലെ തിരുവിതാംകൂർ പ്രദേശത്തെ ആ സദനത്തിലും അന്വേഷണം നടക്കാൻ അവിടെ ഉത്തരവായിട്ടുണ്ട്. ഇതൊന്നും കേട്ട് പരിഭ്രമിക്കേണ്ട. വാസവമേനോനുമായി ബന്ധമില്ലെന്നു നിങ്ങൾ ഒരു സ്റ്റേറ്റ്മെന്റ് തന്നാൽ രക്ഷയുണ്ടാവാൻ വഴിയുണ്ട്.

ഭാനുമതി തളർന്നിരുന്നു. ഭയംകൊണ്ടല്ല താങ്ങാൻ വയ്യാത്ത ഓരോന്ന് പുറകേ പുറകേ വരുന്നു.

"സമാജത്തിൽ ആരെയെല്ലാമാണ് അറസ്റ്റു ചെയ്തത്?"

"ഒരു രജനി. ഒരു നീലാംബിക. അവരെ ഉപദ്രവിക്കുകയോ ഭീഷണിപ്പെടുത്തുകയോ ചെയ്യരുതെന്ന് ഞാൻ പ്രത്യേകം ചട്ടം കെട്ടിയിട്ടുണ്ട്."

"ഞാൻ എങ്ങനെ സ്റ്റേറ്റ്മെന്റ് തരും സാർ?" അവൾ എഴുന്നേറ്റ് ജനാലയ്ക്ക് അരികിലേക്ക് നിന്നു. "ഞാൻ അദ്ദേഹത്തെ അച്ഛനെപ്പോലെ സ്നേഹിക്കുന്നു. ആരാധിക്കുന്നു. അദ്ദേഹം എന്നെ മകളെപ്പോലെ കരുതുന്നു. അദ്ദേഹം എന്റെ ഗുരുവാണ്. സർവവുമാണ്."

"സർക്കാരിനു ഹൃദയമില്ലെന്നു മനസിലാക്കണം. മേനോൻ കുറച്ചുനാൾ ഒളിവിൽ കഴിയാൻ തീരുമാനിച്ചാൽ, അദ്ദേഹത്തെ കാണുന്നിടത്തുവച്ച് വെടിവയ്ക്കാൻ രാജ്യത്തെ പൊലീസിനു കൽപ്പന കൊടുക്കും. അത്രകണ്ട് അപകടകാരിയെന്ന് സർക്കാർ കരുതിയിട്ടുള്ള ഒരാളുമായുള്ള ബന്ധമാണ് പ്രശ്നം. തിരുവിതാംകൂർ, കൊച്ചി, മലബാർ എന്നീ മൂന്നു പ്രദേശങ്ങളിലെയും പ്രവർത്തനങ്ങളെ സംബന്ധിച്ച വിവരങ്ങൾ ഞങ്ങളുടെ കൈവശമുണ്ട്. സദനത്തിന്റെ ചീഫായ സന്ധ്യാദേവിയും അറസ്റ്റു ചെയ്യപ്പെടാൻ സാധ്യതയുണ്ട്. ഉടനെ നിങ്ങൾ എന്തെങ്കിലും ചെയ്യണം."

അവളുടെ കണ്ണുകൾ നിറഞ്ഞു. അവൾ ദൂരത്തേക്ക് നോക്കിനിന്നു.

കാപ്പി കൊണ്ടുവന്നു. അദ്ദേഹം അതു വാങ്ങിവച്ചു.

"മിസ്റ്റർ ദിവാകരനെ കാണാൻ കഴിഞ്ഞില്ല. ആ മനുഷ്യനെക്കൊണ്ട് നിർബന്ധിപ്പിച്ച് സ്റ്റേറ്റ്മെന്റ് എഴുതിപ്പിക്കാനും എനിക്കിഷ്ടമല്ല. നിങ്ങൾ തീരുമാനിക്കണം."

"ഞാൻ ആലോചിച്ചിട്ടു ചെയ്താൽപ്പോരെ?" അവൾ അദ്ദേഹത്തിന്റെ നേർക്ക് തിരിഞ്ഞു.

"ശരി." ഹരീന്ദ്രൻനായർ എഴുന്നേറ്റു രണ്ടുമൂന്നു നിമിഷത്തേക്ക്

അദ്ദേഹം ഒന്ന് തങ്ങി. അവളെ നോക്കി. ദൃഷ്ടികൾ പിൻവലിച്ചു. അവൾ അത് ശ്രദ്ധിച്ചു. വീണ്ടും അവളുടെ നേർക്ക് കണ്ണുകളയച്ചു.

"ഭാനു നിന്നെ അനിയത്തിയെപ്പോലെ കരുതുന്നവനാണ് ഞാൻ. ഇങ്ങനെ വിളിച്ചതിന്റെ അർഥം പിന്നെപ്പറയാം. നീ എനിക്കുവേണ്ടി ഇത് ചെയ്യണം."

അദ്ദേഹം തിടുക്കത്തിൽ വാതിൽക്കലേക്ക് നടന്നു. ഭാനുമതി മിഴിച്ചുനിന്നു.

ഹരീന്ദ്രൻനായർ പുറത്തേക്കിറങ്ങി.

"സാർ.." അവൾ അദ്ദേഹത്തിന്റെ പുറകേ ചെന്നു.

അദ്ദേഹം നിന്നില്ല. ഗേറ്റുകടന്ന് ജീപ്പിൽ കയറി. ജീപ്പ് അതിവേഗം സ്റ്റാർട്ടു ചെയ്തു. അത് ഇരമ്പിപ്പാഞ്ഞുപോയി.

അവൾ പ്രതിമകണക്ക് നിന്നു. അദ്ദേഹം ഏതോ സ്നേഹിതയുടെ ഭർത്താവാണ്. അല്ലെങ്കിൽ സഹോദരനാണ്. ഏത് സ്നേഹിത? തന്നെ നീയെന്നു വിളിക്കാൻ അടുപ്പമുള്ള ഏത് മനുഷ്യൻ? ഓർമിക്കാൻ ശ്രമിച്ചു. പിടികിട്ടിയില്ല. അദ്ദേഹത്തിന്റെ കണ്ണുകൾ കലങ്ങിയിരിക്കുന്നതുപോലെ തോന്നി. സന്ധ്യാദേവി, രജനി, നീലാംബിക.. വാസവമേനോന് വല്ലതും സംഭവിക്കുമോ? താൻ എന്ത്ചെയ്യണം?

അവൾ ജീവച്ഛവത്തെപ്പോലെ നടന്നു, മുറിയിൽ പോയി കിടന്നു.

എട്ട്

രാവിലെ രണ്ടുമണിക്കൂർനേരം എല്ലാവരും നൂൽ നൂറ്റു. അതിനുശേഷമാണ് കാപ്പി കുടിച്ചത്. നാട്ടിൽപ്പോയ സന്ധ്യാദേവിയുടെ കത്ത് വന്നില്ല. ഒരുവിവരവും അറിയിച്ചില്ല. കീർത്തി അങ്ങോട്ട് ഒരെഴുത്തെഴുതി. അതിൽ സന്ധ്യാദേവി വരാൻ വൈകുന്നതിൽ എല്ലാവർക്കുമുള്ള സങ്കടം അറിയിച്ചിട്ടുണ്ട്. പ്രത്യേകിച്ച് അവളുടെ വ്യസനം ഒരുപാടു വരികളിൽക്കൂടി എഴുതി. എല്ലാ ദിവസവും അവൾ ഗേറ്റിലേക്കു നോക്കി ഒട്ടേറെ സമയം ഇരിക്കും. സന്ധ്യാദേവി വരുന്നതും കാത്തുള്ള ഇരിപ്പാണ്. യോഗമയീദേവി ആത്മാർഥമായി പറഞ്ഞു: "ഈ കുട്ടി ഇങ്ങനെയായാൽ എങ്ങനെയാ!"

വൈകിട്ട് അവൾ അതുപോലെ കാത്തിരിക്കുമ്പോൾ, അരവിന്ദൻ പടി കയറി വന്നു. അവളുടെ ഉള്ളു തെളിഞ്ഞു.

അരവിന്ദന്റെ കയ്യിൽ പത്രമുണ്ട്. അത് കീർത്തിയുടെ കൈയിലേക്ക് കൊടുത്തിട്ട് ഇരുന്നു.

അവൾ അതു നിവർത്തി നോക്കി. മിഴികൾ വിടർന്നു. ചിരിച്ചു. ആദ്യത്തെ പുറത്ത് അവളുടെ വലിയചിത്രം. ഭാരതമാതാവിന്റെ വേഷത്തിലുള്ള അവളുടെ അഭിനയചിത്രം.

ഉള്ളിൽ സന്തോഷം. പക്ഷേ, അവൾ പറഞ്ഞു:

"സംഭവം നടന്നിട്ട് ഒരാഴ്ചയായി ഇപ്പോഴാണ് പടം കൊടുക്കുന്നത്?"

"ഫോട്ടോഗ്രാഫർ ഇപ്പോഴാണ് പടം തന്നത്. പിന്നെ ഉത്തമകല അനശ്വരമാണല്ലോ. ആ ഭാരതമാതാവ് അനശ്വരയാണ്. എപ്പോൾ വേണ മെങ്കിലും കൊടുക്കാം.." അരവിന്ദൻ ന്യായീകരിച്ചു.

"ഓ ഏട്ടൻ കളിയാക്കുന്നു."

കീർത്തി ആ കടലാസുകൊണ്ട് അകത്തേക്കോടി. അവൾ അത് എല്ലാവരേയും കാണിച്ചു.

"ഓ ഇനി ഇവിടെ ആർക്കും കിടക്കപ്പൊറുതി കിട്ടില്ല. റീന കളിയാക്കി."

"പോടീ അസത്തേ!" കീർത്തി ആ ചിത്രം റീനയുടെ മുഖത്തേക്ക് ചേർത്തുപിടിച്ചു. റീന പെട്ടെന്ന്, അതിന് ഒരു ഉമ്മ കൊടുത്തു.

"പെണ്ണ് അലവലാതിയാണെങ്കിലും അഭിനയിക്കാനറിയാം." റീന കീർത്തിയുടെ മൂക്കിൽ പിടിച്ചു കുലുക്കി.

യോഗമയീദേവി അരവിന്ദന്റെ അടുക്കലേക്കു ചെന്നു. സന്ധ്യാദേവി യെപ്പറ്റി അന്വേഷിക്കുംമുമ്പ് അയാൾ നടന്നതെല്ലാം പറഞ്ഞു. അവർക്കെല്ലാം സന്തോഷമായി. അൽപ്പം സമാധാനത്തോടെ അവർ തിരിച്ചുവരുമല്ലോ.

കീർത്തിയും അരവിന്ദനും ഒറ്റയ്ക്കായപ്പോൾ അവൾ ചോദിച്ചു:

"ഈ പടത്തിന്റെ കീഴിലെ വരികൾ ആരെഴുതിയതാണ്?"

"ആരോ എഴുതി." അയാൾ അലസമായി മറുപടി പറഞ്ഞു.

"ഓ എന്നെ കളിപ്പിക്കേണ്ട. ഏട്ടൻ എഴുതിയതല്ലേ?"

"പിന്നല്ലാതെ ഈ ഒന്നിനും കൊള്ളാത്ത നൃത്തത്തെപ്പറ്റി ഇത്ര പുകഴ്ത്തി ആരെഴുതും?"

അവളുടെ മുഖം പെട്ടെന്നു കറുത്തു. അയാൾ ഒന്നുമറിയാത്തതു പോലെ മൂളിപ്പാടി. അവൾ ആ കടലാസും പിടിച്ച് മുഖം കുനിച്ചുനിന്നു. അത് അരത്തിണ്ണയിലേക്കു വച്ചു. അകത്തേക്കു നടക്കാൻ ഭാവിച്ചപ്പോൾ വിളിച്ചു:

"കീർത്തീ!"

"തിരിഞ്ഞുനിന്നു."

"പോകുന്നത് കൊള്ളാം. പിണങ്ങിയല്ലെന്ന് പറഞ്ഞേച്ചുപോകണം."

മിണ്ടിയില്ല.

"പറയൂ."

മുഖം തെളിഞ്ഞു.

"പിണങ്ങിയില്ല. പക്ഷേ പറഞ്ഞതു പിൻവലിക്കണം."

"പിൻവലിക്കുകയല്ല ഞാൻ വിശ്വസിക്കുന്നത് വായിച്ചു കേൾപ്പി ക്കാം. അരവിന്ദൻ ആ ചിത്രത്തിനു കീഴിലെഴുതിയ കുറിപ്പു വായിച്ചു: "ഭാരതമാതാ... സേവാസദനത്തിലെ അംഗമായ കീർത്തി എന്ന പെൺ കുട്ടി ഭാരതമാതാവായി അരങ്ങത്തുവന്നു. അത്ഭുതകരമായ അഭിനയ പാടവം കൊണ്ടും രൂപസൗന്ദര്യം കൊണ്ടും കീർത്തി സദസിനെ മാസ്മ രമായ ഒരു അന്തരീക്ഷത്തിൽ പിടിച്ചിരുത്തി."

സന്ധ്യാദേവിയുടെ വിവരങ്ങൾ പറയാനാണ് അരവിന്ദൻവന്നത്. അയാൾ ഒട്ടും വൈകാതെ പോവുകയും ചെയ്തു. അന്നു രാവിലെ ഒരു പയ്യൻ വന്നു. മനോരമയ്ക്ക് ഒരു കത്തുകൊണ്ടു വന്നു കൊടുത്തു. അവൾ

അത് കീർത്തിയെ കാണിച്ചു. ഒരു സ്നേഹിതയുടെ കത്താണ്. അതിൽ ചില കാര്യങ്ങൾ എഴുതിയിട്ടുണ്ട്. കുടുംബകാര്യങ്ങൾ പോലിരുന്നു. ഉച്ചയ്ക്ക് മനോരമ ആ സ്നേഹിതയുടെ വീടുവരെ ഒന്നു ചെല്ലണം. ഉടനെ പോരാം. നിർബന്ധപൂർവമുള്ള അപേക്ഷയാണ്.

മനോരമ കത്ത് യോഗമയീദേവിയെ കാണിച്ചു. ഒരപേക്ഷയും സമർപ്പിച്ചു. കീർത്തിയെ ഒന്ന് കൂടെ അയക്കണം. ഒറ്റയ്ക്ക് പോകാൻ വയ്യ.

ആ സദനത്തിൽത്തന്നെ മറ്റുള്ളവരിൽനിന്ന് വ്യത്യസ്തമായിട്ടാണ് മനോരമയെ കാണാറുള്ളത്. അവളോടുള്ള പെരുമാറ്റത്തിലല്ല. അവൾ ജീവിതത്തിൽ എന്തോ തകർച്ച പറ്റിയവളാണ്. എന്താണെന്ന് അറിയില്ല. അതിൽ നിന്ന് അവൾ മോചനം നേടിയിട്ടില്ല. അതുകൊണ്ട് എല്ലാവർക്കും ഒരു പ്രത്യേക സഹതാപമുണ്ട്. അവളാണെങ്കിൽ മറ്റുള്ളവരെക്കാൾ ഒതുങ്ങിയാണ് കഴിച്ചുകൂട്ടുന്നത്. പുറത്തുനിന്നു വരുന്ന ആരുടെയും മുൻപിൽ ചെല്ലാറില്ല. എപ്പോഴും ഓരോ ജോലിയിൽ വ്യാപൃതയായിരിക്കും. സ്വന്തം ചിന്തകളിൽ മുഴുകിക്കഴിയുന്നതുപോലെയാണ്. കീർത്തിയോടു മാത്രമേ കൂടുതൽ അടുത്തു പെരുമാറുന്നുള്ളൂ. യോഗമയീദേവി ചോദിച്ചു:

"എവിടെയാണ് സ്നേഹിതയുടെ വീട്?"

മനോരമ സ്ഥലം പറഞ്ഞുകൊടുത്തു. ദൂരെയല്ല രണ്ട് മൂന്ന് ഫർലോങ് വരും. പോയി ഒരു മണിക്കൂറുനേരം കൊണ്ട് തിരിച്ചുവരാം.

യോഗമയീദേവി സമ്മതിച്ചു. ഒട്ടും താമസിക്കാതെ വരണമെന്ന് കീർത്തിയോടും നിർദേശിച്ചു.

അവർ ഒരുങ്ങി പുറപ്പെട്ടു.

സാമാന്യം നല്ല ഒരു വീട്. ഗേറ്റു കടന്നു കയറിച്ചെന്നപ്പോൾ വൃദ്ധനായ ഒരു വേലക്കാരൻ വാതിൽ തുറന്നുകൊടുത്തു. രണ്ടുപേരും അകത്തു കയറി. മധ്യവയസ്കയായ ഒരുസ്ത്രീ അവരെ അകത്തേക്ക് കൂട്ടിക്കൊണ്ടു പോയി. കാപ്പി കൊണ്ടുവന്നു. കുടിച്ചു. മനോരമ ആ സ്ത്രീയുമായി അകത്തെ ഒരു മുറിയിലേക്ക് മാറിയിരുന്നു. കുറച്ചുനേരം അവർ സംസാരിച്ചു. അതിനുശേഷം വെളിയിൽ വന്നു.

കീർത്തിയെയും കൂട്ടിക്കൊണ്ട് അവർ അകത്തെ മറ്റൊരു മുറിയിലേക്ക് ചെന്നു. എല്ലാ മുറികളും ആധുനികരീതിയിൽ സജ്ജീകരിച്ചതാണ്. ആ മുറിയുടെ വാതിൽ ചാരിയിട്ടിരുന്നു. ആ സ്ത്രീ അത് തുറന്നു. അവർ അകത്തേക്കു കയറി. മടിച്ചു നിന്ന കീർത്തിയെ അവർ അകത്തേക്ക് ആനയിച്ചു.

കട്ടിലിൽ ഒരു ചെറുപ്പക്കാരൻ കിടക്കുന്നു. അയാൾ എഴുന്നേറ്റിരുന്നു. മനോരമയോട് പരിചയം ഭാവിച്ചു. അയാൾ കീർത്തിയെ തൊഴുതു.

"ഇത് എന്റെ ആങ്ങളയാണ്. ഞങ്ങളുടെ ഒരു കുടുംബകാര്യം സംസാരിക്കാനാണ്. അനിയത്തി ഇരിക്കുന്നതുകൊണ്ട് ഒന്നുമില്ല." ആ സ്ത്രീ പറഞ്ഞു.

"ഞാൻ അപ്പുറത്തിരിക്കാം." കീർത്തി മര്യാദകാട്ടി.

"വേണ്ട, ഇരുന്നോളൂ." അവർ അവളെ പിടിച്ചിരുത്തി.

വാതിൽ അടച്ചിട്ട്, അവർ ഇരുന്നു. തൊട്ടടുത്ത് മനോരമയും.

അവർ മൂന്നുപേരും വീട്ടുകാര്യം സംസാരിക്കാൻ തുടങ്ങി. കീർത്തി ടീപ്പോയിൽ കിടന്ന ഒരു വാരികയെടുത്ത്, വായിച്ചു കൊണ്ടിരുന്നു.

അരമണിക്കൂർ നേരം സംഭാഷണം തുടർന്നു.

"അടുപ്പത്തു കിടക്കുന്നത് ഒന്നു നോക്കിയിട്ടു വരാം." ആ സ്ത്രീ എഴുന്നേറ്റു പുറത്തേക്കു പോയി. വാതിൽ ചാരി.

മനോരമയും ചെറുപ്പക്കാരനും സംസാരം തുടർന്നു. ഒരു പ്രമാണ ത്തെപ്പറ്റി അവർ പറഞ്ഞു. "അത് ചേച്ചിക്കേ അറിയാവൂ." അയാൾ പറ ഞ്ഞു. ആ പ്രമാണത്തിന്റെ അത്യാവശ്യകത അവർ ചർച്ച ചെയ്തു.

"ഞാനൊന്നു ചേച്ചിയോടു ചോദിക്കട്ടെ ആ പ്രമാണം ആരുടെ കൈയിലാണെന്ന്." മനോരമ തിടുക്കത്തിൽ എഴുന്നേറ്റ് പുറത്തേക്കു പോയി. വാതിൽ ചാരി.

കീർത്തി ഒറ്റയ്ക്കായപ്പോൾ വല്ലായ്മ തോന്നി. അവൾ എഴു ന്നേൽക്കാൻ ഭാവിച്ചു. അപ്പോൾ അയാൾ പറഞ്ഞു.

"ഇരിക്കൂ. മനോരമ ഇപ്പോൾ വരും."

അവൾ ഒതുങ്ങി ഇരുന്നു, വായന തുടർന്നു.

"പേര് കീർത്തി എന്നാണ് അല്ലേ?"

"അതെ."

"ഞാൻ അന്നു സ്കൂളിലെ ഫങ്ഷന് വന്നിരുന്നു. ആ നൃത്തവും അഭിനയവും കണ്ടു. ഗംഭീരമായിരുന്നു."

അവൾ അഭിവന്ദനം നിശ്ശബ്ദമായി സ്വീകരിച്ചു.

"സദനത്തിൽത്തന്നെയാണ് താമസം അല്ലേ?"

അതെ."

"ഏതുവരെ പഠിച്ചു?"

"സ്കൂൾ ഫൈനൽ പാസായതാണ്."

"ഞങ്ങൾക്ക് ഒരു കുടുംബപ്രശ്നമുണ്ട്. മനോരമയുടെ ഒരു ബന്ധു അതിൽ എതിർഭാഗത്തുചേർന്നിട്ടുണ്ട്. ഉടനെ തീർക്കാവുന്ന കാര്യമേ ഉള്ളൂ. അത് കഴിഞ്ഞിട്ട് ചില കാര്യങ്ങൾ ചെയ്യാനുണ്ട്. ഞാനും ചേച്ചിയും മാത്രമേ ഇവിടെ ഉള്ളൂ. ചേച്ചിയുടെ ഭർത്താവ് പുറംനാട്ടിലാണ് ഈ പ്രശ്നം തീർത്തിട്ട് എനിക്ക് വിവാഹം കഴിക്കണം. ചേച്ചിക്ക് കൂട്ടിന് ഒരാൾ വേണമല്ലോ ആളെയൊന്നും തീരുമാനിച്ചിട്ടില്ല."

അവൾകേട്ടുകൊണ്ടിരുന്നു.

അയാൾ എഴുന്നേറ്റ് ജനാലയ്ക്കരികിലേക്ക് നടന്നു.

"കയ്മൾ" വിളിച്ചു.

"എന്താ.."

ഒരു മധ്യവയസ്കൻ കയറി വന്നു. ചെറുപ്പക്കാരൻ അലമാരി തുറന്ന് നൂറുരൂപയുടെ ഒരുകെട്ടെടുത്ത് അതിൽ നിന്ന് കുറെ എണ്ണി വലിച്ചെ ടുത്ത് കെട്ടു അലമാരിയിൽവച്ചു.

"ദാ ഇത് കടയിൽ മാനേജരുടെ കൈയിൽ കൊടുത്തിട്ട് വരൂ."

ജോലിക്കാരൻ അത് വാങ്ങിപുറത്തേക്ക് പോയി. വാതിൽ ചാരി.

ചെറുപ്പക്കാരൻ സാവധാനം നടന്ന് കീർത്തിയുടെ സെറ്റിയിൽ അവളുടെ അരികിലിരുന്നു. അവൾ പെട്ടെന്ന് എഴുന്നേറ്റു.

"ഇരിക്കൂ. പേടിക്കണ്ട.." അയാൾ പറഞ്ഞു.

അവൾ ഇരുന്നില്ല. പുറത്തേക്ക് നടക്കാൻ തുടങ്ങി. പെട്ടെന്ന് അവൾ അയാളുടെ കരവലയത്തിലായി. കുതറി വാതിൽക്കലേക്കോടി. കതകു തള്ളി. അത് പുറത്തുനിന്ന് തഴുതിട്ടിരിക്കുന്നു.

"അയ്യോ.." അവൾ വിളിച്ചുപോയി. സംഭ്രമം. ഞരമ്പുകളെ പിച്ചിച്ചീന്തുന്ന ഭീതി. അവൾ കതകിൽ ഇടിച്ചു.

"മനോരമേ... മനേരമേ.." അവൾ ഉറക്കെ വിളിച്ചു മറുപടിയില്ല.

അയാൾ അവളുടെ കൈ രണ്ടും പിടിച്ചുവലിച്ച്, കട്ടിലിനരികിലേക്ക് കൊണ്ടുപോയി. പ്രാണന്റെ എല്ലാ ബലവുമെടുത്ത് അവൾകുതറി. അവൾ ഞെരിയുകയാണ്. കരഞ്ഞുവിളിച്ചു. ഒച്ചയുണ്ടാക്കി. തുറന്നു കിടന്ന ജനാല പുറത്തുനിന്ന് അടയുന്നത് ബഹളത്തിനിടയ്ക്ക് അവൾ കണ്ടു. കരുതിക്കൂട്ടിയുണ്ടാക്കിയ കെണിയാണ്.

കട്ടിലിൽ കിടക്കാതിരിക്കാൻ പൊരുതി. അങ്ങോട്ട് വീണപ്പോൾ ശരീരത്തിൽ ആക്രമിക്കാതിരിക്കാൻ മല്ലുപിടിച്ചു.

"എന്നെ വിടൂ.. വിടൂ.." അവൾ ഗർജിച്ചു, അപേക്ഷിച്ചു, ആക്രോശിച്ചു.

"എന്റമ്മേ!" അവൾ വിളിച്ചുപോയി.

ഒരു നിമിഷം ഒരു ബോധം തലച്ചോറിൽക്കൂടി പാഞ്ഞുപോയി.

"എന്നെ വിട്ടാൽ.. എന്നെ വിട്ടാൽ.... ഞാൻ.... ഞാൻ നിങ്ങളെ അനുസരിക്കാം." കിടന്ന് കുതറുന്നതിനിടയ്ക്ക് അവൾ പറഞ്ഞു.

ബലമായി പിടിച്ചമർത്തിവച്ച് അയാൾ ചോദിച്ചു.

"സത്യമാണോ?"

"നിങ്ങൾ വിടൂ ഞാൻ പറഞ്ഞില്ലേ?"

അയാൾ പിടിവിട്ടു. അവൾ എഴുന്നേറ്റു. പെട്ടെന്ന് അഴിഞ്ഞ മുടികെട്ടി. സാരി ശരിക്കിട്ടു. നിമിഷങ്ങൾ കൊണ്ട് അവൾ നിയന്ത്രണം പ്രാപിച്ചു.

അവൾ അയാളെ തുറിച്ചു നോക്കി.

"ഇങ്ങനെയാണോ വേണ്ടത്? ആദ്യമായിട്ടു കാണുന്ന ഒരു പെണ്ണിനോട് ഇങ്ങനെയാണോ പെരുമാറുന്നത്? നിങ്ങൾക്ക് പെൺകുട്ടികളോട് സൗമ്യമായി പെരുമാറാൻ അറിഞ്ഞുകൂടേ? എനിക്ക് നിങ്ങളോട് ശത്രുതയൊന്നുമില്ല. എന്നിട്ട് എന്താണ് കാട്ടിയത്. ചാടിവീണാൽ ആരാ പേടിക്കാത്തത്? കഷ്ടമാണ്." അവൾ സെറ്റിയുടെ അടുക്കലേക്കുപോയി, ഇരുന്നു. എന്നിട്ട് അയാളെ വിളിച്ചു.

"വരൂ. ഇവിടെ ഇരിക്കൂ. പക്ഷേ, ഞാൻ പറയാതെ എന്നെ തൊടരുത്. ക്ഷമ ഞാൻ പഠിപ്പിക്കാം."

അയാളുടെ ഉള്ളിൽ പ്രകാശം വീണതുപോലുണ്ട്. പതുക്കെ നടന്ന് സെറ്റിയിൽ ഇരുന്നു.

അവൾ മന്ത്രിക്കുംപോലെ ചോദിച്ചു:

"നിങ്ങൾ വലിയ ആളാണ്. പണക്കാരൻ. നിങ്ങൾക്ക് എന്നോട് ഇഷ്ടം തോന്നിയെന്നുവയ്ക്കുക. എന്നെ കല്യാണം കഴിക്കാൻ ആഗ്രഹിച്ചു വെന്നും വയ്ക്കുക. പക്ഷേ, ആദ്യം കാണുമ്പോൾ തന്നെക്കൊന്നുകള യുമല്ലോ. ഒരു ഭാര്യവന്നാൽ എന്തായിരിക്കും സ്ഥിതി?"

അയാൾ ജാള്യതപ്പെട്ട് ഇരുന്നു.

"ക്ഷമിക്കൂ.." അയാൾ അപേക്ഷിച്ചു.

"എനിക്കു സംസാരിച്ചിരിക്കാൻ ഇഷ്ടമാണ് ചേട്ടാ. ചേട്ടന് തിടുക്കമി ല്ലെങ്കിൽ ഞാൻ എത്രനേരം വേണമെങ്കിലും ഇവിടെ കഴിച്ചുകൂട്ടാം.." അവൾ അയാളുടെ കാതിലേക്ക് മന്ത്രിച്ചു. "ചേട്ടന് വേണ്ടത് തരാതെ ഇവിടെ നിന്നു പോവുകയില്ലെന്ന് ഞാൻ ഉറപ്പു തരുന്നു."

അയാൾ അവളുടെ കൈകൾ ഗ്രഹിച്ചു. അവൾ അനുസരണയോടെ ഇരുന്നു.

"മനോരമയ്ക്ക് വല്ലതും തോന്നുമോ?" അവൾ ചോദിച്ചു.

"ഓ ഒന്നുമില്ല അവളോട് ഞാൻ സൂചിപ്പിച്ചിട്ടല്ലേ, നിന്നെ കൂട്ടി ക്കൊണ്ടു വന്നത്."

"ചേച്ചിക്കോ?"

"ഒന്നുമില്ലെന്ന്."

അയാൾ എഴുന്നേറ്റു. വാതിൽക്കൽച്ചെന്നു. "ചേച്ചീ" അവൾ വിളിച്ചു.

അൽപ്പസമയം, വാതിൽ തുറന്നു. മനോരമയാണ് വന്നത്.

കീർത്തി ഓടിച്ചെന്ന് മനോരമയോട് പറഞ്ഞു.

"ഞങ്ങൾ കുറച്ചുനേരം ഇവിടെ സംസാരിച്ചിരിക്കട്ടെ. വിരോധ മുണ്ടോ?"

ഒരു വിരോധവുമില്ല. ഞാൻ പോയേക്കാം. അവൾ കളിയാക്കുന്ന സ്വരത്തിൽപ്പറഞ്ഞു. പിന്നെ നിന്നില്ല പുറത്തേക്ക് പോയി.

അയാൾ വാതിൽ ചാരി.

അവൾ മുറിയാകെ ചുറ്റിനടന്നു. മേശപ്പുറത്തു പുസ്തകങ്ങൾ നോക്കി അലമാരയുടെ അരികിൽച്ചെന്നു നിന്ന് ചോദിച്ചു.

"ഒന്ന് നോക്കിക്കോട്ടെ."

"ഓഹോ." കട്ടിലിൽ ചാരിക്കിടന്നുകൊണ്ട് അയാൾ സന്തോഷ ത്തോടെ സമ്മതിച്ചു.

അവൾ അലമാര തുറന്നു. അയാളുടെ പാന്റ്സുകളും ഷർട്ടുകളും നോക്കി.

ഒരു നിമിഷം ഉറയിട്ട ഒരു കത്തി. അതെടുത്തു ബ്ലൗസിനുള്ളിൽ ഒളിച്ചു.

വീണ്ടും മേശയ്ക്കരികിൽ വന്നു ഭിത്തിയിലെ ചിത്രങ്ങൾ നോക്കി. നഗ്നചിത്രങ്ങൾ. അവിടെ നിന്നുകൊണ്ടു പറഞ്ഞു:

"കണികാണാൻ വച്ചിരിക്കുകയായിരിക്കും."

അയാൾ ചിരിച്ചു.

അവൾ വികാരപൂർവം അയാളെ നോക്കി. മെല്ലെ നടന്നു കട്ടിലിൽ ഇരുന്നു കൈയിൽ തലോടി. അയാൾ കണ്ണടച്ച് ലഹരിയിൽ മുഴുകിക്കിടന്നു.

ഒരു നിമിഷംപോലും വേണ്ടിവന്നില്ല. അവൾ കത്തിവലിച്ചെടുത്ത് അയാളുടെ കൈയിൽക്കുത്തി.

"അയ്യോ!" അയാൾ പ്രാണവേദനപൂണ്ട് നിലവിളിച്ചു.

അവൾ ഓടി മുറിയിൽനിന്നിറങ്ങി. മുറ്റത്തേക്ക് ചാടി. ഗേറ്റ് കടന്നു. അതിവേഗം നടന്നു.

ആത്മധൈര്യം എവിടെ നിന്നോ കൈവരുന്നുവെന്നറിയില്ല. നിരാശതയിൽനിന്നും നിസ്സഹായതയിൽനിന്നും അത് ഉണ്ടാവുമെന്ന് തോന്നുന്നു. സദനത്തിന്റെ പടികടന്ന് ഒരു ഇൻസ്പെക്ടറും പൊലീസുകാരും വന്നപ്പോൾ കീർത്തി അടിമുടി വിറച്ചു നിന്നു. ഉച്ചതിരിഞ്ഞു അവൾ മടങ്ങിയെത്തിയപ്പോൾ എല്ലാവരും ഭക്ഷണം കഴിഞ്ഞ് മയങ്ങുന്നു. കാലൊച്ച കേൾപ്പിക്കാതെ മുറിയിൽച്ചെന്ന് കിടന്നു. ആരോടും ഒന്നും പറയേണ്ട. വരുന്നതുവരട്ടെ. കീർത്തി ഉണർന്നപ്പോൾ അഞ്ചുമണിയായി. "മനോരമ എവിടെ?" അംബികത്തമ്പുരാട്ടി ചോദിച്ചു "അവർ വരും." രണ്ടു വാക്കുകൾ മാത്രം മുൻവശത്തുപോയി ഇരുന്നു അൽപ്പസമയം കഴിഞ്ഞ് പൊലീസുകാർ വന്നു.

അവർ തിണ്ണയിലേക്ക് കയറി.

കീർത്തി അകത്തേക്ക് പോകാൻ തുടങ്ങി.

"നിൽക്കൂ, കുട്ടി സെക്രട്ടറിയെ ഒന്നു വിളിക്കൂ." ഇൻസ്പെക്ടർ പറഞ്ഞു.

"സന്ധ്യാദേവിയെയല്ലേ?" അവർ "ഇവിടെയില്ല." "മറ്റൊരാളുണ്ട്. വിളിക്കാം."

"അവർ എവിടെ പോയി?"

"നാട്ടിൽപോയിരിക്കുകയാണ്."

"കള്ളം പറയരുത്." ഇൻസ്പെക്ടർ താക്കീതു നൽകി.

"കള്ളമല്ല സാർ. സത്യമാണ്."

അവൾ അകത്തുപോയി. യോഗമയീദേവി പുറത്തേക്ക് വന്നു.

"എന്റെ പേർ യോഗമയീദേവി. സന്ധ്യയാണ് ഇവിടത്തെ ചുമതലക്കാരി."

"അവരെയാണ് ഞങ്ങൾക്ക് കാണേണ്ടത്."

"അവർ രണ്ടുദിവസത്തിനകം വരും."

"സ്ഥലത്തില്ലെന്നുള്ളത് സത്യമാണോ?"

"അകത്തു കയറി നോക്കിക്കൊള്ളൂ. ഞങ്ങൾ കള്ളം പറയുകയില്ല എന്തു സംഭവിച്ചാലും പറയുകയില്ല."

"പരിശോധിക്കേണ്ടത് ഞങ്ങളുടെ ആവശ്യമാണ്."

"ആയിക്കൊള്ളൂ."

അവർ എല്ലാ മുറികളും കയറിയിറങ്ങി. പിൻമുറ്റവും പരിശോധിച്ചു മടങ്ങിവന്നു. യോഗമയീദേവി കൂടെ ഉണ്ട്.

സദനത്തിലെ അംഗങ്ങളുടെ പേരുവിവരങ്ങൾ അവർ കുറിച്ചെടുത്തു. പ്രതീക്ഷിച്ച ഒരു ചോദ്യം ചോദിച്ചില്ല. വാസവമേനോനെപ്പറ്റി, അവർ പോയി.

ഒതുക്കിപ്പിടിച്ച ഭീതി അവിടെ തങ്ങിനിന്നു. യോഗമയീദേവി എല്ലാവരെയും വിളിച്ചു ചില ചിട്ടകൾ പറഞ്ഞു. ആരും വെളിയിൽ പോകണ്ട. പരിചയമില്ലാത്ത ആരു കയറിവന്നാലും തന്നെ വിളിക്കണം. സംസാരിക്കുന്നത് താനായിക്കൊള്ളാം.

കീർത്തി പിന്നാലെ പറമ്പിലേക്കു നടന്നു. കുളക്കടവിൽ ഇരുന്നു. മനോരമയുടെ മുഖം തെളിഞ്ഞു വന്നു. ആ ഹിംസ്രമൃഗത്തിന്റെ കൂട്ടിലേക്ക് കൊണ്ടുപോകാൻ അവൾക്ക് എങ്ങനെ മനസുവന്നു? അവളോട് എന്തുതെറ്റുചെയ്തു? ഒരുപക്ഷേ അവളുടെ തൊഴിൽ ഇതാണോ? ഈ സഹായത്തിന് അവൾക്ക് പണം കിട്ടുന്നുണ്ടാവുമോ? ആ ജന്തുവിന്റെ പിടിയിൽപ്പെട്ട് ശരീരം ഇപ്പോഴും നോവുന്നു. ചെയ്ത കൃത്യത്തെപ്പറ്റി ഒരു വിഷമവും തോന്നുന്നില്ല. ആ കത്തി ഒന്ന് തിളങ്ങി. ചോര തെറിച്ചുവീണു. സാരിയിൽ ചോരപ്പാടുകൾ ഉണ്ടായിരുന്നു.

ഇനിയും ആ സംഭവം മറ്റുള്ളവരെ അറിയിക്കാതിരിക്കുന്നതു ശരിയല്ല. യോഗമയീദേവി മഹാത്മാഗാന്ധിയുടെ *സത്യാന്വേഷണ പരീക്ഷകൾ* വായിച്ചുകൊണ്ടിരുന്നു. അവരുടെ വേദപുസ്തകം അതാണ്. അരികിൽച്ചെന്നിരുന്നു. സാവകാശമായി നടന്നതെല്ലാം പറഞ്ഞുകേൾപ്പിച്ചു.

അവൾ ഒട്ടുനേരം ആലോചിച്ചിരുന്നു. എന്നിട്ട് അവളെ സമാധാനിപ്പിച്ചു.

"പോകട്ടെ എന്തുംവരട്ടെ. നിനക്കു അങ്ങനെ രക്ഷപ്പെടാനുള്ള ആത്മധൈര്യം ദൈവം തന്നല്ലോ. അതിന് അവിടെത്തന്നെ പ്രാർഥിക്കൂ. മനോരമയെ എനിക്ക് എന്നും സംശയമായിരുന്നു. അവളുടെ പെരുമാറ്റങ്ങളിൽ ഒന്നും കാണാനില്ല. എന്നാലും അവളുടെ യഥാർഥരൂപം നമുക്ക് മനസിലായിട്ടില്ലെന്ന് തോന്നിയിരുന്നു. എനിക്ക് ഒരു തെറ്റുപറ്റി. കീർത്തിയെ അവളുടെ കൂടെ അയക്കരുതായിരുന്നു. അത്രയ്ക്ക് ബുദ്ധി പോയില്ല. അത്രയും വിചാരിച്ചില്ല."

മറ്റുള്ളവരും ആ സംഭവം അറിഞ്ഞു. റീനയും ഉഷയും ഞെട്ടിപ്പോയി. പാർവതിയമ്മയും അംബികത്തമ്പുരാട്ടിയും സുമതിയും അന്തിച്ചു നിന്നു. അവർക്ക് കീർത്തിയോട് മതിപ്പുതോന്നി. അവിടെ നിന്നു രക്ഷപ്പെട്ടുപോരാൻ കഴിഞ്ഞല്ലോ. അത്രയും വേദന അനുഭവിക്കേണ്ടി വന്നതിൽ സഹതാപവും.

സന്ധ്യാദേവിക്ക് അടിയന്തരമായി കത്തിട്ടുകഴിഞ്ഞു. സദനത്തിലേക്ക് വരുന്നത് സൂക്ഷിച്ചുവേണം. നേരിട്ടു വരരുത്. ഏതെങ്കിലും വീട്ടിൽ ചെന്നിട്ട് ആളെ അയക്കണം അല്ലെങ്കിൽ, ഇങ്ങോട്ട് ഉടനെ വരിക തന്നെ വേണ്ടാ. ആലോചിച്ചു വേണം യാത്ര പുറപ്പെടാനും മറ്റും. പൊലീസിന്റെ അന്വേഷണം തീരുംവരെ, വല്ലയിടത്തും ഒളിച്ചു താമസിക്കുന്നതാണ് നല്ലത്. എല്ലാ വിവരങ്ങളും ഇങ്ങോട്ടറിയിക്കണമെന്ന് പ്രത്യേകം എഴുതി.

അരവിന്ദൻ പത്രമാഫീസിൽ തിരക്കിട്ട ജോലിയിലാണ്. സുഭാഷ് ചന്ദ്രബോസിന്റെ നേതൃത്വത്തിൽ സംഘടിപ്പിച്ച ഇന്ത്യൻ നാഷണൽ ആർമിയുടെ നേതാക്കളെ വിചാരണ ചെയ്തുകൊണ്ടിരിക്കുന്നു. അതാണ് ദിവസവും പ്രധാന വാർത്ത. ബ്രിട്ടീഷ് അധികാരികൾ അവരെ തൂക്കി ക്കൊല്ലാൻ വിധിക്കുമെന്നാണ് പൊതുവെയുള്ള സംസാരം. ദേശീയ ബോധത്തിന്റെ ചൂട് ഉച്ചത്തിലെത്തിക്കൊണ്ടിരിക്കുകയാണ്. ഐ എൻ എ നേതാക്കളെ അങ്ങനെ ശിക്ഷിച്ചാൽ രാജ്യത്ത് കലാപമുണ്ടാവും. ആക്രമണവും തീവയ്പും നടക്കും. പട്ടാളവും പൊലീസും ജാഗ്രതയോടെ നഗരങ്ങളിലും മറ്റുപ്രധാന കേന്ദ്രങ്ങളിലും കാവൽ നിൽക്കുന്നുണ്ട്.

അന്നും വാർത്തകൾ വരുന്നുണ്ട്. ധൃതിയിൽ അതു എഴുതിക്കൊടു ത്തു. സന്ധ്യകഴിഞ്ഞപ്പോൾ സദനത്തിൽ നിന്നു പറഞ്ഞയച്ച ഒരു പയ്യൻ വന്നു. അവൻ ഒരു കുറിപ്പുകൊടുത്തു വായിച്ചുനോക്കി. പൊലീസ് സന്ധ്യാദേവിയെ തിരക്കിച്ചെന്നതും അവർ പേരുവിവരങ്ങൾ കുറിച്ചെടു ത്തതും അതിൽ എഴുതിയിട്ടുണ്ട്.

വാർത്തകളെല്ലാം കൊടുത്തുകഴിഞ്ഞ്, ആലോചിച്ചു. അവർ ഇപ്പോൾ ഇങ്ങോട്ടു വരേണ്ടാ. കൊച്ചിയിൽ ഭയപ്പെടാനൊന്നുമില്ല. വാസ വമേനോൻ അതുകൊണ്ടാണല്ലോ അവിടെ താവളമാക്കിയത്. പക്ഷേ, അദ്ദേഹം അവിടെ അടങ്ങിയിരിക്കുകയില്ലെന്നു മാത്രം.

മേനോനെ കാണുന്നില്ല. വരുമെന്നു പറഞ്ഞ തീയതി കഴിഞ്ഞു. സന്ധ്യാദേവിയുടെ കാര്യം എഴുതിയിരുന്ന കാര്യത്തിൽ, നാലഞ്ചു ദിവ സങ്ങൾക്കകം എത്തുമെന്ന് എഴുതിയിരുന്നു. ഒരു പക്ഷേ, പരിപാടികൾ മാറ്റിയോ?

വൈകുന്നേരത്തെ പോസ്റ്റിൽ തനിക്കു വന്ന കത്തുകൾ പൊട്ടിച്ചിട്ടില്ല. അപ്പോഴാണ് ഓർമിച്ചത് ഓരോന്നും തുറന്നു നോക്കി. ഭാനുമതിയുടെ എഴുത്ത്.

താൽപ്പര്യത്തോടെ വായിച്ചു. ആശങ്കിച്ചിരുന്നതുപോലെയെല്ലാം സംഭവിച്ചിരിക്കുന്നു. വാസവമേനോൻ അപകടമേഖലയിലേക്ക് സഞ്ചരി ച്ചെത്തുകയാണെന്ന് ഊഹിച്ചിരുന്നു. പല രാഷ്ട്രീയപ്രവർത്തകരും അതു പ്രതീക്ഷിച്ചുകൊണ്ടിരുന്നു. അദ്ദേഹം ഒളിവിലായി. സ്വാഭാവികമായും അദ്ദേഹവുമായി ബന്ധപ്പെട്ടവരെ അന്വേഷിക്കും. ഭാനുമതി, ഉൽകണ്ഠ യൊന്നും കാട്ടിയിട്ടില്ല. എന്തു ചെയ്യണമെന്ന് ചോദിച്ചിരിക്കുന്നു. സദന ത്തിൽ വേണ്ട കരുതലുകൾ ചെയ്യണമെന്നും പറഞ്ഞിരിക്കുന്നു.

പൊലീസ് ആഫീസർ ഹരീന്ദ്രൻനായരെപ്പറ്റി പറയുന്നുണ്ട്. ആരാ ണദ്ദേഹം? നേരിട്ടു കണ്ടാൽ അറിയാവുന്ന ആളാണോ?

പത്രം അടിച്ചുവന്നു. ആകെ ഒന്നു നോക്കി. ഒപ്പിട്ടുകൊടുത്തു.

പുറത്തേക്കിറങ്ങി താമസസ്ഥലത്തേക്ക് നടക്കുമ്പോൾ അടുത്തു ചെയ്യേണ്ട കാര്യങ്ങളെപ്പറ്റി ആലോചിക്കുകയായിരുന്നു. സന്ധ്യാദേവിക്ക് രാവിലെ ഒരു കമ്പിയടിക്കണം. ഭാനുമതിക്ക് രാത്രിയിൽത്തന്നെ കത്തെ ഴുതാം. സദനത്തിൽ വേണ്ട കരുതലുകൾ ചെയ്തിട്ടുണ്ട്. എന്നാലും

രാവിലെ ഒന്നുകൂടി കാര്യങ്ങൾ ഓർമപ്പെടുത്താം.

ഇരുട്ടുള്ള വഴി, സമയം പന്ത്രണ്ടുമണി കഴിഞ്ഞു. പുറകിൽ ആരോ വരുന്നുവെന്ന് തോന്നി. തിരിഞ്ഞു നോക്കി. ആരേയും കണ്ടില്ല. തന്റെ പുറകേയും സി ഐ ഡി നടക്കാവുന്നതാണ്. പത്രവും താനും അവരുടെ നോട്ടപ്പുള്ളികളാണ്.

അത് ഒരു ലോഡ്ജാണ്. അരവിന്ദന്റെ മുറി പ്രത്യേകം വിട്ടുമാറിയുള്ളതാണെന്ന് മാത്രം. അകത്തുകയറി വിളക്കു കത്തിച്ചു. ഒരു ബീഡി കൊളുത്തി വലിച്ചു.

സംഭവങ്ങൾ ഒഴുകി. ചുഴിയും മലരിയുമുള്ള ഒരുകയത്തിലെത്തിയിരിക്കുകയാണ്. സ്വന്തം വഴിക്ക് പ്രയാണം തുടങ്ങിയവർ അവിടെ വന്നു ചേർന്നിരിക്കുന്നു. വാസവമേനോൻ, സന്ധ്യാദേവി, ഭാനുമതി, സദനം, വനിതാസമാജം കൂട്ടത്തിൽ താനും. സ്നേഹത്തിന്റെ താമരനൂലുകൊണ്ട് ബന്ധിക്കപ്പെട്ട ഏതാനും ആത്മാക്കൾ. മറ്റുള്ളവരെ വെടിഞ്ഞ്, ഈ ഓളത്തല്ലിൽ നിന്നു ഒഴിഞ്ഞു പൊയ്ക്കൊള്ളാൻ ആരും തയാറില്ല. വിവാഹം കഴിച്ച് കുടുംബമെന്ന സത്യത്തിൽപ്പെട്ടിരിക്കുന്ന ഭാനുമതിപോലും വാസവമേനോനെ തള്ളിപ്പറഞ്ഞു തയാറില്ല. ആ കത്തിലെ സൂചന അതാണ്. ആര് ആരെ ഉപേക്ഷിക്കും? ഒരുമിച്ച് മുങ്ങാനും പൊന്താനും വ്രതമെടുത്ത മനസുകൾ.

പ്രഭാതത്തിൽ എഴുന്നേറ്റപ്പോൾ ജനാലയിൽക്കൂടി കീഴോട്ടെറിഞ്ഞ ഒരു കത്ത് കിടക്കുന്നു. "അരവിന്ദന്" എന്ന് അതിന്റെ പുറത്തെ കണ്ടു. കവറാണ്. ഇന്നലെ രാത്രിയിൽ പുറകേ ആരോ ഉണ്ടെന്ന് തോന്നിയത്, ഓർമിച്ചു. അതു ഇതുമായി ബന്ധം വേണമെന്നില്ല. എങ്കിലും...

ഒൻപത്

കത്ത് വായിച്ചുനോക്കി.

"പ്രിയ സുഹൃത്തേ, അജ്ഞാതനായി നിൽക്കാൻ ആഗ്രഹിക്കുന്ന ഒരാളാണ് ഈ കത്തെഴുതുന്നത്. ഇത് വായിച്ചിട്ട് ഭയപ്പെടേണ്ട. കാരണം, ഞാൻ കഴിയുന്നത്ര നിങ്ങളെ സൂക്ഷിക്കുന്നുണ്ട്. എപ്പോഴും, എന്നല്ല, കഴിയുന്നത്ര, എന്നുമാത്രം നേരിട്ടു കണ്ടു, നേരിൽ സംസാരിച്ച്, നിങ്ങളുടെ ഒരു രക്ഷിതാവാവാൻ എനിക്കാഗ്രഹമില്ല. അതിൽ ഒരു അൽപ്പത്വം അന്തർഭവിച്ചിട്ടുണ്ടെന്ന് എനിക്ക് തോന്നുന്നു.

"ഇന്നലെ രാവിലെയാണ് എനിക്ക് ഒരു സംഗതി അറിവു കിട്ടിയത്. നിങ്ങളുടെ ജീവൻ സുരക്ഷിതമല്ലാത്ത ഒരു അന്തരീക്ഷത്തിലാണ് നിങ്ങൾ കഴിഞ്ഞുകൂടുന്നത്. നിങ്ങൾക്ക് അത് അറിഞ്ഞുകൂടായിരിക്കാം. അതിന്റെ വിശദാംശങ്ങൾ അറിയുകയും വേണ്ടാ. ഒരു സംഘം ആളുകൾ നിങ്ങളെ ആക്രമിക്കാനും കൊല്ലാനും നടക്കുന്നുണ്ട്. അവർ അങ്ങനെ ചെയ്യാൻ മടിക്കുകയില്ല. അത് രാഷ്ട്രീയമാണ്. സംശയിക്കേണ്ടാ. അതിന് അവർപറയുന്ന പല കാര്യങ്ങളുമുണ്ട്. ഒന്നാമത് സദനവുമായുള്ള

നിങ്ങളുടെ ബന്ധം. അതിനെക്കുറിച്ച് അവർ സമർഥമായി അപവാദങ്ങൾ പ്രചരിപ്പിക്കാൻ തുടങ്ങിയിട്ടുണ്ട്. ചോരയും നീരുമുള്ള പെൺകുട്ടികളെ സ്വഭാവ ദൂഷ്യമുള്ള ചെറുപ്പക്കാരിയായ ഒരു വിലാസിനിയെ പാർപ്പിച്ചിരിക്കുന്നു എന്നാണ് അവരുടെ പറച്ചിൽ. അതിന്റെ ഉദ്ദേശ്യം മറ്റു തരത്തിലുള്ളതാണെന്നും, നിങ്ങൾ അവിടെ ചെല്ലുന്നത് അത്തരം താണ വികാരങ്ങളുമായിട്ടാണെന്ന്, അവർ പ്രചരണം നടത്തുന്നു. അങ്ങനെ അവർ ഈ നാട്ടിലെ സംസ്കാരത്തിന്റെ രക്ഷിതാക്കളാകാൻ തീരുമാനിച്ചിരിക്കുന്നു. നിങ്ങളെ അപമാനിക്കുക, ആക്രമിക്കുക, നശിപ്പിക്കുക എന്നിങ്ങനെ ഏതു ഘട്ടങ്ങളും ഉപയോഗിക്കണമെന്നാണ് അവരുടെ ഉന്നം.

എന്റെ ഒരു ഉറ്റ സുഹൃത്താണ് എന്റെ ശ്രദ്ധ ഇതിലേക്കു കൊണ്ടുവന്നിട്ടുള്ളത്. നിങ്ങളുടെ രാഷ്ട്രീയം അദ്ദേഹത്തിനും എനിക്കും അറിയാം. അതിനോടു ഞങ്ങളുടെ മനോഭാവം എന്തുമാവട്ടെ, നിങ്ങൾ അറിയേണ്ടാ. ഒരു സമർഥനായ കവിയെന്നനിലയ്ക്ക്, നിങ്ങൾ ഞങ്ങൾക്കു പ്രിയപ്പെട്ടവനാണ്. ആ ആദരം ഞങ്ങൾക്കുണ്ട്. ഇന്നത്തെ കാലാവസ്ഥ മാറുമ്പോൾ നിങ്ങൾ ഈ നാടിനുവേണ്ട വിലപ്പെട്ട ഒരു മനുഷ്യനായി അംഗീകരിക്കപ്പെടുമെന്ന് ഞങ്ങൾക്ക് ഉറപ്പുണ്ട്. അതുകൊണ്ടാണ് ഈ കത്തെഴുതുന്നത്.

ഇന്നലെ രാത്രിയിൽ ഞാൻ നിങ്ങളുടെ പിന്നാലെ ഉണ്ടായിരുന്നു. നിങ്ങൾ കവല കടന്നപ്പോൾ അവിടെ അഞ്ചാറുപേർ നിന്നത് ശ്രദ്ധിച്ചു കാണുകയില്ല. വഴിപോക്കരെന്നേ കരുതിയിരിക്കൂ. അതുപോലെ ഈ വഴിയിലേക്കു കയറുന്ന മുക്കുതിരിഞ്ഞപ്പോഴും രണ്ടുമൂന്നുപേർ നിൽപ്പുണ്ടായിരുന്നു. രണ്ടുസ്ഥലത്തുവച്ചും രണ്ടുകൂട്ടരും എന്നെക്കണ്ടു. അതുകൊണ്ടാവണം അവർ ഒതുങ്ങിമാറിക്കളഞ്ഞത് കാരണം, ഞാൻ അവർക്ക് പരിചിതനാണ്. എനിക്ക് അവരും. അവർ ദുരുദ്ദേശ്യത്തോടെ കാത്തുനിന്നവരാണെന്ന് വ്യക്തമാണ്.

നിങ്ങൾ ദയവായി ഒരു കാര്യം ചെയ്യണം. പത്രമാഫീസിൽ നിന്ന് രാത്രിയിലെ വൈകിയ വേളകളിൽ ഇറങ്ങി ഒറ്റയ്ക്ക് നടക്കരുത്. പലപ്പോഴും പല നേരങ്ങളിൽ നിങ്ങൾ താമസസ്ഥലത്തേക്കു പോകുന്നതു ഞാൻ കണ്ടിട്ടുണ്ട്. പത്തുമണി കഴിഞ്ഞാൽ അങ്ങനെ ഒറ്റയ്ക്ക് നടക്കരുത്. ആപ്പീസിൽത്തന്നെ കിടന്ന് ഉറങ്ങിയാലും വേണ്ടില്ല, അങ്ങനെ വരാൻ വൈകുന്ന ദിവസങ്ങളിൽ. ഈ സാഹചര്യങ്ങളിൽ നിങ്ങളെ രാഷ്ട്രീയ ക്കാരണങ്ങളാൽ അറസ്റ്റു ചെയ്തു തടവിൽ വച്ചാൽപ്പോലും എന്റെ സുഹൃത്തും ഞാനും സന്തോഷിക്കും. കാരണം അവിടെ നിങ്ങളുടെ ജീവൻ സുരക്ഷിതമായിരിക്കും.

ഏതായാലും ഈ കത്ത് എഴുതുന്നതിന്റെ താൽപ്പര്യം മനസിലാക്കുമെന്ന് വിശ്വസിക്കുന്നു. ഇതിൽ പറഞ്ഞിരിക്കുന്ന കാര്യങ്ങൾ ശ്രദ്ധിക്കണമെന്ന് അഭ്യർഥിക്കുന്നു— എന്ന് നിങ്ങളുടെ അജ്ഞാതരായ രണ്ടു സുഹൃത്തുക്കൾ, ആരാധകർ."

വിചിത്രമായി തോന്നി. പക്ഷേ, സത്യമാവാം. ഇതിൽ ആത്മാർഥതയുടെ സ്വരമുണ്ട്. വെറുതെ ഒരു കത്തെഴുതി ആവശ്യമില്ലാത്ത ഭീതി

ജനിപ്പിക്കാൻ ആരും മെനക്കെടുകയില്ല. ഇതിൽ സത്യമുണ്ട്. സദനത്തെക്കുറിച്ച് അപവാദങ്ങൾ പറയുന്നവരുണ്ട്. താൻ അവിടെ പോകുന്നത് ഇഷ്ടമില്ലാത്തവരുമുണ്ട്. പത്രത്തോടും പലർക്കും എതിർപ്പുണ്ട്. രാഷ്ട്രീയമായി തന്നോട് നീരസമുള്ളവരും ഉണ്ട്. ഇത്രയും ഗൗരവം അതേക്കുറിച്ച് ഇതുവരെ തോന്നിയിട്ടില്ല.

കുളിച്ചു വേഷം മാറി പുറത്തിറങ്ങി സദനത്തിലേക്കു ചെന്നു. ഭാനുമതിയുടെ കത്തിനെപ്പറ്റി യോഗമയീദേവിയോട് സംസാരിച്ചു. ഭാനുമതിക്ക് കത്തെഴുതിയിട്ടുണ്ട്. രാവിലെ തപാലിലിട്ടു കഴിഞ്ഞു. സന്ധ്യാദേവിക്ക് കമ്പിയടിക്കാൻ പോകുകയാണ്. സദനത്തിൽ കാര്യങ്ങൾ നല്ല കരുതലോടെ ചെയ്യണമെന്ന് ഒരിക്കൽക്കൂടി അറിയിച്ചു. വാസവമേനോനെ സംബന്ധിച്ച കാര്യങ്ങൾ സദനത്തിലുള്ളവരെ വ്യാകുലപ്പെടുത്തി.

ഉച്ചയ്ക്കു മുൻപ് ഒരു കമ്പി വന്നു, തുറന്നു നോക്കി.

“മീറ്റ് ക്രാംഗനൂർ റ്റ്വൽത്ത് മേനോൻ”

വാസവമേനോന്റെ കമ്പിയാണ്.

* * * * * *

ആറ്റുതീരത്തെ ആ കൊച്ചുവീട്ടിൽ വാസവമേനോൻ ഇരിക്കുന്നു. അരവിന്ദനും മറ്റു രണ്ടുപേരും ചുറ്റും ഇരിപ്പുണ്ട്. വാസവമേനോൻ ഒരു ആശയം അരവിന്ദന്റെ മുമ്പിൽ അവതരിപ്പിച്ചിട്ടുണ്ട്. സദനത്തിലുള്ളവരും വനിതാസമാജത്തിലുള്ളവരും അരവിന്ദൻ തന്നെയും താനുമായി പ്രത്യേകിച്ചൊരു ബന്ധവുമില്ലെന്ന് പൊലീസിനോടു പറയുക. അതിൽ വ്യക്തിപരമായ വികാരത്തിന് സ്ഥാനമില്ല. ഇത് സർക്കാരും അതിനെതിരായി പ്രവർത്തിക്കുന്ന ദേശീയവാദികളും തമ്മിലുള്ള സമരമാണ്. അതിൽ പിടികൊടുക്കാതിരിക്കാനുള്ള എല്ലാ അടവുകളും പ്രയോഗിക്കണം. “ബന്ധമുണ്ടെന്ന്, പറഞ്ഞിട്ട് എന്തു നേടാനാണ്? അദ്ദേഹം ചോദിച്ചു. മറിച്ച് അതു നിഷേധിച്ചാൽ കൂടുതൽ പ്രയോജനമുണ്ട്. ഒന്നാമത് അവർക്കെല്ലാം സ്വതന്ത്രമായി എന്തെങ്കിലും പ്രവർത്തിക്കാം. രണ്ടാമത്, അങ്ങനെ നിന്നുകൊണ്ട് ആവശ്യം വരുന്ന സന്ദർഭത്തിൽ മേനോന് വിവരങ്ങൾ എത്തിച്ചുകൊടുക്കുക തുടങ്ങിയ സഹായങ്ങൾ ചെയ്യാം. എന്തുകൊണ്ടും അതാണു നല്ലത്.”

അതുയുക്തിയാണ്. പക്ഷേ, ബന്ധമില്ലെന്നു എഴുതികൊടുക്കേണ്ടി വരും. എന്നാലെന്ത്? അതിലും തെറ്റില്ല. അരവിന്ദൻ ആ വാദഗതിയോട് യോജിച്ചു.

മധുരയിൽ പണിമുടക്കത്തെത്തുടർന്ന് ചില സംഭവ വികാസങ്ങൾ ഉണ്ടായിട്ടുണ്ട്. പോലീസും ഗുണ്ടകളും ചേർന്ന് കയ്യേറ്റവും തീവയ്പും എല്ലാം നടത്തി. കേസുകൾ തൊഴിലാളി പ്രവർത്തകരുടെയും തൊഴിലാളികളുടെയും പേരിലാണ് ഒന്നുരണ്ടു കൊലപാതകങ്ങൾ നടന്നിട്ടുണ്ട്. ഒന്നാംപ്രതി മേനോനാണ്.

ഇപ്പോൾ അപരിചിതരായ രണ്ടുമൂന്നുപേർ കൂടെയുള്ളത് മധുരയിലെ

സഹപ്രവർത്തകരാണ്. തൽക്കാലം അവരെ കുറെ ദിവസത്തേക്ക് ഇവിടെ പാർപ്പിക്കാൻ ഉദ്ദേശിക്കുന്നു. അരവിന്ദനെ എല്ലാക്കാര്യങ്ങളും പറഞ്ഞു മനസിലാക്കിക്കൊടുക്കാനാണ് വിളിപ്പിച്ചത്.

മറ്റുള്ളവർ ഉറങ്ങാൻ കിടന്നു. അതിനുശേഷം വാസവമേനോൻ പറഞ്ഞു:

"ഞാൻ ഒരുകടുംകൈ ചെയ്തിട്ടുണ്ട്. അതു അരവിന്ദനെക്കൂടി അറിയിക്കണമെന്നും ഈ വരവിൽ ഉദ്ദേശ്യമുണ്ട്."

അരവിന്ദൻ സംശയിച്ചു നോക്കി.

"എന്താണാവോ, അത്?"

അദ്ദേഹം ചിരിച്ചു.

"ഞാൻ ഒരു ലഘുഗ്രന്ഥം തയാറാക്കിയിരിക്കുന്നു."

അരവിന്ദനും ചിരിച്ചു.

"അതാണോ കടുംകൈ? ഗവേഷകരും പ്രൊഫസറുമായിരുന്ന ഒരാൾക്ക്, ഗ്രന്ഥം രചിക്കാൻ കഴിയില്ലേ? ഞാൻ അത്ഭുതപ്പെടുന്നില്ല."

"അതെ അങ്ങനെ തോന്നും. എന്റെ ആശയങ്ങളും അവതരിപ്പിക്കുന്ന രീതിയും ചിലപ്പോൾ വിചിത്രമായിരിക്കും. നിങ്ങളുടെ അഭിപ്രായം അറിയുകയും ചെയ്യാല്ലോ."

വാസവമേനോൻ തന്റെ സഞ്ചിയിൽനിന്ന് ഒരു നോട്ടുബുക്ക് എടുത്ത് വിളക്കിരുന്ന സ്റ്റൂൾ കുറച്ചുകൂടി അടുപ്പിച്ചിട്ട് ബുക്കു തുറന്നു.

"പുരുഷാർഥം, അൽപ്പം പുതിയ ചിന്തകൾ എന്നാണ് ഇതിന് പേരിട്ടിരിക്കുന്നത്. ആ പേരുകൊണ്ട് വ്യക്തമാകുന്നതുതന്നെ, ഉള്ളടക്കവും തുടക്കവും ഒന്നു വായിക്കാം."

അദ്ദേഹം ആദ്യഭാഗം വായിച്ചു.

"ഭഗവത്ഗീതയിൽ സത്വം, രജസ്സ്, തമസ്സ് എന്ന മൂന്ന് ഗുണങ്ങളെപ്പറ്റി പറയുന്നുണ്ട്. ഓരോ മനുഷ്യനും ചെയ്യുന്ന കർമമാണ് ഈ ഗുണങ്ങൾക്ക് അടിസ്ഥാനം. ഉദ്ധവരുമായി സംഭാഷണം നടത്തുമ്പോൾ ശ്രീകൃഷ്ണൻ ഇത് വിശദീകരിക്കുന്നുണ്ട്. സ്വാർഥം കൂടാതെ സ്വന്തം കർത്തവ്യം ചെയ്യുന്നവൻ സാത്വികൻ. സ്വന്തം ആഗ്രഹങ്ങൾക്കുവേണ്ടി, സ്വത്തിനും അനുഗ്രഹങ്ങൾക്കും വേണ്ടി പ്രവൃത്തി ചെയ്യുന്നവൻ രജോഗുണമുള്ളവൻ. മറ്റുള്ളവർക്ക് ദ്രോഹം ചെയ്യാൻവേണ്ടി പ്രവർത്തിക്കുന്നവൻ തമോഗുണമുള്ളവൻ. അപ്പോൾ കർമം മനുഷ്യന്റെ അടിസ്ഥാന മനോഭാവങ്ങളെ നിർണയിക്കുന്നു. നിസ്വാർഥമായ കർമം മനുഷ്യനെ ശ്രേഷ്ഠനാക്കുന്നു. ധർമവും അർഥവും കാമവും മോക്ഷവും പുരുഷാർഥങ്ങളാണ്. എന്നാൽ ഈ അർഥങ്ങൾക്കും അടിസ്ഥാനകാരണമായ കർമമാണ് ഏറ്റവും പ്രധാനമായ പുരുഷാർഥം."

മേനോൻ ചോദിച്ചു. "എന്താ യോജിക്കുന്നോ?"

"യോജിക്കുന്നു." അരവിന്ദൻ മറുപടി പറഞ്ഞു.

വീണ്ടും വായിച്ചു.

"മറ്റു മനുഷ്യർക്ക് പ്രയോജനകരമായ കർമം ചെയ്യുന്നവനാണ്

സാത്വികൻ. ജനനവും മരണവും സ്വന്തം കർമങ്ങളല്ല. ജീവിതമാണ് സ്വകീയമായ ധർമങ്ങൾക്ക് ആധാരവസ്തു. അവിടെ മനുഷ്യൻ തനിക്കുവേണ്ടി പ്രവർത്തിക്കുന്നോ എന്നാലോചിക്കണം. രണ്ടിലൊന്നു തെരഞ്ഞെടുക്കണം. മറ്റുള്ളവർക്കുവേണ്ടി തെരഞ്ഞെടുക്കാൻ തീരുമാനിച്ചാൽ. ആത്മാർഥമായി അതു സ്വീകരിച്ചാൽ ജീവിതത്തിന് ഏറ്റവും മഹത്തായ അർഥം കിട്ടുന്നു. അതാണ് ഗീത പറയുന്നത്. രാഷ്ട്രീയ പ്രവർത്തകർക്കു വേണ്ടത് യഥാർഥമായ സാത്വിക ചേതനയാണ്."

അരവിന്ദൻ മൗനം പൂണ്ടിരുന്നു.

"എന്താ പറയൂ." മേനോൻ അഭിപ്രായമാരാഞ്ഞു.

"ഈ പഴയ ശൈലി എനിക്ക് ഇഷ്ടപ്പെട്ടില്ല. മാസ്റ്ററെ."

"ശരി എനിക്കതറിയാം. എന്നാൽ അടുത്ത ഭാഗം കേട്ടോളൂ." അദ്ദേഹം ബുക്കിൽ നോക്കി തുടർന്നു വായിച്ചു:

"ജീവിതത്തെ അഭിമുഖീകരിക്കുക എന്നൊരു ചൊല്ലുണ്ട്. കൺഫ്രണ്ടേഷൻ. ചെറുപ്പക്കാരോടാണ് എനിക്കു സംസാരിക്കാനുള്ളത്. നിങ്ങൾക്ക് അഭിമുഖീകരിക്കാനുള്ളത് നിലവിലുള്ള യാഥാസ്ഥിതിക സ്ഥാപനങ്ങളെയാണോ? ആണെന്നു നിങ്ങൾ പറയുന്നു. വിദ്യാഭ്യാസത്തിലും മതത്തിലുമുള്ള പഴയ വിഗ്രഹങ്ങളെയാണോ? ആണെന്നു നിങ്ങൾ പറയുന്നു. അല്ല. ആലോചിച്ചു നോക്കൂ. നിങ്ങളെത്തന്നെയാണ് നിങ്ങളുടെ സ്വഭാവത്തെയാണ്. നിങ്ങൾക്ക് അയഥാർഥങ്ങളായ ആഗ്രഹങ്ങൾ വരാറില്ലേ? തെറ്റായ ധാരണകൾ ഉണ്ടാവാറില്ലേ? നിങ്ങൾക്ക് നിരാശബാധിക്കാറില്ലേ? നിങ്ങൾ അനിശ്ചിതത്വത്തിൽപ്പെടാറില്ലേ? നിങ്ങൾ ദുർബലതകൾക്ക് വശംവദരാകാറില്ലേ? ആ സന്ദർഭങ്ങളിൽ നിങ്ങൾ എന്തു ചെയ്യുന്നു? നിങ്ങൾ വഴങ്ങുന്നു. നിങ്ങൾ അവയെ അഭിമുഖീകരിക്കുന്നില്ല. എന്നുവച്ചാൽ, നിങ്ങൾ നിങ്ങളെ അഭിമുഖീകരിക്കാൻ തയാറല്ല. അങ്ങനെ തയാറല്ലെങ്കിൽ എങ്ങനെ നിങ്ങൾക്കു ജീവിതത്തിന് ഒരർഥം കൊടുക്കാൻ കഴിയും? അങ്ങനെ ഒരർഥം കൊടുക്കാൻ കഴിഞ്ഞില്ലെങ്കിൽ ക്രിയാത്മകമായി പ്രവർത്തിക്കാൻ ജീവിതത്തിൽ എന്തെങ്കിലുമായിത്തീരാൻ എങ്ങനെ കഴിയും? അപ്പോൾ കർമമെന്ന പുരുഷാർഥത്തിന്റെ മഹത്വത്തെപ്പറ്റി പറഞ്ഞതുകൊണ്ടായില്ല. നിങ്ങളെ അഭിമുഖീകരിക്കാൻ കഴിഞ്ഞെങ്കിലേ, നിങ്ങൾക്കു മറ്റുള്ളവരെ ഫലപ്രദമായി അഭിമുഖീകരിക്കാൻ സാധിക്കൂ. ഏറ്റവും വലിയ കൺഫ്രണ്ടേഷൻ അതാണ്. അങ്ങനെ സ്വയം വിമർശനം ചെയ്യാൻ കഴിയാത്ത രാഷ്ട്രീയ പ്രവർത്തകന് ശരിയായ കർമാനുഷ്ഠാനം സാധ്യമല്ല."

അരവിന്ദന് തൃപ്തിയായി.

"ശൈലി മാറി. പക്ഷേ, ആശയമോ?"

"ശൈലിയും ആശയവും ഞാൻ അംഗീകരിക്കുന്നു."

"എന്നാൽ ഇത് മുഴുവനും ഞാൻ വായിച്ചു കേൾപ്പിക്കുന്നില്ല. ഈ ആശയം സ്ഥാപിക്കാൻ വേണ്ടിയാണ്. ഈ ഗ്രന്ഥം, ഇതിന്റെ ഇംഗ്ലീഷ് പതിപ്പ് വിശ്വഭാരതി ക്വാർട്ടർലിയിലേക്ക് അവരുടെ ആവശ്യപ്രകാരം

ഞാൻ അയച്ചിട്ടുണ്ട്. ഇത്, ഇവിടെ പ്രസിദ്ധീകരിക്കാമെന്ന് കരുതുന്നു. അരവിന്ദൻ ഇത് ഒന്നു വായിക്കണം. സ്വീകാര്യമല്ലാത്ത ഭാഗങ്ങൾ നോട്ടു ചെയ്യണം."

"ശരി മാസ്റ്റർ."

അദ്ദേഹം പുസ്തകം താഴെവച്ചു.

മേനോൻ ക്ഷീണിച്ചിരിക്കുന്നു. അരവിന്ദന് കണ്ടപ്പോൾത്തന്നെ അത് തോന്നി. ഉറക്കവും ഊണും വിശ്രമവുമില്ലാത്ത മനുഷ്യൻ. ഇദ്ദേഹം ഏകാകിയെപ്പോലെ നടക്കുന്നുവെന്നു പലപ്പോഴും വിചാരിച്ചുപോയിട്ടുണ്ട്. സത്യത്തിൽ അങ്ങനെയല്ല. ദേശീയ പ്രസ്ഥാനത്തിലെ തീവ്രവാദികളായ കുറെപ്പേരുടെ കൂടെയാണ് അദ്ദേഹം. പല നേതാക്കളെയും കണ്ടിട്ടുണ്ട്. ഇദ്ദേഹം അവരിൽ നിന്നെല്ലാം വ്യത്യസ്തനാണ്. ശാന്തിനികേതനിൽ നിന്നു കിട്ടാവുന്ന ഒരു ആത്മീയഭാവം അദ്ദേഹത്തിന്റെ സംസാരത്തിലും പെരുമാറ്റത്തിലും കാണാം. അതേസമയം ഒരിക്കലും അവിടെ പൊരുത്തപ്പെടാത്ത തീവ്രങ്ങളായ ആശയങ്ങൾകൊണ്ടു നടക്കുന്നു. ആ ആശയങ്ങളാണ് അദ്ദേഹത്തിന്റെ പ്രവർത്തനത്തിന് ശൈലി പകരുന്നത്. ഒരിക്കൽപ്പോലും നിരാശനായി കണ്ടിട്ടില്ല. മഹാത്മജിക്ക് അദ്ദേഹത്തെ വലിയ ഇഷ്ടമായിരുന്നു. മേനോന്റെ ഒരു ഡയറിയിൽ ഇങ്ങനെ കുറിച്ചിരിക്കുന്നു. "യു കാൻ ഫേസ് എ ഹൊളാകാസ്റ്റ് വിത് എ സ്മൈൽ; ഇറ്റ് ഈസ് പ്യൂവർ മെറ്റൽ, ആൻഡ് സ്ട്രോങ്ങ് എന്തൊരു വലിയ സർട്ടിഫിക്കറ്റ്! ഏതോ ദേശീയ നേതാവ് കുറിച്ചതാണ്."

വ്യക്തിപരമായി പലതും ചോദിക്കണമെന്നു ആഗ്രഹിച്ചിട്ടുണ്ട്. സന്ദർഭം കിട്ടിയിട്ടില്ല. ഇപ്പോൾ അങ്ങനെയൊരു സംഭാഷണം ആരംഭിക്കാമെന്നു കരുതി. അപ്പോൾ അദ്ദേഹം പറഞ്ഞു.

"കഴിഞ്ഞ ഒരു ദിവസം ഞാൻ അരവിന്ദനോട് ഒരുകാര്യം സൂചിപ്പിച്ചു. സന്ധ്യാദേവിയുടെ കാര്യം നിങ്ങൾ വിവാഹം കഴിക്കുന്നത് എനിക്ക് സന്തോഷമാണ്."

"എനിക്കും അതു തോന്നിയിട്ടുണ്ട്. മാസ്റ്റർ.." അരവിന്ദൻ അതു സമ്മതിച്ചു. നിശ്ശബ്ദനായിരുന്നശേഷം ആലോചനയിൽനിന്നും ഉണർന്ന് മേനോൻ പറഞ്ഞു. "ഞാൻ എന്റെ അനുഭവം പറയാം. ആരോടും ഞാൻ പറഞ്ഞിട്ടില്ല. നിങ്ങൾ കേൾക്കുന്നത് നല്ലതാണ്. യോഗമയീദേവിയും ഞാനും തമ്മിലുള്ള ബന്ധം അറിയാമോ?"

അരവിന്ദൻ അദ്ദേഹത്തെ സൂക്ഷിച്ചുനോക്കി.

"അറിയില്ല."

അദ്ദേഹം പുഞ്ചിരിച്ചു. അതിൽ ഓർമയുടെ അസ്വസ്ഥമായ ഒരു ഛായ നിഴലിച്ചിരുന്നു.

"ഞങ്ങൾ സ്നേഹബദ്ധരായിരുന്നു. ഇന്ന് നിങ്ങൾക്ക് അതു വിശ്വസിക്കാൻ പോലും കഴിഞ്ഞെന്നുവരില്ല. പക്ഷേ, അങ്ങനെയായിരുന്നു. ഞാൻ ലക്നൗവിൽ എം എ യ്ക്കു പഠിക്കുമ്പോൾ അവർ ബി എ ജൂനിയർ വിദ്യാർഥിനിയാണ്. ഞങ്ങൾ അടുത്തു. അടുപ്പം സ്നേഹമായി. ഞാൻ

അന്നുതന്നെ മഹാത്മജിയുടെ തത്വങ്ങളിൽ വിശ്വസിച്ചിരുന്നു. അവരും ഗാന്ധിജിയുടെയും നെഹ്റുവിന്റെയും മറ്റും ആരാധികയായിരുന്നു. ഞാൻ ജയിച്ച് വിശ്വഭാരതിയിലേക്കു പോയി. ഞങ്ങൾ ഇടയ്ക്കു കാണും. കത്തെഴുതും. അവർ എം എ ജയിച്ച് ബനാറാസിൽ ജോലിയിൽ പ്രവേശിച്ചു. ഞാൻ പ്രൊഫസറും സജീവരാഷ്ട്രീയ പ്രവർത്തകനുമായി. അവരും സൗകര്യം കിട്ടുമ്പോഴെല്ലാം ദേശീയ പ്രസ്ഥാനത്തോടു സഹകരിച്ചു."

"ഞാൻ ആയിടയ്ക്ക് രണ്ടുതവണ ജയിലിൽ പോവുകയും പുറത്തു വരികയും ചെയ്തു. അതോടെ കൂടുതൽ രാഷ്ട്രീയത്തിൽ മുഴുകി. വാർധായിലേക്ക് പോയി. യോഗമയീദേവിയും ഞാനും വല്ലപ്പോഴും കാണുന്ന അവസ്ഥയിലായി. എന്നാലും കത്തെഴുതും. എനിക്കു മഹാത്മജിയുടെ സംഘത്തിൽ നിന്ന് വിട്ടുപിരിയാൻ സാധിച്ചില്ല. മറ്റെല്ലാം മറന്നതുപോലെയായി. യോഗമയീയോടുള്ള സ്നേഹം മനസിൽ സൂക്ഷിച്ചു. ഒരു കാലത്ത് വിവാഹം കഴിക്കാമെന്നായി ഞങ്ങളുടെ കത്തുകളിലെ ഉള്ളടക്കം. ഒരിക്കൽ ഒരു അഭിവന്ദ്യനായ ദേശീയ നേതാവ് എന്നോട് പറഞ്ഞു. "മിസ്റ്റർ മേനോൻ, രാഷ്ട്രീയപ്രവർത്തകന് വിവാഹം ബുദ്ധിമുട്ടാണ്. മഹാത്മജിയും പണ്ഡിറ്റ്ജിയും ഭാഗ്യവാന്മാരാണ്. അങ്ങനെയുള്ള സഹധർമിണികളെ അവർക്ക് കിട്ടി. പിന്നെ രാഷ്ട്രീയപ്രവർത്തകന്റെ ജീവൻ എപ്പോഴും അപകടത്തിലല്ലേ? ഒരുപാവപ്പെട്ട സ്ത്രീയെക്കൂടി അയാൾ എന്തിന് വലയ്ക്കുന്നു? അത് ശരിയാണെന്ന് എനിക്കു തോന്നി. ഞാൻ യോഗമയീദേവിയെ കണ്ടപ്പോൾ ഇത് സംസാരിച്ചു. എന്തും സഹിക്കാൻ അവർ സന്നദ്ധയായിരുന്നു. പക്ഷേ, ഞാൻ ദിവസംചെല്ലുന്തോറും അധീരനായി.

വർഷങ്ങൾ പോയി. ഞങ്ങൾ പിന്നീട് കണ്ടപ്പോൾ യോഗമയീദേവി പറഞ്ഞു. "അങ്ങ് പ്രവർത്തിക്കുക. ഞാൻ സന്തുഷ്ടയാണ്. എന്നും വിവാഹം കഴിക്കാത്ത കാമുകീകാമുകന്മാരായി നമുക്ക് കഴിയാം." എന്തൊരു ധീരതയാണ് അവരെക്കൊണ്ട് ആ തീരുമാനമെടുപ്പിച്ചതെന്ന് എനിക്കറിയില്ല. അത് തീരുമാനമായിരുന്നു. വീണ്ടും വരുമെന്ന് പറഞ്ഞ് ഞാൻ പോന്നു.വാർധായിലെത്തി അധികം കഴിയും മുമ്പ് പൊലീസിന്റെ കൈയിലായി. ഏഴെട്ടുമാസം അവിടെ കഴിയേണ്ടിവന്നു.

ഒരു ദിവസം യോഗമയീദേവി ജയിലിൽ വന്നു. വെളുത്ത വസ്ത്രം, കഴുത്തിൽ ഒരു രുദ്രാക്ഷമാല. അവർ പറഞ്ഞു: "ഞാൻ ഇപ്പോൾ കാശിയിലെ ഒരാശ്രമത്തിലാണ്. ദേശീയപ്രസ്ഥാനക്കാരായ സന്യാസിമാരും സന്യാസിനിമാരുമാണ് അവിടെ ഉള്ളത്. നമ്മൾ രണ്ടുപേരും പൂർണമായും ഒരിടത്തെത്തിയിരിക്കുന്നു."

പിന്നെ ഞങ്ങൾ ഒരുമിച്ചു പ്രവർത്തിച്ചിട്ടുണ്ട്. വർഷങ്ങളായി കാണാതിരുന്നിട്ടുണ്ട്. കണ്ടുമുട്ടുമ്പോൾ പഴയതുപോലെ ആശയവിനിമയം ചെയ്യാറുണ്ട്. പക്ഷേ, ഞങ്ങൾ വ്യക്തിജീവിതത്തിൽ സന്യാസിനിയുമായിപ്പോയി.

"ഞാൻ എന്തിന് ഈ കഥ പറഞ്ഞു? മനസിലായോ കാലം കടന്നുപോകുമ്പോൾ ആശയങ്ങൾ മാറി. ഒരു വിവാഹത്തെപ്പറ്റി ആലോചിക്കേണ്ടെന്ന് തോന്നിപ്പോകാം. ഏതായാലും അരവിന്ദൻ ആലോചിക്കൂ. യുക്ത

മെന്നു തോന്നുംപോലെ പ്രവർത്തിക്കൂ."

നാനാചിന്തകളായിരുന്നു മനസിൽ. കഴിഞ്ഞകാലത്തെപ്പറ്റിയുള്ള ഒരു വിഷാദം മേനോന്റെ ശബ്ദത്തിൽ അയാൾക്ക് അനുഭവപ്പെട്ടു. അത് സ്വാഭാവികമാണ്. അദ്ദേഹം മനുഷ്യവികാരങ്ങളുടെ ഒന്നാംതരം പ്രതീകമാണ്.

അരവിന്ദൻ ഒന്നും പറഞ്ഞില്ല. പെട്ടെന്ന് തീരുമാനം ചെയ്യാൻ പ്രയാസമാണെന്ന് മേനോനും അറിയാം.

"ഇത് നമ്മെ പരീക്ഷിക്കുന്ന ഘട്ടങ്ങളിലൊന്നാണ്." മേനോൻ പറഞ്ഞു. "നമ്മെ മാത്രം ബാധിക്കുന്ന കാര്യമല്ല മറ്റൊരാളെക്കൂടി നേരിട്ടു ബാധിക്കുന്നു. അതോടൊപ്പം വിശ്വസിച്ചുപോന്ന തത്വങ്ങളും പ്രസ്ഥാനവും എല്ലാം അതിൽ കടന്നുവരുന്നു. സ്നേഹത്തിനുവേണ്ടി പ്രസ്ഥാനത്തെയോ പ്രസ്ഥാനത്തിനുവേണ്ടി സ്നേഹത്തെയോ ബലികഴിക്കാൻ നാം ഇഷ്ടപ്പെടുന്നില്ല. രണ്ടും തെറ്റാണ്. പക്ഷേ, ഏതെങ്കിലും ഒന്നിൽ ചെന്നെത്തുകയെന്നതാണ് പലപ്പോഴും സംഭവിക്കുക. അതിന്റെ മാനസികത്തകർച്ച ചെറുതല്ല."

മേനോൻ രാത്രിയിൽത്തന്നെ സ്ഥലത്തുനിന്നും പോവുകയാണ്. വള്ളം ഏർപ്പാടു ചെയ്തിട്ടുണ്ട്. ആ വിഷയം തൽക്കാലം അവർ അങ്ങനെ ഉപസംഹരിച്ചു. അദ്ദേഹം യാത്രയ്ക്ക് ഒരുക്കം ചെയ്ത് അരവിന്ദനുമായി കടവിലേക്കു നടന്നു.

* * *

രാത്രി നല്ല ഇരുട്ടുണ്ട്. സദനം ഉറക്കത്തിലേക്ക് പ്രവേശിച്ചിരിക്കുന്നു.

പൊടുന്നനെ, പുരമുകളിൽ ഒരു വലിയ കല്ലു വന്നു വീണു. യോഗമയീദേവി ശബ്ദംകേട്ടു ഞെട്ടി ഉണർന്നു.

"എന്താ ആ കേട്ടത്?" അവർ ആരോടെന്നില്ലാതെ ചോദിച്ചു. അടുത്ത് താഴെ കിടക്കുന്നത് സുമതിയും അംബികത്തമ്പുരാട്ടിയുമാണ്.

അൽപ്പസമയം വീണ്ടും അതുപോലൊരു ശബ്ദം.

അവർ എഴുന്നേറ്റു ചെവിയോർത്തിരുന്നു. പിന്നെ വിളിച്ചു:

"അംബികേ, സുമതി!"

അംബികത്തമ്പുരാട്ടി ഉണർന്നു. പുറകെ സുമതിയും.

"എന്താ വിളിച്ചത്?"

"എന്തോ പുരപ്പുറത്തു വീഴുന്നതു കേട്ടു. രണ്ടുതവണയായി." അവർ പറഞ്ഞു.

അതു പറഞ്ഞു നിർത്തുംമുമ്പ് മൂന്നാമതും ശബ്ദം.

അവർ എഴുന്നേറ്റ് വിളക്കു കൊളുത്തി. തമ്പുരാട്ടിയും സുമതിയും എഴുന്നേറ്റു.

നിമിഷങ്ങൾക്കൊണ്ട് പുരമുകളിൽ തുരുതുരാ കല്ലുകൾവന്നുവീഴാൻ തുടങ്ങി. നിറുത്താത്ത ശബ്ദം. മഴപെയ്യുംപോലെ കീർത്തി ഉണർന്ന് ഓടി വന്നു. റീനയും പാർവതിയും ഉഷയും ഭയന്നുവിറച്ചു, ഓടിയെത്തി.

അപ്പോഴും കല്ലുകൾ വന്നുവീഴുകയാണ്.

അവരെല്ലാം വെറങ്ങലിച്ച് ശ്വാസമടക്കിപ്പിടിച്ച് ആ മുറിയിൽ നിന്നു. എന്തുചെയ്യണമെന്ന് അറിഞ്ഞുകൂടാ.

"ആരോ. കരുതിക്കൂട്ടി ചെയ്യുകയാണ്." കീർത്തി പറഞ്ഞു. അവളുടെ ചുണ്ടുകൾ വിറയ്ക്കുന്നുണ്ട്. എല്ലാവരും സ്തംഭിച്ചുനിന്നു.

അനവധി ആളുകൾ ചേർന്ന് കല്ലെറിയുന്നു.

ചെവി അടഞ്ഞുപോകുമ്പോലെ. ഒരു ആക്രമണത്തിന്റെ രീതിയാണ്. തൽക്കാലം ആരും തുണയ്ക്കില്ല. കുറച്ചുകഴിയുമ്പോൾ കല്ലേറു നിൽക്കും. അവർ പോയിക്കൊള്ളും എന്ന് സമാധാനിച്ചു.

പക്ഷേ, കല്ലേറ് നിൽക്കുംമുമ്പ്, ഗേറ്റിൽ ശബ്ദം. അട്ടഹാസം, ഗേറ്റ് പൂട്ടിയിട്ടുണ്ട്. അതിൽ ആഞ്ഞടിക്കുകയും പിടിച്ച് ഊക്കോടെ കുലുക്കുകയും ചെയ്യുന്നു. ഇടയ്ക്ക് കല്ലേറ്. ആരോ ഗേറ്റ് ചാടിക്കടന്നു. പെട്ടെന്ന്, സദനത്തിന്റെ വാതിലിൽ ശക്തിയായി മുട്ടുന്ന ശബ്ദം.

കീർത്തിയും റീനയും പൊട്ടിക്കരഞ്ഞു. അവർ യോഗമയീദേവിയെ കെട്ടിപ്പിടിച്ചു. അംബികത്തമ്പുരാട്ടി വിറയ്ക്കുന്ന കൈകളോടെ റീനയെ പിടിച്ചു. പാർവതി കീർത്തിയേയും, ഉഷയും കരയുകയാണ്.

വഴിയിൽ പുലഭ്യങ്ങൾ വിളിച്ചു പറയുന്നു. വാതിലിൽ മുട്ടുന്നു.

"തുറക്കെടീ, തുറക്കെടീ.. കളെ!" ഒരുത്തൻ വിളിച്ചു പറയുന്നു.

കുറേനേരം വാതിലിൽ മുട്ടി ആരോ വടികൊണ്ട് അതിൽ അടിച്ചു. പെട്ടെന്ന് യോഗമയിയും സുമതിയും തമ്പുരാട്ടിയും അങ്ങോട്ടോടി. വാതിൽ അകത്തുനിന്നും ശക്തിയായി തള്ളിപ്പിടിച്ചു. സ്വീകരണമുറിയിൽ കിടന്ന മേശപിടിച്ച് വാതിലിനോട് ചേർത്തിട്ടു.

വഴിയിൽ ആളുകൾ ഓടുന്ന ശബ്ദം. എന്തോ ഒക്കെ വിളിച്ചു പറയുന്നു. ശബ്ദം നിലയ്ക്കുന്നു. വാതിലിലെ മുട്ടൽ നിന്നു. തിണ്ണയിൽനിന്നും. മുറ്റത്തേക്കു രണ്ടുപേർ ചാടി ഓടുന്നു. എല്ലാ ശബ്ദവും അൽപ്പനേരം കൊണ്ടു നിലയ്ക്കുന്നു.

യോഗമയീദേവി മേശപ്പുറത്തേക്കു കയറി. വാതിലിനു മീതെയുള്ള ചില്ലുപൊക്കി. പുറത്തേക്കു നോക്കി അവർ പറഞ്ഞു:

"എല്ലാവരും പോയി."

കീഴേ നിന്നവർക്ക് ആശ്വാസം തോന്നി.

വഴിവിളക്കിന്റെ വെളിച്ചത്തിൽ ഗേറ്റിനുപുറത്ത് ഒരു ഇൻസ്പെക്ടറും പൊലീസുകാരും നിൽക്കുന്നു. മേശ മാറ്റി യോഗമയീദേവി വാതിൽ തുറന്നു. വിളക്കു കൊണ്ടുവന്നു. അവർ ഗേറ്റിലേക്ക് നടന്നു.

"എന്റെ സാറെ, ഞങ്ങളെ ഇവിടെ കിടത്തുകയില്ലെന്നായല്ലോ." അവരുടെ കണ്ഠം ഇടറുന്നുണ്ടായിരുന്നു.

"സാരമില്ല ഞങ്ങൾ നോക്കിക്കൊള്ളാം. നിങ്ങൾ പോയികിടന്നോളൂ." ഇൻസ്പെക്ടർ പറഞ്ഞു.

സമാധാനമായി അവർ തിരിച്ചു നടക്കുമ്പോൾ ഇൻസ്പെക്ടർ പൊലീസുകാർക്ക് നിർദേശം നൽകുന്നു.

"വെളുക്കുംവരെ നിങ്ങൾ രണ്ടുപേർ ഈ പ്രദേശത്ത് ബീറ്റു ചെയ്യണം."

പിറ്റേന്ന് സദനം മൂകമായി കഴിഞ്ഞുകൂടി. രാത്രിയെപ്പറ്റി അവർ ഭയപ്പെട്ടു. ഉച്ചയ്ക്കുമുമ്പ് യോഗമയീദേവി പുറത്തേക്കുപോയി. അവർ സ്ഥലത്തെ ചില നേതാക്കന്മാരെ കണ്ടു തലേന്നത്തെ സംഭവം പറഞ്ഞു. ആ സന്ദർഭത്തിൽ രക്ഷപ്പെടുത്തിയതു പൊലീസാണ്. പക്ഷേ, അവരെ നമ്പാൻ നിവൃത്തിയില്ല. കാരണം, സദനം ഭരണകൂടത്തിന് എതിരായ സ്ഥാപനമെന്ന് മുദ്രയടിക്കപ്പെട്ടിട്ടുണ്ട്. അവിടെ ബന്ധപ്പെട്ടിട്ടുള്ളവരെല്ലാം രാഷ്ട്രീയമായി, ഭരിക്കുന്നവരുടെ പ്രതിയോഗികളാണ്. സൗകര്യം കിട്ടുമ്പോൾ അതിനെ ഞെരുക്കുകയും അതിന്റെ പ്രവർത്തനം സ്തംഭിപ്പിക്കുകയും ചെയ്യാനാണ് പൊലീസിന് സർക്കാരിന്റെ നിർദേശം. ആത്മരക്ഷയ്ക്ക് സ്വന്തമായി ഏർപ്പാടുകൾ ഉണ്ടാക്കുകയേ മാർഗമുള്ളൂ. നേതാക്കന്മാർ ആലോചിച്ച് തൽക്കാലത്തേക്ക് ഒരു സംവിധാനമുണ്ടായി. ദിവസവും രാത്രിയിൽ നാലുപേർ സദനത്തിന്റെ പരിസരങ്ങളിൽ റോന്തു ചുറ്റണം.

ഏതാണ്ടൊരു ആത്മധൈര്യം തിരിച്ചുകിട്ടി.

അന്നുകീർത്തിക്കു നേരിട്ട ആപത്തിനുശേഷം അതേക്കുറിച്ച് ഒരനക്കവും കേട്ടില്ല. അങ്ങനെയൊരു കാര്യം പുറത്തുപറയാൻ ആ ചെറുപ്പക്കാരനോ അയാൾക്കു വേണ്ടപ്പെട്ടവരോ തയാറാവുകയില്ല. അതുകൊണ്ടാവണം അതു നിശ്ശബ്ദമായി പര്യവസാനിച്ചത്. എന്നാൽ, സദനത്തിന്റെ നേർക്കു നടന്ന ആക്രമണവും ആ സംഭവവുമായി ബന്ധമുണ്ടെന്നു കീർത്തിക്കു തോന്നി. അവൾ അതു കൂട്ടുകാരോടു പറയുകയും ചെയ്തു. അവർക്കും ആ ധാരണയുണ്ടായി. ആ ചെറുപ്പക്കാരന് പണമുണ്ട്. അതുകൊണ്ട് ആൾസ്വാധീനവും. റൗഡികളെ പണം കൊടുത്തു പറഞ്ഞയച്ചതാവും.

സദനത്തിന്റെ നേർക്ക് ഗുണ്ടകൾ നടത്തിയ ആക്രമണത്തെപ്പറ്റി, *സ്വതന്ത്രദേശം* പത്രത്തിൽ വലിയ പ്രാധാന്യം കൊടുത്തു. വാർത്ത വന്നു. പ്രാമാണികരായ രാഷ്ട്രീയ പ്രവർത്തകരും സാംസ്കാരിക പ്രവർത്തകരും ചേർന്ന് ഒരു പ്രസ്താവനയും പ്രസിദ്ധീകരിച്ചിരുന്നു. അവർ അതിൽ പറഞ്ഞു: “ഇത് ഫാസിസമാണ്. സമാധാനപരമായി പ്രവർത്തിക്കുന്ന ഒരു സ്ഥാപനത്തെ, പണംകൊടുത്ത് റൗഡികളെവിട്ട് തല്ലിത്തകർക്കുക. അതും സ്ത്രീകൾ നടത്തുന്ന ഒരു സദനത്തെ. ഈ രാഷ്ട്രീയം, ഇത് രാഷ്ട്രീയമാണെങ്കിൽ വച്ചുപൊറുപ്പിക്കാൻ പാടില്ല. ഈ നീചമായ ആക്രമണം നമ്മുടെ സ്ത്രീത്വത്തോടുള്ള ക്രൂരമായ മര്യാദലംഘനവും സാധാരണ മനുഷ്യത്വത്തോടുള്ള വെല്ലുവിളിയുമാണ്...”

ക്ഷേത്രമൈതാനത്ത്, ഒരു യോഗം കൂടി. യോഗമയീദേവി, അവിടെ നടന്ന സംഭവങ്ങൾ വിവരിച്ചു. അരവിന്ദൻ പ്രസംഗിച്ചപ്പോൾ ഇത്രയും പറഞ്ഞു:

“മരിക്കാൻ പോകുന്ന ഒരു വർഗത്തിന്റെ ലക്കില്ലായ്മ ഈ സംഭവത്തിലുണ്ട്. രാഷ്ട്രീയമായി എതിർപ്പുണ്ടെങ്കിൽ അന്തസ്സോടെ വരട്ടെ. ആശയങ്ങൾ പ്രചരിപ്പിച്ച് പ്രവർത്തിച്ച് എതിർക്കട്ടെ. ഇതു ഭീരുത്വമാണ്. ഒളിച്ചിരുന്ന് ആക്രമിക്കാൻ ആർക്കും കഴിയും. ഭീരുത്വത്തിന്റെ മറ്റൊരു മുഖ

മാണ് അതിലുള്ളത്. പക്ഷേ, ഈ ഭീരുക്കൾ സാമൂഹ്യദ്രോഹികളാണ്. പണമുള്ളതുകൊണ്ട്, അവർക്ക് വിഹരിക്കാൻ കഴിയുന്നു. നാളെ നേരം പുലരും. സാഹചര്യങ്ങൾ മാറും. അന്ന് ജനങ്ങൾ ഇവരെ പട്ടികളെപ്പോലെ തെരുവിലിട്ടു തല്ലും..."

പത്ത്

ആ സംഭവത്തിന്റെ ചൂട് മെല്ലെ മാറി.

സന്ധ്യാദേവിയുടെ കത്ത് വന്നതിൽ, അവർ തിരിച്ചു വരുന്നുവെന്നാണു പറഞ്ഞിട്ടുള്ളത്. പൊലീസിൽ നിന്നു മാറിനിൽക്കണമെങ്കിൽ ഇവിടങ്ങനെ വല്ലയിടത്തും രഹസ്യമായി കഴിഞ്ഞു കൂടാം.

അരവിന്ദനും കത്തുകിട്ടി. സൗകര്യപ്പെടുമെങ്കിൽ അവിടം വരെ ഒന്നു കൂടി ചെല്ലണം. ചില പ്രശ്നങ്ങളുണ്ട്.

രണ്ടുമൂന്നു ദിവസങ്ങൾ. ഒരു മനുഷ്യൻ സദനത്തിൽ വന്നു. അയാൾ സ്വയം പരിചയപ്പെടുത്തി. "ഞാൻ റീനയുടെ അമ്മാവനാണ്. അവളെ കാണാൻ വന്നതാണ്."

യോഗമയീദേവി അയാളെ ബഹുമാനപൂർവം ഇരുത്തി. റീന കുളി കഴിഞ്ഞു വന്നപ്പോൾ വിവരം പറഞ്ഞു. ആ മനുഷ്യന്റെ രൂപവും രീതിയുമൊക്കെ പറഞ്ഞു. എല്ലാം കരുതലോടെ ചെയ്യുന്നതുകൊണ്ട് ബോധ്യമുണ്ടെങ്കിൽ മാത്രമേ കുട്ടികളെ മുൻവശത്തേക്ക് വിടാറുള്ളൂ. കാറിലാണ് ആ മനുഷ്യൻ വന്നിരിക്കുന്നത്. റീനയ്ക്കു ആളെ മനസിലായി. അമ്മാവനാണ്. അവൾ അമ്മാവനെ കണ്ടിട്ട് കുറേ നാളുകളായി. ഉത്സാഹം തോന്നി.

ചായ കൊടുത്തത് അയാൾ കുടിച്ചു.

റീന വസ്ത്രങ്ങൾ മാറിവന്നു. അമ്മാവനെ കണ്ടു. അവൾക്ക് എന്തെന്നില്ലാത്ത സന്തോഷമാണ് തോന്നിയത്. അമ്മാവൻ വലിയ പണക്കാരനാണ്. ചാക്കോ എന്നാണ് പേർ. അവളുടെ അമ്മയും കുടുംബവും കഷ്ടിച്ച് ജീവിക്കുന്നു. റീനയുടെ അച്ഛൻ രോഗശയ്യയിലാണ്. അത് വളരെനാളായി. അമ്മാവനിൽ നിന്ന് സഹായങ്ങൾ വാങ്ങുന്നത് അച്ഛന് ഇഷ്ടമല്ല. അമ്മാവനോട് സ്നേഹക്കുറവ് ഉണ്ടായിട്ടല്ല. അച്ഛന്റെ അഭിമാനബോധം അത് സമ്മതിച്ചില്ലെന്ന് മാത്രം. അമ്മാവന് റീനയെ ജീവനെപ്പോലെ സ്നേഹമാണ്. അയാൾക്ക് പെൺമക്കളില്ല.

"എന്താ ഇങ്ങോട്ട് വരാൻ തോന്നിയത്?" എപ്പോഴും പുഞ്ചിരിക്കുന്ന അവൾ തുറന്നു ചിരിച്ചുകൊണ്ട് ചോദിച്ചു. അമ്മാവന്റെ മുമ്പിൽ അവൾ സ്വതന്ത്രയാണ്.

"മനസില്ലാഞ്ഞിട്ട്, എന്തുവേണം ഇപ്പോൾ?" ചാക്കോയും രസം പറഞ്ഞു.

വീട്ടുകാര്യങ്ങൾ. മകൻ അമേരിക്കയിലേക്ക് പോയത്. ഭാര്യ എപ്പോഴും ചാക്കോയെ ശകാരിച്ചുകൊണ്ടു നടക്കുന്നത്. ഒരു ജോലിക്കാരി ചാക്കോയുടെ രണ്ടു മുണ്ടു എടുത്തുകൊണ്ട് പൊയ്ക്കളഞ്ഞത്. അവൾ

മറ്റൊന്നും എടുക്കാതെ പോയതിലുള്ള സങ്കടം! അങ്ങനെ ആ മനുഷ്യൻ പലതും സംസാരിച്ചു. റീനയുടെ വീട്ടിൽ പോയിരുന്നു. അച്ഛനുമായി ദീർഘനേരം വർത്തമാനം പറഞ്ഞിരുന്നു. റീനയുടെ അനുജത്തിയുടെ ചെവിക്കു പിടിച്ചു തിരുമ്മി!

എല്ലാം സംസാരിച്ചുകഴിഞ്ഞു. ചാക്കോ അടക്കത്തിൽ ഒരു കാര്യം പറഞ്ഞു:

"മോളേ, ഞാൻ വന്നത് മറ്റൊരു കാര്യം പറയാനാണ്. നിന്നെ കെട്ടിക്കാൻ അമ്മാവൻ തീരുമാനിച്ചാൽ നിനക്കത് ഇഷ്ടമാണോ?"

ഞെട്ടിപ്പോയി. സത്യമാണോ പറയുന്നത്? ഗൗരവമായിട്ടാണോ?

"ഇത് കാര്യമായിട്ട് ചോദിക്കുകയാണോ?"

"അതെ. പറയൂ."

അവൾ മിണ്ടിയില്ല. മുഖം കുനിച്ചുനിന്നു. നല്ല ഉദ്ദേശ്യത്തോടെ നല്ല കാര്യം പറയുകയാണ്. ജീവിതത്തിൽ എന്നായാലും അതു വേണം. പക്ഷേ, ഇവിടത്തെ ജീവിതവുമായി ഇണങ്ങിച്ചേർന്നുപോയി. എങ്ങനെ വിട്ടുപിരിഞ്ഞുപോകും? മറ്റൊരു കഥകൂടി അവൾക്കുണ്ട്. ഫിഫ്ത്തുഫോറത്തിൽ തോറ്റ് പഠിത്തം നിറുത്തി നിന്നപ്പോഴാണ് സന്ധ്യാദേവി അവളെ കണ്ടുമുട്ടിയത്. അച്ഛനോടും അമ്മയോടും പറഞ്ഞ് സദനത്തിലേക്ക് കൂട്ടിക്കൊണ്ടുവന്നു. തുടർന്നു പഠിക്കാൻ അവളെ നിർബന്ധിച്ചു. ആദ്യം മടിയായിരുന്നു. അവർ ശാസിച്ച് പിന്നെയും സ്കൂളിലേക്കയച്ചു. ഇവിടെ താമസിച്ച് രണ്ടുവർഷം പഠിച്ചു. സ്കൂൾ ഫൈനൽ ജയിച്ചു. ആ പഠിത്തത്തിന്റെ ചെലവെല്ലാം ഈ സ്ഥാപനമാണ് വഹിച്ചത്. ജയിച്ചപ്പോൾ സന്ധ്യാദേവി പറഞ്ഞു: "ഇവിടെത്തന്നെ കഴിയുക പ്രവർത്തിക്കുക. റീനയ്ക്ക് ഒരു ജോലിയോ തൊഴിലോ ഉണ്ടാക്കാൻ ഞാൻ ശ്രമിക്കുന്നുണ്ട്." അങ്ങനെ കഴിയുന്നു. ഇപ്പോൾ ഇതും പിരിഞ്ഞുപോകാൻ വയ്യാത്ത ഒരു കുടുംബമായിക്കഴിഞ്ഞിരിക്കുന്നു.

ഒന്നും പ്രതിവചിക്കാൻ തോന്നാതെ അവൾ നിന്നു. ചാക്കോ പറഞ്ഞു:

"നിന്റെ വിഷമം എനിക്ക് ഊഹിക്കാൻ കഴിയും. ഇവരെയൊക്കെ വിട്ടുപിരിയേണ്ടിവരുമല്ലോ എന്ന വിചാരമാണ് അല്ലേ? അത് ഉണ്ടാവും. പക്ഷേ, മറ്റൊന്നാലോചിക്കണം. അപ്പൻ കിടപ്പിലാണ്. നിനക്ക് താഴെ മൂന്നു പിള്ളേരുണ്ട്. അമ്മയ്ക്ക് ഒന്നും ചെയ്യാൻ കഴിയില്ലല്ലോ. നീ അവർക്ക് ഒരു ഭാരംതന്നെയാണ്. ഇപ്പോൾ എന്റെ മനസിൽ ഒരു നല്ല ആലോചന വന്നിട്ടുണ്ട്. അത് കേൾക്കുമ്പോൾ നിനക്ക് അത്ഭുതം തോന്നും."

അവളുടെ കണ്ണുകൾ അമ്മാവന്റെ മനസിലേക്ക് പരതിനോക്കി. ആരെയാണ് അമ്മാവൻ അവിടെ ഒളിച്ചുപിടിച്ചിരിക്കുന്നത്?

അവൾ ചോദിച്ചില്ല. അറിയാൻ ഉൽക്കണ്ഠ കാട്ടിയുമില്ല.

ചാക്കോ ചോദിച്ചു.

"ഇവിടെ ഉഷാമേനോൻ എന്നൊരു കുട്ടി ഉണ്ടോ?"

"ഉണ്ട്."

"ആ കുട്ടിയുടെ അച്ഛൻ കൽക്കത്തയിലാണോ?"

"അതെ. ബിസിനസാണ്."

"ആ കുട്ടിക്ക് കൽക്കത്തയിൽ അച്ഛന്റെ കൂടെ താമസിക്കുന്ന ഒരു സഹോദരനുണ്ടോ?"

"ഉണ്ട്."

ചാക്കോ ആലോചിക്കുന്നതുപോലിരുന്നു. പിന്നെ പറഞ്ഞു.

"ആ കൊച്ചനാ ചെറുക്കൻ."

റീനയുടെ കണ്ണുകൾ മിഴിച്ചു നിന്നു. ഭ്രാന്തു പറയുന്നോ? എന്തെല്ലാം അർഥമില്ലായ്മ ഈ പറഞ്ഞതിലുണ്ട്! അവർ നായന്മാരാണ്. താൻ ക്രിസ്ത്യാനി. അവർ വലിയ ബിസിനസുകാർ. ആ കൊച്ചൻ എഞ്ചിനീയറിങ്ങിനു പഠിക്കുന്നു. വലിയ വല്ല കുടുംബത്തിലും നിന്ന് കെട്ടാനുള്ളവൻ. അമ്മാവനു ഭ്രാന്താണ്!

"അമ്മാവന് എന്തുപറ്റി?"

അയാൾ ചിരിച്ചു.

"ഇപ്പോൾ ഈ ഒരൊറ്റക്കാര്യമേ പറ്റിയിട്ടുള്ളൂ. ഞാനീ കല്യാണം നടത്തിക്കൊടുക്കണം."

"ഏതു കല്യാണം?" അവൾ പരിഹസിച്ചു ചോദിച്ചു.

"നീയും രവികുമാർ എന്ന പയ്യനും തമ്മിലുള്ള കല്യാണം. അതാണ് ആ കൊച്ചന്റെ പേര്."

അവളുടെ മനസ്സ് പരിഹാസത്തിൽ നിന്നു പിൻവാങ്ങാൻ തുടങ്ങി. ഇതിൽ ഗൗരവമുള്ള എന്തോ കാര്യമുണ്ടെന്ന് ഒരു തോന്നൽ വന്നു.

ചാക്കോ തുടർന്നു:

"നീ ആ കൊച്ചനെ കണ്ടിട്ടുണ്ടോ?"

"ഉണ്ട്. രണ്ടുതവണ ഉഷയെക്കാണാൻ ഇവിടെ വന്നിട്ടുണ്ട്."

എന്നാൽ ഞാൻ ഒരു സംഗതി പറയാം. "അയാൾ നിന്നെക്കണ്ടു. ശ്രദ്ധിച്ചു. നിന്നെ അയാൾക്ക് ഇഷ്ടപ്പെട്ടു. ഈ വർഷം എൻജിനീയറിങ് പാസ്സായി. ജോലിയും കിട്ടി. അയാൾ അച്ഛനോട് ആഗ്രഹം പറഞ്ഞു. അദ്ദേഹം വളരെ വിശാലമനസ്കനാണെന്നു തോന്നുന്നു. അദ്ദേഹം സമ്മതം മൂളി. നിന്റെ വീട്ടിലേക്ക് എഴുതി. അവർ എന്നെ വിളിപ്പിച്ചു. കാര്യം പറഞ്ഞു എന്നോടാലോചിച്ച് വേണ്ടതു ചെയ്യാൻ. അച്ഛൻ കൽക്കത്തയിലേക്ക് എഴുതി. പിന്നെ എഴുത്തുകുത്ത് ഞാനുമായിട്ടായി. ദാ ഇപ്പോൾ കത്തു വന്നിരിക്കുന്നു. കല്യാണം നടത്തിക്കൊള്ളാൻ. ഉഷ എന്ന കുട്ടിക്ക് അദ്ദേഹം ഇതോടൊപ്പം കത്തയച്ചിട്ടുണ്ടെന്ന് എഴുതിയിട്ടുണ്ട്. ഇന്നു രാവിലെയാണ് എനിക്ക് കത്തു കിട്ടിയത്. അതിന് നാളെ കിട്ടുമായിരിക്കും."

വിശ്വസിക്കാൻ കഴിഞ്ഞില്ല. ആ കൊച്ചൻ രണ്ടു തവണയും തന്നെ ശ്രദ്ധിച്ചതായി തോന്നിയിരുന്നു. പക്ഷേ, അപ്പോൾ ഒന്നും വിചാരിച്ചില്ല. ഇപ്പോൾ ഒരു സ്വപ്നം പോലെ തോന്നുന്നു.

"നീ എന്തു പറയുന്നു?"

"ഞാൻ എന്തു പറയാനാണ്?"

അവൾ അകത്തേക്കു പോയി മറ്റുള്ളവരെ വിളിച്ചു. അവൾ പുറ

ത്തേക്കു വന്നു. റീന അമ്മാവനെ എല്ലാവർക്കും പരിചയപ്പെടുത്തി. ഉഷാമേനോനെ അയാൾ നോക്കി ചിരിച്ചു. ആർക്കും അപ്പോൾ കാര്യം മനസിലായില്ല.

ചാക്കോ ആ കഥ വിശദമായി പറഞ്ഞു. താൻ വന്നത് അതിനാണെന്ന് അറിയിച്ചു. ഉള്ളിൽ സന്തോഷം തിങ്ങുന്ന ഒരു നിശ്ശബ്ദത അവിടെ വ്യാപിച്ചു.

യോഗമയീദേവി പറഞ്ഞു.

"നല്ല കാര്യം ഞങ്ങളെല്ലാം സന്തോഷിക്കുന്നു?"

ചാക്കോ ചോദിച്ചു:

"റീന എന്തു പറയുന്നു."

മുഖം കുനിച്ചു നിന്നു. അവൾ മിണ്ടിയില്ല.

"എനിക്ക് സമ്മതമാ..." ഉഷാമേനോൻ പെട്ടെന്നു പ്രഖ്യാപിച്ചു.

"എന്തു സമ്മതം?" കീർത്തി ഉടനെ കളിയാക്കി ചോദിച്ചു.

"എന്റെ ആങ്ങള ഈ പെണ്ണിനെ കെട്ടുന്നത്.." ഉഷ അതേപോലെ മറുപടി പറഞ്ഞു. ആ രംഗം ആ വിവാഹത്തിന്റെ സമ്മതം മൂളലായിരുന്നു.

ചാക്കോ പോയി. അയാൾ അടുത്ത ഒരു ദിവസം വരും.

സന്ധ്യക്ക് അവർ കൂട്ടമായി പിൻമുറ്റത്തിരുന്നപ്പോൾ അകത്തിരുന്നുകൊണ്ട് കീർത്തി വിളിച്ചു!

"പാർവതീ!"

"എന്താടീ?"

"നിനക്ക് ആങ്ങളമാര് വല്ലോരുമുണ്ടോ?"

"ഇല്ലല്ലോടീ."

"അല്ല എനിക്ക് കെട്ടാൻ ഒരാള് വേണമായിരുന്നു."

* * * * * *

കൽക്കത്തയിലെ തിരക്കുള്ള ഒരു തെരുവിനു പിന്നിൽ നാലു നിലയിലുള്ള ഒരു കെട്ടിടത്തിന്റെ ഏറ്റവും മുകളിലത്തെ ഒരു ചെറിയ മുറി. അവിടെ ഒരു സംഘം ചെറുപ്പക്കാർ കൂടിയിട്ടുണ്ട്. മങ്ങിയ ഒരു വൈദ്യുത വിളക്കു കത്തുന്നു. പ്രധാന പാതയിൽ നിന്ന് ഒരു ഇടുങ്ങിയ വഴിയിൽക്കൂടിയാണ് ഈ കെട്ടിടത്തിലെത്തേണ്ടത്. വിളക്കുകാലുകൾക്ക് കീഴിൽ നാനാതരം ചപ്പും ചവറും കിടപ്പുണ്ട്. ഇരുപുറത്തുനിന്നും വെള്ളം ഒലിക്കുന്ന ചാലുകൾ. വണ്ടികൾ, കടകൾ ആളുകളുടെ നിലയ്ക്കാത്ത ശബ്ദം.

മുറിയിൽ അഞ്ചാറു ബഞ്ചുകളുണ്ട്. ഒരു പഴയ മേശയും കസേരയും. ബഞ്ചെല്ലാം ഒരു ഭാഗത്തേക്ക് മാറ്റിയിട്ട്, നിലത്ത് പായ്‌വിരിച്ചാണ് അവർ ഇരിക്കുന്നത്. ആ സംഘത്തിലെ പ്രധാനി ഉഷാമേനോന്റെ സഹോദരൻ രവികുമാറാണ്. രണ്ടു മൂന്നു ബംഗാളി സുഹൃത്തുക്കൾ. ബാക്കിയെല്ലാം മലയാളികൾ. ഒരാൾ കസേരയിലിരുന്ന് സൈക്ലോസ്റ്റൈൽ ചെയ്യാനുള്ള കടലാസിൽ എഴുതുന്നുണ്ട്.

സൈക്ലോസ്റ്റൈൽ മെഷീനിൽ അവർ എന്തോ ഒന്നിന്റെ പകർപ്പു

കൾ എടുത്തുകൊണ്ടിരിക്കുന്നു. രവികുമാറാണ് ആ കൃത്യത്തിൽ ഏർപ്പെട്ടിരിക്കുന്നത്. മറ്റുള്ളവർ ആ പകർപ്പുകൾ കുറെയെണ്ണമാവുമ്പോൾ അടുക്കുന്നു. ചുരുട്ടുന്നു ബ്രൗൺ പേപ്പറിൽ പൊതിയുന്നു. ട്വയിൻ നൂലുകൊണ്ടു കെട്ടുന്നു. അതിനു പുറമേ, കടലാസുചുറ്റി പശതേച്ച് ഒട്ടിക്കുന്നു. എല്ലാം തിടുക്കത്തിലാണ് ചെയ്യുന്നത്. ഇടയ്ക്ക് വാതിൽക്കൽ നിൽക്കുന്ന ഒരു പയ്യനെ വിളിച്ച് രണ്ടു ചുരുളുകൾ ഏൽപ്പിച്ച് എന്തോ ചട്ടം കെട്ടുന്നു. അവൻ പുറത്തേക്കു പോകുന്നു.

രവികുമാർ ജോലിതീർത്ത് ചുമരിൽ ചാരി ഇരുന്നു.

വേഗത്തിൽ, അവർ പല ചുരുളുകളായി അത് കെട്ടി പശയൊട്ടിച്ച് മൂലയിലേക്കു വെച്ചു.

"എത്ര കോപ്പിയാ?" ഒരുത്തൻ ചോദിച്ചു.

"ആയിരം." രവികുമാർ പറഞ്ഞു.

"മേരാ സുന്ദര സപ്നാ ബീത്ഗയി..." ഒരുത്തൻ പാടി.

"ഇവൻ ഈ സ്വപ്നവും കൊണ്ട് എങ്ങോട്ടു സഞ്ചരിക്കുകയാണോ ആവോ..." രവികുമാർ കളിയാക്കി.

"അവൻ ഇടയ്ക്കൊന്ന് സുഖിച്ചോട്ടെ." മറ്റൊരുത്തൻ പറഞ്ഞു.

"ഇനി മറ്റേതുകൂടി നമുക്ക് കോപ്പിയെടുക്കണം." രവികുമാർ എഴുതുന്ന ആളെ നോക്കി. "തീരാറായോടൊ?

"ദാ ഇപ്പം..." അവൻ പറഞ്ഞു.

"ആണുങ്ങളെഴുതിയതാ. നീ തെറ്റു പകർത്തിവയ്ക്കരുത് പോക്കരെ" രവികുമാർ ഫലിതരൂപത്തിൽ ഓർമിപ്പിച്ചു.

"ഓ, ഇത് വേണമെങ്കിൽ ഞാൻ എഴുതാമായിരുന്നു.." എഴുത്തിനിടയ്ക്ക് അയാൾ വച്ചു പറഞ്ഞു.

"ശരിയാ." രവികുമാർ തിരിച്ചടിച്ചു. "അക്ഷരാഭ്യാസം ഉണ്ടായിരുന്നെങ്കിൽ! അത് ഇല്ലാതെ പോയി. എന്തുചെയ്യാം."

മറ്റുള്ളവർ ചിരിച്ചു

അയാൾ പേന താഴെവച്ചു.

"എന്താ സംശയമുണ്ടോ?"

"നീ എഴുതെടാ സമ്മതിച്ചു. നീ ദീ പേശ് മുക്കർജിയേക്കാൾ വലിയ കവിതന്നെ!" രവികുമാർ അവന്റെ നേർക്ക് തൊഴുതു. "ഇപ്പോൾ അതങ്ങു പകർത്തിയാട്ടെ."

അവൻ വീണ്ടും പേനയെടുത്ത് എഴുതാൻ തുടങ്ങി.

പുറത്തേക്കു പോയ പയ്യൻ വന്നു.

"ബക്കൂ, ചാ.." രവികുമാർ പറഞ്ഞു. അവൻ ഓടിയിറങ്ങിപ്പോയി.

അവൻ കുറച്ചു സമയത്തിനുള്ളിൽ ചായയുമായി വന്നു. അവർ അതു കുടിച്ചു.

"നീ എഴുതിക്കഴിഞ്ഞിട്ട് കുടിച്ചാൽ മതി, പോക്കരെ..." രവികുമാർ.

പോക്കർ ചായ കയ്യിലെടുത്തു.

"തനിക്ക് നസ്റൂൾ ഇസ്ലാമിനെ അറിയാമോ?"

"നേരിട്ടു പരിചയില്ല."

"എന്നാൽ എനിക്ക് പരിചയമുണ്ട് അദ്ദേഹം എന്താ പറഞ്ഞതെന്ന റിയാമോ?"

"ഓ, അദ്ദേഹം ഒന്നും പറഞ്ഞില്ല!" ഒരുത്തൻ.

"പറഞ്ഞു. ഈ പോക്കറോട് പറഞ്ഞു... മിസ്റ്റർ പോക്കർ, നീ.. നീ ഭാരതത്തിലെ ഏറ്റവും വലിയ കവിയാകാൻ പോകുന്നു. സൂക്ഷിച്ചിരുന്നോ എന്ന് പറഞ്ഞു. അദ്ദേഹം ഗദ്ഗദം ചൊരിയുകയായിരുന്നു. അറിയാമോ... എന്തറിയും. മൈനേഴ്സ്" ചായ കുടിച്ചു.

"അദ്ദേഹം കരഞ്ഞുപോയി. ഇല്ലേ പോക്കരേ? മറ്റൊരുത്തൻ.

മലയാളം അൽപ്പം വശമുള്ള ബംഗാളി ഇടപെട്ടു.

"പക്ഷേ, ടാഗോറ് പോക്കരെ അറിയിച്ചിട്ടുണ്ട്, പോക്കർ നിങ്ങൾ വളരെ കവിത ഇങ്ങനെ പകർത്തും എന്ന്."

ചിരി.

പോക്കർ അരമണിക്കൂർകൊണ്ട് അത് എഴുതിത്തീർത്തു. അച്ചടി പോലെ എഴുതണം. അതാണ്. അത്രയും സമയം വേണ്ടി വന്നത്.

"നമുക്ക് ജോലി തുടങ്ങുംമുമ്പ് അത് ഒന്ന് വായിക്കാം..." ഒരാൾ അഭിപ്രായപ്പെട്ടു.

"അതെ..." മറ്റു ചിലർ.

"നമ്പൂതിരി വായിക്കെടാ."

നമ്പൂതിരിയുടേത് നല്ല ശബ്ദമാണ്. ഈണമുണ്ട്. വീര്യവും അദ്ദേ ഹത്തിന് കൂടുതലുണ്ട്.

വിപ്ലവ കവിയായ ദീപേശ് മുക്കർജിയുടെ ബംഗാളി കവിത മലയാ ളത്തിൽ പരിഭാഷപ്പെടുത്തിയതാണ്. നമ്പൂതിരി കവിതകളെഴുതിയ കട ലാസ് വാങ്ങിവായിച്ചു:

"ദീപമേ തെളിയൂ വിശക്കുന്ന കൂരകളിൽ,
പട്ടിയും മനുഷ്യരും ഒരുമിച്ചു ആഹാരം കഴിക്കുന്ന
തെരുവുകളിൽ, ദീപമേ, തെളിയൂ!
ഇന്നലെ ഇതിലെ കടന്നുപോയത് ആരാണ്?
ബൂട്ട്സിട്ട പാദങ്ങളുടെ ശബ്ദം ഞാൻ കേട്ടു.
ഇന്ന് ഈ വഴിക്ക് നടന്നുനീങ്ങിയത് ഏതൊരാളാണ്?
തോക്കിന്റെ കാഞ്ചി വലിക്കുന്നത് ഞാൻ കേട്ടു
ഇന്ന് തെരുവുകളിൽ ഞാൻ ശവങ്ങൾ കണ്ടു
എനിക്ക് സന്തോഷം തോന്നി.
ശവങ്ങൾ വിശക്കുന്നുവെന്നു പറഞ്ഞില്ല.
വയറ്റത്തടിച്ചു പാടിയില്ല.
കണ്ണുകൾ കൊണ്ട് കദനകഥ പറഞ്ഞില്ല.
വിശപ്പില്ലാത്ത ആ ശവങ്ങളുടെ മുഖമൊന്നു കാണട്ടെ.
ദീപമേ തെളിയൂ!
എനിക്ക് സങ്കടം തോന്നി.

നീലത്തോട്ടത്തിലെ ആ സുന്ദരി പ്രസവിച്ചപ്പോൾ
അതു ചാപിള്ളയായിരുന്നു. അത് വെളുത്ത -
കുഞ്ഞായിരുന്നു.
അവൾ അതിനെ കൊന്നതാണ്!
വയറ്റിലിട്ടു കൊന്നതാണ്!
കൽക്കത്തയുടെ വയറ്റിൽ പുഴുക്കൾ അരിക്കുമ്പോൾ,
കാളിഘട്ടിലെ ജലത്തിലേക്ക്
മനുഷ്യരക്തം ഒലിച്ചിറങ്ങുമ്പോൾ, ഞാൻ ഉറങ്ങിപ്പോയി.
ഗവർണറുടെ വീട്ടിലെ മദ്യത്തിന് എന്തൊരു ലഹരി!
എന്റെ കൺപോളകൾ ഒന്നുണരട്ടെ.
ദീപമേ, തെളിയൂ!
അവളുടെ ചുണ്ടുകൾ വിളറിയതെങ്ങനെ?
അവളുടെ മാറ് കാറ്റില്ലാത്തബ്ലാഡർപോലെ! കഷ്ടം!
അവളുടെ കൈകൾക്ക് പണം എണ്ണാൻ പോലും
ശക്തിയില്ല, വിറയ്ക്കുന്നു.
ഞാൻ ലജ്ജിക്കുന്നു. കൽക്കത്തയിൽ സൗന്ദര്യം–
വറ്റിപ്പോയോ?
കൽക്കത്താ, നീ കരയൂ
ഞാൻ മാസംതോറും ശമ്പളം കൊടുക്കുന്ന
എഴുത്തുകാർ എവിടെ?
ഞാൻ പിയാനോയിലിരുന്ന് പഠിപ്പിച്ച
പാട്ടുകൾ എവിടെ?
ഞാൻ അത്താഴമേശകളിലേക്കു വിളിച്ചു
വരുത്തിയ നർത്തകികൾ എവിടെ?
വരൂ, എഴുതൂ, പാടൂ, നൃത്തം വയ്ക്കൂ!
ദീപമേ, ഇവർക്കുവേണ്ടി തെളിയൂ!
എന്ത്? വിഡ്ഢികളേ, നിങ്ങൾ
എന്ത്? പറഞ്ഞു? എന്തു പറഞ്ഞു?
പട്ടിയും മനുഷ്യനും തോക്കെടുത്തെന്നോ?
ശവങ്ങൾ സംസാരിച്ചെന്നോ?
ചാപ്പിള്ളകൾ കരഞ്ഞെന്നോ?
ഗവർണറുടെ മന്ദിരത്തിലെ തൂണുകൾ
അടർന്നുവീഴുന്നുവെന്നോ?
കാളിഘട്ടിലെ ദേവത ശൂലവും പേറി,
കൽക്കത്തയിലെ തെരുവുകളിൽ ഇറങ്ങിയെന്നോ?
വിളറിയ ചുണ്ടുകളുടെ വേശ്യകൾ, ദുർഗയുടെ പിന്നാലെ
സഞ്ചരിക്കുന്നെന്നോ?
വിഡ്ഢികൾ! വിശക്കുന്ന, പുഴുക്കളരിക്കുന്ന–
വിഡ്ഢികൾ!

നുണ പറയുന്ന ഇവരുടെ മുഖം ഞാൻ കാണട്ടെ
ദീപമേ, തെളിയൂ!

ആ ചെറുപ്പക്കാർ നിശ്ശബ്ദരായി ആ കവിത കേട്ടു. ആരും ഒരക്ഷരം ഉരിയാടിയില്ല. രവികുമാർ മെഷീനിൽ കടലാസ് ഒപ്പിച്ചുവച്ച് പകർപ്പുകൾ എടുക്കാൻ തുടങ്ങി. ഓരോരുത്തർ ബീഡിയും സിഗരറ്റും കത്തിച്ചു.

അപ്പോൾ, കോണിപ്പടിയിൽ കാലൊച്ച കേട്ടു. ശ്രദ്ധിച്ചു. ഒരു ചെറുപ്പക്കാരി കയറിവന്നു.

"രവികുമാർ നിങ്ങളുടെ അച്ഛനെ പൊലീസുകാർ പിടിച്ചുകൊണ്ടുപോയി."

രവികുമാർ അതു കേട്ടു. അയാൾ തന്റെ ജോലി നിറുത്തിയില്ല. തുടർന്നുകൊണ്ടിരുന്നു. അയാളുടെ ദൃഷ്ടികൾ ആ ചെറുപ്പക്കാരിയിൽ തങ്ങിനിന്നു.

"നിങ്ങൾ എങ്ങനെ അറിഞ്ഞു. അപർണാ?" ഒരുത്തൻ ചോദിച്ചു.

"ഞാൻ കണ്ടു. അദ്ദേഹത്തെ കടയിൽ നിന്നാണ് അറസ്റ്റു ചെയ്തുകൊണ്ടുപോയത് ഇപ്പോൾ..... അൽപ്പം മുമ്പ്.

അവൾ അറിയിച്ചു.

"അപർണാ" രവികുമാർ ജോലിക്കിടയിൽ പറഞ്ഞു. "ഇത് ഏതു നിമിഷവും സംഭവിക്കുമെന്ന് പ്രതീക്ഷിച്ചിരുന്നതാണ്. ഭയപ്പെടേണ്ട അവർ മിനഞ്ഞാന്ന് വന്നിരുന്നു. ഇന്നലെ വന്നിരുന്നു. നിങ്ങളെ ഞങ്ങൾ കൊണ്ടുപോകുമെന്ന് അച്ഛനോട് പലതവണ പറയാറുണ്ട്. ആവശ്യമുള്ളപ്പോൾ വരൂ, ഞാൻ കൂടെ പോരാം, എന്ന് അച്ഛനും പറയാറുണ്ട്. അച്ഛനെ അവർ ഒന്നും ചെയ്യുകയില്ല. പൊലീസ് കമ്മീഷണർ അച്ഛന്റെ സുഹൃത്താണ്. കമ്മീഷണർക്ക് പല സഹായങ്ങളും അച്ഛൻ ചെയ്തുകൊടുത്തുകൊണ്ടിരുന്നു. നമ്മൾ സാവധാനം അങ്ങോട്ടു ചെന്നാൽ മതി. എന്നെ അവർ പിടിക്കുകയില്ല. കാരണം, അപർണാ, അറിയുമോ എന്നെ ബ്രിട്ടീഷ് ഗവൺമെന്റിനും ഭയമാണ്. എന്റെ പേരുകേട്ടാൽ, ചക്രവർത്തി നടുങ്ങിപ്പോകാറുണ്ട്!"

അപർണ ചിരിച്ചുപോയി. അയാൾ ജോലി തുടർന്നുകൊണ്ടിരുന്നു. അവൾ ഇരുന്നു.

പതിനൊന്ന്

"**ഇ**ന്ന് കോളേജ് ഇല്ലായിരുന്നോ?" രവികുമാർ അന്വേഷിച്ചു.

"ഉണ്ടായിരുന്നു. വൈകുന്നേരം സ്പെഷ്യൽ ക്ലാസും. അതുകഴിഞ്ഞു വരുമ്പോഴാണ് ഈ സംഭവം കണ്ടത്."

"താങ്ക്യൂ ഫോർ ദി ഇൻഫർമേഷൻ" രവികുമാർ തമാശ പറഞ്ഞു.

അപർണ, കാളിഘട്ടിലെ ഒരു കമ്പനിയിൽ ക്ലാർക്കായ ദത്തമംജുദാരുടെ മകളാണ്. അവളുടെ അനിയനാണ്, ആ ചെറുപ്പക്കാരുടെ സഹായിയായി നിൽക്കുന്ന ബക്കു എന്ന പയ്യൻ. അവൻ ഫിഫ്ത് ഫോറത്തിൽ പഠിക്കുന്നു. അപർണ ബി എ രണ്ടാം വർഷം വിദ്യാർഥിനിയാണ്.

രവികുമാറിന്റെ തെരുവിൽ, തൊട്ടടുത്ത വീട്ടിലാണ് അപർണയും കുടുംബവും താമസിക്കുന്നത്. അവർ കുടുംബസുഹൃത്തുക്കളാണ്.

രവികുമാർ ഒരു മണിക്കൂർ കൊണ്ട് സൈക്ലോസ്റ്റൈൽ ചെയ്തു തീർത്തു. മറ്റുള്ളവർ അത് ചുരുളുകളാക്കി കടലാസുപൊതിഞ്ഞ് പശ തേച്ച് ഒട്ടിച്ചു.

“ഇത് നാളെ ഓരോ സ്ഥലത്ത് എത്തിച്ചാൽ മതി, അല്ലേ?” രവികുമാർ ചോദിച്ചു.

“മതി.” കൂട്ടുകാർ സമ്മതിച്ചു.

അവരെല്ലാവരും കൂടി പുറത്തേക്കിറങ്ങി. അപ്പോൾ ഒരാൾക്കൂട്ടം. വഴിയിൽ എന്തോ സംഭവിച്ചിരിക്കുന്നു. അവൾ ആൾക്കൂട്ടത്തിനിടയിൽക്കൂടി എത്തിനോക്കി. ഒരു സ്ത്രീ, ഒരു പുരുഷനെ കുത്തിയിട്ടിരിക്കുന്നു. അവൾ വിളിച്ചു പറയുന്നു: “കാണ് നിങ്ങൾ കാണ്. ഇയാളും രണ്ടുപേരും ചേർന്ന് ഇന്നലെ രാത്രിയിൽ എന്നെ ബലാൽസംഗം ചെയ്തു. ഞാൻ വേശ്യയാണ്. എന്നുവെച്ച് എന്നെ ബലാൽസംഗം ചെയ്യാമോ? അതുകഴിഞ്ഞ് വ്യഭിചരിച്ചു. എനിക്കു കിട്ടിയ പൈസ കൊടുത്ത് ഞാൻ ഈ കത്തി വാങ്ങി. പറയൂ, ഇവനെ കൊല്ലേണ്ടതല്ലേ?”

രവികുമാറും കൂട്ടുകാരും പിൻവാങ്ങി. അപർണയും ബക്കുവുമൊരുമിച്ച് അവർ നടന്നു.

* * *

പതിവിലധികം സന്തോഷം ദിവാകരന്റെ മുഖത്തു കാണായി. എന്താണ് കാരണമെന്ന് ഭാനുമതിക്ക് മനസിലായില്ല. ദിവാകരൻ ഒരിക്കലും കറുത്ത മുഖം കാണിക്കാറില്ല. അവളോട് ശുണ്ഠിയെടുക്കാറില്ല. എന്തെങ്കിലും കാര്യത്തിൽ അപ്രിയം പ്രകടിപ്പിക്കാറുമില്ല. പൊലീസ് ഉദ്യോഗസ്ഥനായ ഹരീന്ദ്രൻ നായർ വന്നകാര്യം അറിഞ്ഞപ്പോൾ അയാൾ ഒന്ന് ചിരിച്ചു. എന്നിട്ട് പറഞ്ഞു. “രാഷ്ട്രീയപ്രവർത്തകരെ അങ്ങനെ പൊലീസ് അന്വേഷിച്ചെന്ന് വരും. സർക്കാർ തടവിൽ വച്ചുവെന്നു വരും. ഭർത്താക്കന്മാർ അവരുടെ തിരിച്ചുവരവും കാത്ത് ഇരിക്കേണ്ടിവന്നുവെന്നും വരും.” അവൾ ആ കളിയാക്കലിൽ രസിച്ചിരുന്നു. “എന്നെ ആരു പിടിച്ചുകൊണ്ടു പോവുകയില്ല.” അവൾ പറഞ്ഞു. പെട്ടെന്ന് ദിവാകരന്റെ പ്രതികരണം. “ശരിയാ അയ്യോ ഞാൻ പാവമാണേ. എന്നെ ഉപദ്രവിക്കരുതേ. ഞാൻ ഇനി ഒരു പ്രവർത്തനത്തിനും പോവുകയില്ലേ എന്ന് എഴുതിക്കൊടുത്താൽ പിന്നെ, സർക്കാരു വിളിച്ചുകൊണ്ട് പോവുകില്ല.” അവൾ തിരിച്ചടിച്ചു. “ഞാൻ അങ്ങനെ ആർക്കും എഴുതിക്കൊടുത്തില്ലല്ലോ.” ദിവാകരൻ പറഞ്ഞു. കാണാം. കഷ്ടം മാപ്പെഴുതുന്നത് ഞാനും കൂടി കാണണമല്ലോ.

അങ്ങനെ ആ സംഭാഷണം തീർന്നു. ഭാനുമതി ഹരീന്ദ്രൻ നായരെ കാത്തിരുന്നു. ആ മനുഷ്യൻ വന്നില്ല. അന്വേഷണവും നടപടിയും എന്തായെന്നു. അറിഞ്ഞില്ല.

നാലഞ്ചുദിവസം മുൻപ് അരവിന്ദന്റെ കത്തുവന്നു. വാസവമേനോൻ

നിർദേശിച്ചതനുസരിച്ചുള്ള കത്താണ്. ദിവാകരനാണ് കത്തയച്ചിരുന്നത്. അയാൾ അതു ഭാനുമതിയുടെ കൈയിൽ കൊടുത്തു. വായിച്ചിട്ട് അവൾ വളരെനേരം മൗനത്തിലിരുന്നു. ജീവിതത്തിലെ ഒരധ്യായം അവസാനിക്കുന്നതായി തോന്നി. അത്, തന്നെ സംബന്ധിച്ചിടത്തോളം പ്രകാശം നിറഞ്ഞതായിരുന്നു. കത്തിൽ പറയുന്നത് അനുസരിച്ചു കഴിയുമ്പോൾ, തന്നെ വിശ്വസിച്ച എല്ലാവരുടെയും മുൻപിൽ താൻ ഒന്നുമല്ലാതായിത്തീരുന്നു.

ദിവാകരൻ ആ കത്തിനെപ്പറ്റി പിന്നീട് ഒന്നും സംസാരിച്ചില്ല. അവളും മൗനം ദീക്ഷിച്ചതേയുള്ളൂ. പക്ഷേ, ഒന്നും ചെയ്യേണ്ടിവന്നില്ല. വനിതാസമാജത്തിൽ നിന്ന് രജനിയെയും നീലാംബികയെയും പിടിച്ചുകൊണ്ടുപോയിട്ട് എന്തായി എന്നറിഞ്ഞില്ല. അവരെക്കുറിച്ചുള്ള വിചാരം അലട്ടിക്കൊണ്ടിരുന്നു.

ഇന്ന് ദിവാകരന്റെ സന്തോഷംകണ്ടിട്ട് ഭാനുമതി ചോദിച്ചു.

“എന്താ ഒരു പുതിയ ഉത്സാഹം?”

“ബിസിനസുകാരന് സന്തോഷത്തിന് എന്താ വേണ്ടത്? നല്ല ബിസിനസ് കിട്ടണം. ഇന്ന് കിട്ടി. അതിന്റെ ഉത്സാഹമാണ്.” അയാൾ സെറ്റിയിൽ നിവർന്നിരുന്നു.

അവൾ മറുപടി പറയാതിരുന്നപ്പോൾ അയാൾ വിട്ടില്ല.

“എന്ത് ബിസിനസെന്ന് ചോദിക്കാത്തതെന്താ?”

“ചോദിച്ചിരിക്കുന്നു.”

“അത് പറയാം. എന്റെ ഭാര്യയ്ക്കുവേണ്ടി ഞാനിന്ന് അവളുടെ സുഹൃത്തുക്കളെ കാണാൻ പോയി. അപ്പോൾ സുഹൃത്തുക്കളുടെ വീട്, ക്ലോസ്. കട അടപ്പ്. രണ്ടു സ്നേഹിതകൾ ലോക്കപ്പിൽ കിടപ്പുണ്ടെന്നു കേട്ടു. അവിടെ പോയി. അപ്പോഴേക്കും അവർ രണ്ടുപേരും വീട്ടിൽ പോയെന്നറിഞ്ഞു. ആ വീടുകളിൽ പോയി. അവരെ രണ്ടുപേരെയും കണ്ടു സംസാരിച്ചു. അവർ രണ്ടുപേരും സുഖമായിരിക്കുന്നു എന്ന് എന്റെ ഭാര്യയെ അറിയിക്കണമെന്ന് അവർ പറഞ്ഞയച്ചു.

ഭാനുമതി മുന്നോട്ടാഞ്ഞിരുന്നു.

“ഇത് സത്യമാണോ?”

“സത്യം. രജനിയും നീലാംബികയും അല്ലേ? ചോദ്യം ചെയ്തിട്ട് അവരെ വിട്ടു. പക്ഷേ വനിതാസമാജം അടച്ചിട്ടിരിക്കുകയാണ്.”

“അത് പിന്നെയും തുറക്കാം. ആ പെങ്കൊച്ചുങ്ങളെ വിട്ടല്ലോ.. അവരെ ഉപദ്രവിച്ചില്ലല്ലോ.”

“ഇല്ല മാന്യമായി പെരുമാറി എന്നാണ് അവർ തന്നെ പറഞ്ഞത്.”

“എന്താ ഇങ്ങനെ പോകാൻ തോന്നിയത്?”

“എനിക്ക് ഹരീന്ദ്രൻനായരെ കാണണമെന്നുണ്ടായിരുന്നു. നിങ്ങളുടെ ആ വഴിക്കാണ് പോകേണ്ടിയിരുന്നത്. അപ്പോൾ ഇക്കാര്യം അന്വേഷിക്കാമെന്നു വിചാരിച്ചു. നമ്മുടെ ഭാര്യയും അതേ കേസിൽ പ്രതിയാണല്ലോ.”

“സമാധാനമായി.”

"എന്നിട്ട് ഹരീന്ദ്രൻനായരെ കാണുവാൻ കഴിഞ്ഞുമില്ല."

"എന്തുപറ്റി?"

"അദ്ദേഹം സ്ഥലത്തില്ല. പൊലീസ് ഉദ്യോഗസ്ഥന്മാരുടെ ഒരു കോൺഫറൻസിനു പോയിരിക്കുന്നു. രാഷ്ട്രീയക്കാരെ അമർച്ച ചെയ്യാനുള്ള പുതിയ പരിപാടികൾ ആസൂത്രണം ചെയ്യുകയാണെന്നാണ് പറഞ്ഞുകേട്ടത്."

അത്താഴം കഴിച്ചു കുറച്ചുനേരംകൂടി അവർ ഓരോന്നു പറഞ്ഞുകൊണ്ടിരുന്നു. ഈ ദിവസങ്ങളിലെല്ലാം ഭാനുമതിയെ ശല്യപ്പെടുത്തിക്കൊണ്ടിരിക്കുന്ന ഒരു ചിന്തയുണ്ട്. അത് ഹരീന്ദ്രൻനായർ തന്നെയാണ്. അദ്ദേഹം അന്ന് ഇറങ്ങിപ്പോകുമ്പോൾ പറഞ്ഞത്. എന്താണതിന്റെ അർഥം? പല രൂപത്തിലും ആലോചിച്ചുനോക്കി. ഒരെത്തും പിടിയുമില്ല. ദിവാകരനോട് അതു പറഞ്ഞില്ല. അവർ തമ്മിൽ കാണുമ്പോൾ അത് പരാമർശിക്കുമെങ്കിൽ, ആവട്ടെ.

സ്വസ്ഥതയുള്ള ഒരു രാത്രികൂടി കടന്നുപോയി. സുഖമായി ഉറങ്ങി.

നേരം പുലർന്നു. കണികണ്ടത് അരവിന്ദനെയാണ്.

ദിവാകരനും ഭാനുമതിയും ചേർന്ന് അരവിന്ദനെ സ്നേഹപൂർവം സ്വീകരിച്ചു. അവരുടെ കുടുംബത്തിലേക്ക് അയാൾ ആദ്യമായി വരികയാണ്. ഒരു ആവശ്യം എന്ന നിലയ്ക്കാണ് അരവിന്ദൻ അങ്ങോട്ടു ചെല്ലാൻ നിശ്ചയിച്ചത്. ദിവാകരനെക്കുറിച്ച് മനസിൽ കിടക്കുന്നത് മോശപ്പെട്ട ചിത്രമാണ്. ആ വിവാഹം കഴിഞ്ഞപ്പോൾ, ഭാനുമതി സന്തോഷമായി ജീവിക്കാൻ ഇടവരട്ടെ എന്ന് ആഗ്രഹിക്കുക മാത്രം ചെയ്തു. ഇപ്പോൾ ഭാനുമതിയെ നേരിട്ടു കാണേണ്ടത് അവരുടെ സമാധാനത്തിന് ആവശ്യമാണ്. തന്റെ കർത്തവ്യവുമാണ്.

"കത്തു കിട്ടി." ചായ കൊണ്ടുവന്നു കൊടുത്തുകൊണ്ട് ഭാനുമതി അറിയിച്ചു.

"അതിന്റെ ഒരു സമാധാനത്തിലാണ് ഭാനു ഇപ്പോൾ നടക്കുന്നത്.." ദിവാകരൻ ചിരിച്ചുകൊണ്ട് പറഞ്ഞു.

മൂന്നുപേരും ഇരുന്നു. സംഭാഷണം തുടർന്നു. സദനത്തിലെ വിവരങ്ങൾ ഭാനുമതി ചോദിച്ചറിഞ്ഞു. അവിടത്തെ സംഭവങ്ങൾ കേട്ട് അവൾക്ക് വിഷമം തോന്നി. സന്ധ്യാദേവിയുടെ വീട്ടിലെ സ്ഥിതിയും മറ്റും അരവിന്ദൻ പറഞ്ഞുകേൾപ്പിച്ചു. റീനയുടെ കല്യാണാലോചന അറിയിച്ചു. അത് കേട്ടപ്പോൾ സന്തോഷമായി. കീർത്തിയെപ്പറ്റി ഭാനുമതി പ്രത്യേകം ചോദിച്ചു. അവൾ പഴയതുപോലെ കുസൃതിയായിട്ടുതന്നെ കഴിയുന്നു. ഭാനുമതിയുടെ ഉള്ളിൽ പലപ്പോഴും തോന്നിയിട്ടുണ്ട്. അരവിന്ദന് കീർത്തിയെ കല്യാണം കഴിക്കരുതോ? അവർ തമ്മിൽ നല്ലതുപോലെ ചേരും.

ഇപ്പോഴും അതോർമിച്ചു.

അരവിന്ദൻ വന്ന കാര്യം വെളിവാക്കി.

"വാസവമേനോൻ ഒരു കാര്യം അറിയിച്ചിട്ടുണ്ട്. വടക്കു നിന്ന് ഒരു സന്യാസി ഇങ്ങോട്ടു വരുന്നുണ്ട്. അദ്ദേഹം തിരുവിതാംകൂറിലും കൊച്ചി

യിലും മലബാറിലുമായി ഒരു മാസക്കാലം കഴിച്ചുകൂട്ടും. ക്ഷേത്രദർശന മാണ് ഉദ്ദേശ്യം. അക്കൂട്ടത്തിൽ അദ്ദേഹമെഴുതുന്ന ഒരു ഗ്രന്ഥത്തിന് സഹായകരമായ വസ്തുതകൾ ശേഖരിക്കുകയും, അപ്പോൾ അദ്ദേഹ ത്തിന് ഈ പ്രദേശത്തിൽ സഞ്ചരിക്കാനും താമസിക്കാനുമുള്ള സൗക ര്യങ്ങൾ മിസ്റ്റർ ദിവാകരൻ ചെയ്തു കൊടുക്കണം. ഇത് എന്നെ അറിയി ക്കാൻ കാരണമുണ്ട്. മേനോൻ മാസ്റ്റർ ഇങ്ങോട്ട് കത്തെഴുതി എന്നു വരേ ണ്ടെന്നു വിചാരിച്ചതാണ്. സൂചനപ്പേരുവച്ചെഴുതിയാൽ മിസ്റ്റർ ദിവാകരന് മനസിലായില്ലെന്നുവരാം. സന്യാസി അപകടകാരിയൊന്നുമല്ല. ശാന്ത നാണ് ഗവൺമെന്റ് വിരുദ്ധനല്ല. എന്നുള്ള വികാരങ്ങളൊക്കെ ധരിക്ക ണമെന്നും എഴുതിയിട്ടുണ്ട്. മറ്റൊന്നുകൂടി, ഈ സന്യാസി മലയാളിയാ ണ്. ചെറുപ്പത്തിൽ ഹിമാലയത്തിലേക്കു പോയതാണ്. വർഷങ്ങളോളം അവിടെ ഗുഹകളിൽ കഴിച്ചുകൂട്ടി പുറത്തുവന്നു. ഒരു ആശ്രമം സ്ഥാപി ച്ചു. ഇപ്പോൾ യൂറോപ്പിലും മറ്റും ശിഷ്യന്മാരുണ്ട്."

ഭാനുമതിക്ക് ചിരിവന്നു. അവൾ ചോദിച്ചു:

"ഈ മേനോൻ മാസ്റ്റർക്ക് ഏതെല്ലാം തരം ആൾക്കാരാണ് കൈവ ശമുള്ളത്?"

ദിവാകരൻ ഉടനെ പറഞ്ഞു.

"ഞാനും അതുതന്നെയാണ് ആലോചിച്ചുകൊണ്ടിരുന്നത്. അത്ഭു തപ്പെട്ട മനുഷ്യൻ തന്നെ. അദ്ദേഹം എന്തുപറഞ്ഞാലും അതുപോലെ നിർവഹിക്കാൻ എനിക്ക് സന്തോഷമേയുള്ളൂ. എന്നാണ് സന്യാസി വരിക?"

"രണ്ടുദിവസത്തിനകം അദ്ദേഹം എറണാകുളത്തെത്തിയേക്കും. അവിടെ സ്വീകരിക്കാൻ ആളുണ്ട്. അടുത്ത വ്യാഴാഴ്ച തൃശൂരെത്തും. അവിടെ നിന്ന് മിസ്റ്റർ ദിവാകരൻ വിളിച്ചുകൊണ്ടുപോരണം. അതാണ് നിർദേശം."

"എന്താണ് സന്യാസിയുടെ പേര്?" ഭാനുമതി അന്വേഷിച്ചു.

"ശിവാനന്ദഭാരതി. ഒരു കാര്യം കൂടി മനസിലാക്കണം. ഓക്സ് ഫോർഡിൽ നിന്ന് ഫിസിക്സ് ഐഛിക വിഷയമായെടുത്ത് എം എസ്സി പാസായശേഷമാണ് അദ്ദേഹം ഹിമാലയത്തിലേക്ക് പോയത്. അപ്പോൾ ചെറിയ മനുഷ്യനല്ല."

"നമുക്ക് വേണ്ടതു ചെയ്യാം മിസ്റ്റർ അരവിന്ദൻ"..... ദിവാകരൻ കാര്യം ഏറ്റു. ശിവാനന്ദഭാരതി വന്നെത്തുന്ന ട്രെയിൻ തുടങ്ങിയ വിശദാംശങ്ങളും ചോദിച്ചു മനസിലാക്കി.

അരവിന്ദൻ പോകാൻ ഭാവിച്ചു. ദിവാകരൻ സമ്മതിച്ചില്ല. പോകു ന്നത് തിടുക്കമാണെങ്കിൽ, ഉച്ചതിരിഞ്ഞ് ഊണുകഴിഞ്ഞ്. അതല്ല, കുറ ച്ചെങ്കിലും സൗകര്യമുണ്ടെങ്കിൽ ഒരു ദിവസം താമസിച്ച്, പിറ്റേന്നു പോക ണം. ഭാനുമതിയും അതേ സ്വരത്തിൽ നിർബന്ധിച്ചു. ഒടുവിൽ ഊണു കഴിച്ച് പോകാമെന്നു സമ്മതിച്ചു.

രാജകീയമായ സ്വീകരണമാണ് അവർ അരവിന്ദനു നൽകിയത്. ഉച്ച

ഭക്ഷണത്തിന്റെ വിഭവങ്ങൾ കണ്ട് അതിഥി അന്തിച്ചിരുന്നു. ഊണുകഴിച്ചുകൊണ്ടിരിക്കുമ്പോൾ അയാൾ ഒരു ഫലിതം പറഞ്ഞു:

"പണക്കാർക്ക് പ്രമേഹം തുടങ്ങിയ രോഗങ്ങൾ വരുന്നത് വെറുതേയല്ല."

ഉച്ചതിരിഞ്ഞ്, ദിവാകരൻ അരവിന്ദനെ കാറിൽ വണ്ടി ഓഫീസുവരെ കൊണ്ടുവന്നു. കാറിലിരിക്കുമ്പോൾ ദിവാകരൻ ചോദിച്ചു:

"രാഷ്ട്രീയം അവിടെയൊക്കെ എങ്ങനെയായിത്തീരും."

"തിരുവിതംകൂറിലോ?"

"അതെ."

"ദിവാൻഭരണം ഇനി അധികം നിൽക്കുകയില്ല. ബ്രിട്ടീഷ് ഭരണം തന്നെ അവസാനിക്കാറായി. അതാണ് എന്റെ കാഴ്ചപ്പാട്."

മനഃപൂർവമാണ് അങ്ങനെ പൊതുവായ ഒരു ഉത്തരം പറഞ്ഞത്. ദിവാകരൻ ദേശീയ പ്രസ്ഥാനത്തിന്റെ എതിരാളിയാണെന്ന് അരവിന്ദനറിയാം.

വണ്ടിയിൽ നിന്നിറങ്ങി, ബസിൽ കയറുന്നതിനുമുൻപ് ദിവാകരൻ പറഞ്ഞു:

"മിസ്റ്റർ അരവിന്ദൻ, എനിക്ക് നിങ്ങളെ സൗകര്യമായി ഒന്നുകാണണമെന്നുണ്ട്. രാഷ്ട്രീയമൊന്നുമല്ല. വ്യക്തിപരമായ കാര്യമാണ്. എനിക്ക് ഒന്നു സംസാരിക്കണം. നിങ്ങൾക്ക് അറിഞ്ഞുകൂടാ. നിങ്ങളുടെ രാഷ്ട്രീയം എനിക്കിഷ്ടമല്ല. എന്നാലും നിങ്ങളെ ഇഷ്ടമാണ്. നിങ്ങൾ മനുഷ്യരുടെ മനസ്സ് അറിയാവുന്ന ആളാണ്. ഞാൻ ജീവിതത്തിൽ ഏറ്റവും വലിയ മാനസികത്തകർച്ചയുമായി നടക്കുന്ന ആളാണ്. ഞാൻ ഭാനുമതിയെ വിവാഹം കഴിച്ചു. ഇപ്പോൾ എനിക്കു തോന്നുന്നു അത് വേണ്ടായിരുന്നെന്ന്. അവൾ നല്ലവളാണ് അവളുടെ പൂർവകഥകൊണ്ടുമാത്രം പറയുകയല്ല. ഒരുമിച്ച് ജീവിച്ച് ഇത്രയും നാൾകൊണ്ടുമാത്രം ഞാൻ അവളെ മനസിലാക്കിയിരിക്കുന്നു. ഇത്രയും നല്ല ഒരു ഭാര്യയെ എനിക്കു വേണ്ടായിരുന്നു. ഇത്രയും നല്ല ഒരു പെണ്ണിനെ ഞാൻ വലയ്ക്കരുതായിരുന്നു..."

അയാൾ പൊടുന്നനെ നിറുത്തി. എന്നിട്ട് അപ്പോൾ തോന്നിയതുപോലെ ചോദിച്ചു:

"മിസ്റ്റർ അരവിന്ദൻ. ഞാൻ.. ഞാനപേക്ഷിക്കുന്നു ഈ കാറിൽ നമുക്ക് ഒരു സ്ഥലംവരെ പോകാം. അവിടെയിരുന്ന് എനിക്കൊന്നു സംസാരിക്കണം. അത് നിങ്ങളൊന്ന് കേൾക്കണം എന്നെ നിങ്ങൾക്ക് ഇഷ്ടമില്ലെങ്കിൽക്കൂടിയും കേൾക്കണം. ഞാൻ, നിങ്ങളെ എവിടെ വേണമെങ്കിലും കൊണ്ടുപോയി വിടാം."

അരവിന്ദൻ ആ മനുഷ്യനെ നോക്കി. പെട്ടെന്ന് അയാളുടെ രീതിയും ശബ്ദവും മാറിപ്പോയിരിക്കുന്നു. അയാളുടെ മനസിൽ വ്യഥയുണ്ട്. ആ വാക്കുകൾ ആത്മാർഥമാണ്. സംശയമില്ല അയാൾക്കുവേണ്ടി കുറെ സമയം ചെലവഴിക്കാൻ തീരുമാനിച്ചു. അപ്പോൾ ഭാനുമതിയുടെ മുഖമാണ് അരവിന്ദന്റെ മനസിലുണ്ടായിരുന്നത്.

കുന്നിൻചരിവിലെ ടി ബിയിൽ ഒരു മുറിക്കകത്ത് അവർ ഇരുന്നു. സന്ധ്യയോടടുക്കുന്നു. വൈകുന്നേരത്തെ പ്രകാശം മുറ്റത്തും മുറിയിലും വീഴുന്നു. താഴ്വാരങ്ങളിൽ അത് നിഴലും വെളിച്ചവും ചേർന്ന് പല ചിത്രങ്ങൾ വരയ്ക്കുന്നു. ഉണങ്ങിയ മണ്ണിന്റെ ഗന്ധം മൂക്കിലേക്ക് വന്നു കയറുന്നു. ദൂരെ ഒരു പാതയിൽക്കൂടി കാളവണ്ടികൾ പോകുന്നു. ആ വഴിക്കാണ് കുന്നിൻ ചരിവിലേക്ക് വന്നത്. പകലിന്റെ ചൂടിൽ വൃക്ഷങ്ങൾ വാടിത്തളർന്നു നിൽക്കുന്നു. ചൂട് ഇപ്പോഴും അന്തരീക്ഷത്തെ പൊതിഞ്ഞു പിടിച്ചിട്ടുണ്ട്.

ജനാലയിൽക്കൂടി പിൻപുറത്തേക്കു നോക്കിയപ്പോൾ കുറെ സ്ത്രീകളെ കണ്ടു. അവർ പകലത്തെ ജോലികൾ കഴിഞ്ഞ് മറ്റൊരു കുന്നുകയറി പോവുകയാണ്. അവരുടെ നീണ്ട നിഴലുകൾ അവർക്ക് മുൻപേ പോകുന്നതു കാണാൻ ഭംഗി തോന്നി.

വാച്ചർ പുറത്തിരുന്ന്, റാന്തലുവിളക്ക് തുടച്ചു വൃത്തിയാക്കുന്നു. ഇവിടെ സാധാരണയായി ആളുകൾ വരാറില്ലെന്ന് അയാൾ പറഞ്ഞു. അതുകൊണ്ട് വിളക്ക് കൊളുത്തേണ്ടി വരാറില്ല. വിളക്കിൽ കരിയേക്കാൾ പൊടിയാണുള്ളത്. കാറ്റത്തടിച്ചു കയറുന്ന ചുവന്ന ധൂളി. ഭിത്തിയിലും തറയിലും മേശയിലും കസേരയിലും എല്ലാമുണ്ട്. ഒരു പഴയ ചാക്കുകൊണ്ട് വാച്ചർ ഇരിപ്പിടങ്ങളും മേശയും തുടച്ചു. പിന്നെയാണ് ഇരുന്നത്. രാത്രിയിൽ താമസമുണ്ടെങ്കിൽ, ആഹാരം ഒരു മൈലകലെ നിന്ന് വാങ്ങിക്കണമെന്ന് അയാൾ നേരത്തെ അറിയിച്ചു. അത് വേണ്ട. പാലില്ലാത്ത കാപ്പി ഉണ്ടാക്കാൻ സൗകര്യമുണ്ട്. അത് മതിയെന്ന് അയാളെയും അറിയിച്ചിട്ടുണ്ട്.

ദിവാകരൻ ചിന്തയിൽ മുഴുകി, പുറത്തേക്കു നോക്കി ഇരുന്നു. അയാൾക്ക് സംസാരിക്കാൻ പ്രയാസമുണ്ട്. വിവാഹത്തിനുമുൻപ് പത്രമാഫീസിൽ കയറിവന്നത് അരവിന്ദൻ ഓർമിച്ചു. അന്നും അയാൾ അസ്വസ്ഥനായിരുന്നു. സംസാരിച്ചത് വിക്കിവിക്കിയാണ്. ഇപ്പോൾ സംസാരിക്കാൻ തന്നെ ബുദ്ധിമുട്ടുള്ളതുപോലെ.

"മിസ്റ്റർ അരവിന്ദൻ.." അയാൾ പറഞ്ഞുതുടങ്ങി. "ഞാൻ എന്തിനു നിങ്ങളെ വിളിച്ചുകൊണ്ടുവന്നു എന്ന് ഇപ്പോൾ ആലോചിക്കുകയാണ്. കാരണം, എന്റെ കാര്യങ്ങൾ കേൾക്കാൻ ഇത്രയും നിങ്ങളെ ബുദ്ധിമുട്ടിക്കണോ? ഒരുപക്ഷേ, എന്റെ ഉള്ളിലെ നിലയ്ക്കാത്ത വേദനകളും ആശങ്കകളും കൊണ്ടായിരിക്കാം ഇതു തോന്നുന്നത്. ഏതായാലും നിങ്ങൾ കേൾക്കുക. എന്റെ മനസിലെ സംഘട്ടനം ഒന്നറിയുക. പ്രതിവിധി പറയാൻ വേണ്ടിയിട്ടല്ല. എനിക്ക് ഒരു സമാധാനത്തിനുവേണ്ടി."

അയാൾ ഒരു സിഗരറ്റു കത്തിച്ചു. അരവിന്ദൻ അതിൽ പങ്കുചേർന്നില്ല.

അയാൾ തുടർന്നു:

"ഞാൻ ബിസിനസ് ചെയ്യുന്നുണ്ട്. ഇതു തുടങ്ങിയിട്ട് ഇപ്പോൾ പതിനെട്ടു വർഷമാകുന്നു. ഇതിലേക്ക് വരാൻ കാരണം കർണാടകത്തിലുള്ള ഒരു ഗൗണ്ടറാണ്. ആ മനുഷ്യൻ ഇപ്പോൾ ജീവിച്ചിരിപ്പില്ല. രണ്ടു വർഷ

ങ്ങൾക്കു മുൻപ് മരിച്ചു. തടി ബിസിനസ് ചില കാലഘട്ടങ്ങളിൽ ലാഭകരമാണ്. അങ്ങനെ എനിക്ക് വളരെയധികം പണം കിട്ടി. ഞാൻ വിവാഹം കഴിച്ചു. കുറേനാൾ ഞങ്ങൾ ഒരുമിച്ചു ജീവിച്ചു. പിന്നെ അവർ മരിച്ചു ഞാൻ ഒറ്റയ്ക്കായി.

"ഇത്രയും പറയുമ്പോൾ ഒരു സാധാരണ കഥ. എന്നാൽ ഇതിന്റെ പിന്നിൽ ഒരു അസാധാരണ കഥ നടന്നു. നടക്കുന്നു. ഗൗണ്ടർ രണ്ടാമത് ഒരു വിവാഹം കഴിച്ചിരുന്നു. അത് അദ്ദേഹത്തിന് അറുപത്തഞ്ച് വയസ്സ് പ്രായമുള്ളപ്പോഴാണ്. അവൾ ചെറുപ്പക്കാരിയായിരുന്നു. ലീലാംബാൾ എന്നാണ് അവളുടെ പേര്. ഇനി പറയുന്ന ഭാഗം കേട്ടിട്ട് എന്നോട് ക്ഷമിക്കണം. തുറന്നുപറയുകയാണ്. ഗൗണ്ടറും ഞാനും വളരെ അടുപ്പമാണല്ലോ. മാസത്തിൽ രണ്ടുമൂന്നുദിവസമെങ്കിലും ഞാൻ വയനാട്ടിലുള്ള അയാളുടെ ബംഗ്ലാവിൽപ്പോയി താമസിക്കും. അപ്പോഴാണ് ഞങ്ങൾ ബിസിനസു കാര്യങ്ങൾ ആലോചിക്കുക. അങ്ങേര് മുടക്കിയ പണം തിരിച്ചു കൊടുത്തുകൊണ്ടിരിക്കുകയാണ്. അതേസമയം അങ്ങേരുടെ ബിസിനസിൽ ഞാൻ ശാരീരികമായ സഹായങ്ങൾ ചെയ്യുന്നുണ്ട്. നാളുകൾ പോയി. ഗൗണ്ടർ ബാംഗ്ലൂർക്കും മറ്റും പോകുമ്പോൾ ഞാൻ അവിടെ ചെല്ലാറുണ്ട്. എന്തിനു പറയുന്നു. ലീലാംബാളും ഞാനും അടുപ്പമായി. അടുത്തപ്പോൾ, അവൾ വൃദ്ധനായ ഗൗണ്ടറിൽ തൃപ്തനല്ലെന്ന് മനസിലായി. അവൾ അത് തുറന്നു പറയുകയും ചെയ്തിട്ടുണ്ട്. അവൾ ഗർഭിണിയായി. അപ്പോൾ മുതൽ ഗൗണ്ടർക്ക് സംശയം തുടങ്ങി. കാരണം ആദ്യഭാര്യയിൽ അങ്ങേർക്ക് മക്കളില്ലായിരുന്നു. താൻ അതിന് കഴിവില്ലാത്തവനാണെന്നുതന്നെ അങ്ങേർ വിശ്വസിച്ചിരുന്നിരിക്കണം. അതിനുശേഷവും ഒരു മുടക്കവും കൂടാതെ ഞാൻ അവിടെ പോകും. ആ മനുഷ്യന്റെ സംശയം എന്നോട് അവൾ പറഞ്ഞു. എന്നിട്ടും പോയി. അത് അറിഞ്ഞുവെന്ന് വരുത്താൻ പാടില്ലല്ലോ. ഗൗണ്ടർ എന്നോട് യാതൊരു ഭാവവ്യത്യാസവും കാട്ടിയില്ല. പക്ഷേ, അങ്ങേർ കൂടുതൽ തവണ ബാംഗ്ലൂർക്ക് പോകാൻ തുടങ്ങി. അവിടെ കൂടുതൽ ദിവസം താമസിച്ചു. അവളോടുള്ള താൽപ്പര്യം കുറഞ്ഞുവരുന്നു എന്നതിന്റെ ലക്ഷണമായിരുന്നു അത്. അവൾ പ്രസവിച്ചു. ആ കുഞ്ഞിനോട് അങ്ങേർ അത്ര മമത കാണിച്ചില്ല.

രണ്ടുവർഷം മുമ്പ് അങ്ങേർ മരിച്ചു. ബാംഗ്ലൂരിൽ കിടന്നാണ് മരിച്ചത്. അപ്പോൾ ഞാൻ പോയി. അവിടെത്തന്നെ ശവസംസ്കാരം നടത്തി. തിരിച്ചു വയനാട്ടിലേക്കു പോന്നത് അവളും ഞാനും കൂടിയാണ്. രണ്ടുദിവസം അവിടെ കഴിച്ചുകൂട്ടി. ഏതെല്ലാംരീതിയിൽ പ്രവർത്തിക്കണമെന്ന് ഗൗണ്ടറുടെ മാനേജർക്ക് നിർദേശം നൽകിയിട്ട്, ഞാൻ പോന്നു. പോരാൻ സമയം അവൾ എന്നോട് അഭ്യർഥിച്ചു. മാസംതോറും ചെല്ലണമെന്ന് അത് അപകടമായിരുന്നു. അങ്ങനെയൊരു ബന്ധം സംഭവിച്ചുപോയെങ്കിലും ഗൗണ്ടർ മരിച്ചശേഷം ഞാൻ അവിടെ തുടർച്ചയായി പോകുന്നതു ശരിയല്ലെന്നു എനിക്ക് തോന്നി. ആ ബന്ധം അവസാനിച്ചു കഴിഞ്ഞിരിക്കുന്നുവെന്ന് ഞാൻ നിശ്ചയിച്ചു.

ഗൗണ്ടർ മരിച്ച് രണ്ടുമൂന്നു മാസം കഴിഞ്ഞപ്പോൾ അവളുടെ ഒരു കത്തുവന്നു. അത് എനിക്ക് അൽപ്പം വിഷമമുണ്ടാക്കി: ഗൗണ്ടർ അവസാനക്കാലത്ത് ഒരു വിൽപ്പത്രമെഴുതി. അതിൽ വയനാട്ടിലെ ആ ബംഗ്ലാവും പത്തേക്കർ സ്ഥലവുമൊഴിച്ച് ബാക്കിയെല്ലാം അങ്ങേരുടെ സഹോദരിക്കു കൊടുത്തു. വയനാട്ടിലെ ബംഗ്ലാവ് ലീലാംബാളിനും. ആ ബംഗ്ലാവും ആ സ്ഥലവും ഒരു ഭാരം മാത്രമാണ്. ബംഗ്ലാവ് അറ്റകുറ്റപ്പണികൾ നടത്തി സൂക്ഷിച്ചു കൊണ്ടുപോകാൻ വലിയ തുക വേണം. പത്തേക്കർ സ്ഥലത്തിൽ കുറെ വൃക്ഷങ്ങളുണ്ട്. നിരന്തരമായി ആദായം കൊടുക്കുന്ന ഒന്നുമില്ല. ഭംഗിക്കുവേണ്ടി വച്ച ബംഗ്ലാവാണ്. ഞാൻ ചെല്ലണമെന്നാണ് അവൾ എഴുതിയിരുന്നത്. ഞാൻ ചെന്ന്, രക്ഷിക്കണമെന്ന്. ഗൗണ്ടറുടെ വീട്ടുകാരെല്ലാം അവൾക്ക് എതിരായിരുന്നു. ആ രണ്ടാം വിവാഹം അവർക്ക് ഇഷ്ടമല്ലായിരുന്നു. അങ്ങേർ മരിച്ചപ്പോൾ പിന്നെ ചോദിക്കേണ്ടല്ലോ.

ഞാൻ പോയില്ല. ആ എഴുത്തും മറക്കാൻ ഞാൻ ശ്രമിച്ചു.

രണ്ടുമൂന്നു മാസം കൂടി കഴിഞ്ഞു. വീണ്ടും കത്തുവന്നു. അതുപരിഭവിച്ചും ശകാരിച്ചും ഉള്ള കത്തായിരുന്നു. ഒരു ഭീഷണിയുടെ അംശവും അതിൽ ഉണ്ടായിരുന്നു. ഗൗണ്ടർ അവളുമായി അകന്നത് ഞാൻ മൂലമാണ്. അതുകൊണ്ടാണ് അങ്ങേർ സ്വത്തെല്ലാം മറ്റുള്ളവർക്ക് കൊടുത്തത്. കുട്ടി എന്റേതാണ്. ഗൗണ്ടർ തന്നെ ഉപേക്ഷിച്ചത് ഞാനും അവളും തമ്മിലുള്ള ബന്ധം കൊണ്ടാണെന്നതിനും കുട്ടി എന്റേതാണെന്നുമുള്ളതിനും തെളിവുകളുണ്ട്. ഗൗണ്ടർ, ബാംഗ്ലൂർനിന്നും എഴുതിയ പല കത്തുകളാണത്. അതെല്ലാം അവൾ സൂക്ഷിച്ചിട്ടുണ്ട്. കുട്ടികളുണ്ടാകാത്ത ഗൗണ്ടറുടെ ഭാര്യക്ക് ഗർഭമായത് ഞാൻ മൂലമാണെന്നു വിശ്വസിക്കുന്നതായി ഗൗണ്ടർ ഒന്നിലധികം തവണ എഴുതിയിട്ടുണ്ട്. അതും അവളുടെ കൈയിൽ ഇരിപ്പുണ്ട്. ഇതായിരുന്നു അവളുടെ കത്ത്.

ഞാൻ തെല്ലു പരിഭ്രമിക്കാതിരുന്നില്ല. എന്നാലും അനങ്ങിയില്ല. മാസങ്ങൾ കഴിഞ്ഞു. എന്റെ ഭാര്യ എന്നെ വിട്ടുപിരിഞ്ഞു. ലീലാംബാളുടെ അനക്കമുണ്ടായിരുന്നില്ല.

ഭാനുമതിയുമായുള്ള കല്യാണം നിശ്ചയിച്ചതിനുശേഷം ഒരു ദിവസം ലീലാംബാൾ എന്റെ വീട്ടിൽ വന്നു. ഞാൻ അവിടെ ഉണ്ടായിരുന്നില്ല. ജോലിക്കാർ എന്നെ വിവരമറിയിച്ചു. അതിനിടയ്ക്കാണ് ഞാൻ അവിടെ വന്നു നിങ്ങളെ കണ്ടത്. പിന്നെ ഞാൻ അവൾക്ക് ഒരു കത്തയച്ചു. അതിനു മറുപടിയും വന്നു. അവൾ ഒരു ശല്യവും ഉണ്ടാക്കുകയില്ലെന്നും ഒന്നു വെറുതെ കാണാൻ വന്നതാണെന്നും അവൾ എഴുതിയിരുന്നു. ഞാൻ വിവാഹം കഴിക്കുന്നു എന്ന് അവൾക്ക് അറിഞ്ഞുകൂടായിരുന്നല്ലോ.

വിവാഹം കഴിഞ്ഞ് രണ്ടാഴ്ചയായപ്പോൾ വീണ്ടും അവളുടെ കത്തു വന്നു. അതിൽ അവൾ ക്ഷോഭിച്ച് പലതുമെഴുതിയിരുന്നു. എന്റെ വിവാഹം അവൾ അറിഞ്ഞിരുന്നു. ആരോ മുഖാന്തരം അറിഞ്ഞു. അവൾ എന്നെ സംബന്ധിച്ച് എപ്പോഴും തിരക്കാറുണ്ടെന്ന് എനിക്ക് ബോധ്യമുണ്ട്. പ്രത്യേകിച്ചും തടി ബിസിനസുമായി ബന്ധപ്പെട്ട പലരെയും അവൾക്കു

പരിചയമുണ്ട്. ഞാൻ ചെന്നില്ലെങ്കിൽ അവൾ കോടതിയിൽ കേസുകൊടുക്കുമെന്ന്. ഗൗണ്ടറുടെ കത്തുകൾ അവൾ അവിടെ ഹാജരാക്കും.

ഇതിനിടയ്ക്ക് ഒരു കച്ചവടത്തിൽ ഭീമമായ നഷ്ടം വന്നു. ഞാനിപ്പോൾ കുറേ ലക്ഷം രൂപ കടത്തിലായിരിക്കുന്നു. ആരെയും അറിയിച്ചിട്ടില്ല. അവൾ ഒരു പ്രത്യേക സ്വഭാവക്കാരിയാണ്. ക്രൂരമായ ഒരു വശം അവളിലുണ്ടെന്ന് എനിക്കറിയാം. അവൾ എന്തിനും മടിക്കുകയില്ല. കേസു കൊടുക്കും. വേണ്ടിവന്നാൽ ഇങ്ങോട്ടു വരും. ഗൗണ്ടറുടെ കത്തുകൾ സൂക്ഷിച്ചിട്ടുണ്ടെങ്കിൽ അവൾ കോടതിയിൽ ഹാജരാക്കും. അവൾക്ക് അതിനു മടിയൊന്നുമില്ല. അപരാധബോധവുമില്ല. ഇതൊക്കെ ഉടനെ സംഭവിക്കാം. ബാങ്കുകാർ വസ്തുക്കൾ ജപ്തിചെയ്യുമെന്നും നോട്ടീസ് തന്നിട്ടുണ്ട്. ഇനി അവളുടെ നോട്ടീസും കൂടി വന്നാൽ മതി.

"ഇതിന്റെ അർഥം മിസ്റ്റർ അരവിന്ദനു മനസിലായോ? ഇപ്പോൾ ഞാൻ ബാങ്ക്റപ്റ്റാണ്. വെറും പാപ്പർ. കടംവീട്ടാൻ പണമില്ല. വസ്തുക്കൾ മുഴുവൻ കൊണ്ടുപോയാലും കടം ബാക്കി കിടക്കും. എവിടെയെങ്കിലും പോകേണ്ടിവരും. അവൾ കേസുകൊടുത്താൽ അവളെയും കുഞ്ഞിനെയും ഞാൻ സ്വീകരിക്കേണ്ടി വരും. കാരണം, അവൾക്കു സ്വത്തും പണവുമാണ് വേണ്ടത്. അത് എനിക്കില്ലെന്നു കോടതി മനസിലാക്കും. പിന്നെ എന്തു ചെയ്യണം? അവളെയും കുഞ്ഞിനെയും ഞാൻ സംരക്ഷിക്കണം..."

അരവിന്ദൻ കഥ കേട്ടു. അയാൾക്കു സഹതാപം തോന്നി. ലീലാംബാളുമായുള്ള ബന്ധത്തെപ്പറ്റി ഒന്നും തോന്നിയില്ല. അതു ശരിയാണെന്നല്ല. സംഭവിച്ചുപോയി. അയാളുടെ ദുർബലതമൂലം. ഇന്ന് അയാൾ തകർന്നിരിക്കുന്നു. അവൾ അയാളെ വേട്ടയാടുകയും ചെയ്യുന്നു. അതിന്റെ പര്യവസാനം എന്തായിരിക്കും? അതിൽ ഏറ്റവും കൂടുതൽ ദണ്ഡിക്കാൻ പോകുന്നത് ആരാണ്? ഭാനുമതിയായിരിക്കും.

"നിങ്ങൾ ഉടനെ എന്തെങ്കിലും ഒരു പോംവഴി ഉണ്ടാക്കുമെന്ന് വിചാരിച്ചല്ല ഞാനിത് പറഞ്ഞത്. അങ്ങനെ പോംവഴിയില്ലല്ലോ. ഞാൻ ഇതെല്ലാം അനുഭവിക്കേണ്ടവനാണെന്ന് എനിക്കറിയാം, അനുഭവിക്കുന്നു. എന്നോട് ആരും സഹതപിക്കുകയില്ല അതും എനിക്കറിയാം, ഭാനുവിനെപ്പറ്റി എനിക്കു ദുഃഖമുണ്ട്. അവളെ ക്ലേശിപ്പിക്കാൻ എനിക്കിഷ്ടമില്ല. അവൾ ഇതെന്തെങ്കിലും അറിയുന്നതുപോലും എനിക്ക് സങ്കടമാണ്."

ഇനിയും അരവിന്ദന്റെ യാത്ര വൈകിക്കേണ്ടെന്ന് ദിവാകരനു തോന്നി. അയാൾ അരവിന്ദനെ കാറിലേക്കു കൂട്ടിക്കൊണ്ടു പോയി. തൃശൂർവരെ കാറിൽ കൊണ്ടുചെന്നുവിട്ടു. യാത്രയ്ക്കിടയിൽ അവർ ഒന്നും സംസാരിച്ചില്ല.

പന്ത്രണ്ട്

ദിവാകരൻ നേരെ വീട്ടിലേക്കല്ല പോയത്. റോബർട്ടിന്റെ എസ്റ്റേറ്റിലെ വീട്ടിലേക്കാണ്. സമയം കുറേ വൈകിയിരുന്നു. പക്ഷേ, റോബർട്ട്

ഉറങ്ങിയിട്ടില്ല. ദിവാകരനെ കണ്ടപ്പോൾ അയാൾ പറഞ്ഞു:

"വന്നതു വളരെ നന്നായി ഞാൻ നിങ്ങളെ കാണാനിരിക്കുകയായിരുന്നു."

"എന്താ കാര്യം?" ദിവാകരന് ഇപ്പോൾ എന്തു കേട്ടാലും ഉൽക്കണ്ഠയാണ്. അതു പുറത്തു കാണിക്കാറില്ലെന്നേയുള്ളൂ.

"ഇരിക്കൂ." അയാൾ പറഞ്ഞു. രണ്ടുപേരും അടുത്തടുത്ത് ഇരുന്നു.

"നിങ്ങൾ പറഞ്ഞതനുസരിച്ച് ഞാൻ ബാങ്കിന്റെ ഹെഡ്ഡാഫീസിൽ പോയിരുന്നു. മാനേജിങ് ഡയറക്ടറുമായി സംസാരിച്ചു. ബിസിനസിൽ നിങ്ങളോട് വളരെ അടുത്തു നിൽക്കുന്നു. ആരോ ഒക്കെ ബാങ്കിൽ ചില അറിയിപ്പുകൾ കൊടുത്തിട്ടുണ്ട്. അതിൽ വിചിത്രമായ ഒരു കാര്യമുണ്ട്. നിങ്ങൾ മനഃപൂർവമായി ഒഴിഞ്ഞു മാറുന്നു എന്നാണ് മാനേജിങ് ഡയറക്ടറുടെ വാദം. നഷ്ടം വന്നു എന്നു പറയുന്നത് വെറുതെയാണ്. നിങ്ങളുടെ കയ്യിൽ പണമുണ്ട്. ബാങ്കുകാർ ജപ്തിചെയ്യും. ചെയ്താൽ അവർക്ക് മുഴുവൻ തുകയും ഈടാകുകയില്ല. നിങ്ങളെ ജയിലിലേക്ക് അയക്കുമായിരിക്കും. എന്നാലും നിങ്ങൾക്ക് ലാഭമാണ്. നിങ്ങൾ ഇങ്ങനെ വിചാരിക്കുന്നുവെന്നാണ് ആരോപണം. ഞാൻ വളരെയധികം സംസാരിച്ചുനോക്കി. ഫലമില്ല. അവർ വഴങ്ങുന്നില്ല."

ദിവാകരൻ കേട്ടുകൊണ്ടിരുന്നതല്ലാതെ, ഒന്നും മറുപടി പറഞ്ഞില്ല. എന്തുപറയാനാണ്? വെളുപ്പാൻകാലം വരെ അയാൾ അവിടെ ഉറങ്ങാതെ കിടന്നു. പുലരുന്നതിനുമുൻപ് വീട്ടിലേക്കു മടങ്ങി.

ദിവാകരന് എന്തോ കാര്യമായ മനഃപ്രയാസമുണ്ടായിട്ടുണ്ടെന്ന് ഭാനുമതി മനസിലാക്കിയിരിക്കുന്നു. അയാൾ ചിരിക്കാൻ ശ്രമിച്ചിട്ടും ചിരി വരുന്നില്ല. അവളെ സന്തോഷിപ്പിക്കാൻ പലതും പറയുമ്പോഴും ആലോചന മറ്റു വല്ലയിടത്തുമാണ്. കാര്യം എന്താണെന്ന് അങ്ങോട്ടു ചോദിക്കാൻ ധൈര്യം വന്നില്ല. മുൻപത്തേക്കാളും സ്നേഹത്തോടെയാണ് അയാൾ അവളോടു പെരുമാറുന്നത്. കൂടുതൽ സമയം അവളുടെ കൂടെയിരുന്നു സംസാരിക്കാനും അയാൾ താൽപ്പര്യം കാണിക്കുന്നുണ്ട്. പക്ഷേ, പല രാത്രികളിലും അവൾ ഉണർന്നു നോക്കുമ്പോൾ അയാൾ സിഗരറ്റും കത്തിച്ചു പിടിച്ച് ചിന്തയിൽ മുഴുകിയിരിക്കുന്നതു കാണാം. അവളുടെ മനസ്സ് അതുമൂലം ഒരുതരം മൂകതയിലേക്കു വീഴുകയാണ്. അരവിന്ദനെ കൊണ്ടുവിട്ടിട്ട് രാത്രിയിൽ വന്നില്ല. രാവിലെ ക്ഷീണിച്ചു തളർന്ന് വന്നു കയറി. അപ്പോൾ അവൾ ഒന്നും ചോദിച്ചില്ല. പക്ഷേ, അയാൾ പറഞ്ഞു.

അരവിന്ദൻ നല്ല മനുഷ്യനാണ്. ഭാനൂ, കുറച്ചു മണിക്കൂറുകളേ ഞാൻ അയാളുടെകൂടെ കഴിച്ചുള്ളൂ. അതിനിടയ്ക്ക് അയാളെ എനിക്ക് മനസിലാക്കാൻ കഴിഞ്ഞു. അധികം സംസാരിക്കില്ല. എന്നാലും മറ്റുള്ളവരുടെ ഹൃദയമറിയാൻ അയാൾക്കു കഴിയും. അതറിയുന്നുവെന്ന്, അധികം സംസാരിക്കാതെ ബോധ്യപ്പെടുത്താനും ആ മനുഷ്യന് സാധിക്കും. അയാൾ വലിയ കവി മാത്രമല്ല, വലിയ മനുഷ്യനുമാണ്."

ഇപ്പോൾ ഇത്രയും സ്തുതി പറയാൻ കാരണമെന്ത്? രാത്രി കുറേ

വൈകുംവരെ അവർ ഒരുമിച്ചുണ്ടായിരുന്നുവെന്നും തൃശൂർ കൊണ്ടു ചെന്നു വിട്ടുവെന്നും സൂചിപ്പിച്ചു. അതിനിടയ്ക്ക് ഇത്ര മതിപ്പു തോന്നാൻ എന്തുണ്ടായി?

എന്തുമാവട്ടെ ഒരാളെപ്പറ്റി നല്ലതുപറഞ്ഞാൽ എന്തുകൊണ്ടു പറഞ്ഞുവെന്ന് ചോദിക്കേണ്ട കാര്യമുണ്ടോ?

അരവിന്ദൻ പോയി രണ്ടുമൂന്നു ദിവസങ്ങളിലാണ് ദിവാകരന്റെ മാറ്റം പ്രത്യക്ഷമായത്. തനിക്കു ഊഹം കിട്ടിയിട്ടുള്ള വിഷയമാണോ ഭർത്താവിനെ അലട്ടുന്നത്? അതു സംബന്ധിച്ചു വല്ലതും ഉണ്ടായിട്ടുണ്ടോ?

മൂന്നാം ദിവസം രാവിലെ ദിവാകരൻ ഇറങ്ങി.

"ഭാനൂ ഞാൻ രണ്ടു ദിവസം കഴിഞ്ഞേ വരൂ."

"ശരി."

എവിടെ പോകുന്നുവെന്ന് ഒരിക്കലും അവൾ ചോദിക്കാറില്ല. ഇങ്ങോട്ടു പറഞ്ഞാൽ മാത്രം കേൾക്കും.

വസ്ത്രങ്ങൾ ഒരുക്കിവച്ച പെട്ടി അവൾ തന്നെ കാറിൽ കൊണ്ടു ചെന്നുവച്ചു. വണ്ടി സ്റ്റാർട്ടുചെയ്തു നിർത്തിക്കൊണ്ട് അയാൾ പറഞ്ഞു.

"ഞാൻ മടങ്ങിവരും വരെ നീ സമാധാനമായിട്ടിരിക്കണം. ബിസിന സുപരമായി നമുക്കു കുറച്ചു ക്ഷീണങ്ങൾ പറ്റിയിട്ടുണ്ട്. ചിലപ്പോൾ അതു സംബന്ധമായിട്ടു വല്ലവരും എന്നെതിരക്കി വരികയോ മറ്റോ ചെയ്താൽ, വിഷമിക്കേണ്ട കേട്ടോ."

പതിവില്ലാത്ത വാക്കുകൾ. അവൾ തലകുലുക്കി. കാറു നീങ്ങി. അവൾ നോക്കിനിന്നു. കഴിഞ്ഞ ദിവസങ്ങളിലെ വ്യാകുലതയുടെ അർഥം മനസിലായി. അവൾ സമാധാനിച്ചു. എന്തും വരട്ടെ, പണത്തിനു കുറവോ ഞെരുക്കമോ വരുമെന്നല്ലേ ഉള്ളൂ. ഉള്ളതുപോലെ ജീവിക്കും. നേരത്തെ ഈ വാക്കുകൾ കേട്ടിരുന്നെങ്കിൽ അങ്ങോട്ടു സമാധാനിപ്പിക്കാമായിരുന്നു. തന്നെ വിഷമിപ്പിക്കേണ്ടെന്നു കരുതിത്തന്നെ ഒന്നും മിണ്ടാത്തതാണ്. ഇപ്പോൾ ഇത്രയും പറഞ്ഞല്ലേതീരൂ.

ഭർത്താവിന് ബുദ്ധിമുട്ടുകളുണ്ടാവില്ല, എന്നു മനസാ പ്രാർഥിച്ചു. ദൈവം കാത്തുരക്ഷിക്കുമെന്ന് ആശ്വസിച്ചു.

സമയം അഞ്ചുമണിയായിട്ടുണ്ട്. മുറ്റത്ത് ഒരു കസേരയിട്ട് ഭാനുമതി ഇരുന്നു. വനിതാസമാജവും സദനവുമൊക്കെയായിരുന്നു ചിന്താവിഷയം. സന്ധ്യാദേവിയെ കാണണമെന്ന് ഇന്ന് അതിയായ ആഗ്രഹമുണ്ട്. വനിതാ സമാജത്തിലെ കുട്ടികളെയും കാണണം. ചിന്തിച്ചിരിക്കുമ്പോൾ ഒരു ചെറുപ്പക്കാരൻ ഗേറ്റിൽ വന്നു നിന്നു. അതു മെല്ലെ തുറന്നു സംശയിച്ച്, അകത്തേക്കു കടന്നുവന്നു നിന്നു.

"വരൂ." അവൾ എഴുന്നേറ്റു.

ഒരു കസേര എടുത്തുകൊണ്ടു വന്നിട്ടു.

"ഇരിക്കൂ."

അയാൾ ഇരുന്നു.

"എവിടെ നിന്നാണ്?"

"ഭാനുമതി അല്ലേ?" അയാൾ അന്വേഷിച്ചു.

"അതെ."

ഒരു ചെറിയ പുഞ്ചിരിയോടെ അയാൾ സ്വയം പരിചയപ്പെടുത്തി.

"എന്നെ അറിയാം പണ്ട് ചേച്ചി ഞങ്ങളുടെ വീട്ടിൽ താമസിച്ചിട്ടുണ്ട്. കൊച്ചുന്നാളിൽ."

എല്ലാ ഓർമകളും കൂടി പ്രവഹിച്ചു. അയാളെ സൂക്ഷിച്ചു നോക്കി. രത്നമ്മയുടെ വീട്ടിൽ നിന്നാണ്. അവളുടെ സഹോദരൻ. അതേ, സഹോദരനായിരിക്കും. അന്നു കൊച്ചുകുട്ടിയായിരുന്ന അയ്യപ്പൻ. വലിയ മാറ്റമുണ്ട്.

"അയ്യപ്പനല്ലേ?" ഭാനുമതി ചോദിച്ചു.

"അതെ." അയാളുടെ മുഖം വികസിച്ചു.

ദിവാകരന്റെ അളിയൻ. രത്നമ്മയുടെ മരണം കൊണ്ട് ആ കുടുംബം ദുഃഖത്തിലാണ്ടിരിക്കും. അവൾ ഒരു പെണ്ണേയുള്ളൂ. അവളെപ്പറ്റി എന്തെല്ലാം വേദന ആ കുടുംബക്കാർ അനുഭവിച്ചു! അവസാനം ഇങ്ങനെയും......

പെട്ടെന്ന് മറ്റൊരു തോന്നൽ. എന്നിട്ട് താൻ ആ മനുഷ്യന്റെ ഭാര്യയായിരിക്കുന്നു. ഇത് എപ്പോഴും ആലോചിച്ചു പോകാറുണ്ട്. ഇപ്പോൾ സഹോദരൻ മുമ്പിലിരിക്കുമ്പോൾ അത് വല്ലാത്ത ഒരു ജാള്യതയായി.... കുറ്റബോധമായി, അനുഭവപ്പെടുന്നു.

എന്നിട്ട് ഈ കൊച്ചൻ എന്തിന്, എങ്ങനെ ഇവിടെ വന്നു?

സ്വയം നിയന്ത്രിക്കാൻ നോക്കി അകത്തേക്കു വിളിച്ചു.

"രാജമ്മേ!"

രാജമ്മ വന്നു. കാപ്പിക്കു പറയാൻ തുടങ്ങിയപ്പോൾ അവളുടെ മുഖം ഇരുണ്ടതു കണ്ടു. അവൾ അയ്യപ്പനെ നോക്കുന്നു. അയ്യപ്പൻ അവളെയും. അയാൾ ചിരിക്കാൻ ശ്രമിക്കുന്നു. അവർ കണ്ടിട്ടുള്ളവരാണ്, സംശയമില്ല. രാജമ്മയുടെ മുഖത്ത് ഭീതി. അയ്യപ്പൻ വിഷാദത്തോടെ മുഖം താഴ്ത്തി.

"കാപ്പി കൊണ്ടുവരൂ..." പറഞ്ഞൊപ്പിച്ചു.

"വേണ്ട, കേട്ടോ."

രാജമ്മ പോയി.

ഒരിക്കൽക്കൂടി മനസ്സ് നിയന്ത്രിച്ചു പിടിച്ചു.

"വരുന്ന വഴിയാണോ?"

"അതെ."

"ഇങ്ങോട്ടു തന്നെ വന്നതാണോ?"

"അതെ."

അവൾക്ക് അടക്കം വന്നില്ല.

"അയ്യപ്പൻ എന്നോട് പൊറുക്കണം. നിങ്ങളെല്ലാം എന്നോട് പൊറുക്കണം. ഞാൻ തെറ്റുകാരിയാണ്."

അവളുടെ കണ്ണുകൾ നിറഞ്ഞുനിന്നു.

ഭാനുമതി കാര്യങ്ങൾ അറിഞ്ഞിരിക്കുന്നുവെന്ന് അയ്യപ്പന് ബോധ്യമായി.

“നിങ്ങൾ എന്തു തെറ്റു ചെയ്തു? നിങ്ങളോടു ഞങ്ങൾക്ക് ഒരു വിരോധവുമില്ല. നേരത്തെ ഒന്നും അറിയാതെയല്ലേ ഇതുണ്ടായത്. നിങ്ങൾ എല്ലാം അറിഞ്ഞിട്ടു ചെയ്തതല്ലല്ലോ. പക്ഷേ, എന്റെ പെങ്ങളുടെ അനുഭവം ഓർമിക്കുമ്പോൾ, നിങ്ങളെക്കുറിച്ച് ഞങ്ങൾക്കു ഭയവും സഹതാപവുമുണ്ട്. നല്ലതുവരട്ടെ എന്ന് ഞങ്ങൾ പ്രാർഥിക്കുകയാണ്.”

അവൾ തേങ്ങിക്കരഞ്ഞു. പിന്നെ, അടക്കിപ്പിടിച്ചു.

“ഞങ്ങൾക്ക് ഒരു ദുഃഖമേ ഉള്ളൂ. എന്റെ സഹോദരി പലവട്ടം ഞങ്ങളോട് അവരുടെ വൈഷമ്യങ്ങൾ പറഞ്ഞതാണ്. ഞങ്ങൾ അതൊന്നും കാര്യമായെടുത്തില്ല. ഒടുവിൽ അങ്ങനെ സംഭവിച്ചു. നിങ്ങൾ അതറിഞ്ഞിട്ടുണ്ടെന്ന് വിശ്വസിച്ചാണ് ഞാനിതു പറയുന്നത്. ഞങ്ങളുടെ അശ്രദ്ധകൊണ്ടാണ് അവർക്ക് ഈ അന്ത്യം വന്നത്.”

ചൂടുപിടിച്ച നിമിഷങ്ങൾ ഉരുകിയൊലിക്കുകയായിരുന്നു.

“സാധാരണ ഗതിയിൽ ഞങ്ങൾ ഇവിടെ വരരുതാത്തതാണ്. ഈ വീട് ഞങ്ങളുടെയെല്ലാം മനസിന്റെ ശവകുടീരമാണ്. പക്ഷേ, വരാതെ നിവൃത്തിയില്ലെന്നുവന്നു. അതുകൊണ്ടാണ് ഇറങ്ങിത്തിരിച്ചത്. മിസ്റ്റർ ദിവാകരനെക്കണ്ട് ഒരു കാര്യം പറയേണ്ടതുണ്ട്.”

“അങ്ങേര് ഇന്നുരാവിലെ എവിടെയോ പോയിരിക്കുകയാണ്. എവിടെയാണെന്നു പറഞ്ഞില്ല. രണ്ടു ദിവസം കഴിയും വരാൻ. എന്താണ് കാര്യമെന്ന് എന്നോട് പറയാമോ?”

അയാൾ മടിച്ചു മിണ്ടാതിരുന്നു.

“രഹസ്യമാണോ?”

അയാൾ മ്ലാനതയോടെ അവളെ നോക്കി.

“അയ്യപ്പാ നിങ്ങൾ എന്റെ സഹോദരനെപ്പോലെയാണ്. എന്നെ വളർത്തി കണ്ണു തെളിച്ചുവിട്ടത് അയ്യപ്പന്റെ കുടുംബമാണ്. രത്നമ്മയും ഞാനും തമ്മിൽ യാതൊരു വ്യത്യാസവുമില്ല.വിധി ഇങ്ങനെയും കൂടി, അവൾ കടന്നുപോയ സ്ഥലത്ത് എന്നെ പറഞ്ഞയച്ചിരിക്കുന്നു. ദിവസവും ഓരോ നിമിഷവും ഞാൻ അവളെയോർത്ത് കണ്ണീരൊഴുക്കുന്നുണ്ട്. പക്ഷേ, ഞാൻ ഈ തടവിലായിപ്പോയി. ഇതിൽനിന്ന് എങ്ങനെ മോചനം നേടും? അനുഭവിക്കാമെന്നു വിചാരിച്ച് കടിച്ചുപിടിച്ചു ധൈര്യമായി കഴിയുന്നു.” വീണ്ടും തേങ്ങിപ്പോയി. ഒരുവിധം ഒതുക്കിപ്പറഞ്ഞു. “അതുകൊണ്ടു എന്നെ ഒളിച്ചുവയ്ക്കേണ്ട കാര്യമില്ല. അല്ല, എന്നെ നിങ്ങൾ ഒന്നും ഒളിക്കാൻ പാടില്ല. എല്ലാം അനുഭവിക്കേണ്ടതിൽ ഒരാളല്ലേ ഇപ്പോൾ ഞാനും? നിങ്ങളുടെക്കൂടെത്തന്നെ ഞാനും ഈ ദുഃഖം അനുഭവിക്കുകയല്ലേ?”

ശരിയാണെന്ന് അയാൾ ആലോചിച്ചു. ഭാനുമതിക്ക് തീർച്ചയായും രത്നമ്മയുടെ കുടുംബത്തോട് സ്നേഹമായിരിക്കും. അതു പ്രത്യേകം പറഞ്ഞാണ്, വീട്ടിൽ നിന്നും അയച്ചതും. അവരിൽ നിന്നും ഒന്നും മറച്ചുപിടിച്ചിട്ടു കാര്യമില്ല. ഇങ്ങനെവന്നുപ്പെട്ടെങ്കിലും അവർ തങ്ങളിലൊരാ

ളാണ്. ഇന്നു പറഞ്ഞില്ലെങ്കിൽ നാളെ അവർ അറിയുമല്ലോ.

അയ്യപ്പൻ സാവധാനം പറഞ്ഞു.

"വടക്കുനിന്ന് ഒരു സ്ത്രീ രണ്ടുതവണ ഞങ്ങളുടെ വീട്ടിൽ വന്നു. ഇനിയും വരുമെന്ന് അവരുടെ എഴുത്തുണ്ട്. അവർക്ക് ഒരു കുട്ടിയുമുണ്ട്. അവർ കർണാടകക്കാരിയാണെന്നു തോന്നുന്നു. മലയാളം സംസാരിക്കും. അത്ര നല്ല മലയാളമല്ലെന്നു മാത്രം. ആ കുട്ടി മിസ്റ്റർ ദിവാകരന്റേതാണെന്ന് അവർ പറഞ്ഞു. ഒരു ധനികനായ ഗൗണ്ടറുടെ ഭാര്യയായിരുന്ന അവരെ ദിവാകരൻ സ്വാധീനിച്ചുവെന്നും ഗർഭമായതോടെ ഗൗണ്ടർ അവരെ ഉപേക്ഷിച്ചെന്നുമാണ് പറഞ്ഞത്. അവർ ഞങ്ങളെ ശല്യപ്പെടുത്തുന്നു. എങ്ങനെയോ അഡ്രസും വീടുമൊക്കെ മനസിലാക്കി വന്നതാണ്. ഞങ്ങൾ ദിവാകരന്റെ എതിരാളികളാണല്ലോ. അവർ അവരുടെ കേസിൽ ഞങ്ങളെ സാക്ഷികളാക്കും. ഞങ്ങൾ അവർക്കുവേണ്ടി സംസാരിക്കണം. സത്യത്തിൽ അതു ബുദ്ധിമുട്ടുള്ള കാര്യമാണ്. മൊഴി കൊടുക്കുന്നതല്ല. ഈ കാര്യത്തിനുവേണ്ടി കോടതിയിലേക്ക് പോകാൻ വയ്യ. സഹോദരിയെപ്പറ്റി അവിടെ സംസാരിക്കാൻ വയ്യ. അന്ന് ഞങ്ങൾ പൊലീസിൽ പോയില്ല. ഞാനും മറ്റും നിർബന്ധിച്ചതാണ്. പക്ഷേ, കേസ് കോടതിയിൽവരുമ്പോൾ എന്റെ പെങ്ങൾ മറ്റൊരാളുടെ കൂടെ കഴിഞ്ഞുകൂടുന്നതു കണ്ടുവെന്ന് ദിവാകരൻ ഒരാൾ മുഖാന്തരം പറഞ്ഞയച്ചു. പിന്നെ തന്റെ മുഖത്തു നോക്കാൻ ധൈര്യമില്ലാത്തതുകൊണ്ട് അവിവേകം പ്രവർത്തിച്ചുവത്രെ. ആ മനുഷ്യനു പണമുണ്ട്. ഒരു കൃത്രിമജാരനെ ഉണ്ടാക്കി കോടതിയിൽ ഹാജരാക്കുവാൻ കൂടി മടിക്കുകയില്ല. എന്റെ പെങ്ങൾ മരിച്ചുകഴിഞ്ഞ് അങ്ങനെ ഒരപമാനം പരസ്യമായി ഞങ്ങൾ ഉണ്ടാക്കിത്തീർക്കണോ? നിസ്സഹായരായി ഞങ്ങൾ പിൻവാങ്ങി. ഇപ്പോൾ ആ സ്ത്രീ വിടാതെ കൂടിയിരിക്കുന്നു. ദിവാകരനോട് ഞങ്ങൾക്ക് ഒന്നേ പറയാനുള്ളൂ. ഇതിൽ എന്തെങ്കിലും കഥ കാണും. ഞങ്ങളെ അതും കൂടി ചുമപ്പിക്കരുത്. ആ സ്ത്രീ ഇനി അവിടെ വരാതിരിക്കാൻ ഏർപ്പാടു ചെയ്യണം."

താൻ സ്വയം തണുത്തുറഞ്ഞുപോകുകയാണെന്നു ഭാനുമതിക്കു തോന്നി. ഇനി അങ്ങനെയുംകൂടി ഒന്നിനെ നേരിടേണ്ടതുണ്ടോ? മറ്റൊരു സ്ത്രീയെ അവരുടെ കുഞ്ഞിനെ?

നിയന്ത്രിച്ചിട്ടും നിന്നില്ല. അവൾ മുഖംപൊത്തി കരഞ്ഞു. അയ്യപ്പനും വിവശനായിപ്പോയി. യഥാർഥത്തിൽ അവർ രണ്ടുപേരും നിസ്സഹായരാണെന്ന് അയാൾക്ക് അനുഭവപ്പെട്ടു. തന്റെ സഹോദരി മുൻപിലിരുന്നു കരയുന്നതുപോലെ തോന്നി. അയാളുടെ കണ്ണുകളും നനയുകയാണ്. അന്യോന്യം സമാധാനിപ്പിക്കാൻപോലും കഴിഞ്ഞില്ല. ദിവാകരനെ കാണാൻ കഴിഞ്ഞിരുന്നെങ്കിൽ ഈ അവസ്ഥ ഒഴിവാക്കാമായിരുന്നു. സന്ധ്യമയങ്ങിയപ്പോഴും അവർ രണ്ടുപേരും അങ്ങനെ ഇരിക്കുകയായിരുന്നു.

* * * * * *

യഥാർഥമായ പരീക്ഷണത്തിനുത്തന്നെ അവിടെ കൊണ്ടു ചെന്നെ

ത്തിയതാണെന്ന് അരവിന്ദനു തോന്നി. തൃശൂരുനിന്ന് സന്ധ്യാദേവിയെ കാണാനാണ് പോയത്. അവിടെ ചെല്ലണമെന്ന് അവർ എഴുതിയിരുന്നല്ലോ. വാസവമേനോന്റെ വീട്ടിലേക്കു ചെന്നു. അവർ അവിടെയായിരിക്കാനാണ് സാധ്യത. ഇപ്പോൾ അവിടെ ആരുമില്ല. നാരായണമേനോന്റെ അമ്മ മരിച്ചു. എല്ലാവരും അങ്ങോട്ടു പോയിരിക്കുന്നു. മേനോന്റെ അമ്മയും പോയിട്ടുണ്ട്. വിവരം അയൽപക്കത്തെ രാധയാണ് പറഞ്ഞത്. പക്ഷേ, അവരിൽ ആരെങ്കിലും സന്ധ്യകഴിഞ്ഞു വരുമെന്നു പറഞ്ഞിട്ടാണ് പോയത്.

സന്ധ്യകഴിയുംവരെ വഴിയിലും ചായപ്പീടികയിലും സിനിമാക്കൊട്ടക വാതിൽക്കലും കഴിച്ചുകൂട്ടി. പിന്നെ മടങ്ങിവന്നു. ആരും എത്തിയിട്ടില്ല. രാധ ഒരു വിളക്കുകൊളുത്തി വാതിൽക്കൽ വച്ചു. കുറച്ചു കഴിഞ്ഞ് ഒരു റാന്തൽ കത്തിച്ച് അരത്തിണ്ണയിലും വച്ചു. അവൾ അവളുടെ വീട്ടിൽനിന്ന് അരവിന്ദനു ചായ കൊണ്ടുവന്നു കുടിച്ചു. എട്ടുമണിയായപ്പോൾ വേലിക്കരികിലേക്കു നീങ്ങി അറിയിച്ചു. “രാധേ, ഞാൻ കാപ്പി കുടിച്ചിട്ടു വരാം.” അവൾ ഓടി വന്നു. “അയ്യോ ഇവിടെ കഴിക്കാം.” “വേണ്ട..” അയാൾ സ്നേഹപൂർവം പറഞ്ഞ്, പുറത്തിറങ്ങി വെറുതെ കുറേനേരം കഴിച്ചുകൂട്ടി. പത്തുമണിക്കാണ് തിരിച്ചുവന്നത്. അപ്പോൾ സന്ധ്യാദേവി കാത്തിരിക്കുന്നു.

“മറ്റാരും വന്നില്ലേ?” അരവിന്ദൻ അന്വേഷിച്ചു.

“എന്റെ ഇളയ അനിയത്തിമാത്രം വന്നു. മറ്റുള്ളവർ നാളെ വരും. അരവിന്ദൻ അത്താഴം കഴിച്ചോ?”

“കഴിച്ചു. സന്ധ്യാദേവിയോ?”

“ഞങ്ങൾ ആഹാരം കഴിഞ്ഞാണ് ഇങ്ങുപോന്നത്. ഇവിടെ വന്നു ചായ കുടിച്ചു, വേണോ?”

”വേണ്ട വേണ്ട, വയറു നിറച്ച് ഭക്ഷണം കഴിച്ചു...”

തെക്കേമുറിയിൽ പായ് വിരിക്കുകയും അയാൾ കട്ടിലിൽച്ചാരി ഇരിക്കുകയും അവർ പഴയതുപോലെ ആ കസേരയിൽ വന്നിരിക്കുകയും ചെയ്തപ്പോഴാണ് അരവിന്ദന് ആ തോന്നൽ ഉണ്ടായത്. പരീക്ഷണത്തിനാണ് ഇവിടെ കൊണ്ടു ചെന്നെത്തിച്ചിട്ടുള്ളത്.

അവർ ഓരോ തവണയും തമ്മിൽ കാണുമ്പോൾ ആകർഷണത്തിന്റെ ചൂട് വർധിച്ചു വരികയാണ്. അതു രണ്ടുപേർക്കും അനുഭവപ്പെടുന്നുണ്ട്. അപകടത്തിലേക്കു ചെന്നുവീഴുന്ന മുഹൂർത്തം എപ്പോഴാണെന്നു മാത്രമേ രണ്ടുപേരും ഭയപ്പെടുന്നുള്ളൂ. ഈയിടെയായി അതിനുള്ള സന്ദർഭങ്ങൾ നിനച്ചിരിക്കാതെ വന്നുകൊണ്ടുമിരിക്കുന്നു. കുറച്ചു ദിവസം സദനത്തിലേക്കു ചെല്ലാതെ ഇവിടെ കഴിച്ചുകൂട്ടണമെന്ന് അവിടെ നിന്നുള്ള കത്തു വായിച്ചുകേട്ടപ്പോൾ അമ്മയും വല്യമ്മയും അവരുടെ ഭർത്താവും എല്ലാം ഉപദേശിച്ചു. അതു തിരസ്കരിച്ചിട്ട് ഉടനെ ഇറങ്ങി പുറപ്പെടേണ്ടെന്നു വിചാരിച്ചു. അവിടത്തെ കാര്യങ്ങളെക്കുറിച്ച് ഉൽക്കണ്ഠയുണ്ടെങ്കിലും അപ്പോഴാണ് അരവിന്ദന് കത്തയച്ചത്. ഇവിടെവരെ വരണമെന്നു എഴുതി. അത് അത്യാവശ്യമായിരുന്നോ? ചില പ്രശ്നങ്ങ

ളുണ്ട്. എന്നാലും പെട്ടെന്ന് വരേണ്ടുന്ന കാര്യമുണ്ടായിരുന്നോ? അത് പലവുരു ചിന്തിച്ചു. നിയന്ത്രിക്കാൻ കഴിയാഞ്ഞ ഒരു പ്രേരണ അതിന്റെ പിന്നിലുണ്ടായിരുന്നു. അതിനെക്കുറിച്ചു പശ്ചാത്തപിക്കുകയും ചെയ്തു.

ഭാനുമതിയുടെ വിവരങ്ങൾ അരവിന്ദൻ പറഞ്ഞു. ദിവാകരൻ തന്നെ വിളിച്ചുകൊണ്ടുപോയി സംസാരിച്ചത്, റീനയുടെ വിവാഹാലോചന, അവിടെ നിന്നും സന്ധ്യാദേവിയെ എഴുതി അയച്ചിരിക്കുന്നു. ദിവാകരന്റെ കഥ അവരെ ഉൽക്കണ്ഠപ്പെടുത്തി. വാസവമേനോന്റെ സുഹൃത്ത് സന്യാസി വരുന്ന കാര്യവും അറിയിച്ചു. സന്ധ്യാദേവിയും ചിരിച്ചുപോയി. സന്യാസി!"

അങ്ങനെ എല്ലാവിഷയങ്ങളും സംസാരിച്ചു തീർത്തു. പിന്നെ ഒന്നുമില്ല. അരവിന്ദൻ ചോദിച്ചു:

"ഇനി എന്തുപറയാൻ?"

"ഇനി.." സന്ധ്യാദേവി ആലോചിച്ചു. "ഒന്നുമില്ല."

"എനിക്കാണെങ്കിൽ പറയാൻ മനസ്സ് നിറയെ കാര്യങ്ങളുണ്ട്." അരവിന്ദൻ അലസമായി പ്രസ്താവിച്ചു.

"ഓഹോ.." അവരുടെ വിടർന്ന മിഴികൾ അയാളുടെ നേർക്ക് ചെന്നു. മനസുനിറയെ ഉണ്ടെങ്കിൽ, കുറെ ഇങ്ങോട്ടു തൂവിത്തരാൻ ദയവുണ്ടായാലും."

"ഇല്ല. ഭക്തി ഇനിയും തെളിയിക്കുന്നവർക്കേ അനുഗ്രഹത്തിന്റെ പുഷ്പങ്ങൾ കിട്ടൂ." അയാളുടെ സ്വരം ശാന്തമായൊഴുകി.

"ഒരുപാടു തപസ്സ് ചെയ്യേണ്ടിവരുന്ന മട്ടുണ്ട്." അവരുടെ സ്വരം കളിയാക്കുന്ന മട്ടിലായിരുന്നു.

"വേണ്ടിവരും.." അരവിന്ദൻ പറഞ്ഞു: "ആത്മജ്ഞാനം നേടാൻ വളരെ സഞ്ചരിക്കേണ്ടിവരും."

"എത്ര മൈലുകൾ?"

"ഇന്ന് ഞാൻ ഒരുപാടു മൈലുകൾ സഞ്ചരിച്ചാണ് ഇവിടെ, ഈ ആത്മജ്ഞാനത്തിന്റെ മുൻപിലെത്തിയത്."

അവർ മുഖം താഴ്ത്തിക്കളഞ്ഞു. മിണ്ടിയില്ല. അങ്ങനെയാണ്. അവരെ നേരിട്ട് സ്പർശിക്കുന്ന എന്തെങ്കിലും സൂചിപ്പിച്ചുപോയാൽ ഉടൻ അവർ വാടിപ്പോകും.

"ഇന്നു ഞാൻ അറിയാനും കൂടി വന്നതാണ്." അയാൾ നിവർന്നിരുന്നു.

"എന്തറിയാൻ?"

"മനസ്സും മനസിലിരിക്കുന്നതും എന്താണെന്ന്."

"ഇനിയും അറിഞ്ഞിട്ടില്ലേ?"

"ഇല്ല."

"ഞാൻ ഒന്നും പറയാത്തതിനു കാരണമുണ്ട്. ഒരു തരത്തിൽ ഞാൻ നിസ്സഹായയാണ്, അരവിന്ദൻ എന്റെ ജീവിതത്തിന് എന്തെങ്കിലും മാറ്റമുണ്ടായാൽ, സദനത്തിലുള്ളവരുടെ മനോഭാവം മാറും. അവരുടെ

താൽപ്പര്യം നഷ്ടപ്പെടും. ഞാൻ എന്റെ സ്വാർഥ ജീവിതത്തിലേക്ക് ഒതുങ്ങിക്കൂടിയെന്നു വിചാരിക്കും."

"ഇതിന്റെ അർഥം തെളിച്ചുപറയൂ." അരവിന്ദൻ അൽപ്പം അക്ഷമ കാട്ടിയതുപോലെ.

"അർഥം." അവർ മുഴുമിപ്പിക്കാതെ നിറുത്തി.

"ഇങ്ങനെ കാലം കഴിച്ചുകൂട്ടുക. വാസവമേനോൻ അതു പറഞ്ഞു."

"എന്തു പറഞ്ഞു?" അവർ ഉദ്വേഗത്തോടെ ചോദിച്ചു.

"കുറെ കഴിയുമ്പോൾ ഈ ഉറപ്പുള്ള വികാരങ്ങൾ പോകുമെന്ന്. മനസ്സ് തണുത്ത് തടാകമാകുമെന്ന്. അപ്പോൾ ഇപ്പോഴത്തെ വിചാരങ്ങളിൽനിന്ന് മോചനം കിട്ടുമെന്ന്. ശരിയാണ്. അദ്ദേഹം പറഞ്ഞത് ശരിയാണ്.

സന്ധ്യാദേവി നടുങ്ങിയതു കണക്കുനോക്കി. ഒരു പുതിയ കാര്യം കേൾക്കുന്നു. കാലം ആത്മാവിൽക്കൂടി അതിവേഗം പറന്നുപോകുന്നു. അതിന്റെ ചിറകടിയൊച്ചകൾ. ദിനരാത്രങ്ങൾ, വരുന്നു പോകുന്നു. ശിരസിൽ വെളുത്ത മുടികൾ കാണുന്നു. കൈകാലുകൾക്ക് തളർച്ച. ശബ്ദത്തിന്റെ ഭംഗി മായുന്നു. ശരിയാണോ? ഇത് സംഭവിച്ചുകൊണ്ടിരിക്കുകയാണോ? അരവിന്ദൻ മുഷിച്ചിലോടെ സംസാരിക്കുന്നു. ഈ പറഞ്ഞത് പുരുഷവാക്കുകളാണ്.

തുടർന്ന് അരവിന്ദന്റെ ശബ്ദം.

"അപ്പോൾ സ്വന്തം സൗന്ദര്യം ഉലഞ്ഞുപോകാതെ സൂക്ഷിക്കാം. വാർധക്യത്തിലും യൗവനത്തിലും പൊടിപറ്റാത്ത മുഖവുമായി ഭൂമിയിൽക്കൂടി നടക്കാം. മനുഷ്യർ പറയും. ഐശ്വര്യമുള്ളകന്യക..."

കുത്തുവാക്കുകൾ സന്ധ്യാദേവിയുടെ ഉള്ളിൽ നിരാശയും അതിൽ നിന്നുള്ള ക്ഷോഭവും പതഞ്ഞുപൊന്തി. പെട്ടെന്ന് അവരുടെയിടയിൽ ഒരു തീ കത്തിപ്പടർന്ന്, പരസ്പരം മുഖം കാണാൻ വയ്യാതാക്കിയതുപോലെ. അവരുടെ ശബ്ദം പൊട്ടിത്തെറിച്ചു.

"ഇതൊക്കെ യഥാർഥമായി വിശ്വസിച്ചു. പറയുകയാണോ?"

"നൂറിന് നൂറും വിശ്വസിച്ചു. ഞാൻ ഇരുട്ടിൽ തപ്പിത്തടയുന്നതുപോലെ എനിക്കു തോന്നുന്നു."

അവർ ഒന്നിളകി, ചൊടിച്ച് എഴുന്നേറ്റു. അയാൾ അതേപടി ഇരുന്നു. അവർ വാതിൽക്കലേക്കു നടന്നു, പുറത്തിറങ്ങി. തിണ്ണയിൽക്കൂടി നടന്ന്, മുറിയിൽ കയറുന്നത് അരവിന്ദൻ കണ്ടു.

അയാൾ കിടന്നു.

കുറേസമയത്തേക്ക് ബോധം നശിച്ചതുപോലിരുന്നു. പിന്നെ അതിന്റെ ഓരോ അംശങ്ങൾ ഉയർന്നു വന്നു. എല്ലാം ഒരുമിച്ചുകൂടി അവരുടെ രൂപം. ക്ഷോഭിച്ച മിഴികൾ. പൊട്ടിത്തെറിച്ച ശബ്ദം. പെട്ടെന്നുള്ള ഇറങ്ങിപ്പോക്ക്. അയാൾ മൂഢതയുടെ താഴ്വാരങ്ങളിലേക്ക് ചവിട്ടിയിറങ്ങാൻ തുടങ്ങി. അപരാധബോധത്തിന്റെ തണുത്ത കാറ്റ് ഉള്ളിലേക്കു വീശുന്നു. പെട്ടെന്ന് എന്തു സംഭവിച്ചു? എന്തിനാണ് അങ്ങനെ സംസാരിച്ചത്? അയാൾക്ക് അതറിയാം. കുറച്ചു നാളുകളായി അതുണ്ട്. ഉപ

ബോധത്തിന്റെ അടിത്തട്ടിൽ അതൃപ്തി കിടക്കുന്നു. അവരുടെരൂപവും ശബ്ദവും ചലനവും മനസിനെ കൊത്തിവലിക്കുന്നു. അവർ ദൂരെയാണെന്ന ബോധം ചേതനയിൽ ഉഷ്ണജലപ്രവാഹം സൃഷ്ടിക്കുന്നു. അവരുടെ ഉള്ളിന്റെ കാണാത്ത ഭാഗങ്ങൾക്കുവേണ്ടി ആവശ്യമില്ലാത്ത ദാഹം വളരുന്നു. ഈ ചൂടും നൊമ്പരവും ഒതുക്കിപ്പിടിച്ചു നടക്കുകയാണ്. ഇപ്പോൾ... ഇപ്പോൾ അത് അറിയാതെ പൊട്ടിത്തെറിച്ചുപോയി... ഒരു ചെറിയ സ്പർശനം മതിയായിരുന്നു. അവർക്കും തനിക്കുമിടയ്ക്ക് സദനം നിൽക്കുന്ന ചിത്രം, മനസിൽക്കൊണ്ടു. അത് വെടിമരുന്നു ശാലയിലേക്കു നീട്ടിപ്പിടിച്ച തിരിയായിരുന്നു.. പൊട്ടിത്തെറിച്ചു.

അങ്ങനെ പൊട്ടിത്തെറിക്കരുതായിരുന്നു, പാവം സ്ത്രീ.

തിരിഞ്ഞും മറിഞ്ഞും കിടക്കുന്നു. ഉള്ളിൽ ഉഷ്ണം തിളച്ചുമറിയുന്നു. ഇറങ്ങി ഓടിയാലോ? അർഥമില്ല. എവിടെയെങ്കിലും ചെന്നെത്താനല്ല ഈ നൊമ്പരം, ഈ പ്രയാണം, ഒന്നിൽ എത്തിപ്പിടിക്കാനാണ് ഒന്നിൽമാത്രം...

അതു അടുത്തുണ്ട് അതോ അകലയോ?

യാമങ്ങൾ കടന്നുപോയി. തളർന്നു. ഓർമകൾ സാവധാനം താണടിയുന്നു മയക്കം കണ്ണുകളെ തഴുകി.

അടുത്ത് തേങ്ങിക്കരയുന്ന ശബ്ദം. മുറ്റത്ത് കിളികൾ ചിലയ്ക്കുന്നു. കണ്ണു തുറന്നു. തിരിഞ്ഞു നോക്കി. സന്ധ്യാദേവി കട്ടിലിൽ, അരികത്തിരുന്ന് കരയുന്നു. തിരിഞ്ഞുകിടന്നു ഇടതുകൈ അവരെ വലയം ചെയ്തു. അവരുടെ കൈകൾ തന്റെ കൈയിൽ ചേർന്നിരുന്നു. കവിതയിൽ താനെഴുതിവച്ച ചന്ദനലതപോലെ അവർ തന്റെ ശരീരത്തിലേക്ക് പടർന്നു. കണ്ണുനീരിന്റെ ഉപ്പുരസം, അയാൾക്ക് അനുഭവപ്പെട്ടു.

"ക്ഷമിക്കണം.." അവരുടെ ശ്വാസധാര അയാളുടെ മുഖത്തെ തലോടി നിന്നു.

"തെറ്റുചെയ്തത് ഞാനാണ്. എന്നോടു പൊറുക്കണം." അയാൾ മന്ത്രിച്ചു.

"ഞാൻ എന്നും അരവിന്ദന്റേതാണെന്ന് ഇനിയും പറയണോ?"

"വേണ്ട."

"ഞാൻ ഇനിയും മാപ്പുചോദിക്കണോ?"

"വേണ്ട."

"അകന്നിരിക്കുന്നതിൽ എനിക്കും വേദനയുണ്ടെന്ന് അറിഞ്ഞുകൂടേ?"

"അറിയാം."

"എന്നെ മനസുകൊണ്ട് വെറുക്കുമോ?"

"ഇല്ല."

"ഭൂമിയിലേക്കു കടന്നുവന്ന പകൽവെളിച്ചം അവരെ ആ വിസ്മൃതിയിൽനിന്ന് നുള്ളി ഉണർത്തി.

സന്ധ്യാദേവി അകത്തുപോയി കാപ്പി കൊണ്ടുവന്നു. അത് അവർതന്നെ

അയാളുടെ ചുണ്ടിനോട് അടുപ്പിച്ചുകൊടുത്തു. അയാൾ അതു കുടിച്ചു.

പതിമൂന്ന്

സന്ധ്യാദേവി സദനത്തിലേക്കു മടങ്ങിവന്നു. കീർത്തിക്ക് അത് ഉത്സവം പോലെയായിരുന്നു. അവൾക്ക് നൂറു പരാതികളുണ്ട്. ഒന്നാമത് സന്ധ്യാദേവി അവൾക്കുമാത്രം കത്തെഴുതിയില്ല. അവൾ രണ്ടുകത്തുകളെഴുതിയിട്ടുണ്ട്. യോഗമയീദേവിയുടെ കത്തിന്റെ കീഴിൽ മാത്രമേ അവൾക്കു വേണ്ടി രണ്ടുവരികൾ കുറിച്ചുള്ളൂ. സദനത്തിലുള്ളവരെല്ലാം അവളെ കളിയാക്കിക്കൊണ്ടിരുന്നു. തള്ളയെപ്പിരിഞ്ഞ ആട്ടിൻകുട്ടിയെപ്പോലെ അവൾ കരഞ്ഞുകൊണ്ട് നടക്കുകയാണെന്ന്, അങ്ങനെപോയി, പരാതികൾ. സന്ധ്യാദേവിയും അവരുടെ മുൻപിൽ അൽപ്പം ദുർബലയാണ്. അതുകൊണ്ട് ഈ ചെറിയ കാര്യങ്ങളിൽപ്പോലും അവർ അവളെ സമാധാനിപ്പിച്ചു.

ആദ്യത്തെ സന്തോഷപ്രകടനങ്ങൾ കഴിഞ്ഞു. അപ്പോൾ യഥാർഥ പ്രശ്നം പൊന്തിവന്നു. സന്ധ്യാദേവി പൊലീസിന്റെ അന്വേഷണത്തിലിരിക്കുകയാണ്. അവർ വന്നു എന്നറിഞ്ഞാൽ പൊലീസ് വരാൻ സാധ്യതയുണ്ട്. അരവിന്ദനുമായി അതേപ്പറ്റി ആലോചിച്ചിരുന്നു. പ്രത്യേകിച്ച് കേസൊന്നുമില്ല. ചോദ്യം ചെയ്തെന്നുവരും. വാസവമേനോനായിരിക്കും വിഷയം. അദ്ദേഹവുമായി നമുക്കാർക്കും ബന്ധമില്ല. എഴുതിക്കൊടുക്കണമെങ്കിൽ അങ്ങനെ ചെയ്യണം.

സന്ധ്യാദേവി ഇത് സദാനാംഗങ്ങളോട് വിശദീകരിച്ചുപറഞ്ഞു. ഭീതിയുടെ കനം തെല്ലൊന്നു കുറഞ്ഞു. അവർ പഴയതുപോലെ തന്റെ കൃത്യങ്ങളിൽ വ്യാപൃതരായി.

നാലഞ്ചുദിവസങ്ങൾ കഴിഞ്ഞു. അധികാരികൾ സദനത്തിന്റെ ചീഫിനെ അന്വേഷിച്ചില്ല. അതിനിടയ്ക്ക് അവിടെ ചില ഒരുക്കങ്ങൾ ചെയ്തു. വാസവമേനോന്റെ സുഹൃത്തായ സന്ന്യാസിയോഗി ശിവാനന്ദഭാരതി സദനം സന്ദർശിക്കുവാൻ താൽപ്പര്യം പ്രകടിപ്പിച്ച വിവരം അറിയിച്ചു. അദ്ദേഹത്തെ സ്വാഗതം ചെയ്തുകൊണ്ട് മറുപടി അയച്ചു. സന്ദർശനത്തിന്റെ തീയതി നിശ്ചയിച്ചുവന്നു. പൊതുജനങ്ങളെക്കൂടി പങ്കെടുപ്പിച്ച് അതുപ്രയോജനമുള്ള ഒരു സന്ദർഭമാക്കണം. യോഗമയീദേവിയും സന്ധ്യാദേവിയും അങ്ങനെ തീരുമാനിച്ചു. കത്തുകൾ എഴുതി. കുറേപ്പേരെ ക്ഷണിച്ചു. പരിചയക്കാരോടു പറഞ്ഞു. വിദ്യാഭ്യാസസ്ഥാപനങ്ങളിൽ മുഖ്യാധ്യാപകരെ സമീപിച്ച്, ക്ലാസുകളിൽ നോട്ടീസ് വായിപ്പിച്ചു.

അന്ന് നേരത്തെ അറിയിച്ചിരുന്നതുപോലെ, കൃത്യം അഞ്ചുമണിക്ക് ശിവാനന്ദജി സദനത്തിലെത്തി. സന്ധ്യാദേവിയും മറ്റും ചേർന്ന് അദ്ദേഹത്തെ സ്വീകരിച്ചു. നല്ല ഒരു സദസ്സ്, വരാന്തയിൽ ഒരു മേശയിട്ടു. അതിൽ വിരിപ്പു വിരിച്ചു. സ്വാമിജിക്ക് വേണമെങ്കിൽ അതിലിരുന്നു സംസാരിക്കാം. മുറ്റത്ത് ആളുകൾക്കിരിക്കാൻ ബഞ്ചുകളിട്ടു.

സ്വാമിജി എല്ലാവരുടേയും സവിശേഷമായ ശ്രദ്ധയെ ആകർഷിച്ചു കഴിഞ്ഞിരുന്നു. അത്രയ്ക്കു കാന്തിയുള്ള മുഖം. അൻപത്തഞ്ചുവയസ്സ് പ്രായം തോന്നിക്കും. പക്ഷെ മുടി നരച്ചിട്ടില്ല. വടിവൊത്ത ശരീരം. പ്രകാശമുള്ള കണ്ണുകൾ പ്രൗഢിയുള്ള നടത്തം. അരവിന്ദനാണ് സ്വാമിജിയെ സദസിന് പരിചയപ്പെടുത്തിക്കൊണ്ട് സ്വാഗതം പറഞ്ഞത്. ശിവാനന്ദജിയെപ്പറ്റിയുള്ള വിവരങ്ങൾ അയാൾ സംഭരിച്ചിരുന്നു. സദസിലുള്ളവർ നേരത്തെതന്നെ സ്വാമിജിയുടെ പ്രഭാഷണത്തെപ്പറ്റി പലതും പരസ്പരം പറഞ്ഞു. സ്വാമിജി ഗീതയെക്കുറിച്ചു പറയും. ഉപനിഷത്തിനു വ്യാഖ്യാനം നൽകും. മതത്തിന്റെ ആവശ്യകത ചർച്ച ചെയ്യും. യോഗത്തെപ്പറ്റി ഉപന്യസിക്കും. ഭാരതീയ സംസ്കാരത്തിന്റെ അടിസ്ഥാനതത്വങ്ങൾ പറയും. അങ്ങനെ നാനാതരം അഭിപ്രായങ്ങൾ.

സ്വാഗതത്തിനു ശേഷം സ്വാമിജി സംസാരിക്കാൻ എഴുന്നേറ്റു.

“അടിമകളാക്കപ്പെട്ട സുഹൃത്തുക്കളേ..” അദ്ദേഹം അങ്ങനെയാണ് മുൻപിലിരുന്നവരെ അഭിസംബോധന ചെയ്തത്. സദസ്സ് ഒന്ന് ഞെട്ടിയതുപോലുണ്ട്. അദ്ദേഹം പ്രസംഗമാരംഭിച്ചു; “വർഷങ്ങൾക്കുമുമ്പ് കൽക്കത്തയിലെ ഒരു ഗൂഢാലോചനക്കേസിൽ ഞാൻ അറസ്റ്റ് ചെയ്യപ്പെട്ടപ്പോൾ, അവിടുത്തെ പ്രസിഡൻസി മജിസ്ട്രേറ്റിനോട് ഞാൻ ചോദിച്ചു. “പത്തു പേരെ തടവിൽ വച്ച്, അല്ലെങ്കിൽ ഇരുപതുപേരെ തൂക്കിക്കൊന്ന് ഒരഭിപ്രായത്തെ ഇല്ലാതാക്കാൻ കഴിയുമോ? നിറവും ഭംഗിയുമുള്ള ഒരു റോസാപ്പൂവിനെ നിങ്ങൾക്കു ചവിട്ടിത്തേച്ചു കളയാം. പക്ഷേ, റോസാപ്പൂവിന്റെ നിറത്തോടും ഭംഗിയോടുമുള്ള മനുഷ്യന്റെ ഇഷ്ടത്തെ അതുകൊണ്ടു നശിപ്പിക്കാൻ കഴിയുമോ?” അൽപ്പം വിവേകമുള്ള ആ മജിസ്ട്രേറ്റ് ഇങ്ങനെ മറുപടി പറഞ്ഞു. “ഇല്ല. മിസ്റ്റർ ശിവശങ്കരൻ — അന്ന് എന്റെ പേര് അതായിരുന്നു. മുന്നിൽക്കാണുന്ന കൈയിൽ കിട്ടുന്ന റോസാപ്പൂ നശിപ്പിക്കാമെന്നേ ഈ നീതിപീഠത്തിലിരിക്കുന്ന ഞാൻ ഏറ്റിട്ടുള്ളൂ. മറ്റേത്, ബ്രിട്ടീഷ് സാമ്രാജ്യം ഏറ്റിരിക്കുന്ന കാര്യമാണ്. യഥാർഥത്തിൽ ആ സായ്പ് പറഞ്ഞത്, സ്വന്തം യജമാനന്മാരുടെ നേർക്കുള്ള പരിഹാസമായിരുന്നു. ആ പരിഹാസം തന്നെ എനിക്ക് ഇന്നു തോന്നുന്നു. അതേ ബ്രിട്ടീഷ് സാമ്രാജ്യത്തോട്, അതിന്റെ പ്രതിനിധികളായ നാട്ടുരാജ്യങ്ങളിലെ ഭരണാധികാരികളോട്.

ഞാൻ രാഷ്ട്രീയമല്ലേ പറയുന്നത്. ‘തമസോമാ ജ്യോതിർഗമയ’ എന്ന് നമ്മുടെ ഏറ്റവും വലിയ വിജ്ഞാന പൈതൃകമായ ഉപനിഷത്തിൽ പറഞ്ഞിരിക്കുന്നു. ഇരുട്ടിൽനിന്നും എന്നെ വെളിച്ചത്തിലേക്ക് നയിക്കേണമേ, എന്നാണതിനർഥം. അതുപോലെതന്നെയാണ് അടിമത്തത്തിൽനിന്ന് എന്നെ സ്വാതന്ത്ര്യത്തിലേക്കു നയിക്കേണമേ എന്നു പറയുന്നതും. അടിമത്തം ഇരുട്ടാണ്. സ്വാതന്ത്ര്യം വെളിച്ചവും. സ്വാതന്ത്ര്യം വേണമെന്നു ഞാൻപറയുന്നത് ഒരു ആധ്യാത്മിക കാര്യമാണ്. കാരണം, സ്വാതന്ത്ര്യമില്ലെങ്കിൽ നമുക്ക് നമ്മുടെ സാംസ്കാരിക സമ്പത്തുകൾ മനസിലാക്കാൻ കഴിയുകയില്ല. വേദം പഠിക്കാൻ, ഉപനിഷത്തു വായിക്കാൻ ഗീത

വ്യാഖ്യാനിക്കാൻ ശങ്കരാചാര്യരുടെ അദ്വൈതവാദം അറിയാൻ സാധിക്കുകയില്ല. ഇതെല്ലാം പ്രചരിപ്പിക്കാനാണ് ഞാൻ ഇറങ്ങി സഞ്ചരിക്കുന്നത്. എന്നെയോ നിങ്ങളെയോ തടവിലാക്കിയാൽ, നാം എങ്ങനെ ഇതെല്ലാം പരസ്പരം പറയുകയും പഠിക്കുകയും ചെയ്യും? അതുകൊണ്ട്, നമുക്ക് സ്വാതന്ത്ര്യം വേണം.

മഹാത്മജിക്ക് ഏറ്റവും പ്രിയപ്പെട്ട ഒരു ഗീതമുണ്ട്. നരസിംഹമേത്ത എഴുതിയതാണത്. അത് ഇങ്ങനെ ആരംഭിക്കുന്നു. "അന്യരുടെ യാതനകൾ അറിയുകയും ആത്മവഞ്ചന കൂടാതെ അവർക്കുവേണ്ടി ദയാമയമായ കരുണാമയമായ പ്രവൃത്തികൾ നിർവഹിക്കുകയും ചെയ്യുന്നവനാണ് യഥാർഥഭക്തർ. എന്റെ മാർഗം ഭക്തിയാണ്. പക്ഷേ, എനിക്കു സ്വാതന്ത്ര്യമില്ലെങ്കിൽ എങ്ങനെ ഞാൻ എന്റെ സഹോദരങ്ങളോടു ദയകാട്ടും? കരുണാപൂർവം പ്രവർത്തിക്കും? അതുകൊണ്ട് നമുക്ക് സ്വാതന്ത്ര്യം വേണം."

ദീർഘമായ ആ പ്രസംഗം ഒരു ഗംഗാപ്രവാഹം പോലെ നീങ്ങി. ഭക്തിയും സ്വാതന്ത്ര്യവും സ്നേഹവും സമരവും ഭാരതവും ലോകവും എല്ലാം അതിൽ തുടിച്ചു നിന്നു. ഉപസംഹരിക്കുമ്പോൾ അദ്ദേഹം പറഞ്ഞു: "എനിക്ക് ഭൂമിയിൽ ഏറ്റവും വലിയ പുരുഷൻ ബ്രിട്ടീഷ് ചക്രവർത്തിയല്ല, ശ്രീകൃഷ്ണപരമാത്മാവാണ്. എനിക്ക് പ്രിയപ്പെട്ട രാജ്യം ഇംഗ്ലണ്ടല്ല ഭാരതമാണ്. എനിക്ക് ബൈബിളിനോട് സ്നേഹമാണ്. അതുകൊണ്ട് ബ്രിട്ടീഷ് സാമ്രാജ്യത്തോട് വിരോധമാണ്."

ഒതുക്കിപ്പിടിച്ച പുതിയ ആവേശവുമായിട്ടാണ് സദസ്യർ അവിടെ നിന്നുംപോയത്. ഈ സ്വാമിജി വിപ്ലവകാരിയായ സന്യാസിയാണെന്ന് ചിലർ പറഞ്ഞു. സ്വാമിജി പറഞ്ഞതിനെല്ലാം രണ്ട് അർഥമുണ്ടെന്ന് മറ്റു ചിലർ അഭിപ്രായപ്പെട്ടു. ശിവാനന്ദഭാരതിയുടെ വാക്കുകൾ ഏവരുടെയും മനസിൽ പതിഞ്ഞു എന്നുള്ളതാണ് സത്യം.

ശിവാനന്ദജി വാസവമേനോന്റെ സുഹൃത്തായതിൽ അത്ഭുതമില്ലെന്ന് അരവിന്ദനു തോന്നി. സദനത്തിലുള്ളവരുമായി സ്വാമിജി പരിചയപ്പെട്ടു. യോഗമയീദേവി ബനാറസിൽവെച്ച് സ്വാമിജിയെ കണ്ടിട്ടുണ്ട്. പ്രസംഗം കേട്ടിട്ടുണ്ട്. വർഷങ്ങൾക്കു മുമ്പ്.

എറണാകുളത്തുനിന്നും മൂന്നാലുപേർ സ്വാമിജിയുടെകൂടെ വന്നിട്ടുണ്ട്. അവരും സ്വാമിജിയും അത്താഴം കഴിച്ചു. ചെറിയ ഒരു വിശ്രമത്തിനുശേഷം സ്വാമിജിയും സംഘവും യാത്ര പുറപ്പെട്ടു.

അരവിന്ദന്റെ പത്രത്തിൽ, പിറ്റേന്ന് സ്വാമി ശിവാനന്ദഭാരതിയുടെ ചിത്രവും അദ്ദേഹത്തിന്റെ പ്രസംഗം ഏതാണ്ടു പൂർണരൂപവും പ്രസിദ്ധീകരിച്ചിരുന്നു. "ഞങ്ങൾക്ക് സ്വാതന്ത്ര്യം വേണം! എന്നാണ് ആ പ്രസംഗത്തിനു തലക്കെട്ടു കൊടുത്തിരുന്നത്. ഒരു സന്യാസിയുടെ പ്രസംഗമെന്ന നിലയ്ക്ക് ആളുകൾ അത് താൽപര്യപൂർവം വായിച്ചു. ആ പ്രഭാഷണം പട്ടണത്തിലെ സംസാരവിഷയമായി. പൊതുമൈതാനത്ത് അദ്ദേഹം പ്രസംഗിക്കേണ്ടതായിരുന്നു എന്ന് പലരും അഭിപ്രായപ്പെട്ടു.

അന്നുതൊട്ടു രഹസ്യപൊലീസുകാർ അരവിന്ദന്റെ പിന്നാലെ കൂടി.

അവരിൽ പലരും പരിചിതരാണ്. അവരുടെ മേധാവികൾക്ക് ഒരു ധാരണ ഉണ്ടായിരിക്കുന്നു. സ്വാമി ശിവാനന്ദഭാരതിയെ മലയാള പ്രദേശത്തേക്ക് കൊണ്ടുവന്നത് അരവിന്ദനാണ്. ഗവൺമെന്റിന്റെ റിപ്പോർട്ടും അങ്ങനെ തന്നെയാണെന്നു സുഹൃത്തായ സി ഐ ഡി ഉദ്യോഗസ്ഥൻ പറയുകയും ചെയ്തു.

രണ്ടു ദിവസം കഴിഞ്ഞ് അരവിന്ദൻ സദനത്തിൽ ഇരിക്കുന്നു. ഒരു പൊലീസ് ജീപ്പുവന്നു നിന്നു. ഇൻസ്പെക്ടർ ഇറങ്ങിവന്നു.

"അരവിന്ദൻ നിങ്ങളല്ലേ?" അയാൾ ചോദിച്ചു.

"അതെ." അരവിന്ദൻ പ്രത്യേകിച്ചൊരു ഭാവവും കൂടാതെ പറഞ്ഞു.

"യോഗമയീദേവി ആരാണ്? അവരെ ഒന്നു വിളിക്കണം."

സന്ധ്യാദേവി പുറത്തേക്കു വന്നു. ഇൻസ്പെക്ടറുടെ സംസാരം കേട്ടുകൊണ്ടാണ് അവർ കടന്നുവന്നത്.

"യോഗമയീദേവിയെ എന്തിന് കാണണം?" അവർ ചോദിച്ചു.

"ഇവർക്ക് രണ്ടുപേർക്കും വാറണ്ടുണ്ട്." ഉദ്യോഗസ്ഥൻ പറഞ്ഞു.

കുറേ നിമിഷങ്ങൾ നിശ്ശബ്ദമായി നീങ്ങി.

അരവിന്ദൻ എഴുന്നേറ്റു. യോഗമയീദേവി വാതിൽക്കൽ വന്നു കഴിഞ്ഞിരുന്നു. ഇൻസ്പെക്ടർ അവരെ നോക്കി.

അകത്തെ മുറിയിൽ കീർത്തിയും പാർവതിയും തമ്പുരാട്ടിയും റീനയും എല്ലാം വന്നുകൂടിയിരുന്നു. ഇൻസ്പെക്ടർ സന്ധ്യാദേവിയെ ശ്രദ്ധിച്ചതേയില്ല.

"വേഗമാകട്ടെ. വരൂ." അയാൾ ദൃഢമായി ആവശ്യപ്പെട്ടു.

പരസ്പരം ആലോചിക്കാൻ സമയം കിട്ടിയില്ല. അരവിന്ദൻ ഒരു നിമിഷം ചിന്തിച്ചു. എതിർത്തിട്ടു കാര്യമില്ല. സാഹചര്യം അതല്ല; അവർ ബലം പ്രയോഗിക്കും. സ്ത്രീകൾ മാത്രമുള്ള സ്ഥലത്ത് അത് വളരെ വിഷമം പിടിച്ച രംഗം സൃഷ്ടിക്കും.

"സന്ധ്യാദേവി ഞങ്ങൾ ചെല്ലാം."

സന്ധ്യാദേവി മിണ്ടാതെ നിന്നു.

യോഗമയീദേവി മുന്നിലും അരവിന്ദൻ പിന്നിലുമായി ഗേറ്റിലേക്കു നടന്നു. അവരെ ജീപ്പിന്റെ പിന്നിൽ കയറ്റിയിരുത്തി. ഇൻസ്പെക്ടറും കയറി. ജീപ്പു വിട്ടുപോയി

കീർത്തിയും റീനയും ഉഷയും സുമതിയും കരഞ്ഞു.

"നിങ്ങൾ അകത്തുപോയിരിക്കൂ." സന്ധ്യാദേവി നിർദേശിച്ചു.

അവർ ഇരുന്നു. അടുത്തപടി എന്തുചെയ്യണമെന്ന് ആലോചിച്ചു.

ഡി എസ് പി യുടെ വസതിയിലേക്കാണ് അവരെ ആദ്യം കൊണ്ടുപോയത്. ഡി എസ് പി അവിടെ ഉണ്ട്. അദ്ദേഹം ഒറ്റയ്ക്കു പിന്നിൽ ഇരിക്കുന്നു. ഒരുവശത്ത് കിടന്ന കസേര ചൂണ്ടിക്കാണിച്ചു. അദ്ദേഹം പറഞ്ഞു:

"ഇരിക്കൂ."

യോഗമയീദേവിയും അരവിന്ദനും ഇരുന്നു

ഡി എസ് പി സംസാരിച്ചു.

"ഞാൻ അധികം പറഞ്ഞ് എന്റെ സമയം കളയുന്നില്ല. നിങ്ങളെ ബുദ്ധിമുട്ടിക്കുന്നുമില്ല. നിങ്ങൾക്കു രണ്ടുപേർക്കും സ്വാമി ശിവാനന്ദഭാരതിയുമായി ദീർഘകാലത്തെ ബന്ധമുണ്ടെന്ന് ഗവൺമെന്റിന് റിപ്പോർട്ട് കിട്ടിയിട്ടുണ്ട്." അദ്ദേഹം യോഗമയീദേവിയുടെ നേർക്ക് നോക്കി. "നിങ്ങൾ ബനാറസിൽവച്ച് ആ മനുഷ്യനുമായിചേർന്ന് ഗവൺമെന്റ് വിരുദ്ധ പ്രവർത്തനങ്ങളിൽ ഏർപ്പെട്ടിരുന്നതായി അറിവുണ്ട്. മിസ്റ്റർ അരവിന്ദനാണ് ശിവാനന്ദജിയെ ഈ ഭാഗത്തേക്ക് കൊണ്ടുവന്നതെന്നും അറിവുണ്ട്. ശിവാന്ദജി സർക്കാർ വിരുദ്ധരായ പണക്കാരിൽനിന്നും പിരിക്കുന്ന പണം കൊണ്ടാണ് നിങ്ങളുടെ പത്രം നടത്തുന്നതെന്നും റിപ്പോർട്ടുണ്ട്. പല പ്രവിശ്യകളിലും അങ്ങനെ പത്രങ്ങൾ നടത്തുന്നുണ്ട്. എനിക്ക് ഒറ്റ വാക്കിൽ മറുപടി കിട്ടണമെന്നാണ് ആഗ്രഹം. ഇതെല്ലാം ശരിയല്ലേ?"

"ശരിയല്ല." അരവിന്ദൻ പറഞ്ഞു.

"ഒട്ടും ശരിയല്ല." യോഗമയീദേവിയും അറിയിച്ചു.

"സത്യം പറഞ്ഞാൽ അത് പറയിക്കാൻ വേണ്ടി ഞങ്ങൾ ബുദ്ധിമുട്ടേണ്ടി വരികയില്ല. സർക്കാരിനെതിരായി യുദ്ധം പ്രഖ്യാപിക്കുന്നവരോട് വലിയ സൗജന്യമൊന്നും കാട്ടുകയില്ലെന്ന് അറിയാമല്ലോ." ഡി എസ് പി ചുരുട്ടു വലിച്ചുകൊണ്ടിരുന്നു.

"ഞങ്ങൾ സത്യമാണ് പറഞ്ഞത്. ബാക്കികാര്യങ്ങൾ നിങ്ങൾക്ക് തീരുമാനിക്കാം." അരവിന്ദൻ പ്രതിവചിച്ചു.

"നിങ്ങൾ പാടെ നിഷേധിക്കുന്നു. അല്ലേ?" ഡി എസ് പി യുടെ ചോദ്യം.

"അതെ."

"ശരി."

ഇൻസ്പെക്ടറോട് അരവിന്ദനെ കൊണ്ടുപോകാൻ നിർദേശിച്ചു.

അരവിന്ദനെ മറ്റുതടവുകാരുടെ കൂടെ ഒരു മുറിയിലാക്കി യോഗമയീദേവിയെ മറ്റൊരു മുറിയിൽ ഒറ്റയ്ക്കും.

പതിനാല്

യോഗമയീദേവിയെയും അരവിന്ദനെയും അറസ്റ്റു ചെയ്തതിൽ പ്രതിഷേധിച്ച്, ഒരു മഹായോഗംകൂടി സന്ധ്യാദേവി ഉൾപ്പെടെ പലരും പ്രസംഗിച്ചു. അവരെ രണ്ടുപേരെയും ഉടനടി മോചിപ്പിക്കണമെന്ന പ്രമേയം പാസാക്കി. അധികാരസ്ഥാനത്തേക്ക് കമ്പിയടിച്ചു. പക്ഷേ, മൂന്നുനാലുദിവസത്തേക്ക് ഒരനക്കവും ഉണ്ടായില്ല. കോടതിയിൽ കൊണ്ടുപോയില്ല ആരും ഒന്നും ചോദിച്ചില്ല. എന്തു ചെയ്യാൻ പോകുന്നുവെന്ന് ഒരു വിവരവും കിട്ടിയില്ല. നാലാംദിവസം രണ്ടുപേരെയും ലോക്കപ്പിൽ നിന്നിറക്കി. അവരെ ബസിൽ രണ്ടു പൊലീസുകാരുടെ അകമ്പടിയോടെ എറണാകുളത്തേക്ക് കൊണ്ടുപോയി. അവിടെ രണ്ടു തിരുവിതാംകൂർ

പൊലീസുകാരുകൂടി കാത്തുനിന്നിരുന്നു. ഇതിനിടയ്ക്ക് പൊലീസുകാരുമായി അരവിന്ദൻ സംസാരിച്ചു. അവരെ മദ്രാസിലേക്ക് കൊണ്ടുപോവുകയാണ്. സ്വാമി ശിവാനന്ദഭാരതിയെ മലബാറിൽ വച്ച് അറസ്റ്റ് ചെയ്ത്, മദ്രാസിലേക്ക് കൊണ്ടുപോയിട്ടുണ്ട്. ഒരു മാസക്കാലത്തിനുമുൻപ് ശിവാനന്ദഭാരതി അവിടം സന്ദർശിച്ചിരുന്നു. അന്ന് അവിടെയുണ്ടായ ഒരു ഏറ്റുമുട്ടലിന് രഹസ്യമായ നേതൃത്വം നൽകിയതു വാസവമേനോനും സ്വാമിജിയും കൂടിയാണ്. ആ കേസ് സംബന്ധിച്ചാണ് ഇപ്പോഴത്തെ അറസ്റ്റ്. അരവിന്ദനെ കൊണ്ടുപോകുന്നത്, സ്വാമിയുമായുള്ള ബന്ധത്തിന്റെ അടിസ്ഥാനത്തിലാണ്.

'സ്വതന്ത്രഭൂമി' ആഫീസ് അടച്ചു മുദ്രവച്ചു കഴിഞ്ഞുവെന്ന് പൊലീസുകാർ അരവിന്ദനെ അറിയിച്ചു.

യോഗമയീദേവിയെ മദ്രാസിലേക്ക് എന്തിനു കൊണ്ടുപോകുന്നുവെന്ന് അവർക്ക് അറിഞ്ഞുകൂടാ. അവരെ അവിടത്തെ പൊലീസിനെ ഏൽപ്പിക്കുക എന്നുള്ളതാണ് തിരുവിതാംകൂർ പൊലീസിന്റെ കർത്തവ്യം.

രണ്ടു തടവുകാരും നാലു പൊലീസുകാരും മദ്രാസിലേക്കുള്ള തീവണ്ടിയിലെ മൂന്നാംക്ലാസ് മുറിയിൽ കയറി.

തിരക്കുള്ള കമ്പാർട്ടുമെന്റ്, കഷ്ടിച്ച് ഇരിക്കാൻ സ്ഥലം കിട്ടി. പൊലീസുകാർ പല സ്ഥലങ്ങളിലായിട്ടാണ് ഇരുന്നത്.

അരവിന്ദൻ പുറത്തേക്കുനോക്കി ഇരുന്നു. ദുഃഖിക്കുന്ന രണ്ടു കണ്ണുകൾ തന്നെ പിൻതുടരുന്നതുപോലെ, ഇരുട്ടിൽക്കൂടി വണ്ടി അതിവേഗം പോകുന്നു. ദൂരെ പ്രകാശങ്ങളുണ്ട്. തന്നെപ്പറ്റി ഒരു വിഷമവും തോന്നിയില്ല. യോഗമയീദേവി, അവർ മുഖം കുനിച്ച്, ചിന്തയിലാണ്ട് ഇരിക്കുന്നു. എന്തും ധീരമായി നേരിടുന്ന സ്ത്രീ. പക്ഷേ, മദ്രാസിൽ ചെന്നാൽ, അവരെ എങ്ങോട്ട് കൊണ്ടുപോകും എന്നറിയില്ല അതാണ് ഉൽക്കണ്ഠ. പെട്ടെന്നാലോചിച്ചു. എന്തിന് മദ്രാസ് വരെ പോകണം?

രാത്രി ഭക്ഷണം കഴിക്കാമെന്ന് പൊലീസുകാർ പറഞ്ഞു. വേണ്ട. യോഗമയീദേവിയും ആഹാരം കഴിച്ചില്ല. പൊലീസുകാർ ഭക്ഷണം വരുത്തിക്കഴിച്ചു. വണ്ടി പുറപ്പെട്ടു.

ഇരുട്ടുനിറഞ്ഞ വിശാലമായ ലോകത്തിലേക്ക് നോക്കിക്കൊണ്ട് അരവിന്ദൻ സമയം കഴിച്ചുകൂട്ടി. യാത്രക്കാർ സീറ്റുകളിൽ ഇരുന്ന് ഉറങ്ങിത്തുടങ്ങി. കുറേപ്പേർ താഴെക്കിടന്നു. ഒന്ന് ബാത്ത്റൂം വരെ പോകാൻ ഇടമില്ല. അരവിന്ദൻ ജനൽത്തട്ടിലേക്കു തലവെച്ചു. തണുപ്പുള്ള കാറ്റ്. അത് സുഖമായിത്തോന്നി. സ്റ്റേഷനുകൾ കടന്ന് വാഹനം കൂടുതൽ വേഗത്തിൽ കുതിക്കുന്നു.

ഇടയ്ക്ക് യോഗമയീദേവി മുഖമുയർത്തിയപ്പോൾ, അരവിന്ദൻ ഒരു സൂചന നൽകി. അവർ പെട്ടെന്ന് അതു മനസിലാക്കി.

രാത്രി ഓടിക്കിതച്ച് മുൻപോട്ടു പോകുന്നു. എല്ലാവരും ഉറക്കമായി. ചിലർ സീറ്റുകളിലിരുന്നുള്ള ഉറക്കത്തിൽ വണ്ടിയുടെ ചുമരിൽ തലയിട്ടു തല്ലുന്നു.

ഒരു മണി, വണ്ടി ഒരു സ്റ്റേഷനിൽ നിന്നു പൊലീസുകാർ അപ്പോഴും ചോദിച്ചു.

"ചായ കുടിക്കുന്നോ?"

വേണ്ടെന്നറിയിച്ചു. യോഗമയീദേവി അത് ശ്രദ്ധിച്ചതേയില്ല.

അന്ധകാരത്തെ മുറിച്ചുകൊണ്ട് നീണ്ട ചൂളങ്ങൾവിളിച്ച് വണ്ടി പാഞ്ഞുപോയി. ഇനി വെളുക്കുംവരെ, ലക്ഷ്യത്തിലെത്താൻ വേണ്ടിയുള്ള തിടുക്കമാണ്. എഞ്ചിൻ ക്യാബിനിൽ നിൽക്കുന്ന ഡ്രൈവറുടെയും സഹായികളുടെയും ചിത്രം മനസിൽ കണ്ടു. തീയും ചൂടും. വെന്തു ചുവന്ന കൽക്കരി നിരന്തരം കോരിയിടുന്ന മനുഷ്യർ. ആയിരക്കണക്കിനാളുകളെയും കൊണ്ട് സഞ്ചരിക്കുന്ന വണ്ടിയുടെ ചുക്കാൻ പിടിക്കുന്ന ഡ്രൈവർ. തീവണ്ടിക്ക് ഒരു സംഗീതമുണ്ട്. ഓളങ്ങൾ. പലമാത്രകളിൽ വീഴുന്ന താളമുണ്ട്. അത് പുതിയ കവിതയ്ക്കുള്ള 'ബിറ്റു'കൾ നൽകുന്നുവെന്നു തോന്നി.

രണ്ടുമണി.

പിന്നെ നിമിഷങ്ങൾ എണ്ണുകയായിരുന്നു. വണ്ടിയുടെ താളവും നിമിഷങ്ങളുടെ സ്പന്ദവും ഒരുമിച്ചു ലയിക്കുന്നതായി അനുഭവപ്പെട്ടു.

മൂന്നു മണിയായപ്പോൾ തല ഉയർത്തി പുറത്തേക്കു നോക്കി. ദൂരെ ഒരു വെളിച്ചം കാണുന്നു. ഒരു ചെറിയ ഗ്രാമം അല്ലെങ്കിൽ പട്ടണം. ഇരുട്ടിൽക്കൂടി അടുത്തു വരികയാണ്. യോഗമയീദേവിയുടെ മെയ്യിൽ ഒന്നു സ്പർശിച്ചു. അവർ മുഖമുയർത്തി നോക്കി. കുറെ മിനിട്ടുകൾകൂടി. വണ്ടി അതേ വേഗത്തിൽ പോകുന്നു. ഒടുവിൽ ദൂരെക്കണ്ട വെളിച്ചം അടുത്തേക്കുവന്നു. വണ്ടിയുടെ വേഗം കുറഞ്ഞു. ഒരു ചെറിയ സ്റ്റേഷനിലേക്ക് താളംപിടിച്ച് അതു ചെന്നു കയറുന്നു. തളർന്ന സഞ്ചാരിയെപ്പോലെ വണ്ടി സ്റ്റേഷൻമാസ്റ്റർ കാട്ടിയ വിളക്കിൽ നോക്കി, സാവധാനംനിന്നു.

അരവിന്ദൻ രണ്ടു നിമിഷം കൂടി കാത്തിരുന്നു. എന്നിട്ട് എഴുന്നേറ്റു. യോഗമയീദേവിയും എഴുന്നേറ്റു. ക്ലേശിച്ച് വാതിലിലേക്ക് നടന്നു. അവരും ആളുകളെ കടന്ന് പുറകിൽ വന്നു നിന്നു. വാതിൽ തുറന്നു. യോഗമയീദേവി ആദ്യം താഴെയിറങ്ങി. പുറകെ അരവിന്ദനും അവർ അതിവേഗം നടന്നു. സ്റ്റേഷനിലെ മങ്ങിയ വെളിച്ചത്തിൽ നിന്ന് ഇരുട്ടിലേക്കു നീങ്ങിയപ്പോൾ വണ്ടി അനങ്ങി. ചൂളം വിളിച്ചു. അത് നീണ്ട നിശ്വാസങ്ങൾ പുറപ്പെടുവിച്ചുകൊണ്ട് നീങ്ങി. മുമ്പോട്ടു പോയിത്തിരിഞ്ഞു നോക്കിയപ്പോൾ പുറകിലത്തെ ചുവന്ന വെളിച്ചം ദൂരെക്കണ്ടു.

റെയിൽപ്പാളത്തിൽക്കൂടി വേഗം നടന്നു. യോഗമയീദേവിയുടെ കൈയിൽ ഇറുകെപ്പിടിച്ചു. "വല്ല കല്ലോ കമ്പിയോ കാണും." അരവിന്ദൻ പറഞ്ഞു. നാട്ടുവെളിച്ചം. അതിൽക്കൂടി റെയിൽപ്പാളം നീണ്ടുകിടക്കുന്നതു കാണാം. വിജനമായ പ്രദേശം. ഒരു കുഗ്രാമമാണ്. അവിടെ ആകെക്കൂടി കിട്ടിയ ഒരു ഭാഗ്യം ഈ കൊച്ചുറെയിൽവേ സ്റ്റേഷനാണെന്നു തോന്നുന്നു. ഇപ്പോൾ വഴി കാണാം. നാട്ടുവെളിച്ചവുമായി കണ്ണുകൾ പൊരുത്തപ്പെട്ടിരിക്കുന്നു. ഉറക്കം തൂങ്ങിയിരുന്ന പൊലീസുകാരെപ്പറ്റി

ഓർമിച്ചു. അവർ എന്തു സംഭ്രമത്തിലാണ് അകപ്പെടുക!

സമാധാനമുണ്ട്. നേരം പുലരാൻ മൂന്നു മണിക്കൂർ മതി. അതുവരെ നടന്നാലും വേണ്ടില്ല. കുറച്ചുകൂടി പോയി ഒരു റെയിൽവേ ക്രോസിൽ വന്നെത്തി. വലത്തോട്ടു തിരിഞ്ഞു അത് റോഡാണ്. അൽപ്പം നടന്നു.

അവിടെ പല കടകളും ഒരു വണ്ടിപ്പേട്ടയുമുണ്ട്. കുറച്ചു നേരം ആ വണ്ടിപ്പേട്ടയിൽ ഇരിക്കാൻ നിശ്ചയിച്ചു. അവിടെ കാളവണ്ടികളിട്ടുകൊണ്ട് ചിലർ ഉറങ്ങുന്നുണ്ട്. ഒരു ചെറിയ ചായക്കട തുറന്നുവച്ചിരിക്കുന്നു. കടക്കാരൻ മേശപ്പുറത്ത് തല വെച്ച് ഉറങ്ങുന്നു. യോഗമയീദേവിയുടെ കൈവശം പതിനഞ്ച് ഉറുപ്പികയുണ്ട്. സന്ധ്യാദേവി ലോക്കപ്പിൽ വന്നു കണ്ടപ്പോൾ കൊടുത്തതാണ്. വല്ലതും പുറത്തുനിന്നു വാങ്ങിപ്പിക്കാൻ കഴിഞ്ഞാൽ, അതിനുവേണ്ടി, പുറത്തുനിന്ന് ആഹാരം വാങ്ങിക്കൊടുക്കാൻ സന്ധ്യാദേവിക്ക് അനുമതി നൽകിയില്ല. അരവിന്ദന്റെ കൈയിലും അൽപ്പം പൈസയുണ്ട്.

കിഴക്കുനിന്നു പ്രകാശം കണ്ടുതുടങ്ങി. ചായക്കടക്കാരൻ ഉണർന്നു. അയാൾ കടയുടെ ഓരത്ത് ഇരിക്കുന്ന അപരിചിതരെ സൂക്ഷിച്ചു നോക്കി. എന്നിട്ട് ചായപ്പാത്രത്തിനുകീഴെ തീ കൂട്ടി.

ചൂട് ചായ കഴിച്ച്, ചായക്കടക്കാരനോടു കുശലങ്ങൾ ചോദിച്ചു. അരവിന്ദന് തമിഴ് വശമാണ്. അതുകൊണ്ട് കടക്കാരന് സന്തോഷവും തോന്നി. രണ്ടു മൈലുകൾക്കപ്പുറം സിമന്റ് ഉണ്ടാക്കുന്ന ഒരു ഫാക്ടറിയുണ്ട്. അവിടെ ധാരാളം ജോലിക്കാരുണ്ട്. അവിടെ അന്വേഷിച്ചാൽ ഒരു ജോലി കിട്ടിയെന്നുവരും. ഒരു തൊഴിൽ കണ്ടുപിടിക്കാൻ അമ്മയും മകനും കൂടി കോയമ്പത്തൂരുനിന്ന് ഇറങ്ങിത്തിരിച്ചിരിക്കുകയാണ്. ഒരു സ്റ്റേഷൻ തെറ്റായിറങ്ങിപ്പോയി. പക്ഷേ, അതിൽ കുഴപ്പമില്ല. രണ്ടു മൈൽ നടന്നാൽ സിമന്റ് കമ്പനിപ്പടിക്കലെത്താമല്ലോ.

നല്ല വെളിച്ചം വീണുകഴിഞ്ഞപ്പോൾ, ചായക്കടക്കാരനോട് നന്ദിയും യാത്രയും പറഞ്ഞ് നടന്നു. കമ്പനിപ്പടിക്കലെത്തി. തൊഴിലാളികൾ ധാരാളം അകത്തേക്കു കയറിക്കൊണ്ടിരിക്കുന്നു. നല്ല വസ്ത്രങ്ങളണിഞ്ഞ മറ്റുജോലിക്കാരും ജോലിക്കു കയറാൻ വേണ്ടി പടിക്കൽ നിൽക്കുന്നു. ആരെയോ തിരക്കിവന്ന രീതിയിലാണ് അരവിന്ദനും യോഗമയീദേവിയും കമ്പനിപ്പടിക്കൽ നിന്നത്. ചിലർ അവരെ ശ്രദ്ധിച്ചു. ജോലിക്കാരിൽ പലരും മലയാളികളാണ്. കണ്ടാലറിയാം. അവരാണ് ശ്രദ്ധിച്ചത്. ഒരാൾ അരവിന്ദന്റെ അടുത്തു വന്നു.

"ആരെ കാണാനാ നിങ്ങൾ നിൽക്കുന്നത്?"

എന്തുപറയും? ആരുടെ പേരു പറയും? പെട്ടെന്ന് ബുദ്ധിതോന്നി.

"എനിക്ക് മാനേജരെ ഒന്നു കാണണം."

"മാനേജരും മലയാളിയാണ്. അദ്ദേഹം പത്തര മണിക്ക് വരും. നിങ്ങൾ അകത്തേക്കു വരൂ. സൗകര്യമായി ഇരുത്താം."

ആ മനുഷ്യൻ അവരെ അകത്തേക്ക് കൂട്ടിക്കൊണ്ടുപോയി. സന്ദർശകർക്ക് സ്വസ്ഥമായി ഇരിക്കാനുള്ള ഒരു മുറി കാട്ടിക്കൊടുത്തു. അയാൾ പോയി. അൽപ്പം കഴിഞ്ഞപ്പോൾ ചായ വന്നു. അതു കുടിച്ചു. മാനേജർ

വരുമ്പോൾ കൂട്ടിക്കൊണ്ടുപോകാമെന്ന് വാക്കു കൊടുത്തു. എന്നിട്ടാണ് അയാൾ അകത്തേക്ക് പോയത്.

പത്തേകാൽ മണിയായപ്പോൾ അയാൾ വന്നു. പത്തര മണിക്ക് മാനേജരുടെ കാറു വന്നപ്പോൾ, അയാൾ ചെന്ന് വിവരം പറഞ്ഞു. അവരെ തന്റെ മുറിയിലേക്ക് കൂട്ടിക്കൊണ്ടു ചെല്ലാൻ നിർദേശിച്ചു.

മാനേജരുടെ മുൻപിൽ ഇരുന്നു. പേരു ചോദിച്ചു. എന്തിന് വന്നു വെന്നു തിരക്കി. അരവിന്ദൻ മാനേജരെ പരിചയപ്പെടാൻ ശ്രമിച്ചു. അദ്ദേഹത്തിന്റെ പേര് പി ആർ മേനോൻ, സ്ഥലം തൃശൂർ.

"അരവിന്ദൻ എന്നൊരു കവിയുണ്ട്. കേട്ടിട്ടുണ്ടോ? നിങ്ങളുടെ പേരു കേട്ടപ്പോഴാണ് ഞാനോർമിച്ചത്." മേനോൻ ചോദിച്ചു.

യോഗമയീദേവി ചിരിയടക്കി. അരവിന്ദനെ നോക്കി. അയാൾ രണ്ടു നിമിഷം ഓർത്തിരുന്നു.

"ഉണ്ട്. കേട്ടിട്ടുണ്ട്."

"അയാൾ എന്റെ ഒരു ബന്ധുവാണ്." അദ്ദേഹം തുടർന്നു പറഞ്ഞു.

അരവിന്ദനും യോഗമയീദേവിയും പരസ്പരം നോക്കി.

"എങ്ങനെ ബന്ധം?" അയാൾ തിരക്കി.

"അയാളുടെ അമ്മയുടെ ഒരു സഹോദരിയുടെ മകനാണു ഞാൻ."

"ഡൽഹിയിലായിരുന്ന സഹോദരിയുടെ...?"

"അതെ.." മേനോന്റെ ദൃഷ്ടികൾ ഉത്സാഹം കാട്ടി. "നിങ്ങൾ അവരെ അറിയുമോ?"

"അറിയും. മിസ്റ്റർ മേനോൻ ഇന്ത്യയ്ക്കു പുറത്തായിരുന്നു അല്ലേ?"

"അതെ. ഇന്ത്യയ്ക്കു പുറത്താണ് ജനിച്ചതും വളർന്നതും. നാടുമായി ബന്ധമൊന്നുമില്ല. അരവിന്ദൻ വലിയ കവിയാണെന്നു കേട്ടിട്ടുണ്ട്. അത്രയേയുള്ളൂ. ഞാൻ അയാളെ കാണുന്നുണ്ട്. ഞാൻ ഈ ജോലി രാജിവച്ച് മദ്രാസിലേക്കു പോവുകയാണ്. അവിടെ ഒരു പത്രം തുടങ്ങണം. എല്ലാ ഏർപ്പാടുകളും ചെയ്തു കഴിഞ്ഞു. സ്ഥലം, കെട്ടിടം, പ്രസ്... എനിക്ക് വളരെ നാളായിട്ടുള്ള ഒരു ആഗ്രഹമാണ്. ഏപ്രിൽ മാസത്തിൽ ആരംഭിക്കണമെന്നാണ് ആഗ്രഹിക്കുന്നത്."

ഇനിയും മറച്ചുവയ്ക്കുന്നതു ശരിയല്ല.

"ഞാൻ പറയുമ്പോൾ അത്ഭുതപ്പെടരുത്." അയാൾ പറഞ്ഞു: "അരവിന്ദൻ ഞാനാണ്."

മേനോൻ ഉള്ളാലെ നടുങ്ങിപ്പോയി. സൂക്ഷിച്ചുനോക്കി. അദ്ദേഹത്തിനു വിശ്വസിക്കാൻ കഴിയുന്നില്ല. കുറച്ചുനേരം നോക്കിയിരുന്നിട്ടു പറഞ്ഞു:

"ഉണ്ട്. ഛായയുണ്ട്. എനിക്ക് അത്ഭുതം തോന്നുന്നു. ദൈവം നമ്മളെ കൂട്ടിമുട്ടിച്ചതുപോലെ, നീ വലിയവനായതിൽ സന്തോഷിക്കുന്നവനാണ് ഞാൻ. ഇനി ഇവർ ആരാണെന്നു സത്യം പറയൂ."

അരവിന്ദൻ എല്ലാം പറഞ്ഞു കേൾപ്പിച്ചു. കേട്ടിട്ട്, മേനോൻ ചിരിച്ചു;

"ഒട്ടും ഭയപ്പെടേണ്ട. ഞാൻ നിങ്ങളെപ്പോലെ ദേശീയ പ്രസ്ഥാന

ത്തിൽ അടിയുറച്ചു വിശ്വസിക്കുന്നവനാണ്. ഞാൻ പത്രമാരംഭിക്കുന്നത്, ആ പ്രസ്ഥാനത്തെ പിന്താങ്ങാനാണ്." അദ്ദേഹം യോഗമയീദേവിയുടെ നേർക്കു തിരിഞ്ഞു: "അമ്മയെ കാണാൻ കഴിഞ്ഞതിൽ എനിക്കു വലിയ സന്തോഷമുണ്ട്."

ആഹ്ലാദം നിറഞ്ഞ അവരുടെ സ്വരം പുറത്തുവന്നു:

"ഈ കൂടിക്കാഴ്ചയ്ക്ക് ദൈവത്തെയാണ് സ്തുതിക്കേണ്ടത്." സുരക്ഷിതമായ ഒരു സ്ഥലത്തു വന്നെത്തിയ ആശ്വാസത്തോടെ അവർ മേനോന്റെ കൂടെ അദ്ദേഹത്തിന്റെ വീട്ടിലേക്കു പോയി. മേനോന് ഭാര്യയും ഒരു കുട്ടിയുമുണ്ട്. ഭാര്യയ്ക്കും അരവിന്ദനെ കണ്ടപ്പോൾ അത്ഭുതമായി. അയാൾ ആ വീട്ടിലെ എപ്പോഴത്തെയും സംസാരവിഷയമാണ്. അങ്ങനെയുള്ള ആൾ ദാ, നേരിട്ടുവന്നിരിക്കുന്നു. ആ സ്ത്രീയും, വിദ്യാഭ്യാസവും ദേശീയബോധവുമുള്ളവരാണ്. യോഗമയീദേവിയെ അവർക്ക് നന്നേ ഇഷ്ടപ്പെട്ടു. സ്വന്തം അമ്മയെപ്പോലെയാണ് അവർ പെരുമാറിയത്. അന്നുരാത്രി മുഴുവനും അവർ സംസാരിച്ചുകൊണ്ടിരുന്നു. പത്രം തുടങ്ങുന്നതിന്റെ വിശദാംശങ്ങളാണ് അവർ ചർച്ച ചെയ്തത്.

* * *

ദിവാകരൻ ഭാനുമതിയിൽ കണ്ണുംമർപ്പിച്ച് വളരെ നേരമായി ഇരിക്കുന്നു. അയാളുടെ മനസ്സ് അടിയോടെ പിഴുതുമറിഞ്ഞു കിടക്കുന്നതുപോലെ ഉണ്ട്. രത്നമ്മയുടെ സഹോദരൻ വന്നതും ലീലാംബാളിനെപ്പറ്റി പറഞ്ഞതുമെല്ലാം യാതൊരു ക്ഷോഭവും കൂടാതെയാണ് അവൾ ദിവാകരനെ അറിയിച്ചത്. ക്ഷോഭിക്കരുതെന്നും അതുംവച്ചുകൊണ്ട് അയാളെ വേദനിപ്പിക്കരുതെന്നും അവൾ തീരുമാനിച്ചിരുന്നു. ആ മനുഷ്യൻ ജീവിതത്തിൽക്കുറേ തെറ്റുകൾ ചെയ്തിട്ടുണ്ട്. പലതും സഹിക്കാൻ വയ്യാത്ത തെറ്റുകളാണ്. എന്നാലും അദ്ദേഹം തന്റെ ഭർത്താവാണ്. എന്തു വന്നാലും ഇനി അത് അല്ലാതാവുകയില്ല. അദ്ദേഹത്തിന്റെ പ്രവൃത്തിയുടെ ഫലങ്ങൾ താൻ പങ്കിട്ടെടുക്കണം. അദ്ദേഹത്തിന്റെ ദുഃഖങ്ങൾ കുറയ്ക്കാൻ ചെയ്യാവുന്നതൊക്കെ ചെയ്യണം. ഭാനുമതി വലിയ ചില തീരുമാനങ്ങൾ ചെയ്തിരിക്കുകയാണ്. ആലോചിച്ച്, തന്നെ അത് അറിയിക്കുവാനുള്ള സമയം കാത്തിരിക്കുകയായിരുന്നു. ഇന്നാണ് ഭർത്താവ് അൽപ്പം സ്വസ്ഥനായത്.

കഴിഞ്ഞകാലത്തിന്റെ പ്രേതങ്ങൾ തന്റെ ആത്മാവിൽ ഉണർന്നെഴുന്നേൽക്കുന്നതായി ദിവാകരനു തോന്നി. അവ വാ പിളർന്ന്, തന്നെ വിഴുങ്ങാൻ നിൽക്കുന്നു. ആ ഗൗണ്ടറെ കണ്ടുമുട്ടിയ ദിവസം തന്റെ ആപത്തിന്റെ ആരംഭമായിരുന്നുവെന്ന് ഓർമിച്ചു. അത് ചെന്നു കലാശിച്ചത് അങ്ങനെയൊക്കെയാണ്. പണവും സ്വത്തും ഉണ്ടായി. എന്നിട്ട് അതൊക്കെ എവിടെ? അപമാനത്തിന്റെ ഇരുണ്ട കോലങ്ങൾ ഭീഷണിപ്പെടുത്തിക്കൊണ്ടു നിൽക്കുന്നു. പലരോടും സഹായങ്ങൾ തേടിനോക്കി. അടഞ്ഞു കിടക്കുന്ന വാതിലുകൾ...

"ഭാനുമതി." അയാൾ വിളിച്ചു.

"എന്താ" അവൾ വിളികേട്ടു.

"ഞാൻ നിന്നെ ഒരിക്കലും ദുഃഖിപ്പിക്കുകയില്ല."

"അങ്ങനെ ഒരാൾമാത്രം ദുഃഖത്തിൽനിന്ന് രക്ഷപ്പെടുന്ന പ്രശ്നമില്ല. എന്തുവന്നാലും ഒരുമിച്ചു നേരിടണം."

അൽപ്പം ആലോചിച്ച് അയാൾ പറഞ്ഞു:

"നമുക്ക് ഇവിടെ നിന്നു മാറണം. കാരണം, ബാങ്കുകാർ ജപ്തിചെയ്യുമ്പോൾ നാം ഇവിടെ ഉണ്ടാവാൻ പാടില്ല."

"കുറെ ദൂരെ എവിടെയെങ്കിലും ഒരുചെറിയ വീട് അന്വേഷിക്കൂ. ഉടനെ നമുക്ക് അങ്ങോട്ടുമാറാം. നമുക്ക് രണ്ടുപേർക്ക് കഴിയാൻ ജോലിക്കാരും ആവശ്യമില്ല."

അയാൾ നെടുവീർപ്പിട്ടു. സിഗരറ്റിന്റെ പുക അയാളുടെ മുഖത്തെ മറച്ചു.

"പിന്നെ ആ നശിച്ചവളാണ്. അവൾ എന്നെ നശിപ്പിച്ചേ അടങ്ങൂ."

"ഇല്ല." പെട്ടെന്നാണ് ആ മറുപടി വന്നത്.

"ഭാനൂ നിനക്കറിഞ്ഞുകൂടാ. അവൾ മടങ്ങിപ്പോകുന്ന സ്വഭാവക്കാരിയല്ല. അവൾ രണ്ടിലൊന്നു കാണാൻ നിശ്ചയിച്ചേ വരൂ."

"ഞാനൊന്നു പറയട്ടെ?" ഭാനുമതി കസേര അയാളുടെ മുൻപിലേക്കു വലിച്ചിട്ടു.

അയാൾ അവളെ ഉറ്റുനോക്കി.

"എന്താണ്? പറയൂ."

"നിങ്ങൾക്കു ഒന്നും തോന്നരുത്. എന്നെ സംശയിക്കുകയും ചെയ്യരുത്."

"ഇല്ല പറയൂ."

"ഞാൻ പറയുന്നത് വിശ്വസിക്കുമോ?"

"തീർച്ചയായും പറയൂ."

"അവൾ സ്വരമടക്കിപ്പറഞ്ഞു."

"നിങ്ങൾ അവളെ തിരിച്ചയക്കേണ്ട."

ദിവാകരൻ മിഴിച്ചിരുന്നു.

"ഭാനൂ.." അയാൾ പൊട്ടിത്തെറിച്ചതുപോലെ വിളിച്ചു.

"ശാന്തമായി കേൾക്കൂ. അവൾക്ക് സമ്മതമാണെങ്കിൽ അവൾ നമ്മുടെ കൂടെ താമസിക്കട്ടെ. എനിക്ക് സമ്മതമാണ്. നിങ്ങൾ വിശ്വസിക്കണം. ആ കുട്ടി നിങ്ങളുടേതാണെന്ന് ഇപ്പോൾ നിങ്ങൾ പറഞ്ഞു. നിർബന്ധമായും നിങ്ങളുടെ കുട്ടിക്കുവേണ്ടി അവൾ ഗൗണ്ടറെ തൊടാതെ മാസങ്ങൾ കഴിച്ചുവെന്നു പറഞ്ഞു. അവളെ ഉപേക്ഷിക്കരുത്. അവളെ ഞാൻ എന്റെ സഹോദരിയായി കരുതും. പത്തു ദിവസം ലീലാംബാൾ എന്റെ കൂടെ വന്നുകഴിഞ്ഞുകൂടാനുള്ള സന്ദർഭം ഉണ്ടാക്കിയാൽ മതി. അവൾ ഇണങ്ങും. അവളും സ്ത്രീയാണ്. അവളുടെ ദുഃഖം നമുക്ക് ഒരു കാലത്തും നല്ലതായിരിക്കുകയില്ല."

ദിവാകരന്റെ സിരകളിൽ കത്തുന്ന കീടങ്ങൾ അരിച്ചു കയറുന്നു.

കണ്ണുകളിൽ ചുവന്ന പൂച്ചികൾ ആർത്തു പറക്കുന്നു. ശ്വാസം തടയും പോലെ ഭാനുമതിയുടെ രൂപം അയാളെ വിഴുങ്ങുന്നു! അയാൾ മരിച്ച ഒരു പ്രാണിയായി കിടക്കുന്നു. മനുഷ്യൻ ചെയ്യുന്ന തെറ്റുകൾ ഇത്ര ഭീകരമായി തിരിച്ചുവരുമോ? ഒരു ഭാര്യയും പറയാത്ത വാക്കുകൾ. ഒരു ഭർത്താവ് എങ്ങനെ ഇതിനു മറുപടി പറയും? മരിക്കുകയാണ് ഭേദം. ഇത് സമ്മതിക്കുന്നത് ആത്മഹത്യയാണ്. ഈ ഭീകരമായ നാടകത്തിന് സ്വയം തിരശ്ശീല ഇടുന്നതല്ലേ നല്ലത്?

"ഭാനൂ. നീ അത് പറയരുത്." അയാൾ വിങ്ങിപ്പൊട്ടി.

"ഞാൻ പറയുന്നത് നിങ്ങൾ കേൾക്കണം." അവളുടെ സ്വരം ദൃഢമായിരുന്നു.

"ഞാൻ മനുഷ്യനല്ലാതെയാണ് ജീവിച്ചത്. ഇനി ഇതുംകൂടി ചെയ്ത് ഞാൻ കാടനാണെന്ന് ലോകത്തിന്റെ മുമ്പിൽ വിളിച്ചു പറയണോ?"

"മറ്റു തരത്തിലാണെങ്കിലും ലോകം നിങ്ങളെ പുച്ഛിക്കും. ഇത്, നമ്മൾ മാത്രം ഏറ്റെടുക്കുന്ന കാര്യമാണ്. മറ്റേത് സമുദായം ഏറ്റെടുക്കും. നിങ്ങൾക്കു ചുറ്റുമുള്ളവർ തീകൂട്ടും. നിങ്ങളെ ചുടാൻ ശ്രമിക്കും. എനിക്കതു കണ്ടു നിൽക്കാൻ സാധ്യമല്ല."

അയാൾ കമിഴ്ന്നുകിടന്ന് തേങ്ങിക്കരഞ്ഞു. അവൾ അടുത്തു ചെന്നിരുന്ന് അയാളെ തലോടി.

അനേകം സാന്ത്വനവാക്കുകൾ അവൾ അയാളുടെ ചെവിയിലേക്കു മന്ത്രിച്ചു. ജീവിതത്തെപ്പറ്റിയുള്ള ധൈര്യം കൊടുക്കാൻ ശ്രമിച്ചു. അവളിലുള്ള വിശ്വാസ്യത ഉറപ്പിച്ചുകൊടുക്കാൻ യത്നിച്ചു. ആ ദിവസം അങ്ങനെ ഞെരുങ്ങി, വേദനിച്ച് ഇഴഞ്ഞുപോയി.

രണ്ടു ദിവസത്തേക്ക് അവർ തമ്മിൽ ഒന്നും സംസാരിച്ചില്ല. മൂന്നാം ദിവസം പ്രഭാതത്തിൽ, വീട്ടിന്റെ മുൻവശത്ത് ഒരു സ്ത്രീ വന്നിരിക്കുന്നുവെന്ന്. രാജമ്മ കിടക്കമുറിയുടെ വാതിൽക്കൽനിന്ന് അറിയിച്ചപ്പോൾ, അത് ലീലാംബാളായിരിക്കുമെന്ന് ഭാനുമതി നിശ്ചയിച്ചു. അവളെ നേരിടാനുള്ള മനസ്സാന്നിധ്യം വരുത്തിയിട്ടാണ് അങ്ങോട്ടു നടന്നത്. അവൾ ഏതുസമയത്തും വരുമെന്ന് ഭാനുമതി പ്രതീക്ഷിച്ചു. ദിവാകരൻ കുളിച്ചു കൊണ്ടിരിക്കുകയാണ്.

ഭാനുമതി മുൻവശത്തെ വരാന്തയിലെത്തി. കസേരയിൽ അവൾ ഇരിക്കുന്നു. കയ്യിൽ കുഞ്ഞുമുണ്ട്. "അകത്തേക്കു വരൂ." ഭാനുമതി സൗമ്യമായി ക്ഷണിച്ചു. അതിനിടയ്ക്ക് അവർ പരസ്പരം അടിമുടി നോക്കി. കണ്ണുകൾ തമ്മിൽ ഇടഞ്ഞു. ഭാനുമതിയുടെ സ്നേഹപൂർണമായ മുഖവും ക്ഷണവും അവളെ സ്പർശിച്ചുവെന്നു തോന്നുന്നു. ലീലാംബാളിന്റെ കണ്ണുകളിലെ ഗൗരവം പൊടുന്നനെ അലിഞ്ഞുപോയി...

പതിനഞ്ച്

രണ്ടുപേരും അഭിമുഖമായി സ്വീകരണമുറിയിലെ സെറ്റിയിലിരുന്നു. "വരുന്നവഴിയാണോ?" ഭാനുമതി സംഭാഷണമാരംഭിച്ചു.

"അതെ."

"കൂടെ ആരെങ്കിലുമുണ്ടോ?"

"ഇല്ല. ഒറ്റയ്ക്കാണ്."

ഭാനുമതി അവളെ കാണുകയായിരുന്നു. കൂർഗ്ഗനാട്ടിലെ സുന്ദരികളെപ്പറ്റി കേട്ടിട്ടുണ്ട്. മനോഹരമായ ആ താഴ്വാരങ്ങളുടെ ഭംഗി, ഈ സ്ത്രീക്കുണ്ട്. അവർ കുട്ടിയെ വിളിച്ചു അത് അമ്മയുടെ മടിയിൽ പറ്റിപ്പിടിച്ചിരുന്നു.

"മലയാളം ഒരു മാതിരി നല്ലപോലെ സംസാരിക്കുന്നല്ലോ."

"അതെ. എന്റെ അമ്മ. ഒരു മലയാളി സ്ത്രീയായിരുന്നു. കാസർകോട്ട്, ഒരു നമ്പ്യാരുടെ മകൾ. ഞാൻ കൂർഗിലാണ് വളർന്നത്."

"എനിക്ക് ഒരപേക്ഷയുണ്ട്."

"എന്താണ്?"

"ഞാൻ പറഞ്ഞാൽ കേൾക്കുമോ?"

"പറഞ്ഞോളൂ."

"നിങ്ങൾ വന്ന കാര്യം എനിക്കറിയാം. എല്ലാക്കാര്യവും ഞാൻ മനസിലാക്കിയിട്ടുണ്ട്. എന്റെ ഭർത്താവ് അകത്തുണ്ട്. നിങ്ങൾ അദ്ദേഹവുമായി ഒന്നും സംസാരിക്കരുത്. ഇവിടെ അസുഖകരമായ അന്തരീക്ഷം ഉണ്ടാവാൻ ഇടവരുത്തരുത്. എല്ലാം ഞാൻ സംസാരിച്ചുകൊള്ളാം. എല്ലാറ്റിനും നമുക്കു പരിഹാരമുണ്ടാക്കാം. എന്താ സമ്മതമാണോ?"

"ഞാൻ മിണ്ടാതിരിക്കാം." ലീലാംബാൾ കൂടുതലൊന്നും പറഞ്ഞില്ല.

ഭാനുമതി ഒന്നാശ്വസിച്ചു. അവൾ എഴുന്നേറ്റ്, അകത്തേക്കുപോയി.

ദിവാകരൻ കുളിച്ചു പുറത്തുവന്ന്, വേഷം മാറുന്നു. ഭാനുമതി വിവരം അറിയിച്ചപ്പോൾ, അയാൾ പ്രതിമകണക്കെനിന്നു.

"നിങ്ങൾ അവരോട് സംസാരിക്കരുത്."

അയാളുടെ ചുണ്ടുകൾ അനങ്ങി.

"ഇല്ല."

ഭാനുമതി പുറത്തേക്കു വന്നു. ലീലാംബാളിന്റെ അടുത്തു ചെന്നിരുന്നു. അവൾ പറഞ്ഞു:

"ഞാൻ മറ്റൊരപേക്ഷ നിങ്ങളുടെ മുൻപിൽ വയ്ക്കുന്നു. നിങ്ങളുടെ കുട്ടിയുടെ അച്ഛനെ നിങ്ങൾക്കുകിട്ടണം അല്ലേ?"

"ആ മനുഷ്യൻ ക്രൂരനാണ്. എന്നെ വഞ്ചിച്ച ആളാണ്. ഈ കുട്ടിയുടെ മുഖത്തേക്ക് നിങ്ങൾ നോക്കൂ." ലീലാംബാളുടെ സ്വരം പരുഷമായിരുന്നു. വേദനയാണ് അതിൽ ധ്വനിച്ചു കേട്ടത്.

"ആ മനുഷ്യൻ നിങ്ങളുടേതായിരിക്കും."

"എങ്ങനെ? എനിക്കു മനസിലാവുന്നില്ല."

"നിങ്ങൾക്കിഷ്ടമെങ്കിൽ നിങ്ങൾ ഇവിടെ താമസിച്ചു കൊള്ളൂ."

ലീലാംബാൾ ഭാനുമതിയെ തന്റെ ദൃഷ്ടികൾകൊണ്ട് അടിമുടി അളക്കുന്നതുപോലെ തോന്നി. അവളുടെ വാക്കുകൾ മനസിലാവാത്തതുപോലെ.

"നിങ്ങൾ എന്താണു പറഞ്ഞത്?"

"ഒന്നുകൂടി വ്യക്തമായി പറയാം. നിങ്ങൾക്ക് അദ്ദേഹത്തിന്റെ ഭാര്യയായി ഇവിടെ ജീവിക്കാം."

അവിശ്വാസത്തിന്റെ നിമിഷങ്ങൾ.

അവൾ ചോദിച്ചു.

"നിങ്ങൾ അയാളുടെ ഭാര്യയല്ലേ?"

"എന്നെ അദ്ദേഹം കല്യാണം കഴിച്ചുകൊണ്ടുവന്നതാണ്."

"പിന്നെ, നിങ്ങൾ പറഞ്ഞതിന്റെ അർഥം?"

"അതുതന്നെ. നിങ്ങൾക്കിഷ്ടമെങ്കിൽ, ഞാൻ ഇവിടെ ഒരു മൂലയിൽ കഴിഞ്ഞുകൂടിക്കൊള്ളാം. അല്ലെങ്കിൽ നിങ്ങൾക്കു വേണ്ടി ഞാൻ വഴിമാറിത്തരാം."

അതു പെട്ടെന്നു തോന്നിയതാണ്. ആ തോന്നൽ നാവിൽ വന്നതാണ്. ഇല്ല തെറ്റില്ല. തന്റെ മനസ്സ് അവിടംവരെ പോകാൻ തയാറാണ്. അവിടംവരെ അതു ചെന്നെത്തി നിൽക്കുകയാണ്. ജീവിതത്തിൽ മറ്റൊരു പുരുഷനെ സ്വീകരിക്കുകയില്ല. ആ സുഖം ആഗ്രഹിക്കുന്നുമില്ല. പിന്നെ എന്തുകൊണ്ട് അവളോട് ഇത് പറഞ്ഞുകൂടാ.?

"ആ മനുഷ്യൻ എവിടെ?" അവൾ ചോദിച്ചു.

"വരൂ."

ഭാനുമതി അവളേയുംകൂട്ടി അകത്തേക്കു നടന്നു. ബെഡ്റൂമിന്റെ ചാരിക്കിടന്ന വാതിൽ തുറന്നു. ലീലാംബാളെ അകത്തേക്കു ആനയിച്ചു. ദിവാകരൻ കട്ടിലിൽ ചാരിക്കിടക്കുകയാണ്.

ഭാനുമതി സംസാരിച്ചു.

"ഇവർ ഇവിടെ താമസിക്കും. നിങ്ങൾ ഒരു കാര്യം സമ്മതിക്കണം. ഞാൻ പോകുന്നു..."

അയാൾ തുറിച്ചുനോക്കി നിവർന്നിരുന്നു.

"ഇല്ല ഭാനൂ, നീയില്ലാതെ എനിക്ക് ജീവിതമില്ല. മറ്റുതരത്തിൽ എന്ത് അപമാനവും ഞാൻ സഹിച്ചോളാം. അവിടംവരെ നിന്റെ ത്യാഗം എനിക്കാവശ്യമില്ല." ശാന്തമായിട്ടാണ് അയാൾ സംസാരിച്ചത്.

ഭാനുമതി ലീലാംബാളിന്റെ നേർക്കു തിരിഞ്ഞു:

"ഞാൻ ഇവിടെ കഴിഞ്ഞുകൂടാൻ സമ്മതമാണോ?"

ലീലാംബാൾ ആകെ നോക്കി. ആലോചിച്ചു. എന്നിട്ടു പറഞ്ഞു:

"ഈ മുറി എന്റേതാണ്. എന്റേതും ഈ മനുഷ്യന്റേതും. അത് അംഗീകരിക്കുമെങ്കിൽ നിങ്ങൾ ഇവിടെ താമസിക്കുന്നതിൽ എനിക്ക് വിരോധമില്ല."

ആ സ്ത്രീ കസാലയിൽ ഇരുന്നു.

ഭാനുമതി സാവധാനം വെളിയിലേക്ക് നടന്നു.

"ഭാനൂ.." അയാളുടെ ശബ്ദം ഉയർന്നു.

അവൾ തിരിഞ്ഞുനിന്നില്ല.

ദിവാകരൻ എഴുന്നേറ്റു പുറത്തേക്കു നോക്കിനിന്നു.

ലീലാംബാൾ കുട്ടിയെ കൈയിലെടുത്തു. അയാളുടെ മുൻപിലേക്കു

ചെന്നുനിന്നു.

"നിങ്ങൾക്ക് എങ്ങനെ എന്നെ മറക്കാൻ തോന്നി? എന്തുകൊണ്ട് ഒരിക്കൽപ്പോലും എന്നെ വന്നുകാണാൻ തോന്നിയില്ല? ഒരുകാലത്ത് എന്റെ ശരീരത്തെ നിങ്ങൾ ആവേശത്തോടെ ഉപയോഗിച്ചതല്ലേ? അങ്ങനെ അല്ലേ ഈ കുട്ടി ഉണ്ടായത്? ൃഞാൻ നിങ്ങളെ ശല്യപ്പെടുത്തുകയില്ലായിരുന്നു. നിങ്ങളെ കാണാൻ ഞാൻ കാത്തിരുന്നു. എന്നെ ഒന്നു കാണണമെന്ന് നിങ്ങൾക്ക് തോന്നിയില്ല. ആ ക്രൂരതയ്ക്ക് പകരം വീട്ടണമെന്ന് എനിക്ക് തോന്നി. നിങ്ങളുടെ സ്വത്തിനുവേണ്ടി ഞാൻ ബഹളം കൂട്ടുകയാണെന്ന് നിങ്ങൾ വിചാരിച്ചു. അങ്ങനെ നിങ്ങൾ പലരോടും പറഞ്ഞതായിട്ടും ഞാനറിഞ്ഞു. എന്റെ വൈരാഗ്യം വർധിക്കുകയായിരുന്നു. അങ്ങനെയാണ് ഞാൻ നിങ്ങളുടെ ആദ്യഭാര്യയുടെ വീട്ടിൽപ്പോയത്. നിങ്ങൾക്ക് എത്ര കത്തുകൾ ഞാനെഴുതി? ആദ്യമാദ്യം സ്നേഹമില്ലാത്ത ഒരൊറ്റ വാചകം ഞാൻ കുറിച്ചിരുന്നോ? ഞാൻ ഇപ്പോൾ, ഇന്ന് തോറ്റിരിക്കുന്നു. എവിടെയാണ് തോറ്റതെന്നറിയാമോ? നിങ്ങളുടെ മുൻപിലല്ല, ആ സാധുസ്ത്രീയുടെ മുൻപിൽ പാവം! അതിനെ വേദനിപ്പിക്കാനും എനിക്കു വയ്യ. അതുകൊണ്ട്, ഞാൻ തോറ്റു. നിങ്ങൾക്ക് സ്ത്രീയെ അറിഞ്ഞുകൂടാ. മനുഷ്യനെ അറിഞ്ഞുകൂടാ. നിങ്ങൾ ഓർമിക്കുന്നുണ്ടോ? അന്ന് ആദ്യമായിട്ട് ഞാൻ ഒറ്റയ്ക്കുകിടന്ന മുറിയിലേക്കു നിങ്ങൾ കയറിവന്നപ്പോൾ ഞാൻ ഭയപ്പെട്ടുപോയി. എന്റെ ശരീരത്തിൽ തൊട്ടപ്പോൾ അരുതേ എന്നു ഞാൻ അപേക്ഷിച്ചു. എന്റെ അച്ഛനും അമ്മയും കൂടിയാണ് വൃദ്ധനായ ആ മനുഷ്യന്റെ കൈയിൽ എന്നെ പിടിച്ചുകൊടുത്തത്. നിങ്ങൾ എന്നെ ആക്രമിച്ചു കീഴടക്കുകയായിരുന്നു. പിന്നെ ദുർബലയായിപ്പോയി. രണ്ടുപേരെ ഒരുപോലെ സ്നേഹിക്കാൻ ഞാൻ ശ്രമിക്കുകയായിരുന്നു. നടന്നില്ല ആ മനുഷ്യൻ വേദനിച്ചു മരിച്ചു. ഉടനെ എന്തിനു നിങ്ങൾ ഒളിച്ചോടിപ്പോന്നു. ഞാൻ നിങ്ങളെ തടവിലാക്കുമെന്നു വിചാരിച്ചോ? എന്നെ സ്വീകരിക്കാമെന്നു നിങ്ങൾ പറഞ്ഞിരുന്നെങ്കിൽ ഞാൻ സ്നേഹപൂർവം അതു നിരസിക്കുമായിരുന്നു. എല്ലാം നഷ്ടപ്പെട്ടാൽ ഈ കുട്ടിയെ ഞാൻ വേല ചെയ്ത്, പോറ്റിവളർത്തുമായിരുന്നു. അതാണ് നിങ്ങൾക്ക് മനുഷ്യനെ അറിഞ്ഞുകൂടെന്ന് ഞാൻ പറഞ്ഞത്. ആ മനുഷ്യന്റെ ഭാര്യയായിരുന്ന ഞാൻ അദ്ദേഹത്തിന്റെ കൂട്ടുകാരന്റെ ഭാര്യയായിത്തീർന്നാൽ എനിക്കുമാത്രമാണോ, ആ കൂട്ടുകാരനും കൂടി അപമാനമാകും, അതൊക്കെ കഴിഞ്ഞ് രഹസ്യമായി എന്നെയും ഈ കുഞ്ഞിനേയും ഒന്നു കാണാൻ നിങ്ങൾക്ക് ആഗ്രഹമില്ലെന്നറിഞ്ഞപ്പോഴാണ് ഞാൻ എന്തിനും തയാറായത്. സ്ത്രീ സാധുവാണ് പക്ഷേ, സ്ത്രീക്കു വൈരാഗ്യം വന്നാൽ, അവൾ എന്തും ചെയ്യും. ഇല്ല, ഞാൻ കൂടുതലൊന്നും പറയുന്നില്ല. ഞാൻ പോകുന്നു. ഞാൻ ഭീകരയാണെന്നു നിങ്ങൾ വിശ്വസിക്കുന്നു. പക്ഷേ, എന്തുകൊണ്ടോ എന്റെ വൈരാഗ്യത്തിൽ എനിക്കു പിടിച്ചു നിൽക്കാൻ കഴിഞ്ഞില്ല. രണ്ടു ദിവസം മുമ്പ് വീണ്ടും കാണണമെന്ന് എനിക്കുതോന്നി. കാണണം, നിങ്ങൾക്കു നഷ്ടം

വന്നിരിക്കുന്നുവെന്നും ബിസിനസ് കുഴപ്പത്തിലായെന്നും ഞാനറിഞ്ഞു. എന്റെ ദേഷ്യമെല്ലാം പോയി. നിങ്ങൾ ബുദ്ധിമുട്ടുന്നുവെന്നറിഞ്ഞുകൊണ്ട് എനിക്ക് അടങ്ങിയിരിക്കാൻ കഴിഞ്ഞില്ല. അങ്ങനെ ഞാൻ തോറ്റാണ് ഇങ്ങോട്ട് പോന്നത്. നമ്മൾ ഒരുമിച്ചു കഴിഞ്ഞുകൂടിയവരാണ്. എന്നോട് അണുവിടയെങ്കിലും സ്നേഹമുണ്ടെങ്കിൽ, ഞാൻപറയുന്ന ഒരു കാര്യം കേൾക്കുക. വയനാട്ടിലെ വീടും വസ്തുവും എന്റേതാണ്. എനിക്ക് അതു വേണ്ട. അതു ഞാൻ വിൽക്കാം. കടം വീട്ടൂ. എനിക്ക് എവിടെയെങ്കിലും ഒരു കൊച്ചുവീട് ഞാൻ വാങ്ങിച്ചോളാം. ദയവുചെയ്ത് അത് സമ്മതിക്കൂ. ഒരു മനുഷ്യൻ അറിയാതെ നിങ്ങളുടെ ഭാര്യപോലും അറിയാതെ ഞാനതു ചെയ്തുതരാം.

ദിവാകരന്റെ കണ്ണുകളിൽക്കൂടി കണ്ണുനീർ ധാരയായി ഒഴുകി. അപ്പോൾ മരിക്കണമെന്നുതോന്നി. താൻ കൃമിയാണ്, വൃത്തികെട്ട കൃമി.

എല്ലാ ശബ്ദവും തന്നെ കൈവിട്ടുപോയിരിക്കുന്നു.

ആ കുഞ്ഞ് അയാളുടെ നേർക്ക് കൈനീട്ടി. അയാൾ അതിനെ എടുത്തു.

* * * * * *

സംസ്ഥാനത്തെ പൊലീസ് കമ്മീഷണർ വന്നിട്ടുണ്ട്. പട്ടണത്തിൽ നിന്നും ഒന്നുരണ്ട് മൈൽ ഉള്ളിലേക്ക് മാറി, വലിയ ഒരു ബംഗ്ലാവ്. അത് ഗവൺമെന്റ് മന്ദിരമാണ്. ഏറ്റവും ഉന്നതരായ ഉദ്യോഗസ്ഥന്മാർക്കുമാത്രം യാത്രയ്ക്കിടയ്ക്ക് പാർക്കാനും വിശ്രമിക്കാനുമുള്ള സങ്കേതം. അപ്പോൾ അവിടെ പൊലീസ് കാവൽ കാണും. ഇപ്പോൾ കമ്മീഷണറാണ് വന്നിരിക്കുന്നത്. കീഴുദ്യോഗസ്ഥന്മാരുടെ ഒരു വലിയകൂട്ടം തന്നെ അവിടെയുണ്ട്. അദ്ദേഹം രണ്ടുദിവസം അവിടെ ഉണ്ടാവും. രാഷ്ട്രീയ പരിതസ്ഥിതികൾ ചൂടുപിടിച്ചിരിക്കുന്നതുകൊണ്ട് ഓരോ ഡിസ്ട്രിക്റ്റ് തലസ്ഥാനങ്ങളിലും അദ്ദേഹം ക്യാമ്പ് ചെയ്യുന്നു. ഉദ്യോഗസ്ഥന്മാർക്ക് നിർദേശങ്ങൾ നൽകുന്നു.

സന്ധ്യാദേവി കമ്മീഷണറെ കാണാൻ പോവുകയാണ്. യോഗമയീദേവിയെ അറസ്റ്റ് ചെയ്തതും അനന്തര സംഭവങ്ങളും അദ്ദേഹത്തെ അറിയിക്കണം. സദനത്തിലെ അംഗമെന്ന നിലയ്ക്ക് അവരെ മോചിപ്പിക്കാനുള്ള ഉത്തരവിനുവേണ്ടി അപേക്ഷിക്കണം. ഇപ്പോൾ അവരെ മദ്രാസിലേക്ക് കൊണ്ടുപോയിട്ട് ദിവസങ്ങളായി. വിവരങ്ങൾ ഒന്നുമില്ല. അരവിന്ദന്റെ കാര്യം തനിക്കു സംസാരിക്കാമോ എന്നു സംശയമാണ്. എങ്ങനെയെങ്കിലും അതു സൂചിപ്പിക്കണമെന്ന് ആഗ്രഹമുണ്ട്.

കമ്മീഷണറെ കാണുന്നത് സംബന്ധിച്ച് ചില നേതാക്കന്മാരുമായി സംസാരിച്ചു. അവർ ഇക്കാര്യത്തിനുവേണ്ടി അദ്ദേഹത്തെ പ്രത്യേകം കാണാം, ആദ്യം സന്ധ്യാദേവി തന്നെ കാണുന്നതാണ് കുറച്ചുകൂടി നല്ലത്. സദനത്തിന്റെ ചുമതലക്കാരി എന്ന നിലയ്ക്ക് അവരോടു കാട്ടാവുന്ന അനുകൂല മനോഭാവം ഒന്നുവേറെയാണ്. മറ്റേത് വെറും രാഷ്ട്രീയ കാര്യമെന്നുവരും. സദനം രാഷ്ട്രീയസേവികകളുടെ സ്ഥാപനമാണ്. എന്നാലും

അതിനുവേണ്ടി രാഷ്ട്രീയക്കാർ ഇടപെടുന്നത് അധികാരികൾ എപ്പോഴും നീരസത്തോടെയേ കാണുകയുള്ളൂ.

സന്ധ്യാദേവി കീർത്തിയെക്കൂടി കൂടെ കൊണ്ടുപോകാൻ നിശ്ചയിച്ചു. ഒറ്റയ്ക്കു പോകേണ്ട. രാവിലെ പത്തു മണിക്ക് പുറപ്പെട്ടു. പത്തരയ്ക്ക് ഗവൺമെന്റ് ഹൗസിന്റെ മുൻപിലെത്തി. അവിടെ, ധാരാളം പൊലീസ് ആഫീസർമാരും പൊലീസുകാരും മറ്റു ചില പ്രമുഖന്മാരും ഉണ്ട്. സന്ധ്യാദേവി കാത്തിരുന്നു. ഒരു ഇൻസ്പെക്ടറെ കണ്ട് കാര്യം പറഞ്ഞു. ആ മനുഷ്യൻ ഒരു ചിറ്റുവാങ്ങി. അകത്തുപോയി അധികം താമസിച്ചില്ല. ഇൻസ്പെക്ടർ പുറത്തേക്കുവന്നു. അവരെ വിളിച്ചു. സന്ധ്യാദേവിയും കീർത്തിയും പോകാൻ ഭാവിച്ചപ്പോൾ ഇൻസ്പെക്ടർ പറഞ്ഞു: "ഒരാൾ മാത്രം."

കീർത്തിയെ താഴത്തെ നിലയിലിരുത്തിയിട്ട് സന്ധ്യാദേവി ഇൻസ്പെക്ടറുടെ മുകളിലത്തെ നിലയിലേക്കു പോയി. അവിടെ അകത്തെ മുറിയുടെ വാതിൽക്കൽ ചെന്നുമുട്ടി. "കമിൻ" അകത്തു നിന്നു ശബ്ദം. അകത്തേക്ക് ചെല്ലാൻ ഇൻസ്പെക്ടർ ആംഗ്യം കാട്ടി.

ഉള്ളിലേക്കു കയറി, പുതിയ ധൈര്യം സമാഹരിച്ചുകൊണ്ടാണ് കടന്നത്. വലിയ മേശയ്ക്കു പിന്നിൽ ഉയരം കൂടിയ ഒരു മനുഷ്യൻ ഇരിക്കുന്നു. ചീകിവച്ച മുടി, ചെറിയ മീശ, നീണ്ട കൈയുള്ള ഷർട്ട്, ടൈ, ട്രൗസേഴ്സ്, ഗൗരവം പ്രകടമായ മുഖം അദ്ദേഹം ഏതോ കടലാസുകൾ നോക്കുകയായിരുന്നു. സന്ധ്യാദേവി മാറിനിന്നു. കുറച്ചുകഴിഞ്ഞ് അദ്ദേഹം മുഖമുയർത്തി നോക്കി.

"കമോൺ പ്ലീസ് സിറ്റ് ഡൗൺ" ക്ഷണിച്ചു.

"അവർ ഇരുന്നില്ല."

"സിറ്റ് പ്ലീസ്"

വളരെ മര്യാദയുള്ള സ്വരം അവർ ഭവ്യതയോടെ ഇരുന്നു.

"എന്താണ്, എന്താണ് കാര്യം?"

സന്ധ്യാദേവി കാര്യം വിശദീകരിക്കുകയും തയാറാക്കിക്കൊണ്ടുപോയിരുന്ന പെറ്റിഷൻ കൊടുക്കുകയും ചെയ്തു. അതേപ്പറ്റിയുള്ള എല്ലാ വിവരങ്ങളും അറിയാവുന്ന രീതിയിലാണ് അദ്ദേഹം മറുപടി നൽകിയത്. കമ്മീഷണർ പറഞ്ഞു.

"നിങ്ങൾക്ക് ഇതിന്റെ ഗൗരവം മനസിലായിട്ടില്ലെന്ന് തോന്നുന്നു. ഗവൺമെന്റിനെതിരായി പ്രവർത്തിക്കുന്ന വ്യക്തികളോടും സംഘടനകളോടും ഗവൺമെന്റിന് ചില പ്രത്യേക നയങ്ങളുണ്ട്. അത് അവർ മാറ്റുകയില്ല. ഈ കേസ് ഇപ്പോൾ സംസ്ഥാന ഗവൺമെന്റിന്റെ കൈവശമില്ല. അത് മദ്രാസിലേക്ക് മാറ്റിയിരിക്കുന്നു. അത് ആ ഗവൺമെന്റിന്റെ അപേക്ഷാപ്രകാരമാണ്. നിങ്ങൾ അവരെ സമീപിക്കുകയേ ഇനി നിവൃത്തിയുള്ളൂ."

അങ്ങോട്ട് കൂടുതലൊന്നും ചോദിക്കാനില്ല. ഈ സർക്കാരിന്റെ കൈയിൽ നിന്ന് പോയെങ്കിൽ, ഇവരോട് പറഞ്ഞിട്ടെന്തു കാര്യം?

പതിനാറ്

പൊടുന്നനെ കമ്മീഷണർ ചോദിച്ചു:

"സ്വാമി ശിവാനന്ദഭാരതിയെ നിങ്ങൾ ക്ഷണിച്ചു വരുത്തിയതാണോ?"

"അല്ല സാർ" സന്ധ്യാദേവി പ്രതിവചിച്ചു. "സദനം സന്ദർശിക്കണമെന്ന് ആഗ്രഹിക്കുന്നുവെന്ന് അദ്ദേഹം അറിയിച്ചു. ഞങ്ങൾ അനുകൂലമായി മറുപടി അയച്ചു."

"സദനത്തെപ്പറ്റി അദ്ദേഹത്തിന് എങ്ങനെ അറിയാം?"

"അത് ഞങ്ങൾക്ക് മനസിലായില്ല, സാർ?"

"ആരെങ്കിലും അദ്ദേഹത്തെ പറഞ്ഞു മനസിലാക്കിക്കൊടുത്തിരിക്കുകയില്ലേ?"

സംഗതികൾ അറിയാൻ വേണ്ടിത്തന്നെ ചോദ്യങ്ങൾ ചോദിക്കുകയാണെന്ന് സന്ധ്യാദേവിക്കു മനസിലായി.

"കാണും, സാർ."

"അത് ആരാണെന്നാണ് ഊഹിക്കുന്നത്?"

"അറിയില്ല സാർ."

"അറിയില്ലേ?" നിമിഷംകൊണ്ട് കമ്മീഷണറുടെ മുഖം ചുവന്നു. കണ്ണുകൾ രൂക്ഷമായി.

"അറിയില്ല സാർ." സന്ധ്യാദേവി വിനയത്തോടെ ദൃഢമായി മറുപടി നൽകി.

"ഞാൻ പറയട്ടെ?" അതും പരുഷമായ ശബ്ദത്തിലായിരുന്നു.

അവർ മിണ്ടിയില്ല.

"നിങ്ങളുടെ പേരെന്താ?"

"സന്ധ്യാദേവി."

"നിങ്ങളുടെ സദനത്തിലെ എല്ലാവരേയും ഇവിടെ കൊണ്ടുവരാൻ ഞാൻ എന്റെ ജീവനക്കാരെ അയച്ചിട്ടുണ്ട്. അതിനിടയ്ക്കാണ് നിങ്ങൾ ഇവിടെ വന്നുവെന്നറിഞ്ഞത്. ഞങ്ങളുടെ ഉദ്യോഗസ്ഥന്മാർ വരുംമുൻപ് നിങ്ങൾ പോന്നു. ഞങ്ങൾ എല്ലാ വിവരങ്ങളും ശേഖരിക്കും. ദാക്ഷിണ്യം കാണിക്കുന്ന പ്രശ്നമില്ല. എല്ലാം നിങ്ങൾതന്നെ തുറന്നു പറഞ്ഞാൽ നിങ്ങളുടെ പ്രവർത്തകർക്കുകൂടി ബുദ്ധിമുട്ടില്ലാതിരിക്കും. മനസിലായോ?"

സന്ധ്യാദേവിയുടെ മുഖം വിളറി. ഉള്ളിൽ തീപിടിച്ചതുപോലെ, തന്നെ ഓർത്തല്ല. സദനത്തിലെ കുട്ടികളുടെ സ്ഥിതി എന്തായിരിക്കും?

വാതിൽക്കൽ ഒരു കോൺസ്റ്റബിൾ വന്നു. സല്യൂട്ടു ചെയ്തു.

"എന്ത്?"

"അവരെ കൊണ്ടുവന്നിട്ടുണ്ട്."

"യെസ് അവിടെ നിർത്തിക്കോളൂ."

"നിങ്ങളുടെ ആളുകളെ കൊണ്ടുവന്നിട്ടുണ്ട്. എങ്ങനെയും ഞങ്ങൾ

വിവരങ്ങൾ ശേഖരിക്കും. പറയൂ. ആരാണ് നിങ്ങളെപ്പറ്റിയുള്ള അറിവ് ശിവാനന്ദഭാരതിക്കു കൊടുത്തത്?"

ഇനി മറച്ചുവെച്ചാൽ താഴെ കൊണ്ടുവന്നിരിക്കുന്ന കുട്ടികളെ ഇവർ ദണ്ഡിക്കും. സന്ധ്യാദേവിയുടെ കരുത്ത് നഷ്ടപ്പെടുന്നത് അവർക്കു അനുഭവപ്പെട്ടു.

"സാർ, അങ്ങ് ചോദിക്കുന്നതിന്റെ അർഥം എനിക്കു മനസിലായി. ഇത് നേരത്തെതന്നെ പൊലീസിൽനിന്ന് അന്വേഷിക്കുന്നുണ്ട്. വാസവമേനോനുമായി ഞങ്ങൾക്ക് ബന്ധമുണ്ടോ എന്ന്."

"ബന്ധമുണ്ടോ? പറയൂ."

"പ്രത്യേകിച്ച് ബന്ധമൊന്നുമില്ല സാർ."

"അത് അവ്യക്തമായ മറുപടിയാണ് തെളിച്ചുപറയൂ."

"അദ്ദേഹം ഒന്നുരണ്ടു തവണ അവിടെ വന്നിട്ടുണ്ട്. അങ്ങനെ പരിചയമുണ്ട്."

"അദ്ദേഹം വിപ്ലവകാരിയാണെന്ന് നിങ്ങൾക്കറിഞ്ഞുകൂടെ?"

"അറിയാം."

"അദ്ദേഹത്തെ സ്വീകരിച്ച നിങ്ങൾ അദ്ദേഹത്തിന്റെ ആശയങ്ങളെ അനുകൂലിക്കുന്നു എന്നല്ലേ ധരിക്കേണ്ടത്?"

"ഞങ്ങൾ അങ്ങനെയുള്ള കാര്യങ്ങൾ നോക്കിയില്ല സാർ. ഞങ്ങൾ ഗാന്ധിഭക്തരാണെന്നുള്ളതു സത്യമാണ്. ചർക്ക സംഘപ്രവർത്തകരുമാണ്. വിപ്ലവകാരികളല്ല, സാർ."

"വാസവമേനോൻ ഏറ്റവും ഒടുവിൽ അവിടെ വന്നത് എന്നാണ്?"

"സദനത്തിന്റെ വാർഷികത്തിനായിരുന്നു സാർ."

"അതു കഴിഞ്ഞ്."

"വന്നില്ല സാർ. സത്യം പറയുകയാണ്."

കമ്മീഷണർ മേശപ്പുറത്തുനിന്ന് ഒരു ഫയൽ എടുത്തുതുറന്ന് അതിൽനിന്ന് രണ്ടുമൂന്നു കത്തുകൾ എടുത്ത്, സന്ധ്യാദേവിയുടെ മുൻപിലേക്ക് നീക്കിവച്ചു.

"അതു നോക്കൂ."

സന്ധ്യാദേവി കത്തുകൾ ഓരോന്നു നോക്കി. വാസവമേനോൻ അരവിന്ദനെഴുതിയ കത്തുകളാണ്. അവയിലെല്ലാം സദനത്തിന്റെ കാര്യങ്ങൾ എഴുതിയിരിക്കുന്നു. അവർ കത്തുകൾ കമ്മീഷണറുടെ അടുക്കലേക്കു തിരിച്ചുവച്ചു.

"ഇനിയും ബന്ധം നിങ്ങൾ നിഷേധിക്കുന്നുണ്ടോ?"

വല്ലായ്മയോടെ അറിയിച്ചു:

"സാർ അദ്ദേഹം താൽപ്പര്യമെടുത്തു എന്നുള്ളതു സത്യമാണ്. അത് ഞങ്ങൾ ആവശ്യപ്പെട്ടിട്ടില്ല. അദ്ദേഹത്തെ വ്യക്തിപരമായി ഞങ്ങൾ ബഹുമാനിക്കുന്നു എന്നേയുള്ളൂ."

കമ്മീഷണർ ആലോചിച്ചു.

"ശരി. നിങ്ങളുടെ മേൽ കേസ് ചുമത്താനുള്ള കാര്യങ്ങൾ ഞങ്ങ

ളുടെ കൈയിലുണ്ടെന്നു മനസിലായല്ലോ?"

"അതെ. സാർ."

"വാസവമേനോനെ കാണുന്നിടത്തുവച്ചു വെടിവയ്ക്കാൻ ഇന്ത്യയിലെ എല്ലാ സംസ്ഥാനാധികാരികൾക്കും ഗവൺമെന്റ് കൽപ്പന കൊടുത്തിട്ടുണ്ട്. അറിയാമോ?"

"ഇപ്പോൾ അറിയുന്നു സാർ."

"നിങ്ങൾ വിദ്യാഭ്യാസമുള്ള ചെറുപ്പക്കാരിയാണ്. നിങ്ങളുടെ സദനത്തിൽ ഉള്ളവരും കൊച്ചു പെൺകുട്ടികളും യുവതികളുമാണ്. നിങ്ങളെ ഉപദ്രവിക്കണമെന്ന് ഞങ്ങൾക്ക് ആഗ്രഹമില്ല. പക്ഷേ, നിങ്ങൾ ചില കാര്യങ്ങൾ ചെയ്യണം."

"സാറ് പറയൂ ഞങ്ങൾ.."

പെട്ടെന്നു കമ്മീഷണർ പറഞ്ഞു:

"നിങ്ങൾ സദനം പിരിച്ചുവിടണം."

ഒരു പ്രഹരമേറ്റതു കണക്കായിരുന്നു. അവർ തളർന്ന കണ്ണുകളോടെ അദ്ദേഹത്തെ നോക്കി.

"എന്തു പറയുന്നു?"

"സാർ..."

"മറ്റൊന്നും കേൾക്കണ്ടാ., ഒറ്റവാക്കിൽ മറുപടി പറയൂ."

"ക്ലേശിച്ചു വളർത്തിക്കൊണ്ടുവന്ന സ്ഥാപനമാണ് സാർ."

"സർക്കാരിനെ അട്ടിമറിക്കാൻ അല്ലേ?"

"അല്ല, സാർ."

"പിന്നെന്തിന്? ദേശീയപ്രവർത്തനമെന്നു പറയുന്നതിന്റെ അർഥമെന്താണ്? മഹാത്മാഗാന്ധിയുടെ അഭിപ്രായമെന്താണ്? നിങ്ങൾ കൊച്ചുകുഞ്ഞിനെപ്പോലെ എന്നോട് സംസാരിക്കാൻ ശ്രമിക്കുന്നു.. നിങ്ങൾ തയാറുണ്ടോ?"

"സാർ."

"ശരി. തയാറില്ല. അല്ലേ?"

"അങ്ങ് അതുമാത്രം പറയരുത്." അവരുടെ ആത്മാവിൽ ഏതോ ഒരു ശക്തി ഉയർന്നുവരുന്നു. അത് അനുഭവപ്പെടുന്നു.

"നിങ്ങൾ അനുസരിക്കുകയില്ല?"

"ഞാൻ ജീവിതം ഇതിന് ഉഴിഞ്ഞുവച്ചവളാണ്."

"റൈറ്റ്, ആവട്ടെ."

"കാളിങ് ബെല്ലടിച്ചു, ഇൻസ്പെക്ടറാണ് വന്നത്.

"ഇവരെ കൊണ്ടുപോകൂ."

സന്ധ്യാദേവി എഴുന്നേറ്റു കമ്മീഷണറെ തൊഴാനെടുത്ത കൈ, അവർ പെട്ടെന്ന് താഴ്ത്തി, ഇൻസ്പെകടർ അവരെ പുറത്തേക്കു കൊണ്ടുപോയി.

താഴത്തെ നിലയിൽ സദനത്തിലെ എല്ലാവരേയും കൊണ്ടുവന്നു നിറുത്തിയിരിക്കുന്നു. അവരുടെ അടുക്കലേക്ക് നടക്കാൻ തുടങ്ങി.

ഇൻസ്പെക്ടർ തടഞ്ഞു. ജീപ്പിനരികിലേക്ക് കൊണ്ടുപോയി. കീർത്തിയും റീനയും ഉഷയും എല്ലാം കരയുന്നത് അവർ കണ്ടു.

"കയറൂ."

ജീപ്പിൽ കയറി. ഇൻസ്പെക്ടർ മുൻപിൽ കയറി. ജീപ്പ് വിട്ടുപോയി.

തന്റെ കുട്ടികളെ അവർ എന്തു ചെയ്യാൻ പോകുന്നു? അവരുടെ കണ്ണുകൾ നിറഞ്ഞു.

കണ്ടുപരിചയമില്ലാത്ത വഴിയിൽക്കൂടി ജീപ്പുപോയി. അൽപ്പം ചെന്ന് ഒരു കോമ്പൗണ്ടിൽക്കയറി. അവിടെ അഴിയിട്ട ഒരു ചെറിയ വീട്. ജീപ്പ് അതിന്റെ മുൻപിൽ നിറുത്തി. പൂട്ടിയിരിക്കുന്ന അഴിവാതിൽ തുറന്നു. സന്ധ്യാദേവിയെ ഇറക്കി. അകത്തേക്കു കയറ്റി. അകത്തെ വാതിൽ തുറന്നു. ഒരു വലിയ മുറി. നല്ല വെളിച്ചമില്ലാത്ത മുറിയാണ്. അതിനകത്താക്കി വാതിലടച്ചു. ഇൻസ്പെക്ടർ ഇറങ്ങി, പുറത്തെ വാതിലും അടച്ചുപൂട്ടി. ജീപ്പിൽ കയറി സ്ഥലംവിട്ടു.

ഒരു മൂലയിൽ കുത്തിയിരുന്നു. തലച്ചോറിൽ ആയിരം പഴുതാരകൾ ഒരുമിച്ചു കത്തുന്നതുപോലെ തടഞ്ഞുനിർത്തിയിട്ടും കരച്ചിൽ നിൽക്കുന്നില്ല. കരയുകയല്ലാതെ എന്തു ചെയ്യാൻ കഴിയും?

എങ്കിലും ആത്മധൈര്യം കൈവെടിയരുതെന്ന് തീരുമാനിച്ചു.

എതിർവശത്തെ വാതിൽ തുറക്കുന്നു. ആരാണത്? നല്ല ഉയരവും തടിയുമുള്ള ഒരു സ്ത്രീ കടന്നുവന്നു. തെല്ലൊരു സമാധാനം തോന്നി. പക്ഷേ, അടുത്ത നിമിഷം അതു മാറി. അവൾ പറഞ്ഞു.

"എഴുന്നേൽക്കെടീ!"

മിഴിച്ചിരുന്നു.

"എഴുന്നേൽക്കാൻ!"

അതേപടി ഇരുന്നു.

ആ സ്ത്രീ ചാടി അടുത്തെത്തി. മുടിക്കു കുത്തിപ്പിടിച്ചു. കുതറിനോക്കി. രക്ഷയില്ല. ഇരുമ്പുപോലുള്ള കൈകാലുകൾ അവൾക്കു താടിക്കു തട്ടി. കാലെടുത്ത് നാഭിയിൽ ചവിട്ടാൻ ഭാവിച്ചു. എഴുന്നേറ്റുപോയി. ഒരു ഞൊടിക്കുള്ളിൽ അവൾ സാരിക്കു കടന്നുപിടിച്ചു. താൻ അതോർമിക്കുംമുമ്പ് ഒരുകൈകൊണ്ട് അതിന്റെ ചുറ്റും മറ്റേ കൈകൊണ്ട് കുത്തും അഴിച്ചു. കുത്തിയിരുന്നു. അവൾ മറിച്ചിട്ടു ബലം പ്രയോഗിച്ച് സാരി വലിച്ചഴിച്ച് അടുത്ത മുറിയിലേക്കിറങ്ങി.

അടുത്തപടി എന്തെന്ന് ഊഹം കിട്ടി. തറയോട് അള്ളിപ്പിടിച്ചു കമിഴ്ന്ന് കിടന്നു. അവൾ എന്തോ സാധനം കൊണ്ട് ബ്ലൗസിന്റെ പിൻഭാഗം മുഴുവൻ കീറിവിടുവിച്ചു. പിന്നെ ബോഡീസും. വാവിട്ടു കരഞ്ഞു. അവൾ ബ്ലൗസ് വലിച്ചുകീറി. ഞൊടിയിടയിൽ കെട്ടിയ പാവാടയും ചരടുമുറിച്ച് കുത്തിക്കീറിവലിച്ചുമാറ്റി...

നഗ്നത, തറയിലേക്ക് കൂടുതൽ ചേർന്നു. മൂലയിലേക്ക് ചുരുണ്ടുകൂടി. "അമ്മേ.." സന്ധ്യാദേവി ഉറക്കെ വിളിച്ചു.

അവൾ അകത്തുപോയി മടങ്ങിവന്നു. കൈകൾ പിടിച്ചു വച്ചു കുട

ഞ്ഞുനോക്കി. പക്ഷേ, അവ അവളുടെ കൈപ്പിടിയിലമർന്നു. കൈകൾ ചേർത്തുവച്ചു കെട്ടി.

കാൽപ്പെരുമാറ്റം. രണ്ടു പുരുഷന്മാർ പുറകിലേക്കു പിടിച്ചകൈകളുമായി വരുന്നു. സന്ധ്യാദേവി ഉറക്കെ കരഞ്ഞു.

വളരെ വേഗമാണ് അവർ അതെല്ലാം ചെയ്തത്. അവരെ പിന്നിലേക്ക് ജനാലയിലേക്ക് പുറംതിരിച്ചു നിറുത്തി. ആ പുരുഷന്മാർ ചൂരൽവടികൊണ്ട് അവരുടെ പുറത്തും പിൻതുടയിലും അടിക്കാൻ തുടങ്ങി.

നിസ്സഹായമായ മിഴി, കുറെ നിമിഷങ്ങൾ കഴിഞ്ഞപ്പോൾ സന്ധ്യാദേവിക്ക് ബോധമില്ലാതായി.

* * * * * *

നാലഞ്ചു മാസങ്ങൾ കടന്നുപോയി. മദ്രാസിലെ കീഴ്പ്പാക്കം പ്രദേശത്ത് ഹൈവേയിൽ നിന്നുമുള്ള ഒരു ഇടവഴിയുടെ ഒരു വശത്ത് *വന്ദേമാതരം* വാരിക എന്ന ബോർഡ് തൂങ്ങുന്നുണ്ട്. ഒരു നല്ല കെട്ടിടം. അകത്ത് ഒരു വശത്തുള്ള മുറിയിൽ അരവിന്ദൻ കടലാസുകൾ നോക്കിക്കൊണ്ടിരിക്കുന്നു. എതിർവശത്തെ മുറിയിൽ പി ആർ മേനോൻ ഒരു സന്ദർശകനുമായി സംസാരിക്കുന്നു. അകത്ത്, പ്രസ് ശബ്ദിക്കുന്നു. പി ആർ മേനോന്റെ ആശയം രൂപംകൊണ്ടിരിക്കുകയാണ്. അതാണ് 'വന്ദേമാതരം വാരിക' അരവിന്ദൻ അതിൽ പ്രവർത്തിക്കുന്നു.

യോഗമയീദേവി ഒരു മാസം അവിടെ താമസിച്ചു. പിന്നെ കൽക്കത്തയിലേക്കുപോയി. അവിടെവച്ച് അവരെ അറസ്റ്റ് ചെയ്തതായി അറിവുകിട്ടി. ആറുമാസത്തേക്ക് ശിക്ഷിച്ചു. ഇപ്പോൾ ആലിപ്പൂർ ജയിലിൽ കിടക്കുകയാണ്.

സ്വാമി ശിവാനന്ദഭാരതിയെ മലബാറിൽ പൊന്നാനിയിൽ വച്ചാണ് അറസ്റ്റ് ചെയ്തത്. മദ്രാസിൽ കൊണ്ടുവന്നു. അവിടെ ഒരു കേസുണ്ട്. അവിടെ നിന്ന് ഡൽഹിയിലേക്ക് കൊണ്ടുപോയി. പിന്നെയുള്ള വിവരങ്ങൾ അറിഞ്ഞിട്ടില്ല. ഡൽഹിയിലെ സുഹൃത്തുക്കളോട് എഴുതി ചോദിച്ചു. ഒരു വിവരവുമില്ല. ഇപ്പോഴും അദ്ദേഹത്തെപ്പറ്റി അന്വേഷിക്കുന്നുണ്ട്.

വാരികയുടെ കാര്യങ്ങളിൽ അഹോരാത്രം മുഴുകി. അതൊരശ്വാസമായിരുന്നു. എങ്കിലും എപ്പോഴും മനസിൽ സന്ധ്യാദേവിയാണ്. പല ദിവസം രാത്രിയിൽ മേനോനുമൊരുമിച്ച് മറീനാ കടൽപ്പുറത്തു പോകും. നക്ഷത്രങ്ങളുള്ള ആകാശത്തേക്കു നോക്കി മലർന്നു കിടക്കും. ഇരമ്പുന്ന കടലിന്റെ സംഗീതം ശ്രവിക്കും. അപ്പോൾ ഉള്ളിൽ കവിതയുടെ വരികൾ ഉണർന്നു വരും. ജീവിതത്തിലെ കയ്പുകളെയും മധുരങ്ങളെയും കുറിച്ചു മേനോനോട് അവസാനമില്ലാതെ സംസാരിച്ചുകൊണ്ടിരിക്കും. ചന്ദ്രൻ ഉദിച്ചു നിൽക്കുന്ന നിശീഥിനികളിൽ, സന്ധ്യാദേവിയുടെ രൂപം അരികിൽ മണൽത്തരികൾക്കുമീതെ വരച്ചുനോക്കും. ചിലപ്പോൾ, നോക്കെത്താത്ത, കടലിനക്കരെ, അങ്ങേത്തീരത്ത് സ്നേഹിച്ചും കലഹിച്ചും ജീവിക്കുന്ന മനുഷ്യരെക്കുറിച്ച് ഓർമിക്കും. കാണാത്ത സഹോ

ദരങ്ങൾ. ആ കറുത്ത വർഗക്കാരെപ്പറ്റി താൻ കവിതയെഴുതിയിട്ടുണ്ട്. എല്ലാം ഓർമകളായി പിൻവാങ്ങിപ്പോകുന്നതുപോലെ പുറകോട്ടു തിരിഞ്ഞിരുന്ന് മരുപ്പച്ചകളെ നോക്കി മനസ്സ് നിശ്വാസങ്ങൾ ഉതിർക്കുന്നു...

ഒരിക്കൽ ഒരു കവിതയെഴുതി ഓർമിക്കൂ..
താരകങ്ങളാൽ മുത്തുമാലകൾ കോർക്കും മുഗ്ദ്ധ
ശാരദാംബത്തിന്റെ കീഴിലാമലർക്കാവിൽ
ഒരു പാതിരാക്കാറ്റിലലിയും മനസിന്റെ
മധുരോദാര സ്വരരാഗത്തിൻ ലഹരിയിൽ
ഓർമിക്കൂ, കുറുമൊഴിപ്പൂങ്കുല പൊട്ടിച്ചു നി-
ന്നോമൽകാർകൂന്തൽക്കെട്ടിലണിയിച്ചൊരു രാത്രി!
എന്റെ ദാഹത്തിൽ തിരക്കൈകളിൽക്കിടന്നു നീ
ചന്ദനലതപോലെ തുടിച്ചു നീന്തവേ
സുന്ദരസ്മിതവുമായ് ദൂരെനിന്നിടയ്ക്കിടെ
ചന്ദ്രലേഖവന്നെത്തിയൊളിച്ചു നോക്കീടവേ,
ഓർമിക്കൂ, പുലർക്കാലം താമസിച്ചെത്താൻ നമ്മൾ
പ്രാർഥിച്ചു നിമിഷങ്ങളെണ്ണി നിന്നൊരാ രാത്രീ!
മഞ്ഞുനീരോരോ തുള്ളിയിറ്റിറ്റു വീണാമാറിൽ
പൂന്തുകിൽ പറ്റിച്ചേർന്നു കുളിരുകോരും നേരം
അധരങ്ങളിൽ ചൂടുപകർന്നു രോമാഞ്ചത്താ-
ലൊരുപൂവനികയായ് നാം തന്നെ മാറുംനേരം,
ഓർമിക്കൂ പിരിയരുതെന്നു ചൊല്ലിയില്ലീലോകം
സാക്ഷിവന്നപ്പോൾ, നൊന്തു യാത്രയോതിയരാത്രി!

* * *

വാരികയുടെ മുൻപുറത്ത് ഈ ദീർഘമായ കവിത അച്ചടിച്ചുവന്നു. അത് വീണ്ടും വായിച്ചപ്പോൾ, ആ പുറങ്ങളിൽനിന്ന് മറ്റൊരാത്മാവ് തന്നെ നോക്കി തേങ്ങിക്കരയുന്നതായി തോന്നി. ദൂരമല്ല, തന്നെയും ആ ഹൃദയശാലിനിയെയും അകറ്റിയിരിക്കുന്നത് മറ്റു ചിലതാണ്. പലവുരു കത്തെഴുതി. അതെല്ലാം കീറിക്കളഞ്ഞു. തന്റെ കത്ത് അവിടെച്ചെന്നാൽ അവർക്കു അത് ആപൽക്കരമാവാം.

തന്റെ രഹസ്യമായ ആ സ്നേഹകഥ അരവിന്ദൻ മേനോനെ പറഞ്ഞുകേൾപ്പിച്ചു. ബന്ധുക്കളെങ്കിലും അവർ സുഹൃത്തുക്കളെപ്പോലെയാണ്. ബന്ധം തങ്ങൾ കണ്ടുപിടിച്ച ഒരു കാര്യമെന്നാണ് അവർക്കു രണ്ടുപേർക്കും തോന്നിയിട്ടുള്ളത്. മേനോൻ ആ കഥകേട്ട് ഒന്നും പറയാതിരിക്കും. അദ്ദേഹത്തിൽനിന്നു ചില വാക്കുകളെങ്കിലും പ്രതീക്ഷിച്ച് അരവിന്ദന്റെ കാത്തിരിപ്പും. എന്താ ഒന്നും മിണ്ടാത്തത്? അയാൾ ചോദിക്കും അപ്പോൾ മേനോൻ പറയും. ഞാൻ കേൾക്കുകയായിരുന്നു നിങ്ങൾക്ക് നന്മവരട്ടെ...

മൂന്നുമാസം കൂടി അങ്ങനെ കഴിഞ്ഞു. ഒരുദിവസം പ്രഭാതത്തിൽ അരവിന്ദൻ പത്രമാഫീസിനു പിന്നിലുള്ള തന്റെ മുറിയിൽ ഉണർന്നപാടെ

ഇരിക്കുന്നു. ഒരു ചെറുപ്പക്കാരൻ വാതിൽക്കൽ വന്നുനിന്നു. "അരവിന്ദൻ സാറ്? അയാൾ ചോദിച്ചു. "അതെ." അരവിന്ദൻ മറുപടി നൽകി. അത് രവികുമാറാണ്. ഉഷാമേനോന്റെ സഹോദരൻ. അയാൾ അതു പറഞ്ഞു സ്വയം പരിചയപ്പെടുത്തി. രവികുമാറും അരവിന്ദനും തമ്മിൽ കത്തിട പാടുകൾ നടത്തിയിട്ടുണ്ട്. നേരിട്ടു കണ്ടിട്ടില്ല. ദീപേശ് മുക്കർജിയുടെ കവിതകൾ രവികുമാറിന് തർജമ ചെയ്തു അയച്ചുകൊടുത്തിട്ടുള്ളത് അരവിന്ദനാണ്. രവികുമാറിന്റെ ആവശ്യപ്രകാരം, ആ ചെറുപ്പക്കാരനെ നേരിൽ കണ്ടതിൽ അരവിന്ദനു സന്തോഷമായി.

യോഗമയീദേവി കൽക്കത്തയിൽ എത്തിയപ്പോൾ രവികുമാറിന്റെ വീട്ടിൽ ചെന്നു. അച്ഛൻ ഭാസ്കരമേനോനെ അറസ്റ്റുചെയ്ത് എഴുതിവ യ്പിച്ചു വിട്ടിരിക്കുകയായിരുന്നു. യോഗമയീദേവിയാണ് അരവിന്ദൻ മദ്രാ സിലെത്തിയ വിവരം അറിയിച്ചത്. രണ്ടാഴ്ചമുമ്പ്, *വന്ദേമാതരം* വാരിക, യുടെ ആദ്യലക്കം അയച്ചതുകിട്ടി. രണ്ടാമത്തേതു കണ്ടില്ല. പോകാനുള്ള തിടക്കുംമൂലമാണ് കാണാഞ്ഞത്. ഇപ്പോൾ നാട്ടിലേക്കു പോവുകയാണ്. റീനയെ വിവാഹംചെയ്തിട്ടു മടങ്ങണം.

"അപ്പോൾ അച്ഛൻ വരുന്നില്ലേ?" അരവിന്ദൻ തിരക്കി.

"വരും. പോകുംവഴി അരവിന്ദേട്ടനെ കണ്ടിട്ടുപോകാമെന്നു ഞാൻ വിചാരിച്ചു. അപ്പോൾ, കല്യാണത്തിന് ഏട്ടനു വരാൻ സാധിക്കില്ലല്ലോ?"

"വരുന്നത് അപകടമാവും. എന്റെ പേരിൽ അവിടെ കേസുണ്ട്. പത്ര സംബന്ധമായും മറ്റും."

പല കാര്യങ്ങളും പിന്നെ അവർ സംസാരിച്ചു. ഉച്ചയൂണു കഴിഞ്ഞി രിക്കുമ്പോൾ രവികുമാർ ഒരു വിഷയം അവതരിപ്പിച്ചു.

"ഏട്ടനുവേണ്ടി ഞാൻ ഒരുകാര്യം കൊണ്ടുവന്നിട്ടുണ്ട്."

"എന്താണത്?"

"സാധനമല്ല ഒരു പ്രൊപ്പോസൽ."

"പ്രൊപ്പൊസലോ?" അരവിന്ദൻ പുഞ്ചിരിച്ചു.

"കല്യാണപ്രൊപ്പോസലല്ല, ഏട്ടാ, സിനിമാ പ്രൊപ്പോസൽ. ഏട്ടന് അത് കഴിയും. ജീവിതമുള്ള സിനിമകളുണ്ടാക്കണം! ഏട്ടനോട് സംസാ രിക്കാൻ അച്ഛൻ പറഞ്ഞയച്ചു. ചില ബംഗാളി ചിത്രങ്ങൾ കണ്ടപ്പോഴാണു അച്ഛന് ഈ ആശയം തോന്നിയത്. എനിക്കും തോന്നി ഞങ്ങൾ ആലോ ചിച്ചു. ഏട്ടനെ ഓർമിച്ചു. ഞങ്ങൾ തീരുമാനിച്ചു. ഏട്ടനു വേണ്ട പണം അച്ഛൻ തരും. എന്റെ കല്യാണം കഴിഞ്ഞ് ഇതിലേ ഞങ്ങൾ വരുമ്പോൾ, ഇത് ഫൈനലൈസ് ചെയ്യാം."

കുറെ നാളുകളായി മനസിൽക്കിടന്ന ഒരു ചിന്തയ്ക്ക് ഒരാഗ്രഹത്തിന് ഒരു നിമിഷത്തിൽ ഭൗതികരൂപം കിട്ടിയതുപോലെ തോന്നി.

മേനോൻ വന്നു രവികുമാറുമായി പരിചയപ്പെട്ടു.

അന്നു വൈകുന്നേരം അരവിന്ദനും മേനോനും രവികുമാറിനെ കൂട്ടി ക്കൊണ്ടു കടൽപ്പുറത്തുപോയി. രവികുമാർ നിർബന്ധിച്ചിട്ടാണ് പോയത്? "കൊച്ചനല്ലേ? കടൽപ്പുറം കണ്ടോട്ടെ." മേനോൻ തമാശ പറഞ്ഞു.

അപ്പോൾ രവികുമാർ നിവർന്നുനിന്ന് ഇങ്ങനെ പ്രഖ്യാപിച്ചു. "എന്നാൽ ഞാൻ നിങ്ങളെ ഇന്ന് ഒരത്ഭുതം കാട്ടിത്തരും. കണ്ടുകഴിഞ്ഞ്, നിങ്ങൾ എനിക്കു അഭിനന്ദനം നൽകും." അവർക്ക് രണ്ടുപേർക്കും മനസിലായില്ല. വെറും വാക്കായി മാത്രം കരുതി മറീനാ കടൽപ്പുറത്ത് എന്തത്ഭുതം കാണാനാണ്? കുറേ ആളുകളെ ഒഴിച്ച്?

കടൽപ്പുറത്തു ചെന്ന് ഒരു സ്ഥലത്ത് ഇരിക്കാമെന്ന് മേനോൻ നിർദേശിച്ചു. അപ്പോൾ രവികുമാർ ശഠിച്ചു.

"വേണ്ട. ഇരിക്കേണ്ട. സ്ഥലം ഞാൻ നിശ്ചയിക്കാം. നിങ്ങൾക്ക് അത്ഭുതം കാണേണ്ടേ? എങ്കിൽ നിശ്ചയിക്കുന്നിടത്ത് ഇരിക്കുകയും വേണം."

അവർ വഴങ്ങി. രവികുമാർ ബ്രിട്ടീഷ് രാജാവിന്റെ പ്രതിമയ്ക്കരികിലെത്തി. അവിടെ കടലിലേക്കു നോക്കി ഇരുന്നു. മറ്റു രണ്ടുപേരെയും ക്ഷണിച്ചു.

ഇരുന്നു കഴിഞ്ഞപ്പോൾ മേനോൻ കളിയാക്കി.

"കേട്ടോ അരവിന്ദൻ, ബ്രിട്ടീഷ് രാജാവിന്റെ പാദങ്ങൾക്കുകീഴെ ഇരിക്കാനാണ് ഇപ്പോഴും വാസന."

അരവിന്ദൻ ചിരിച്ചു.

രവികുമാർ തിരിച്ചടിച്ചു.

"അതെ സാറേ, ഞങ്ങൾ അങ്ങനെയാണ്. പക്ഷേ, ഞങ്ങൾ അങ്ങനെയിരിക്കുന്നത് അയാളുടെ പീഠത്തിനു കീഴിലെ മണ്ണുമാന്തി അതോടെ അയാളെ മലർത്തിയിടാനാണ്.

"വെരിഗുഡ്" മേനോൻ അഭിനന്ദനം രേഖപ്പെടുത്തി.

അവർ സംസാരിച്ചു. കടലിനെപ്പറ്റി. അതു രവികുമാറാണ് തുടങ്ങിയത്.

"കരയുടെ വിസ്തീർണം മനുഷ്യൻ അളന്നു പറഞ്ഞിട്ടുണ്ട്. കടലിന്റെ ആകെ വിസ്തീർണം എത്രയാണ്?"

അരവിന്ദനും മേനോനും മിണ്ടിയില്ല.

"ആകട്ടെ അതറിഞ്ഞുകൂടാ. കടലിൽ ആകെ എത്ര ടൺ ഉപ്പു കാണും?"

അവർ അപ്പോഴും മിണ്ടിയില്ല.

മറ്റൊരു ചോദ്യം. "കടലിലെ ഏറ്റവും ചെറിയ മീൻ ഏതാണ്?"

മേനോൻ എല്ലാറ്റിനുംകൂടി മറുപടി നൽകി:

"ഇതെല്ലാം കടലിനോടുതന്നെ ചോദിക്കുകയാണു ഭേദം."

"അല്ല, സമയം പോകാനാണ്. അത്ഭുതം വരുന്നുവെന്നു തോന്നുന്നു." എങ്ങും പ്രത്യേകിച്ചു നോക്കാതെയാണ് രവികുമാർ അതു പറഞ്ഞത്.

നീണ്ട താടിയുമായി പ്രായം ചെന്ന ആൾ അങ്ങോട്ടു നടന്നുവന്നു. നീണ്ട കുപ്പായം കൈയിൽ ഒരു ബാഗും. അയാൾ ഒന്നും ചോദിക്കാതെ അവരുടെ കൂടെ ഇരുന്നു.

"മനുഷ്യരെ ഇത്ര പെട്ടെന്ന് മറന്നാലെങ്ങനെയാണ്. അരവിന്ദൻ?" ആ മനുഷ്യൻ ചോദിച്ചു.

അരവിന്ദൻ അത്ഭുതപ്പെട്ടുപോയി. വാസവമേനോൻ!

രവികുമാർ പറഞ്ഞു.

"ഇതാണ് അത്ഭുതം. ഞങ്ങൾ കൽക്കത്തയിൽവച്ച് ഈ അത്ഭുതത്തെപ്പറ്റി പറഞ്ഞുപിരിഞ്ഞതാണ്."

മേനോൻ ആ ആളെ സൂക്ഷിച്ചുനോക്കി.

"എന്നെ അറിയുമോ?" വാസവമേനോനോട് ചോദിച്ചു.

"ഒരിക്കൽ തിരുച്ചിക്കടുത്തുള്ള സിമന്റ് ഫാക്ടറിയിൽ വച്ച്, നമ്മൾ പരിചയപ്പെട്ടിട്ടുണ്ട്. ഞാൻ ഡയറക്ടർമാരിൽ ഒരാളായി, യഥാർഥനോർത്ത് ഇന്ത്യനായി, അവിടെ വന്നു, ഓർമിക്കുന്നു. എന്നെ ഓർമിച്ചതിനു നന്ദി."

പതിനേഴ്

ഈ മനുഷ്യൻ എവിടെയെല്ലാം പോകും? അരവിന്ദൻ ആലോചിച്ചുപോയി.

അയാൾ ചുറ്റും നോക്കി. പതുക്കെ സംസാരിച്ചു.

"ഇങ്ങനെ നടന്നാലോ?"

"തലയ്ക്ക് അയ്യായിരമാ വില!" രവികുമാറും സ്വരമടക്കിപ്പിടിച്ചു.

"ഹേയ് ഒന്നുമില്ല. ഇവിടെ കുറെ ജോലിയുണ്ട്. അതുകൊണ്ടു വന്നതാണ്. അടങ്ങിയിരിക്കാനാണെങ്കിൽ ഇതിനു വല്ലതിനുംപോണോ? അരവിന്ദൻ എനിക്ക് രസം തോന്നാറുണ്ട്. നമ്മുടെ മേൽ നൂറ്റിനാൽപ്പത്തിനാല് പ്രഖ്യാപിച്ചിരിക്കുന്നു. അതുകൊണ്ട് ഞാൻ പോകുന്നിടത്തെല്ലാം നൂറ്റിനാൽപ്പത്തിനാലാണ് ഇരിക്കുന്നിടത്തും നിൽക്കുന്നിടത്തും എല്ലാം! നോക്കണേ, എന്റെ ഒരു ഭാഗ്യം. ഇതു പറഞ്ഞിട്ട് സഞ്ചിയിൽ നിന്ന് ഒരു ബംഗാളി ദിനപത്രം എടുത്തു നിവർത്തിക്കാട്ടി അതിൽ മേനോന്റെ ചിത്രം! പിടിച്ചുകൊടുക്കുന്നവർക്ക് അയ്യായിരംരൂപ!

"ഒരുത്തനും അങ്ങനെ അതു വാങ്ങിച്ച് ധനികനാകണ്ട!" അദ്ദേഹം ഒരു ഫലിതം പൊട്ടിച്ചു.

പിന്നെ, കുറെ മാസങ്ങളിലെ സംഭവങ്ങൾ പറഞ്ഞു. മധുരയിൽ നിന്ന് അഹമ്മദാബാദിലും ബംഗാളിലുംപോയി. മില്ലുകളിൽ പ്രവർത്തനം കേന്ദ്രീകരിക്കുകയായിരുന്നു. ഒരേ തൊഴിലിൽപ്പെട്ട തൊഴിലാളികളെ അഖിലേന്ത്യാടിസ്ഥാനത്തിൽ ഒരേ സമയത്ത് സമരത്തിനിറക്കിയാൽ അത് ഒരു വലിയ മൂവ്മെന്റിന്റെ ഫലമുണ്ടാക്കും. അതാണ് ശാസ്ത്രീയമായ തന്ത്രം. പ്രശ്നങ്ങൾക്കു സാമ്യമുണ്ട്. പരസ്പരധാരണയ്ക്കും എളുപ്പമുണ്ട്. അപ്പോൾ ഒരു പൊതുപണിമുടക്കിന്റെ ഛായ കൈവരും.

യോഗമയീദേവിയുടെ വിവരങ്ങൾ അരവിന്ദൻ പറഞ്ഞു. തങ്ങളെ അറസ്റ്റുചെയ്തതും മറ്റും അതൊക്കെ കേട്ടിട്ട്, മേനോൻ തിടുക്കപ്പെട്ടറിയിച്ചു:

"നമുക്ക് ഉടനെ ഇവിടെനിന്ന് പോകണം. ഒരു കാര്യം ഉണ്ട്. അത് ഇപ്പോൾ കാണാം."

അദ്ദേഹം എഴുന്നേറ്റു. കൂടെ മറ്റുള്ളവരും നടക്കുമ്പോൾ അദ്ദേഹം വ്യക്തമാക്കി.

“ഇപ്പോൾ ദാ ബീച്ചിന്റെ അങ്ങേയറ്റം മുതൽ ഇങ്ങേയറ്റം വരെ കുറെ നോട്ടീസുകൾ എറിയും. ആര് വിതറിയെന്ന് അറിയില്ല. മിക്കവാറും പൊലീസ് വരും. ബഹളമുണ്ടാക്കും. നമ്മളെന്തിനാ ഇങ്ങനെയുള്ളിടത്തു ഇരിക്കുന്നത്?;

അത് ഒരു പദ്ധതിയാണെന്ന് അരവിന്ദനും മേനോനും മനസിലായി. അവർ നടന്ന് റോഡിന്റെ മറുപുറത്ത് മാറി നിന്നു. പത്തുമിനിറ്റ്. ബീച്ചിലാകെ ബഹളം. നോട്ടീസുകൾ വാരിവിതറുകയാണ്. എല്ലാവരും എത്തിപ്പിടിക്കുന്നു. ഓടിച്ചെന്നു എടുക്കുന്നു. പിള്ളേര് എടുത്ത് ഉറക്കെ വിളിച്ചു പറയുന്നു. തമിഴിലാണ് സംഗതി ഇതാണ്.

ബ്രിട്ടീഷ് വാഴ്ചക്കെതിരായി മധുരയിലും അഹമ്മദാബാദിലും ബംഗാളിലും പഞ്ചാബിലും ആസ്സാമിലും മിൽത്തൊഴിലാളികൾ സമരത്തിൽ. ക്രൂരമായ ബ്രിട്ടീഷ് സാമ്രാജ്യാധികാരികൾ സമരം ചെയ്യുന്ന തൊഴിലാളികളെ വെടിവെച്ചു കൊല്ലുന്നു.

അധികം താമസിച്ചില്ല. പൊലീസുകാർ ഓടിയെത്തി. നോട്ടീസുകൾ പിടിച്ചുവാങ്ങുന്നു. ചിലർക്ക് ലാത്തിയടി. കുറച്ചു സമയം കൂടി. ഒരു വാൻ പൊലീസ് വരുന്നു.ചാടിയിറങ്ങുന്നു. കടൽപ്പുറത്ത് ഭയങ്കരബഹളം. അടി നടക്കുന്നു. ഓട്ടവും കരച്ചിലും.

മേനോനും മറ്റും നടന്നു. അപ്പോൾ മേനോൻ പറഞ്ഞു.

“ഇതിൽ വല്ല ടെററിസവുമുണ്ടോ? വെറും ടെററിപോലുമില്ല. സാധാരണ ബഹളം അതുതന്നെ.”

* * * * * *

ഒരു കൊച്ചുവീട് പട്ടണത്തിൽനിന്നു കുറച്ചുമാറിയാണ്. ദിവാകരനും ഭാനുമതിയും ഇപ്പോൾ അവിടെയാണ് താമസിക്കുന്നത്. അത് അവളുടെ നിർബന്ധമായിരുന്നു. അയാൾ വഴങ്ങി. ബാങ്കുകാർ ജപ്തിയും ലേലവും നടത്തുന്നതിനുമുൻപ് മാറിയതാണ്. പഴയ വീടുപോയി. കാറുപോയി. തന്റെ പതനം ഭീകരമാണെന്നു ദിവാകരന് കാണാൻ കഴിഞ്ഞു. അയാൾ അതെല്ലാം മനസിലൊതുക്കി. ഭാനുമതിയാണ് അതിനുള്ള ബലം അയാൾക്ക് നൽകിയത്.

അയാൾ പുറത്തിറങ്ങാറില്ല. ആരെയും കാണാറില്ല. ആരും ആ വീട്ടിൽ വരാറുമില്ല. ബാങ്കുകാർ ലേലത്തിൽ കിട്ടിയ പണം കൊണ്ട് തൃപ്തിപ്പെട്ടു. കൂടുതൽ ഉപദ്രവിച്ചില്ല. റോബർട്ടിന്റെയും മറ്റും തീവ്രമായ ശ്രമംകൊണ്ടാണ് അത്രയും കാര്യമായ സൗജന്യബുദ്ധി ബാങ്കിൽ നിന്നുണ്ടായത്. റോബർട്ടു മാത്രം വല്ലപ്പോഴും അവിടെ വന്ന് കൂട്ടിക്കൊണ്ടു പോകും. അയാളുടെ വീട്ടിൽ കുറേ നേരം കഴിച്ചുകൂട്ടും. തിരിച്ച് വീട്ടിൽ കൊണ്ടുചെന്നാക്കും.

ദിവാകരന്റെ ഉള്ള് ശാന്തമായിട്ടില്ല. അവിടെ ഒരു സംഘർഷം അവ

ശേഷിക്കുന്നു രത്നമ്മ. ജീവിതത്തിലെ യഥാർഥ രഹസ്യം അതാണ്, അതു തീർന്നിട്ടില്ല. തലയ്ക്കു മുകളിൽ ഒരു വാളു പോലെ അതു തൂങ്ങുന്നു. ആത്മാവിലെ തീയായി അത് കത്തി നിൽക്കുന്നു. പാപബോധത്തിന്റെ അഗ്നിയിൽനിന്നും തെല്ലൊരു മോചനം കിട്ടാൻ ഇപ്പോൾ അയാൾ ഉറ്റുനോക്കുന്നത് ഭാനുമതിയെയാണ്.

ക്ഷീണിതനായി അയാൾ കട്ടിലിൽ കിടന്നു. ഭാനുമതി എന്തോ തച്ചുകൊണ്ടിരുന്നു. സമയം രാത്രി പതിനൊന്നു മണിയായി. ദിവാകരൻ എഴുന്നേറ്റിരുന്നു. അയാൾ അവളെ വിളിച്ചു. അവൾ തയൽ നിറുത്താതെ വിളി കേട്ടു. അയാൾ ചോദിച്ചു.

"ഭാനൂ ഇപ്പോൾ ഞാൻ നിന്നോട് എന്തെങ്കിലും കള്ളം പറയുമെന്ന് നീ വിചാരിക്കുന്നുണ്ടോ?"

"എന്താ ഇങ്ങനെ ചോദിക്കുന്നത്?"

"അർഥമുണ്ട്. പറയാം. നീ വിചാരിക്കുന്നുണ്ടോ?"

"ഇല്ല."

"ഞാൻ ഒരു സംഗതി പറഞ്ഞാൽ നീ വിശ്വസിക്കുമോ?"

"തീർച്ചയായും വിശ്വസിക്കും."

അയാൾ കട്ടിലിൽ ചാരി.

"ഇങ്ങ് അടുത്തിരിക്കൂ."

അവൾ കസേര കട്ടിലിനരികിലേക്കു വലിച്ചിട്ടു.

"ഭാനൂ, രത്നമ്മ സത്യത്തിൽ ആത്മഹത്യ ചെയ്യുകയായിരുന്നു."

ആദ്യത്തെ ഭാര്യയെക്കുറിച്ച് അന്ന് ആദ്യമായി അയാൾ മിണ്ടുകയാണ്. അവരെ സംബന്ധിച്ച കഥകൾ ആദ്യമായി അവർക്കിടയിൽ ശബ്ദം കൊള്ളുകയാണ്.

ഭാനുമതി, ഇമയിളകാതെ ദിവാകരന്റെ മുഖത്ത് ദൃഷ്ടി ഉറപ്പിച്ചു.

"അവളെ ഞാൻ കൊന്നുവെന്നാണ് പലരും വിചാരിച്ചിട്ടുള്ളത്. അങ്ങനെയാണ് പ്രചരിപ്പിച്ചിട്ടുള്ളത്. പക്ഷേ, അവൾ സ്വയം ജീവിതത്തിന് വിരാമമിടുകയായിരുന്നു. നീ ഇതു നേരത്തെ കേട്ടിട്ടുണ്ടോ?"

"ഉണ്ട്, ഞാൻ കേട്ടിരുന്നു."

"എന്നിട്ട് നീ എന്തുകൊണ്ട് അതേപ്പറ്റി ചോദിച്ചില്ല?"

"വേണ്ടെന്നുവച്ചു. പാടില്ലെന്നു തോന്നി. നിങ്ങൾ എന്റെ സ്ഥാനത്തു നിന്നുകൊണ്ട് ആലോചിച്ചു നോക്കൂ. എന്തുവന്നാലും നേരിടാൻ ഞാൻ നിശ്ചയിച്ചു. പിന്നെ എന്തിന് ചോദിക്കുകയും കൂടുതൽ അറിയുകയും ചെയ്യണം? അതുമൂലം ഇനിയും നിങ്ങൾക്ക് ആപത്തൊന്നും വരുത്തരുതേ എന്ന് ഞാൻ പ്രാർഥിക്കുന്നുണ്ട്."

"ഇല്ല അതു തീർന്നിട്ടില്ല. അതുമൂലമുള്ള ആപത്ത് പതിയിരിപ്പുണ്ട്. എപ്പോൾ വേണമെങ്കിലും അത് എന്നെ ആക്രമിച്ചേക്കാം. അതു നിശ്ശബ്ദമായി എന്നെ പിന്തുടരുകയാണ്."

അവൾ തയ്യൽ നിറുത്തി. ചിന്തയിൽ മുഴുകി അയാൾ തുടർന്നു:

"സത്യം നിന്നോടു പറയണമെന്ന് കുറച്ചുനാളായി ആഗ്രഹിക്കുന്നു.

സാധിച്ചില്ല. സന്ദർഭം വന്നില്ല. ഇന്ന് നീ അതു കേൾക്കണമെന്ന് ഞാൻ അപേക്ഷിക്കുന്നു. അവളെ ഞാൻ വിവാഹം കഴിച്ചുകൊണ്ടുവന്നു. നിന ക്കറിയില്ല അത് യഥാർഥത്തിൽ ഒരു വിവാഹമായിരുന്നില്ല. അവൾ പഠി ച്ചുകൊണ്ടിരുന്നപ്പോൾ, എന്റെ സ്നേഹിതനായ ഒരു ചെറുപ്പക്കാരൻ അവളെ തട്ടിക്കൊണ്ടുപോന്നതാണ്. തട്ടിക്കൊണ്ടുപോന്നോ അവൾ കൂടെ ഇറങ്ങി വന്നോ എന്നെനിക്കറിയില്ല. ഞാനത് ചോദിച്ചിട്ടില്ല. അവർ സ്നേഹത്തിലായിരുന്നു എന്നു എനിക്കറിയാം. അവർ അങ്ങനെ പോന്ന പ്പോൾ അയാൾക്ക് ഒരു പ്രശ്നമുണ്ടായിരുന്നു. അവളെ അയാളുടെ വീട്ടിൽ കൊണ്ടുപോകാൻ നിവൃത്തിയില്ല. വീട്ടുകാർ ആ ബന്ധത്തിന് എതിരായിരുന്നു. അയാൾ വല്ലാത്ത വിഷമത്തിലായി. ഏറ്റവും അടുത്ത സുഹൃത്തെന്ന നിലയിൽ എന്നോടാലോചിച്ചു. അവർ തമ്മിൽ സ്നേഹ മാണെന്ന് എനിക്ക് അറിയാമായിരുന്നതിനാൽ അന്നു ഞാൻ ഒരു ചെറിയ വീടെടുത്ത് ഒറ്റയ്ക്ക് താമസിക്കുകയായിരുന്നു. അയാളും അവളും അവിടെ വന്നു താമസിച്ചുകൊള്ളാൻ ഞാൻ പറഞ്ഞു. ഭാവികാര്യം പിന്നെ ആലോചിക്കാം. അങ്ങനെ അവർ അവിടെ വന്നു താമസമായി. അയാൾക്ക് അന്ന് അത് വലിയ ഒരു കാര്യമായിരുന്നു. കാരണം, അയാൾക്ക് തൊഴിലില്ല. അതിനുവേണ്ടി അന്വേഷണവും ശ്രമവും തുടങ്ങി. ഞാൻ തടി ബിസിന സിലേക്കു പ്രവേശിച്ച കാലമാണ്. എനിക്ക് പൈസ വരാൻ തുടങ്ങിയിരു ന്നു. അതുകൊണ്ട് ബുദ്ധിമുട്ടു കൂടാതെ മുൻപോട്ടു നീങ്ങി. എന്റെ പൈസ അയാൾക്കും ഭാര്യയ്ക്കും വേണ്ടി ചെലവാക്കുന്നു എന്ന വിചാരമേ ഉണ്ടാ യിരുന്നില്ല. ഞങ്ങൾ അത്രയ്ക്ക് ഉറ്റ സുഹൃത്തുക്കളായിരുന്നു.

കുറേ അങ്ങനെ കഴിഞ്ഞു. വർഷം ഒന്നായിട്ടും അയാൾക്ക് ജോലി കിട്ടിയില്ല. അവൾക്ക് എന്റെ പണം അങ്ങനെ ചെലവാക്കുന്നതിൽ പ്രയാ സവും കുറെയൊക്കെ ജാള്യതയും ഉണ്ടായിരുന്നു. ഒരിക്കൽ അയാൾ ജോലിയന്വേഷിച്ച് ഇറങ്ങി. ഞാൻ വല്ലപ്പോഴുമേ അവിടെ പോകാറുള്ളൂ. കാട്ടിലും ലോറിയിലും വണ്ടിപ്പേട്ടയിലും ഒക്കെയായിരിക്കും. കുറച്ചു ദിവസം കഴിഞ്ഞ് ഞാൻ തിരിച്ചു ചെന്നപ്പോഴാണറിയുന്നത് അയാൾ തിരിച്ചു വന്നിട്ടില്ലെന്ന്, എന്തിനു പറയുന്നു. പിന്നെ അയാൾ മടങ്ങിവന്ന തേയില്ല.

അവളെ കാത്തുസൂക്ഷിക്കേണ്ട ചുമതല എന്റേതായി. ഒരു വർഷ ത്തോളം അങ്ങനെ കഴിഞ്ഞു. ഞാൻ അവളുടെ മുഖത്തു നോക്കുക പോലും ചെയ്തിട്ടില്ല. ഒരു ദിവസം അവളുടെ വേദന എന്നോടു പറ ഞ്ഞു. മറ്റൊരർഥത്തിലല്ല. സ്വാഭാവികമായും മനസിലാക്കാൻ കഴിയുന്ന അവളുടെ നിസ്സഹായത. ഞാൻ അവളെ സംരക്ഷിച്ചുകൊള്ളാമെന്ന് ഉറ പ്പുനൽകി. അന്ന് ഞങ്ങൾ ഒരു മുറിയിൽ ഒരു കട്ടിലിൽ കിടന്നു. അങ്ങനെ അവളെന്റെ ഭാര്യയായി.

രത്നമ്മ നല്ലവളായിരുന്നു. എന്റെ ബിസിനസ് വളർന്നു. വീടായി, കാറായി, ബാങ്ക് ബാലൻസായി. അതിനിടയ്ക്ക് ലീലാംബാളുമായുള്ള ബന്ധമുണ്ടായി. അത് അവൾ അറിഞ്ഞു. ഒന്നും മിണ്ടിയില്ല. കുറേ കഴി

ഞ്ഞപ്പോൾ എതിർക്കാൻ തുടങ്ങി. ഞാൻ അന്നത്തെ സ്വഭാവത്തിന് അവളെ വകവയ്ക്കാതായി. എന്തെങ്കിലും മിണ്ടിയാൽ പിണങ്ങി ഇറങ്ങിപ്പോകും. വല്ലപ്പോഴും തോന്നുമ്പോഴേ പിന്നെ വരികയുള്ളൂ.

ഒരു ദിവസം പ്രതീക്ഷിച്ചിരിക്കാതെ അവളുടെ ആ ഭർത്താവ് എന്റെ സ്നേഹിതൻ തിരിച്ചുവന്നു. അയാൾ തളർന്ന ഒരു മനുഷ്യനായിട്ടാണ് വന്നത്. ആ രൂപവും വേഷവും കണ്ട് എനിക്കു ദുഃഖം തോന്നി. അവൾ മരിച്ചതുപോലെയായി. ഞങ്ങൾ എന്തുചെയ്യും? അയാൾ എന്നോട് ശത്രുത പോലെയാണ് പെരുമാറിയത്. അത് എനിക്കു മനസിലാക്കാൻ കഴിഞ്ഞു. അയാൾ അവിടെ വരികയും പോവുകയും ചെയ്യാൻ തുടങ്ങി. അയാൾ അവളെ സ്വീകരിക്കുന്നതിൽ എനിക്ക് വിരോധമില്ലായിരുന്നു. പക്ഷേ, അതിനൊന്നും അയാൾ തയാറായിട്ടില്ല. ഒരു പ്രേതത്തെപ്പോലെ ചുറ്റിക്കൂടി അവളെ വിഷമിപ്പിച്ചു. ഒരു ദിവസം ഞാൻ വീട്ടിൽ ചെന്നപ്പോൾ അവൾ മരിച്ചുകിടക്കുന്നു.

വിഷം കഴിച്ചാണ് മരിച്ചത്. പക്ഷേ, അത് പുറത്തുവരാതെ ഞാൻ സൂക്ഷിച്ചു. ഞാൻ കൊന്നുവെന്ന് ആദ്യം പറഞ്ഞത് അയാളായിരുന്നു. അയാൾ അധികനാൾ ഈ നാട്ടിൽ നിന്നില്ല. അയാളുടെ കൂടെ പോകാൻ അവൾ തയാറായതുകൊണ്ട് ഞാൻ അവളെ കൊന്നു എന്നാണ് എന്റെ ശത്രുക്കൾ പ്രചരിപ്പിച്ചത്. പെട്ടെന്ന് വിശ്വസിക്കാൻ തോന്നുന്ന പ്രചരണമായിരുന്നു അത്. അവളുടെ വീട്ടുകാർപോലും അങ്ങനെ വിശ്വസിച്ചു. വിശ്വസിക്കുന്നു.

ഇതാണ് സത്യം. ഞാൻ നല്ലവനല്ല. അത് എന്റെ ജീവിതകഥ തന്നെ വിളിച്ചു പറയുന്നുണ്ട്. പക്ഷേ, ഞാനവളെ കൊന്നില്ല."

ഒന്നു നിറുത്തിയിട്ട് ദിവാകരൻ ചോദിച്ചു:

"ഇത് നീ വിശ്വസിക്കുന്നുണ്ടോ?"

"ഉണ്ട്. നിശ്ചയമായും ഉണ്ട്. നിങ്ങൾ സംശയിക്കേണ്ട." അവൾ അയാളുടെ മുഖത്തുതന്നെ കണ്ണുകൾ നട്ടുകൊണ്ട് ഉറപ്പിച്ചുപറഞ്ഞു.

ഭാനുമതിയുടെ കണ്ണുകൾ നനഞ്ഞിരിക്കുന്നത് അയാൾ കണ്ടു. ആ കഥ കേട്ടതിന്റെ ദുഃഖമായി അയാൾ അത് കരുതി. അവൾ അറിയിച്ചു.

"നിങ്ങൾക്ക് മറ്റൊരു കാര്യം അറിയാമോ?"

"എന്താണ്?"

"രത്നമ്മയും ഞാനും ഒരുവീട്ടിൽ ഒരുമിച്ചു വളർന്നവരായിരുന്നു."

അയാൾ ഏതോ ഭയങ്കരമായ ഒന്നു കേട്ടതുപോലെ നോക്കി.

"എങ്ങനെ?"

ഭാനുമതി ആ കഴിഞ്ഞകാല കഥ അയാളെ പറഞ്ഞു കേൾപ്പിച്ചു. അയാൾ കട്ടിലിലേക്ക് ശിരസ്സ് കുനിച്ചുവച്ച് കുറേനേരം ഇരുന്നു. പിന്നെ നിവർന്നു.

"അപ്പോൾ നീ എന്നെക്കാളും ദുഃഖം അനുഭവിക്കേണ്ടി വന്നു. ഭാനൂ നീ എന്നോട് ക്ഷമിക്കണം." അയാളുടെ ശബ്ദം തകർന്നു.

"ഇനി അതോർത്ത് ദുഃഖിക്കരുത്." അവൾ അപേക്ഷിച്ചു.

"അല്ല ഭാനു, ആ ഭീകരമായ സംഭവത്തിന്റെ കാറ്റ് അവസാനിച്ചിട്ടില്ല."

"എന്താ അത്? ഇനിയും കേസു വരുമോ എന്ന് ഞാൻ ഭയപ്പെടാറുണ്ട്.

അയാൾ കരുതലോടെ പറഞ്ഞു.

"ഒരാൾ – ഒരാൾ മാത്രം അതു വീണ്ടും കുത്തിപ്പൊക്കിക്കൊണ്ടുവരാൻ നിശ്ചയിച്ചിട്ടുണ്ട്. അയാൾ ഇപ്പോൾ നിന്റെ സഹോദരനാണെന്നു പറയുന്നു. അതു ശരിയുമാണെന്ന് ഞാൻ അന്വേഷണത്തിൽ മനസിലാക്കി.

അവൾ വിസ്മയവും ഉൽക്കണ്ഠയും കാട്ടി.

"എന്റെ സഹോദരനോ? ആരാണത്?"

"പൊലീസ് ഉദ്യോഗസ്ഥനായ ഹരീന്ദ്രൻനായർ."

ഓർമ. അയാൾവന്നത്. സംസാരിച്ചത്. ഒടുവിൽ നീ എന്നു വിളിച്ചത്. ഒരിക്കൽ അങ്ങനെ വിളിച്ചതിന്റെ കാരണം പറയാമെന്നു പറഞ്ഞത്....

ദിവാകരൻ വിശദീകരിച്ചു:

"നിങ്ങൾ രണ്ടു ജാതിക്കാരാണല്ലോ, പക്ഷേ, അയാളുടെ അച്ഛൻ വലിയ ജന്മിയാണ്. അദ്ദേഹം ഈയിടെ മരിച്ചു. ആ മനുഷ്യനാണ് നിന്റെ അച്ഛൻ. അത് അവിടെ ചിലർ പറയുന്നുണ്ട്."

"ഞാൻ കേട്ടിട്ടില്ലല്ലോ!"

"നിന്റെ നാട്ടിലല്ലല്ലോ നീ ജീവിച്ചതും വളർന്നതും പ്രവർത്തിച്ചതും. ചുരുക്കം ചിലർക്കേ അറിയാവൂ."

"എന്റെ സഹോദരനാണെങ്കിൽ എന്റെ ഭർത്താവിനെ ഉപദ്രവിക്കുമോ?"

"ഞങ്ങൾ പണ്ടേ ശത്രുക്കളാണ്? ബിസിനസ് കാര്യത്തിൽ എന്നെ ഒരുപാട് ദ്രോഹിച്ചിട്ടുണ്ട്. രത്നമ്മയുടെ മരണം സംബന്ധിച്ച് ഒരു കേസ് രജിസ്റ്റർ ചെയ്തിരുന്നു. അത് അവളുടെ ആ ഭർത്താവിന്റെ പെറ്റീഷനെ അടിസ്ഥാനപ്പെടുത്തിയായിരുന്നു. രഹസ്യമായി ചില്ലറ അന്വേഷണവും നടന്നു. അത് എഴുതിത്തള്ളിക്കാൻ ശ്രമിച്ചുകൊണ്ടിരിക്കുമ്പോഴാണ് ഹരീന്ദ്രൻ നായർ പ്രമോഷൻ കിട്ടി വന്നത്. അദ്ദേഹത്തിന്റെ ചില ഉറ്റ സ്നേഹിതന്മാർ പറഞ്ഞതുകൊണ്ട് പിന്നെ അത് പിന്തുടർന്നില്ല. ഇപ്പോൾ, നിന്നെ ഞാൻ തുലച്ചു എന്ന് അദ്ദേഹം കരുതുന്നുണ്ടാവും."

ദിവാകരൻ തളർന്നവനെപ്പോലെ ചാരിക്കിടന്നു. ഭാനുമതി ആകെ വിഭ്രമത്തിലകപ്പെട്ടിരിക്കുന്നു. ബന്ധശൈഥില്യങ്ങളും ബന്ധങ്ങളും ഒരുപോലെ അവൾക്ക് വീർപ്പുമുട്ടിക്കുന്ന പരീക്ഷണങ്ങളായിത്തീരുന്നു.

ഒരു ദിവസം കഴിഞ്ഞതേയുള്ളൂ പൊലീസുകാർ വന്നു. അവർ ദിവാകരനെ സ്റ്റേഷനിലേക്ക് വിളിച്ചുകൊണ്ടുപോയി. ഭാനുമതി ഉമ്മറത്ത് ബോധമില്ലാതെ വീണു.

പതിനെട്ട്

രവികുമാർ സദനത്തിലേക്ക് കയറിച്ചെന്നു. മുൻവശത്ത് ആരെയും കണ്ടില്ല. അരത്തിണ്ണയിൽ ഒരു സിഗരറ്റും പുകച്ച് ഇരുന്നു.

എപ്പോഴും പുഞ്ചിരിക്കുന്ന ആ മുഖം അയാൾ കണ്ടു. റീന. അവ

ളുടെ കവിളുകളിൽ റോസാപ്പൂക്കൾ വിരിയുന്നുണ്ടെന്നും അവളുടെ ഉള്ളിൽ പനിനീരു പെയ്തുനിൽക്കുന്നുണ്ടെന്നും ഒക്കെ അയാൾ വെറുതെ സങ്കൽപ്പിച്ചു. ജീവിതത്തെ വളരെ ഗൗരവത്തോടെ കാണുന്ന രവികുമാർ എപ്പോഴും ലാഘവത്തോടെ എല്ലാറ്റിനേയും പറ്റി ചിന്തിക്കും, പറയും. അവൾ വരുമ്പോൾ ആദ്യം എന്തു പറയണം?

ആരെയും കാണുന്നില്ല. ശ്രദ്ധിച്ചു. അസാധാരണമായ ഒരു നിശ്ശബ്ദത. എഴുന്നേറ്റു പകുതി ചാരിയ വാതിലിൽക്കൂടി അകത്തേക്കു നോക്കി. ആരുമില്ല. പിന്നെ ഒന്നു ചുമച്ചു. ഒരുത്തരുംവന്നില്ല. പിന്നെ കതകിൽ മുട്ടി. കുറേനിമിഷങ്ങൾക്കുശേഷം സുമതി പുറത്തേക്കു തലകാട്ടി.

അവൾക്ക് ആളെ മനസിലായി. രണ്ടുതവണ അവൾ രവികുമാറിനെ കണ്ടിട്ടുണ്ട്.

“ഇവിടെ ആരുമില്ല. ഞാൻ മാത്രമേയുള്ളൂ.” സുമതി അറിയിച്ചു.

“എല്ലാവരും എവിടെപ്പോയി?” രവികുമാർ ചോദിച്ചു.

“സന്ധ്യാദേവിക്കൊച്ചമ്മ ആശുപത്രിലാ. എല്ലാവരും അങ്ങോട്ടു പോയിരിക്കുവാ.”

“സന്ധ്യാദേവിക്ക് എന്താണസുഖം?”

സുമതി ഒന്നു മടിച്ചു. പിന്നെ പരുങ്ങലോടെ പറഞ്ഞു.

“പൊലീസുകാര് ഉപദ്രവിച്ചതാ.”

രവികുമാർ പകച്ചു നിന്നു.

“ഏതാശുപത്രിയിലാണ്?”

“വലിയ ആശുപത്രീലാ.”

“ശരി ഞാൻ പോയിട്ടുവരാം.”

“ഓ...”

അയാൾ ഇറങ്ങി മനസ്സ് ഇരുണ്ടതുപോലെ. പൊലീസ് അവരെ ഉപദ്രവിച്ചോ? കുലീനയായ സാത്വികയായ ആ സ്ത്രീയെ. ഉള്ളിൽ രോഷത്തിന്റെ ഒരിരമ്പലുണ്ടായി.

കാലുകൾ താനറിയാതെ ധൃതികൂട്ടി. ആശുപത്രിപ്പടി കടന്ന് റിസപ്ഷനിൽ അന്വേഷിച്ചു. അവർ സ്ഥലം പറഞ്ഞുകൊടുത്തു അങ്ങോട്ടു ചെന്നു.

എല്ലാവരും അവിടെയുണ്ട്. പ്രത്യേകമുറിയാണ്. സന്ധ്യാദേവി കിടക്കുന്നു. മയങ്ങുകയാണ്. കീർത്തിയും റീനയും അംബികത്തമ്പുരാട്ടിയും പാർവതിയും ഉണ്ട്.

“എന്താണ് സംഭവം?”

“ഒരു മാസമായി.” അംബികത്തമ്പുരാട്ടി പ്രതിവചിച്ചു.

“ഇപ്പോഴും സുഖമില്ലേ?”

“ഭേദമുണ്ട്. കുറച്ചുദിവസം കൂടി ഇവിടെ കിടക്കണമെന്നാണ് ഡോക്ടറന്മാർ പറഞ്ഞിരിക്കുന്നത്.”

“ഉറങ്ങട്ടെ വിളിക്കേണ്ട.”

അയാൾ പുറത്തേക്കിറങ്ങി.

എപ്പോഴും പ്രകാശിക്കുന്ന റീനയുടെ മുഖം അയാൾ മറന്നു. വാടി ത്തളർന്ന സന്ധ്യാദേവിയുടെ മുഖം മുൻപിൽ കാണുന്നു. ചന്ദ്രോദയ ങ്ങളെ ഓർമിപ്പിക്കാറുള്ള അവരുടെ മുഖവും ചിരിയും മാഞ്ഞ് വിളറി പ്പോയിരിക്കുന്നു. അവർ നന്നേ ക്ഷീണിച്ചിട്ടുണ്ട്.

ഒരുമാസം മുൻപ് രണ്ടാമത്തെ തവണയും അവർ പൊലീസിന്റെ കയ്യിലായി. ആദ്യം ഒരു സായാഹ്നം മുതൽ വെളുക്കും വരെ അവരെ പ്രഹരിക്കുകയും ഉപദ്രവിക്കുകയും ചെയ്തു. എന്നിട്ട് സദനത്തിൽ കൊണ്ടുചെന്ന് വിട്ടു. ഒരു കേസും ചാർജ് ചെയ്തില്ല. കേസെടുക്കാതെ നോവിച്ചുവിടുക. അതായിരുന്നു കമ്മീഷണറുടെ പരിപാടി. ഒരു മാസ ക്കാലം ആശുപത്രിയിൽ കിടന്നു. പുറത്തുവന്നപ്പോൾ അവരുടെ സ്വഭാ വത്തിന് മാറ്റം വന്നിരുന്നു. മുൻപ് ഒരിക്കലും അവർ രാഷ്ട്രീയ കാര്യ ങ്ങൾ പറഞ്ഞ് ക്ഷോഭിക്കാറില്ല. തർക്കിക്കാറില്ല. ആ സംഭവത്തിനുശേഷം പ്രത്യക്ഷമായി അതെല്ലാം കാണായി. ഒരു സഹിഷ്ണുവിനെപ്പോലെ അവർ പൊതുരംഗങ്ങളിൽ പ്രത്യക്ഷപ്പെട്ടു. മുറിവേറ്റ സിംഹിയെപ്പോലെ ഭരണാധികാരികളുടെ നേർക്ക് അവർ സ്വന്തം രോഷം കാട്ടി. സദനത്തിൽ അവർ കുറേക്കൂടി മാർദവമുള്ള നായികയായി. കീർത്തി കുറച്ചുകൂടി അവരോടടുത്തു. മുൻപു അവർ അവരോട് സംസാരിക്കാറില്ല. അവൾ നിശ്ശബ്ദമായി അവരുടെ അരികിൽ വന്നിരിക്കാറേ ഉള്ളൂ. മിണ്ടുന്നത് വല്ല പ്പോഴുമായിരിക്കും. അതും മാറി. രാത്രിയിൽ അവർ അവളെ അടുത്തു കിടത്തും. മണിക്കൂറുകളോളം അവർ അവളോട് ഓരോ കാര്യം പറയും. ഒരിക്കൽ അങ്ങനെ അവർ രണ്ടുപേരും മാത്രം ഉറങ്ങാൻ കിടക്കുമ്പോൾ സന്ധ്യാദേവി അവളോട് പറഞ്ഞു:

"എനിക്ക് ഒരുപാട് ആഗ്രഹങ്ങളുണ്ട്. എല്ലാം നമ്മുടെ സദനത്തെ സംബന്ധിച്ചുള്ളതാണ്. നമുക്ക് ഒരു വസ്തു വാങ്ങണം. സ്വന്തമായി കെട്ടി ടവും ഒരു ഹാളും ഉണ്ടാവണം. എന്നിട്ട് പാഠശാലകൾ തുടങ്ങണം. ഹിന്ദി പഠിപ്പിക്കാനും പാട്ടുപഠിപ്പിക്കാനും നൃത്തം പഠിപ്പിക്കാനുമൊക്കെ ഓരോ വിഭാഗം ഉണ്ടായിരിക്കണം. നല്ല അധ്യാപകരെ അതിനൊക്കെ വയ്ക്ക ണം. നമുക്ക് ഒരു ഗാനസംഘം തന്നെ വേണം. കുറേക്കാലം കഴിയു മ്പോൾ നമുക്ക് സ്കൂൾ തുടങ്ങാൻ സാധിക്കണം. അങ്ങനെ സദനം വലിയ സ്ഥാപനമായിത്തീരും. ഇന്ന് നമ്മൾ രാഷ്ട്രീയക്കാരാണെന്നു പറഞ്ഞ് ആളുകൾ മാറിനിൽക്കുന്നു. അന്ന് അങ്ങനെ മാറിനിൽക്കുകയില്ല. എല്ലാവരും നമ്മുടെ സ്ഥാപനത്തിലേക്കു വരും..."

അവരുടെ സ്വപ്നം കീർത്തിയെ ആകർഷിച്ചു. ഇതെല്ലാം ചെയ്യാൻ അവർക്കു കഴിവുണ്ട്. ഇതിലേക്കു മനുഷ്യരെ ആകർഷിക്കാൻ അവർക്ക് സാമർഥ്യമുണ്ട്. പക്ഷേ, ഹൃദയമില്ലാത്ത കുറേ മനുഷ്യർ ഈ സ്ഥാപ നത്തെ അപമാനിക്കുന്നു. അധികാരികൾ ഇതിനെ ആക്രമിക്കുന്നു. അതി ന്റെയെല്ലാം മുൻപിൽ പിടിച്ചു നിൽക്കാൻ കഴിയണം. അതു ചെറിയ കാര്യമല്ല. സന്ധ്യാദേവിയുടെ തന്റേടം ഒന്നുകൊണ്ടു മാത്രമാണ്, ഈ സ്ഥാപനം ഇങ്ങനെ പിടിച്ചുനിൽക്കുന്നത്. എല്ലാ വശത്തുനിന്നുമുള്ള ശര

ങ്ങളെ അവർ നിവർന്നുനിന്ന് ഏറ്റുവാങ്ങുന്നു.

മറ്റൊരിക്കൽ അതുപോലെ കീർത്തി അരവിന്ദനെപ്പറ്റി ഒരുപാടു സ്തുതിച്ചു സംസാരിച്ചു. അത് ആരാധനയുടെ ശബ്ദമായിരുന്നു. അവളുടെ ഹൃദയം അയാളിൽ അലിഞ്ഞുചേർന്നതു പോലിരുന്നു. അവൾ ഇത്രയുംകൂടി പറഞ്ഞു. “ആ ഏട്ടൻതന്നെ ഒരു കവിതയാണ്. പൗരുഷവും സൗന്ദര്യവുമുള്ള കവിത.” പിന്നെകുറച്ചുനേരം അവൾ മിണ്ടാതെ കിടന്നു. അയാളെപ്പറ്റിയുള്ള ഓർമയുടെ ലഹരിയിൽ ഒഴുകിപ്പോയി.

അരവിന്ദനോട് ആർക്കും അങ്ങനെ മമത തോന്നും.

പക്ഷേ, തന്റെ ആ ബന്ധത്തിന് എന്താണർഥം? അവർ ആലോചിച്ചുപോയി. വിവാഹം കഴിഞ്ഞ് ഭാര്യയായി, അമ്മയായി, കുടുംബിനിയായി ജീവിക്കാൻ വേണ്ടിയാണോ താൻ ജനിച്ചത്? അങ്ങനെ ഒരു ജീവിതം തനിക്ക് വിധിക്കപ്പെട്ടിട്ടുള്ളതായി തോന്നുന്നില്ല. യുക്തികൊണ്ട് വാദം കൊണ്ട് അതു സമർഥിക്കാൻ കാരണമൊന്നും കാണുന്നില്ല. എന്നാൽ, സ്വന്തം മനസിനെ സ്വയം നോക്കിക്കാണാൻ ശ്രമിക്കുമ്പോഴെല്ലാം ആ തോന്നലാണ്. ഇന്നു വിശ്വസിക്കുന്ന ജീവിതത്തെ അവിടെ ഇട്ടെറിഞ്ഞുകളഞ്ഞിട്ടല്ലാതെ, ഒരു ഭാര്യയും അമ്മയും കുടുംബിനിയുമാവാൻ കഴിയുകയില്ല. അല്ലെങ്കിൽ സ്വയം സ്വീകരിച്ച് പൊരുത്തക്കേടുകളുടെ നടുവിൽക്കിടന്ന് തനിക്കും മറ്റുള്ളവർക്കും സുഖം നൽകാൻ കഴിയാത്ത ഒരു ജീവിതം നയിക്കേണ്ടിവരും.

അങ്ങനെയൊക്കെ ആലോചിച്ചു അൽപ്പനിമിഷങ്ങൾക്കുള്ളിൽ പ്രിയപ്പെട്ട ഓർമകളുടെ ഒരു തിരക്കൈ വന്നു തഴുകി. ആ വിചാരങ്ങൾ മാഞ്ഞുപോവുകയും ചെയ്തു.

മാസങ്ങൾ ഇഴഞ്ഞു നീങ്ങി. ഒരു ദിവസം വീണ്ടും അവരെ പൊലീസ് സ്റ്റേഷനിൽ കൊണ്ടുപോയി. അക്കുറി മൂന്നു ദിവസം ലോക്കപ്പു മുറിയിലിട്ടിരുന്നു. നാലാം ദിവസം അവരെ അജ്ഞാതമായ ഒരു താവളത്തിലേക്കു മാറ്റി. രണ്ടാഴ്ച കഴിഞ്ഞ് തിരിച്ചുകൊണ്ടു വരികയുംചെയ്തു. അത് അടിച്ചേൽപ്പിച്ച ഒരു ഏകാന്തവാസമായിരുന്നു. ആരും അവരെ ശാരീരികമായി ശല്യപ്പെടുത്തിയില്ല. മാനസികമായി താങ്ങാൻ വയ്യാത്ത ഒരു ബന്ധമായിരുന്നു അത്. മനസ്സ് മാറ്റിയെടുക്കാനുള്ള ശ്രമത്തിൽ അധികാരികൾ പരാജയപ്പെട്ടു. ഒരു ശബ്ദവുമുണ്ടാക്കാതെ അവരെ തടവിൽ നിന്നു പുറത്തേക്കിറക്കി വിട്ടു.

ആദ്യത്തെ ശാരീരിക ദണ്ഡത്തെ അവർ അതിജീവിച്ചു. കുറേക്കൂടി വീറും വാശിയും സ്നേഹവും എല്ലാം അവരിൽ ഉണർന്നു. ഇപ്പോൾ മൗനത്തിന്റെ ഒരു ആവരണത്തിനുള്ളിലേക്ക് അവർ പിൻവലിക്കുകയാണുണ്ടായത്. ആ മാറ്റം എല്ലാവരേയും ഉൽക്കണ്ഠപ്പെടുത്തി. ആരോടും മിണ്ടാത്ത ദിവസങ്ങളിൽക്കൂടി ഒന്നു ചിരിക്കാൻപോലും ഉത്സാഹം കാട്ടാത്ത വിമുഖതകളിൽക്കൂടി, അവർ നടന്നു നീങ്ങുന്നത് മറ്റുള്ളവർ ഹൃദയവ്യഥയോടെ നോക്കി നിന്നു. കീർത്തി, സന്ധ്യാദേവിക്ക് ഒഴിച്ചുകൂടാൻ വയ്യാത്ത ഒരു വസ്തുവായിത്തീർന്നു. അവൾ അരികിൽ നിന്നു

പോയാൽ, അപ്പുറത്തെങ്ങാനും കൂടുതൽ സമയം കഴിച്ചുകൂട്ടിയാൽ അവർ വിളിക്കും. ഒന്നുംപറയാനില്ല, ചോദിക്കാനില്ല, അത് മനസിന്റെ ഒരാവശ്യമാണെന്നു കണ്ടു നിന്നവർക്കു മനസിലായി.

എന്നിട്ടും സദനത്തിലെ കാര്യങ്ങൾക്കു മുടക്കമില്ല. എല്ലാം ഓർമിച്ചുവച്ച് ചെയ്തുകൊണ്ടിരുന്നു. അതിഥികളെ സ്വീകരിച്ചു. കത്തുകൾക്ക് മറുപടി അയച്ചു. ചർക്കാ സംഘത്തിന്റെ പ്രവർത്തനങ്ങൾക്ക് ഭംഗംവരാതെ സൂക്ഷിച്ചു.

നാലഞ്ചാഴ്ച കഴിഞ്ഞപ്പോൾ അവർ കിടപ്പിലായി. തീ ചിന്തുന്ന പനി. ആശുപത്രിയിലേക്ക് മാറ്റേണ്ടിവന്നു. ശരീരത്തിന് പറ്റിയ ആഘാതമാണ് രോഗകാരണമെന്ന് ഡോക്ടർമാർ പറഞ്ഞു.

രവികുമാറും മിക്കവാറും ആശുപത്രിയിലുണ്ട്. മറ്റു ജോലികളില്ല. പലരേയും കാണണമെന്ന് ആഗ്രഹിച്ചിരുന്നു. സന്ധ്യാദേവി രോഗശയ്യയിൽ കിടക്കുമ്പോൾ അവിടം വിട്ടു പോകാൻതോന്നിയില്ല. ദിവസങ്ങൾ കഴിഞ്ഞപ്പോൾ അവർക്ക് ആശ്വാസം കിട്ടിത്തുടങ്ങി. ജ്വരത്തിന്റെ കടുത്ത പിടിയിൽ നിന്നും രക്ഷപ്പെട്ടു. ബോധത്തിന്റെ ചാലുകൾ സാവധാനം തെളിയുന്നു. രവികുമാറിനെ അവർ മനസിലാക്കി.

അരവിന്ദൻ ഒരു കത്തു കൊടുത്തയച്ചിട്ടുണ്ട്. ഏതാനും ദിവസങ്ങൾക്കൂടി കഴിഞ്ഞ്, അത് കൊടുത്താൽ മതിയെന്ന് രവികുമാർ നിശ്ചയിച്ചു.

കീർത്തിക്കും റീനയ്ക്കും മറ്റും നേരിയ ഉത്സാഹം തിരിച്ചുകിട്ടി. അവർ മനസ്സുഖത്തോടെ പരസ്പരം മിണ്ടി. ആഴ്ചകൾ കൂടിയിട്ട് ചിരിച്ചു. അവർ രവികുമാറിനെ കളിയാക്കാൻ സന്ദർഭം കണ്ടെത്തി. കീർത്തി ചോദിച്ചു:

"എന്തിനാ ഇവിടെയൊക്കെ ചുറ്റിപ്പറ്റി നടക്കുന്നത്? കൽക്കത്തയ്ക്കു തിരിച്ചുപോകരുതോ?"

ആശുപത്രിയിൽ ഒരുമിച്ചുകഴിഞ്ഞ് അകൽച്ച നീങ്ങിയിരുന്നു. അവർ അയാളുമായി അനേക ദിവസങ്ങളിൽക്കൂടി അടുത്തുകഴിഞ്ഞിരുന്നതുകൊണ്ടാണ് കീർത്തി ആ ധൈര്യം കാട്ടിയത്.

രവികുമാർ പാന്റ്സിന്റെ പോക്കറ്റിൽ കൈയിട്ട് അലസമായിനിന്ന് മറുപടി നൽകി.

"സദനത്തിലെ കുട്ടികൾക്ക് ഒരു കൂട്ടുണ്ടായിരിക്കട്ടെ എന്നു വിചാരിച്ചു. സന്ധ്യാദേവിക്ക് അസുഖമായിരിക്കുമ്പോൾ അവർക്കു പിന്നെ ആരുണ്ട്?"

"ഞങ്ങളുടെ ആവശ്യം കഴിഞ്ഞു. ഇനി നിങ്ങൾക്കുപോകാം." കീർത്തി സ്വരത്തിൽ ഗൗരവം വരുത്തി.

"യെസ്. പക്ഷേ, ഒറ്റയ്ക്കു മടങ്ങാൻ ഒരു മെന്റൽ അൺ ഈസിനസ്."

"ഇങ്ങോട്ട് ഒറ്റയ്ക്കല്ലേ വന്നത്?"

"അതെ. പക്ഷേ, തിരിച്ചുപോക്ക് ഒരു പ്രശ്നമാണ്. സഹോദരീ. ഒരു തത്വം തന്നെയുണ്ട്. ഒരു യാത്രയിൽ, അങ്ങോട്ടോ ഇങ്ങോട്ടോ ഒരു കൂട്ടു

വേണം. മാത്രമല്ല സഹോദരീ, ഒരു വഴിക്കുപോയാൽ എന്തെങ്കിലും ഒരു ധനവും കൊണ്ടുവേണം മടങ്ങിവരിക."

കീർത്തി ചിരിച്ചിട്ടു കളിയാക്കി.

"ഓ, ധനം തേടി ഇറങ്ങിയതാണ്! ആ ധനം ഇവിടെയെങ്ങാനും നിൽപ്പുണ്ടോ?"

അതുവരെ ഒളിഞ്ഞുനിന്ന റീന ഒന്നുകൂടി നാണിച്ച് പിൻവാങ്ങി നിന്നു.

"യെസ്, യു ആർ ദെയർ! ഇവിടെ, ഇവിടെത്തന്നെയുണ്ട്. എ സ്മൈലിങ് പോട്ട് ഓഫ് ഗോൾഡ്! എന്നുവച്ചാൽ മലയാളത്തിൽ പുഞ്ചിരിക്കുന്ന പൊന്നിൻകുടം!"

"എടീ പൊൻകുടമോ ഇങ്ങോട്ട് മാറിനിക്കെടീ.." കീർത്തി റീനയെ പിടിച്ചു മുൻപോട്ടു നിറുത്താൻ ശ്രമിച്ചു. അവൾ കുതറിമാറി പൊയ്ക്കളഞ്ഞു.

സന്ധ്യാദേവി കുറേക്കൂടി ആശ്വാസം നേടി എഴുന്നേറ്റിരുന്ന ദിവസം രവികുമാർ അരവിന്ദന്റെ കത്തുകൊടുത്തു. അരവിന്ദൻ മദ്രാസിലുണ്ടെന്നും പത്രം നടത്തുന്നുണ്ടെന്നും കേട്ടപ്പോൾത്തന്നെ അവരുടെ ക്ഷീണിച്ച മിഴികൾ വിടർന്നു. യോഗമയീദേവിയുടെ വിവരവും അറിയിച്ചു. കത്തു കൊടുത്തശേഷം രവികുമാർ പുറത്തേക്കുപോയി. അവർ അതുവായിച്ചു.

"പ്രിയപ്പെട്ട സന്ധ്യാദേവി, അങ്ങോട്ട് എന്റെ വിവരങ്ങൾ അറിയിക്കാഞ്ഞതിൽ പരിഭവിക്കരുത്. മനഃപൂർവം അത് വേണ്ടെന്നുവച്ചതാണ്. കാലാവസ്ഥ അങ്ങനെയായതുകൊണ്ട്. ഞാൻ, എന്റെ ബന്ധുവായ മേനോൻ പ്രസിദ്ധീകരിക്കുന്ന വാരികയിൽ പ്രവർത്തിക്കുന്നു. യോഗമയീദേവി ആലിപ്പൂർ ജയിലിലാണ്. കഴിഞ്ഞ ഒരു ദിവസം വാസവമേനോനെ കണ്ടു. അദ്ദേഹം വീണ്ടും ഇവിടെ നിന്നും പോയി. അത്ഭുതമനുഷ്യൻ..

ഓരോ ദിവസവും, ഓരോ നിമിഷവും, ഞാൻ അവിടത്തെ കാര്യങ്ങൾ ഓർക്കുന്നു. എനിക്ക് ഓർമിക്കാനുള്ള ഏറ്റവും പ്രിയപ്പെട്ട കാര്യങ്ങൾ അതൊക്കെയാണല്ലോ. ആൾക്കൂട്ടത്തിലും ഞാൻ ഏകാകിയാണെന്നു തോന്നിപ്പോകുന്നു. കഴിഞ്ഞകാലം എന്റെ വിചാരത്തിന്റെ താഴ്വാരങ്ങളിലേക്ക് കൂട്ടിക്കൊണ്ടുപോകുന്നു! എത്ര ഭംഗിയുള്ള പുൽപ്പറമ്പുകൾ! എന്തുനിറമുള്ള ഉദ്യാനങ്ങൾ! എത്ര മധുരമായ ശബ്ദങ്ങൾ... ഞാൻ അവയെല്ലാം പിന്നിട്ട് എവിടെ എത്തിയിരിക്കുന്നുവെന്ന് ആലോചിച്ച് പോകാറുണ്ട്. അറിഞ്ഞുകൂടാത്ത ആളുകൾ തിങ്ങി ഞെരുങ്ങി സഞ്ചരിക്കുന്ന വലിയ തെരുവുകൾ ചെറിയ ഇടനാഴികൾ നഗരത്തിന്റെ തിരക്കിൽ ഔപചാരികമായിമാത്രം കണ്ടുപിരിയുന്ന ചുരുക്കം ചില മനുഷ്യർ.. ജീവിതം ചുരുങ്ങിക്കൂടി ഒരു പുഴുവിന്റെ വലുപ്പത്തിലായിപ്പോയിരിക്കുന്നു....

ഒന്ന് കാണാൻ ആഗ്രഹമുണ്ട്. ദിവസവും എത്ര തവണ മനസിൽ ചിത്രങ്ങൾവരച്ചു സമാധാനിക്കും?

ഞാൻ വരും. എന്റെ കേസ് സംബന്ധമായ കുഴപ്പമുണ്ടെങ്കിൽ അത് അന്വേഷിക്കുവാൻ രവികുമാറിനോട് പറഞ്ഞിട്ടുണ്ട്.

ഈ ശൂന്യതയിൽനിന്ന് ഒരു നിമിഷം മാറിനിൽക്കാൻ എനിക്ക് ഒരു കത്തയച്ചു തരിക. ആ രൂപം കണ്ടുകൊള്ളാം. ആ ചൂടുള്ള സ്പർശം അനുഭവിച്ചുകൊള്ളാം.

ഓർമിക്കുക

സ്നേഹത്തിന്റെ പൂക്കൾ,

അരവിന്ദൻ"

അനവധി മാസങ്ങൾക്കുശേഷം ആത്മാവിൽ മഞ്ഞുപെയ്യുകയായിരുന്നു. താനറിയാതെ കണ്ണുകൾ നിറഞ്ഞൊഴുകിയത് ആ കത്തിലേക്ക് ഇറ്റുവീണു. ശരീരത്തിന്റെയും മനസിന്റെയും തളർച്ച അലിഞ്ഞുപോയതുപോലെ. പൊടിയിൽ വീണടിഞ്ഞു കിടന്ന പ്രത്യാശകൾ ജീവനജലമേറ്റ് ഉണർന്നെഴുന്നേൽക്കുന്നു. അകന്നുപോയ ഒരു ലോകം തിരിച്ചു വന്നിരിക്കുന്നു. ഇനി എന്നു കാണാൻ കഴിയും? ചിറകിട്ടടിക്കുന്ന മനസിനെ പിടിച്ചു നിർത്താൻ കഴിയുന്നില്ല.

ചിന്താധീനയായി കിടന്നു.

വൈകുന്നേരം സദനത്തിൽ വന്ന ഒരു കമ്പിയുമായി സുമതി വന്നു. സന്ധ്യാദേവിയുടെ കൈയിൽ കൊടുത്തു. രവികുമാറും കീർത്തിയും തമ്പുരാട്ടിയും അടുത്തുണ്ട്. കമ്പി പൊട്ടിച്ചു.

"Yogamayidevi Expired Yesterday night Alipur Central Jail, Bhaskara Menon."

സന്ധ്യാദേവി ജീവച്ഛവത്തെപ്പോലെ ഇരുന്നു. കീർത്തിയും തമ്പുരാട്ടിയും സ്തബ്ധരായി നിന്നു. രവികുമാറിന്റെ അച്ഛൻ അയച്ച കമ്പിയാണ്.

സന്ധ്യാദേവി ചുമരിലേക്ക് ചാരിയിരുന്നു.

പത്തൊൻപത്

റീനയുടെ വിവാഹം സദനത്തിൽ വച്ചുതന്നെ ആർഭാടരഹിതമായി നടത്താൻ നിശ്ചയിച്ചു. സന്ധ്യാദേവി ആശുപത്രിയിൽ നിന്നു വന്നിട്ടുണ്ട്. പഴയ ഉന്മേഷത്തിലേക്ക് അവർ തിരിച്ചു വന്നു. സദനം പണ്ടത്തെപ്പോലെ ശബ്ദമുള്ളതായി. ചലനമുള്ളതായി. വരാൻപോകുന്ന വിവാഹത്തിന്റെ അന്തരീക്ഷം നേരത്തെ അനുഭവപ്പെടുന്നു. പക്ഷേ, രഹസ്യമായി സന്ധ്യാദേവി അസ്വസ്ഥയാണ്. ഒരുപുതിയ പ്രശ്നം വന്നിരിക്കുന്നു. അവിടെ നിന്ന് ഇറങ്ങിക്കൊടുക്കേണ്ടിയിരിക്കുന്നു. ആ ഭവനത്തിന്റെ ഉടമസ്ഥൻ നിയമപരമായ അറിയിപ്പും കൊടുത്തുകഴിഞ്ഞു. ഞെരുക്കാൻ തുടങ്ങിയിട്ട് നാളുകളായി പലരുടെയും എതിർപ്പും വൈരാഗ്യവും ഇഷ്ടക്കേടും ഒരുമിച്ചുചേർന്ന് ഒരു കുടിയിറക്കായി മാറിയിരിക്കുകയാണ്.

എങ്ങോട്ടു മാറും? അതു പ്രശ്നമാണ്. ഭയപ്പെട്ടിട്ട് ആരും സ്ഥലം കൊടുക്കില്ല. പ്രത്യേകിച്ചും അടുത്ത കാലത്തെ സംഭവങ്ങൾ അറിഞ്ഞവർക്കെല്ലാം ഭീതിയാണ്. എല്ലാ യാതനകളും അനുഭവിച്ചുകഴിഞ്ഞ് ഇപ്പോൾ ഇറങ്ങിക്കൊടുക്കണം... ഇനി വാദിക്കാൻ വഴിയില്ല. പിടിച്ചു

നിൽക്കാൻ അടിസ്ഥാനമില്ല. സദനത്തിൽ എല്ലാവരെയും ഇത് അറിയിച്ചിട്ടില്ല. കുട്ടികളോട് പറഞ്ഞിട്ട് എന്തു കാര്യം? അംബികത്തമ്പുരാട്ടിക്കു മാത്രം അറിയാം. മുതിർന്ന ഒരു സ്ത്രീ അവർ മാത്രമേ ഉള്ളൂ. റീനയുടെ വിവാഹം നടക്കാൻ പോകുന്നു. അപ്പോൾ ഈ സംഗതി തീർച്ചയായും പുറത്തു പറയാൻ പാടില്ല.

ഒരു ഞായറാഴ്ച ദിവസം രാവിലെ, വിളക്കു കൊളുത്തിവച്ച്, അതിന്റെ മുൻപിലിരുന്ന്, റീനയുടെ കഴുത്തിൽ രവികുമാർ താലികെട്ടി, ഒരു ചെറിയ സംഘം ആളുകൾ മാത്രം കൂടിയിരുന്നു. സദനത്തിലുള്ളവരും റീനയുടെ അച്ഛനും അമ്മയും അമ്മാവനും പിന്നെ സ്ഥലത്തെ നാലഞ്ചു രാഷ്ട്രീയ പ്രവർത്തകരും എഴുത്തുകാരും. രവികുമാറിന്റെ അച്ഛൻ രണ്ടുദിവസം മുൻപ് വന്നു.

അരവിന്ദന്റെയും പി ആർ മേനോന്റെയും കമ്പിസന്ദേശങ്ങൾ വന്നു. വധൂവരന്മാർക്ക് ഭാവുകങ്ങൾ. ഭാനുമതിയുടെ കത്തുണ്ടായിരുന്നു. വരാൻ തരപ്പെട്ടില്ല. റീനയ്ക്കും ഭർത്താവിനും നന്മ നേരുന്നു..... മൂന്നാമതൊരു..... കമ്പി വന്നപ്പോൾ ആരുടേതെന്നു സംശയിച്ചു. 'റീനയ്ക്കും രവികുമാറിനും ഭാവുകങ്ങൾ ഭവിക്കട്ടെ. നിങ്ങളുടെ ജീവിതം രാഷ്ട്രീയത്തിനു നല്ലതായിരിക്കട്ടെ- മേനോൻ.' ആ വാചകം വായിച്ചപ്പോൾതന്നെ അത് വാസവമേനോന്റേതായിരിക്കുമെന്ന് സന്ധ്യാദേവി വിചാരിച്ചതാണ്. കമ്പിയടിച്ചിരിക്കുന്നത് നാഗപ്പൂരിൽ നിന്നാണ്.

അന്നു രാത്രിയിൽത്തന്നെ രവികുമാറും അച്ഛനും റീനയും കൽക്കത്തയിലേക്കു യാത്രപുറപ്പെടുകയാണ്. റീനയെ ഇവിടെ നിറുത്തിയിട്ടു പോകാൻ അവർ തയാറാണ്. പക്ഷേ, സന്ധ്യാദേവി അതു സമ്മതിച്ചില്ല. അവർ ഒരുമിച്ചു കഴിഞ്ഞുകൂടണം. മറ്റെല്ലാ പരിഗണനകളും തെറ്റാണ്

വണ്ടിയാപ്പീസിൽ അവരെല്ലാവരും കൂടി നിന്നു. പലരും ഫലിതങ്ങൾ പറഞ്ഞു പരസ്പരം കളിയാക്കി. കഥകൾ പറഞ്ഞു. എന്നാലും എല്ലാവരുടെയും മനസ്സ് മൂകമായിരുന്നു. മുഖങ്ങളിൽ മ്ലാനത ഉണ്ടായിരുന്നു. റീന പിരിഞ്ഞു പോകുന്നുവെന്ന സത്യം അത്രയ്ക്കു ദുഃഖമുണ്ടാക്കി. അവൾക്ക് പിരിയാൻ മനസില്ല.

കീർത്തിപറഞ്ഞു.

"നീ ഞങ്ങളെ മറന്നാല്, കൽക്കട്ടയിൽവന്ന് നിന്നെ ഇടിക്കും. കേട്ടോടി പെണ്ണേ!"

"നീ എന്നെ മറക്കാതിരുന്നാൽ മതി." റീന തിരിച്ചടിച്ചു.

ഒരു ഏങ്ങലടി കേട്ടു. എല്ലാവരും നോക്കി. കളിയാക്കിയ കീർത്തി പൊട്ടിക്കരയുകയായിരുന്നു. മറ്റുള്ളവർ നിശ്ചലരായി നിന്നുപോയി. രവികുമാർ മുഖം കുനിച്ചുകളഞ്ഞു.

റീന കീർത്തിയുടെ തോളിലേക്ക് തല ചായ്ച്ചു. അവളുടെ കണ്ണുകൾ നിറഞ്ഞൊഴുകി.

സമനില തിരിച്ചുകിട്ടാൻ കുറച്ചുസമയം വേണ്ടിവന്നു. അവർ കണ്ണുകൾ തുടച്ചു. പിന്നെയും സംസാരിച്ചു.

വണ്ടി വന്നു. ആയിരം യാത്രാമൊഴികൾ. തുടച്ചിട്ടും തീരാത്ത കണ്ണുനീർ. സന്ധ്യാദേവി റീനയുടെ ശിരസിൽ ചുംബിച്ചു. അവരും വിവശയായിരുന്നു.

റീന ഉഷയോടു യാത്രപറഞ്ഞു. അവളും പ്രയാസമടക്കിപ്പിടിച്ചു നിൽക്കുകയായിരുന്നു.

വണ്ടി നീങ്ങിയപ്പോൾ ഫ്ളാറ്റ്ഫോറത്തിൽ ഒരു സംഘം പ്രതിമകൾ നിന്നു കൈവീശുന്നതുപോലിരുന്നു.

എട്ടുപത്തു ദിവസങ്ങൾ കഴിഞ്ഞു. അതിനിടയ്ക്ക് റീനയുടെ കത്തു വന്നു. അവർ മദ്രാസിൽ ഇറങ്ങി അരവിന്ദനെ കണ്ടു. അന്നുതന്നെ കൽക്കത്തയ്ക്ക് വണ്ടി കയറി സുഖമായി വന്നെത്തി. അവിടെ പുതിയ ഒരു ജീവിതം ആരംഭിച്ചിരിക്കുന്നു. രവിയേട്ടൻ ഇവിടെ ചെറുപ്പക്കാരുടെയിടയിലെ വലിയ രാഷ്ട്രീയ പ്രവർത്തകനാണ്. ദിവസവും സി ഐ ഡി പുറകേയുണ്ട്.

കീർത്തി മറ്റുള്ളവർക്കുവേണ്ടി അവൾക്ക് മറുപടി അയച്ചു.

സദനത്തിൽ വരുന്നവർ ഒരുചോദ്യം ചോദിക്കാൻ തുടങ്ങി. "നിങ്ങൾ ഇവിടെനിന്നു മാറുകയാണ് അല്ലേ?" സന്ധ്യാദേവി പല മറുപടികൾ പറയും ചിലർ ചോദിക്കും. "നിങ്ങളെ ഇറക്കി വിടാൻ പോകുന്നെന്ന് കേട്ടല്ലോ." അതിന് അവർ ഒരുപുഞ്ചിരികൊണ്ട് സമ്മാനം നൽകും. അവർ വീട്ടുടമസ്ഥനെ കണ്ടു. അയാൾ ക്ഷോഭിച്ചു സംസാരിച്ചു. സാവകാശം നൽകാൻ തയാറായില്ല. ഒടുവിൽ അവർ പറഞ്ഞു: "ഞങ്ങൾക്ക് ആറു മാസം കൂടി സമയം അനുവദിക്കണം. നിങ്ങൾ അത്രയുംകൂടി ദയ കാട്ടണം" അയാൾ വഴങ്ങിയില്ല.

അന്നുരാവിലെ ഒരു പൊലീസ് വാൻ സദനത്തിന്റെ മുൻപിൽ വന്നു നിന്നു. ഇൻസ്പെക്ടറും വലിയ ഒരു സംഘം പൊലീസുകാരും അതിൽനിന്നിറങ്ങി. അവർ മുറ്റത്തുനിന്നു. ഇൻസ്പെക്ടർ വരാന്തയിലേക്ക് കയറി. സന്ധ്യാദേവി അവിടെ നിൽപ്പുണ്ട്. ഇൻസ്പെക്ടർ പറഞ്ഞു.

"നിങ്ങളുടെ കൂടെ ഇവിടെ താമസിക്കുന്ന എല്ലാവരേയും വിളിക്കണം."

"എന്തിനാണു സാർ?" സന്ധ്യാദേവി ചോദിച്ചു.

"അത് വിശദീകരിക്കേണ്ട കാര്യം ഞങ്ങൾക്കില്ല. സർക്കാരിന്റെ കൽപ്പനയുമായി വന്നവരാണ് ഞങ്ങൾ. അവരെ വിളിക്കണം."

"കാര്യം എന്നോടു പറഞ്ഞുകൂടേ? ഞാൻ ഈ സ്ഥാപനത്തിന്റെ ചുമതലക്കാരിയാണ്."

"നിങ്ങൾ എന്തുമാകുന്നതിൽ ഞങ്ങൾക്കു വിരോധമില്ല. ബലം പ്രയോഗിക്കാതിരിക്കാൻ വേണ്ടിയാണ്. ഞാൻ മര്യാദ പറഞ്ഞത്. ഇല്ലെങ്കിൽ, ഞങ്ങൾ അവരെ കൊണ്ടുപോകും."

തർക്കിച്ചിട്ടു കാര്യമില്ല. അവർ അധികാരത്തിന്റെ പ്രതിനിധികളാണ്. രണ്ടുതവണ അതിന്റെ ഭീകരത നേരിട്ടു കണ്ടു. അനുഭവിച്ചു. പക്ഷേ, തന്റെ കുട്ടികളെ പിടിച്ചുകൊണ്ടു പോകുന്നത് എങ്ങനെകണ്ടുകൊണ്ടു നിൽക്കും? അവർ പറഞ്ഞു.

"സാർ നിങ്ങൾ അവരെ കൊണ്ടുപോകേണ്ട. എല്ലാറ്റിനും ഉത്തരവാദി ഞാനാണ്. എന്നെ കൊണ്ടുപോവുക. ദാ ഞാൻ തയാറാണ്."

ഇൻസ്പെക്ടർ അവരെ അടിമുടി നോക്കി.

"ആരെ കൊണ്ടുപോകണമെന്ന് തീരുമാനിക്കേണ്ടത് ഞങ്ങളല്ലേ? അതു നിങ്ങൾ ഉപദേശിച്ചുതരേണ്ട കാര്യമില്ല." അയാൾ നിലത്തു ചവിട്ടി. "ആകട്ടെ, അവരെ വിളിക്കുന്നോ ഞങ്ങൾ അകത്തുകടന്നുപിടിച്ചിറക്കണോ."

കീർത്തിയും മറ്റുള്ളവരും വാതിലിനു പിന്നിൽ എത്തിയിരുന്നു. മനസ്സ് തകർന്ന ജീവികളെ കണക്കു അവർ നിന്നു. അവർകരയാൻ പോലും മറന്നു നിൽക്കുകയാണ്.

സന്ധ്യാദേവി ആ വാതിൽക്കലേക്ക് ചെന്നു. അവരുടെ മുഖത്തു നോക്കാൻ സന്ധ്യാദേവിക്കു കഴിഞ്ഞില്ല.

"ഇറങ്ങ്. എന്താ നിൽക്കുന്നത്?" ഇൻസ്പെക്ടറുടെ ചോദ്യം.

വെറങ്ങലിച്ച നാലു മനുഷ്യപ്രതിമകൾ പുറത്തേക്കുവന്നു. ഇൻസ്പെക്ടർ ആംഗ്യം കാട്ടി. അവർ പുറത്തേക്കിറങ്ങി. ഇൻസ്പെക്ടറും ഇറങ്ങി. സന്ധ്യാദേവി പുറകെ ചെന്നു.

അവരെ വാനിലേക്ക് കയറ്റി. സന്ധ്യാദേവിയും കയറാൻ ഭാവിച്ചു. സദനം തുറന്നു കിടക്കുന്നു. ആരുമില്ല. അതെല്ലാം അവർക്ക് ഓർമയുണ്ട്. പക്ഷേ, ഇപ്പോൾ എല്ലാം നഷ്ടപ്പെട്ട നിലയിലാണ്. പിന്നെ സദനത്തിലെ സാധനങ്ങളെക്കുറിച്ച് ആലോചിച്ചു നടന്നിട്ട് കാര്യമെന്ത്?

ഇൻസ്പെക്ടർ തടഞ്ഞു:

"വേണ്ട നിങ്ങൾ തൽക്കാലം ഇവിടെ കാവലിരുന്നോളൂ. ഇവരെ ഞങ്ങൾ അവരുടെ വീടുകളിൽ കൊണ്ടുചെന്നാക്കാൻ പോകുന്നു. നിങ്ങൾ ആരോട് പരാതിപ്പെട്ടിട്ടും കാര്യമില്ല. അവരുടെ ഭദ്രതയെപ്പറ്റി നിങ്ങൾ വിഷമിക്കുകയും വേണ്ട, ഇതു സർക്കാരിന്റെ ആജ്ഞയാണ്."

വാനിന്റെ പിന്നിലെ കതകടച്ചു.

ഇൻസ്പെക്ടർ വണ്ടിയുടെ മുൻപിൽ കയറി. അത് ഇരമ്പി, അതിവേഗം പാഞ്ഞുപോയി.

സന്ധ്യാദേവി പ്രേതത്തെപ്പോലെ നോക്കി നിന്നു. പിന്നെ അവർ അകത്തേക്കു കടന്നു. വരാന്തയിൽക്കയറി അരത്തിണ്ണയിൽ ഇരുന്നു. വഴിയിൽ കുറച്ച് ആളുകൾ കാഴ്ചക്കാരായി കൂടിയിരുന്നു. അവർക്ക് പരിചയമുള്ളവരും ഇല്ലാത്തവരും. അവരെല്ലാം പതുക്കെ അങ്ങോട്ടുമിങ്ങോട്ടും പോയി. എല്ലാവർക്കും ഭയമാണ്. സംഗതി ചോദിക്കാൻ പോലും അവർക്കെല്ലാം ഭീതിയാണ്. തന്നോട് മിണ്ടിയാൽ സർക്കാരിന്റെ നോട്ടപ്പുള്ളികളാകാൻ സാധ്യതയുണ്ട്.

വളരെനേരം അങ്ങനെയിരുന്നു. എന്തു ചെയ്യണമെന്ന് അറിയില്ല. ഇറങ്ങിപ്പോകാൻ കാര്യമെന്ത്? പരാതിപ്പെടാൻ സ്ഥലമില്ല. സദനത്തിന്റെ സുഹൃത്തുക്കളായ നേതാക്കന്മാരോട് പറഞ്ഞാലോ? അതാണു നല്ലതെന്നു അവർ നിശ്ചയിച്ചു. എഴുന്നേറ്റു അകത്തുചെന്ന് താക്കോൽ എടു

ത്തുകൊണ്ടു വന്നു വീടു പൂട്ടി. ഇറങ്ങി ഗേറ്റിലെത്തി.

അപ്പോൾ ഒരു ജീപ്പുവന്നു. അതും പൊലീസിന്റേതാണ്. രണ്ടു പൊലീസുകാർ ഇറങ്ങി ജീപ്പുപോയി.

"നിങ്ങൾ എവിടെപ്പോകുന്നു?" അവർ ചോദിച്ചു.

"പുറത്തു പോകുന്നു. എന്തുവേണം?"

"പോകാൻ പാടില്ല."

"എന്ത്?"

"പോകാൻ പാടില്ല. നിങ്ങളെ വിടാതിരിക്കാനാണ് ഞങ്ങളെ അയച്ചിരിക്കുന്നത്."

ഇതൊരു പ്രഹരംപോലെ തോന്നി. ഒന്നും പറഞ്ഞില്ല. അവർ തിരിച്ച് വരാന്തയിലേക്കു കയറി. താക്കോലെടുത്ത് വാതിൽ തുറന്ന് അകത്തു കയറി വാതിലടച്ചു തഴുതിട്ടു. എന്നിട്ട് മുറിയിലെ കട്ടിലിൽ കിടന്നു.

ഒടുവിൽ താൻ ഏകാകിയായി. ആ വീട് വാടകയ്ക്കെടുത്ത്, ആദ്യമായി ഒരു സംഘം സ്ത്രീകളോടുകൂടി അവിടേക്കു കയറിവന്ന ദിവസം സന്ധ്യാദേവി ഓർമിച്ചു. ഒട്ടേറെ സ്വപ്നങ്ങളുമായിട്ടാണ് അന്ന് കടന്നുവന്നത്. ഒരു മഹത്തായ പ്രസ്ഥാനത്തിന്റെ ആരംഭം. അന്ന് ഉണ്ടായിരുന്നതിൽ അംബികത്തമ്പുരാട്ടിയും സുമതിയും മാത്രമേ ഇന്നുള്ളൂ. യോഗമയീദേവിയും ഉണ്ടായിരുന്നു. അവർ എന്നെന്നേക്കുമായി ഭൂമിയിൽ നിന്നു യാത്ര പറഞ്ഞു അഞ്ചുവർഷം പ്രവർത്തിച്ചു. ഇതിനിടയ്ക്ക് പലരും വന്നു പോയി. പോയവരെല്ലാം അവരുടെ സ്നേഹം പകർന്നിട്ടാണ് ഈ പടി കടന്നത്. എല്ലാവരും നല്ല നിലയിലേക്ക് തന്നെ പോയി. ഇവിടെ എന്തു ബഹളവും ചൈതന്യവുമായിരുന്നു. അടുത്തകാലത്താണ് അത് പോയിത്തുടങ്ങിയത്. ഇപ്പോൾ ഇതിനെ തകർക്കുവാനുള്ള ശ്രമങ്ങൾ പൂർത്തിയായിരിക്കുന്നു. ശാരീരികമായും മാനസികമായും നോവിച്ച്, ആത്മബലം നഷ്ടപ്പെടുത്തിയിരിക്കുന്നു. ഇന്ന്, ദാ, താൻ മാത്രം.. ഒരു കാൽപ്പെരുമാറ്റമില്ല. ഒരു സംസാരമില്ല. ആ കുട്ടികളെ എങ്ങോട്ടുകൊണ്ടുപോയി? ആ മനുഷ്യൻ പറഞ്ഞത് സത്യമാണോ? അവരെ ഭദ്രമായി അവരുടെ വീടുകളിലെത്തിക്കുമോ? ഉഷയെ എവിടെയാക്കും? അവൾക്ക് ഇവിടെ വീടില്ല. തൃശൂര് കൊണ്ടുചെന്നു വിടുമോ?

ഇത് ഏറ്റവും പുതിയ തന്ത്രമാണ്. തന്നെ ഒറ്റപ്പെടുത്തുക. അത് സാധിച്ചിരിക്കുന്നു. ഭാവിയിൽ നടക്കാവുന്നത് സന്ധ്യാദേവി കണ്ടു. ഇവിടെ കടന്നുവരാൻ ആളുകൾ മടിക്കും. ആരെങ്കിലും വരാൻ തയാറായാൽ അവരെ ഭീഷണിപ്പെടുത്തും.

അവർ ആലോചിച്ചാലോചിച്ച് തേങ്ങിക്കരഞ്ഞു. ആരും കേൾക്കാനില്ലാത്തതുകൊണ്ട് അടക്കിയില്ല. നിയന്ത്രണംവിട്ടു കരഞ്ഞു.

എത്രസമയം കഴിഞ്ഞുവെന്നറിയില്ല. എഴുന്നേറ്റ് പുറത്തെ ജനാലയിൽക്കൂടി നോക്കി. നേരം ഇരുട്ടി. മേശപ്പുറത്തിരുന്ന വാച്ചുനോക്കി. എട്ടുമണി. വീണ്ടും കിടന്നു. ഭീകരമായ ഒരു സ്വപ്നത്തിൽപ്പെട്ടിരിക്കുന്നതുപോലെ മയങ്ങുകയും ഞെട്ടി ഉണരുകയും ചെയ്യുന്നു.

മുൻവശത്ത് കാൽപ്പെരുമാറ്റം കേട്ടോ? ഉള്ളിൽ ഭയം തോന്നി. ഒറ്റയാണെന്നുള്ള ബോധം അപ്പോഴാണ് വന്നത്. എഴുന്നേറ്റിരുന്നു. ശ്രദ്ധിച്ചു ഒരു ശബ്ദവും കേട്ടില്ല. കിടന്നു.

അൽപ്പം കഴിഞ്ഞപ്പോൾ മുൻവശത്തെ വാതിലിൽ സാവധാനം മുട്ടുന്ന ശബ്ദം.

ആരാണ്? പൊലീസായിരിക്കുമോ? അന്നത്തെ അനുഭവങ്ങൾ ഓർമിച്ചു. ഞെട്ടിവിറച്ചുപോയി. യഥാർഥമായ ഭയം ഞരമ്പുകളിൽക്കൂടി അരിച്ചു കയറിക്കൊണ്ടിരിക്കുന്നു. ശരീരമാകെ വിറയ്ക്കുകയാണ്. എഴുന്നേറ്റിരുന്നു.

വീണ്ടും മുട്ടുന്ന ശബ്ദം.

ഇരിക്കാനുംവയ്യ. എഴുന്നേറ്റു ചെല്ലാനും വയ്യ. സന്ധ്യാദേവി മനസ്സു മുട്ടി ചോദിച്ചു പോയി. "ദൈവമേ ഞാൻ ഇത്രക്രൂരമായ അനുഭവങ്ങളുണ്ടാകാൻ എന്തു തെറ്റു ചെയ്തു?"

"കതക് തുറക്ക്.." പുറത്തു നിന്ന് ആരോ ആവശ്യപ്പെടുന്നു.

ധൈര്യം അവലംബിച്ചു വിളക്കുകൊളുത്തി. അതുമായി അങ്ങോട്ടു ചെന്നു വാതിലിന്റെ തഴുതെടുത്തു ഒരു പാളി തുറന്നു. രണ്ടുമൂന്നുപേർ നിൽക്കുന്നു.

പെട്ടെന്ന് അവരെ തള്ളിമാറ്റിക്കൊണ്ട് അവർ അകത്തു കയറി കതകടച്ചു തഴുതിട്ടു.

"നിങ്ങൾ പുറത്തേക്കുപോകണം." സന്ധ്യാദേവി ഉച്ചത്തിൽ വിളിച്ചു പറഞ്ഞു.

ഒരുത്തൻ വിളക്കു പിടിച്ചു പറിച്ച് ഊതിക്കെടുത്തി. എല്ലാം അതിവേഗം നടന്നു. അവരുടെ വായിൽ എന്തോ കയറുന്നു. തുണിയാണെന്ന് പിന്നെ മനസിലായി.

അനങ്ങാൻ നിവൃത്തിയില്ല. ഉരുക്കുപോലുള്ള പിടി.

ഒട്ടുനേരം കഴിഞ്ഞ്, അവർ ബോധരഹിതയായി.

ഇരുപത്

ദിവാകരൻ ഒരു ജോലിക്ക് പലയിടത്തും അന്വേഷിച്ചു. ബിസിനസ്സ് തുടങ്ങാനുള്ള യത്നങ്ങൾ പരാജയപ്പെട്ടപ്പോഴാണ് ജോലിയെപ്പറ്റി ആലോചിച്ചത്. ബുദ്ധിമുട്ടുകൾ നിത്യജീവിതത്തെ അള്ളിപ്പിടിച്ചുകൊണ്ടിരിക്കുമ്പോൾ അഭിമാനം നോക്കിയിട്ടു കാര്യമില്ല. അങ്ങനെയാണ് പലയിടത്തും ചെന്നുമുട്ടിയത്. മുമ്പ് തടിക്കച്ചവടം നടക്കുമ്പോൾ പരിചയമുള്ള അതേ ബിസിനസുകാരിൽ ചിലരെ കണ്ടു. അവർക്ക് സഹതാപമുണ്ട്. പക്ഷേ, എന്തു ജോലിയാണുള്ളത്? അയാൾക്ക് ചെയ്യാൻ തക്കവണ്ണമുള്ള ജോലി? പലദിവസങ്ങളിലും കടുത്ത നിരാശയോടെയാണ് വീട്ടിലേക്ക് മടങ്ങിയെത്തുക. അപ്പോൾ ചിരിച്ച മുഖവുമായി നിൽക്കുന്ന ഭാനുമതിയെക്കണ്ട്, അയാൾ സമാധാനിക്കും. ഒരു ദിവസം അയാൾ അവരോട് പറഞ്ഞു.

"ഭാനൂ എനിക്കു പണ്ടത്തെ കഥ ഓർമ വരുന്നു. രത്നമ്മയെ ഭാര്യ

യാക്കിക്കൊണ്ടുവന്ന എന്റെ ചങ്ങാതി ഇങ്ങനെയാണ് ജോലിയന്വേഷിച്ചു നടന്നത്. ഇപ്പോൾ എനിക്ക് ആ സ്ഥിതി വന്നിരിക്കുന്നു."

അയാളുടെ വേദന അവൾ മനസിലാക്കുന്നുണ്ട്. അവൾ പറഞ്ഞു.

"അങ്ങനെയൊക്കെ ആലോചിച്ച് വേദനിക്കരുത്."

പരിചയക്കാരുടെ ഇടയിൽ ദിവാകരനെപ്പറ്റി പെട്ടെന്ന് ഒരു സംശയവും അത്ഭുതവും ഉണ്ടായിട്ടുണ്ട്. ആ അറസ്റ്റും മോചനവുമാണ് അതിനടിസ്ഥാനം. വാസവമേനോന്റെ നിർദേശപ്രകാരം ദിവാകരൻ തന്റെ കാറുമായി ചെന്നു. സ്വാമി ശിവാനന്ദഭാരതിയെ കൂട്ടിക്കൊണ്ടുവന്നു. പല സ്ഥലങ്ങളിലും പോയി. പെരിന്തൽമണ്ണയിൽ വന്നപ്പോൾ മറ്റാളുകൾ അദ്ദേഹത്തെ സ്വീകരിച്ചുകൊണ്ടുപോയി. ദിവാകരൻ വീട്ടിലേക്ക് മടങ്ങി. സ്വാമിയെ ശ്രദ്ധിച്ച പൊലീസ് ദിവാകരനെയും ശ്രദ്ധിച്ചു. ദിവാകരൻ ഗവൺമെന്റിന്റെ ബന്ധുവാണ്. അങ്ങനെയാണ് അയാൾ അതുവരെ അറിയപ്പെടുന്നത്. പിന്നെ ഇതെങ്ങനെ സംഭവിച്ചു? സ്വാമിയുടെ സന്ദർശനവും വാസവമേനോനുമായി ബന്ധമുണ്ടെന്ന് പൊലീസിന് ഊഹമുണ്ട്. അങ്ങനെയാണ് ദിവാകരനെ കസ്റ്റഡിയിലെടുത്തു ചോദ്യം ചെയ്തത്. അയാൾ മറുപടികൾ പറഞ്ഞു രക്ഷപ്പെട്ടു.

പക്ഷേ, ആളുകൾ പറഞ്ഞു. ഈ ഒളിവിൽ നടക്കുന്നവരോട് ആർക്കൊക്കെയാണ് ബന്ധമെന്ന് ആർക്കറിയാം.

ദിവാകരൻ അൽപ്പം ദൂരെയെങ്ങോ പോയിരിക്കുകയാണ്. ഉച്ചയായപ്പോൾ ഒരു കാറ് വീട്ടുപടിക്കൽ വന്നുനിന്നു. ഉമ്മറത്ത് കിടന്ന ഭാനുമതി എഴുന്നേറ്റു നോക്കി. ഹരീന്ദ്രൻനായരാണ്.

ആ മനുഷ്യനെപ്പറ്റി അവളുടെ മനസിൽ ഒരകൽച്ചയാണ് ഇപ്പോഴും. അദ്ദേഹത്തെപ്പറ്റി ദിവാകരൻ പറഞ്ഞ കഥ ശരിയാണെന്ന് അവൾക്കു തോന്നിയിട്ടില്ല. അതുകൊണ്ട്, അങ്ങനെയൊരു ബന്ധത്തിൽ ഉണ്ടാകാവുന്ന മമത ഉദിച്ചിട്ടുമില്ല. പക്ഷേ, ആ ഒരു ദിവസം കണ്ടപ്പോൾ അദ്ദേഹത്തെപ്പറ്റി മതിപ്പു തോന്നി. ആ സംസാരം, പെരുമാറ്റം... അവസാനം നീ എന്നു വിളിച്ചപ്പോൾപോലും സ്നേഹമാണ് തോന്നിയത്. വെറുതെ അങ്ങനെ വിളിക്കുമോ?

ബഹുമാനപൂർവം സ്വീകരിച്ചു. കസാല വലിച്ചിട്ടു കൊടുത്തു. ഹരീന്ദ്രൻനായർ ഇരുന്നു. കുറെ നിമിഷത്തേക്ക് ഒന്നും മിണ്ടിയില്ല. പിന്നെ ചോദിച്ചു.

"ഇന്നും ദിവാകരൻ ഇല്ല അല്ലേ?"

"പുറത്തു പോയിരിക്കുകയാണ്."

"ഞാൻ വീണ്ടും വരുമെന്നു പ്രതീക്ഷിച്ചില്ല അല്ലേ?"

"വരികില്ലെന്ന് വിചാരിച്ചില്ല. കാരണം, വരുമെന്ന് ഒരു സൂചന തന്നിട്ടാണല്ലോ പോയത്."

"അതെ ജോലിത്തിരക്കുകൊണ്ടാണ് വരാത്തത്. ഇതിനിടയ്ക്ക് നിങ്ങൾക്ക് ഇങ്ങനെ ഒരു മാറ്റം വന്നുവെന്ന് അറിഞ്ഞു. അതൊന്നും ഓർമിച്ചു വിഷമിക്കേണ്ട. ജീവിതത്തിൽ അങ്ങനെ പലതും ഉണ്ടാവും.

എല്ലാറ്റിനേയും അഭിമുഖീകരിക്കണം."

അവൾ മൗനമായി നിന്നു.

"ഭാനുമതീ" അദ്ദേഹം തുടർന്നു: "അന്നു ഞാൻ സൂചിപ്പിച്ചത് മുഴുവൻ പറയാം. നീ എന്റെ സഹോദരി തന്നെയാണ്. ഇത് അവിടെ നാട്ടുകാർക്കറിയില്ല. ഞാനത് ഒരിക്കൽ ചോദിച്ചു. അപ്പോൾ അച്ഛൻ എന്നോട് ചില കാര്യങ്ങൾ പറഞ്ഞു. ജീവിതത്തിലൊരിക്കൽ അങ്ങനെ ഒരു തെറ്റു പറ്റി. അതിനു പ്രായശ്ചിത്തം ചെയ്യാൻ അച്ഛൻ തയാറായിരുന്നു. പക്ഷേ, നിന്റെ അമ്മ അങ്ങനെ യാതൊരു സൗജന്യവും സ്വീകരിക്കാൻ തയാറായിരുന്നില്ല. അങ്ങനെ നിന്നെയും കൊണ്ട് മറ്റൊരു നാട്ടിലേക്കു പോന്നു. അതൊക്കെ രഹസ്യമായിട്ടാണ് നടന്നത്. കുറെ പരസ്യമായി പോയെന്നു മാത്രം. അച്ഛൻ മരിക്കുവോളം ഞാൻ നിന്നെ കാണരുതെന്നും നീ എന്റെ സ്വന്തമാണെന്ന് ലോകത്തോടു പറയരുതെന്നും അദ്ദേഹം എന്നോടഭ്യർഥിച്ചു. ഞാൻ ആ വാക്കു പാലിച്ചു. അച്ഛൻ മരിച്ചു. നിന്നെ വന്നുകാണണമെന്ന് ആഗ്രഹിച്ചിരിക്കുമ്പോൾ ഈ വിവരത്തെപ്പറ്റി കേട്ടു."

ഭാനുമതി ആ കഥകേട്ട് അതിലുപരി അവൾ ആ മനുഷ്യനെ കാണുകയായിരുന്നു. ഉള്ളിൽ അദ്ദേഹത്തെപ്പറ്റി സ്നേഹം ഉടലെടുക്കുന്നതും അത് അവളെ ദുർബലയാക്കുന്നതും അവൾക്കനുഭവപ്പെട്ടു. അത് തന്റെ ചേട്ടനാണ്. ചേട്ടൻ.. തനിക്കു ആരുമില്ല. ആരുമില്ലാതെ വളർന്നു. ആരുമില്ലെന്ന വിശ്വാസത്തിൽത്തന്നെ ജീവിച്ചു. അനാഥയെന്ന് എല്ലാവരും കരുതി. ഇപ്പോൾ തനിക്കു ഒരാളുണ്ടായിരിക്കുന്നു. വെറും ആളല്ല. ഒരച്ഛന്റെ മകൻ.

"എന്റെ ചേട്ടൻ തന്നെയാണോ?" ഒരു കൊച്ചു കുഞ്ഞിനെപ്പോലെ അവൾ ചോദിച്ചുപോയി. അവളുടെ തൊണ്ട ഇടറി. ഇനി, ചേട്ടനല്ലെന്നു കേൾക്കരുതെന്ന അത്യുൽക്കടമായ വികാരം കൊണ്ട് ചോദിച്ചുപോയതുപോലെ.

"അതെ ഭാനു ഞാൻ എന്തിനു കെട്ടുകഥ ഉണ്ടാക്കണം?" അയാൾ ചോദിച്ചു. "നീ മറ്റൊന്നുകൂടി മനസിലാക്കണം. എനിക്ക് സഹോദരിമാരില്ല. ഒരു സഹോദരൻ മാത്രമേ ഉള്ളൂ. ആ സ്ഥിതിക്ക് എനിക്ക് നിന്നോട് എന്ത് സ്നേഹമുണ്ടായിരിക്കണമെന്ന് ആലോചിച്ചു നോക്കൂ. ഞാൻ നിന്നെ എന്റെ വീട്ടിലേക്ക് കൂട്ടിക്കൊണ്ടു പോകുമായിരുന്നു. പക്ഷേ, ഒരു കാര്യം തടസമായി നിന്നു. ദിവാകരന്റെ പേരിൽ ഒരു കേസുണ്ടായത് നിനക്കറിയില്ലേ?"

"അറിയാം. ഞാനുദ്ദേശിക്കുന്നത് തന്നെയല്ലേ?"

"അതെ. ആദ്യത്തെ ഭാര്യയെ സംബന്ധിച്ച കേസ്. ഇന്ന് അത് നിലവിലില്ല. വീണ്ടും അത് പൊന്തിവരുമായിരുന്നു. ഞാൻ രത്നമ്മയുടെ ആദ്യത്തെ ഭർത്താവായിരുന്ന മനുഷ്യനെ തേടിപ്പിടിച്ചു. അയാളെ കർശനമായി ചോദ്യം ചെയ്തു. ദിവാകരൻ തെറ്റുകാരനല്ലെന്നു മനസിലാക്കി. ചാർജ് ചെയ്തിട്ടില്ലായിരുന്ന ആ കേസിനെപ്പറ്റി ഇനി ഒന്നും വരാൻ പോകുന്നില്ല. ഒരു പൊലീസ് ഉദ്യോഗസ്ഥനെന്ന നിലയ്ക്ക് എന്റെ മനഃ

സാക്ഷിക്കൊപ്പിച്ച് അത്രയും ഞാൻ ചെയ്യേണ്ടിയിരുന്നു. ഇന്ന് നിന്നെ വിളിച്ചുകൊണ്ടു പോകുന്ന കാര്യത്തിൽ ഞാൻ സ്വതന്ത്രനാണ്. ദിവാകരന്റെ അഭിപ്രായമറിഞ്ഞേ എന്തെങ്കിലും ചെയ്യാവൂ. അയാൾ വരുമ്പോൾ ഈ കേസ് നിലനിൽക്കുന്നില്ലെന്നു പറയണം. ഞാൻ അയാളുടെ ശത്രുവല്ലെന്നു ധരിപ്പിക്കണം. പണമുണ്ടായപ്പോൾ അയാൾ കുറെ ധിക്കാരങ്ങൾ കാട്ടിയിട്ടുണ്ട്. മനഃപൂർവമല്ല. അതെനിക്കറിയാം. അയാൾ സാധുവാണ്. ദുർബലനായ ഒരു മനുഷ്യനെന്നേ ഞാൻ കാണുന്നുള്ളൂ."

ഭാനുമതിക്ക്, എത്രയോ നാളുകളായി അലട്ടിയിരുന്ന ഒരു ഭീഷണിയിൽനിന്നു പുറത്തുവന്നതായി തോന്നി. ദിവാകരൻ വന്നാടുലൻ ഇതറിയിക്കണം. ആ സാധു മനുഷ്യന് ജീവിതത്തിലെ ഏറ്റവും വലിയ ആശ്വാസം കൈവരും."

ഹരീന്ദ്രൻനായർ അരമണിക്കൂർ കൂടി ഇരുന്നു. എന്നിട്ടു പോയി. രണ്ടുവിലപ്പെട്ട ധനങ്ങൾ കിട്ടി. ആരുമില്ലാത്തവളായ തനിക്ക് ഒരു സഹോദരനുണ്ടായി. കുറ്റവാളിയെന്ന് എല്ലാവരും വിചാരിച്ചിട്ടുള്ള തന്റെ ഭർത്താവ് അതല്ലെന്നു വന്നു..

വൈകുന്നേരം വരെ കാത്തിരുന്നിട്ടും ദിവാകരൻ വന്നില്ല. അത്താഴം പാകം ചെയ്തു വീണ്ടും കാത്തിരുന്നു. രാത്രി വളരെ വൈകുംവരെ ഉറങ്ങിയില്ല. പക്ഷേ, അയാൾ വന്നില്ല.

പിറ്റേന്നു പകൽ മുഴുവനും കഴിഞ്ഞപ്പോൾ, അവൾ അസ്വസ്ഥയായി വീട്ടിനുചുറ്റും നടന്നു. ഇരുന്നും കിടന്നും ആ രാത്രിയും കടന്നുപോയി. മൂന്നാം ദിവസം അന്നും ദിവാകരൻ വന്നില്ല.

അയൽക്കാരോട് പറഞ്ഞു. അതുകൊണ്ട് എന്തുപ്രയോജനം? പട്ടണത്തിലേക്ക് പോകുന്ന ചിലർ അവിടെ അന്വേഷിക്കാമെന്നു മാത്രം പറഞ്ഞു. റോബർട്ട് വളരെ ദൂരെയാണ്. ആ മനുഷ്യനെ ഒന്നുകണ്ടിരുന്നെങ്കിൽ എന്നു വിചാരിച്ചു. പിന്നെയാണ് ഓർമ വന്നത്. തന്റെ ചേട്ടനോടു തന്നെ വിവരം പറയുക. ഒരിക്കലും അങ്ങനെ പറയാൻഒരാളില്ലാതിരുന്ന അവൾക്ക് അത് ഓർമിക്കുവാൻ അത്രയും സമയം വേണ്ടിവന്നു.

ഭാനുമതി പട്ടണത്തിലേക്കു നടന്നു. ഹരീന്ദ്രൻനായർ അന്നു പോകും മുമ്പ് ആ സ്ഥലം പറഞ്ഞു കൊടുത്തിരുന്നു. അങ്ങോട്ടു പോകേണ്ട. സ്റ്റേഷനിൽച്ചെന്ന് കണ്ടാൽ മതി. അതിനടുത്താണ് ആഫീസ്. അങ്ങോട്ട് കയറിച്ചെന്ന് പൊലീസുകാരോട് വിവരം പറഞ്ഞു.

ഹരീന്ദ്രൻനായർ പുറത്തേക്കു വന്നു. അയാളുടെ മുഖംവാടിയിരിന്നു. അവളെ കണ്ടപ്പോൾ ഒന്നുപകച്ചതുപോലെ ഉണ്ട്.

"ഭാനൂ.." അയാളുടെ ശബ്ദം പതറിയിരുന്നു.

"എന്താ.." അവളും ഹരീന്ദ്രൻ നായരുടെ ഭാവഭേദം കണ്ട് അങ്ങോട്ടൊന്നും പറയാതെ നിൽക്കുകയായിരുന്നു.

"നീ വിഷമിക്കരുത്. ദിവാകരൻ വിഷം കഴിച്ചു മരിച്ചു. ശവശരീരം ഇന്നാണ് ഒരു ഹോട്ടൽമുറിയിൽ നിന്നുകണ്ടെടുത്തത്. പോസ്റ്റ്മോർട്ടത്തിന് അയച്ചിരിക്കുന്നു. നിന്നെ വിളിക്കാൻ ഞാൻ പുറപ്പെടുകയായിരുന്നു."

അവൾക്ക് ആ ആഘാതം താങ്ങാൻ കഴിഞ്ഞില്ല. വീഴാൻ തുടങ്ങിയപ്പോൾ ഹരീന്ദ്രൻനായർ താങ്ങിപ്പിടിച്ച് സ്വന്തം മുറിയിൽ കൊണ്ടുചെന്നു കിടത്തി. മുഖത്തു വെള്ളം തളിച്ചു. മെല്ലെ ഉണർന്ന് തേങ്ങിക്കരഞ്ഞുകൊണ്ടു കിടന്നു.

ദിവാകരൻ ഹരീന്ദ്രൻ നായർക്ക് ഒരു കത്തെഴുതിവച്ചിട്ടാണ് മരിച്ചത്. ഹരീന്ദ്രൻ നായർ അത് വീണ്ടും എടുത്തു നോക്കി.

"ഭാനുവിനു കത്തെഴുതാൻ ധൈര്യമില്ലാത്തതുകൊണ്ടാണ് നിങ്ങൾക്കു എഴുതുന്നത്. നിങ്ങൾ അവളുടെ സഹോദരനാണെന്ന് എനിക്കറിയാം.

നല്ല നിലയിൽ ജീവിച്ചിട്ട് പിന്നീട് അപമാനവും അവഗണനയും സഹിച്ച് ഈ ഭൂമിയിൽ കഴിയേണ്ടെന്നുവച്ചാണ് ഞാൻ ഈ ക്രൂരമായ കൃത്യം ചെയ്യുന്നത്. ജീവിതത്തിൽ ഞാൻ ഒരാളോടാണ് തെറ്റു ചെയ്തത്. ഭാനുവിനോട്. അതിന് ആരും തെറ്റുകാരല്ല, ഞാൻ മാത്രം തെറ്റുകാരനാണ്.

ഈ വാർത്ത അറിയുമ്പോൾ അവിവേകമൊന്നും കാണിക്കാതെ അവളെ കാത്തുസൂക്ഷിക്കണം. അതാണ് എന്റെ ആത്മാവിന് ശാന്തികിട്ടാനുള്ള ഏകമാർഗം.

അവൾ ജീവിക്കണം. ഒരു സഹോദരന്റെ ലാളനമെങ്കിലും അവൾക്കു കിട്ടുമല്ലോ എന്ന സമാധാനത്തോടെയാണ് ഞാൻ പോകുന്നത്.

ഒരു കാര്യം നിങ്ങളെ ഈ അവസരത്തിൽ ഞാൻ അറിയിച്ചു കൊള്ളട്ടെ. നിങ്ങൾ അതു വിശ്വസിക്കണം. ഞാൻ രത്നമ്മയെ കൊന്നില്ല. അവൾ ആത്മഹത്യ ചെയ്തതാണ്. ഇനി എനിക്കു കേസിനെ ഭയപ്പെടേണ്ടല്ലോ. നിങ്ങളോട് സത്യം അറിയിക്കാൻവേണ്ടി പറഞ്ഞതാണ്.

സ്വന്തം, ദിവാകരൻ"

ദിവാകരന്റെ ജഡം കൊണ്ടുവന്നപ്പോൾ ഭാനുമതി അതിൽ കെട്ടിപ്പിടിച്ചുകിടന്നു കരഞ്ഞു. അഴുകിത്തുടങ്ങിയ മൃതദേഹം പൊതുസ്ഥലത്ത് അതു ദഹിപ്പിച്ചു.

അന്നു രാത്രിയിൽ ഭാനുമതിയെ ഹരീന്ദ്രൻനായരുടെ വീട്ടിലേക്ക് കൂട്ടിക്കൊണ്ടുപോയി.

ഇരുപത്തിഒന്ന്

രണ്ടു മാസമായി ഒരിടത്തുനിന്നും ഒരു വിവരവും അറിഞ്ഞില്ല. അരവിന്ദൻ സന്ധ്യാദേവിക്കയച്ച കത്തുകൾക്കു മറുപടിയില്ല. വാസവമേനോൻ കൽക്കത്ത തുടങ്ങിയ പ്രദേശങ്ങളിലേക്കു പോയിട്ട് മടങ്ങിവന്നില്ല. പത്രത്തെ സംബന്ധിച്ച കേസു നിലവിലുണ്ടെന്നും വാറണ്ട് പിൻവലിച്ചിട്ടില്ലെന്നും രവികുമാറിന്റെ അന്വേഷണത്തിൽ അറിഞ്ഞിട്ടുണ്ട്. എന്നാലും നാട്ടിലേക്ക് ഒന്നു പോകണമെന്ന് അരവിന്ദൻ ആഗ്രഹിച്ചു. ഒളിവിലുള്ള ഒരു യാത്ര അതാണ് മനസിൽ കണ്ടത്.

നാടുമായുള്ള ബന്ധങ്ങൾ അറ്റുപോയതുപോലെയാണ്. സദന

ത്തിൽനിന്നോ ഭാനുമതിയിൽനിന്നോ ശബ്ദമൊന്നും കേട്ടില്ലെങ്കിൽ, തന്നെ സംബന്ധിച്ചിടത്തോളം നാട് മൂകമായ ഒരു പ്രദേശമാണ്. തന്നെ സ്നേഹിക്കുന്ന അനേകായിരം മനുഷ്യർ അവിടെയുണ്ട്. മുഖരായ അറിഞ്ഞുകൂടാത്ത സുഹൃത്തുക്കൾ. ദേശീയ പ്രസ്ഥാനത്തിൽപ്പെട്ട സഹപ്രവർത്തകരുണ്ട്. അവരുമായും ഇന്നു ബന്ധമൊന്നുമില്ല. താൻ മദ്രാസിൽ ഉണ്ടെന്ന് അവരിൽ കുറേപ്പേർക്കറിയാം. അത്രതന്നെ. അവർ 'വന്ദേമാതരം' വാങ്ങുന്നുണ്ടെന്നു മാത്രം മനസിലായിട്ടുണ്ട്.

നാട്ടിലേക്കു തിരിക്കാൻ തീരുമാനിച്ചു മേനോനെ അറിയിച്ചു. അദ്ദേഹത്തിനു സന്തോഷം തന്നെ. മേനോൻ ഒരു ഫലിതം മാത്രംപറഞ്ഞു. "അങ്ങോട്ടു പോകാൻ ഇതുവരെ തിടുക്കം കാട്ടാഞ്ഞതിൽ ഞാൻ അത്ഭുതപ്പെട്ടിരിക്കുകയാണ്. ഇനിയും വൈകിക്കേണ്ട." മേനോന് വാറണ്ടും അറസ്റ്റും കേസുമൊക്കെ വലിയ കാര്യങ്ങളല്ല. അതെല്ലാം ധാരാളം കഴിഞ്ഞിട്ടാണ് അദ്ദേഹം കമ്പനി ഉദ്യോഗസ്ഥനായത്. രാജിവച്ചു പത്രം തുടങ്ങുമ്പോൾ പഴയ അനുഭവങ്ങളൊക്കെ വീണ്ടും സ്വീകരിക്കാൻ തയാറായിരുന്നു താനും.

യാത്രയ്ക്കു നിശ്ചയിച്ച ദിവസം രാവിലെ ഒരാൾ വന്നു. മാന്യനായ ഒരു മധ്യവയസ്കൻ. പരിചയമില്ല. കണ്ടിട്ടില്ല. തന്റെ മുറിയിൽ അദ്ദേഹത്തെ സ്വീകരിച്ചു. വളരെ ഒതുക്കി, വിനയം ദ്യോതിപ്പിക്കുന്ന ശബ്ദത്തിൽ സംസാരിക്കുന്ന ആ മനുഷ്യൻ തന്നെ സ്വയം പരിചയപ്പെടുത്തി.

"ഞാൻ ഒരു പൊലീസ് ഉദ്യോഗസ്ഥനാണ്, തിരുവിതാംകൂറിൽ നിന്നാണ് വരുന്നത്. എന്നെ മനസിലാക്കാൻ ഒരു മാർഗം പറയാം. ഒരിക്കൽ പത്രം ആഫീസിൽ നിന്നു മടങ്ങി വന്ന നിങ്ങളുടെ പുറകേ ഞാൻ വന്നിരുന്നു. പല ദിവസവും അങ്ങനെ വന്നിരുന്നു. അജ്ഞാതനായ ഒരു സ്നേഹിതൻ എന്ന നിലയ്ക്ക് ഞാൻ നിങ്ങൾക്ക് ഒരു കത്തയച്ചിരുന്നു. ഓർക്കുന്നോ?"

ഒട്ടും ആലോചിക്കേണ്ടിവന്നില്ല. ആ മനുഷ്യൻ ആരെന്ന് മനസ്സുകൊണ്ട് അനേകകാലം അന്വേഷിച്ചു. ഒരെത്തും കിട്ടിയില്ല. സംശയിച്ചിട്ടു കാര്യമില്ല. ആ മനുഷ്യൻ ഇദ്ദേഹം തന്നെയാവണം പൊലീസ് ഉദ്യോഗസ്ഥനെന്ന് നേരത്തെ പറയുകയും ചെയ്തിരിക്കുന്നു.

"കണ്ടതിൽ സന്തോഷം... ഞാൻ നിങ്ങളെ കുറേക്കാലം തേടി നടന്നിരുന്നു. പിന്നെ ആ അന്വേഷണം ഉപേക്ഷിച്ചു."

ആ മനുഷ്യൻ തുടർന്നു പറഞ്ഞു:

"മിസ്റ്റർ അരവിന്ദൻ, ഇപ്പോഴും എന്റെ ഐഡന്റിറ്റി വെളുപ്പെടുത്തണമെന്ന് ഞാൻ വിചാരിച്ചിരുന്നതല്ല. രണ്ടു കാരണങ്ങളാൽ അത് ചെയ്യാമെന്നുവച്ചു. ഒന്നാമത്, അത്യാവശ്യമാണെന്നു തോന്നി. രണ്ടാമത് മറുനാട്ടിൽവച്ച് നിങ്ങളെപ്പോലെയൊരാളോട് ആൾമാറാട്ടം കാട്ടിപ്പോകാൻ എനിക്ക് മനസ്സു വന്നില്ല. അദ്ദേഹം ചിരിച്ചു. വീണ്ടും സംസാരിച്ചു. മി. ഹരീന്ദ്രൻനായർ എന്റെ സീനിയർ ആഫീസറായിരുന്ന ആളാണ്. അദ്ദേഹം നിങ്ങളുടെ നാട്ടുകാരനാണ്. അറിയാമല്ലോ? അദ്ദേഹമാണ്

ആദ്യം നിങ്ങളെ സദനത്തിനടുത്തുവച്ച് എന്നെ കാട്ടിത്തന്നത്. നിങ്ങൾ അന്ന് ഞങ്ങളെ കണ്ടില്ല. നേരത്തെതന്നെ എനിക്ക് ബഹുമാനമുള്ള ഒരു കവിയെ നേരിട്ട് കാണാൻ കഴിഞ്ഞതിൽ ഞാൻ സന്തോഷിച്ചു. നിങ്ങളെപ്പറ്റി താൽപ്പര്യപൂർവം സംസാരിച്ചതും നിങ്ങളെ ഞങ്ങളുടെ പരിധിയിൽ നിന്നുകൊണ്ട് കാത്തുസൂക്ഷിക്കണമെന്ന് ആവശ്യപ്പെട്ടതും മിസ്റ്റർ ഹരീന്ദ്രൻനായരാണ്. ഞാൻ ആ കത്തിൽ സൂചിപ്പിച്ചിരുന്നതും അദ്ദേഹത്തെപ്പറ്റിത്തന്നെ. ഇന്ന് നമ്മുടെ സദനം അവിടെയില്ല. അറിഞ്ഞോ?"

അരവിന്ദൻ അതുകേട്ട് മനസൊന്നു പകച്ചു.

"എന്ത്? എന്തു സംഭവിച്ചു?"

"അറിഞ്ഞില്ല, അല്ലേ?"

"ഇല്ല."

"രണ്ടിലധികം മാസങ്ങൾക്കുമുമ്പ് ഞങ്ങളുടെ ആൾക്കാർ സർക്കാരിന്റെ പരോക്ഷമായ നിർദേശപ്രകാരം സദനത്തിൽ ഒരാക്രമണം നടത്തി. എന്നുവച്ചാൽ അന്തേവാസികളെയൊക്കെ ബലമായി അവരുടെ വീടുകളിൽ കൊണ്ടുചെന്നാക്കി. സന്ധ്യാദേവി എവിടെയാണെന്ന് ഇപ്പോൾ ആർക്കുമറിഞ്ഞുകൂടാ. അവരെപ്പറ്റി അന്വേഷിക്കാൻപോലും ആളുകൾക്കെല്ലാം ഭയമാണ്. അതു സ്വാഭാവികമാണല്ലോ. ആ സദനം, ഉടമസ്ഥൻ പൊളിച്ചു കളഞ്ഞു. അവിടെ ഒരു പുതിയ കെട്ടിത്തിന്റെ പണി ആരംഭിച്ചിരിക്കുന്നു."

അരവിന്ദൻ നിശ്ശബ്ദനായി കുറച്ചു നേരമിരുന്നു. മനസ്സ് മറിഞ്ഞുകൊണ്ടിരുന്നു. സമനിലയ്ക്കുവേണ്ടി ശ്രമിച്ചു. ഒരു കുറ്റബോധം പതഞ്ഞുപൊന്തുന്നു. താൻ രക്ഷപ്പെട്ടു മറ്റൊരിടത്തേക്കു പോരുകയായിരുന്നു എന്നൊരു തോന്നൽ. സ്നേഹിച്ചവരെപ്പറ്റി ആലോചിച്ചില്ല. അവരുടെ ആപത്തുകളിൽ കൂടെ നിൽക്കാൻ കഴിഞ്ഞില്ല. സദനം തന്റെ കുടുംബം പോലായിരുന്നു. അതിൽ നായികയായ സ്ത്രീ തനിക്ക് ജീവസർവസ്വവുമായിരുന്നു. എന്നിട്ടും അവരെ കൈവിട്ടുപോന്നതുപോലല്ലേ താൻ പെരുമാറിയത്?

സദനത്തിന്റെ ചിത്രം തെളിഞ്ഞുവന്നു. തിരക്കിട്ട പ്രവർത്തനങ്ങൾക്ക് കേന്ദ്രമായിരുന്നു ഭവനം. എല്ലാവരും സഹോദരങ്ങളെപ്പോലെ കഴിഞ്ഞു. എപ്പോഴും സന്തോഷമുള്ള അന്തരീക്ഷം പ്രയാസങ്ങൾ വരുമ്പോൾ, എല്ലാവരും അത് പങ്കിട്ടെടുത്തിരുന്നു. ആത്മാർഥതയും ഐക്യവും കൊണ്ടുമാത്രം ചൈതന്യത്തോടെ ജീവിച്ച ആ ഭവനം ഇല്ലാതായി. ആ ചുമരുകളും വാതിലും എല്ലാം അന്തർധാനം ചെയ്തിരിക്കുന്നു. അവിടെ പുതിയ കെട്ടിടം തല ഉയർത്താൻ പോകുന്നു.

ആത്മാവിൽ അഗാധമായ വിഷാദം ബാധിച്ചു. ഇനി അങ്ങോട്ട് പോയിട്ടെന്തു കാര്യം?

"ഞാൻ നാട്ടിലേക്ക് പുറപ്പെടാൻ തീരുമാനിച്ചിരിക്കുകയായിരുന്നു." അരവിന്ദൻ അറിയിച്ചു: "സദനത്തിൽ പോവുകയായിരുന്നു. പ്രധാന ഉദ്ദേശ്യം. ഇനി അതിനർഥമില്ല. സന്ധ്യാദേവി എവിടെയെന്ന് ആർക്കും ഊഹമില്ലോ?"

"ഇല്ല, മിസ്റ്റർ അരവിന്ദൻ. അദ്ദേഹം പറഞ്ഞു: അവരെ ഗുണ്ടകൾ കൊന്നുവെന്ന് ആദ്യം കേട്ടിരുന്നു. അതു സംബന്ധിച്ച് ഞങ്ങൾക്ക് പരാതികൾ കിട്ടി. ബഹുജനങ്ങൾതന്നെ സമർപ്പിച്ച പരാതികൾ. പക്ഷേ, ശരിയായ അന്വേഷണം നടന്നില്ല. അങ്ങനെ അന്വേഷണം വേണ്ടെന്നായിരുന്നു മുകളിൽ നിന്ന് പരോക്ഷമായി കിട്ടിയ നിർദേശം. അത് അതുപോലെ തേഞ്ഞുമറഞ്ഞുപോവുകയും ചെയ്തു.

മറന്നുപോയ ഒരു കാര്യം ചോദിച്ചു:

"നിങ്ങളുടെ പേര്?"

"സദാനന്ദൻ."

നിമിഷങ്ങൾക്കുശേഷം മുഖമുയർത്തി സദാനന്ദനെ നോക്കി.

"മി. സദാനന്ദൻ നിങ്ങൾ എന്നെ സഹായിക്കുമോ? നിങ്ങൾ ഒരു പൊലീസ് ഓഫീസറാണ്. കൃത്യമായി പറഞ്ഞാൽ ഞാൻ അധികാരമുള്ള പ്രദേശത്തെ പിടികിട്ടാത്ത ഒരു പ്രതിയുമാണ്. എങ്കിലും നിങ്ങൾ കുറെ മനുഷ്യത്വം കാട്ടി. അതിന്റെ പേരിലാണ് ചോദിക്കുന്നത്. നിങ്ങൾ എന്നെ ഒന്നു സഹായിക്കുമോ?"

"എന്താണ് പറയൂ."

"ആ സ്ത്രീയെ എങ്ങനെയും തേടിപ്പിടിച്ചേ തീരൂ. അവരെ കണ്ടെത്താൻ കഴിഞ്ഞില്ലെങ്കിൽ, എന്റെ ജീവിതത്തിൽ ഒരു സ്വസ്ഥതയും കിട്ടുകയില്ല."

"ഞാനതു മനസിലാക്കുന്നു. പക്ഷേ..."

"എന്താണ് സംശയിക്കുന്നത്?"

"ഞാൻ വിശ്വസിക്കുന്നതു പറയട്ടെ? നിങ്ങൾ വിഷമിക്കരുത്."

"പറയൂ."

"ആ സ്ത്രീ ജീവിച്ചിരിക്കുന്നില്ല."

"പൊടുന്നനെ പ്രകാശം മങ്ങിയ മുഖം കുനിച്ചുകളഞ്ഞു. ഇതു സത്യമെങ്കിൽ തന്റെ മുൻപിൽ നിത്യദുഃഖത്തിന്റെ ഒരു കറുത്ത ലോകം തുറക്കപ്പെടുകയാണ്."

"എനിക്കു വിശ്വസിക്കാൻ കഴിയുന്നില്ല. മിസ്റ്റർ സദാനന്ദൻ."

"അതു സത്യമാകാതിരിക്കാൻ ഞാനും പ്രാർഥിക്കുകയാണ്."

രണ്ടുപേരും മൗനത്തിൽ മുഴുകിയിരുന്നപ്പോൾ അവർ പുതിയ അന്വേഷണം ആരംഭിച്ചു കഴിഞ്ഞിരുന്നു. മരണത്തെപ്പറ്റി പറഞ്ഞതും കേട്ടതും രണ്ടുപേരും മായ്ച്ചുകളയാൻ ശ്രമിക്കുകയായിരുന്നു. റെയിൽവേസ്റ്റേഷനുകൾ, നിരത്തുകൾ, കടൽത്തീരങ്ങൾ, കാടുകൾ... രണ്ടു മനസുകൾ അവിടെയെല്ലാം സഞ്ചരിക്കുന്നു. ആ സ്ത്രീ ലോകത്തോട് അന്ത്യയാത്ര പറഞ്ഞുവെന്നു വിശ്വസിക്കാൻ തോന്നുന്നില്ല.

മദ്രാസിലേക്കുള്ള തന്റെ വരവിന്റെ ഉദ്ദേശ്യം സദാനന്ദൻ പറഞ്ഞു. അത് അരവിന്ദനെ ഒരിക്കൽക്കൂടി ഞെട്ടിച്ചു. ദിവാകരൻ ആത്മഹത്യ ചെയ്തത് അപ്പോഴാണറിയുന്നത്. ഭാനുമതി, ഹരീന്ദ്രൻനായരുടെ അച്ഛന്റെ മകളാണ്. കുറച്ചുനേരം ഇരുന്നാലോചിച്ചുപോയി. അത്ഭുത

മൊന്നും തോന്നിയില്ല. തനിക്ക് അറിഞ്ഞുകൂടാത്ത കാര്യങ്ങൾ എന്തിന് അത്ഭുതങ്ങളായി കരുതണം?

"ഭാനുമതി, ഹരീന്ദ്രൻനായരുടെ കൂടെ ആയിരുന്നു. പക്ഷേ, ഏതാനും ആഴ്ചകളേ അവിടെ കഴിഞ്ഞുകൂടിയുള്ളൂ. അവർ സമാധാനം നഷ്ടപ്പെട്ട സ്ത്രീയാണല്ലോ. അവിടെനിന്ന് അദ്ദേഹത്തോട് പറയാതെ ഇറങ്ങിപ്പോയി. സദനത്തിലേക്ക് ചെന്നതായി അറിവുണ്ട്. അവിടെ ആരുമില്ല. സദനവുമില്ല. പിന്നെ എങ്ങോട്ട് പോയെന്നറിയില്ല. ഞങ്ങൾ അന്വേഷിച്ചു. മദ്രാസിലേക്ക് പോന്നതായിട്ടാണ് മനസിലായത്. ഇവിടെ നിങ്ങളെ വന്നു കാണാനാണ് സാധ്യതയെന്ന് ഹരീന്ദ്രൻനായർ എന്നെ അറിയിച്ചു. അദ്ദേഹത്തിന് സംസ്ഥാനം വിട്ടുപോകാൻ നിർവാഹമില്ല. അതുകൊണ്ട് ഞാൻ പോന്നതാണ്.

ഒരു സംഘം മനുഷ്യർ അനാഥരായിപ്പോയ ചിത്രമാണ് മനസിൽ ഉദിച്ചത്. അതിലും പ്രത്യേകിച്ചൊന്നും തോന്നിയില്ല. ഒരു പ്രത്യേക ലക്ഷ്യംവച്ചു ജീവിച്ച കുറേപ്പേർ അതിന്റെ വേദനയിലും കഷ്ടപ്പാടിലും വീണിരിക്കുന്നു. ഭാനുമതിയും അതിലൊരു കഥാപാത്രമാണ്. പക്ഷേ, അവരെന്തിന് മദ്രാസിലേക്കു പോന്നു? ആ വാർത്ത ശരിയാണോ?

"മദ്രാസിലേക്ക് പോന്നുവെന്നു എങ്ങനെയറിയാം."

"അവർ അങ്ങോട്ടുള്ള തീവണ്ടിയിൽ യാത്രചെയ്തത് കണ്ടവരുണ്ട്."

"എന്ന്?"

"നാലഞ്ചു ദിവസങ്ങളായിരിക്കുന്നു."അപ്പോൾ ഒരു ഉൽക്കണ്ഠ തോന്നി. പരിചയമില്ലാത്ത ഈ നഗരത്തിൽ വന്നിറങ്ങിയിട്ട്, അവർ എങ്ങോട്ടു പോയിരിക്കും? പലവിധത്തിലുള്ള ആപത്തുകൾ ഒളിച്ചിരിക്കുന്ന നഗരം...

അരവിന്ദന്റെ ഉൽക്കണ്ഠ മനസിലാക്കി സദാനന്ദൻ പറഞ്ഞു.

"അതേ, മിസ്റ്റർ അരവിന്ദൻ. അവർ എവിടെ പോയിയെന്നു ഞാനും ആലോചിക്കുകയായിരുന്നു. ഇവിടെയില്ലെന്ന് ചോദിക്കാതെതന്നെ എന്തുകൊണ്ടോ എനിക്കു തോന്നി."

പരസ്പരം പിന്നെ അധികമൊന്നും പറയാനില്ല. പിടികിട്ടാത്ത കുറേ കാര്യങ്ങളുമായി രണ്ടുപേർ മുഖത്തോടു മുഖം നോക്കി ഇരുന്നു. സദാനന്ദന് മദ്രാസിൽ പാർത്ത് അന്വേഷണം തുടരാനും ബുദ്ധിമുട്ടുണ്ട്. നാട്ടിൽ ചൂടു നിറഞ്ഞ അന്തരീക്ഷമാണ്. പൊലീസ് ഉദ്യോഗസ്ഥന്മാർക്ക് ഉറങ്ങാൻ പോലും അധികാരികൾ നേരം കൊടുക്കുന്നില്ല. നഗരത്തിലെ പൊലീസ് സ്റ്റേഷനുകളിൽ വിവരമറിയിക്കുകയാണ് ഇനി ചെയ്യാവുന്നത്. അവർ ഒരുപക്ഷേ, ഭാനുമതിയെ കണ്ടുപിടിച്ചേക്കും.

പത്രമാപ്പീസിലെ അത്യാവശ്യജോലികൾ ചെയ്തു തീർത്തു. മേനോനെ വിവരം ധരിപ്പിച്ചു. എന്നിട്ട് അരവിന്ദനും പുറത്തിറങ്ങി.

ഒരുമിച്ച് ആഹാരം കഴിച്ചു. ഒരിക്കൽക്കൂടി ആലോചിച്ചു. പൊലീസിൽ അറിയിക്കണോ?

അല്ലാതെ മറ്റെന്തു മാർഗം?

ഒരുവാടകവണ്ടിയെടുത്ത്, അവർ നഗരത്തിലെ പൊലീസ് അധികാരികളുടെ ആസ്ഥാനത്തെത്തി. അധികാരി അവരെ അകത്തേക്കു വിളി ച്ചു. തിരുവിതാംകൂറിൽ നിന്നുവന്ന പൊലീസ് ഉദ്യോഗസ്ഥനെന്ന നിലയ്ക്ക് സദാനന്ദനെ താൽപ്പര്യപൂർവം സ്വീകരിച്ചു. വിവരങ്ങൾചോദിച്ചു. സദാനന്ദൻ ഭാനുമതിയെക്കുറിച്ച് എല്ലാ രേഖകളും പറഞ്ഞു കേൾപ്പിച്ചു. അവളുടെ രൂപവും നിറവും ശബ്ദവും എല്ലാം വിശദീകരിച്ചുകൊടുത്തു.

"ഈ മനുഷ്യൻ?" അരവിന്ദനെപ്പറ്റി അധികാരി തിരക്കി.

"എന്റെ ഒരു സ്നേഹിതനാണ്."

കൂടുതലൊന്നും അദ്ദേഹം ചോദിച്ചില്ല.

ആ സംഭാഷണത്തിനിടയ്ക്ക് മറ്റൊരു ഓഫീസർ കയറിവന്നു. അധികാരിയും അയാളും തമ്മിൽ ഇംഗ്ലീഷിൽ സംസാരിച്ചു, അവരുടെ ഔദ്യോഗികകാര്യങ്ങൾ. അയാൾ അരവിന്ദനെ സൂക്ഷിച്ചുനോക്കി. വീണ്ടും വീണ്ടും അയാളുടെ കണ്ണുകൾ അരവിന്ദനിലേക്ക് ചെല്ലുകയും നിമിഷങ്ങൾക്കുശേഷം പിൻവലിക്കുകയും ചെയ്യുന്നു. അൽപ്പനേരത്തെ സംസാരത്തിനുശേഷം അയാൾ പുറത്തേക്കുപോയി. അയാൾ കാട്ടിയ ആ ശ്രദ്ധ അരവിന്ദൻ കണ്ടില്ല. പൊലീസ് അധികാരി അത് ശ്രദ്ധിച്ചു.

"ശരി മിസ്റ്റർ സദാനന്ദൻ ഞാൻ ഇപ്പോൾതന്നെ എല്ലാ സ്റ്റേഷനിലും അലർട്ടു ചെയ്യുന്നുണ്ട്. മദ്രാസ് നഗരത്തിൽ ആ സ്ത്രീ ഉണ്ടെങ്കിൽ തേടിപ്പിടിക്കുകതന്നെ ചെയ്യും. അദ്ദേഹം പുഞ്ചിരിച്ചിട്ട് പറഞ്ഞു: "ഞങ്ങൾ മദ്രാസ് പൊലീസുകാർ എഫിഷ്യന്റാണ്. അത് ഞങ്ങൾ അവകാശപ്പെടുന്നു. നിങ്ങളുടെ സംസ്ഥാനത്തെ പൊലീസ് മോശമാണെന്ന് ഇതിൽ സൂചനയില്ല. ഞങ്ങൾ വളരെ കരുതലോടെ പ്രവർത്തിക്കുന്നു എന്നു മാത്രമേ പറയുന്നുള്ളൂ."

അവർ യാത്ര പറഞ്ഞ് ഇറങ്ങി.

അന്നു വൈകുന്നേരത്തെ വണ്ടിക്ക് നാട്ടിലേക്കു മടങ്ങാനാണ് സദാനന്ദൻ തീരുമാനിച്ചത്. ഇവിടെ നിന്നിട്ടു കാര്യമില്ല. ഇനി അതിന്റെ ആവശ്യവുമില്ല. ഭാനുവിനെപ്പറ്റി എന്തെങ്കിലും അറിവു കിട്ടിയാൽ പൊലീസ് അധികാരികൾ ഉടനെതന്നെ അതറിയിക്കും. കൂടാതെ അരവിന്ദൻ ഇവിടെയുണ്ട്. അയാൾ പൊലീസുകാരുമായി അടുത്തു പെരുമാറേണ്ടെന്ന് സദാനന്ദൻ ഉപദേശിച്ചു. തിരുവിതാംകൂറിൽ ഒരു കേസു കിടപ്പുണ്ട്. മലബാർ മദ്രാസിന്റെ കീഴിലാണ്. മലബാറും തിരുവിതാംകൂറും തമ്മിൽ രാഷ്ട്രീയ പ്രവർത്തകരുടെ കാര്യത്തിൽ അധികാരികൾ സമ്പർക്കം പുലർത്തുന്നുമുണ്ട്. അതൊക്കെ അപകടങ്ങളുണ്ടാക്കും. അതുകൊണ്ട് കരുതി കഴിയണമെന്നു പ്രത്യേകം ഓർമിപ്പിച്ചു.

സന്ധ്യ കഴിഞ്ഞ് നാട്ടിലേക്കു പുറപ്പെടുന്ന വണ്ടിയിൽ സദാനന്ദൻ മടങ്ങി. അരവിന്ദൻ റയിൽവേസ്റ്റേഷനിൽച്ചെന്ന് യാത്രയയച്ചു.

മറീനാ കടൽപ്പുറത്ത് സന്ധ്യാകാലത്ത് തിരക്കാണ്. അരവിന്ദൻ ഒരറ്റത്ത് മാറി ഇരുന്നു. കടൽ ഇരുണ്ട് കിടക്കുന്നു. അൽപ്പം കഴിഞ്ഞപ്പോൾ ചന്ദ്രൻ സാവധാനം ചക്രവാളത്തിലേക്ക് ഉയർന്നുവന്നു. കടൽപ്പുറത്ത്

ആ ആകാശദീപത്തിന്റെ ഹൃദയസ്പർശിയായ പ്രകാശം പരക്കുന്നു. തീരത്തിൽ വന്നലയ്ക്കുന്ന തിരകളുടെ ശബ്ദം ശാന്തമായ ഒരു ഗീതം പോലെയാണ് അനുഭവപ്പെട്ടത്. നിലാവ് തെളിഞ്ഞുവീണപ്പോൾ, കടലിലാകെ മാലാഖമാർ നീന്തിനടക്കുംപോലെ ഏതോ കവിയുടെ വരികൾ മനസിൽ ഒഴുകിയെത്തുന്നു. ഓർമകൾ ഉണർത്തപ്പെടുന്നു. അസ്വസ്ഥതയുടെ ചൂടുനിറഞ്ഞ ഓർമകൾ... സന്ധ്യാദേവിയുടെ രൂപം നിലാവു കാണുമ്പോഴേക്കും അവരെ ഓർമിക്കും. നല്ല പൂക്കൾ അവരുടെ ഗന്ധം മനസിലേക്കു കൊണ്ടുചെന്നെത്തിക്കും. സ്വപ്നങ്ങളുടെ കലവറകൾ അപ്പോഴേക്കും തുറക്കപ്പെടുകയാണ്. ആ സ്വപ്നങ്ങളിലെല്ലാം കണ്ണുനീരിന്റെ നനവു പറ്റിയിരുന്നു. തനിക്കു ജീവിതത്തെപ്പറ്റി ബോധമുണ്ട്. തൊഴിലാളിവർഗത്തിന്റെയും കൃഷിക്കാരുടെയും അധ്വാനിക്കുന്നവന്റെയും സമരാനുഭവങ്ങളുടെ ഊഷ്മാവ് തന്റെ സിരകളിൽ ഉണ്ട്. രാജ്യം അന്ധകാരത്തിൽ കിടക്കുന്നുവെന്ന വിവരവുമുണ്ട്. പക്ഷേ, അവയ്ക്കെല്ലാമിടയിൽ മനസ്സ് അനവദ്യങ്ങളായ ചില ജ്ഞാനങ്ങളുടെ ലഹരിയിൽ മയങ്ങിപ്പോകുന്നു. ഹേമന്തചന്ദ്രികയും കുറുമൊഴിമുല്ലയും വാനസരോവരവും അവിടെ മാദകാനുഭൂതികൾ പകർന്നു നിൽക്കുന്നു. അതൊക്കെ ആത്മാവിന്റെ ഈണങ്ങളാണ്. ആ അനുഭൂതികളില്ലെങ്കിൽ താനെവിടെ? തന്റെ കവിതയെവിടെ? തന്റെ ആത്മസ്വപ്നങ്ങൾ തന്നെ എവിടെ? പ്രാണനിൽ പ്രകാശം പരത്തുന്ന അനുഭൂതികൾ...

കടൽപ്പുറത്ത് തിരക്കുമാറി. അവസാനത്തെ ആളും പോയിക്കഴിഞ്ഞിരിക്കുന്നു. നിലാവ് പരന്നൊഴുകുന്നു. സന്ധ്യാദേവിയും ഭാനുമതിയും ഏകാന്തതയുടെ ഭാരവും മനസിൽ തങ്ങിനിന്നു. അയാൾ എഴുന്നേറ്റു ദൂരെ ചക്രവാളത്തിലേക്കു നോക്കി. ലോകം അനന്തമായ ഒരുപ്രദേശമാണെന്നു തോന്നി, മറീനാ കടൽപ്പുറത്തെ ശൂന്യത, അസഹ്യമായിരുന്നു. അൽപ്പ സമയത്തിനുമുൻപ് അവിടെ കടലിനേക്കാൾ ഇരമ്പമായിരുന്നു ചലനമായിരുന്നു. മനുഷ്യന്റെ ചലനം മനുഷ്യന്റെ ഇരമ്പം...

നടന്നു. വഴിവിളക്കുകൾ തന്റെ നടത്തത്തെ മൂകമായി ഉറ്റുനോക്കുന്നു. തന്റെ നിഴൽ നീളുകയും കുറയുകയും വീണ്ടും വീണ്ടും ചെയ്യുന്നതു കണ്ടു. ചിലപ്പോൾ വൃക്ഷച്ചില്ലകൾക്കിടയിലേക്ക് അത് ലയിച്ചുപോകുന്നു. വീണ്ടും അതിനുള്ളിൽനിന്ന് പുറത്തേക്കുവരുന്നു.

വളരെ ദൂരം ചെന്നപ്പോഴും കടലിന്റെ അലർച്ച കേൾക്കുന്നു. സൗമ്യമായിക്കിടന്ന അത് ക്ഷോഭിച്ചിരിക്കുന്നു. അതിന്റെ ശബ്ദമാണ്.

മുറിയിൽ കയറി. വിളക്കുകൊളുത്തി. മേശപ്പുറത്തു കിടന്ന പുസ്തകം കൈയിലെടുത്തു വായിച്ചു. അർഥമുള്ള വരികൾ.

ഉപബോധമനസിലേക്ക് താണിറങ്ങി. ഒളിഞ്ഞു കിടക്കുന്ന അനുഭവങ്ങളും ധാരണകളും മോഹങ്ങളും ഉറക്കത്തിൽ ഉണർന്ന് എഴുന്നേൽക്കുന്നു. അവയാണ് സ്വപ്നങ്ങളായി നമുക്കനുഭവപ്പെടുന്നത്...

ഫ്രോയിഡിന്റെ മാനസികാപഗ്രഥനം. ക്ഷീണം തോന്നി. പുസ്തകം അടച്ചുവച്ചു.

വെളുപ്പാൻകാലമായപ്പോഴാണ് മയങ്ങിയത്. മുറിയുടെ വാതിൽ ചാരിയിരുന്നു.

കതകിൽ മുട്ടുന്നതുകേട്ടാണ് ഉണർന്നത്. പ്രകാശം വീണിരിക്കുന്നു. എഴുന്നേറ്റു നോക്കി. രണ്ട് പൊലീസുകാർ നിൽക്കുന്നു.

“മിസ്റ്റർ അരവിന്ദൻ. നിങ്ങളെ കൂട്ടിക്കൊണ്ടു പോകാനാണ് ഞങ്ങൾ വന്നത്. ഉടനെ തയാറാവൂ.”

മനസ്സ് അപ്പോഴാണ് മുഴുവനും ഉണർന്നത്.

ഇരുപത്തി രണ്ട്

ഒളിവിൽ പ്രവർത്തിക്കുന്ന വിപ്ലവകാരികളുമായി ബന്ധം പുലർത്തുകയും അവരെ സഹായിക്കുകയും ചെയ്യുന്നു. സ്വന്തം നിലയിൽ അട്ടിമറി പ്രവർത്തനങ്ങൾ രഹസ്യമായി സംഘടിപ്പിക്കുന്നു. തെളിവിൽ ആപൽക്കരമായ രീതിയിൽ പത്രപ്രവർത്തനം നടത്തി അതിൽക്കൂടി ഗവൺമെന്റിനെ തകിടം മറിക്കാൻ ഉദ്ദേശിച്ചുകൊണ്ടുള്ള വിധ്വംസകങ്ങളായ ആശയങ്ങൾ പ്രചരിപ്പിക്കുന്നു. കവിതയിൽക്കൂടി വിപ്ലവാഹ്വാനം നിരന്തരം നൽകുന്നു. ഇതെല്ലാമാണ് അരവിന്ദന്റെ പേരിൽ ചുമത്തപ്പെട്ട കുറ്റങ്ങൾ. അറസ്റ്റു ചെയ്യപ്പെട്ട ശേഷമാണ് ചില കാര്യങ്ങൾ അയാളറിഞ്ഞത്. സദാനന്ദനുമായി മദ്രാസിലെ പൊലീസ് അധികാരിയുടെ മുറിയിലിരുന്നപ്പോൾ കയറിവന്ന കീഴുദ്യോഗസ്ഥൻ മലബാറുകാരനായിരുന്നു. അയാൾക്ക് അരവിന്ദനെ അറിയാം. അരവിന്ദന്റെ പേരിൽ ഉണ്ടായിട്ടുള്ള കേസുകളും മനസിലാക്കിയിരുന്നു. അങ്ങനെയാണ് അറസ്റ്റുനടന്നത്.

ഒന്നരവർഷത്തേക്കു ശിക്ഷിച്ചു. തിരുവിതാംകൂറിലേക്കു കൊണ്ടുപോന്നു. ഇവിടെവച്ചാണ് വിചാരണയും ശിക്ഷയും ഉണ്ടായത്. അരവിന്ദനെ വിയ്യൂർ സെൻട്രൽ ജയിലിലേക്ക് അയച്ചു.

ജയിൽമുറി പുതിയ ലോകമായിരുന്നു. മുൻപ് ചെറിയ സമരങ്ങൾക്ക് ലോക്കപ്പിൽ കിടന്നിട്ടുണ്ട്. വലിയ ശിക്ഷ ഉണ്ടായിട്ടില്ല. ഇപ്പോൾ, മറ്റൊരു ലോകത്തിലേക്കു ചെന്നുകയറുകയായിരുന്നു. ജയിലിലേക്കു കയറ്റി അതിന്റെ അഴിവാതിലടച്ചിട്ട് പൊലീസുകാരൻ പിൻവാങ്ങിയപ്പോൾ, യഥാർഥത്തിൽ ആശ്വാസം തോന്നി. ഇനി ഒരുതരം വിശ്രമമാണ്. പുറംലോകവുമായി ബന്ധമില്ലാത്ത വിശ്രമം. ഇവിടെ മനുഷ്യരുണ്ട്. ജീവിതത്തിലെ പല തുറകളിൽനിന്ന് കയറിവന്നിട്ടുള്ള കുറ്റവാളികൾ. അവരുടെ ലോകം പരിചയപ്പെടാൻ കൊള്ളാവുന്നതാണെന്നു പറഞ്ഞു കേട്ടിട്ടുണ്ട്.

ആ മുറിയിൽ അഞ്ചാറുപേരുണ്ട്. ആദ്യത്തെ ദിവസം ആരുമായും മിണ്ടിയില്ല. താൻ ശ്രദ്ധിക്കുന്നുവെന്നറിയാതെ അവരെയൊക്കെ ഇടയ്ക്കിടയ്ക്കു നോക്കി, രൂപങ്ങളും രീതികളും കണ്ടുവച്ചു. അവർ അരവിന്ദനെത്തന്നെ നോക്കിക്കൊണ്ടിരുന്നു. പുതിയ സഖാവ്, രാഷ്ട്രീയക്കാരനാണെന്ന് അവർ നേരത്തേ അറിഞ്ഞിട്ടുണ്ട്, അങ്ങനെയാണ്. പാറാവുകാരനിൽനിന്ന് അത്തരം വാർത്തകൾ കാലേക്കൂട്ടി കിട്ടുന്നു. ആളിന്റെ നില

യനുസരിച്ച് പുതിയ കൂട്ടുകാരനെ നോക്കുകയും കാണുകയും അയാളോടു പെരുമാറുകയും ചെയ്യുന്നു.

കയറിച്ചെന്ന ദിവസം രസമുള്ള അനുഭവമുണ്ടായി. അന്ന് അന്തേവാസികളിൽ ഒരാൾ മോചിപ്പിക്കപ്പെടുന്നു. അരവിന്ദൻ ചെന്ന് മണിക്കൂറുകൾ കഴിഞ്ഞതേ ഉള്ളൂ. അധികാരികൾ അയാളെ വാതിൽതുറന്നു പുറത്തേക്കിറക്കിയപ്പോൾ അയാൾ തിരിഞ്ഞു നിന്നു. അരവിന്ദനെ നോക്കി തൊഴുതു. എന്നിട്ടു പറഞ്ഞു: "ക്ഷമിക്കണം സാർ, പരിചയപ്പെടാനും ഒരുമിച്ചു കഴിഞ്ഞുകൂടാനും സാധിച്ചില്ല. ഞാൻ എന്റെ ഭാര്യയെ കൊന്നതിന് ഏഴുവർഷം കിട്ടി. ഇവിടെ വന്നതാണ്. ഇനി വല്ലപ്പോഴും കാണാം."

അരവിന്ദൻ മിഴിച്ചിരുന്നുപോയി. ആ വിനയപൂർവമുള്ള യാത്രാമൊഴി! അരവിന്ദൻ താനറിയാതെന്നപോലെ കൈകളുയർത്തി പ്രത്യഭിവാദനം ചെയ്തു.

അയാൾ ഇറങ്ങിപ്പോയി. അപ്പോൾ തന്റെ ചിരകാല സുഹൃത്തുക്കളോടെല്ലാം തലകുലുക്കി, ഒന്നു ചിരിച്ചു യാത്രചോദിച്ചു.

അരവിന്ദൻ മുറിയിലവശേഷിച്ചവരുടെ മുഖങ്ങളിലേക്ക് നോക്കി. ഒന്നും പ്രത്യേകിച്ചു കണ്ടില്ലെങ്കിലും, അത്യന്തം അവ്യക്തമായ ഒരു വിഷാദഛായ ഉണ്ടായിരുന്നു. കൂട്ടുകാരൻ പോയതിന്റെ വിഷാദമാണ്. ഒപ്പം തങ്ങൾക്ക് ഇനിയും കിടക്കേണ്ടിയിരിക്കുന്നു എന്ന വിഷാദവും.

ഒരാൾമാത്രം അങ്ങനെ നോക്കിയില്ല. ദീക്ഷ വളർന്ന് നഖം വളർന്നു പ്രാകൃത മനുഷ്യനെപ്പോലെ അയാൾ മൂലയിലിരുന്ന് ചുവന്ന കണ്ണുകൾ കൊണ്ട് ഇറങ്ങിപ്പോയ ആളെ തുറിച്ചുനോക്കി. അയാൾ അനങ്ങാതിരുന്നു.

രാത്രിയിൽ ഒരു പായ് നീർത്തു കിടന്നു, ഉറക്കം വന്നില്ല. വല്ലാത്ത അസ്വസ്ഥത. വീർപ്പുമുട്ടുംപോലെ. ഇനി പ്രഭാതം പുലരുമോ? ഈ രാത്രിക്ക് എത്ര നീളമുണ്ട്? അടുത്ത് കൂർക്കംവലികൾ കേൾക്കുന്നു. പുറത്തു പാറാവുകാരൻ എന്തു ചെയ്യുന്നു? അയാൾ ഉറങ്ങുകയാണോ? ആ വാതിൽക്കലേക്ക് നീങ്ങിയിരുന്നാൽ അവരോട് സംസാരിക്കാൻ കഴിയുമോ?

അപ്പോൾ തൊട്ടടുത്ത പായയിൽ നിന്ന് ഒരു ആ മന്ത്രണം കേൾക്കുന്നു. "മനോരമേ... എന്റെ മനോരമേ.."

തുടർന്ന് ഒരു ദീർഘനിശ്വാസം.

പുറത്തെ വെളിച്ചം അകത്തേക്കു മങ്ങിവീശുന്നുണ്ട്. അതിൽക്കൂടി നോക്കി. ഒരു ചെറുപ്പക്കാരനാണത്. വെളുത്ത് അൽപ്പം താടിമീശ വളർന്ന അയാളെ നേരത്തെ ശ്രദ്ധിച്ചിരുന്നു. ആവർത്തിച്ച് അയാൾ ആ പേര് ഉരുവിട്ടു.

രണ്ടുമൂന്നു ദിവസം കടന്നുപോയി. മിക്ക ദിവസങ്ങളിലും രാത്രിയിൽ ആ ചെറുപ്പക്കാരൻ അങ്ങനെ മന്ത്രിക്കും.

അപ്പോഴേക്കും അരവിന്ദൻ എല്ലാവരുമായി പരിചയപ്പെട്ടു. എല്ലാവർക്കും അയാളോട് മതിപ്പാണ്. ആ ചെറുപ്പക്കാരൻ മാത്രം അരവിന്ദന്റെ മുഖത്തുനോക്കിയിട്ടില്ല. അയാളുമായി മിണ്ടിയിട്ടില്ല. ഒരു ദിവസം അരവിന്ദൻ അങ്ങോട്ടു മിണ്ടി.

"എന്താണ് പേര്?"

അയാൾ മിഴിച്ചുനോക്കി.

"എന്താണ്?"

"ചാക്കോ."

"വീട്..."

മറുപടി പറഞ്ഞില്ല. അയാൾ ഭയപ്പെടുന്നതുപോലെ തോന്നി ഒഴിഞ്ഞുമാറി. ഒന്നും ചോദിക്കാതെ അകന്ന മൂലയിൽ ഇരുന്നു. അരവിന്ദൻ പിന്നെ അയാളോടു സംസാരിക്കാൻ ശ്രമിച്ചില്ല.

മറ്റൊരു തടവുകാരൻ അരവിന്ദനോട് പറഞ്ഞു

"സാറേ അയാളുടെ വീട് കോട്ടയത്താ. അയാള് ഒരു പെണ്ണിന് വിഷം കൊടുത്ത കേസാ. ആ പെണ്ണിന്റെ പേര് മനോരമയെന്നാ...."

പെട്ടെന്നു അരവിന്ദൻ എന്തോ ഓർമിച്ചു. അയാളെ ഓർമവരികയാണോ? തെല്ലു കഴിഞ്ഞപ്പോൾ അയാളെപ്പറ്റിയുള്ള സംശയം പൊന്തിവന്നു. മുൻപൊരിക്കൽ കീർത്തിയെ തന്റെ വീട്ടിലേക്ക് വിളിപ്പിച്ചു. മാനഭംഗം ചെയ്യാൻ ശ്രമിച്ച ആ ചെറുപ്പക്കാരനല്ലേ അയാൾ? സദനത്തിലെ അന്തേവാസിയായി താമസിച്ച്, കീർത്തിയെ വിളിച്ചുകൊണ്ടുചെന്ന മനോരമയുടെ പേരല്ലേ അയാൾ എല്ലാ രാത്രികളിലും മന്ത്രിക്കുന്നത്?

അതെ അതുതന്നെ തോന്നുന്നു.

ഒരു രാത്രിയിൽ ഒരു കുസൃതി കാട്ടി. എല്ലാവരും ഉറങ്ങാൻ കിടന്നു. കുറച്ചുകഴിഞ്ഞ് അരവിന്ദൻ ശ്വാസധാരയിൽക്കൂടി വിളിച്ചു

"കീർത്തി... എന്റെ കീർത്തി..."

കുറച്ചകലെ കിടക്കുന്ന അയാളെ നോക്കിക്കൊണ്ടാണ് അരവിന്ദൻ ആ പേരു വിളിച്ചത്. പെട്ടെന്ന് ആ ചെറുപ്പക്കാരൻ തല ഉയർത്തി അരവിന്ദനെ നോക്കി. അയാൾ എഴുന്നേറ്റു. ഭിത്തിയിൽ ചാരി കുത്തിയിരുന്നു. അയാളുടെ ദൃഷ്ടികൾ അരവിന്ദനിലാണെന്ന് കാണാൻ കഴിയും. അരവിന്ദൻ വീണ്ടും വിളിച്ചു:

"കീർത്തീ..."

തടവുമുറിയിൽ അതു മുഴങ്ങി.

"നിമിഷങ്ങൾ അരവിന്ദൻ ഉറക്കം നടിച്ചു. കിടന്നു. അപ്പോൾ, അയാൾ ഭിത്തിയിലേക്കു ചാരിയിരുന്ന് തേങ്ങിക്കരയുന്നു.

മറ്റൊരോർമ. പിറ്റേന്നു രാവിലെ ആ ഓർമ വച്ചുകൊണ്ട് അയാളെ നോക്കി. അയാളുടെ വലതു കൈത്തണ്ടയിൽ മുറിവു പറ്റി ഉണങ്ങിയ വലിയ പാട്... പിന്നീട് അയാൾ താൻ കാണാതെ, തന്നെ തുറിച്ചുനോക്കിയിരിക്കാറുള്ളത്. അരവിന്ദൻ കണ്ടു.

പകൽ ജയിലിന്റെ പറമ്പിൽ മൺവെട്ടിയും തൂമ്പയും കൊണ്ട് കിളച്ചു. അപ്പോഴൊക്കെ ഉത്സാഹമാണ് തോന്നിയിരുന്നത്. ആ ജീവിതവുമായി പൊരുത്തപ്പെടാൻ മനഃപൂർവം ശ്രമിച്ചു. ആ മനുഷ്യരുമായി ധാരാളം സംസാരിച്ചു. വേനൽ പോയി വർഷം വന്നു. വർഷം കടന്നുപോയി. തണുപ്പുള്ള രാത്രികൾ വന്നു. എന്നിട്ടും ഋതുഭേദങ്ങൾ അനുഭവപ്പെട്ടില്ല. അവ

ജയിൽ വളപ്പിനു പറത്തുകൂടി വരികയും പോവുകയും ചെയ്യുന്നു. ഇവിടെ എല്ലാം നിറമില്ലാത്ത ഗന്ധമില്ലാത്ത സൗന്ദര്യമില്ലാത്ത രാത്രികളും പകലുകളുമാണ്. ഒരുകാര്യം ഓർമിച്ചു. സ്വാതന്ത്ര്യമില്ലാത്തപ്പോൾ ഋതുക്കൾക്കും ഭംഗിയില്ല. എല്ലാം മനസിന്റെ ആശ്വാസത്തിൽ തങ്ങിനിൽക്കുന്നു. നിറവും ഗന്ധവും സൗന്ദര്യവും എല്ലാം...

മാസങ്ങൾ. ഇവിടെ ജീവിതത്തിന് ഒരു വേഗവുമില്ല. ഇവിടെ കാലം നിശ്ചലമായി നിൽക്കുന്നു. ദിവസങ്ങൾക്കു തമ്മിൽ ഒരു വ്യത്യാസവുമില്ല. എല്ലാം ഏകരൂപം. ഇത് മാറ്റമില്ലായ്മയുടെ ചലനമില്ലായ്മയുടെ താവളമാണ്....

എല്ലാ നിമിഷങ്ങളിലും സന്ധ്യാദേവി മനസിന്റെ മുൻപിൽ നിന്നു അവരുടെ ചന്ദനലതപോലുള്ള സൗന്ദര്യത്തിന് ആയിരം മടങ്ങ് ആകർഷണം വർധിച്ചതുപോലെ. കേസുവിചാരണ നടന്നുകൊണ്ടിരുന്നപ്പോൾ ചില സുഹൃത്തുക്കൾ വന്നു കണ്ടു. അവരുമായി അധികം സംസാരിക്കാൻ സമ്മതിച്ചില്ല. എങ്കിലും സന്ധ്യാദേവിയെപ്പറ്റി അവരോടു ചോദിച്ചു. ആർക്കും അറിഞ്ഞുകൂടാ. നാടുവിട്ടതാണെന്ന് ചിലർ പറഞ്ഞു: മരിച്ചതാണെന്ന്, മറ്റു ചിലർ പറഞ്ഞു. ആത്മഹത്യ ചെയ്തിരിക്കുമെന്ന് ഇനിയും ചിലർ പറഞ്ഞു.

ഇടയ്ക്ക് ഭാനുമതിയെ ഓർമിക്കും. അവർ എവിടെയാണ് മദ്രാസ് എന്ന നഗരത്തിൽ അവർ മുങ്ങി മരിച്ചോ?

വായിക്കാൻ അധികാരികൾ സമ്മതിച്ചില്ല. എഴുതാൻ സൗകര്യം കൊടുത്തില്ല. ജയിലറും വാർഡർമാരും മറ്റു പൊലീസുകാരും ഇപ്പോൾ അരവിന്ദന് അടുപ്പമുള്ളവരാണ്. പക്ഷേ, അയാളെ സഹായിക്കാൻ അവർക്കാർക്കും അനുവാദമില്ല. അത് അവരുടെ ചോറാണ്. ഒന്നും ചെയ്യാൻ നിവൃത്തിയില്ല. തനിക്കു കൂട്ടുകാരായി രണ്ടുമൂന്നു രാഷ്ട്രീയത്തടവുകാർ ഉണ്ടായിരുന്നെങ്കിൽ എന്ന് അയാൾ ആഗ്രഹിച്ചു. കുറച്ചുപേർ ഉണ്ടായിരുന്നു. അവരെ തിരുവനന്തപുരത്തേക്കും മറ്റും കൊണ്ടുപോയി.

വീണ്ടും മാസങ്ങൾ കൊഴിഞ്ഞുവീണുകൊണ്ടിരുന്നു.

അരവിന്ദൻ ഇപ്പോൾ പതിനൊന്നു മാസക്കാലം ജയിലിൽ തള്ളിനീക്കിയിരിക്കുന്നു. ഒരു ദിവസം രാവിലെ ഒരു പൊലീസുകാരൻ വന്നു. നല്ല പരിചയമുള്ള മനുഷ്യനാണ്. അയാൾ പറഞ്ഞു:

"സാറേ, സാറിനെ കാണാൻ ഒരു യോഗിനിയമ്മ വന്നിരിക്കുന്നു. അവർ സൂപ്രണ്ടദ്ദേഹവുമായി സംസാരിക്കുകയാണ്. ഇപ്പോൾ ഇങ്ങോട്ടു വരും."

ഉള്ളിൽ ഒരു ഉഷ്ണക്കാറ്റ് അടിച്ചുയർന്നു. യോഗിനിഅമ്മ... ആരാണത്? ജയിലിൽവന്നിട്ട് ആദ്യമായി ഒരാൾ തന്നെ കാണാൻ വരികയാണ്. യോഗമയീദേവിയുടെ രൂപം ആദ്യം മനസിൽ തെളിഞ്ഞുവന്നു. അവരുമായി പിരിഞ്ഞ ദിവസം... ആലിപ്പൂരിലെ ജയിലിൽ കിടന്ന് ആരുമറിയാതെ അവർ അന്ത്യശ്വാസം വലിച്ചു. അമ്മയെപ്പോലെ സ്നേഹിച്ച മഹാമനസ്വിനി. പിന്നെ ഒരു യോഗിനിയെയും താൻ കണ്ടിട്ടില്ല. അങ്ങനെ ആരു

മായും പരിചയപ്പെട്ടിട്ടില്ല. ഇപ്പോൾ ഒരുയോഗി അമ്മ വന്നിരിക്കുന്നു.

ആ പൊലീസുകാരൻ പോയി.

അയാൾ ആകാംക്ഷയോടെ കാത്തുനിന്നു. സമയം നീങ്ങുന്നില്ല. അവർ വരുന്നില്ല.

ഒരു മണിക്കൂറോളം കഴിഞ്ഞുകാണും. അപ്പോൾ ഒരു പൊലീസുകാരന്റെ അകമ്പടിയോടെ അവർ ജയിലിന്റെ വിശാലമായ മുറ്റം കടന്ന് നടന്നുവരുന്നു. സൂര്യപ്രകാശത്തിൽ ആ രൂപം കണ്ടു. നടുങ്ങി. കണ്ണുകൾ വിശ്വസിക്കുന്നില്ല. എല്ലാ സംശയങ്ങളും തീർന്നു. അത് സന്ധ്യാദേവിയാണ്.

അവരുടെ മുഖത്ത് പ്രകാശം വെട്ടിത്തിളങ്ങുന്നു.

ഇടതൂർന്ന മുടി മുകളിലേക്ക് കെട്ടിവച്ച്, അതിനു ചുറ്റും വെളുത്ത പൂമാല ചൂടിയിരിക്കുന്നു. നെറ്റിയിൽ പ്രസാദക്കുറി. വെളുത്ത സാരി തോളിലൂടെ ചുറ്റിവലിച്ചിട്ട് ഒതുക്കി കുത്തിയിരിക്കുന്നു. അരയിൽ ഒരു കറുത്ത ചരട് കെട്ടിയിട്ടുണ്ട്. കഴുത്തിൽ രുദ്രാക്ഷമാല...

പൊലീസുകാരൻ, അവരെ വരാന്തയിൽക്കൂടി ജയിൽമുറിയുടെ അഴിവാതിലിനു മുമ്പാകെ കൊണ്ടുവന്നു നിറുത്തി. അരവിന്ദൻ അഴികളിൽ പിടിച്ച്, സന്ധ്യാദേവിക്ക് അഭിമുഖമായി നിൽക്കുകയാണ്...

അവരുടെ കണ്ണുകൾ തമ്മിലിടഞ്ഞു. കുറച്ചുനേരം നിശ്ചലമായി നിന്നു. രണ്ടുപേരും ഒന്നും മിണ്ടിയില്ല. അവരുടെ കണ്ണുകൾ നിറഞ്ഞു. അരവിന്ദന്റെ ചുണ്ടുകൾ വിറച്ചു. അൽപ്പസമയം കൊണ്ട് രണ്ടുപേരും സ്വയം നിയന്ത്രിച്ചു.

"അരവിന്ദൻ" അവരുടെ ശബ്ദം ആത്മാവിന്റെ ഒരു ദീർഘ നിശ്വാസമായിരുന്നു.

"സന്ധ്യാദേവി.." അത് പതറിപ്പോകാതിരിക്കാൻ അരവിന്ദൻ ശ്രമിച്ചിരുന്നു.

"അവർ പതിനഞ്ചു മിനിട്ടാണ് ഈ കൂടിക്കാഴ്ചയ്ക്കു തന്നിരിക്കുന്നത്."

"എനിക്കു കണ്ടാൽ മതി."

"ദയവു ചെയ്ത് അരവിന്ദൻ എന്നോട് ഒന്നു ചോദിക്കരുത്."

"ഇല്ല, എനിക്കു കണ്ടാൽ മതി."

അയാളുടെ തൊണ്ട ഇടറിപ്പോയി."

"ഞാൻ ചിലതു പറയാനാണ് വന്നത്."

"പറയൂ."

"എങ്ങനെ പറയും? ഇവർ നിൽക്കുന്നു." സന്ധ്യാദേവി പാറാവുകാരനേയും കൂടെ വന്ന പൊലീസുകാരനേയും നോക്കി പുഞ്ചിരിച്ചു.

അവർ, അവിടെ ഒരു മര്യാദ കാട്ടി. പാറാവുകാരൻ പത്തു ചുവടു നടന്നു. കൂടെ ആ പൊലീസുകാരനും.

സന്ധ്യാദേവി തുടക്കത്തിൽ സ്വരം താഴ്ത്തി പറഞ്ഞു:

"വയനാട്ടിൽ സുൽത്താൻബത്തേരിക്ക് കിഴക്കേ അറ്റം, ഒരാശ്രമമു

ണ്ട്. ശിവാനന്ദജി..." അവർ തിരിഞ്ഞ് പൊലീസുകാരനോടും പാറാവുകാരനോടുമായി അറിയിച്ചു. അത്ര ദൂരം പോകണ്ടേ കേട്ടോ..."

അവർ അവിടെ നിന്ന്, അവരെ നോക്കിച്ചിരിച്ചു.

"അരവിന്ദൻ" അവർ മറയ്ക്കാതെ പറഞ്ഞു. "എന്നെപ്പറ്റി അരവിന്ദൻ ഇനി ഓർമിച്ചു. ദുഃഖിക്കരുത്. എന്റെ ജീവിതത്തിന്റെ വഴിത്താര ഞാൻ സ്വീകരിച്ചു കഴിഞ്ഞു. എനിക്ക് ഒരപേക്ഷയുണ്ട്. അത് എന്നെ സ്നേഹിക്കുന്ന അരവിന്ദൻ കൈക്കൊള്ളണം."

"എന്താണ്? പറയൂ. അയാൾ ഉൽക്കണ്ഠ കാട്ടി.

"പറയാം. ആശ്രമത്തിൽ ഭാനുമതിയുണ്ട്. കീർത്തി ഉണ്ട്. പിന്നെ ചിലരും. ഞങ്ങൾ കോയമ്പത്തൂർ വച്ചാണ് സന്ധിച്ചത്. എല്ലാം അദ്ദേഹത്തിന്റെ നിർദേശമനുസരണം തന്നെ. മനസിലായോ? അങ്ങനെ വീണ്ടും ഒരു താവളത്തിലെത്തി. പുതിയ അന്തരീക്ഷം. പുതിയ രൂപങ്ങൾ പുതിയ മനസും. അതാണ് പ്രധാനം. കീർത്തിയെ ഞാനാണ് വരുത്തിയത്. അവളുടെ മനസും എനിക്കറിയാം. ഇനി അവൾക്ക് തുണയായിരിക്കേണ്ടത് അരവിന്ദനാണ്. ഞാനത് നിശ്ചയിച്ചു. എനിക്ക് അങ്ങനെയൊരു ജീവിതമില്ല. അവൾക്ക് അതുണ്ടാവണം. നിങ്ങളിൽ അലിഞ്ഞു ചേർന്ന ഒരാത്മാവുമായി അവൾ എത്രയോ നാളായിട്ട് കഴിഞ്ഞുകൂടുകയാണ്. അത് ഞാൻ കണ്ടിരുന്നു. മനസിലാക്കിയിരുന്നു. അന്നു ഞാൻ വേദനിച്ചു. ഇന്നു ഞാൻ സന്തോഷിക്കുന്നു. എനിക്കുവേണ്ടി അരവിന്ദൻ ഈ ഭൂമിയിൽ നിർവഹിക്കേണ്ട കടമയാണിത്. അഞ്ചു മാസം കഴിയുമ്പോൾ നിങ്ങൾ സ്വതന്ത്രനാകും. അപ്പോൾ അങ്ങോട്ടു പോകണം. അവൾ നിങ്ങളെ സ്വീകരിക്കാൻ കാത്തുനിൽപ്പുണ്ടാവും. ആ കനകം പോലുള്ള തെളിനീരു പോലെയുള്ള പെൺകുട്ടി.

വിതുമ്പുന്ന മനസോടെ, അരവിന്ദൻ ചോദിച്ചുപോയി.

"സന്ധ്യാദേവി എന്തർഥത്തിലാണ് ഇതു പറയുന്നത്."

"അരവിന്ദൻ എന്നെ അനുസരിക്കുമെന്ന വിശ്വാസത്തിൽ എന്റെ വാക്കുകളിലെ ആഗ്രഹവും അർഥവും അതാണ്."

"അപ്പോൾ സന്ധ്യാദേവി?"

"ഞാൻ... ഞാൻ. സമ്മതം വാങ്ങിക്കൊണ്ടുപോകാൻ വന്നു. അതു കണ്ട് സന്തോഷിക്കാൻ കഴിയുമെന്ന വിശ്വാസത്തോടെ പോകും."

"എന്നെ ഉപേക്ഷിക്കാൻ എങ്ങനെ കഴിഞ്ഞു?"

"ജീവിതത്തിൽ അത് ചെയ്യില്ല. പക്ഷേ എന്നെ സ്വീകരിക്കാൻ സാധ്യമല്ല. ഞാനതു സമ്മതിക്കുകയും ഇല്ല. അങ്ങനെയൊരു ജീവിതം എനിക്കു വേണ്ട. എന്നെ എന്റെ കീർത്തിക്ക് കൊടുത്തിരിക്കുന്നു. ഇനി എന്നിലവശേഷിച്ചിട്ടുള്ള എല്ലാം അവളിലാണ്. ഞാൻ ഒരു പ്രേതം മാത്രം. അവൾ... അവൾ എത്ര ഹൃദയശാലീനയായ പെൺകുട്ടിയാണ്. അരവിന്ദനറിഞ്ഞുകൂടെ? എനിക്കുവേണ്ടി അവളെ സ്വീകരിക്കുക. അവളെ, എന്റെ കീർത്തിയെ."

അരവിന്ദൻ ജയിലഴികളിലേക്ക് തല ചേർത്ത് കുനിഞ്ഞു നിന്നു.

"നോക്കൂ..." സന്ധ്യാദേവി വിളിച്ചു.

അയാൾ മുഖം തെല്ലുയർത്തി ദൃഷ്ടികൾ അവരുടെ നേർക്കുപിടി

ച്ചു. അയാളുടെ നനഞ്ഞകണ്ണുകൾ അവർ കണ്ടു.

"ഞാൻ ജീവിച്ചിരിക്കണോ?"

"വേണം."

"എങ്കിൽ എനിക്കുവേണ്ടി ഇത് ചെയ്യണം."

"സന്ധ്യാദേവി."

"എനിക്കു വാക്കു തരൂ."

"അവർ കൈകൾ അഴികൾക്കു നേർക്കു നീട്ടി.

"ഈ കൈയിൽ തൊട്ടു വാക്കുതരൂ."

പാറാവുകാരനും പൊലീസുകാരനും അടുത്തുവന്നു.

"സാറേ സമയം.." പൊലീസുകാരൻ മര്യാദപൂർവം അറിയിച്ചു.

"വാക്കുതരൂ."

അരവിന്ദന്റെ കരങ്ങൾ സാവധാനം പുറത്തേക്ക് നീണ്ടു ചെന്നു.

"എങ്കിൽ ഞാൻ ജീവിക്കും."

ആ കൈകൾ സന്ധ്യാദേവിയുടെ കൈതലങ്ങളെ സ്പർശിച്ചു. അയാൾ തകർന്നവനെപ്പോലെ മുഖം താഴ്ത്തി.

"ഞാൻ പോകുന്നു." അവർ അറിയിച്ചു.

അവരുടെ കണ്ണുകൾ നിറഞ്ഞു. അത് കവിളുകളിലേക്ക് ഒഴുകി.

"ഇനി എന്നു കാണും."

"എന്റെ ആത്മാവ് എപ്പോഴും അരവിന്ദന്റെ കൂടെ ഉണ്ട്."

അവരുടെ ഇരുണ്ട മിഴികൾ അയാളിൽ തങ്ങിനിന്നു അൽപ്പസമയം അവർ തിരിഞ്ഞു. പൊലീസുകാർ അടുത്തുവന്നു. സന്ധ്യാദേവി നടന്നു. മുറ്റത്തേക്കിറങ്ങി. സൂര്യപ്രകാശത്തിൽക്കൂടി അവർ ജയിൽമുറ്റം വഴി നടന്നുനീങ്ങുന്നത് അരവിന്ദൻ നോക്കിനിന്നു. അവർ തിരിഞ്ഞുനോക്കാതെ ആ ഉയർന്ന ചുമരുകൾക്കപ്പുറത്തേക്കു മറഞ്ഞു.

അരവിന്ദൻ തളർന്ന് ജയിൽമുറിയുടെ തറയിൽ ചാരി ഇരുന്നു. മറ്റുള്ളവർ അയാളിൽത്തന്നെ ദൃഷ്ടികളർപ്പിച്ചിരിക്കുകയായിരുന്നു.

ഇരുപത്തിമൂന്ന്

അന്നുരാത്രി വളരെ വൈകിയപ്പോഴും ഉറങ്ങാതെ കിടന്നു. രാഷ്ട്രീയക്കുറ്റത്തിന്റെ പേരിൽ ശിക്ഷിക്കപ്പെട്ടു. അങ്ങനെ ഇവിടെ വന്നു. പക്ഷേ, ഇന്ന് ജീവിതത്തിലെ ഏറ്റവും വലിയ ശിക്ഷ കിട്ടിയതുപോലെ ജീവിതത്തിൽ കഴിയുന്നിടത്തോളം യാഥാർത്ഥ്യബോധം നിലനിറുത്താൻ ശ്രമിച്ചിരുന്നു. ആകാശ പുഷ്പങ്ങളെ നിഷേധിക്കുന്ന എല്ലാ തത്വസംഹിതകളോടും ഇഷ്ടമായിരുന്നു. അങ്ങനെയാണ് തൊഴിലാളിവർഗത്തെ, കൃഷിക്കാരനെ അധ്വാനിക്കുന്ന മനുഷ്യന്റെ ആശാഭംഗങ്ങളെ സ്വച്ഛമായി കാണാൻ ശ്രമിച്ചത്. ഇടയ്ക്ക് ഒരു മോഹം മനസിൽ വളർന്നു. അത് കാണാവുന്ന സ്പർശിക്കാവുന്ന ചൂടുള്ള ശ്വാസധാരയിൽക്കൂടി അനുഭവിക്കാവുന്ന ഒരഭിനിവേശമായിരുന്നു. ആ മോഹം എല്ലാ സിരകളിലേക്കും

ഒഴുകിച്ചെന്ന്, പ്രാണന്റെ ഒരു പ്രവാഹതാളമായിത്തീർന്നു.. അത് മാത്രമാണ് ഇടയ്ക്ക് സ്വപ്നം കാണാൻ പ്രേരിപ്പിക്കുന്ന ഒരു സത്യമായിരുന്നത്. അകന്നുപോയപ്പോഴും അജ്ഞാതമായ ഏതോ ഭൂമിയിൽ മറഞ്ഞു നിന്നപ്പോഴും, ആ വികാരം വളരുകയായിരുന്നു. ഇന്ന്, ആ സ്വപ്നം നഷ്ടപ്പെട്ടിരിക്കുന്നു. അത് വെറുമൊരു യാത്രാമൊഴിയല്ല. താൻ മറ്റൊരു സ്വപ്നത്തെ ആത്മാവിലേക്ക് ഏറ്റെടുത്തുകൊള്ളുവാൻ കൽപ്പിച്ചുകൊണ്ടുള്ള പിൻവാങ്ങലാണ്.

സന്ധ്യാദേവിക്ക് എന്തു സംഭവിച്ചു?

അവർ സന്യാസിയായിരിക്കുന്നു. സർവസാധകയായ പ്രകൃതി കൊടുത്ത അഴകിന് തരിവളയും സ്വർണഹാരവും മാത്രമല്ല, തുളസിപ്പൂവും ഭസ്മവും അലങ്കാരമാണ്. അവരുടെ സൗന്ദര്യം ഇപ്പോൾ കുറച്ചുകൂടി ശുദ്ധീകരിക്കപ്പെട്ടിരിക്കുന്നു. കണ്ണുകൾക്കു ദീപ്തികൂടിയിരിക്കുന്നു.

ആ കൈകൾക്കു ചൂടുണ്ടായിരുന്നു. സന്യാസിയുടെ ചൂട്...

പ്രപഞ്ചമാകെ ഉഷ്ണത്തിൽപ്പെട്ടിരിക്കുന്നതുപോലെ വിയർക്കുന്നു. ശരീരത്തിലാകെ അസ്വസ്ഥത പടരുന്നതുപോലെ, ഇനി സന്ധ്യാദേവിയെ എന്നു കാണും?

"എന്റെ ആത്മാവ് എപ്പോഴും അരവിന്ദന്റെ കൂടെയുണ്ട്..." ആ വാക്കുകൾ ഉള്ളിൽ മുഴങ്ങുന്നു. മനസ്സു നിറച്ചു. കൺഠിതം താൻ ഒന്നും പറഞ്ഞില്ല. അങ്ങോട്ട് പലതും അപേക്ഷിക്കാമായിരുന്നു. അത് ചെയ്തില്ല. അർഥമില്ലാത്ത നിൽപ്പു നിന്നു. എല്ലാം സമ്മതിച്ചതു കണക്കെ നിന്നു.

"സാർ.." കാതിനരികിൽ അടക്കിപ്പിടിച്ച ഒരു വിളി.

പെട്ടെന്ന് മനസിലായി അതെ അയാൾ തന്നെ. ചാക്കോ. മങ്ങിയ വെളിച്ചത്തിൽക്കൂടി അയാളുടെ മുഖം കണ്ടു.പ്രത്യേകിച്ച് ഒന്നും തോന്നിയില്ല. സ്വന്തം ഹൃദയഭാരത്തിനിടയ്ക്ക് അയാളോട് തോന്നിയിരുന്ന വെറുപ്പ് ഇപ്പോൾ അനുഭവപ്പെട്ടില്ല.

"എന്താ?"

"ഞാനൊന്ന് ചോദിച്ചാൽ പറയുമോ?" അയാളുടെ കണ്ണുകൾ തിളങ്ങിയിരിക്കുന്നതുകണ്ടു.

"ചോദിക്കൂ." അലസമായി പറഞ്ഞു.

"ഇന്ന് വന്നിരുന്നത്, ആ സദനത്തിലുണ്ടായിരുന്ന സ്ത്രീയല്ലേ സാർ?"

അയാൾ ഭയചകിതനായിരിക്കുന്നു. അങ്ങനെയായിരുന്നു അയാളുടെ ചോദ്യം. ശ്വാസവേഗം വർധിച്ചിരുന്നു. അത് ഭയമാണെങ്കിൽ അതിന്റെ അർഥം മനസിലാക്കാവുന്നതേയുള്ളൂ.

അയാളോട് അധികം സംസാരിക്കാൻ തോന്നിയില്ല. ഒന്നും പറയാൻ തോന്നിയില്ല. കണ്ണുമടച്ചു കിടന്നു. അയാൾ വീണ്ടും ആ ചോദ്യം ചോദിച്ചില്ല.

ഒട്ടുനേരം കഴിഞ്ഞ് ആ ശബ്ദം കേൾക്കുന്നു. അരവിന്ദൻ നോക്കി. അയാൾ തേങ്ങിക്കരയുന്നു. അപ്പോഴും അരവിന്ദൻ അനങ്ങാതെ കിടന്നു.

ആ രാത്രിയും കടന്നുപോയി.

ആ മുറിയിൽക്കിടന്ന തടവുകാർക്ക് ഒരു ജിജ്ഞാസയുണ്ടെന്ന് അര

വിന്ദനു മനസിലായി. ആ സ്ത്രീ ആരാണ്? അയാളെ കാണാൻ വന്ന ആ സന്യാസിനി? ആരും ചോദിച്ചില്ല. രണ്ടു മൂന്നു ദിവസം കഴിഞ്ഞപ്പോൾ പ്രശ്നം എല്ലാവരുടെ മനസിൽ നിന്നും മാഞ്ഞുപോയിരിക്കുമെന്ന് അയാൾ കരുതി. പക്ഷേ, ഒരു ദിവസം ഉച്ചയ്ക്ക് ചാക്കോയുടെ വിവരങ്ങൾ ധരിപ്പിച്ച ആ കൂട്ടു തടവുകാരൻ ജയിലിലെ തോട്ടത്തിൽ പണിയെടുക്കുന്നതിനിടയ്ക്ക് അരവിന്ദന്റെ അടുക്കൽ വന്ന് രഹസ്യമായി ചോദിച്ചു.

"എന്നോട് പരിഭവിക്കരുത്. ആ സന്യാസിനിയും സാറുമായിട്ട് സ്നേഹമായിരുന്നു, അല്ലേ? സാറ് വലിയ ആളാണല്ലോ. അതുകൊണ്ട് ഇത്തരം കാര്യങ്ങൾ ചോദിച്ചാലും പരിഭവിക്കുകയില്ലെന്നു വിചാരിച്ച് ചോദിച്ചതാണ്."

അരവിന്ദൻ അയാളെ നോക്കി. മൗനമായി മന്ദഹസിച്ചു. കൂട്ടുതടവുകാരനും പുഞ്ചിരിച്ചു. അത് സത്യമാണെന്ന് അരവിന്ദന്റെ മുഖത്തുനിന്ന് മനസിലാക്കുകയായിരുന്നു.

"ഇത് ആരു പറഞ്ഞു?" അൽപ്പംകഴിഞ്ഞ് അരവിന്ദൻ ചോദിച്ചു.

കൂട്ടുതടവുകാരൻ പതുക്കെ അറിയിച്ചു. "ചാക്കോ."

അരവിന്ദൻ മിണ്ടിയില്ല.

അയാൾ മറ്റൊരു കാര്യം കൂടി മെല്ലെ ചോദിച്ചു:

"അവരിൽ സാറിന് ഒരു കുട്ടിയുണ്ട്, അല്ലേ?"

അരവിന്ദൻ മിഴിച്ചു നിന്നു. താൻ ചോദിച്ചത് അവിവേകമായിപ്പോയോ എന്ന് വിഷമിച്ച് ആ തടവുകാരൻ നിന്നു.

വയനാടൻ മലകളുടെ തലയിലേക്ക് കയറിച്ചെല്ലുകയാണെന്നുതന്നെ തോന്നി. സമയം പകൽ നാലുമണി കഴിഞ്ഞിരുന്നു. വണ്ടിയിറങ്ങി കുറെയധികം നടന്നിരിക്കുന്നു. വഴിക്ക് കിട്ടിയ അറിവനുസരിച്ച് ഇനിയും കുറേ നേരം നടക്കണം. പക്ഷേ, അതൊരു ക്ലേശമായി അനുഭവപ്പെട്ടില്ല. ജീവിതത്തിലെ ഒരു ലക്ഷ്യത്തിലേക്ക് നടന്നു കയറുകയാണ്. കുറേ കാതങ്ങൾക്കപ്പുറം ഒരു ലോകം തന്നെ കാത്തിരിക്കുന്നു. സന്ധ്യാദേവിയുടെ ലോകം. മനുഷ്യമോചനത്തിൽ വിശ്വസിക്കുന്ന ഏതാനും കർമാപാസകരുടെ തപോവനം.

പിന്നെയും ഒരു മണിക്കൂർകൂടി നടന്നപ്പോൾ ചാഞ്ഞും ചരിഞ്ഞും കിടന്ന ഭൂമി. ഒരു സമതലത്തിലേക്ക് ചെന്നെത്തി.

ആളുകൾ പാർക്കുന്ന ഒരു സ്ഥലമാണത്. പണക്കാരെന്നു തോന്നിക്കുന്ന കുറേ മനുഷ്യർ. അങ്ങോട്ടുമിങ്ങോട്ടും പോകുന്നു. അവിടെ സൂര്യന്റെ ചുവന്ന വെളിച്ചം വീഴുന്നു. വൃക്ഷങ്ങൾ ആകാശത്തിലേക്ക് തൊട്ടുരുമ്മി നിൽക്കുന്നു. നടപ്പാതയിൽ അൽപ്പം വലുതായ വഴിയിൽക്കൂടി ഒരു ലക്ഷ്യംവച്ചുപോയി. ദൂരെ മലകൾ പിന്നെയും കാണാം. ഇത് അവിടെ ഒരു താഴ്വാരമാണ്. അവിടെയുമിവിടെയും ചെറിയ കുടിലുകളുണ്ട്. അവയിൽ നിന്നിറങ്ങി വന്ന മനുഷ്യൻ അയാളെ നോക്കി. അവർ ഒരു പുതിയ മനുഷ്യനെ കണ്ടു.

തെല്ലകലെ, വൃക്ഷക്കൂട്ടങ്ങൾക്കിടയിൽ വിളക്കുകൾ കാണുന്നു.

സന്ധ്യ കടന്നുവന്നതുതന്നെ അയാൾ അറിഞ്ഞില്ല. ആ ദീപങ്ങൾ ആശ്രമത്തിലേതാണ്. അവിടെ നിന്നും ചിലർ ഇങ്ങോട്ടു വരുന്നു. അവർ നടന്നുപോകുമ്പോൾ അയാളെ ശ്രദ്ധിക്കുന്നു. കുറച്ചുകൂടി നടന്നടുത്തു. അപ്പോൾ, ആ ഭവനം ഒട്ടു വ്യക്തമായി കാണാൻ കഴിഞ്ഞു. വേഗത്തിൽ അവിടെയെത്താൻ കാലുകൾ കുതിച്ചുപോകുന്നു. ഇരുവശവും മരങ്ങൾ നിൽക്കുന്ന ഒരു കൊച്ചുവഴിയിലേക്ക് പ്രവേശിച്ചു. അതിന്റെ അറ്റത്തെത്തിയപ്പോൾ മുറ്റം... ആശ്രമത്തിന്റെ മുറ്റം.

പുറത്ത് ആരേയും കണ്ടില്ല അയാൾ തുറന്നുകിടന്ന വാതിലിനകത്തേക്കു കയറി. അൽപ്പം വിസ്താരമുള്ള ഒരു പ്രവേശനമുറിയാണത്. നേരെ ഒരു വാതിൽ, ഇടത്തും വലത്തും രണ്ടു മുറികൾ. ആശ്രമത്തിന്റെ പുറത്ത് ഇരുപുറത്തും പനിയോല കെട്ടിയ ചാർത്തുകളുമുണ്ട്. പുറത്ത് കത്തിച്ച രണ്ടു തൂക്കുവിളക്കുകൾ. അകത്തെ വാതിൽക്കൽ കൊളുത്തിയ ഒരു നിലവിളക്ക്. മുറിയുടെ നടുക്ക് ഒരു റാന്തൽ കത്തിച്ചു തൂക്കിയിരിക്കുന്നു. അരവിന്ദൻ ഒന്നു ചുമച്ചു. ബഞ്ചിലിരുന്നു.

നിമിഷങ്ങൾക്കകം അകത്തുനിന്ന് ജടാധാരിയായ മനുഷ്യൻ ഇറങ്ങിവന്നു. കണ്ട മാത്രയിൽ അരവിന്ദന് ആളെ മനസിലായി. അദ്ദേഹം തുറന്നു ചിരിച്ചു.

"ഗുഡ് ഈവനിങ്, പൊയറ്റ് അദ്ദേഹം അരവിന്ദനെ സ്വാഗതം ചെയ്തു."

"ഗുഡ് ഈവനിങ്, ശിവാനന്ദജി." അരവിന്ദൻ എഴുന്നേറ്റു തൊഴുതു.

രണ്ടുപേരും ഇരുന്നു. ശിവാനന്ദജി അകത്തേക്കു വിളിച്ചു

"ഭാനുമതീ, കീർത്തി, ദാ ഇത് ആരെന്നു നോക്കൂ."

"ഭാനുമതി, വിളികേട്ടു പുറത്തേക്കു വന്നു. പുറകെ കീർത്തിയും.

"ദാ, ജയിലിൽനിന്നുവരുന്ന കവിയെ കണ്ടുമുട്ടുക." ശിവാനന്ദജി പറഞ്ഞു.

ഭാനുമതി മെലിഞ്ഞിരിക്കുന്നു. അവരുടെ പിന്നിൽ നിന്ന കീർത്തി മുമ്പത്തേക്കാൾ രൂപവതിയായി കാണപ്പെട്ടു.

അരവിന്ദന്റെ കണ്ണുകൾ പരതി നടക്കുകയായിരുന്നു. സന്ധ്യാദേവി എവിടെ? ശങ്കിച്ചിരുന്നിട്ട് അയാൾ ചോദിച്ചു.

"അപ്പോൾ സന്ധ്യാദേവി?"

ആരും മിണ്ടിയില്ല. അയാൾ ഓരോരുത്തരെയും മാറി മാറി നോക്കി. അപ്പോഴേക്കും റീന ഒരുവശത്തെ വാതിൽക്കൽ വന്നുനിന്നു. അത് അയാൾക്ക് അത്ഭുതമായിത്തോന്നി. പഴയ സദനത്തിലേക്ക് മടങ്ങിവന്നതുപോലെ.

"റീന?" അയാൾ ചോദിച്ചു.

"അവൾ ഇന്നലെ കൽക്കത്തയിൽ നിന്നുവന്നു. രവികുമാറിനേയും അറസ്റ്റു ചെയ്തു ശിക്ഷിച്ചു. അപ്പോൾ അവളെ ഇങ്ങയക്കുകയാണ് നല്ലതെന്ന് മിസ്റ്റർ മേനോനു തോന്നി."

അദ്ദേഹം തുടർന്നു.

"അരവിന്ദൻ, സന്ധ്യാദേവി രണ്ടുമാസം മുൻപ് ഇവിടെ നിന്നുംപോ

യി, അന്നു ഞാൻ ഇവിടെ ഉണ്ടായിരുന്നില്ല. ആന്ധ്രവരെ പോയിരുന്നു. അവർ ഒരു കത്തെഴുതിവച്ചിട്ടാണ് പോയത്. അവർ ഇനി ഒരിക്കലും ഇങ്ങോട്ടു മടങ്ങിവരികയില്ലെന്ന് അതിൽ പറഞ്ഞിരുന്നു. അവരും കുട്ടിയും ഈ ഭൂമിയിൽ എവിടെയെങ്കിലും ജീവിക്കുമെന്നും ഒരിക്കലും അവരെ രണ്ടുപേരെയും അന്വേഷിക്കരുതെന്നും അവർ അഭ്യർഥിച്ചിരുന്നു."

അരവിന്ദൻ കണ്ണും നട്ടിരുന്നു ചോദിച്ചു:

"കുട്ടിയോ? ആരുടെ കുട്ടി?"

ശിവാനന്ദഭാരതി താടി തടവി. അദ്ദേഹം സാവധാനം പറഞ്ഞു:

"അരവിന്ദൻ, നിങ്ങൾ ആ കഥയൊന്നും അറിഞ്ഞില്ല. അല്ലേ? സദനത്തിന്റെ അവസാനത്തെ ദിവസങ്ങൾ ഏറ്റവും ദുഃഖകരമായിരുന്നു. എല്ലാവരെയും ബലം പ്രയോഗിച്ചു ഓരോ സ്ഥലത്തു കൊണ്ടുചെന്നുവിട്ടല്ലോ. സന്ധ്യാദേവിയെ അവർ ഒറ്റയ്ക്ക് അവിടെ തടഞ്ഞുവച്ചു. അന്നു രാത്രിയിലുണ്ടായ സംഭവങ്ങൾ അവരെ ശാരീരികമായും മാനസികമായും തകർത്തുകളഞ്ഞു. വാസവമേനോൻ വളരെ ക്ലേശിച്ചാണ് ആളെ അയച്ച് അവരെ കണ്ടുപിടിച്ചതും കോയമ്പത്തൂരെത്തിച്ചതും. ഭാനുമതി നേരത്തെ അവിടെ ചെന്നിരുന്നു. അന്ന് മേനോൻ കോയമ്പത്തൂരിൽ ക്യാമ്പായിരുന്നു. സന്ധ്യാദേവിയെയും ഭാനുമതിയെയും അവിടെ ഒരു ഗൃഹത്തിൽ പാർപ്പിച്ചു. കുറെ മാസങ്ങൾ കഴിഞ്ഞ് അവർ പ്രസവിച്ചു. അന്നു മുതൽക്ക് അവരുടെ സ്വഭാവം മാറി. അവരുടെ ജീവിതം ഒരു വൈരാഗ്യത്തിന്റെ പ്രതീകമായിത്തീർന്നുവെന്നു പറയാം. സാഹസികമായ വൈരാഗ്യമല്ല, ആത്മനശീകരണത്തോടൊപ്പം വരുന്ന ജീവിത നിരസനമാണത്. നമുക്കത് മനസിലാകും. അതെല്ലാം കഴിഞ്ഞാണ് വാസവമേനോനും ഞാനും തമ്മിൽ കണ്ടത്. ഞങ്ങൾ ആലോചിച്ച് ഇവിടെ ഇങ്ങനെയൊരു താവളമുണ്ടാക്കാൻ നിശ്ചയിച്ചു. നമുക്ക് ഇവിടെ ചില സഹായികളൊക്കെ ഉണ്ടായിരുന്നു. അങ്ങനെ നമ്മുടെ ഈ കർമാശ്രമം സ്ഥാപിച്ചു. സന്ധ്യാദേവിയെയും ഭാനുമതിയെയും ഇങ്ങോട്ടു കൊണ്ടുവന്നു. സന്ധ്യാദേവി തന്നെയാണ് കീർത്തിയെ വിളിച്ചു കൊണ്ടുവന്നത്. ഇവിടെയും അവർ മൗനവ്രതത്തിൽ മുഴുകിയ ജീവിതമാണ് കഴിച്ചിരുന്നത്. രണ്ടുപേരുകൾ മാത്രമേ അവർ ശബ്ദിച്ചു കേട്ടിട്ടുള്ളൂ. ഒന്ന് കീർത്തി. ഒന്ന് ദ്രൗപതി. അത് കുട്ടിയുടെ പേരാണ്. അർഥമില്ലാത്ത ഒരു വാക്കു പറയുകയോ എഴുതുകയോ ചെയ്യാത്ത അവരെ അന്വേഷിച്ചിട്ടു കാര്യമില്ലെന്നാണ് എനിക്കു തോന്നിയത്. ഇതിനിടയ്ക്കാണ് സന്ധ്യാദേവി നിങ്ങളെ ജയിലിൽ വന്നു കണ്ടത്, എന്നോടു പറഞ്ഞു. അവർ ചില നിശ്ചയങ്ങൾ ചെയ്തുപോവുകയാണുണ്ടായത്. നമുക്കെല്ലാം അവർ മനസിലെ തീരാത്ത ദുഃഖമായി."

അവിടെയാകെ നിശ്ശബ്ദത തങ്ങിനിന്നു. എല്ലാവരും ഓർമകളുടെ കയങ്ങളിലേക്കു വീണുപോയി. റീന മുഖം കുനിച്ചു. ഭാനുമതിയും കീർത്തിയും വിദൂരതയിലേക്കു നോക്കിനിന്നു.

എങ്ങും ശൂന്യത വ്യാപിച്ചതുപോലെ, മനസ്സു ഒന്നുമില്ലാത്ത പ്രദേശമായിപ്പോയതുപോലെ. അവരെ കാണാതായപ്പോൾ ദുഃഖിച്ചു നാളുകൾ

കഴിച്ചുകൂട്ടി. പക്ഷേ, അന്ന് എപ്പോഴെങ്കിലും കണ്ടെത്താമെന്ന ഒരു ആഗ്രഹം അവശേഷിച്ചിരുന്നു. ഇന്ന് കാണാത്ത ഭൂമിയിലേക്ക് അവർ പൊയ്ക്കളഞ്ഞിരിക്കുന്നു. അവർ മടങ്ങിവരികയില്ലെന്നത്, സഹിക്കാൻ കഴിയുന്നില്ല. എന്തിന് ഇത്ര മാത്രം സ്നേഹിച്ചു? എന്തിന് ജീവന്റെ അണുക്കളിൽ ഒരു ഓർമയും ഒതുക്കിപ്പിടിച്ച് ഇത്രനാളും നടന്നു?

മനസിൽ ആയിരം അണക്കെട്ടുകൾ ഒരുമിച്ചു പൊട്ടിയിരിക്കുന്നു. കാലങ്ങളായി അഹോരാത്രം പണിഞ്ഞുണ്ടാക്കിയ സ്നേഹത്തിന്റെ സംരക്ഷണവലയങ്ങൾ.

എല്ലാ ശബ്ദങ്ങളുടെയും കവാടങ്ങൾ അടഞ്ഞുപോയി. അരവിന്ദൻ ശിരസിൽ കൈക്കൊടുത്തു മൂകനായി ഇരുന്നു.

രണ്ടുനാഴിക നേരത്തിനു ശേഷമാണ് അയാൾ ആ വിസ്മൃതിയിൽ നിന്ന് ഉണർന്നത്. അത്രയും സമയം എല്ലാവരും അയാളുടെ മുൻപിൽ നിന്നുപോയി. ഒടുവിൽ ശിവാനന്ദജി വിളിച്ചു.

"അരവിന്ദൻ."

"സ്വാമിജി."

"വരൂ."

അയാൾ എഴുന്നേറ്റു. അവർ ആശ്രമത്തിന്റെ പിന്നിലേക്കു നടന്നു. അവിടെയും മരങ്ങളും അവയ്ക്കിടയിൽക്കൂടി വഴികളുമുണ്ട്. അവർ അതിലേ നടന്നു. ശിവാനന്ദജി മൗനം ദീക്ഷിച്ചു. നിലാവ് തെളിഞ്ഞു തുടങ്ങിയിരുന്നു. മഞ്ഞുമൂടി മനോഹരമായി നിൽക്കുന്ന സഹ്യപർവതം. അതിനപ്പുറത്ത് താഴ്വാരങ്ങൾ. ആ പ്രകൃതിയാകെ അയാൾക്ക് ശൂന്യതയുടെ വരകളും രൂപങ്ങളുമായിത്തോന്നി. ആ പാറക്കെട്ടിൽ അവർ ഇരുന്നു. ശിവാനന്ദജി സാവധാനം സംസാരിച്ചു.

"അരവിന്ദൻ ദേശസ്നേഹം പലപ്പോഴും ആത്മഹൂതി തന്നെ ആവശ്യപ്പെടുന്നില്ലേ? അവിടെ ദുർബലതയ്ക്ക് സ്ഥാനമില്ല. ദുഃഖം തന്നെ ബലഹീനതയല്ല മഹത്തായ വികാരമാണവിടെ രക്തസാക്ഷികളിൽ നിന്നും നാം ആത്മാവേശം കൈക്കൊള്ളുന്നത് അങ്ങനെയാണ്. മരിച്ചവരെപ്പറ്റി നമുക്ക് ദുഃഖമില്ലേ? നമ്മുടെ സമരസഖാക്കളെപ്പറ്റി? ഉണ്ട്. പക്ഷേ, അത് നാം കരയാനുള്ള ശവകുടീരങ്ങളാക്കുകയില്ല. കരുത്തു സമ്പാദിക്കാൻ ഉള്ള ചൈതന്യസ്ഥാനങ്ങളാക്കും. നിങ്ങൾക്ക് വ്യക്തിപരമായി സംഭവിച്ചിട്ടുള്ള നഷ്ടം എനിക്കറിവുണ്ട്. വാസവമേനോൻ അത് എന്നെ അറിയിച്ചിട്ടുണ്ട്. അവിടെ ഒരു തത്വവും മനോവികാരവും തമ്മിൽ ഏറ്റുമുട്ടുന്നു. താൻ ഇനി ഒരു ഭാര്യയാവാൻ പറ്റിയവളല്ലെന്ന് സന്ധ്യാദേവി വിശ്വസിക്കുന്നു. ഒരു പക്ഷേ, എന്തും സഹിക്കാനും സ്വീകരിക്കാനും നിങ്ങൾ മനസാ തയാറാണുതാനും. അതിന് അവർ തയാറല്ല. നിങ്ങൾ ഒരു തെറ്റും ചെയ്തിട്ടില്ല. അവർ നിങ്ങളോടുള്ള സ്നേഹം ഒരു നിമിഷംപോലും നഷ്ടപ്പെടുത്തിയിട്ടുമില്ല. സമാധാനിക്കൂ. അല്ലാതെ നാമെന്തു ചെയ്യും?"

ഈ വാക്കുകൾ കാറ്റിൽ പറത്തിയ അപ്പൂപ്പൻ താടികളാണെന്ന് ശിവാനന്ദജിക്കറിയാം. എങ്കിലും അത്രയും പറഞ്ഞു. അരവിന്ദനും തന്റെ

സമനിലയ്ക്കുവേണ്ടി ശ്രമിക്കുകയായിരുന്നു. ശിവാനന്ദജി അൽപ്പം കൂടി സംസാരിച്ചു.

"നമ്മുടെ മൂകത, ആശ്രമത്തിലെ ആ പെൺകുട്ടികളെ മൂകരാക്കും." അവർക്ക് ആരുണ്ട്? ആരെ വിശ്വസിച്ച് അവർ ഈ പർവതതടത്തിലേക്ക് വന്നിരിക്കുന്നു? നമ്മളെ, നമ്മളെ മാത്രം. അതുകൊണ്ട്, അവരുടെ മുൻപിൽ വ്യക്തിപരമായ ദുർബലതകൾ വേദനകൾ, വിചാരങ്ങൾ, മറച്ചുവയ്ക്കാൻ നമ്മൾ ബാധ്യസ്ഥരായിത്തീരുന്നു. അരവിന്ദന് ഇതൊന്നും അറിയാത്തതല്ല. എന്നെനിക്കു ബോധ്യമുണ്ട്. എങ്കിലും പറഞ്ഞുവെന്നു മാത്രം."

സമയം കുറെ പോയി. അരവിന്ദൻ മൂകതയിൽനിന്ന് മോചനം നേടിയതുപോലുണ്ട്. അയാൾ ചോദിച്ചു.

"സ്വാമിജി, അങ്ങയെ അറസ്റ്റു ചെയ്ത് കൽക്കത്തായിലേക്കു കൊണ്ടുപോയതായിട്ടാണ് ഞാനറിഞ്ഞത്. പിന്നെ എങ്ങനെ ഇവിടെയെത്തി?"

ശിവാന്ദജി ചിരിച്ചു.

"എന്നെ കൽക്കത്തെയിലേക്കു കൊണ്ടുപോയതു ശരിയാണ്. ഞാൻ അവിടെ ചെന്നിറങ്ങിയതും സത്യമാണ്. എന്നെ ജയിലിലാക്കിയതും യാഥാർത്ഥ്യമാണ്. ജയിലിൽ നമുക്കു ധാരാളം ആളുകളുണ്ട്. പക്ഷേ തടവുചാടാൻ എനിക്ക് സൗകര്യമുണ്ടാക്കിത്തന്നത് രവികുമാറാണ്. അയാളെ പിടിച്ചത് ആ കേസിനല്ല, രഹസ്യ ലഘുലേഖകൾ പ്രചരിപ്പിക്കുന്നു എന്ന പേരിലാണ്. അയാളും ഒരു സംഘം കുട്ടികളും ശിക്ഷിക്കപ്പെട്ടിട്ടുണ്ട്?"

"ഇവിടെ പൊലീസിന്റെ കണ്ണ് വന്നെത്തിയിട്ടില്ലേ?"

"തൽക്കാലം ഇല്ലെന്നാണു തോന്നുന്നത്. ഏതായാലും എന്നെ അറിയുകയില്ല. പിന്നെ ഇവിടെ അവർക്ക് വന്നെത്താൻ പ്രയാസമുണ്ട്. വളരെ ദൂരെ അവരെത്തുമ്പോൾ നമ്മെ അറിയിക്കാനുള്ള ആൾക്കാരും ഉണ്ട്. അദ്ദേഹം നിറുത്തിയിട്ട് പറഞ്ഞു: "ഏതായാലും അരവിന്ദൻ ഇന്നുതന്നെ ഇവിടെയെത്തിയതു നന്നായി."

"എന്താണത്?"

"മഹാസന്യാസി ഇന്നു രാത്രിയിൽ വരുന്നുണ്ട്."

വാസവമേനോനെപ്പറ്റിയാണ് അത് പറഞ്ഞതെന്ന് അരവിന്ദനു മനസിലായി.

"ലഘുലേഖകൾ ഉണ്ടാക്കാനും അവയുടെ കോപ്പികൾ എടുക്കാനും കൃഷിക്കാരും മറ്റു ജനങ്ങളുമായി സമ്പർക്കം ഉണ്ടാക്കാനും നല്ല ഒരു സംഘടനയും രീതിയും നമ്മൾ ഇവിടെ ഉണ്ടാക്കിയിട്ടുണ്ട്. അതൊക്കെ നാളെ വിശദീകരിച്ചു തരാം. എന്റെ അഭിപ്രായത്തിൽ അരവിന്ദൻ മദിരാശിയിലേക്കുതന്നെ മടങ്ങിപ്പോകണം. ഇവിടെ തിരുവിതാംകൂറിലും വടക്കൻനാടുകളിലും നമുക്ക് നല്ലതുപോലെ പ്രവർത്തിക്കാൻ ആളുകളുണ്ട്. മദ്രാസിൽ പ്രവർത്തിക്കാൻ ആളു കുറവാണ്. അതുകൊണ്ട് താമസിയാതെ അങ്ങോട്ടുപോകണം."

അരവിന്ദൻ സമ്മതിച്ചു.

അവർ ആശ്രമത്തിലേക്കു തിരിച്ചു നടക്കുമ്പോൾ, ഒരാൾ അങ്ങോട്ടു

വരുന്നു. അടുത്തു വന്നപ്പോൾ ആളെ മനസിലായി. വാസവമേനോൻ.

"നേരത്തെ എത്തിയോ?" ശിവാനന്ദജി അന്വേഷിച്ചു.

"അതെ. വെളുപ്പിന് പോവുകയും വേണം. ലഘുലേഖകൾ തയാറായല്ലോ?"

"തയാറായി. കൊണ്ടുപോകാം."

രാത്രി വളരെ വൈകിക്കഴിഞ്ഞിരുന്നു. ശിവാനന്ദജിയും വാസവമേനോനും അരവിന്ദനും സംസാരിച്ചുകൊണ്ടിരുന്നു. പുറത്ത് തെളിനിലാവ് ഒഴുകി നിൽക്കുന്നു. വാസവമേനോൻ വെളുപ്പിനു യാത്ര തിരിക്കുകയാണ്. അവർ ഉറങ്ങാൻ കിടന്നു. അരവിന്ദൻ വെളിയിലിറങ്ങി. അയാളുടെ മനസിന് സ്വസ്ഥത കിട്ടിയില്ല. സന്ധ്യയ്ക്ക് സ്വാമിജിയുമൊരുമിച്ചിരുന്ന ആ സങ്കേതത്തിലേക്ക് അയാൾ നടന്നു. ഉറക്കം വരാത്ത ആ രാത്രിയിൽ, ഏകാന്തതയിലിരുന്ന് സമാധാനം കണ്ടെത്താമെന്ന് അയാൾ മോഹിച്ചു. വൃക്ഷങ്ങളുടെ നിഴലുകൾപോലും അയാളെ ഒരുതരം വിഭ്രാന്തിയിലേക്കു വലിച്ചുകൊണ്ടുപോയി. ദൂരെ ആകാശവും താഴ്വാരങ്ങളുമെല്ലാം വീണ്ടും ശൂന്യതയുടെ ദൃശ്യങ്ങളായി മാറിയിരിക്കുന്നു. എല്ലാം നഷ്ടപ്പെട്ട ഒരുവന്റെ വ്യർഥതാബോധം അയാളെ ആക്രമിച്ചു കീഴ്പ്പെടുത്തുകയാണ്.

പണ്ട്, ജീവിതത്തിൽ ധാരാളം തളിരുകളും പൂക്കളും ഉണ്ടായിരുന്ന ഒരുകാലത്തു അൽപ്പം മാനസികവ്യഥ വന്നു തൊട്ടപ്പോളെഴുതിയ ചില വരികൾ അയാളുടെ ഓർമയിലേക്കു കടന്നുവന്നു.

ശാരദാകാശത്തിന്റെ ഹൃദയത്തിൽ നിന്നെന്തേ
താരകങ്ങളേ നിങ്ങൾ നോക്കുന്നു, ചിരിക്കുന്നു
ദൂരെയിക്കിനാവിന്റെയേകാന്തഗൃഹത്തിൽ ഞാ–
നാമനോരമണിയെക്കാത്തുകാത്തിരിക്കുമ്പോൾ?
അറിയില്ലല്ലോ നിങ്ങൾക്കൊറ്റയ്ക്കീ നിശീതത്തിൽ
മരുവും ശോകാപ്തനാമെന്റെ ജീവിതദുഃഖം?
ചിരിക്കൂ, വീണ്ടും വീണ്ടും ചിരിക്കൂ, ഞാൻ നിങ്ങൾക്കു
ചിരിക്കാനുള്ളോരൊറ്റക്കളിപ്പാവയാണല്ലോ!

അരവിന്ദൻ ആ പാവയ്ക്കരികിലെത്തി. അയാൾ നിന്നു പോയി. പ്രതീക്ഷിച്ചതല്ല. നാനാവികാരങ്ങളുടെ ഒഴുക്കുത്തിൽ അകപ്പെട്ടതുപോലെ.

കീർത്തി, ആ പാറക്കെട്ടിൽ ഒറ്റയ്ക്കിരിക്കുന്നു. അവൾ കിഴക്ക്, സഹ്യന്റെ താഴ്വാരങ്ങളിലേക്കു നോക്കി. വിസ്മൃതിയിൽപ്പെട്ടിരിക്കുകയാണ്. അയാൾ അവിടെനിന്നു അൽപ്പം സമയം. അവൾ തിരിഞ്ഞുനോക്കി. എന്തോ പ്രേരണ കൊണ്ടെന്നപോലെ അരവിന്ദനെ കണ്ട് അവൾ ഞെട്ടി, എഴുന്നേറ്റു മാറിനിന്നു. അവളുടെ മുഖം ഉയർന്നു. അയാളുടെ കണ്ണുകൾ അവളിൽ തങ്ങിനിന്നു. ആ നിലാവിൽ അവർ പരസ്പരം നോക്കി നിന്നു. അവളുടെ കവിളിലേക്ക് ഒഴുകിയ നീർത്തുള്ളികൾ ചന്ദ്രികയിൽ മിന്നിത്തിളങ്ങി.

www.ingramcontent.com/pod-product-compliance
Lightning Source LLC
LaVergne TN
LVHW060625051026
849519LV00002B/765

* 9 7 8 9 3 8 5 0 1 8 1 0 7 *

9 789385 018107